Marcus Goncalves
Global Markets, Diverse Economies

Marcus Goncalves

Global Markets, Diverse Economies

Integrating Economics, Culture and ESG Strategies

DE GRUYTER

ISBN 978-3-11-151004-0
e-ISBN (PDF) 978-3-11-151028-6
e-ISBN (EPUB) 978-3-11-151163-4

Library of Congress Control Number: 2024944692

Bibliographic information published by the Deutsche Nationalbibliothek
The Deutsche Nationalbibliothek lists this publication in the Deutsche Nationalbibliografie; detailed bibliographic data are available on the internet at http://dnb.dnb.de.

Cover image: brijith vijayan/iStock/Getty Images Plus
Typesetting: Integra Software Services Pvt. Ltd.
Printing and binding: CPI books GmbH, Leck

www.degruyter.com

To my cherished wife, whose endless love and steadfast support are my sanctuary and whose belief in me knows no bounds. To my children, Andrea and Joshua, who shine as stars in heaven and guide me through my darkest times, each word written is a tribute to your lasting impact on my heart. To my son, Samir, whose resilience and kindness inspire daily life, and Betsy, whose presence brought joy and enriched our family. To my granddaughter Olivinha, a beacon of hope and joy, her growth and potential light up our lives. And lastly, glory be to God, whose boundless grace carries me through the trials and triumphs, making each achievement a reason for thanksgiving.

Acknowledgments

Embarking from an initial idea to a published book has involved the pivotal support of many, each with their unique and invaluable contributions. Their guidance has been crucial, and their dedication is exceptional. Some have mainly stood out for their relentless support and wisdom, which has been instrumental in shaping this book.

Above all, I sincerely thank Jaya Dalal, Acquisitions Editor at De Gruyter. Jaya's unwavering confidence in my potential and this project's value has been fundamental to its realization. Being entrusted with this publication under Jaya's guidance has been a privilege. Her continual support and insightful feedback throughout the development from concept to manuscript completion have been vital, enriching this journey tremendously.

I also extend my heartfelt thanks to the production team for their critical and collective roles in bringing this manuscript to life. Their precise attention to detail and unwavering dedication have ensured a smooth transition from manuscript to publication, free of any hurdles. Their expertise in fine-tuning the manuscript's structure and enhancing its aesthetic and coherent presentation has been indispensable. Their collective efforts have significantly improved this book's quality and potential success.

Writing a book is like weaving an intricate tapestry with threads from numerous contributors, each adding their unique strength and color to the overall picture. Amidst all the professional support, my wife's quiet support and patience have been the foundation for this endeavor.

https://doi.org/10.1515/9783111510286-202

Contents

Preface

This book offers an insightful exploration of international business and entrepreneurship, delving into the complex layers of global market dynamics, macroeconomics, cultural challenges, and strategic operations. Designed for academicians and practitioners, it comprehensively analyzes the multifaceted aspects of conducting business across borders. Its rich theoretical frameworks and practical insights illuminate the path to succeeding in today's interconnected world economy.

Chapter 1: Navigating Global Markets: Complexities and Strategies in International Business sets the stage by discussing the critical distinctions between domestic and international business and outlining the global landscape's opportunities and pitfalls. It covers the growth of international business activities, supported by data from the World Trade Organization, and discusses the strategic implications of globalization, cultural differences, language barriers, and geopolitical policies.

Chapter 2: Social Cultural Forces, Natural Resources, and Sustainability focuses on the influence of cultural forces. This chapter examines how culture affects business operations across different geographies. It emphasizes the importance of sustainability in business practices and explores how natural resources impact international trade dynamics.

Chapter 3: Geopolitical Dynamics and Legal Landscapes in Global Trade and Intellectual Property, examines the intricate geopolitical dynamics that shape international trade policies and the complex legal landscapes governing global intellectual property rights. It explores how geopolitical tensions, trade agreements, and international regulations influence business operations and competitive strategies worldwide. The chapter also delves into the critical role of intellectual property management in global commerce, highlighting best practices for protecting patents, trademarks, and copyrights in diverse jurisdictions. This analysis provides readers with an understanding of how legal and geopolitical factors can enable and constrain international business endeavors.

Chapter 4: Global Dynamics: Economic, Socioeconomic, and Financial Forces Shaping the International Monetary System delves into the economic, socioeconomic, and financial forces that shape the international monetary system, presenting an insightful analysis of how global financial architectures and policies influence trade, investment, and economic stability worldwide. It discusses the roles of major international financial institutions like the IMF, World Bank, and regional development banks. It examines the impact of monetary policies, currency exchange systems, and financial crises on global economic relations. Additionally, the chapter addresses the socioeconomic factors that drive financial decisions and outlines the challenges and opportunities within the evolving international financial landscape, providing a nuanced understanding of the interconnectedness of global economies.

Chapter 5: International Competitive Strategy provides an in-depth exploration of international competitive strategy, analyzing how firms develop and sustain competi-

https://doi.org/10.1515/9783111510286-204

tive advantages in global markets. It delves into the frameworks and analytical tools businesses employ to understand competitive landscapes, differentiate themselves, and effectively position their products and services internationally. The chapter covers strategic decision-making processes, including market entry modes, competitive positioning, scaling operations, and strategic alliances. It also discusses the impact of cultural, political, and economic factors on strategic choices and how companies can adapt their strategies in response to dynamic global market conditions. This chapter equips readers with the knowledge to craft robust international strategies that leverage global and local competitive insights.

Chapter 6: International Organizational Design and Control delves into the crucial aspects of international organizational design and control, focusing on how multinational corporations structure and manage their global operations to optimize efficiency and effectiveness. It examines various organizational frameworks and control mechanisms that enable firms to respond swiftly to international market dynamics and manage the complexities of diverse regulatory environments and cultural landscapes. The chapter discusses the balance between centralization and decentralization, the role of technology in streamlining global operations, and the strategies for integrating cross-border teams and processes. It also highlights the challenges of maintaining organizational flexibility while ensuring alignment with strategic objectives across multiple geographies, providing a comprehensive guide for leaders managing international businesses.

Chapter 7: Global Leadership Issues and Practices addresses the vital role of leadership in navigating the complexities of global business environments. It explores leaders' unique challenges when managing culturally diverse teams and operating across legal and economic systems. The chapter discusses critical leadership qualities and practices effective in global settings, such as cultural intelligence, ethical decision-making, and adaptive leadership styles. It also examines case studies of successful global leaders and their strategies to inspire and lead multinational organizations toward achieving their strategic objectives. Through a detailed analysis of contemporary leadership theories and real-world applications, this chapter equips current and aspiring leaders with the tools to excel internationally.

Chapter 8: International Markets: Assessment and Entry Mode offers an analytical approach to assessing international markets, focusing on the methodologies and criteria for market research in selecting potential markets for entry or expansion. It outlines various market assessment techniques, including economic, sociopolitical, and competitive analysis, providing a strategic framework for understanding market attractiveness. The chapter also delves into the different entry modes available to businesses, such as exporting, licensing, joint ventures, and wholly owned subsidiaries, discussing the advantages and risks associated with each. Through a detailed examination of strategic considerations, including market saturation levels, regulatory environments, and cultural compatibility, this chapter provides essential insights for businesses planning to venture into new international markets.

Chapter 9: Marketing Internationally explores the complexities and strategies of marketing in the global arena, emphasizing the need for businesses to adapt their marketing mixes to fit diverse international markets. It discusses the importance of cultural sensitivity, local consumer behavior, and legal regulations influencing marketing tactics abroad. The chapter outlines the steps for creating effective global marketing campaigns, including market segmentation, positioning, and channel strategies, while addressing digital marketing's rising significance in reaching international audiences. Through real-world examples and case studies, this chapter illustrates the dynamic challenges and innovative approaches companies must embrace to succeed in global marketing management.

Chapter 10: Managing Human Resources in an International Context addresses the intricacies of managing human resources within an international framework, emphasizing the strategic importance of adapting HR practices to diverse cultural, legal, and economic environments. It covers effective recruitment, development, and retention strategies across different countries alongside challenges such as expatriate management, cross-cultural team dynamics, and compliance with local labor laws. The chapter also explores the impact of global trends on HR practices, including technological advancements and global demographic shifts, providing insights into creating a resilient and inclusive global workforce that aligns with an organization's international business objectives.

Chapter 11: International Accounting and Financial Management investigates the critical aspects of international accounting and financial management, essential for corporations operating across borders. It discusses the diverse accounting standards and practices, financial reporting requirements, and regulatory environments in different countries. The chapter also covers strategies for managing currency risk, tax implications, and financial planning in an international context. This chapter provides vital insights for financial managers and accountants to optimize financial performance and compliance in the global marketplace through a detailed examination of cross-border financial transactions and the challenges of aligning global financial operations.

Chapter 12: Export, Import Practices, and Global Operations and Supply Chain Management provides a comprehensive look at the export and import practices that underpin successful global trade, alongside an in-depth analysis of global operations and supply chain management. It discusses the logistical, regulatory, and strategic challenges in navigating international markets, including customs, trade barriers, and documentation requirements. The chapter also examines the integration of supply chain strategies with global business objectives, emphasizing the importance of logistics, supplier relationships, and technology in enhancing operational efficiency and competitiveness in the global marketplace. This section is crucial for businesses seeking to streamline their supply chains and optimize their import and export operations.

Chapter 1
Navigating Global Markets: Complexities and Strategies in International Business

Learning Objectives

- Differentiate between domestic and international business
- Analyze the leading international business challenges
- Appraise the main factors impacting international business trade
- Assess the international business investment opportunities and challenges
- Understand the differences between the leading international trade theories

Overview

The distinction between domestic and international business (IB) implies that a business must engage in both to prevail and expand in the market. Both these business forms have advantages and disadvantages, which all organizations that want to succeed in such a global market must cope with and overcome. This chapter is intended to highlight such essential business factors.

All managers need to have a basic knowledge of international business to be able to meet the challenges of global competition, including but not limited to, these ever-evolving trends:

- Firms are increasingly involved in IB.
- Executive management wants employees to have a global business perspective.
- IB skills are essential for both senior executive and entry-level positions.
- IB proficiencies are even more critical for companies anticipating increasing international activities.

Figure 1.1 depicts the growth of IB across the globe, according to the World Trade Organization (WTO). Notice that despite many other schools of thought suggesting the world is in the process of dis-internationalization, WTO data shows that all trends (optimistic, pessimistic, and conservative) show IB continues to grow, despite the global financial meltdown of 2007/08 and the COVID-19 pandemic of 2019.

https://doi.org/10.1515/9783111510286-001

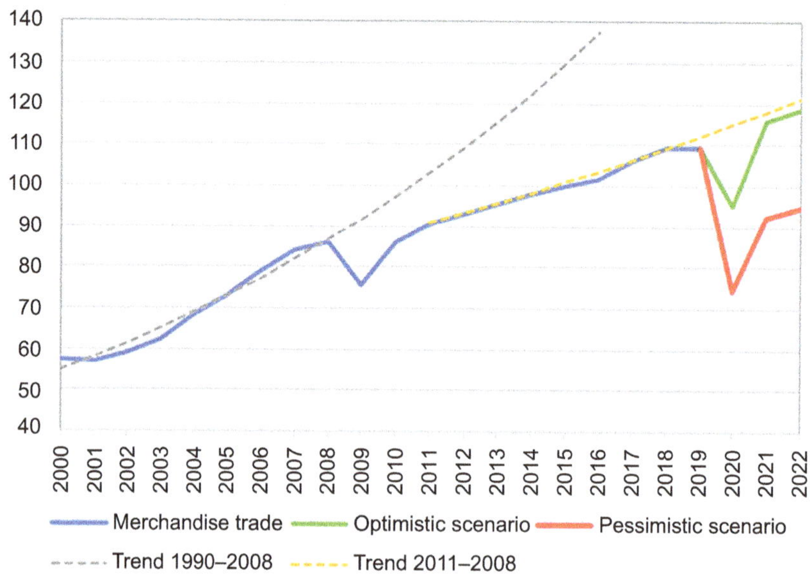

Figure 1.1: Growth of IB across the globe in the past decade, from 2000–22. (SOURCE: WTO, 2021).

Engaging in International Business

International business encompasses the process of production and sale of goods and services among nations abroad, potentially across the globe, where multinational enterprises (MNEs) may:

- Produce goods domestically and sell both domestically and internationally.
- Produce goods in a foreign country but sell them domestically.
- Produce goods in a foreign country and sell both domestically and abroad.

As listed in Figure 1.2, engaging in IB has several advantages. Companies have the opportunity to capitalize on various fronts, including but not limited to:

a. Expanding to markets beyond their domestic frontier, allowing them to tap into new target markets and customer segmentation.
b. Attracting foreign direct investments (FDI) and bring in foreign exchanges.
c. Spreading business risks, as the company can diversify its risks across multiple markets to cope with geopolitical, financial, and monetary forces.
d. Developing economies of scale for their products and services; production costs decrease as markets and customers expand.
e. Tapping onto cost advantages international markets may offer, especially labor costs, taxation, currency exchanges, and many other special incentives or subsi-

dies often provided by foreign governments to stimulate specific industries in their internal markets.

f. Contributing to improving international relations among many countries across the globe as IB development offers incentives and benefits to all sides.
g. Offering outbound and inbound employment opportunities for skilled expats to work abroad and local employment to nationals to participate in the foreign company's operations in their markets.
h. Attaining government support, domestically, with potential incentives or subsidies to stimulate exporting activities and foreign governments to attract foreign companies to boost local markets, foster knowledge and technology transfers, and many other factors.

Figure 1.2: Some of the main benefits offered by international business.

There are several paths a business can follow to become international. Companies generally produce goods overseas due to lower labor costs, tax rates, or both. These companies may sell products and services in the international market as management may seek higher earnings, the prospect of acquiring a more extensive customer base, new consumers, and improved revenues. While an international business can be fascinating, it can also be risky for numerous reasons and circumstances abroad. For instance, foreign nations have their form of governance, distinct trade policies, laws, unique cultures, languages, currency, time zones, geographical challenges (e.g., being landlocked without access to seaports), and inflation rates. Hence, navigating the global business landscape can be challenging. The following are five main challenges to consider:

- **Cultural Differences** – Learning about the cultures of nations where an enterprise plans to expand its businesses is crucial. Just as each country has its own set of languages, they also have specific cultures or a mix of cultures, including arts, foods, traditions, and social norms, to name a few.

When operating offices overseas, managing staff, selling products or services to potential international customers and retailers, or even supervising a production plant abroad, organizations should convey that they have tried to comprehend the local culture. Not only can it facilitate businesses significantly, but it can also project the respect and emotional intelligence necessary to conduct business successfully. Spain and the United States are good examples of such cultural differences. In Spain, business typically opens from 9 a.m. to 1:30 p.m. and then again from 4:30 p.m. to 8 p.m. to allow for a siesta, a time to rest after lunch. Unlike in Spain, In the U.S., working hours are typically from 9 a.m. to 5 p.m., often opening earlier and closing later. Figure 1.3 depicts ways in which cultural differences affect communication.

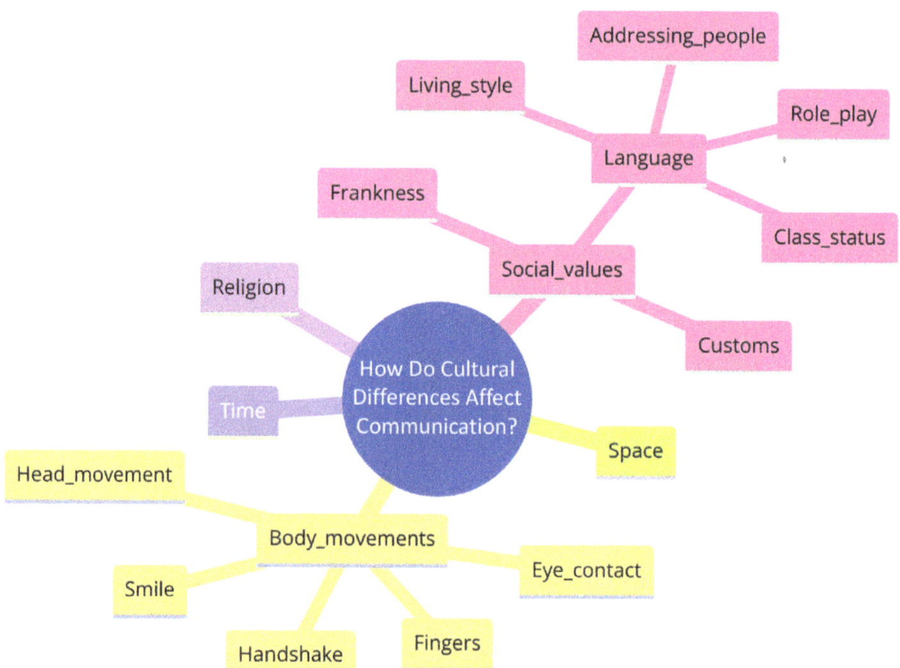

Figure 1.3: Ways cultural differences affect communication when engaged in IB.

– **Language Obstacles** – When engaging in international business, organizations must assess the languages spoken in the nations they want to expand into. Evaluating how the service or product message translates into another language is essential. Enterprises venturing abroad may need to contract interpreting services and rely on a consultant who is a resident and native speaker in the markets they plan to enter. Figure 1.4 depicts six main barriers to communication.

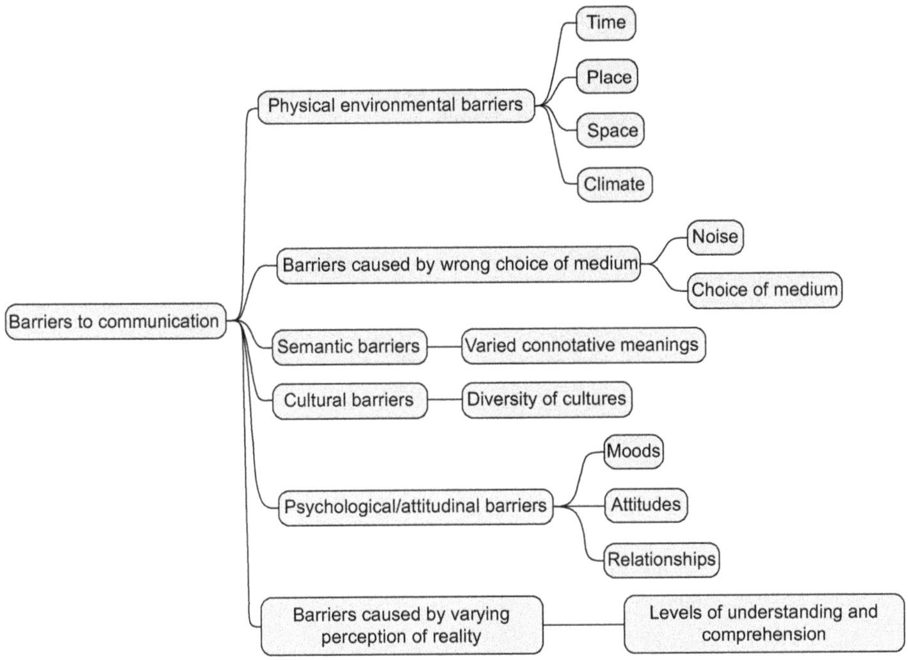

Figure 1.4: Six main barriers to communication when engaging in IB.

– **Legal and Regulatory Requirements** – Compliance is essential for effective business operations in international markets. Every nation has distinct regulations and laws governing business practices, labor rights, taxes, and adherence, encompassing import-export regulations, intellectual property rights, and environmental laws.

– **Political Risks** – The political environment in a foreign market can significantly affect business activities. Political instability, government changes, and policy shifts can lead to unpredictable operating conditions. It is crucial to be mindful of these risks, which may also encompass alterations in trade policies that could impact tariffs or trade barriers.

– **Economic Factors** – The economic situation in the destination nation plays a crucial role in deciding whether business growth is viable. These factors include inflation, forex rates, economic expansion, and general economic steadiness. Changes in these regions can affect expenses, pricing techniques, and business profits.

The following are some examples of blunders committed by well-known international companies:

– **PEPSI** – The lack of professional localization and translation was the leading cause of a failed campaign by one of the world's largest beverage corporations. While entering China's market, the company adopted the well-known slogan in the U.S.,

"Pepsi brings you back to life." But, when the motto is translated into Mandarin, it renders "Pepsi brings your ancestors back from the grave." Not only evoking a deceased person is likely a bad idea in any culture, but in the Chinese one, it is even worse, as they tend to be very sensitive to such remarks regarding their ancestors.
- **KFC** – Similar to PEPSI, KFC tried to approach the Chinese market without doing its homework and, as a result, failed miserably. In 1980, the fast-food giant opened its first outlet in Beijing. The company's world-famous slogan, "finger-lickin' good," literally translates to mean, "It's good to eat your fingers off!"
- **FORD** – Brazil is a growing economy and a desirable market for brands from most industries. Ford expanded its market into Brazil by introducing its newest car, the "Pinto." The company quickly realized how inappropriate the name was as it saw how meager the car's sales numbers were. The reason: "Pinto" in Brazilian Portuguese is a slang word for "small male genitalia." The company had to undergo a costly rebranding quickly.
- **HSBC** – one of the world's leading banks, committed a huge mistake in its 2009 international marketing campaign. Their famous slogan, "Assume nothing," was translated as "Do nothing," a rather pricey mistake that had to be substituted by "The world's private bank." Such a blunder cost the bank about $10 million.
- **ELECTROLUX** – Although committing branding and marketing blunders usually happens when English-speaking brands expand overseas, Electrolux proved that international communication blunders are two-way and can occur even with English-speaking market segments. The Swedish company tried to introduce its new powerful vacuum cleaner into the U.S. market with the slogan, "Nothing sucks like Electrolux." Initial sales were meager until the company rectified the blunder.

These mistakes, summarized in Figure 1.5, clearly show how complex international marketing campaigns and translations can be. In most cases, language is only one factor that needs to be considered during internationalization and international marketing campaigns. Culture, customs, history, and socioeconomic aspects must be considered when introducing a new service or product to a foreign market. Assessing the languages the organization's staff speaks in international branches is essential. Again, hiring interpreters can assist in the smooth business operation abroad.
- **Geopolitics, Policies, and International Relations** – No business exists in a vacuum, and even more so in the case of international business, as they are all influenced by the political environment, policies and regulations, and diplomatic relations between nations. Any decision made by a foreign political leader can impact international business trades, labor laws, taxation, and access to raw materials and infrastructure (i.e., seaports, airports, rail services, etc.), to name a few. Hence, these factors can impose international business challenges without being watched closely.
- **International Team Management** – Another challenge international businesses face is the management of personnel co-located worldwide. It can be challenging

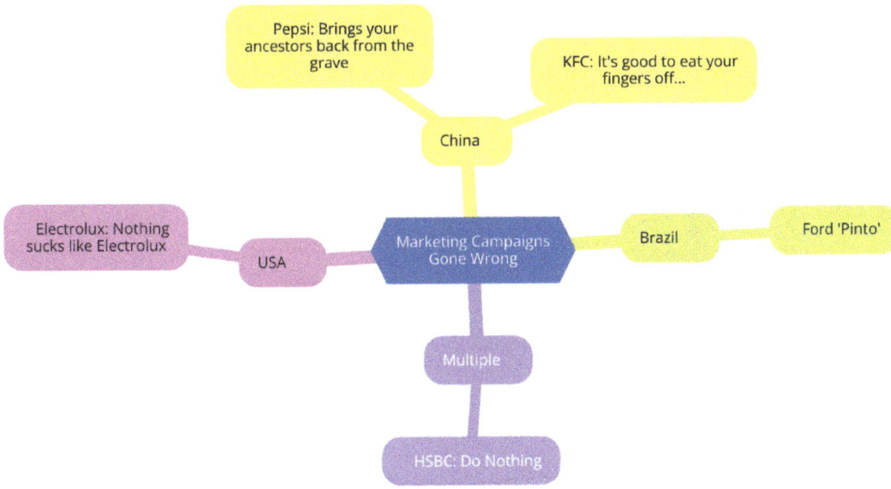

Figure 1.5: Examples of companies' international marketing blunders when entering a new market.

to deal with language barriers when trying to lead a team cohesively, especially when considering the differences in culture, time zones, and inconsistent availability of reliable integrated communication technologies. To develop and sustain a robust working relationship with global teams, it is crucial to encourage them to check in frequently. Ideally, a video conferencing platform, such as Google Meets, Microsoft Teams, Zoom, WebEx, BlueJeans, and many others, allows for real-time interactions. Research conducted by the Gallup group indicates that workers with frequent check-ins with their supervisors are much more inclined to be fully engaged at the job than workers without.

– **Currency Exchange and Inflation Rates** – The value of a local currency will always vary compared to currencies in other nations. Not only will the currency value vary, but also the worth. For example, according to Eurostat, as shown in Figure 1.6, the euro's value between 2011–2021 depreciated by 15.2% against the pound sterling, 15.0% against the U.S. dollar, and 12.3% against the Swiss franc. The exchange rate is the comparative value between two countries' currencies. Companies expanding abroad should familiarize themselves with the exchange rates between their country and the markets they plan to enter. These exchange rates should be monitored frequently, as they do fluctuate often.

It is also necessary to watch inflation rates, which correspond to the rates at general price levels in an economy that tends to increase annually. These rates differ from country to country and may impact expenses, cost of materials, labor costs, and pricing. Figure 1.7 depicts a projection of the global inflation outlook for 2022, according to Statista, with data from the International Monetary Fund (IMF).

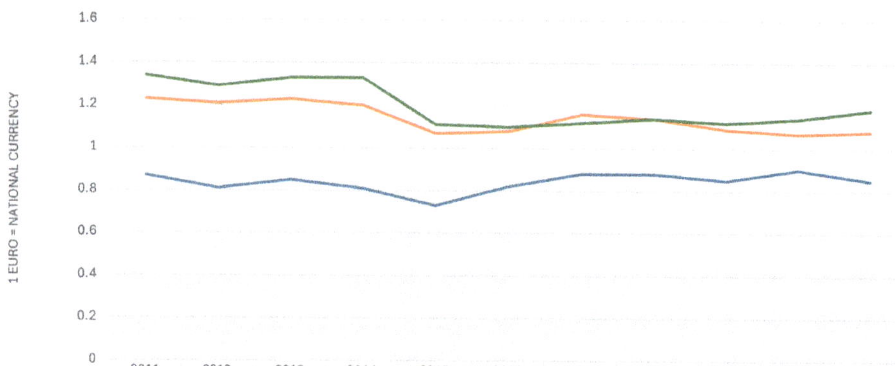

	2011	2012	2013	2014	2015	2016	2017	2018	2019	2020	2021
EUR/GBP	0.87	0.81	0.85	0.81	0.73	0.82	0.88	0.88	0.85	0.9	0.85
EUR/CHF	1.23	1.21	1.23	1.2	1.07	1.08	1.16	1.14	1.09	1.07	1.08
EUR/USD	1.34	1.29	1.33	1.33	1.11	1.1	1.12	1.14	1.12	1.14	1.18

Figure 1.6: The euro's value between 2011–2021 against the pound sterling, the Swiss franc, and the U.S. dollar. (SOURCE: Eurostat, 2021).

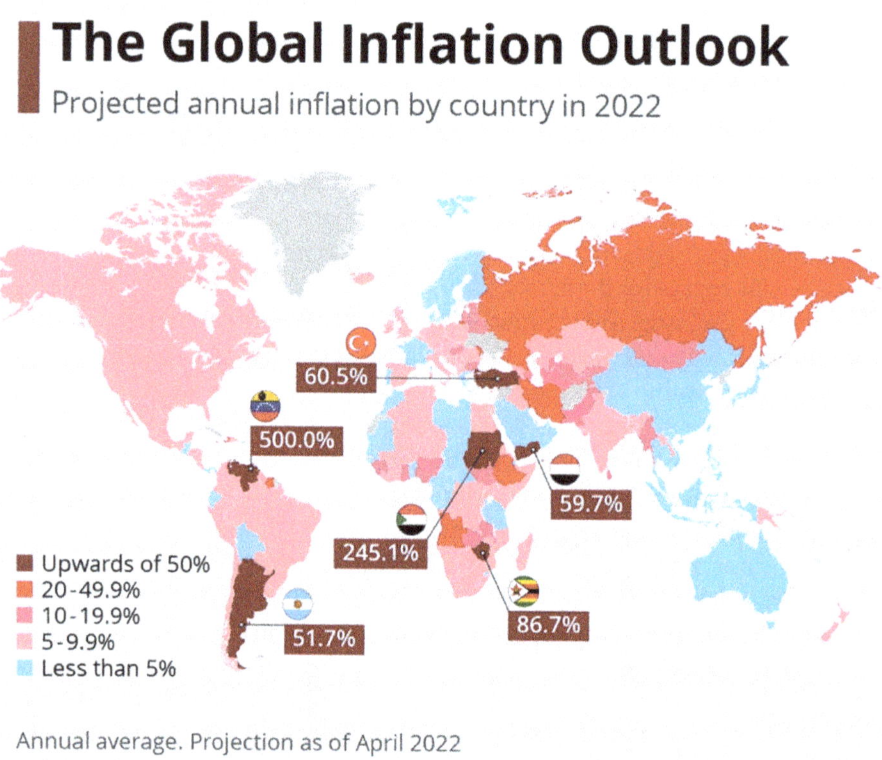

Figure 1.7: A projection of the global inflation outlook for 2022. (SOURCE: IMF, Statista, 2022).

Difference Between Domestic and International Business

Domestic business encompasses economic trades happening inside a country's geographical borders. In this type of business, the shopper and vendor belong to the same nation. Domestic business is also known as internal business or local trade. It is also much easier to conduct market research in domestic businesses than in firms from abroad, and the risk is likewise much lower. The selling process, currency, type of consumers, taxation laws, and other regulations are more or less uniform in a domestic environment, which can significantly benefit any company.

International business involves those commercial transactions taking place beyond the geographical borders of a nation. The customer and the vendor do not necessarily belong to the same country in this type of business. The trade process, currency exchange, type of clients, foreign taxation regulations, and other ordinances are distinct for the customer and vendor, which can restrict a company from conducting trade abroad. Businesses involved in international trade are known as multinational corporations (MNCs), multinational enterprises (MNEs), or transnational companies. It is much more challenging to conduct business market research on international firms than on domestic companies, and the risk is also higher.

Table 1.1 lists the main differences between domestic and international business.

Table 1.1: List of the main differences between domestic and international business.

Category	Domestic Business	International Business
Definition	Domestic business involves those economic transactions that take place within the geographical boundaries of a country.	International business involves those economic transactions that take place outside the geographical boundaries of a country.
Buyer and Seller	Both the buyer and seller belong to the same country in domestic business.	The buyer and seller belong to different countries in international business.
Currency	Domestic businesses deal with the same currency since both the buyer and seller are from the same country.	International businesses deal with different currencies since the buyer and seller are not from the same country.
Customers	There is greater homogeneity in terms of the nature of customers of domestic businesses.	There is greater heterogeneity in terms of the nature of customers of international businesses.
Geographical Boundaries	Geographical boundaries limit domestic businesses.	Geographical boundaries do not limit international businesses.
Business Research	Business research is less complex and relatively cheaper for domestic businesses compared to international organizations.	Business research is more complex and relatively expensive for international businesses compared to domestic companies.

Table 1.1 (continued)

Category	Domestic Business	International Business
Capital Investment	Capital investment is lower for companies that are involved in domestic business.	Capital investment is higher for companies that are involved in international business.
Factors of Production	The domestic business has greater mobility of factors of production compared to international business.	The international business has lesser mobility of factors of production compared to domestic business.
Restrictions	Domestic business involves lesser restrictions than international business.	International business involves greater restrictions than domestic business.
Quality Standards	The quality standards for domestic business tend to be relatively lower than international business.	The quality standards for international business tend to be relatively higher than domestic business.

While Table 1.1 offers a summary of some of the main differences between domestic and international business, the following is a more detailed list of essential distinctions between the two:

1. Domestic businesses are restricted to a single nation or geographical area. In contrast, international business expands beyond national borders and can extend across the globe without being limited to any specific location.
2. A single currency typically operates domestic businesses since nations generally operate under a single national currency. On the other hand, international business requires multi-currency handling and exchange due to different nations holding distinct currencies.
3. A domestic business's product quality and standard tend to be lower than international standards, as domestic firms do not need to pass a high-quality test to enter the international markets.
4. A domestic business typically requires much lower investment than international expansions abroad (there are cases of born-global or new international ventures [NIVs], which are discussed later).
5. Market competition for a local company is relatively low compared to international business ventures.
6. There are very few regulations in the case of domestic business. However, massive rules and restrictions exist in international markets because each of these markets (think of the European Union, which encompasses 27 countries at present) or any specific country has several restrictions and regulations in place to protect their citizens (consumers), businesses, environment, intellectual property, etc.
7. The movement of factors of production, such as goods, human resources, machinery, etc., is relatively inexpensive for a domestic business. Still, the mobility of

aspects of production abroad is much more complex and demanding, often restricted, and requires tax payment.
8. Market research for a local business is comparatively easier than researching abroad in a foreign market. Language, culture, history, and economic conditions abroad can be complex.
9. Domestic businesses' supply chain, logistics, and management are comparatively straightforward compared to international companies, where tariffs, trade barriers, sanctions, geopolitical environments, and many other factors can significantly add to their complexity.
10. Domestic businesses do not have a comparative advantage in production cost, but international trade can use cheap resources, experiences, and expertise.
11. The price of a product or service tends to be similar in the domestic business market, with minor local variations. However, international prices for the same product or service may vary widely from market to market and nation to nation, as each may have its unique economic conditions, purchasing power parity (PPP), and other inherited market idiosyncrasies, which are taken into consideration when price strategies are developed.
12. Domestic businesses' promotional activities are the same as those of domestic industries. However, international trade marketing differs from country to country and requires more comprehensive market research.

Although domestic businesses, in comparison to international business ventures, are easier to start due to relatively lower capital investment and other factors, internationalization strategies can be very complex and expensive, often requiring significant financial support. Table 1.2 offers some additional differentiation between domestic and international business.

Table 1.2: Some additional differentiation between domestic and international business.

Basis	Domestic Business	International Business
Definition	Domestic business can be defined as the business activity that happens within a national boundary.	International business can be defined as the business activity that happens around or across the national boundaries.
Area	Home country	Around the world
Risk	Less	More
Currency	Single currency	Multiple currencies
Product Quality	Low	High
Competition	Low	High
Investment	Low	Vast amount

Table 1.2 (continued)

Basis	Domestic Business	International Business
Rules and Restrictions	Less	Huge
Market Entry	Easy	Difficult
Market Research	Easy	Complex
Mobility of Factors of Production	Free	Not free
Supply Chain	Comparatively easy	Very complex
Management	Comparatively easy	Difficult
Nature of Customer	Homogeneous	Heterogeneous
Form of Products	Both (tangible or intangible)	Both (tangible or intangible)
Cost Advantage	No	Yes
Environment	Linear	Versatile
Level of Progress	Same	Different
Pricing	Same price	Different price
Promotion	Domestic marketing and advertising	Marketing policy varies by country to country
Human Resource	Domestic business can succeed with low skill	Need a high-level of employee skill. Multilingual, multicultural, and multi-strategic skill
Culture	Uniform culture	Varies by country to country
Technology	Average technology	Cutting-edge technology
Political Risk	Risk is low	High political risks because if a country changed by revolutionary force, then the business entity can be confiscated
Communication	Single language and easy to communicate	Multi-language. Must know the different language of different countries
Size of Business	Small	Large

International Business Challenges

Conducting international business is not easy. Advanced economies, such as North America and Europe, have become very competitive, with an enormous footprint of multinational corporations. Entering emerging markets, responsible for more than 50 percent of global gross domestic product (GDP), is difficult. In my experience teaching this topic, consulting for several multinational corporations worldwide, and being a practitioner, I find emerging markets challenging. Government interference, backward infrastructure, and a lack of skilled workers require a lot of patience, perseverance, and specialized assistance. Opportunities in emerging markets come with their own set of challenges. For instance, a lack of education in the workforce often translates into thwarted growth being curbed by a lack of a skilled workforce. Other challenges are legal frameworks concerning trade policies, which may be absent or underdeveloped, or tendencies for political paternalism or blatant interferences, which we see in India and Latin America.

International business managers often become confused and frustrated by these patriarchal decisions. Although many nations have transitioned from autocratic rule to democracies with free markets, some continue to dabble in market interference. Take Argentina as an example. In the summer of 2022, strict currency controls were implemented to prevent an Argentine run on the peso.

Now take India, which is expected to grow by 7.1–7.6 percent in 2022–23 and 6–6.7 percent in 2023–24. The nation will be in crisis if India's economic growth falls below six percent. In contrast, in most advanced economies, such as the United States and Western Europe, if the economy grew at that rate, it would risk overheating. India can barely keep up with educating its rising population. Meanwhile, Mexico is turning out more engineers and engineering technicians yearly than Germany, and it must scramble to ensure they all get jobs. To fail would be to spawn social unrest.

Another critical factor when considering entering new markets is the distance between these markets, which can hamper trade. One study found that a 10 percent increase in distance between north-to-north traders reduces trade by 10 percent; the exact distance between south-to-south traders reduces trade by 17 percent. An improved policy would make an essential difference in resolving such problems, but emerging markets have yet to demonstrate earnest desires for genuine bilateral cooperation.

Public administration in emerging markets has much to be desired. Infrastructure remains a significant problem in most emerging markets, especially African ones, with many frontier economies still in their infancy regarding global trade. China continues to invest heavily in roads, railways, and ports, but the progress is weak elsewhere.

The situation is no different in Latin America. It is arguably worse, as 80 percent of Latin Americans live in cities, compared to fewer than half of Asians. The need for modern urban infrastructure is urgent. Brazil, for instance, wants to improve its infrastructure, which is a bottleneck for the outflow of many of its export products, but it is moving glacially. It has been so slow that Sao Paulo's underground rapid transit system covers only one-tenth of the distance of the one in Seoul, South Korea.

Does all this mean that international business professionals should avoid trading with or investing in emerging markets? On the contrary, any organized program opening to emerging markets must include specialized expertise, on-the-ground knowledge, local partnerships, and patience.

International Business and Entrepreneurship Challenges

International entrepreneurship is a crucial skill in international business. Successful strategies abroad must be used to cope with the development of born-global or NIVs engaging in international trade, thus considering their operational environment internationally from the initial phases of the enterprise's operation. Figure 1.8 depicts the main barriers international entrepreneurship entrepreneurs face when expanding abroad.

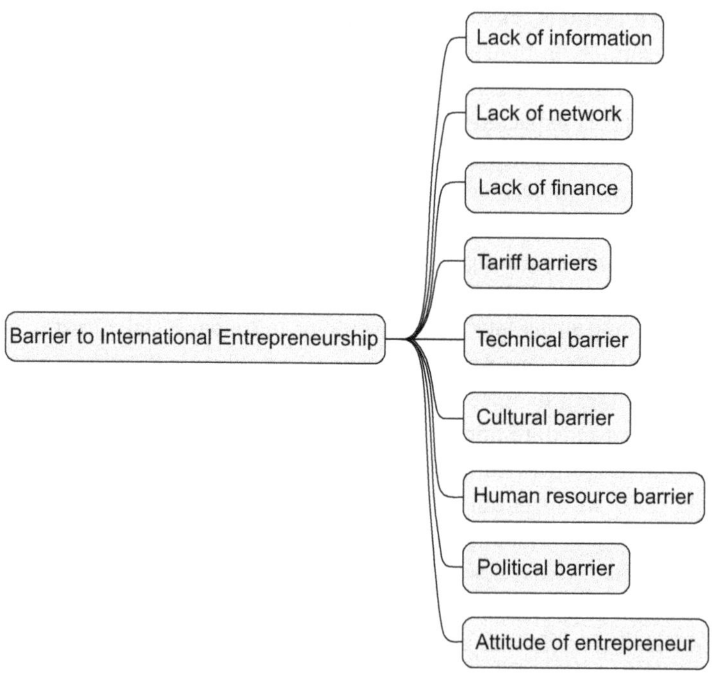

Figure 1.8: Main barriers to international entrepreneurship entrepreneurs face when expanding abroad.

As depicted in Figure 1.8, there are many barriers and challenges to international entrepreneurship and business. The strategy and enterprise structure of born-global /NIVs tend to vary wildly from domestic firms due to such obstacles and challenges.

These born-global companies seek more comprehensive international market-based strategies, seeking a broader market scope through developing and controlling multiple distribution channels, serving various consumers in various market segments, and aiming for high market visibility. These MNCs, or MNEs, also underscore a more aggressive internationalization entry mode built on external financial and production resources to enter multiple geographical markets on a large scale.

Securing intellectual property (IP) rights and patent technologies is often essential to the internationalization strategy. These companies compete by penetrating international markets and industries on large scales, striving to infiltrate numerous markets swiftly, and realizing that many external resources will be necessary to sustain the internationalization process.

Whereas both the domestic and companies that internationalize depict domestic competition as being rather intense, companies engaged in international business compete in markets with higher levels of global competition. International business scholars do not yet agree whether NIVs choose a market abroad with high international competition and respond to it with an international direction because the new venture has an international approach or if they perceive a higher degree of international competition. Another international market distinction NIVs face is the higher degree of restrictiveness due to government regulations. It is unclear, however, whether such restrictiveness encourages NIVs to pursue less-regulated international markets or if, when competing abroad, these NIVs are confronted with increased regulatory conditions.

Conversely, domestic companies are characterized by their focus on a production expansion approach and consumer specialization strategy. The production specialization process concentrates on more local geographical markets, holding excess capacity and seeking forward integration. The consumer specialization strategy combines the production of a specialty product that is infrequently acquired, which requires a persistent closeness between the domestic strategy for both the producer and consumer.

Internal and External Forces Impacting International Business

International business concepts look perfect on paper but may prove imperfect in the real world. Figure 1.9 depicts internal environment factors such as finances, marketing/sales, management, operations, and research and development (R&D) often bring challenges. Notwithstanding, external environment factors surrounding the firm, such as economic, legal, technological, international, social, and competitive, can also be challenging. Understanding how internal and external environmental factors affect the firm can help international businesses succeed.

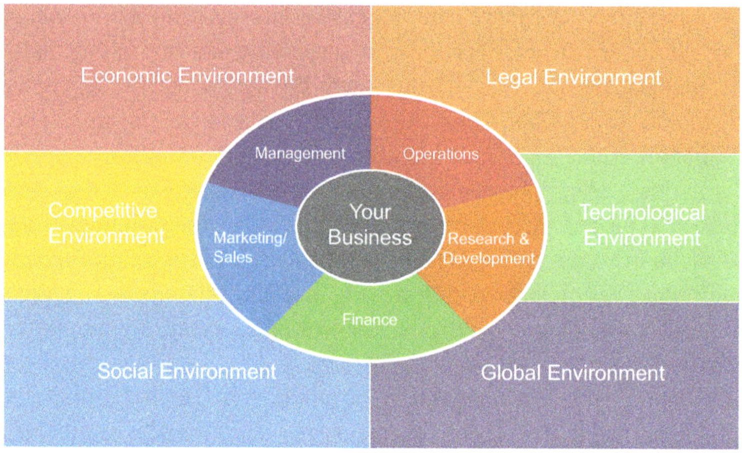

Figure 1.9: Internal and external forces are impacting international business.

External Forces

Economic – Economic factors may affect the performance of firms operating in each market, including interest rates, employment rates, and disposable income. In a bad international economy, even a well-run international firm may face complex challenges to succeed. For instance, consumers and prospects may lose their jobs in a recessionary economy. Customers are also vulnerable to inflationary forces, causing them to spend less on discretionary products and services that are not a priority. International business firms cannot control the global economy, but spotting threats and opportunities is vital for the success of any company operating in foreign environments.

Political and Legal – Political factors may incorporate adaptations in laws, rules, and regulations resulting from the government. These affect how a foreign business can operate within the market and economy. Some examples include trade tariff policies and tax policies. Legal factors incorporate laws and regulations that influence how international companies conduct themselves. Differences in local government policies, laws, and regulations can considerably affect international business. Think of the tobacco industry, which, since the 1950s, international and national companies are required to place warning labels on their packages and are not allowed to advertise on television, not to mention that smokers are restricted to where they can smoke legally.

Technological – Technological factors can affect correlated businesses in any market and their ability to execute well in that market. As newer technological advancements supersede some technologies, it drastically affects the firm's ability to use (or sell!) obsolete technologies. Artificial intelligence (AI), intelligent internet searches through web scrapers and machine learning (ML) algorithms, and other high-tech processes are all kinds of technology that have been at the forefront of many firms engaged in international business.

Global – Environmental factors influence international business operations along the supply chain. Changes in global climate, such as global warming, natural disasters, such as tsunamis in Japan and earthquakes in Indonesia, or biological disasters, such as the COVID-19 pandemic of 2019, will always affect the alternatives international business must make about how it operates.

Social – Sociocultural factors influence how firms present themselves and advertise their products to consumers. Since these factors may include demographics and cultural tendencies, firms will try to position themselves favorably to entice their target audience based on these factors.

Competitive – When firms enter a new market, they must compete against well-established, more experienced businesses in the same industry. Unless the firm offers a unique product/service, competition is inevitable. And even if the firm's offering is unique, it is just a matter of time before new competitors enter the market, trying to slice away the firm's consumers.

Internal Forces

Finances – Even in an exceptional economy, insufficient financial resources and capital can be challenging for firms operating in foreign markets. For instance, limited cash resources can affect the number of employees a firm can hire abroad, the quality of office equipment and technologies, and the amount of advertising it can buy. International business expansion can be capital-intensive. If the firm has the necessary investment requirements, it can be more flexible in developing and expanding abroad in the new market and enduring any international economic downturns.

Marketing/sales – An internal marketing environment should be a factor the firm controls. The primary resources to be considered include the Five M's: Manpower, Materials, Machinery, Minutes, and Money:

1. Manpower is often referred to as workforce or staff.
2. Materials refer to marketing processes, including the marketing supply chain and the marketing assets that sustain the firm's marketing strategy.
3. Machinery is the system utilized to support the firm's operations and marketing activities. This may include workspace applications and software, such as your Customer Relationship Management (CRM) and digital marketing applications.
4. Minutes or time is an asset directly influenced by the firm's marketing planning, strategy, and processes.
5. Money: While the firm may not control all aspects of a marketing campaign budget, it does control how it uses it. Firms that leverage marketing budget instruments have a better chance of understanding how to get the most from their budgets.

Management – Unless the international firm is a one-person entity (a few born-global can be), employees can be essential to the firm's internal environment. Both domestic and international employees must be proficient at their jobs. Managers must be skilled at managing a multicultural staff and supervising different internal environment elements, as even if everyone's competent and qualified, internal politics and contentions can wreck a well-managed firm.

Operations – As discussed earlier in this section, the firm's internal culture consists of the values, mindsets, and prerogatives employees live by. For instance, an aggressive and competitive culture where every worker competes with each other produces a distinct environment compared to a firm that underscores cooperation and teamwork. Commonly, a firm's culture streams from the top, upper management, down through the firm's ranks. The firm's personnel tend to infer values based on the kind of individuals hired, dispensed, or promoted.

Research and development – In such a competitive global marketplace undergoing a digital business transformation for the past decade, international business firms will find it hard to compete abroad unless they invest in R&D and continue to develop new ideas and technologies to fuel their overall success continuously. Fundamentally, R&D must be able to foster innovations and introduce new things into international business offerings. Innovative international firms should be able to bring about productivity, cost reduction, increased competitiveness, and brand value. Firms that fail to invest in innovation will undoubtedly encounter the risks of relinquishing market share to other competitors, underlying profit loss, and losing key staff.

Porter's Diamond Model: A Word About Competitive Advantage

As illustrated in Figure 1.10, Porter's diamond model is a much-adopted tool for this purpose. The Porter Diamond Model is a strategic economic model that attempts to explain why one nation-state is more successful than another for a particular industry. A country's surface features significantly contribute to the economic, cultural, political, and social differences between and within nations. Inland waterways and outlets to the sea are vital to a country's economy.

Porter's diamond is a diamond-shaped framework that describes why distinct industries in a country become internationally competitive while those in other nations do not. This framework examines the company's strategy, structure/rivalry, factors, demand conditions, and related and supporting industries. The model was first published in 1990 in Porter's book, *The Competitive Advantage of Nations.*

The traditional economic approach implies that land, labor, population size and natural resources are critical elements in a country's ability to gain a competitive advantage. However, Porter asserted that this measure was a relatively passive summary of economic potential and that far from creating sustained growth, the abovementioned

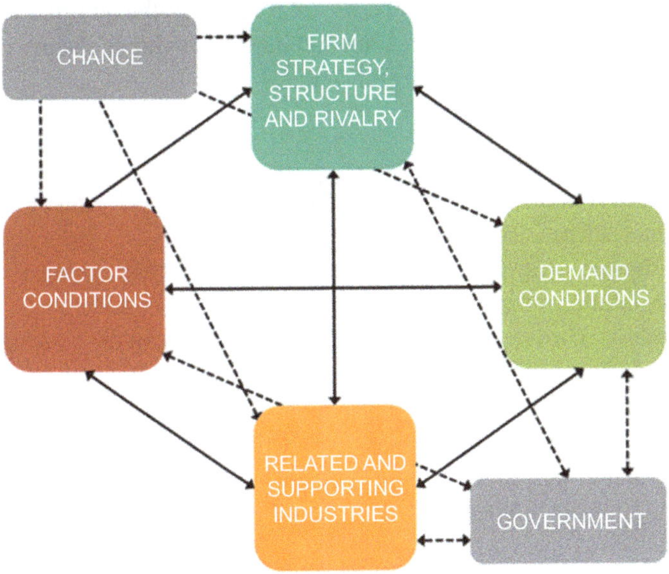

Figure 1.10: The Porter Diamond Model.

factors could *undermine* potential competitive advantage. Instead, he suggested that four other factors could accurately foretell whether a country produced organizations that were competitive enough on the international landscape.

The following are the four characteristics of Porter's diamond model:

1. Firm strategy, structure, and rivalry – This feature encompasses how organizations are structured and managed. It also contains a firm's goals and the existence of competitive rivalries, if appropriate. Rivalry is significant because it compels firms to innovate, equipping them for the international markets. For instance, German auto manufacturers Mercedes-Benz, BMW, and Audi would not have become globally successful without the intense competition they face inside their native Germany.
2. Factor conditions – Factor requirements are more fundamental and refer to unskillful labor, natural resources, and infrastructure. Porter claimed that more advanced factor conditions, such as skilled and specialist knowledge and access to capital, were more critical to competitive advantage.
3. Demand conditions – Demand conditions refer to the level of demand in the industry's home market. Demand produces competition, which in turn develops innovation. Specific demand conditions may comprise market size and sophistication.
4. Interconnected and supporting industries – Most large companies are only as thriving as their supply chains. Undoubtedly, most rely on collaborations and good connections with suppliers to accomplish cost savings transferred to customers. Countries with high concentrations of large, innovative businesses that function close to each other facilitate the spread of innovation. A good example is

companies in Silicon Valley, California, or the RT 128 corridor in the outskirts of Boston, Massachusetts, which promotes creation and innovation due to the proximity of innovative and often supportive organizations.

Criticisms of Porter's Diamond Model

Given that Porter's diamond assesses competition in a relatively broad context of countries, there has been criticism, including:

- **Contradictory evidence** – a large amount of evidence indicates that a country's competitiveness has multiple exogenous forces that Porter did not consider.
- **Industry selectiveness** – Porter's initial investigation concentrated on the banking sector, consultancy companies, and manufacturers. Some IB scholars have challenged whether the framework is relevant enough to the numerous large and influential transnational services companies, such as KFC, McDonald's, and Burger King.
- **Scope** – When the model was conceived in the 1990s, it contained just ten advanced economies. Thus, its applicability has been restricted to emerging and frontier economies.

Primary Factors Impacting International Business and Trade

Several scholars (Pacek and Thorniley, 2007; Estrin et al., 2019) have identified an exhaustive range of factors contributing to international business and trade failure, par-

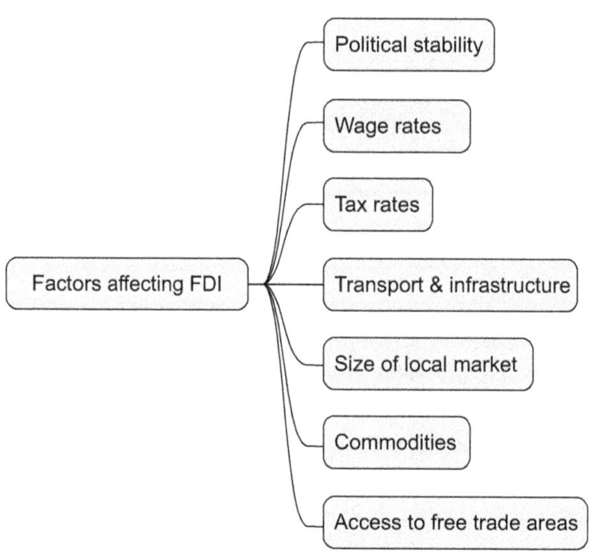

Figure 1.11: Factors affecting FDI in a foreign market.

ticularly in more lucrative emerging markets. These factors are often correlated to foreign direct investments (FDI) and are depicted in Figure 1.11.

Other important factors include a lack of strategy development and proper knowledge regarding the international target market. These factors may be divided into external and internal factors, and almost all are related to strategic and leadership issues:

- Leaders fail to consider international markets as an integral part of a strategy and acknowledge that such markets need to be approached with a distinct set of criteria for judging progress and success.
- Upper management fails to commit sufficient resources to establish and grow businesses abroad or acknowledge that it is never a short-term affair.
- Companies, when internationalizing, fail to appoint a country manager for the foreign markets and often assign this responsibility to an international manager responsible for markets in developed and emerging countries. The problem with this is that operational approaches are distinct in each market.
- Companies fail to understand that business is driven by heads of regions and business units rather than by heads of functional areas. While the former focuses on and appreciates international markets, the latter tends to be interested in developed markets.
- Companies do not acknowledge that international markets operate under distinct business models and structures and often merely transfer practices tested in other global markets without considering adaptation.
- Many companies' board members have limited diversity in terms of culture and ethnic background and do not develop sufficient appreciation for the peculiarities of emerging markets.
- Multinational corporations (MNCs) underestimate the potential and often early competition from smaller multinational enterprises (MNEs) and other international and domestic companies (i.e., born-global or new international ventures), thus never accepting that they may be destined as a follower in emerging markets.
- Economic and political crises also exist in emerging markets, significantly impacting business performance. Top managers need to understand this and be prepared to adapt and introduce new tactics rather than change strategy, which, despite having short-term success, tends to be the wrong approach in the long term.
- Companies get alarmed by short-term slippages and cut costs to attain favorable temporary results, yet this is likely to have a structural impact on strategy implementation and long-term effects.
- Companies set unrealistic targets to achieve, which leave managers with limited maneuvering space and short-lived careers.
- Companies fail to recognize that entering the market early is fundamental to establishing networks, developing brands, and learning the larger context from which it will operate.
- Senior leaders fail to recognize that developing a network of reliable contacts often requires establishing friendships with locals abroad, which requires time and visibility in emerging markets.

- Companies fail to empower regional and country managers and delegate decision-making power to local managers.
- Foreign companies fail to recognize that emerging markets are more price-sensitive than those in advanced economies and often stick to their pricing structures instead of adapting to local sensitivities.
- International firms fail to recognize that their product portfolio is not tailored to emergent markets' lower and middle segments and do not develop context-oriented innovations.
- Foreign companies underestimate the competition from local companies in emergent markets. Local companies understand local markets better than anyone, sometimes employ dubious practices, and often have the support of local governments.
- One of the most significant obstacles foreign companies face may be the unwillingness to change long-standing business practices.
- Another challenge is appointing senior managers unfamiliar with the local market, culture, and language in emerging countries.
- Multinationals that focus too much on the larger emerging markets, such as the former BRICS countries (Brazil, Russia, India, China, and South Africa), and as of January 2024, the expanded one including Egypt, Ethiopia, Iran, Saudi Arabia, and the United Arab Emirates, may neglect more minor needs and miss better-suited opportunities.
- Demand is volatile and unpredictable in emergent markets, which often expect reliable market information, which may discourage multinationals.

The failure factors are numerous and diverse, but it all boils down to inadequate market entry preparation. Preparation requires companies to continuously research the external environment and know how to use internal resources to take advantage of opportunities. Hence, a preliminary audit focusing on external and internal factors is essential. The external factors may be examined by posing questions concerning the market, the political environment, the economic environment, and the business environment, as depicted in Tables 1.3. and 1.4.

Table 1.3: External factors and sample questions.

	Understanding the market
Market potential	– How large and wealthy is the market? – Is there an unsatisfied demand for the product/service?
Understanding local consumers/ customers	– Who are the consumers/customers? What are their characteristics? – How do consumers make their decisions?

Table 1.3 (continued)

Reaching the consumer/customer Competition	– How difficult/easy is it to reach potential consumers/customers? – How do competitors and non-competitors reach their customers? – Which competitors are already operating in the market? – How strong are these competitors?
Lessons learned by noncompetitors	– What do noncompetitors say about the business environment in the country? – What have been the most significant obstacles to successful operations?
Local culture	– What aspects of local culture are relevant to running a successful business?
	Understanding the political and economic environment
Economic outlook	– How sustainable is economic growth? – What is driving economic growth?
Political outlook	– What is the level of political risk, and how will or might it affect the business?
Government policies	– Does the government allow a level playing field? – Is the government in the hands of local lobbies?
	Understanding the business environment
Finance	– Is it possible to finance operations locally? – What access do customers/consumers have to finance?
Labor market	– What are the wage/salary rates for the employees who will be needed? – What are the most effective ways of recruiting local employees?
	Understanding the business environment
Taxation	– What are the current levels of taxation? – What is the outlook for tax incentives?
Legal environment	– How effective and efficient is the local judiciary? – Is there any hope that the legal system will improve?
Bureaucratic obstacles to business	– What are the most common bureaucratic obstacles for business? – How easy or difficult is setting up a business in the country?
Crime and corruption	– Is crime a problem for business? – What is the level of corruption?
Infrastructure	– What is the quality of local transport infrastructure? – And telecommunications?
Foreign trade environment	– Is the country a WTO member? – Does it belong to any trading blocs or regional free-trade areas?
Cost of building a business and brand	– How expensive is it to build a brand? – How much time will it take to do what is necessary to get the business? off the ground?

Table 1.4: Internal factors and sample questions.

Resources	– How much time and money will be required? – Is the CEO committed to supporting business development and providing necessary resources? And the senior managers? – What human resources are needed?
Products	– Is the product portfolio right for the market? – Will investment be available for developing new products?
Organization	– Will existing internal processes and operational practices help or hinder what is planned? – What existing capabilities can be drawn?
Risks	– Can the risks that have been identified be managed? – How would the entry be financed?

Similarly, the internal factors must inquire about resources, products, organization, and risks, as depicted in Table 1.4. After a preliminary external and internal audit, managers must prepare a business proposal describing what to do, how, when, and the resources required. Businesses must then ask themselves whether similar or better opportunities exist in other emerging markets. How, then, can we compare the potential of different emerging markets?

Foreign Business Investment Opportunities and Challenges

As discussed throughout this first chapter, international business, especially in emerging markets, has risen rapidly over the past two decades. During such a period, the BRICS powered the high growth rate in emerging market economies, volatility notwithstanding. The rally, however, has started to trickle down in recent years and came to a screeching halt around 2019 with the COVID-19 global pandemic, mainly due to fears of the U.S. Federal Reserve tapering the stimulus and the slowdown of the Chinese economy.

However, it is essential to note that several investment opportunities still exist in emerging markets, as many of these countries entered the global crisis with varying economic maturity levels and conditions. Thus, they were impacted by the global financial crisis of 2007/08, and now the post-COVID pandemic and breakdown of the worldwide supply chain crisis of 2020/22 to diverse degrees. Some were already dealing with the beginnings of their internal economic crisis associated with these multi-global crises, not to mention the end of unsustainable credit booms or fiscal policies, which left high levels of debt caused mainly by unhedged foreign currency exchange. Other emerging countries were just caught up in the crash.

Latest World Economic Outlook Growth Projections

(real GDP, annual percent change)	ESTIMATE 2021	PROJECTIONS 2022	2023
World Output	5.9	4.4	3.8
Advanced Economies	5.0	3.9	2.6
United States	5.6	4.0	2.6
Euro Area	5.2	3.9	2.5
Germany	2.7	3.8	2.5
France	6.7	3.5	1.8
Italy	6.2	3.8	2.2
Spain	4.9	5.8	3.8
Japan	1.6	3.3	1.8
United Kingdom	7.2	4.7	2.3
Canada	4.7	4.1	2.8
Other Advanced Economies	4.7	3.6	2.9
Emerging Market and Developing Economies	6.5	4.8	4.7
Emerging and Developing Asia	7.2	5.9	5.8
China	8.1	4.8	5.2
India	9.0	9.0	7.1
ASEAN-5	3.1	5.6	6.0
Emerging and Developing Europe	6.5	3.5	2.9
Russia	4.5	2.8	2.1
Latin America and the Caribbean	6.8	2.4	2.6
Brazil	4.7	0.3	1.6
Mexico	5.3	2.8	2.7
Middle East and Central Asia	4.2	4.3	3.6
Saudi Arabia	2.9	4.8	2.8
Sub-Saharan Africa	4.0	3.7	4.0
Nigeria	3.0	2.7	2.7
South Africa	4.6	1.9	1.4
Memorandum			
Emerging Market and Middle-Income Economies	6.8	4.8	4.6
Low-Income Developing Countries	3.1	5.3	5.5

Figure 1.12: World economic outlook growth projections. (SOURCE: IMF, World Economic Outlook Update, January 2022).
Note: For India, data and forecasts are presented on a fiscal year basis, with FY 2021/2022 starting in April 2021. For the January 2022 WEO Update, India's growth projections are 8.7 percent in 2022 and 6.6 percent in 2023 based on calendar year. For India the impact of the Omicron variant is captured in the column for 2021 in the table.

Emerging markets are not in "crisis." Their growth has outpaced that of the United States, Europe, and Japan, as shown in Figure 1.12. Many other emerging markets – such as the "frontier" states – are performing very well economically and deserve investment attention, as projections for 2023 show 4.7 percent growth compared to 2.6 percent for advanced economies and 3.8 percent for the world's output. Progress, however, has not been across the board, with monetary and fiscal policies, FDI flow imbalances, and stock vulnerabilities varying widely across these emerging economies, especially after COVID-19 broke out in 2019.

Despite the slowdown of leading emerging markets, these breeds of countries, often referred to as "frontier" markets due to their small, unpopular, and illiquid economies, are also prone to fast growth, especially on the African continent. Although these countries have not yet joined the global investment community, they have already joined the global economic community. Figure 1.13 shows an impressive performance of Africa's international tourist receipt per capita, adjusted for COVID-19!

Frontier markets are sometimes referred to as "pre-emerging markets." These are countries with equity markets that are less established, such as Bangladesh, Benin, Bosnia and Herzegovina, Botswana, Bulgaria, Burkina Faso, Côte d'Ivoire, and Croatia, as of 2021 data from Morgan Stanley Country Index (MSCI). They tend to be characterized by lower market capitalization, less liquidity, and, in some cases, earlier stages of economic development. However, such markets are not just growth markets in distant places. They represent more than 1.2 billion people. These emerging and frontier countries are also increasing demands on the world's resources as they become intensive consumers of essential commodities to support their infrastructure development and manufacturing. In the 1950s, the U.S. Interstate Highway System was built, and China is building its equivalent now. This trend is echoed in railway construction, power plant construction, and new building and bridge construction. It is not just China either. Developing countries around the world are undertaking such projects.

International Trade Theories

Global competition continues to increase at a rapid pace. The massive increase in imports due to the reduction in trade barriers, coupled with increased foreign investment, means that all firms face competitors from any place in the world. This growing internationalization of business requires managers to gain a global business perspective through experience and education. International trade and foreign direct investment have grown dramatically over the last four decades. The traditional approach to international involvement began with exporting, setting up foreign sales companies, and finally establishing foreign production facilities where the sales volume warranted. Increasingly, because countries have liberalized trade restrictions and information technology has made communication instantaneous, companies are becoming involved in trade and foreign direct investment for many reasons. Exchange rates and currency

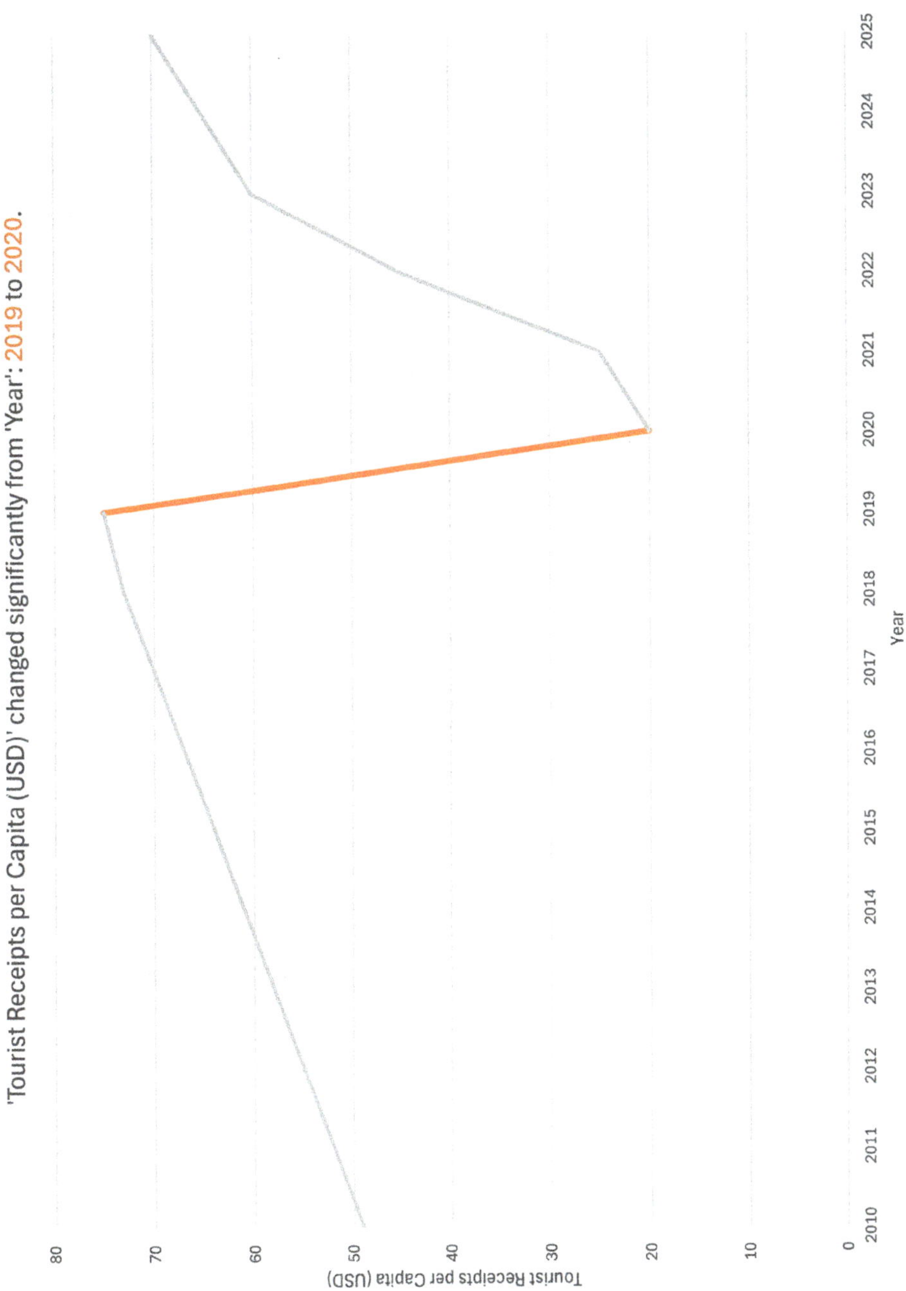

Figure 1.13: Africa's international tourist receipt per capita, adjusted for COVID-19. (SOURCE: Statista, UNWTO, WB, 2022).

devaluations play a crucial role in the direction of trade flows and directly impact the generation of profits from global markets.

Trade generally means exchanging goods and services between two individuals or entities. Individuals or corporations trade because they feel that they profit from the deal. International trade is the exchange between individuals or entities in two or various nations. While this may sound very simple, much theory, policy, and business strategy constitute international trade.

As illustrated in Figure 1.14, international trade theories attempt to explain why nations trade with each other. Mercantilists (1550 to 1800 and perhaps ongoing) believed that trade should be a vehicle for accumulating gold. Displeased with mercantilist ideas, Adam Smith showed that a nation could acquire what it does not produce by employing free, unregulated trade. A nation could gain the most by producing only goods it could make with less labor than other nations. David Ricardo, a British economist in 1817, carried Smith's argument a step further by proving that a country that was less efficient in the production of all goods could still gain from trade by exporting those products in which it was less inefficient.

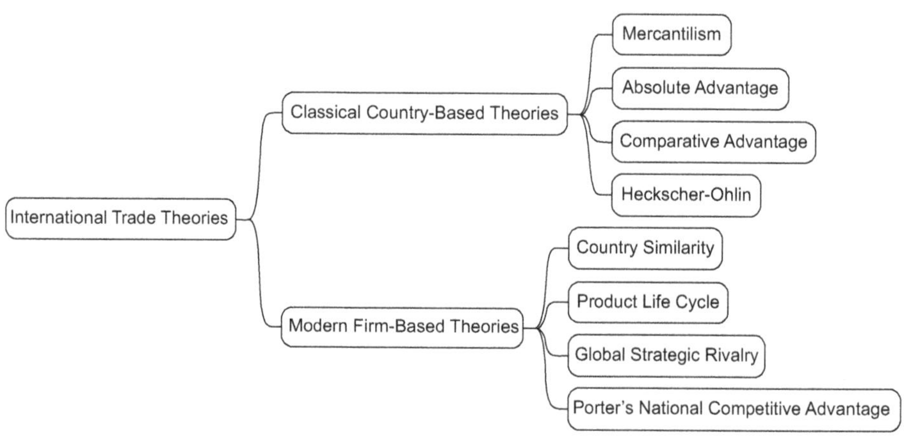

Figure 1.14: Main international trade theories.

International investment theory attempts to explain why foreign direct investment occurs. Product and factor market imperfections provide firms primarily from oligopolistic industries with advantages not open to indigenous companies. The international product life cycle helps explain global investment and trade direction. Some companies follow the industry leader overseas, and the tendency for European firms to invest in the United States and vice versa seems to indicate that this cross-investment is done for defensive reasons. The internalization theory states that international firms will seek to invest in a foreign subsidiary rather than license their superior knowledge to receive a better return on investment used to produce knowledge. Two financially based explanations for foreign direct investment (FDI) are:

1. Foreign exchange market imperfections resulting in overvalued and undervalued currencies may attract investors from nations with overvalued currencies to countries with undervalued currencies and
2. The portfolio theory postulates that international operations are made for risk diversification.

Although theories argue for free trade among nations, tariff and non-tariff barriers to trade still exist. Various arguments are given for their existence, such as the necessity to protect local industry from cheap foreign labor, to protect new initiatives until they are mature, and to ensure that a country will have the needed defense industries. Interestingly, although new trading and investment patterns are emerging, developed nations tend to trade with and invest primarily in other developed nations and less in developing countries.

Main International Trade Theories

In recent centuries, economists have concentrated on understanding and elucidating trade patterns. Thomas Friedman, the international business professor at Brandeis University and author of *The World is Flat*, breaks up history into three stages: from 1492 to 1800, which he called Globalization 1.0; from 1800 to 2000, the 2.0 version; and from 2000 to the present, the 3.0 version of globalization. In Globalization 1.0, he argued, nations dominated global expansion, while in version 2.0, MNCs came to prominence and drove international trade development. Today, the era of Globalization 3.0 is driven by technology. But, to best appreciate and understand how contemporary global trade has developed, it's vital to comprehend how nations traded with each other historically. Over the centuries, economists have developed theories to describe international trade mechanisms. The main historical ideas are called *classical* and are from a nation or nation-based stance. By the mid-twentieth century, these theories began to pivot to describe international trade from an enterprise rather than a nation's viewpoint. These theories are referred to as contemporary and are enterprise-based. Both classical and modern categories consist of several international theories discussed below.

Mercantilism

Mercantilism, one of the earliest endeavors to develop an economic theory, was created in the 16th century. Its premise was that a country's wealth was determined by the amount of its gold and silver holdings. Mercantilists believed that a nation should expand its holdings of gold and silver by encouraging exports and discouraging imports. If countries bought more from your country (exports), they would also sell to your country (imports), and then they would have to compensate your country for the difference in gold and silver. Any country engaged in international trade would want to have a trade surplus. In other words, they export more than they import and have credit with their trading nation, avoiding a trade deficit.

Mercantilism flourished between the 1500s and late 1800s with the rise of new nation-states, as nations wanted to strengthen their global stand by building larger armies and national institutions. Many of these new nations boosted exports by imposing restrictions on imports, a strategy known as protectionism, much in use to this date. As illustrated in Figure 1.15, by increasing exports and trade, rulers and monarchs of these nations could accumulate more gold and wealth for their countries. Many nations grew their wealth by exploiting their colonies, or territories, worldwide to control more trade and amass more riches. Take the British colonial empire as an example, which sought to increase its wealth through raw materials from far distant places, from what is now India and the Americas. The Netherlands, France, Spain, and Portugal successfully built large colonial empires that generated extensive wealth for their governing nations.

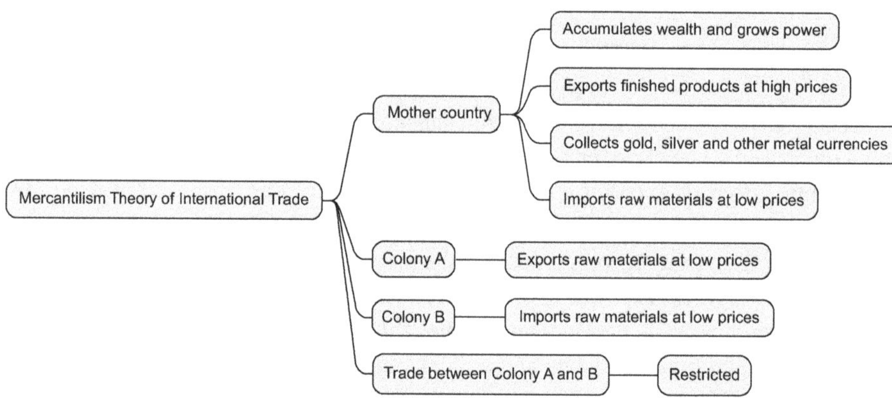

Figure 1.15: Mercantilism theory of international trade.

Although mercantilism is considered one of the oldest trade theories, many nations still embrace its tenets today. China, Japan, Taiwan, Singapore, and, to some extent, Germany still prefer exports. They dissuade imports through neo-mercantilism, in which the nations foster a blend of protectionist policies, restrictions on trade, and domestic industry-based subsidies. Most countries, at some point, have implemented some form of protectionist policy to guard critical industries in their domestic economy. Although export-oriented corporations tend to support protectionist policies that benefit their sector, protectionism negatively impacts others. Taxpayers, for instance, pay for government subsidies of select exports through higher taxes. However, import restrictions tend to increase consumer prices, which results in paying much more for foreign products and services. Free-trade proponents often underscore the benefits of free trade to all parties involved in international trade. Mercantilist, protectionist policies, however, only favor select industries, often at the expense of consumers and other corporations across the industry, domestically and internationally.

Absolute Advantage

Adam Smith challenged the leading mercantile theory in his book, *The Wealth of Nations*, published in 1776. He proposed a new trade theory dubbed *absolute advantage*, which focused on a country's capability to produce a good more efficiently than another. He argued that government intervention or regulations should not control or regulate trade between nations. He argued that trade must flow naturally according to the international market and trade forces.

Countries would develop efficiencies by specializing because their labor force could become better skilled and proficient by doing the same activities. As illustrated in Figure 1.16, production could become more efficient because there would be a motivation to develop faster and better production techniques to increase specialization. Smith's theory reasoned that people in both countries would benefit from increased efficiencies, and trade could be encouraged. Smith also argued that a nation's wealth should not be assessed based on how much gold and silver it holds, but by the living standards of its citizens instead.

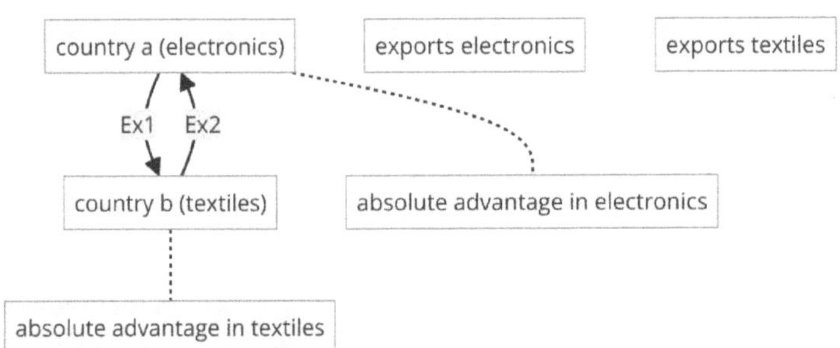

Figure 1.16: Absolute advantage theory of international trade.

Comparative Advantage

The absolute advantage theory challenged some nations, calling for better means of production and allowing them advantages in *many* areas. To address these challenges, Ricardo proposed the theory of comparative advantage. He argued that even if Country A had the absolute advantage in producing *both* products, specialization, and trade could still occur between the two countries. Comparative advantage appears when a country cannot make a product more efficiently than another, as illustrated in Figure 1.17. But it may be able to produce that product much better and more efficiently than other goods. The differentiator between these theories is very subtle. The comparative advantage focuses on the *relative productivity differences*, while the *absolute advantage* focuses on the *absolute productivity*.

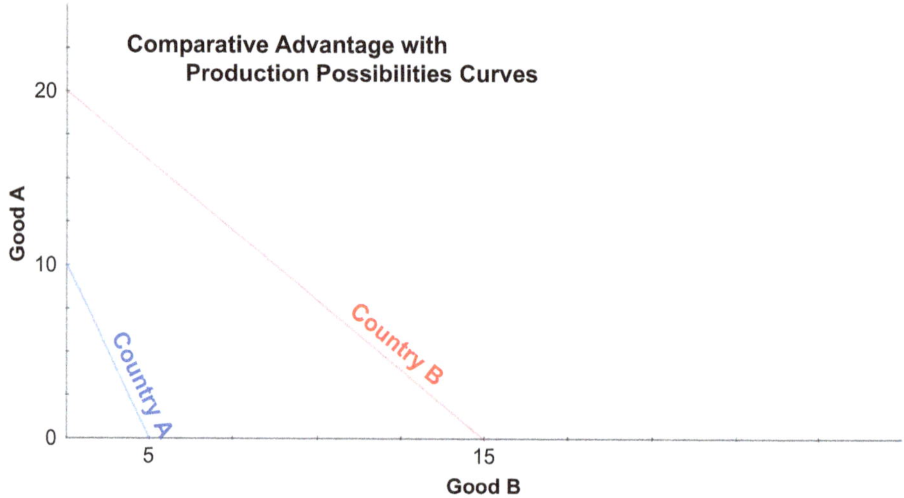

Figure 1.17: Comparative advantage theory of international trade.

Factor Proportions Theory

Smith's and Ricardo's theories did not assist nations in deciding which products could give a country an advantage. Both approaches believed that a free and open international market could lead governments and producers to determine which goods they would be able to produce more efficiently. The Swedish economists Eli Heckscher and Bertil Ohlin, in the early 1900s, began to investigate how a nation could develop a comparative advantage through the development of products adopting factors widely available in the country. Heckscher and Ohlin's theory was based on domestic production factors, including but not limited to land, capital, and labor, which offered the necessary investments in plants, equipment, and supplies. They argued that the cost of any factor or resource was a function of supply and demand. Factors in plentiful supply relative to market would be cheaper; factors in great demand relative to supply would be more expensive.

Their theory also called the *factor proportions theory,* stated that nations could produce and export goods that demanded resources or factors that were in plentiful supply and widely available, enabling cheaper production factors. In contrast, as illustrated in Figure 1.18, countries would import goods that needed resources in short supply but with higher demand. China, Vietnam, Bangladesh, India, and many other Southeast Asian countries (and, more recently, some African countries) are home to cheap, large pools of labor, often becoming the destination of choice for labor-intensive industries like textiles and garments.

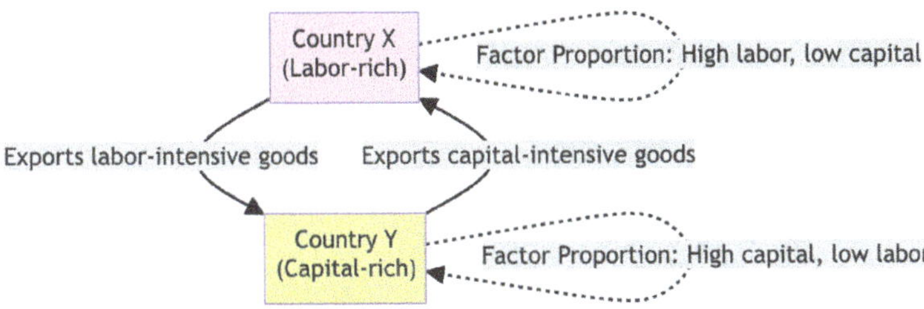

Figure 1.18: Factor proportions theory of international trade.

Firm-Based Trade Theories

In contrast to classical, nation-based trade theories, firm-based theories emerged after World War II. It was built in significant part by business professors, not economists. These firm-based theories evolved with the growth of MNCs. The country-based theories could not sufficiently address the expansion of either MNCs' international trade within the same industry. Japan, for instance, exports Toyota vehicles to Germany and imports Mercedes-Benz automobiles from Germany. Firm-based theories include other product and service factors in understanding trade flows, including brand and customer loyalty, technology, and quality.

The Theory of Global Strategic Rivalry

The theory of global strategic rivalry was developed in the 1980s based on research by economists Paul Krugman and Kelvin Lancaster. Focused on MNCs, their theory called for these international firms to gain a competitive advantage over other multinationals. These MNCs, or MNEs, should assume competition will always be at play in their industries. To succeed, these international companies would have to develop competitive advantages, as illustrated in Figure 1.19.

In such a case, Krugman and Lancaster argued that MNCs/MNEs needed to create sustainable competitive advantages, also known as the industry's entry barriers to other competitors. Barriers to entry may adopt many forms, but the following are some of the leading strategies these companies may adopt to optimize their competitive advantage:

- Investment in research and development (R&D),
- Development and ownership of intellectual property (IP) rights,
- Fostering economies of scale,
- Adoption of unique business processes or methods and
- Implement control of resources or favorable access to raw materials.

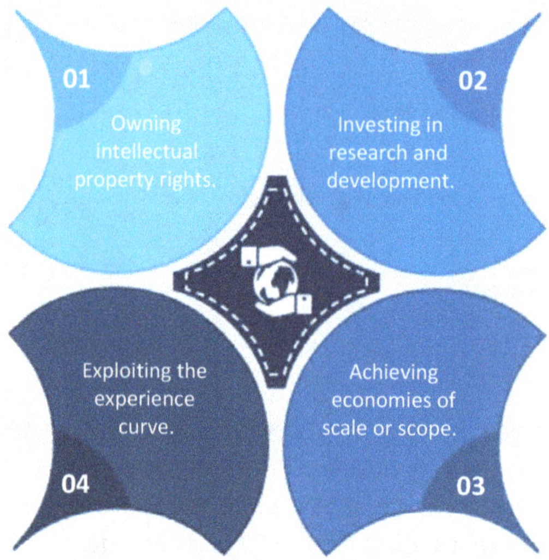

Figure 1.19: Theory of global strategic rivalry.

Exploring the Convergence of International Business and Global Sustainability: ESG Factors

The connection between international business practices and global sustainability is more noticeable in today's global market. This market is characterized by merging economic goals and the necessity for environmental stewardship, social responsibility, and governance (ESG) excellence.

Environmental Stewardship: The Non-negotiable of International Expansion

In international business, environmental factors are now crucial aspects of strategic planning and operational execution rather than being seen as minor concerns. Companies engaged in international business and investments are increasingly expected to take responsibility for their ecological footprint, necessitating a thorough integration of sustainable practices. This shift is motivated by regulations and a strategic initiative to align with the growing consumer demand for environmentally friendly products and services. To enter international markets, companies must adopt tactics that minimize environmental damage, back renewable energy, and uphold sustainable resource usage, making ecological accountability imperative for worldwide prosperity and longevity. It is essential to prioritize environmental stewardship when expanding globally, with no room for compromise.

Environmental factors in global trade have shifted from minor issues to crucial aspects in planning and daily operations. Businesses involved in international trade and investments face heightened scrutiny of their environmental impact, highlighting the importance of fully incorporating sustainable practices. This change results from regulatory requirements and a strategic shift to meet the increasing consumer desire for environmentally friendly products and services. To succeed in global markets, companies must implement strategies that reduce environmental harm, support renewable energy use, and guarantee sustainable resource utilization, highlighting the significance of ecological accountability in worldwide competitiveness and flexibility.

Social Responsibility: Bridging Global Operations and Local Impact

The increasing presence of international and multinational companies worldwide highlights the significance of social accountability, especially in how businesses interact with their employees, suppliers, and the local communities where they are based. A nuanced understanding of cultural differences, labor standards, and socioeconomic contexts of different markets is required in international business. Companies need to work hard to improve the well-being of local communities, promote fair labor practices, and support inclusive growth, showing a dedication to social equality beyond international boundaries. This strategy reduces the dangers linked to social conflict and fosters a favorable brand reputation and customer loyalty worldwide.

Governance: The Keystone of Sustainable International Ventures

Effective governance management is essential for effectively navigating the complexities of global businesses. As companies venture into foreign markets, they encounter a mix of regulatory landscapes, legal structures, and governance criteria. Adhering to stringent governance standards, including transparency, accountability, and ethical practices, is crucial for establishing and maintaining investor confidence and achieving sustainable long-term growth. Furthermore, effective governance frameworks are essential in managing the risks associated with international business activities, including compliance with global trade regulations, anti-corruption measures, and protecting intellectual property rights.

Businesses expanding abroad face many challenges, from cultural and language barriers to geopolitical and economic uncertainties. Integrating ESG principles into the core strategy of international business operations offers a pathway to address these challenges holistically. ESG-focused strategies enable firms to:

- Enhance resilience against global market volatilities through sustainable practices that anticipate environmental risks and regulatory changes.
- Build more robust, more equitable relationships with international partners and local communities, improving social license to operate.
- Establish governance structures that foster transparency, innovation, and adaptability in complex global dynamics.

Understanding the strategic importance of ESG for gaining a competitive edge in the global market should be based on international trade theories and business strategies. In a time when global rivalry involves more than just cost and productivity but also sustainability and ethical behavior, ESG elements become crucial distinguishing factors. Businesses that actively incorporate ESG principles into their global business models can more successfully manage the complexities of the international market, opening opportunities for growth, creativity, and leadership in sustainability.

The coming together of global sustainability and international business marks a crucial change in the worldwide economic scene. When companies expand internationally, incorporating environmental stewardship, social responsibility, and strong governance practices is essential for promoting sustainable growth, resilience, and a competitive edge. In the end, the direction of global business in the future will depend on multinational companies working together to promote sustainability, viewing it not only as a legal obligation or ethical necessity but as a key factor driving innovation, creating value, and achieving long-term success in the global market.

Discussion Questions

1. **Discuss the role of cultural sensitivity in international business. How can a lack of cultural understanding impact a company's global operations? Provide examples from the chapter.**

Multiple-Choice Questions

2. **Which of the following is NOT listed as an internal force impacting international business?**
   A) Currency exchange rates
   B) Marketing and sales strategies
   C) Research and development
   D) Management and operations

3. **According to the chapter, what is one of the major challenges faced by international businesses when managing global teams?**
   A) Finding sufficient investment
   B) Language and cultural barriers
   C) Adapting to local technological standards
   D) Implementing domestic marketing strategies internationally

4. **Political and legal factors do not significantly influence international business operations. True or False?**

5. **Effective governance and adherence to global regulations are crucial for international businesses to gain investor confidence and achieve sustainable growth. True or False?**

Recommended Readings

Chukwu, E., Adu-Baah, A., Niaz, M., Nwagwu, U., & Chukwu, M. U. (2023). Navigating ethical supply chains: the intersection of diplomatic management and theological ethics. *International Journal of Multidisciplinary Sciences and Arts*, 2(1), 127–139.

Joel, O. S., Oyewole, A. T., Odunaiya, O. G., & Soyombo, O. T. (2024). Navigating the digital transformation journey: strategies for startup growth and innovation in the digital era. *International Journal of Management & Entrepreneurship Research*, 6(3), 697–706.

Olutimehin, D. O., Ofodile, O. C., Ejibe, I., & Oyewole, A. (2024). Developing a strategic partnership model for enhanced performance in emerging markets. *International Journal of Management & Entrepreneurship Research*, 6(3), 806–814.

Sun, P., Doh, J. P., Rajwani, T., & Siegel, D. (2021). Navigating cross-border institutional complexity: A review and assessment of multinational nonmarket strategy research. *Journal of International Business Studies*, 52(9), 1818–1853.

Tasheva, S., & Nielsen, B. B. (2022). The role of global dynamic managerial capability in the pursuit of international strategy and superior performance. *Journal of International Business Studies*, 53(4), 689–708.

Chapter 2
Social Cultural Forces, Natural Resources, and Sustainability

Learning Objectives

- Understand the importance of culture in international business
- Assess how culture affects business functions
- Evaluate leading culture frameworks
- Appreciate strategies when doing business across cultures
- Develop awareness of sustainability in international business
- Understand strategies for measuring sustainability
- Develop awareness of ESG and DEI considerations

Overview

You might ask why to incorporate economic, socioeconomic, and geopolitical forces in studying international business. What do location, culture, customs, language, or regional positioning have to do with it? Two parts to the answer need to be contemplated before and then addressed. Here is the first, and it is a sign of something that most individuals and businesses still need to get: You are in international business whether you or your company is large or small or does not sell a single product to another country!

Suppose you ask who the competitors are in the marketplace, no doubt. In that case, there is no need to get too far down the list before names of foreign companies and national companies selling a competitive foreign good/service appear. It is interesting to view large and small firms as composites of power and resources competing for their share and position in the global marketplace, which has become increasingly international throughout the past two decades. Unfortunately, many firms do not appreciate the extent to which the world's markets have been globalized, and they confuse importing and exporting activities with international business.

Unsuspecting domestic firms who do not consider themselves in international business are apt to find that foreign intruders are prepared to allocate substantial resources and use global strategies to steal market space. Undoubtedly, you can recall that the problem encountered by the Big Three automakers during the 1970s was not their international sales. It was a lack of understanding about how to compete against their Japanese competition! As the pace of internationalization escalates, even small companies untrained in the complexities of the international marketplace will find it increasingly difficult to survive.

https://doi.org/10.1515/9783111510286-002

Enterprises go abroad either to increase profits and sales or to protect them from being eroded by competition. To increase profits and sales, they may enter new markets, go to markets that promise to help them obtain greater profits, or enter new markets to test them. The competitive forces are motivated to protect the home market, attack competition in their home market, protect their foreign markets, guarantee the supply of raw materials for geographic diversification, and satisfy management's desire. In summary, enterprises face several social-cultural, geopolitical, and economic forces when internationalizing, not to mention natural resources and sustainability challenges. In this chapter, we will focus more on understanding the progression of multiple internationalization theories and how they were all influenced by the social-cultural and other factors listed above.

The Importance of Culture in International Business

Although various definitions exist, culture refers to a set of learned, persuasive, shared, and interconnected symbols whose meanings provide orientations for society's members. Culture is an individual's acquired knowledge that interprets experience and generates social behavior. Some critical cultural elements are social structure and dynamics, human nature perspective, time and space orientation, religion, gender roles, and language.

It is essential to recognize that culture is learned and helps people in their efforts to interact and communicate with others in society. When placed in a different culture, some individuals may have difficulties adjusting. Cultural differences must be comprehended, and international business managers must be sensitive to them to succeed in the global economy.

Traditionally, international business and trade focus mainly on handling organizational structures, economics, and the legal aspects of business abroad. However, understanding national cultures and broadly understanding the cultural traits of the target country's values, beliefs, norms, and behavioral patterns is imperative. Such awareness has been paramount since Hofstede's classical cultural distance framework in the 1980s. National culture has been shown to impact significant business activities, from capital structure to group performance, and it is only by understanding and analyzing one's own culture that it's possible to understand foreign cultures and succeed in international business. As illustrated in Figure 2.1, cultural differences can influence negotiations in many ways. For instance, as expected, research shows that expatriate experience and host-country language fluency significantly improve the expat adjustment process and their ability to negotiate agreements successfully.

Hofstede, back in 1994, brought an array of symbols, beliefs, values, ideas, and a few other traits into a definition of what he dubbed collective mental programming. Culture is the amalgamation of acquired experience and values that feed into and influence the behavior and responses of distinct groups. Culture is a learned experience,

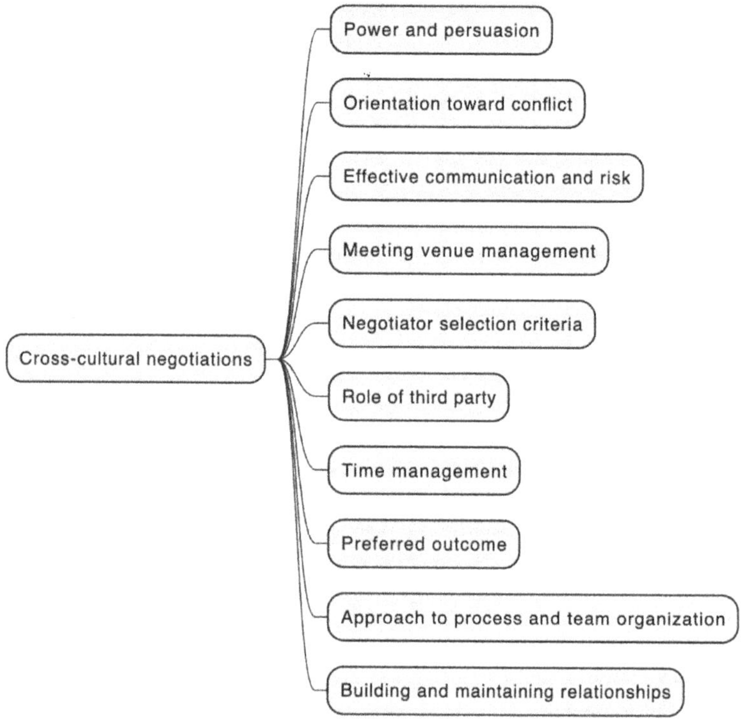

Figure 2.1: Cultural differences can influence negotiations in many ways.

where the outcomes of such transmitted experiences over many years are transferred through many generations. A national culture offers a broad context where other cultural manifestations occur, including regional, religious, organizational, and occupational cultures. Several of those cultural attributes also have a cross-border dimension. For instance, the Christian Catholic denomination is subject to similar influences in Brazil, the United States, Mexico, Italy, and Portugal. However, the effect of these distinctions tends to vary depending on the target country and many compelling cultural attributes.

Culture plays a significant role in international business and trade. Entry into new markets requires understanding the local market's values, beliefs, and customs. For instance, inappropriate advertising language or images can damage initiatives to enter a new target market.

Overcoming Ethnocentricity

Ethnocentricity is the tendency to regard one's race or social group as the model of human experience. Ethnocentricity also includes the perception of internal cultural conflicts as part of the norm. Figure 2.2 describes the steps to flexible ethnocentrism. For instance, women in one cultural convention may suppose that women in other cultures have the same struggles and stresses with their communities and are pursuing the same goals. This inaccurate assumption may lead to misconceptions about international business and trade conduct. Ethnocentricity is perilous in global ethical behavior as it involves contempt and unquestioning beliefs, like self-attributions.

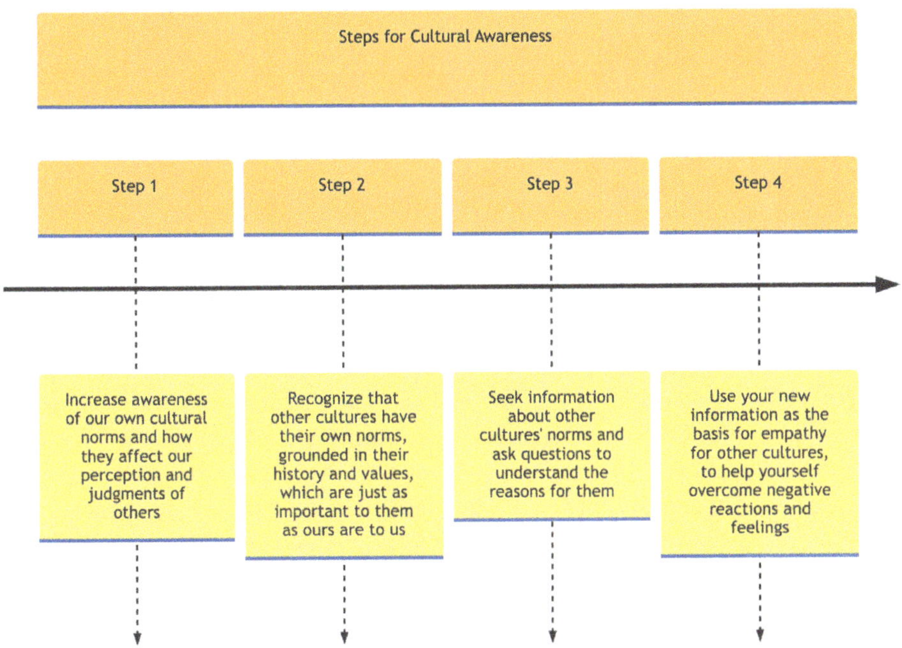

Figure 2.2: Steps to flexible ethnocentrism.

Overcoming ethnocentric attitudes begins with understanding our cultural traits and how they are distinct or similar to other cultures. The focus should be mapping the differences, bridging the gaps, and promoting integration (the MBI model). Global enterprises should focus initially on the target country's cultural environments and incorporate data on subcultures later. Learning to respect the ethnocentricity of others is paramount, as it assists in upholding the equality of people's values and the dignity of their members and those of other societies, as well as dissidents within a community. In sociological terminology, such orientation is dubbed cultural relativism.

Practical Strategies to Adapt to a Target Country's Culture

Many cultural aspects powerfully shape the international business and trade environment. These often exhibit a complex interplay of values, ideas, beliefs, history, customs, practice, etc. MNEs must exhibit culture-appropriate, specific behaviors such as gift-giving, proper greetings and introductions, punctuality, physical contact, physical space between people during conversation, and speaking patterns. For better chances of success in international business trade, MNEs should develop synergies between the home and host country and other global business environments. It will demand adaptations in the home country and across international organizations' cultures, including language and proper communication, politics, and law, values and belief systems, educational programs and training, technology, and other resources. The following are a few strategies MNEs may adopt when adapting to the target country's culture:

- Adapt Through Local Ownership: MNEs can adapt to the local culture by adopting franchising as an internationalization mode of entry. This allows personal creativity to adjust to local circumstances while tightening operating procedures.
- Appoint Protocol Officers: Several multinational corporations hire protocol officers to ensure the company's executives are properly "oriented" during their foreign visits or have the data they need for conducting business there. Such a strategy is typical for government officials traveling abroad and interacting with a foreign government.
- Create a Code of Ethics: Develop a code of ethics that considers the target country's cultural values as a guide for management to drive their operations abroad.
- Develop a Polycentric Orientation: MNEs know that each international operation's environment is distinctive and full of challenges that need to be understood and dealt with from the home base. Thus, each international subsidiary and its functions are allowed a great deal of independence to run its business abroad.
- Formalize Cultural Integration: MNEs should recruit a local management team as much as possible. Such employees will be much more aware of their local culture.
- Six Interacting Processes: Research shows that one of the most effective ways to change or modify a company's culture is via management team interventions through six interactive processes:
  a. The selection and recruiting of people with the necessary cultural values.
  b. Socialization among members of the company during a strategic implementation of cultural change.
  c. Removing personnel who cannot adapt to the new modified culture.
  d. Adapting the firm's communication protocols and standards concerning language, myths, jargon, and corporate traditions.
  e. Appointment of a cultural integration staff to assist with any cultural issues.
  f. Becoming cognizant of local culture and customs.

Cultural Distances Across the Globe

Sixty years ago, we could bypass contact with diverse cultures if we did not step outside our cultural comfort zone, and, at that time, only very few people had to do that. So, we all lived peacefully in our cultural enclaves, where we were safe and comfortable. Then the immigration started. In Western Europe, individuals came from Eastern Europe and Turkey; in the United States, they came from Mexico. Then, the Cold War ended, and individuals could move about more freely for employment and leisure. Many wanted to follow their vision of happiness beyond their cultural comfort zone, and many left while many other new individuals arrived.

Technological development, regional deregulation, and trade agreements unlocked the world. The Western world outsourced production and later services to remain competitive. Suddenly, the nations the Western world had outsourced to wanted independence. Moreover, these countries could because they did well, unlike most countries in the Western world. As a result of these integrations, or attempts to, through these past 60 years, there has been enormous tension between the cultures in both the Western world and the new emerging markets. The Western world is challenged to learn to steer in a globalized world it has created, but where it is no longer in command. The nations in the emerging and, later, the frontier markets are starting to figure out how to deal with the fast economic development without falling apart culturally and socially. Many distinct strategies have been selected – some are successful, while others are disastrous.

An Overview of Hofstede's Cultural Dimensions

Hofstede's cultural dimensions was developed by Geert Hofstede. It is a framework for understanding cultural differences across countries. Hofstede's initial six key dimensions, as illustrated in Figure 2.3, include power distance, uncertainty avoidance, individualism-collectivism, masculinity-femininity, and short- vs. long-term orientation. As far as international business is concerned, the dimensions of culture form an essential facet. Knowing how different MNEs features are viewed in other cultures can help a manager understand and sail successfully across the international business market.

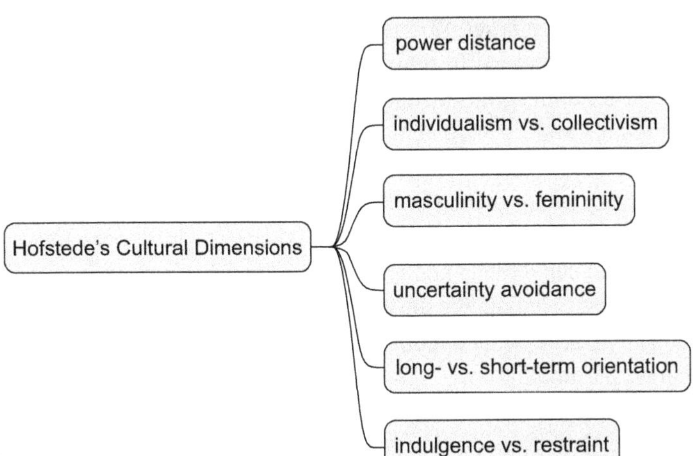

Figure 2.3: Hofstede's cultural dimensions.

The model adopted six classifications that describe national culture:

- Power Distance Index (PDI). The PDI is *the extent to which the less powerful members of organizations and institutions accept and expect that power is distributed unequally.* Higher scores suggest that individuals accept societal hierarchies, while lower scores mean the contrary.
- Collectivism vs. Individualism (IDV). This dimension depicts *how cohesively individuals are incorporated into teams.* Individualistic societies concentrate more on the individual and their immediate family. Collectivist societies integrate extended families and in-groups.
- Uncertainty Avoidance (UA). Those societies with an elevated UA are *opposed to the unfamiliar and the unpredictable.* Hence, they frequently have more rigid behavioral policies and regulations. This index summarizes how much individuals accept ambiguity.
- Femininity vs. Masculinity (MAS). In this model, *masculinity* prizes *achievement, heroism, assertiveness, and material rewards for success. Femininity,* in contrast, favors *cooperation, modesty, caring for the weak, and quality of life.*
- Short-Term vs. Long-Term Orientation (LTO). Nations geared towards a *long-term value transformation and problem-solving,* while those with a short-term emphasis value *commitment and tradition.*
- Restraint vs. Indulgence (IND). The index guides how rigidly a society *controls the fulfillment of human desires.* Those that permit indulgence offer people the liberty to indulge those desires, while their counterparts tend to restrict such behavior.

Leveraging Cultural Diversity

Leveraging cultural diversity, which is the main objective of this section, is an essential element in competing in the global market. Most transnational and multinational corporations have made substantial progress in their globalization efforts. They have installed operations in several nations and offshored specific processes or functions to countries with the credentials and development prospects. Nevertheless, while these more recent internationalization endeavors have their roots in cost arbitrage, today, prosperous organizations must comprehend that international business can be a means for shoring up competitive advantage not only to lower labor costs but, more importantly, to diversify intellectual capabilities and growth, and improve quality enhancement opportunities, in addition to enhancing the ability to get products to market more quickly. Notwithstanding, a greater understanding of culture and multiculturalism and how to leverage it becomes paramount.

Diversity Versus Inclusion

Inclusion and diversity are different concepts, but they are related. The Society for Human Resources Management (SHRM) defines diversity and inclusion as the accomplishment of a work environment in which individuals are regarded and treated equitably and with respect, have equitable access to the same resources and opportunities as everyone else, and can fully contribute to the organization's success.

The objective of the inclusion framework is to improve diversity by creating egalitarian work conditions in which employees feel welcome and included. The framework is based on Marilynn Brewer's theory (1991), which states that individuals in a workgroup have two basic needs: the need to belong and differentiation. Both needs must be met for individuals to feel accepted within the group and their communication capacity to increase.

The following framework, as depicted in Figure 2.4, describes the four dimensions of the individual group interaction:

- Exclusion – occurs when a workgroup perceives the characteristics of other individuals as non-important and insignificant.
- Assimilation – occurs when workgroups have a sentiment of harmony towards new members and avoid stereotyping them.
- Differentiation occurs when workgroup members are mindful that team members have valuable attributes and incorporate them into the workgroup. However, they are still regarded as foreign strangers to the workgroup.
- Inclusion – occurs when people are accepted in the workgroup and the two basic needs are met.

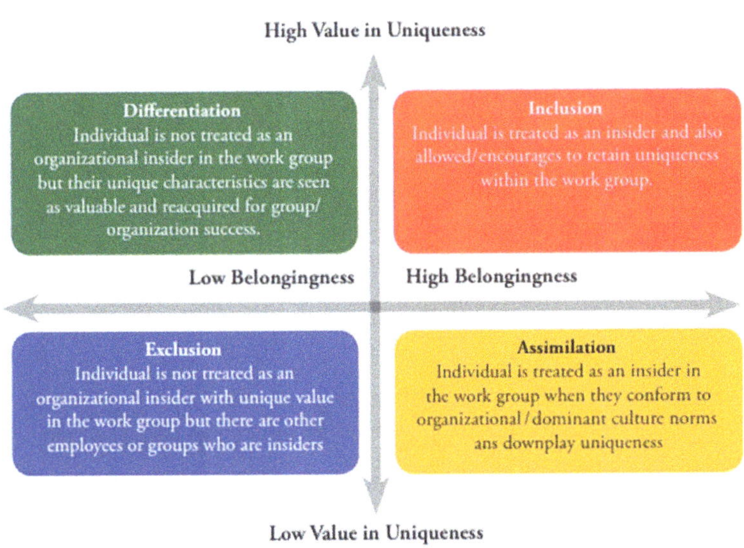

Figure 2.4: Inclusion framework. (SOURCE: USAID's Workplace Diversity Management Module One, 2021).

Awareness of diversity and inclusion is critical, especially in international business interactions. Most individuals still view cultural dissimilarities as a hindrance to success. This section discusses how one can leverage cultural diversity to develop more suitable, more competitive organizations, more suitable leaders, and, hopefully, a safer and more sustainable world.

When a global poll asked individuals to select from groups of people they would not want as neighbors, as depicted in Figure 2.5, the share of people worldwide who indicated "people from another race" was significant. While few of us would challenge the moral rightness of this declaration, the very basis for individualism, we may have misgivings about the offspring. Valuation depends on the speaker's stance, and indeed, aspects of this development are not universally admired, particularly when observing a diminishing sense of community, social obligation, or security as one proceeds along this trajectory.

World's most and least racially tolerant countries.

Region	Color on Map	Percentage of People Who Would Not Want Neighbors of Another Race
North America	Dark Blue	0% - 4.9%
Central America	Blue	5% - 9.9%
South America	Light Blue	10% - 14.9%
Western Europe	Dark Blue	0% - 4.9%
Eastern Europe	Purple	15% - 19.9%
Russia	Dark Purple	20% - 29.9%
Middle East & North Africa	Red	30% - 39.9%
Sub-Saharan Africa	Blue/Red	5% - 9.9% / 30% - 39.9%
South Asia	Orange	40%+
Southeast Asia	Blue	5% - 9.9%
East Asia	Dark Blue	0% - 4.9%
Australia & New Zealand	Dark Blue	0% - 4.9%

Figure 2.5: Race tolerance chart. (SOURCE: *The Washington Post* https://www.washingtonpost.com/news/worldviews/wp/2013/05/15/a-fascinating-map-of-the-worlds-most-and-least-racially-tolerant-countries/ [accessed July 8, 2022|).

Mapping Cultural Distance

Scholars have pinpointed culturally diverse groups of countries. Each cultural cluster echoes a shared past, faith, economic expansion, regional proximity, and other aspects. Within each set, countries are similar in three to four cultural value orientations. The patterning of cultural value priorities in one cluster differentiates it from another. Clustering countries into culturally equivalent classes helps summarize the parallels and distinctions among cultures. Learning about cultural dissimilarities is more efficient than concentrating on societies one at a time.

From a practical standpoint, clustering supplies a framework for addressing cultural diversity. Cluster-based data can assist in evaluating the potential success of sharing human resources, organizational practices, training, or customer products across global societies. Clusters, or groups, are a helpful starting point, but it is too simplistic to say that all nations in a cluster are the same. Differences within each cluster should be appreciated. Although the countries within each cluster emphasize three or four cultural attributes, they can differentiate from other features:

- Africa and the Middle East – Africa and the Middle East group includes the countries of Senegal, South Africa, Nigeria, Uganda, Ghana, Zimbabwe, Ethiopia, Namibia, Iran, Jordan, Cameroon, Egypt, and Yemen. This group emphasizes Doing Orientation, Collectivism, and Short-Term Orientation. This cultural value profile describes societies struggling to overcome poverty, legitimizing active change and exploitation of the environment, and reinforcing group solidarity over individual uniqueness. There is significant variation within this cultural region in all values, but not in collectivism.

- Anglo – The Anglo group comprises Great Britain, Australia, South Africa (White), Canada (English speaking), New Zealand, Ireland, and the United States. This cluster has a cultural focus on Doing Orientation, Individualism, Assertiveness, and Indulgence. And comparable cultural de-emphasis on Power Distance and Uncertainty Avoidance. The U.S. has the highest score on individualism, closely trailed by by other Anglo nations. The Anglo value profile echoes a high individual goal direction, where rewards are founded on merits, and personal achievement objectives take priority over family bonds. Also, the United States has a higher Doing Orientation and Power Distance among the Anglo cluster than other countries. French-Canadian culture is much closer to the culture of Western Europe, especially France, than Anglo-Canadian culture – reflecting its historical and linguistic roots.

- Confucian Asia Region – The Confucian Asia region is a cluster defined by a strong historical influence of the Confucian ideology. Countries in this cluster include Taiwan, Singapore, Hong Kong, South Korea, China, Japan, and Thailand. The Confucian Asia cluster emphasizes Collectivism, Doing Orientation, Power Distance, and Future Orientation, with collective and family-orientated goals and a system of rewards for achieving collective goals. It describes cultures with a pragmatic, entrepreneurial orientation and a strong emphasis on relationships and hierarchy. In this cluster, Japan scores the highest on Being and Individualism but the lowest on Power Distance and Collectivism. China, Japan, Taiwan, South Korea, Singapore, and Hong Kong score high for Future Orientation.

– East Europe – East Europe refers to countries dominated by Soviet communism. Countries in the East European group comprise Hungary, Russia, Kazakhstan, Poland, Greece, Albania, Georgia, and Slovenia. East Europe has strong scores for Being Orientation, Gender Egalitarianism, Collectivism, Future Orientation, and Restraint, and lower scores for Uncertainty Avoidance. The group is low on Collectivism and Power Distance compared with Africa, the Middle East, and South Asia, which are more elevated than West Europe. This cultural value profile depicts an adaptive orientation to a totalitarian communist regime – evading problems and taking many initiatives. The regional area of East Central European and Baltic cultures (Czech Republic, Poland, Estonia, Latvia, Croatia, Hungary, Slovakia, and Romania) is more robust in Being Orientation and Individualism and weaker in Power Distance when compared to Balkan and the Eastern cultures, including Bulgaria, Bosnia-Herzegovina, Macedonia, Georgia, Ukraine, Serbia, and Russia). The Baltic and East Central countries have a cultural profile closer to Western Europe. These echo strong historical and trade connections to Western Europe, weaker penetration, a minor period of totalitarian and communist rule, and a dominant Roman Catholic or Protestant religion. In contrast, the nations in the East European and Balkan regions had historical connections to the Ottoman Empire and more fragile ties to the West. These countries were profoundly infiltrated by communism, and they practiced more conservative and in-group-orientated orthodox religions.

– Germanic Europe – As a subset of the West Europe group, the Germanic Europe cluster consists of societies that persist in using the German language and includes the Netherlands, Austria, Switzerland, former West Germany, and former East Germany. East German culture is much closer to West German culture than Eastern European culture, echoing shared language, history, and traditions not eradicated by communist rule. Even though East Germany underwent a communist regime for 40 years, traditional German values were integral to society. The Germanic Europe cluster displays higher scores for Individualism, Doing Orientation, Uncertainty Avoidance, Assertiveness, and Future Orientation but lower scores for Humane Orientation and Power Distance.

– Latin America – Latin America is a group of nations that share a particular Latin culture influenced by Catholicism, Iberian colonial past, Roman law heritage, and Spanish or Portuguese languages. It includes the countries of Mexico, Peru, Chile, Venezuela, Costa Rica, Ecuador, El Salvador, Bolivia, Columbia, Guatemala, Argentina, and Brazil. Latin America has more substantial scores for Collectivism and Power Distance compared to West Europe and Anglo clusters, although not if compared to

South Asia, Africa, and Confucian nations. It scores low for Doing Orientation, Uncertainty Avoidance, and Future Orientation. Latin American cultures accept life as it is, taking its unpredictability as a way of life and not over-worrying about the future. There is much less concern with institutional goals than with family bonds. Among Latin America, Bolivia, and Peru, there are much higher power distance and collectivism rates than their neighbors, reflecting their relatively low relative exposure to European culture and precarious economic development. Countries with high Indulgence scores include Venezuela, Mexico, Puerto Rico, El Salvador, Colombia, and Trinidad.

– Latin Europe – Another subgroup of the West Europe group, the Latin Europe cluster, consists of the regions affected by Roman culture, which rejected Protestant reforms. It includes Italy, Portugal, Spain, France, French-speaking Switzerland, and Israel. Israel, although not Catholic, is incorporated into this area because it was established by Jews who ended up migrating from Latin Europe to Eastern Europe to escape religious repression. Nevertheless, Israeli Jews maintained their social and business ties to Latin Europe. The Latin European culture has elevated scores for Collectivism and low scores for Humane Orientation.

– Nordic Europe – The highest scores attained for Gender Egalitarianism are from Nordic countries. Nordic Europe clusters the Scandinavian nations of Finland, Sweden, Norway, and Denmark. This group is similar to Germanic Europe, offering solid scores for Uncertainty Avoidance, Future Orientation, Individualism, and Gender Egalitarianism and poor scores for Power Distance and Assertiveness. Nordic societies stress certainty, social unity, and cooperation. They underplay strong and masculine authority.

– Southern Asia – The Southern Asia cluster includes Iran, India, Indonesia, Philippines, Malaysia, Nepal, and Fiji. Despite a diversity of external influences, the nations in this cluster share an inclination to assimilate external and modern influences into their indigenous cultures. They have displayed throughout history a peaceful and interactive coexistence of diversity (for example, in religious beliefs). Southern Asian societies report significantly higher scores for Collectivism, Power Distance, and Humane Orientation. This cultural value profile describes societies emphasizing fulfilling obligations in a hierarchical order and with a deep sense of community orientation. This cluster includes India, which is high on Doing Orientation, and India and Bangladesh, which have higher Restraint scores.

– Sub-Saharan Africa – Within Africa and the Middle East group, the Sub-Saharan African cluster encompasses cultures with slavery history, a distinctive shared philosophy of humaneness, and Christian missionary efforts. Countries in the Sub-Saharan African cluster include Namibia, Zambia, Zimbabwe, Nigeria, and South Africa (Black). Sub-Saharan African societies report more substantial scores for a more Humane Orientation. This trait highlights the humanistic model of these societies, which live a wild and typically rural lifestyle. South Africa is a single African country with a dominant individualist orientation and is part of the Anglo group.

– Middle East – The Middle East cluster mirrors the Arabic Muslim culture and encompasses Morocco, Qatar, Turkey, Kuwait, and Egypt. The Middle Eastern cultures display lower scores on Future Orientation, Uncertainty Avoidance, and Gender Egalitarianism than any other clusters, although with higher scores in Restraint and Collectivism. The Middle East cluster represents cultures that believe the future happens according to Allah and should not be regarded through instrumental means. Turkey is higher in Individualism but lower in Power Distance compared with its Middle Eastern neighbors, which reflects a secular democratic system with historical influences from the Eastern Europe region and its struggle to join the West. The Israeli Jewish culture is closer in values to the Anglo cluster than to its Middle Eastern Muslim neighbors.

– West Europe – The West Europe cluster contains the countries of Germany, Switzerland, Austria, Belgium, Italy, the Netherlands, France, Spain, Portugal, Canada (French speaking), Greece, and the Nordic countries of Sweden, Denmark, Finland, and Norway. In the West Europe group, Greece scores higher on Power Distance, Doing Orientation, and Collectivism, while French-speaking Switzerland and France score higher on Power Distance. Overall, West Europe has a cultural focus on Individualism and Being Orientation and a comparative cultural de-emphasis on Power Distance, typical of democratic welfare states, where regard for the environment is substantial. One of the fascinating conclusions is the cultural distance between the 'Western' industrialized cultures of non–English speaking Western Europe and the Anglo cultures. Treating all developed Western countries under an Individualistic label is too simplistic. Even though West Europe is individualistic in that self-sufficiency is highlighted, it varies from the Anglo group, emphasizing egalitarianism and Being Oriented and a comparative de-emphasis on doing. The West Europe cluster involves a selfless consideration for the welfare of others and conforming to the natural and social world without seeking to alter it. The Anglo cultures, nonetheless, exploited the social and natural environment. In addition, the United States scores higher on Power Distance; in other words, it is less egalitarian.

The Lewis Model

The Lewis Model, illustrated in Figure 2.6, was developed to denote with which cultural grouping a person would have a higher or lower degree of empathy. Lewis broke down his three typologies into Linear-active, Multi-active, and Reactive.

Richard Lewis developed the Lewis Model after visiting 135 countries and working in over 20. It was created in the 1990s and is the latest to gain worldwide recognition, especially after the launch of his well-known book titled *When Cultures Collide* (1996), which won the U.S. Book of the Month Award in 1997. According to him, humans can be

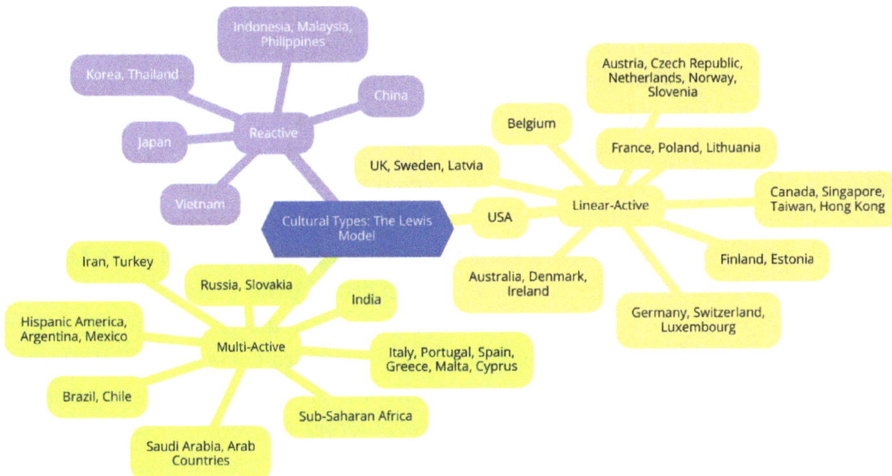

Figure 2.6: The Lewis Model. (SOURCE: Lewis, When Cultures Collide, 1996).

divided into three classes based not on nationality or religion but on behavior. He named these three classes, or typologies as he called them, Linear-active, Multi-active, and Reactive.

Lewis thought that prior cross-culturalists, as they accumulated an assortment of dimensions, ran the danger of developing confusion for those who sought clarity and conciseness, such as business professionals, especially international businesses. In his views, experts' fixation with north/south and mono-chronic/poly-chronic dichotomies had compelled them to miss or disregard the powerful Asian mindset, which comprises about half of the world's population.

Governance Distances and the Impact on Business and Trade

The real-impact consequence caused by the distance between nations or international markets negatively affects international business and trade. Policymakers worldwide are always very concerned about international business and trade volatility since it is a vital channel of transmission of economic shocks and policies, of contagion, as financiers would call it. Does distance matter for the volatility of international business and trade? At first glance, such effects are ambiguous. When faced with challenging conditions, international business managers, especially exporters, tend to pull back from distant markets in terms of CAGE and Lewis models.

According to a European Central Bank report (ECB Working Paper Series No 2252/ March 2019), demand shocks significantly impact international business and trade between more distant countries than those closer to the home market. Intuitively, the demand reduction weighs on profits and leads some exporters to exit the market (de-internationalization or deglobalization). However, as firms withdraw from these international markets, they increase the market strength of the remaining firms and their markups on products and services, especially when there are initially few exporters owing to high trading costs to distant destinations.

The more significant increase in markup prices for products and services in more distant markets leads to a more substantial trade contraction. As evidenced in the ECB's report, during the great trade collapse of 2007–09 (the global financial crisis initiated in the U.S.), as depicted in Figure 2.7, international business and trade fell more between nations farther from each other. The effect of such distance was economically very substantial. According to the ECB report, as discussed earlier in this chapter, an increase in the physical distance between two nations by one standard deviation (SD) decreased trade in goods and services by 23 percent during the great trade collapse; the corresponding decreases for linguistic distance were 5 percent. However, although physical distance has received the bulk of attention in the literature, it is not always the measure with the most significant effects. For instance, virtual distance, the psychological and emotional sense of detachment that may result from a lack of human interactions or the loss of the human moment (think of it as a result of fear, misinformation, fake news, etc.), had a more considerable impact on international business and trade.

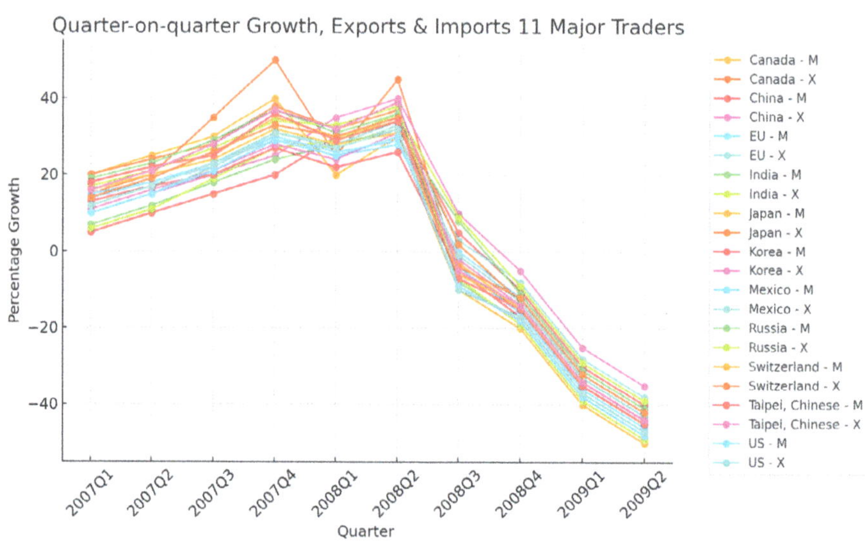

Figure 2.7: The great trade collapse, 2008 to 2009. (SOURCE: WTO, IMF World Economic Outlook, September 2011).

The impact of the various distance measures was not limited to the global crisis initiated by the U.S. The ECB report argues that results from their longitudinal research from 1950 through 2015 confirmed that physical and virtual distances matter, with trade generally more volatile between nations that are farther apart. The two metrics of distance magnified each other's impacts.

Sustainability in International Business

Irrational usage of natural resources in numerous parts of the world impacts public health, population working ability, and macroeconomic performance. It has been found that each global citizen's heavier responsibility and value changes can enhance the current international situation. The general utility function can be improved by rational nature and environmental management and execution of a development process to minimize such harmful risk elements as ecological state deterioration, inefficient healthcare system functioning, exacerbated usage of chemical compounds while making agricultural products, etc.

Equally important is topography, the surface features of a country or region, such as mountains, deserts, plains, etc. It contributes to differences in economies, cultures, politics, and social structures. The same is true for a country's climate or its meteorological conditions. It sets limits on what people can do. Fewer people tend to live in harsher climates, for example.

Environmental control is one of the core social objectives that can extend living standards and ecosystem conditions in case of a well-elaborated approach for further efforts, and it is one of the most crucial environmental healthcare challenges facing the world today. The literature on this topic is vast, but the issue must be fully addressed globally, especially in some emerging and frontier economies. It is constantly becoming more robust and extensive. Monitoring and analyzing human and environmental interaction are background data for developing managerial decisions while implementing the green economy in leading nations in the 21st century. To raise the social and economic impact of production, one should continually control the external environment and minimize unattainable risks without embracing a system for the sustainable use of natural resources. As the climate has limitations and is in short supply, while the target function of manufacturing includes the more efficient application of available resources, steady ecosystem preservation can be considered an optimization problem.

Measuring Sustainability

All United Nations member states conceived the 2030 Agenda for Sustainable Development 2015. It was developed around 17 Sustainable Development Goals (SDGs), as illustrated in Figure 2.8, and 169 targets representing an ambitious strategy for attaining sustainable development and functions as the basis for nations to shape their national policies and priorities. At the project's core is the acknowledgment that genuine development must incorporate economic maturation and poverty relief with strategies that enhance health and education and reduce inequality while mitigating climate change and protecting nature. The interconnected nature of the SDGs charges for an integrated process for policy decision-making. As the global statistical standard for assessing the environment and its relationship with the economy, it is well-placed to sustain integrated policies founded on a more suitable understanding of the inter-relations and trade-offs between the economy and the environment.

Figure 2.8: UN's Sustainable Development Goals (SDGs). (SOURCE: UN).

Sustainable Development Goals (SDGs) have been an enormous success in the industry, from corporate reports to models to improving sustainability. The goals cover the usual sustainability areas defined by the Five P's: people, planet, prosperity, peace, and partnership. These issues are standard components of many sustainability models. The standard extends past the traditional environment, social, and economic triple bottom line approach and is much more detailed.

Continuous development toward the 17 goals, as listed in Figure 2.9, and 169 targets of the 2030 Agenda are being assessed through 244 indicators, entailing the collection of essential data. The UN Statistical Commission (UNSC) has encouraged the Inter-Agency and Expert Group on SDG Indicators (IAEG-SDGs), the institution commissioned to devise and implement the global indicator framework for the 2030 Agenda, to take into consideration existing standards and frameworks that can improve SDG monitoring, including the System of Environmental-Economic Accounting (SEEA).

Figure 2.9: The UN's 17 Sustainable Development Goals. (SOURCE: UNCEEA).

The United Nations Committee of Experts on Environmental-Economic Accounting (UNCEEA), an intergovernmental body established by the UNSC to provide overall vision, coordination, prioritization, and direction in the field of environmental-economic accounting and supporting statistics, has assessed that currently, 40 indicators for nine Sustainable Development Goals can be informed by the SEEA.

A pivotal part of the success of the SDGs is not just the actual coverage but also that they are explicit and visually memorable to ensure they are easily discernible in news, reports, and other sources. These 17 goals cover various issues; the participating countries must achieve the goals by 2030 – more specific targets and indicators back up each general goal. The targets are the standards of improvement, whereas an indicator is the standards by which progress towards the target can be tracked. For instance, Goal 11 has ten detailed targets *to make cities and human settlements inclusive, safe, resilient, and sustainable*. For instance:

- 11.1 By 2030, ensure access for all to adequate, safe, and affordable housing and essential services and upgrade slums (target); 11.1.1 proportion of urban populations living in slums, informal settlements, or inadequate housing (associated indicator), and
- 11.7 By 2030, provide universal access to safe, inclusive, and accessible green and public spaces, in particular for women and children, older persons, and persons with disabilities (target); 11.7.1 Average share of the built-up area of cities that is open space for public use for all, by sex, age and persons with disabilities (associated indicator).

ESG and DEI Considerations

Environmental, social, and governance (ESG) standards are criteria for a firm's conduct adopted by socially mindful investors to screen potential investments. Environmental measures assess how a firm protects the environment, including corporate guidelines and policies handling climate change issues. Social standards analyze how they address relationships with workers, suppliers, consumers, and the societies where it operates. Governance concerns a firm's leadership, upper management compensation, audits, internal controls, and shareholder rights.

Diversity, equity, and inclusion (DEI) are the phrases most often used to depict a training format in the workplace. DEI training promotes a functional understanding of fellow workers' identities and how to steer diversity in an institution. The concept of DEI, however, has a much broader range of applications, as DEI is not just a phrase. Each term conveys specific values. Diversity is the existence of differences or distinctions that enhance the workplace. A few examples of diversity may include gender, age, race, ethnicity, language, religion, religious commitment, sexual orientation, nationality, socioeconomic status, (dis)ability, or political stand among other staff at the workplace. But many more distinctions exist. Equity ensures that access, resources, and prospects are offered for all individuals and staff so they can thrive and evolve. It is mainly true for those who are underrepresented and historically underprivileged. Inclusion is an organization's culture that welcomes all individuals regardless of race, ethnicity, sex, gender identity, age, abilities, and religion; everyone is valued, respected, and able to reach their full potential.

International entrepreneurism can be a catalyst for equitable and sustainable international business development. Research shows the challenges in understanding the business industry without investigating the entrepreneurs' roles and behavior. International entrepreneurial competencies are strongly correlated as predictors of international business success. Such a correlation of international entrepreneurial competencies with success in international business tends to be more assertive when dynamic environments are more challenging. International entrepreneurs are skilled in assuming responsibilities for and decision-makers on various actions and endeavors impacting local and international business operations, environment, organization, use of goods and services, resources, institutions, etc. Entrepreneurs are actors in developing early-stage company startups, mainly digital international entrepreneurship, and they can also be intrapreneur managers within companies.

Often, international and local entrepreneurs are catalysts of change in society. Social entrepreneurs play a critical role in a changing environment, especially in the public sector, influencing institutions, policies, governance, and the awareness of specific societal issues. They also significantly influence reshaping industries towards sustainable development, driving sustainability transitions as they innovate, create, and distribute goods and services, and stimulating and enabling greater sustainability of consumption and behavior. In addition to new offerings, products, and services, international entrepreneurs engage in active entrepreneurial actions, developing or transforming institutions, including but not limited to policies, legal rights, and other legislations supporting sustainable ESG development.

Private entrepreneurship, especially when international, is among the best engines for reducing social and economic inequalities, poverty, and the digital gap. Global entrepreneurs are essential for effective innovation systems worldwide. As a function, they convert the opportunity for novel creation, such as networks, new knowledge, and market niches, into tangible activities made up of experimentations of entrepreneurship and business projects. By doing so, increased local and international business opportunities can be found. Several indicators can be considered to support international entrepreneurial investigations, including those for digital technologies purposes, new pilot project débuts, new market entries, and various other systems' incubations.

The available literature argues that when it comes to international entrepreneurship potential, especially in high-performing markets, the role of entrepreneurs is highly present. It provides relevant data for policymakers, business industry practitioners, academics, and non-governmental organizations (NGOs) on the right path for best practices and business models to be adopted and implemented. Despite such a significant role, the literature is scarce on how international business entrepreneurs could develop new markets, opportunities, and organizations to foster a transformation towards a more equitable, diverse, and sustainable society.

DEI and ESG for Equitable and Sustainable International Business Development

International business ventures can be considered instruments of change, capable of stimulating economic expansion abroad in foreign markets. For the past few years, mainly since the COVID-19 pandemic breakout in 2019, digital technological transformations, especially internet-based ones, have rapidly evolved. Several digital technology innovations and applications have arisen and been broadly embraced worldwide by the private and public sectors.

Digital applications in the manufacturing industry (manufacturing 4.0) across the globe and digital transformations across multiple sectors significantly enhance governance, industry, and business competitiveness. Still, if not planned with ESG and DEI in mind, it can substantially increase the digital divide and sustainability transition efforts. Moreover, it also influences the dispersal of innovative digital applications in foreign markets where multicultural diversity can add to the complexity of compliance with ESG and DEI standards. For digital transformation sustainability to thrive, policymakers worldwide must understand the reasons for stimulating it and offer support by facilitating business and industry competitiveness and using such innovations through socially responsible, equitable, diverse, inclusive, and supportive means.

For instance, in the early summer of 2022, Google Analytics was barred from use in Italy for being perceived as a threat to the privacy rights of its citizens. While in the U.S., it is not an issue, it is a big issue in Italy. Hence, in the age of digitalization of business processes, the arrival of the Metaverse, artificial intelligence (AI), and machine learning neuromarketing algorithms, virtual and augmented reality, a need exists to determine distinctive elements that may impact responsible, sustainable, and inclusive digital transformations and best understand the correlations among these elements. Nevertheless, selecting a series of characteristics affecting transformation sustainability and digital technologies can be challenging.

Environmental, Social, and Governance Criteria

Environmental, social, and governance (ESG) are criteria for international firms' operations that socially mindful investors should adopt when assessing prospective investments. ESG standards consider how enterprises perform as a custodian of the natural environment. Such social standards investigate how the international firms' associations (locally and in target markets) with workers, suppliers, clients, and the communities in which they operate are managed. Governance concerns the firm's management and leadership, policies driving executive compensation, auditing, internal controls, and shareholders' and stakeholders' rights. It evaluates a firm's pooled conscientiousness regarding social and environmental elements. They are often represented as scores assembled from information gathered across the firm encompassing detailed benchmarks associated with the organization's intangible assets, usually regarded as corporate social credit ratings. Researchers argue that these intangible assets constitute an increasing portion of the firm's future valuation. Although numerous ways of considering intangible asset benchmarks exist, these prominent attributes concurrently (ESG) comprise a designation embraced across the financial sector in the U.S. ESG scores have been adopted for some time now for a multitude of specific objectives, with the ultimate goal of calculating factors associated with sustainability, and the social impact of firms in their operations.

In less than two decades, ESG as a movement evolved from a corporate social responsibility (CSR) initiative launched by the United Nations (UN) to an international and highly respected ambition. No business or industry in the global economy is unaffected by technological innovation. All things equal, innovators will concentrate on–and technological innovation will occur – where the returns to innovative capital are the highest. International agencies rating ESG have become influential in the popularization of sustainable investments. Traditionally, they relied on a firm's volunteered disclosure and laborious human analysis to deliver a rating score. The advent of technological innovation and digital business process transformations introduced web data scraping, coupled with machine learning and AI, to virtually eliminate such orthodox approaches. Such technology-driven ESG scoring has become progressively persuasive, although it continues to be overwhelmingly uninvestigated in sustainable transition literature.

The Value of Diversity, Equity, and Inclusion

The increase in disseminated writings and literature materials regarding microaggressions, cultural competency, appraisal of diversity matters, and campaigns for social justice indicates that diversity-related movements across the globe have grown and developed over the past decade. There is also a growth in multicultural and diverse communities locally, nationally, and internationally. DEI, therefore, is described beyond racial and ethnic groupings. An international diversity/inclusion strategy for companies in internationalizing may contain an assertion of diversity values or goals to be incorporated into their internationalization strategy and avoid a situation like Google's in Italy. It may include depicting procedures for recruiting and retaining culturally and ethnically diverse professionals for their projects, designing programs encouraging cultural and ethical sensitivity at the workplace, and other equivalent components.

As briefly described earlier, diversity concerns individuals' differences and preferences and the various attributes that distinguish groups or individuals. Equity ensures fairness in treating someone, including accessibility, equal opportunities, and development for anyone. It identifies and clears any obstacles that may preclude certain groups of individuals from thoroughly engaging. Equity also fosters justice and impartiality among systems or organizations' operations, processes, and allocation of resources. To tackle equity, individuals must comprehend the fundamental causes of societal discrepancies. Inclusion fosters a culture where individuals feel accepted and welcome, actively involving all groups and communities to participate and contribute. Such an inclusive and welcoming atmosphere sustains and welcomes dissimilarities and respects every individual in all manners. An inclusive workplace is respectful, collaborative, and supportive. It strives to move all workers to participate in social activities and collaborate – an inclusive workplace seeks to remove all obstacles, discrimination, and prejudice.

DEI matters because it enables the development of fair societies and offers equal opportunities to every individual. It allows people to coexist, expressing their personal beliefs, perspectives, diversity, and faith to support the creation of more robust ties among people, communities, and organizations. Promoting DEI through international business ventures is critical to reducing disparities among nations and markets and improving business and trade outcomes. Several studies have revealed that a diverse and inclusive team displays enhanced problem-solving capability than more homogeneous ones. Organizations focusing on DEI initiatives benefit from enhanced worker engagement and retention. More diverse executive committees yield improved profitability and overall business success.

In international business, as a discipline, the importance of DEI is still a developing concept, less investigated, though it has been a progressively acknowledged and prioritized theme. It appears rational that the advantage of supporting social diversity, as already documented in the local business landscape, would also extrapolate to international business. Nevertheless, in international business, where cultural differences are prevalent, crucial value dimensions may differ from stakeholders' viewpoints, including consumers, STEM professionals, learners, researchers, and society. These traits improve worker engagement and retention, problem-solving capability, and profitability. Additionally, diversity directly benefits innovation. Researchers have long noted that networking, which in this context can be viewed as gathering diverse viewpoints and association, is two of the five core characteristics of innovators. Through diverse perspectives, diversity can enable innovators to associate novel solutions.

The COVID-19 pandemic has exposed with stark clarity the pressing need for ethical dialogues about how technologies are developed and incorporated into society in ways that respect and foster DEI. Entrepreneurs and other STEM professionals at the forefront of technological innovation are indispensable in influencing the future of global digital transformations and a more responsible and inclusive digital economy. However, there is an inadequate understanding of compelling strategies for incorporating DEI training in STEM academia, both in terms of the training needed and how best to execute these training programs within existing STEM programs. Such negligence poses fundamental challenges for the STEM professions, mainly because it makes it challenging for educators to deliver and assess ethics and DEI training effectively. Going beyond STEM, the effects of this deficiency are significant, as it perpetuates technological bias and inequities, environmental degradation, lack of diversity and inclusion, and a culture apathetic to technological innovation's effects.

The ultimate value of ESG/DEI for international business is the opportunity to improve product-to-market outcomes, reduce digital gaps, and make technology innovation more equitable and inclusive in global societies. Existing discrepancies in approach and results, grounded on varied obstacles found in diversity and inclusion, are numerous. As discussed, cultural and language hindrances prevent certain STEM professionals and market consumers of diverse global backgrounds from accessing employment opportunities, developing inclusive technologies, and accessing products and services. To deliver a genuinely ESG/DEI-centered international business practice, entrepreneurs and STEM professionals should sympathize, perceive, speak, love, and have faith as their consumers do; they should be able to relate. A commonality between international business consumers and their product and service providers enhances decision making, communication, and commitment to a more responsible and inclusive international trade. Researchers have shown that underrepresented minority entrepreneurs and other technological innovation professionals are more likely to relate to and develop innovative products and services for underserved communities. Diversifying the structure of an internationalization strategy to a more responsible and sustainable framework can offer many benefits. It can better support the international business opportunities it fosters so that newly developed products and services reflect international consumers' needs and narrow the social inclusion gap. It can also enhance access to technological innovation while decreasing costs caused by gaps in technology accessibility by some under-represented social strata.

The ethical justification for DEI as part of an internationalization strategy is that everyone has something significant to share. As such, international communities of practice and society must respond to any hindrances and historic aspects potentially inducing unjust circumstances for underrepresented or minority groups. From the economic perspective, DEI should be a strategy MNCs and MNEs should seek when hiring personnel, observing ESG/DEI criteria, and engaging in diversity training. Without DEI, business internationalization implementations will likely lack new perspectives from ESG criteria and the more responsible and inclusive market demands. They will not be as competitive as other organizations embracing DEI. Furthermore, without DEI criteria, workers will likely leave their jobs, feeling unappreciated or underrepresented, taking their valuable talents with them.

Sustainability in Internationalization Strategies

Sustainability is described as a competency to last, remain, or endure in our context of studying international business practices. Sustainability-associated actions are identified as transition processes, including industrial and digital transformations and sustainable transitions in technology and socio-technical transformations. Such socio-technical transformations are encouraged through social and technical transformations and a technology innovation revolution that always co-exists with societal alterations. Sustainable socio-technological transformation critically relies on technological innovation that fosters industrial sustainability.

Three sustainability issues in the international business environment have already been broadly debated: industrial sustainability, manufacturing, and corporate. Industrial sustainability is correlated to the local and target market physical factory in manufacturing, involving a myriad of activities comprising raw materials, process flows, facilities, production systems, and products; in manufacturing, sustainability is often correlated to production and operation systems; and corporate sustainability characterizes an engagement of processes, procedures, and strategies.

Government sectors and enterprises should perform specific supportive measures to ensure and promote digital transformation sustainability during a post-pandemic global recovery. Still, outlining processes to facilitate sustainability in the industrial sector offers many challenges. For instance, when deciding on approaches to promote sustainable digital transformations worldwide, public and private sectors must first comprehend the factors impacting sustainable digital technology and industrial implementations, as the resources available in advanced economies are not the same as those found in emerging markets, and even less so in frontier economies. Only when adopting a more global and holistic approach to sustainability will policymakers be able to offer interconnected metrics for fostering industrial sustainability.

As an accelerated digital transformation occurs worldwide, governments and enterprises face many challenges. In particular, the public and private sector's inadequate capability to incorporate technology into industries and a culturally diverse society lack the talent to foster a digital divide reduction. Thus, it is essential to comprehend the elements that affect sustainable digital transformations and, additionally, to offer guidance for policymakers to define viable approaches for reducing the digital divide.

Discussion Questions

1. **How can understanding cultural dimensions, like those outlined by Hofstede, enhance a manager's ability to navigate international business successfully?**

2. **What does ethnocentricity refer to in the context of international business?**
   A) The economic policies of a country favoring domestic companies.
   B) The perception that one's own culture is superior to others.
   C) The practice of international businesses adapting to local cultures.
   D) The strategies used by businesses to enter foreign markets.

3. **Which of the following is NOT a cultural dimension identified by Hofstede?**
   A) Power Distance Index
   B) Collectivism vs. Individualism
   C) Long-Term vs. Short-Term Orientation
   D) Profitability vs. Sustainability

4. **Sustainability in international business only refers to environmental concerns. True or False?**

5. **Overcoming ethnocentricity is crucial for businesses to succeed in global markets. True or False?**

Recommended Readings

Erdoğan, S., Çakar, N. D., Ulucak, R., Danish, & Kassouri, Y. (2021). The role of natural resources abundance and dependence in achieving environmental sustainability: evidence from resource-based economies. *Sustainable Development*, 29(1), 143–154.

Litvinenko, V., Bowbrick, I., Naumov, I., & Zaitseva, Z. (2022). Global guidelines and requirements for professional competencies of natural resource extraction engineers: Implications for ESG principles and sustainable development goals. *Journal of Cleaner Production*, 338, 130530.

Luna-Nemecio, J., Tobón, S., & Juárez-Hernández, L. G. (2020). Sustainability-based on socioformation and complex thought or sustainable social development. *Resources, Environment and Sustainability*, 2, 100007.

Ruggerio, C. A. (2021). Sustainability and sustainable development: A review of principles and definitions. *Science of the Total Environment*, 786, 147481.

Zhang, Y., Khan, I., & Zafar, M. W. (2022). Assessing environmental quality through natural resources, energy resources, and tax revenues. *Environmental Science and Pollution Research*, 29(59), 89029–89044.

Chapter 3
Geopolitical Dynamics and Legal Landscapes in Global Trade and Intellectual Property

Learning Objectives

- Understand how government and business ownership affect global trade
- Evaluate strategies adopted by governments to foster stability and protection of businesses
- Comprehend government interventions
- Understand tariffs and quotas
- Analyze IP rights and enforcement
- Review the various types of legal systems
- Analyze globalization and its risk assessment process

Overview

You may ask why international business management should be abreast of different global political and legal systems. Primarily, despite the globalization of business and trade, international firms must abide by their target countries' local rules and regulations, or even more so, the countries where they already operate. In Chapter 1, we learned that Google had to deal with the Chinese government's regulations on the freedom of speech to conduct business in that country. China's distinct political and legal policies caused Google to discontinue the mainland Chinese version of its site and redirect mainland Chinese users to a Hong Kong version.

Until recently, governments could directly enforce the rules and regulations based on political and legal philosophies. However, the digitalization of business processes and knowledge management systems has started to change this, as international sellers and buyers now have easier access to each other. Nevertheless, nations can still force strong-arm international firms to conform to their domestic rules and regulations. Hence, international business companies must monitor and assess the political and legal environment in the target countries where they plan or operate.

https://doi.org/10.1515/9783111510286-003

Government and the Ownership of Business

The government can be a business friend, providing financial, advisory, and other services. It can also be a friend of the public, creating and enforcing consumer protection, worker safety, and other laws. However, many sectors of the business world have long complained about government regulation. Corporations and their spokespeople often denounce government rules as irrational impediments to profits, economic efficiency, and job creation. Unsurprisingly, many firms have used loopholes, moved operations abroad, and violated antitrust laws as they attempted to deal with regulations.

Businesses across the globe have both prospered and suffered due to an ever-increasing number of government rules and often complicated tax codes. More importantly, the rules have protected consumers from exploitative practices. As a result, the relationship between businesses and the government can be collaborative or adversarial.

State-Owned Enterprises

The COVID-19 pandemic has underlined the role of the public sector in rescuing human lives and livelihoods, and state-owned enterprises (SOEs) have been part of this effort as public utilities deliver essential services. Often, these SOEs are public banks offering loans to small and medium-sized (SME) businesses. However, others who were not so successful were and continue to struggle as of these writings, adding to the burden on government finances. Such SOEs range from national oil corporations dealing with a significant decline in oil prices to national airlines without enough passengers traveling. Most individuals encounter SOEs daily as these often supply the water they drink, the electricity they use, and the public transportation (bus, metro, or train) they ride to and from work or school. These SOEs come in all forms and sizes, with some wholly owned by the government, while private investors may jointly own others. Figure 3.1 illustrates the number of SOEs per region across the globe.

According to a 2022 Organization for Economic Co-operation and Development (OECD) report, SOEs are becoming increasingly present in the international marketplace, as shown in Figure 3.2, which can have significant implications for fair global competition and leveling the playing field for international business and trade. As of spring 2022, SOEs total 132 out of the world's top 500 most prominent corporations, up from only 32 just two decades ago. Such a trend reflects mainly, but not only, the ascendancy of emerging and frontier economies, most of which have large state-owned sectors.

The OECD's report argues that policymakers and the private international business sector should not be alarmed, as the world could yet see a new wave of mass privatizations. Either way, the trend points to SOEs operating with equally high governance standards, levels of transparency, and commercial orientations, as private companies are expected to do. As the OECD argued in another report, governments are seriously adopting international best practices.

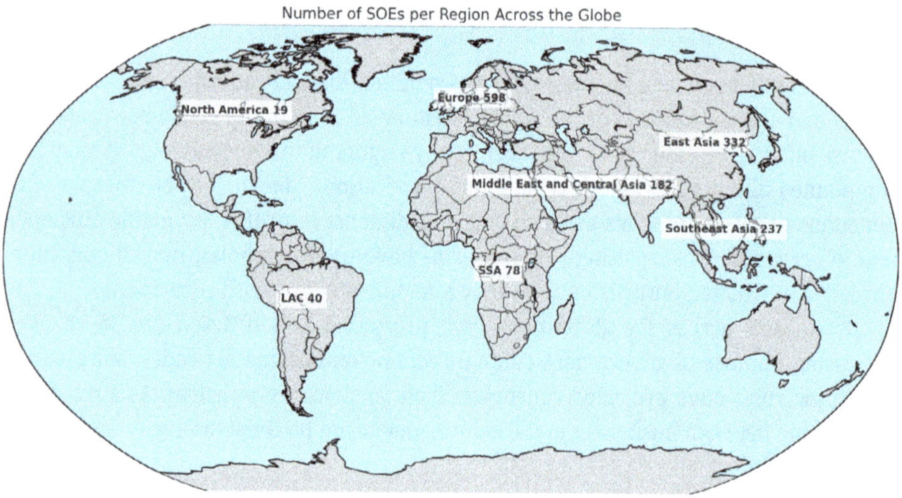

Figure 3.1: Number of SOEs per region across the globe. (SOURCE: Adapted from UNCTAD and IMF, 2020).

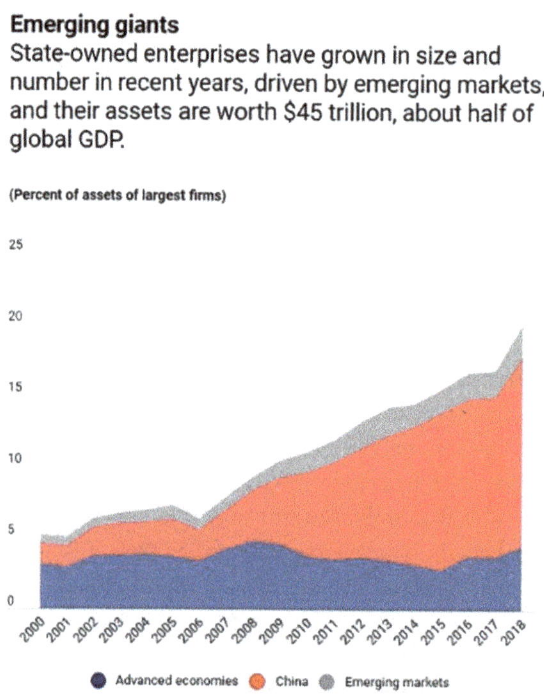

Figure 3.2: Global growth of SOEs from 2000–2018. (SOURCE: IMF, S&P Capital IQ, and UNCTAD).

Nationalizations

Nationalization, or collectivization, transforms a privately owned enterprise or assets into a public asset. The process brings the targeted enterprise, or asset, under the public ownership of a nation's government or state. Nationalization may also apply to private assets or those owned by lower levels of government being transferred to the state. The process typically occurs without compensation for losing the net worth of confiscated assets and possible income. Such action may result from a government's attempt to consolidate power, resentment of foreign ownership of industries representing significant importance to local economies, or it may be triggered by failing sectors.

Below are some reasons for the nationalization of business, which are also illustrated in Figure 3.3:

- Avoidance of foreign dominance of the domestic economy. For example, the government of a hosting country could decide to nationalize foreign enterprises operating in its market to decrease the number of foreigners in their nation, as most foreigners would have to return to their home countries.
- Political: When the relationship between two countries deteriorates, the governments of both nations may decide to nationalize businesses owned by the other country in retaliation and to prevent or reduce the country's national income.
- Prevent wasteful competition among domestic or foreign companies, especially in the service industry.
- Prevention of exploitation by private individuals or companies, foreign or domestic, when a government notices that a business has exploited citizens because of its monopoly.
- Provide uninterrupted services, such as electricity, water supply, etc. Governments may nationalize those services to ensure that citizens obtain better services.
- Raising significant capital: when foreign companies need large amounts of capital, they may entice the local government to nationalize their business and access the capital required.
- Strategic, for instance, is when there is war or the government tries to regulate the economy. For example, if a government decides to engage another country in a war, it may quickly nationalize every business owned by the opposite country to limit its income.

Figure 3.3: Main reasons for nationalization.

Below are some disadvantages of nationalized business:
- Corruption and mismanagement often occur with government-owned and -managed businesses.
- Low productivity and inefficiencies are often caused by the fact that government businesses are usually poorly managed.
- Political interference, which may lead to the misallocation of resources.
- Prevention of private initiatives: as private businesses are nationalized, other private initiatives tend to decrease, fostering a lack of competition.
- The exploitation of consumers is a significant risk. Although nationalization is supposed to be aimed at not making a profit, the government can still exploit its citizens.

Nationalization is more typical in emerging and frontier economies. Conversely, privatization, which transfers government-run operations into the private business sector, occurs more often in advanced economies. Nationalization is also one of the main risks for firms conducting business in a foreign market due to the prospect of having substantial assets confiscated without any compensation. Such risk can be heightened in nations with unstable political governments and stagnant or contracting economies. The critical objective of nationalization is redirecting revenues to the nation's government rather than private operators who may export funds with no local benefit to the host nation.

The oil sector has undergone nationalization actions for decades. These date to Mexico's nationalization of the assets of foreign producers such as Royal Dutch and Standard Oil in 1938, which resulted in the creation of PEMEX, now one of the largest oil producers in the world. Another example is Iran's nationalization of Anglo-Iranian in 1951, right before the country's economy fell into disarray, which allowed the British back into the country as a 50% partner a few years later, and, in 1954, the company was renamed British Petroleum Company.

The Venezuelan government nationalized Exxon Mobil's Cerro Negro Project and other assets in 2007. When Exxon sought $16.6 billion in compensation, a World Bank arbitration panel awarded the company approximately 10% of that amount in 2014.

Privatizations

Privatization of state-owned enterprises was a core recommendation of the Washington consensus that emerged over two decades ago. While governments worldwide followed those recommendations, and several state-owned enterprises were privatized in the process, the discussion over the appropriate role of the government in the economy remains open. Privatization describes transferring ownership, operation, and control of a government or public institution to a non-government or private company. The procedure is typically conducted to ensure the public enterprise or institution becomes more disciplined and efficient concerning its industry and market expectations. There are numerous forms in which privatization could be performed.

Privatization always helps to keep the consumer needs uppermost. It enables governments to pay their debts, helps increase long-term jobs, and promotes competitive efficiency and an open market economy. Privatized assets and institutions are more effective and productive, providing citizens with higher-quality goods and services. Most significantly, privatizations tend to generate more economic activities through increased investments, a welcome undertaking in tough economic times.

The primary objectives of privatization may be summarized as follows:

1. To improve efficiency and decrease the size of the public sector.
2. To lessen public debt/deficit and to raise funds.
3. To bolster the stock markets.

Privatization creates wealth, as production costs are reduced and profits are maximized. It is often a good strategy when the government believes a particular industry can be extended to competition, benefiting the market and the consumer. Contrary to popular belief, privatization cannot reduce business corruption, as it depends on our attitude, needs, self-respect, desires, emotions, financial condition, salary, tax rate, laws, rules and regulations, selfishness, behavior, etc. Figure 3.4 lists the pros and cons of privatization.

Government Stability and Protection

The standard description of political *instability* is the tendency of a government to tumble either because of conflicts or uncontrolled rivalry between many political parties. Government changes also increase the probability of succeeding changes, causing political instability to be persistent. Economic development and political stability are profoundly related. On the one hand, the indecisiveness associated with an unstable

Privatization

Pros

- Private companies often operate more efficiently than public companies
- Acceleration of technological progress
- Less bureaucratic work style
- May attract more highly-qualified people
- Higher wages
- Product quality may improve
- Service quality may get better
- Supervision may be easier
- Lower product prices
- Lower influence of lobbyists
- Additional source of income for governments

Cons

- Privatization may not be suitable for important infrastructure
- Energy supply may be threatened
- Access to medical equipment may no longer be guaranteed
- Education levels may become lower
- Harmful if the business has a monopolistic character
- May not be feasible due to regulatory restrictions
- Public companies may be sold too cheap to private corporations
- One-time payment instead of multiple dividend payments for governments
- Insufficient regulation
- Responsibilities may become unclear
- Fragmentation of public infrastructure may lead to serious problems
- Public vs. private interest

Figure 3.4: Pros and cons of privatization.

political climate may decrease investment and the rate of economic growth. On the other hand, inadequate financial results may lead to government failure and political turmoil. However, although not desirable, political stability can be attained through oppression or holding a political party where it does not have to compete to be re-elected. In such cases, political stability will be a double-edged sword. While a peaceful environment may be a requirement, it could quickly become a breeding ground for cronyism with impunity.

Political stability is by no means the standard in human history. Democratic governments, like all political powers, are flimsy. Irrespective of political regimes, if a nation is not concerned with conflicts and radical government changes, its citizens can focus on working, saving, and investing. The literature on corruption identifies several variables that correlate significantly with bribery and corruption. A decades-long tradition of democracy and political stability is among the characteristics that decrease government corruption. Nowadays, however, many nations incorporate one of these two powerful determinants of bribery with the opposite: politically stable autocracies versus newly instituted and unstable democracies.

Many external environmental factors can impact international business and trade. Common elements assess political, economic, social, technological, ecological,

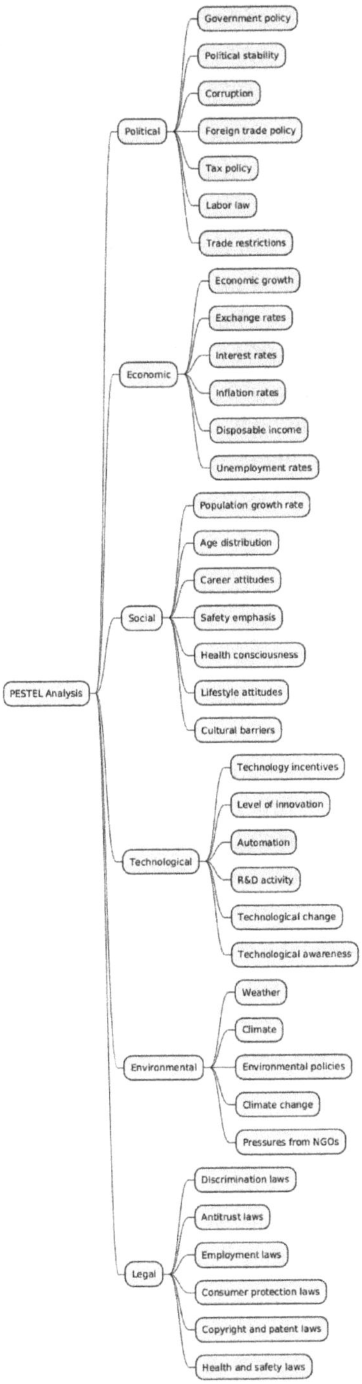

Figure 3.5: PESTEL analysis, a framework to analyze and monitor macro-environmental factors.

and legal factors, also known as PESTEL analysis, as depicted in Figure 3.5. It is common for business leaders to evaluate each of these aspects closely. The objective is often to make more suitable and informed decisions for the company's success in the new market. The political factors impacting international business are often important since several factors related to government policy can affect business, and all firms must follow the law. Management must figure out how some upcoming legislation can impact business activities in the country.

The political environment can also impact business organizations in many ways. For instance, it could add a risk factor leading to a significant loss. Management must understand that political factors have the power to change business results. It can also affect government policies at the local to the federal level. Companies should be ready to deal with politics and regional and international outcomes. Changes in government policy make up the political factors. The difference can range from economic, legal, or social but could also be a combination of these factors.

An increase or decrease in tax could be an example of a political element. Governments may increase taxes for some foreign companies in one industry while lowering them for others in another. Such government decisions directly affect international companies operating in the country. Government interventions like interest rate changes can affect a company's demand patterns. So, foreign companies must constantly stay abreast of such political factors.

Specific characteristics may create interlinkages in many different ways. Here are some examples:

- Political decisions affect the nation's socio-cultural environment.
- Political determinations may impact the economic environment.
- Politicians can influence the endorsement of new technologies.
- Politicians can manipulate the degree of the emergence of new technologies.

The political environment is among the least predictable factors in the international business environment. A cyclical political environment evolves as democratic administrations pursue re-election every few years. This external factor of business comprises the influences of pressure groups, which often tend to alter government policies. As political systems in distinct areas vary, the political influence also differs. In totalitarian regimes, the government's authority derives from a select group. The nation's population democratically elects an open government system.

Lastly, as shown in Figure 3.6, corruption is a barrier to economic growth for many nations. Some foreign firms survive and grow by bribing government officials. Their success and development are not based on the value they deliver to consumers.

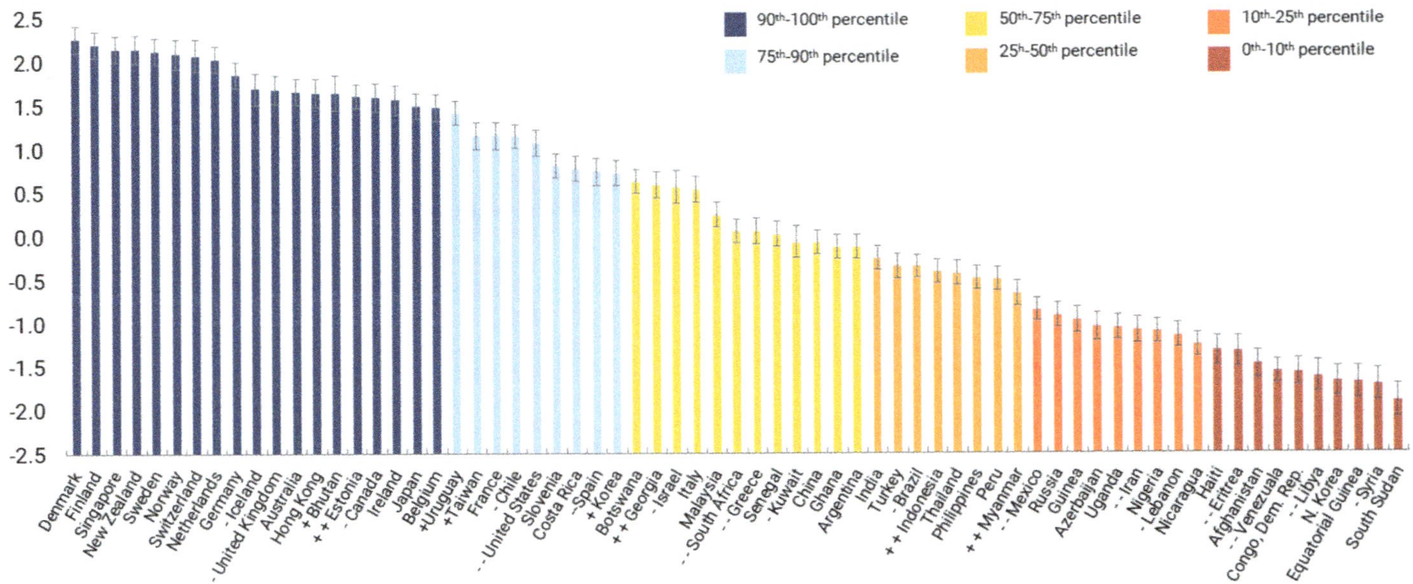

Figure 3.6: Worldwide governance indicators control of corruption. (SOURCE: Brookings, 2020).

Government Protections

A global market economy permits and promotes competition between industrial and commercial international organizations. As global competitors are out to succeed, they may periodically be enticed to adopt malicious means to attain an unfair advantage, such as posing a direct attack against the competition or misleading the general public to the disadvantage of a competitor, which tends to prompt government protections. Self-regulation, via associations of international organizations, can play a significant role in developing a code of conduct or controlling practices, which boosts and facilitates global trade. As Figure 3.7 shows, global trade hit a record high in the first quarter of 2022. However, obstacles and challenges exist, as fair and free trade frequently fails to be respected by parties across the globe or followed by judicial powers. In 1900, at the Brussels Diplomatic Conference for the Revision of the Paris Convention, Article 10 bis was added to the Convention to prevent unfair competition.

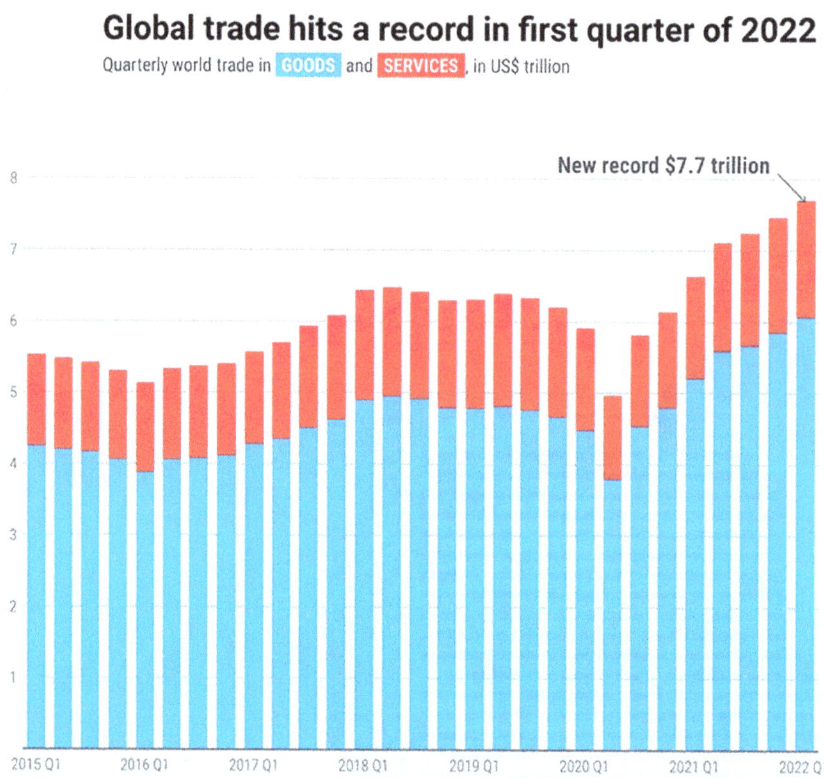

Figure 3.7: shows that global trade hit a record high in the first quarter of 2022. (SOURCE: UN, UNCTAD).
Note: Figures for Q1 2022 are preliminary.
Source: UNCTAD calculations based on national statistics

Generally, any act or practice in the course of industrial or commercial activities, domestic or international, contrary to honest business practices comprises an act of unfair competition, the decisive criterion being "contrary to honest practices." In Belgium and Luxembourg, ethical practices are sometimes referred to as "honest trade practices," in Switzerland and Spain as "the principle of good faith," and in Italy as "professional correctness." Finding a clear-cut and worldwide description of what constitutes an act contrary to honest practices is challenging. Standards of honesty and fairness may vary from nation to nation to mirror a society's economic, sociological, and moral notions. Consequently, the idea of 'honesty' has to be analyzed by the concerned judicial bodies of the nation. Concepts of honest international business practices specified by international trade should also be evaluated, particularly in competition between international firms in distinct countries.

A broad understanding can be an action or business practice contrary to ethical business practices. For instance, an omission to act can be deemed unfair competition. The World Intellectual Property Organization (WIPO) Model Provisions on Protection Against Unfair Competition defines the "failure to correct or supplement information concerning a product test published in a consumer magazine, thereby giving a wrong impression of the quality of the product offered on the market, or failure to give sufficient information concerning the correct operation of a product or concerning possible side-effects of a product,"[1] as an act of unfair competition.

WIPO also notes that failure to abide by honest business practices should arise "during industrial or commercial activities." Government agencies' protection against unfair competition is an ever-evolving concept that must adjust to international trade development and new principles and obligations for actors in the global business market. It can be broadly understood as the actions of business and trade organizations supplying goods or services – especially the selling or buying of such products or services – and the activities of business professionals such as medical doctors or legal experts. Nowadays, laws against unfair competition aim to ensure fair competition in the interests of all concerned. Originally designed to protect the 'honest businessman,' the scope of protection against unfair competition has now been enlarged to include the protection of the customers.

Behaviors Classified as Unfair Competition

To prevent unfair international business practices, explicit activities are limited by law. Article 10 bis of the Paris Convention categorizes unfair business practices into three broad categories:

1 Senftleben, M. (2024). Article 10 bis of the Paris Convention as the common denominator for protection against unfair competition in national and regional contexts. *Journal of Intellectual Property Law and Practice*, 19(2), 81–89.

- **Acts confusing** – An act or practice, in the course of industrial or commercial activities, that drives, or is likely to cause, confusion regarding another's firm or its activities, particularly the products or services offered by such a firm, comprises an act of unfair competition. Even the possibility of confusion having a damaging effect equivalent to actual confusion includes an act of unfair competition, which broadly widens the scope of protection. For example, a brand, whether registered or not, or a product's appearance can lead to confusion. Appearance of a product may include its packaging, shape, or other non-functional characteristic qualities.
- **Misleading acts** – A dishonest act can develop a false image of a competitor's product or services, leading to consumers acting on inaccurate facts and suffering financial harm. Deceptive actions can also be statements that give incorrect indications or allegations about an enterprise or its products or services. For example, misleading statements concerning the development manufacturing process may relate to a product's safety and create a false impression.
- **Acts damaging goodwill or reputation** – Reducing a product's distinctive character, appearance, value, or reputation could harm another's goodwill or repute. For instance, any act that weakens the effect of a brand is deemed unfair as it could destroy a trademark's uniqueness and distinct character.

Other acts that could be categorized as causing unfair competition include:
- Discrediting another's business enterprise or its activities.
- Industrial or commercial espionage, including cyberattacks and terrorism.
- Acting unfairly concerning confidential data, such as an agreement or trust breach.

Under the Paris Convention, member states must protect against unfair competition. This obligation is reinforced by Article 2 of the Trade-Related Aspects of Intellectual Property Rights (TRIPS), which obliges the World Trade Organization's (WTO's) members to comply with the Paris Convention.

Government Interventions

This section discusses how government intervention affects the relationship between a company's information management capability when engaged in international business and the sustainable competitive advantage of such firms. The government plays a critical role in shaping the success of companies involved in international business and trade. The government often intervenes in many ways to assist companies, such as financial assistance, green innovations, policy and incentives, and any government-related intervention and assistance. Government agencies can help by providing financing, promotion, developing capacity, marketing, and other aid programs. Apart from providing direct funds, fiscal measures such as tax reductions or exemptions also play a role.

Companies must be able to develop resources to generate sustained competitive advantages over their rivals to compete abroad successfully. Resources could include value-added products and services, uniqueness of offerings, and barriers to imitability and substitutability. Think back to Porter's diamond, which was discussed in Chapter 2. A sustainable competitive advantage is vital as it offers a long-lasting advantage in implementing unique value-creation strategies not simultaneously implemented by current or potential competitors abroad. Companies expanding abroad should understand the types of resources/capabilities they have and how these resources foster competitive advantage and contribute to sustainable competitive advantage.

Most international business and trade companies, varying by sector, are influenced by government policies. Figure 3.8 illustrates the effects of COVID-19 public intervention indices and specific measures on trade flows according to United States Trade and Development Agency (USTDA) data. Such policies can have a qualitative or quantitative impact on international business and trade to increase their long-term competitive advantage abroad or to protect domestic markets from international trade forces. Governments may intervene in international trade for economic causes. One of the most significant reasons is to protect new industries from fierce international competitors, especially in emerging and frontier economies in sectors that might not survive against more industrialized and advanced economies. However, there are two main reasons governments may intervene in international business and trade: political and economic.

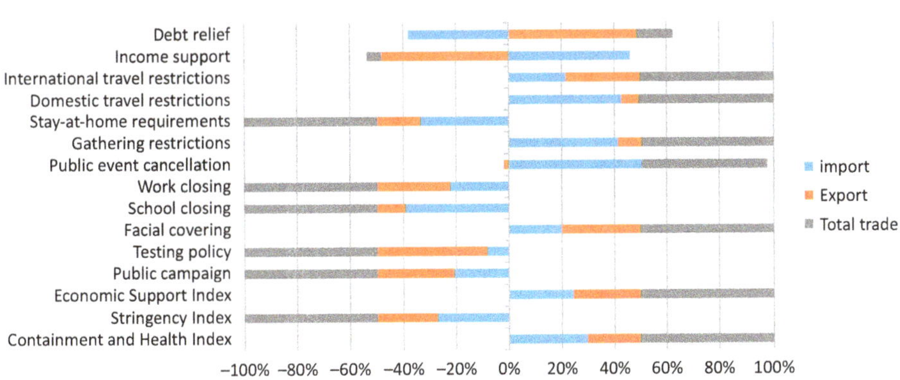

Figure 3.8: The effects of COVID-19 public intervention indices and specific measures on trade flows. (SOURCE: USTDA, 2022).

Political Interventions

There are many political reasons for a government to intervene in international trade to benefit or detriment companies doing business abroad. Often, governments want to protect infant industries and jobs from international business threats. For instance, other nations could attempt to dump (flood) a market with their surplus commodities, such as sugar, wheat, rice, etc., which could cause domestic producers to lose their business. Jobs could also be lost in the sectors affected by the dumping of these commodities, which could be purchased at lower prices from international suppliers.

Another vital reason for political intervention in international trade is to protect national security, such as in the case of military defense-related sectors, semiconductor and telecommunication industries, or aerospace. Political retaliation as part of a foreign policy is a more vengeful reason for intervention. Figure 3.9 offers insight into the G20 tariff weight (2018), which shows there is a trade war, but neither the U.S. nor China started it, although the two countries have been engaged with each other. For example, when the U.S. develops tension with a foreign country over terrorism support or the handling of an international crisis, one weapon in the government's arsenal is to set up trade restrictions to potentially hurt the country's economy.

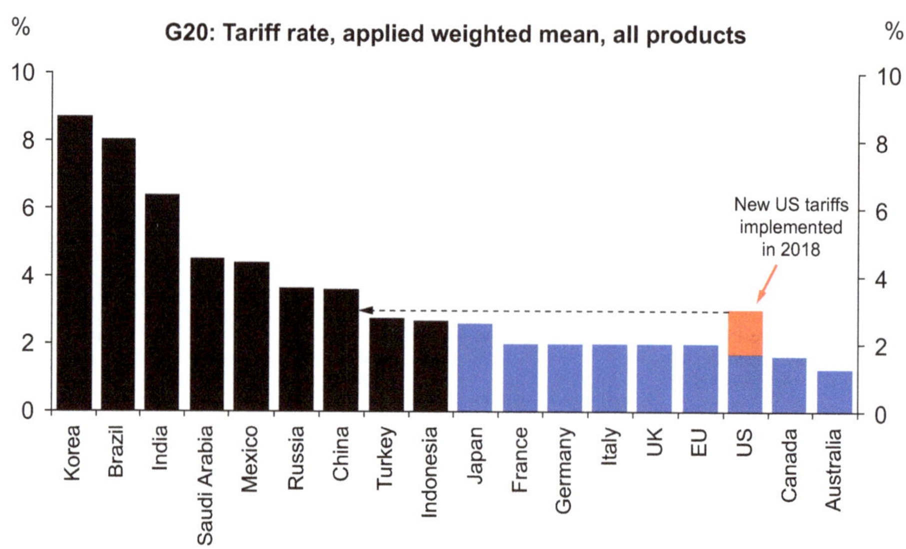

Figure 3.9: The G20 tariff rate shows the U.S. at the emerging market level. (SOURCE: World Bank, DB Global Research, 2018).

The protection of consumers is yet another crucial reason for government intervention. It prevents countries from exporting products that are not up to U.S. standards to the U.S. These products can hurt consumers. An example is the recent China lead paint disaster with children's toys.

Economic Interventions

Governments may intervene in international business and trade for economic reasons, such as to protect new industries from fierce global competition, especially in emerging and frontier economies, which may not survive against much more industrialized and advanced economies. An issue with this premise is that governments may create inefficient sectors and organizations by protecting infant industries. An example is the parastatal or SOE, in which Figure 3.10 depicts the top major SOE global oil companies. The companies are not typically suited to internationalize into foreign markets unless governments continue to support them. For example, due to protectionism, Brazil developed the world's tenth-largest auto industry due to tariff barriers and quotas. Unfortunately, when these protectionary measures were removed, Brazil's imports dramatically increased, and the auto industry could not compete with their competition's products.

Aramco	Saudi Arabia
Gazprom	Russia
China National Petroleum Corp.	China
National Iranian Oil Co.	Iran
Petróleos de Venezuela	Venezuela
Petrobras	Brazil
Petronas	Malaysia

Figure 3.10: The Top Major Global State-Owned Oil Companies. (SOURCE: Energy Intelligence Group, "Petroleum Intelligence Weekly Ranks World's Top 50 Oil Companies"). Source: https://www2.energyintel.com/PIW_Top_50_ranking_about.

The last economic reason for government intervention is based on the strategic trade policy, which cites that, due to scale economies, only a few large global firms would survive if not for government intervention. Many economists are concerned with this type of intervention because it hurts companies that are early entrants into a new product. Also, many economists feel that a government that pushes to have its domestic firm remain in control of an industry is acting selfishly and will end up hurting global competitors and the global economy.

For instance, from 1971 to 1973, former U.S. president Richard Nixon imposed the New Economic Policy to combat an oil crisis due to American foreign oil dependency. For 90 days, wages and prices froze to combat high inflation. While government intervention stabilized external trading forces (the import of oil from foreign markets), inflation quickly became a threat as soon as government controls relaxed. Nixon resigned a few months later, but price controls on oil had to continue, and the government tried to become independent from foreign oil resources through increased domestic oil exploration. The stock market during the 1970s was destabilized, failing about 40% in 18 months.

Take the Philippines, one of the largest rice exporters in Southeast Asia, as another example. The Philippine government has engaged in the rice market using a variety of policy measures, which can be loosely divided into subsidization and taxation. On the one hand, the government gives farmers financial and production aid through price guarantees or input subsidies. At the same time, it imposes tariffs on imported inputs and machinery and regulates prices for consumers.

Knowledge Management as a Catalyst to International Business and Trade

Accelerated by the COVID-19 pandemic, businesses worldwide are increasingly characterized by a pervasive role of business digitalization, redefining domestic and international organizations' management of customer experience efficiencies. In evolving business models, digital transformation challenges enterprises' adaptability, development, technology integration, and resilience. It redefines value-creation strategies. As technologies transform international business processes, knowledge management (KM) catalyzes the changing nature, knowledge assets, and transformation preparedness of enterprises' value drivers. Digital transformation drivers and the role of KM for strategic relevance are underlined through digitalized knowledge processes and customer-centric strategies to access and manage resources, core competencies, and dynamic capabilities.

Today's global business landscape is increasingly characterized by the pervasive role of digital technologies that redefine how enterprises manage their clients' experiences and govern operations. To cope with internet advancements, including 5G infrastructure and the latest integrated communications digital technologies, the race for businesses' digital transformation has accelerated, especially since the global COVID-19 pandemic broke out in 2019. Access to knowledge and the management of information can be a catalyst to sustainable competitive advantage. A KM strategy can enhance a company's information management capability and ability to leverage IT resources to provide accurate and valuable information to improve its competitive advantage when internationalizing. Companies with innovative products or services gain a competitive advantage over other firms, which helps them in internationalization and engagement in foreign collaborative projects. Information and the internet have helped produce innovation in clusters, no longer geographically.

As a global shift into digital transformation occurs, it challenges global enterprises to develop a more holistic integration of business processes, requiring a rethinking of how products and value are delivered to their customers and stakeholders. For this reason, business decision-makers must assess how business data is being created, managed, and shared across the enterprise. The latest digital technologies foster a paradigm shift in how business, as an enterprise asset, is being used to shape value drivers, especially those related to data processing, to manage and access crucial data resources and shape core competencies' dynamic capabilities.

Technological innovations and human ingenuity have persistently contributed to managing strategic data and business capabilities. Indeed, digital technologies now offer ubiquitous and timely access to a vast array of business and market resources, opening significant prospects across the globe and, with it, several business challenges as well. Considering the rising influence and dependence on digital technologies and applications across global markets and business sectors/industries, the ability and level of connectedness of managed business data and strategies encompass a more significant impact on the growth and sustainability of competitiveness. Besides the importance of strategic data, the extant literature on digitally connected conceptualizations, such as big and thick data, cloud computing, deep learning, Internet of Things (IoT), augmented reality, virtual worlds, digital wallets, and applied business analytics highlights several challenges associated with attaining and maintaining business value for customers and stakeholders. While applied business analytics might generate data and business intelligence, the need to understand data inputs and intelligence in a more human sense is still needed. In other words, while big data (quantitative) may offer business insight into *what* is happening in the industry, it does not tell why. For that, we need to analyze the thick data (qualitative). There remains an associate degree of an inherent risk of how decision-makers use, interpret, and apply strategic data effectively in their enterprises to realize and sustain competitive advantage, which is still not clear.

Business decision-makers usually have a limited understanding of the role of strategic data management and its influence on their enterprise's international business and trade competitive advantages. Oversight of strategic data management within the context of the growing stress of digital transformation across numerous industries worldwide generates substantial challenges, such as non-adaptive and dysfunctional data processes, including but not limited to data creation, transfer, use, and application. Consequently, such inefficiencies could result in reinvention and loss of data assets at substantial costs to the enterprise's international competitiveness. Hence, it is crucial that decision-makers better understand the intersection between strategic KM and the need to adopt a digital transformation in the enterprise, especially when competing for a new market abroad where many uncertainties and needs for data exist.

Competing Technologies Accelerating Digital Transformation

If there were any protracted disbeliefs about the need for businesses to engage in digital transformation to extend their lifespan and enhance competitive advantage, the global COVID-19 pandemic has quashed it. As several business sectors across the globe are still deterred from physical contact with supply chains, distribution channels, and especially its customers, most exchanges are being pushed to a virtual platform. Digital operations have become the only alternative for many businesses due to mandated shutdowns and constrained in-person activities. Enterprises face the terrible choices of going digital or going dark.

The pandemic has fast-tracked industries' transformation across the globe, forcing business decision-makers to rethink their business models. As shown in Figure 3.11, commercial organizations expect to face digitally mature competitors in the next five years. Digital transformation has become a megatrend, threatening existing businesses and concurrently promising all-encompassing new opportunities. More than ever before, digital transformation processes are becoming part of every aspect of business worldwide with a significant impact on business growth and sustainability, without restrictions to any industry or business division, affecting cross-divisional or cross-departmental functions that affect businesses. To avoid shrinking profitability and make effective decisions, enterprises worldwide must understand the significance and scale of changes caused by digital transformation. Business models must be adapted to integrate these rapidly developing digital processes and translate them into value and economic success.

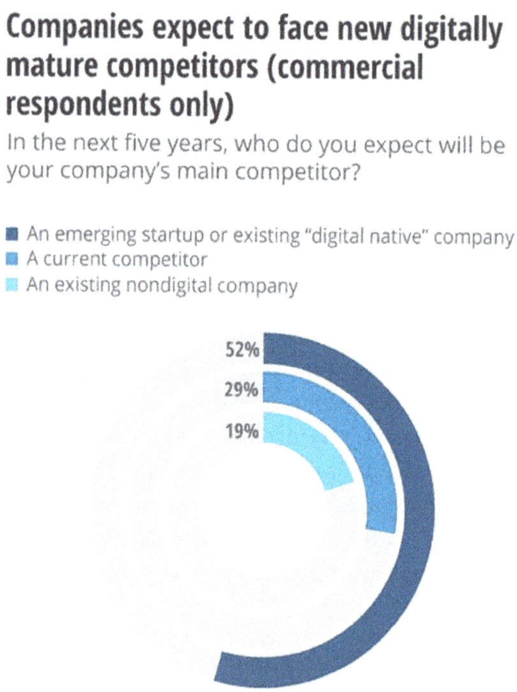

Figure 3.11: Commercial organizations will face digitally mature competitors in the next five years. (SOURCE: Deloitte, 2021).

This digital mandate is not a reaction to the global COVID-19 pandemic, as it has been around since integrated communications technologies (ICT) became a reality in the dot-com era. Such a paradigm shift toward the global economy's digital transformation has existed for quite some time. The pandemic brought the need for businesses' digital transformation into a sharper focus. The global pandemic and the business and economic challenges it has created have accelerated the adoption of such a digital paradigm, as evidenced by the marked shift in digital businesses' spending. This forced shift into business processes digitalization serves as a widespread test case for the effectiveness of digital solutions, as shown in Figure 3.12. In healthcare, telehealth doctor visits are set to replace the traditional annual physical by 2025. Real estate is also changing, with all new construction of multi-family homes beginning in 2021, including coworking spaces. In the financial services industry, integrating tokenization technology to secure better and track individual purchases and transactions began in 2023, while manufacturing's full adoption of supply chain 4.0 might debut by 2025. These digital business transformations will become permanent fixtures and lead to long-term changes for many other interconnected businesses.

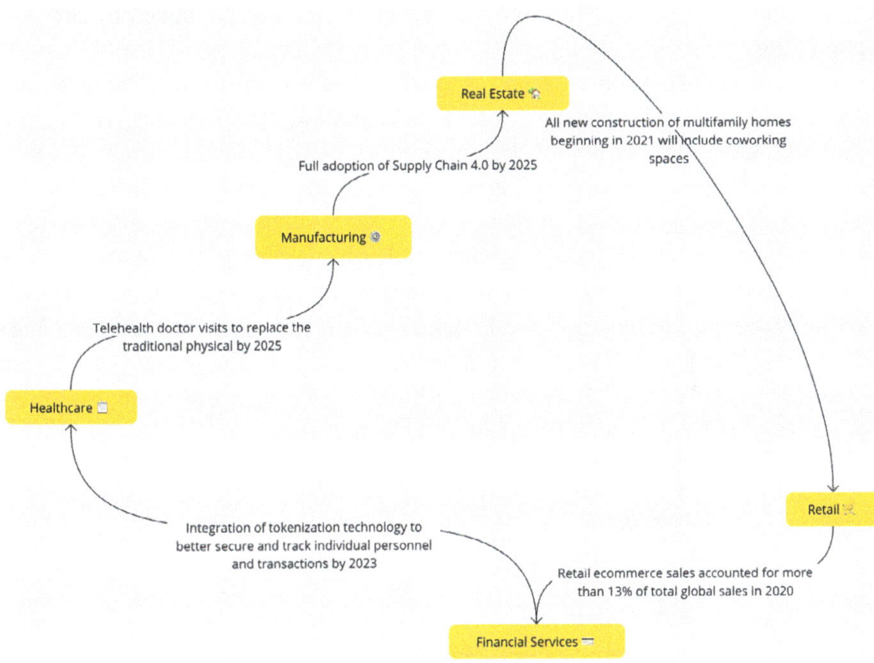

Figure 3.12: Business process digitalization is a widespread test case for the effectiveness of digital solutions. (SOURCE: ARK, 2020).

Digital transformation, speedier changing internal and external structure conditions, and new customer expectations for the fastest delivery and best quality of goods, to list a few, are challenging enterprises to optimize their internal business processes. Driven by the internet, real and virtual worlds have grown further, giving birth to the IoT and cloud computing data importing capabilities. Digital transformation is taking processes and managing processes customarily managed internally by people into the cloud, where they can be adapted and analyzed from anywhere.

Deep learning (DL), as a form of artificial intelligence (AI), has become a driving force for digital transformation across the global markets. Until recently, humans programmed all software, but DL can use data to write software by itself. DL is turbocharging every industry by automating software creation, from object-oriented programming languages and graphical user interfaces to translation systems and intelligent games. Virtual worlds, here defined as a computer-simulated environment that anyone can access at any time, although in their infancy, are undergoing a substantial digital transformation, enabling businesses and consumers to interact daily with platform markets, buying and selling goods. The percentage of global virtual world gaming revenues has been shrinking from 80 percent in 2010 to 25 percent in 2020, while revenues from in-game purchases have grown from only 20% in 2010 to more than 75% in 2020. Digital transformation strategies in virtual worlds are forecasted to generate compound revenues of 17 percent yearly, from about $180 billion in 2020 to $390 billion by 2025 ARK Report (2020).

Digital transformation is having a profound effect on the way international businesses operate and interact with customers abroad. Digital wallets, as shown in Figure 3.13, have become one of the alternatives to digitizing consumer payables and corporate receivables and are becoming increasingly prevalent worldwide. The Cimigo report (2020) found that most leading digital wallet brands offer features similar to those of their users. The global competitive landscape is already crowded, with brands taking dominance in their respective continents, such as Venmo, MOGO, Chime, Robinhood, Sofi, and Cash App in North America; Mercado Pago, Uala, PicPay, Movil, and Albo in Latin America; Lydia, Revolut, Satispay, BN-XT and N26 in Europe; M-Pesa, MTN, TymeBank, KKudo in Africa; and WeChatPay, AlyPay, PayPay, toss, PayTM, PhonePe, GrobPay, and MoMo in Asia.

Region	Digital Wallets
North America	Cash App, Chime, Venmo, Robinhood, SoFi, Mogo
South America	Mercado Pago, Ualá, PicPay, Albo, Nubank, Movi
Europe	Lydia, Revolut, Bnext, N26, Satispay
Africa	M-PESA, Eversend, MTN, Chipper Cash, TymeBank, Kuda
Asia	WeChat Pay, Alipay, Paytm, PhonePe, PayPay, GrabPay, MoMo, Toss

Figure 3.13: Digital wallets have become a global phenomenon. (SOURCE: ARK, 2020).

Despite modest successes, KM has not entirely delivered on the potential of the learning organization. Many organizations lack the basic building blocks in KM. Still, given the latest data transformation trends, including a fluid workforce, KM is getting back the importance it deserves with increasing interest, with the Asia region engaging in several KM initiatives. Companies have understood that retaining their workforce, fostering innovation, and staying ahead of the competition requires effective KM strategies in the high-tech industry. Information systems and technologies researchers have found evidence that digitalization is pivotal in enabling external knowledge acquisition activities.

International Business Cases of KM as Catalyst for Digital Transformation

The recent and rapid proliferation of intelligent digital technologies (e.g., AI and DL) relies on intelligent digital devices and data repositories. Data is extracted automatically through web crawlers and scrapers by analyzing, classifying, labeling, and correlating structured and unstructured data volumes, including free-form text. Structured or not, enterprises are undergoing digital transformation. There is an opportunity to adopt KM as a catalyst for innovation and creativity, showing how innovative ideas can be captured, shared, and leveraged, leading to more innovative ideas. For instance, the medical diagnostic or financial advisory services available through intelligent devices are possible due to their capacity to generate their knowledge base by absorbing automatically significant structured and unstructured datasets and free-form text. Though KM is rarely mentioned explicitly, data science methods are utilized to attain KM objectives.

There has also been a growing interest in augmented and virtual reality and how enterprises may use KM as a competitive advantage. For instance, service engineers and physicians wearing augmented reality goggles can offer consultations and send and receive data regarding a product or service directly overlaid on the device without fumbling for a laptop or tablet, as the necessary information would be readily accessible and manipulated through eye movements. Other real-world applications of KM for international business and trade competitive advantage are exemplified in cases such as Waymo, TikTok, Facebook, the World Bank, and Pratt & Whitney:

- **Waymo** is arguably at an advantage in the race to introduce a driverless car onto the global market. It is ahead of leading international automakers such as American General Motors, German Mercedes-Benz, and Audi by at least a year to announce driverless vehicles to the broader public. The Waymo Open Dataset has been released recently, providing a platform to crowdsource some fundamental challenges for automated vehicles (AVs), such as 3D detection and tracking. The dataset offers much high-quality and multi-source driving information stored in a cloud-based environment. The company is tapping into KM strategies in its digital transformation of self-driving cars by collecting over 20 million real-world driving miles throughout 25 cities in the United States.
- **TikTok** uses DL models such as convolutional neural networks, recurrent neural networks, or graph neural networks to achieve considerable success in various ML tasks for video recommendations over the internet. This enables the company

to outgrow Snapchat and Pinterest combined. The company also uses DL to handle relational data more efficiently and effectively than its competitors.
- **Facebook** (Meta) uses ML to provide a broad range of competencies that direct several user experience characteristics, content understanding, incorporating posts' ranking, object recognition, and trailing for augmented reality, speech recognition, and text translations. While machine learning models are trained on tailored data-center infrastructure, Facebook brings machine learning inference to the edge. The user experience is improved with reduced inference time and becomes less dependent on network connectivity.
- **The World Bank** transformed dramatically from a hierarchical source of low-interest loans to a decentralized organization that uses KM technologies to fight poverty and disease in developing nations. The bank's information infrastructure and communications network had to be overhauled.
- **Pratt & Whitney** has been digitalizing its business processes, enabling its airline engines to constantly transmit data about the status of their parts even when airborne. Simultaneously, on the ground, data recorders at the manufacturer capture this data and compare it to optimum levels to ensure the engines' ongoing health. Data streams are readily made available through a KM Web portal.

Inadvertence towards strategic KM in the growing emphasis on digital transformation across diverse industries and global markets can present enormous concerns, such as non-adaptive and dysfunctional knowledge processes such as creation, transfer, use, and application. Consequently, such inadvertence can result in reinvention, loss of knowledge assets, and massive organizational costs. Considering the rising influence and dependence on digital technologies and applications in many different sectors/industries, the relevance of managing strategic knowledge in learning organizations has a more significant impact than ever before.

When engaging in international business and trade, business decision-makers must beware that not all innovative ideas and digitalization strategies are suitable or ideal at first. By capturing and sharing these ideas with others, they can be developed and used as a springboard for new ones. Digital transformation forces are not evolving exclusively from technology. The challenge faced by global decision-makers is recognizing how digital technologies are changing business logic and strategies across entire industries and learning how to transform associated challenges into innovative business models. The accelerating pace of digital transformation, especially after the breakout of the COVID-19 pandemic in 2019, makes it increasingly important for international business decision-makers to develop innovative digital business models. Research shows that over 80 percent of business decision-makers know the pressure to transform their organizations. However, about a third of them have little confidence in coping with severe challenges, such as the COVID-19 global pandemic.

It's difficult to tell whether government interventions worldwide are always reasonable. Historically, the results of such interventions have been both positive and negative. Still, the president, regardless of the country, is expected to intervene when a problematic situation arises in international trade. In the long run, the impact of that intervention is unpredictable and generally cannot be thoroughly evaluated until time has passed.

Tariffs and Quotas

Now that you understand why governments get involved in trade policies, let us learn about the different instruments governments can use to affect trade. The oldest forms of trade policy are tariffs, aimed at protecting domestic industries from international competition by increasing the cost of imported goods through a tax. Tariffs are also beneficial to the home country as they raise revenue. A negative to tariffs is that consumers in the domestic market usually end up paying more for imports due to the tariffs. For example, the U.S. places a 35% tariff on Chinese auto tires and a 40% tariff on Japanese leather. Figure 3.14 provides an overview of the U.S.-China trade war tariffs from January 2018 through June 2022.

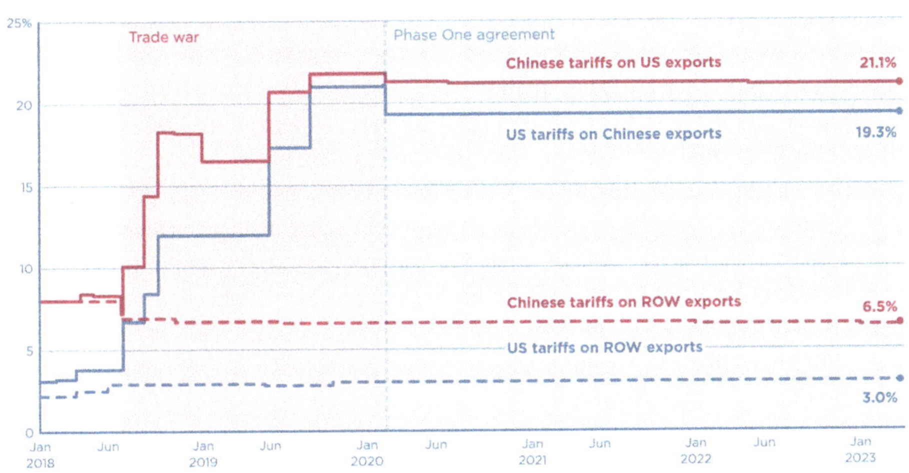

Figure 3.14: An overview of the U.S.-China trade war tariffs from January 2018 to June 2022. (SOURCE: PIIE, 2022).

Quotas and tariffs safeguard domestic industries by artificially inflating costs in the domestic market. Their administration and effects, however, vary in distinct ways. Quotas always restrict the number of goods imported from another nation, while tariffs are charges imposed on the value of goods imported from another country. While tariffs induce revenue disbursed to the importing nation's treasury, the value of a quota, also called "quota rents," typically goes to the international exporters. They can trade goods subject to the quota at higher prices and collect a higher per-unit income. In both cases, domestic buyers in the importing nation pay the tariff costs and quota rents, whereas, with quotas, the government of the importing nation receives no revenue.

Quotas can also be much more complex to administer than tariffs. A customs officer collects tariffs as goods enter a country. With quotas, however, customs officers must either monitor imports directly to confirm that no goods beyond the quota amount are imported or grant licenses to specific firms, giving them the right to import the amount authorized under the quota. Quotas can also be a voluntary export restraint (VER), where the exporting nation administers the quota.

Costs and pricing under tariff control are more transparent and predictable than quotas. For instance, if a good is subject to a 10 percent tariff, it should cost about 10 percent more than before when it was assessed. With quotas, the cost of that same good may increase as long as demand for the good continues and the supply stays restrained, which could mean that quota rents are ultimately more costly to domestic consumers than a tariff. In such a manner, quotas may incentivize international producers to boost the quality standard of their exports, fostering more direct competition with domestic producers and a higher-price product mix for customers. On the other hand, if international producers decide to export low-quality goods within a quota regime, the prices and profits for both foreign and domestic producers of low-quality goods will increase because of quotas. In contrast, domestic consumers are compelled to pay more for lower-quality goods.

Quotas can be tricky to administer. The General Agreement on Tariffs and Trade (GATT) forbids quotas and other quantitative limitations under Article XI (except on particular exceptions, including for "security reasons"), as the GATT parties agreed that quantitative requirements were overly restrictive and distortive compared to duties or taxes, where are permitted. Take, for example, the case of South Korea, Brazil, and Argentina, where each nation agreed to product-specific absolute quotas for 54 distinct steel articles based on each country's average annual steel import volumes from 2015 through 2017. Argentina also accepted product-specific absolute quotas on two aluminum product categories.

The United States administers these quotas to provide exporters with the minimum possible flexibility level and demonstrate how complex quota regimes can be. Specific quotas can be absolute, meaning once a certain quota is reached, no extra amounts are allowed to enter the U.S. for any price unless an exclusion is granted. Some quotas apply to the entire calendar year. But, in reality, these may be filled when the quota is in effect, while others may be subject to similar quarterly limits. Once a quota limit is filled in any given quarter, the importer must hold imports until the next quarter, when the product can again enter the U.S.

The quotas regime has diminished export volumes and total revenue for Brazil, South Korea, and Argentina. For instance, data from the U.S. Department of Commerce shows that the overall quantity of steel Brazil, South Korea, and Argentina exported to the U.S. in 2017 dropped significantly compared to 2015. Regarding value, South Korea and Argentina's steel exports, subject to quotas, declined from 2015 to 2017, while Brazil's steel exports under the quota increased in 2017. Argentina's aluminum exports, subject to the quota, fell from 2015 to 2017. Although South Korea, Brazil, and Argentina have benefitted from generally higher prices in the United States for steel and aluminum, the quotas effectively reduce US imports from these countries.

Intellectual Property Rights and Enforcement

Although often ignored, intellectual property (IP) must be nurtured and safeguarded as valuable corporate assets. Unfortunately, many in-house attorneys do not comprehend the different types of IP or know the proper steps to protect it or inspire its creation. Figure 3.15 depicts the leading IP rights companies and individuals (inventors, creators) that may be granted.

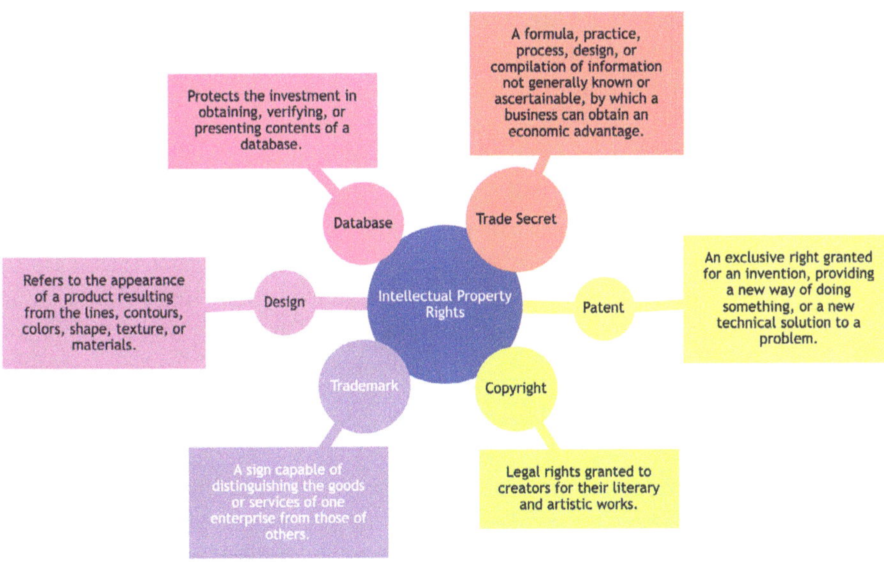

Figure 3.15: Main IP rights companies and individuals (inventors, creators) may be granted.

As depicted in Figure 3.15, IP rights are customarily split into two main sections:
- **Copyright and rights related to copyrights** – The rights of authors of literary and artistic works, including books and other writings, paintings and photographs, musical compositions, sculptures, films, and computer programs, are protected by copyright for at least 50 years after the author's death. Likewise protected via copyright and corresponding rights are the rights of performers such as singers, actors, and musicians, as well as phonograms and sound record-

ings producers and broadcasting organizations. The primary social purpose of protecting copyright and related rights is to stimulate and reward creative and innovative work.

- **Industrial property** – Industrial property can usefully be split into two main areas:
  - *Protecting distinctive signs*, mainly trademarks, differentiates an individual's or enterprise's goods or services from others. It also encompasses the protection of specific geographical signs and indications adopted to identify goods from a particular place where a given characteristic of the good is essentially attributable to its geographical origin. The protection of such distinctive signs seeks to encourage and assure fair competition and to safeguard consumers by allowing them to make educated selections between many goods and services. The protection can last indefinitely as long as the sign remains distinctive.
  - *Other industrial property types* are protected mostly to encourage innovation, novelty designs, and the development of new technologies. Inventions, for example, are typically protected by patents, industrial designs, and trade secrets. The main social objective for these IP protections is to safeguard the outcomes of investments in developing new technologies, thus providing the motivation and means to fund research and development (R&D) activities.

A functioning IP regime should promote technology transfer through foreign direct investment (FDI), joint ventures, and licensing. The protection is typically given for a finite term, usually 20 years, in the case of patents. As summarized in this section, the leading social objectives of IP protection provide exclusive rights. Still, they typically are subject to several restrictions and exceptions aimed at fine-tuning the essential balance between the legitimate interests of right holders and other users. The following are four main types of IP.

Patents

A patent granted by the government allows the grantee to hold a monopoly on developing, commercializing, and using the patented invention while giving rights to prevent competitors from doing the same. Figure 3.16 illustrates the top 25 companies with the newest patents as of 2021.

A patent is usually good for 20 years, but sometimes, patents may only be good for 14 years. Once a patent expires, anyone can copy and use it to build, develop, and commercialize the original invention. In other words, to be granted a monopoly through a patented invention, the author(s) must be willing to disclose the details of the invention through a patent application. If and when granted, the details will become public domain, subject to reverse engineering by others who will attempt to

Rank	Company	Number of Patents	Industry
1	IBM	8,540	Technology
2	Samsung	8,517	Technology
3	LG	4,388	Technology
4	Canon	3,400	Technology
5	Huawei	2,955	Technology
6	Intel	2,835	Technology
7	TSMC	2,807	Technology
8	Toyota	2,753	Consumer Cyclical
9	Raytheon Technologies	2,694	Industrials
10	Sony	2,624	Technology
11	Apple	2,591	Technology
12	Microsoft	2,453	Technology
13	Qualcomm	2,165	Technology
14	BOE Technology	2,141	Technology
15	Amazon	2,110	Consumer Cyclical
16	Dell	2,053	Technology
17	Alphabet (Google)	2,015	Technology
18	Micron	1,798	Technology
19	Panasonic	1,715	Technology
20	Ford	1,675	Consumer Cyclical
21	Johnson & Johnson	1,525	Healthcare
22	Honeywell	1,506	Industrials
23	Hitachi	1,497	Industrials
24	Hyundai	1,483	Consumer Cyclical
25	Fujifilm	1,421	Consumer Cyclical

Figure 3.16: Top global 25 companies with the newest patents as of 2021. (SOURCE: Harrity Patent Analytics, 2021).

launch some copycats of your invention and compete with the original good, but that is another story. To be awarded a patent in the U.S., its author(s) must meet four minimum requirements:

- The subject matter, or nature of the invention, must be patentable, according to the definitions by the U.S. Congress and courts.
- The idea or invention must be entirely new.

- The idea or invention must be helpful.
- The idea or invention must be unique and non-obvious.

Patents are broken up into three categories an author or inventor can apply:
- Design patents may be awarded to any inventor or author of something new and original with ornamental design characteristics. These patents are granted for 14 years.
- A plant patent may be granted to any inventor or author of inventions or discoveries who can reproduce any distinct and unique new type of plant asexually. These patents are granted for 20 years.
- A utility patent may be awarded to any inventor or author of a new and valuable process, new machine or apparatus, article of manufacture, discovery of a unique composition of matter, or helpful innovation or novelty that improves a function. These patents are granted for 20 years.

Patents can be expensive to develop, obtain, and maintain, as annual or regular fees may be required. In addition, patents are only protected within the country in which they were issued and granted. Companies must file for a patent with the government agency of the target country in which they plan to operate to ensure their protection from competitors and other copycat producers.

Trademarks

Any word, symbol, phrase, design, or combination can be a trademark for a firm's goods and services. Customers often recognize companies in the global marketplace through trademarks such as Nike's *Just Do It*. Trademarks are used for goods, while service marks refer to services. Figure 3.17 shows the number of trademark applications in the U.S. as of 2021, which has skyrocketed. China accounts for 25 percent of U.S. filings, and fraudulent applications are abounding.

In general, however, the term trademark refers to both service marks and trademarks and offers many benefits to the holder:
- Identifies the source of the company's goods and services
- Provides legal protection for the company's brand
- Safeguard against counterfeiting copycats and fraudulent claims

However, a trademark does not mean a company owns any particular word or phrase. Instead, the company holding a trademark owns the right to adopt a set of words or phrases regarding specific goods or services. Any company in the U.S. seeking a trademark will need to do the same or, in good faith, demonstrate their intent to do so. For instance, in our international management consulting firm, MGCG LLC, my two partners and I were awarded a trademark in 2001 for the phrase *Turning Knowledge into Action One Client at a Time*. Our methodology was also trademarked and dubbed *The*

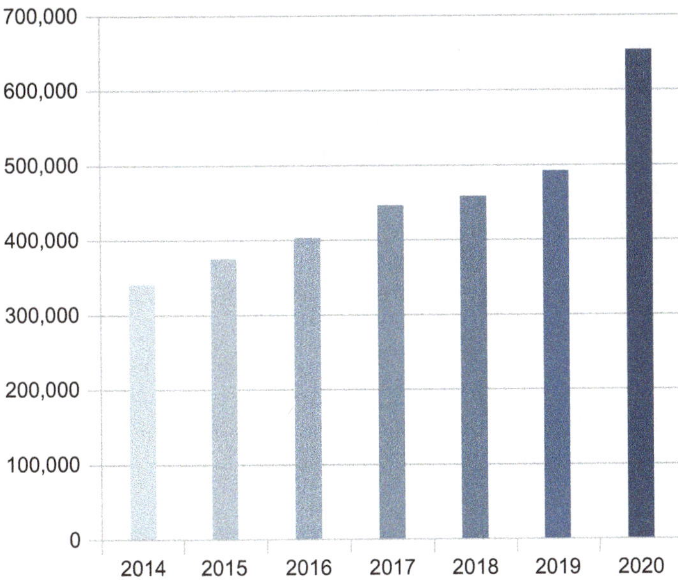

Figure 3.17: Number of trademark applications in the U.S. as of 2020. (SOURCE: Dechert LLP, 2021).

Knowledge Tornado. In obtaining the trademark protection, we had to identify the particular categories of goods and services our consulting practice provided that the trademark would cover. We had to show our company used such goods and services in the chosen categories.

In the U.S., however, a company owns a trademark, known as a common law trademark, when it starts using it in association with its goods or services. It only applies to the geographic region where the company operates and offers its goods or services, not nationwide. The company must apply to register its trademark to obtain nationwide rights. The procedure is simple and can be done online by accessing the United States Patent and Trademark Office (USPTO), filling out a form, and paying a relatively small fee.

Once granted the trademark, every time the company uses it, it can use a symbol for it, such as "TM" for goods, "SM" for services, or "®" for a registered trademark. These symbols "TM" for goods"SM" for services can be used even if the company has not sought to register the trademark. Note that such symbols convey to consumers and competitors the claim the company is making on the mark as its own.

Copyrights

Copyrights protect original works of authorship, such as books, paintings, musical compositions, photographs, sound recordings, blog posts, computer programs, architectural works, plays, and movies. Copyright safeguards expressions, not ideas, systems, methods, processes, principles, concepts, or discoveries.

Therefore, firms may be copyright holders as the law allows ownership through "works made for hire," works developed by employees within the scope of their employment, or through independent contractors. Copyright law grants copyright owners these primary exclusive rights:

- Reproduction of its works
- Preparation of derivative works
- Distribution of copies through the sales, transferring of ownership, or licenses
- Performing or displaying the work publicly

Any works created on or after January 1, 1978, grant copyright owners a term of life of the author and another seventy years past the author's death. For any work originating from works made for hire, the coverage protection is 95 years from the date of publication or 120 years from the creation of the work, whichever is shorter. Although copyrights exist automatically, companies can improve their protection by registering the work, which is not mandatory but allows owners to pursue certain kinds of monetary damages and attorney fees in case of litigation.

Trade Secrets

A trade secret is usually not generally known to the public, but reasonable efforts are made to maintain it confidential. It grants some economic value to the holder because competitors do not understand the data.

In the U.S., the meaning of a trade secret may vary from state to state, even more so from one country to another. The best way to identify a trade secret is to ask yourself what information you would not want competitors to have. Examples may include but are not limited to customer and supplier information, business models, pricing strategies, processes and formulae, marketing strategies, and any other confidential business information.

Figure 3.18 shows reports of filing case decisions involving violations of trade secrets with Westlaw, an online legal research service and proprietary database for lawyers and legal professionals in over 60 countries. The blue bars show all *noncompete decisions*, the red ones show all trade secrets decisions, and the yellow bars show all decisions involving the Defend Trade Secrets Act (DTSA). The DTSA of 2016 is a United States federal law that allows an owner of a trade secret to sue in federal court when its trade secrets have been misappropriated. President Barack Obama signed the act into law on May 11, 2016. As you can see, litigation regarding stealing or misappropriating trade secrets is up significantly across the globe. These are decisions reported on Westlaw only, not including all the decisions in these cases. For instance, U.S. courts often do not report all their choices, and Westlaw may not pick them up.

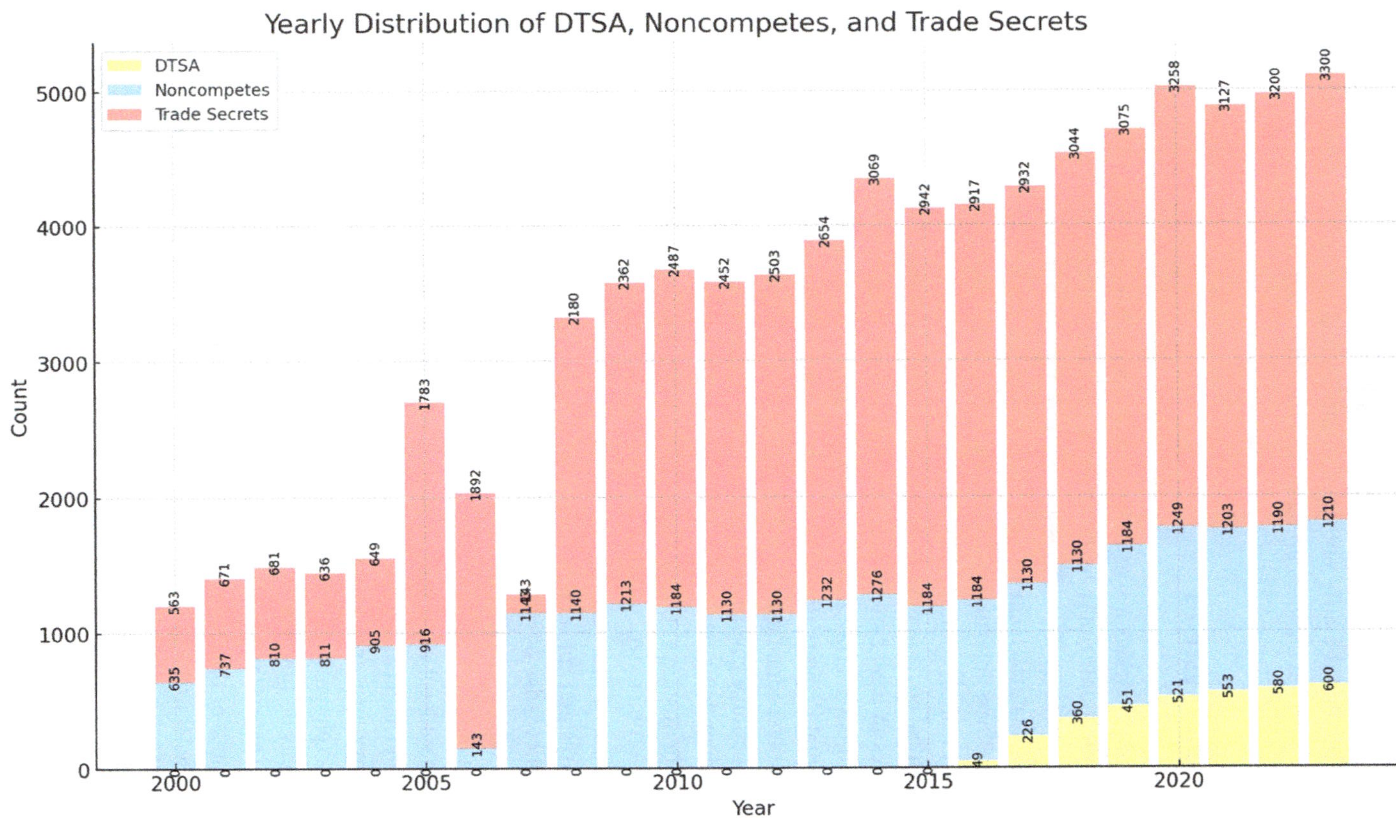

Figure 3.18: shows the number of reports filed of case decisions involving trade secrets violations with Westlaw through 2021. (SOURCE: Westlaw, 2021).

Patents, trademarks, copyrights, and trade secrets are valuable company assets, and understanding how they work and are created is critical to knowing how to protect them. Understanding the different types of intellectual property is essential knowledge that international business professionals should remember.

Types of Legal Systems

Nowadays, global markets are as integrated as ever, where purchasing goods manufactured in one country may be finished or packaged in another. Businesses have crossed the boundaries of countries and expanded globally in search of better opportunities in raw materials, cheap labor, talent, and the market for their goods. However, doing business internationally can be very distinct from doing it domestically. International business professionals must know the target country's culture, people's behavior, political environment, economic conditions, and legal system.

Differences in legal systems can influence the attractiveness of a target country as a market to enter or an investment opportunity. The legal system of a nation is significantly vital to international businesses. A country's local laws regulate business practices and determine business policies, rights, and obligations involved in business transactions. Country governments define their legal framework within which firms must abide when doing business in the country. Therefore, laws differ from country to country. For instance, China has a communist, government-planned economy, where the government strictly controls business laws to control business sectors. Conversely, India has a democratic government, and business laws are made to protect small businesses and consumers. Although various nations have different rules and regulations, knowledge of common law, civil law, contract laws, laws governing property rights, product safety, and liability for a country helps businesspeople to make business decisions.

The business legal environment plays a substantial role in determining the success of any international business trade globally. Government taxes imposed, among other regulatory measures, can also help promote economic growth and protect consumers from exploitation and other illegal factors.

Let us focus on how the political and economic ideologies that define countries impact their legal systems. There are three central legal systems – common law, civil law, and religious or theocratic law. Most countries have combined these systems, creating hybrid legal systems. The University of Ottawa in Canada has a well-designed and informed database that you can access by country when exploring legal systems around the globe. The following are the three central legal systems adopted around the world, as illustrated in Figure 3.19:

- **Civil law** is based on a detailed set of laws and constitutes a set of codes. It focuses on applying the law to specific facts and circumstances. This system is the most widespread legal system worldwide.

- **Common law** is based on traditions and precedence, in which judges interpret the law, and judicial rulings can set a precedent.
- **Religious law**, also known as theocratic law, is based on a set of religious guidelines, with the most common example being Islamic law, also known as Sharia. Islamic law governs several Islamic nations and communities worldwide and is the most widely accepted religious law system.

Jewish Halacha and the Christian Canon systems are also religious law systems, with the latter observed in Vatican City. Neither of these systems is practiced at the national level in a country.

Country/Region	Legal System
United States, Canada, Australia	Common law system
Most of Europe, Latin America	Civil law system
Parts of Africa, Asia	Customary law system
Saudi Arabia, Yemen	Muslim law system
Various countries (combining elements)	Mixed law system

Figure 3.19: Main types of legal systems adopted across the globe. (SOURCE: Juriglobe, 2022).

Islamic law directly impacts international businesses since it is a moral rather than a commercial legal system. Sharia has explicit guidelines for factors of life. For instance, in Islamic law, business is directly affected by the concept of interest since banks cannot charge or profit from interest. Such a condition has developed an entire set of financial products and strategies to emulate interest for an Islamic banking institution without being technically categorized as interest. For instance, some banks may charge a hefty up-front fee, while others can engage in sale-buyback or leaseback of a particular asset. For example, to borrow money from an Islamic bank, a company may sell its assets or products to the bank for a fixed price. Under the agreement, the bank commits to sell back the support to the company later and at a higher price – the difference between the original sale and the later buyback price functions as the interest. Many international businesses and foreign investment banks are discovering creative venues to conduct international business with Islamic banks in ways they can comply with Islamic law while earning profits.

Globalization and Risk Assessment

Political forces often affect global business, constantly generating risks to internationalization and prosperous international trade. Such risks are typically described as the risk of doing business abroad resulting from political instability or changes, often through policies, sanctions, trade barriers, tariffs, etc. Political risk exists in every nation and differs in magnitude and classification from one country to another. Political risks may originate from changes in government policies to adjust foreign trade controls or those imposed on exchange and interest rates. Moreover, the political risk may be driven by efforts of legitimate governments to stabilize their economies, such as controls on prices, output flow, international and domestic activities, currency exchange, and remittance limitations. Such political risk may also result from circumstances beyond government controls of a domestic or geopolitical nature, such as war, terrorism, revolution, labor strikes, and extortion.

Political risk can adversely impact all facets of international business and trade, from exporting or importing goods to the ability or suitability to own or operate a business in the hosting market. These risks can vary widely, but in general, they can be categorized into a few main risks, including but not limited to economic; exchange transfer; strike, riot, or civil commotion; war; terrorism; sovereign non-payment; legal and regulatory; political interference; and supply chain vulnerability.

You might ask why to incorporate economic, socioeconomic, and geopolitical forces in studying international business. The first inquiry you might consider is, what does location, culture, customs, language, or regional positioning have to do with it? Two parts to the answer need to be contemplated before and then addressed. Figure 3.20 illustrates the top four risks of international business.

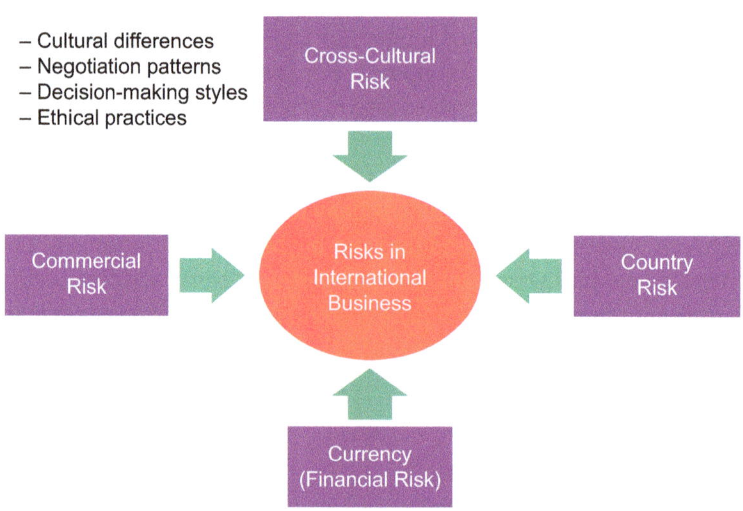

Figure 3.20: The top four risks of international business.

Assessing Country Risks

The IMF's Vulnerability Exercise (VE) is a cross-country exercise that identifies country-specific near-term macroeconomic risks. As a critical element of the Fund's broader risk architecture, the VE is a bottom-up, multi-sectoral approach to risk assessments for all IMF member countries. The VE modeling toolkit is regularly updated in response to global economic developments and the latest modeling innovations. The new generation of VE models used by the IMF leverages machine-learning algorithms. The models can better capture interactions between different parts of the economy and non-linear relationships that are not well measured in *standard times*.

The framework, as shown in Figure 3.21, is multimodal, encompassing a variety of global, regional, and country-specific risks. It spans near-baseline and tail risks and methodologies ranging from simple indicators to large structural models, quantitative empirical work to the narrative, and experiential approaches. Within this architecture, the VE helps to integrate these approaches. It is a bottom-up, country-based approach that yields regional and global insights. It combines cutting-edge quantitative empirical assessments with country-specific details and expert judgment.

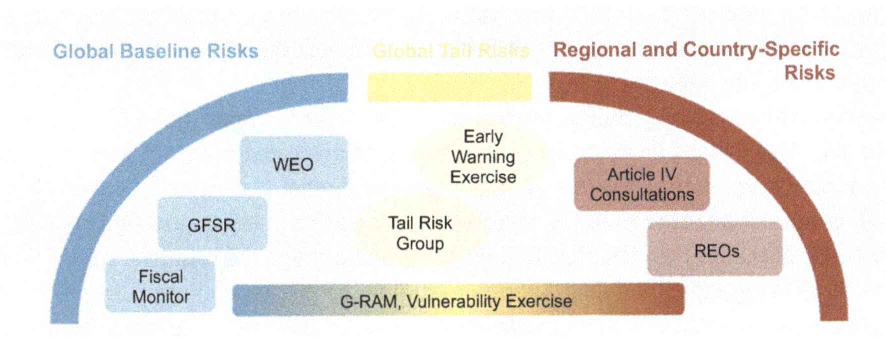

Figure 3.21: IMF's Country Risk Assessment Architecture. (SOURCE: IMF, Ahuja, Syed, and Wiseman (2017).

Machine learning (ML) tools have become well-suited to the challenges of macroeconomic risk assessments. Crises are rare and almost always involve novel features, which makes them challenging to anticipate. When they materialize, they often reveal economic relationships that are not regularly observed in regular times, making it challenging to reach firm conclusions based on any country's history. Looking across countries can help shed additional light on crises, but the degree of heterogeneity across similar countries is daunting. Without sophisticated designs, classical estimation methods, like logistic regressions, may be poorly suited to capture the interactions, nonlinearities, and high degree of cross-country heterogeneity in crisis assessment. ML tools have become increasingly popular in addressing these issues in economics and other fields and have shown promise, specifically in the case of crisis prediction. However, as with other empirical methods that rely on past observations, ML models cannot predict crisis events in which the shocks or transmission channels have not been seen before.

Country-specific risks cover a broad spectrum. When you are ready to explore international investments, you can conduct country risk analyses via qualitative and quantitative assessments or a combination of both. Quantitative research uses an objective analysis of the country's vital data ratios and statistics to determine risks. These assessments may include a country's debt-to-gross domestic product (GDP) ratio or the beta coefficient (a measure of sensitivity or correlation of a security or an investment portfolio to movements in the overall country's market) of the Morgan Stanley Emerging Markets (MSEM) index. Qualitative analysis helps to determine risks based on subjective analysis of political news and market rumors.

International business leaders should assess quantitative information in rating agency reports, online sources, and investment magazines and newspapers, such as *The Economist* and the *Financial Times.* Searching Google World News, other international news aggregators and financial publications for information that can be used in a qualitative assessment is also a good strategy. Sovereign credit ratings, independent assessments of a country's creditworthiness or sovereign entity, are essential resources for international investors – offering an easy way to analyze country risk. Standard & Poor's, Moody's Investor Services, and Fitch Ratings are the three most-monitored rating agencies.

Governments and public resources can be excellent support both at home and abroad. Most nations have branches or institutions dedicated to this. A local government may assist with expansions abroad, and the foreign government can also help in the internationalization of the targeted country. Companies should try contacting the trade bureaus or associations in their home country and the countries where they are considering expanding their operations to find the proper institution. Often, these bureaus and institutions have programs to assist in internationalization and help management contact the right people abroad. These institutions have insider knowledge concerning many economic, political, and other risks involved in international business with specific foreign markets. Including reputable sources of information, like chambers of commerce and trade consulates, in the risk assessment can help companies gather more details about compelling and prosperous business opportunities abroad and learn which markets and business partners to avoid and minimize risk.

Types of Risk in International Business

When considering internationalization strategies, hundreds of characteristics of international business must be considered. Still, these can broadly be classified as economic, political, and social factors.

Tax laws, interest rate increases, political and social turmoil or disruption, and even statements from politicians can affect international business transactions and the firm's associated risk. Specific risks may include oscillations in currency exchange rates, economic or political instability, the prospect of trade sanctions or embargos, and anything else happening in the country that may negatively influence the business environment, trade, and cash flows in and out of that nation.

Economic risks arise from a country's financial circumstances and debt repayment capacity. Political risks also come from the influence of politicians' decisions about investments. Social factors distinctive to a nation – such as belief systems and practices, traditions, customs and behaviors, trends and influences – can all affect the potential risks and successes, as can any significant social turmoil or activities intended to bring about societal transformation. In some cases, these risks can be interwoven. Below are a few of the most important factors to consider in your country's risk analysis.

Economic Risk in International Business Trade

It is essential to consider economic data by country to determine risk levels carefully. No country is immune to economic risk. Even normally stable countries such as the United States and the United Kingdom have faced significant financial consequences. Currency fluctuations due to its proposed and eventual exit from the European Union affected and continue to impact the U.K. The global financial crisis that started in the U.S. in 2008 is another.

Businesses can analyze economic data by country utilizing the following key economic indicators, which provide a snapshot of a country's financial performance and prospects that can assist paint a fuller picture when evaluating country risk:

- Access to affordable capital.
- Currency exchange rates.
- Debt-to-GDP ratio.
- Monetary policy and currency stability.
- Overall government finances.
- Political Risk.
- The short-, medium- and long-term outlook for the country's GDP and GNP.
- The stability and solvency of banks.
- Unemployment rate.

Every country, from the most to the least developed, has some political risk. When deciding to do business in another country, it is wise to look into factors like the stability of all levels of government, the presence or absence of corruption, and the regulatory environment. Obvious signs of instability, like a war or coup, translate to political risks. However, changes to government policies and priorities following a democratic election or leadership change can also significantly influence. A shift from less to more regulation, greater state ownership of specific industries, or more government involvement in the economy also represents political risk. The following are some examples of factors to consider when evaluating political risk:

- Government's attitudes toward foreign investment.
- Government assistance programs for businesses.
- Government stability.
- Immigration and employment laws.
- Information access and transparency.
- Regulatory and policy environment.
- Structural Assessment.
- Terrorism, violence, and crime.
- Workforce freedom and mobility.

The structural factors within a specific country also merit close inspection. Structural factors include any fixed elements within the country that can impact economic performance, including:

- Co-production opportunities with other nations.
- Competitors.
- Demographics.
- Export regulations.
- Import acceptance from other countries.
- Labor force.
- Physical infrastructure.
- Social infrastructure.
- Treaty participation.

Also, it is essential to consider whether the country's infrastructure supports efficient transportation, telecommunications technology, and banking and financial services. Are current and future demographic trends and health and educational systems likely to support a strong labor force? For example, suppose the firm launches operations or partners with a country with an aging population that has not invested enough in its education and healthcare systems. In that case, you may have trouble finding a skilled workforce.

Debt Management

Debt management should be an essential consideration in a country's risk analysis. Debt management deals with how well a country manages its debt load and whether it is growing, static, or declining. High government debt levels can lead to inflation and currency destabilization, which will likely have a real and significant impact on any company doing business in and with that country.

The following are the top three debt management indicators to consider:

- Current account balance to GNP.
- Debt service to exports.
- Total debt stocks to GNP.

Debt currency and interest rate composition can also considerably affect external vulnerability. Still, analysis and indicators of such vulnerability may likewise require a focus on a sectoral level (focus on the industry) or even at the level of individual organizations. External debt's specific foreign currency and interest rate composition may also have important implications. If abrupt shifts are imposed in the exchange rates in which debt is carried, but these rates are not offset by similar changes on the inflow side, such as with exports, considerable income effects can result. Likewise, quick boosts in short-term interest rates, such as those from the early 1980s, may have significant implications for the actual cost of debt, particularly if a considerable share of debt is floating rate.

Developing a country's risk assessment and mitigation plan is essential to internationalization. It allows for identifying the potentially adverse impact of a country's environment on the internationalizing firm and potential cash flows generated by an FDI project. As discussed in this section, country risk analysis is essential for several reasons. First, the MNE can utilize it as a screening instrument to bypass investing in a market with excessive risk. Also, such analysis can help monitor markets where the MNE is already engaged in international business and trade.

ESG Impact on Geopolitical, Legal, and Intellectual Property Dynamics

As discussed in Chapter 2, ESG criteria increasingly influence international business operations, impacting everything from geopolitical dynamics to legal frameworks governing trade and intellectual property. Hence, international business professionals should know how ESG considerations reshape international business landscapes across economic, cultural, and legal dimensions.

Geopolitical Dynamics

Geopolitical dynamics are profoundly affected by ESG criteria, particularly environmental and governance aspects. Countries increasingly leverage their ecological policies as tools in international relations, either as soft power instruments or as prerequisites for entering trade agreements. For instance, the European Union's Green Deal, as illustrated in Figure 3.22, seeks to establish a carbon border adjustment mechanism that could redefine trade dynamics by imposing tariffs on imports from countries with less stringent environmental regulations. This approach forces a reconsideration of trade policies and national environmental strategies globally, pushing countries toward greener practices to maintain competitive access to significant markets.

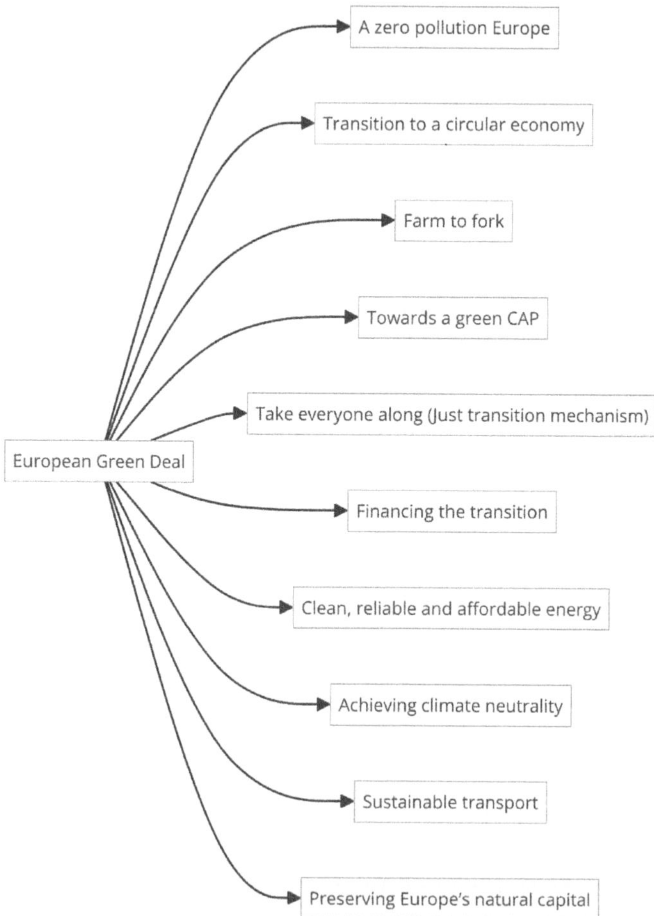

Figure 3.22: The European Union Green Deal. (SOURCE: WEF, 2020).

Moreover, governance in ESG pertains not only to corporate governance but also to political stability and transparency, which are crucial for international trade. International firms, or those contemplating internationalization, are now assessing political risks with an eye on governance indicators, influencing decisions on foreign direct investments and partnerships. Countries with poor governance scores may find themselves disadvantaged in attracting international business, as companies increasingly prefer to operate in stable, transparent regions with robust legal systems to enforce contracts and protect investments.

ESG Scores

Each ESG factor has its own set of measurable criteria contributing to the overall ESG score. Environmental criteria evaluate a company's environmental impacts and efforts to reduce them. Social criteria measure a company's relationship with its social environment, like its employees or local communities. Governance criteria gauge corporate responsibility, which could include the duties of executive management or shareholders' rights. An ESG score should indicate a company's dedication to responsible environmental stewardship, willingness to strengthen existing communities, and corporate governance accountability.

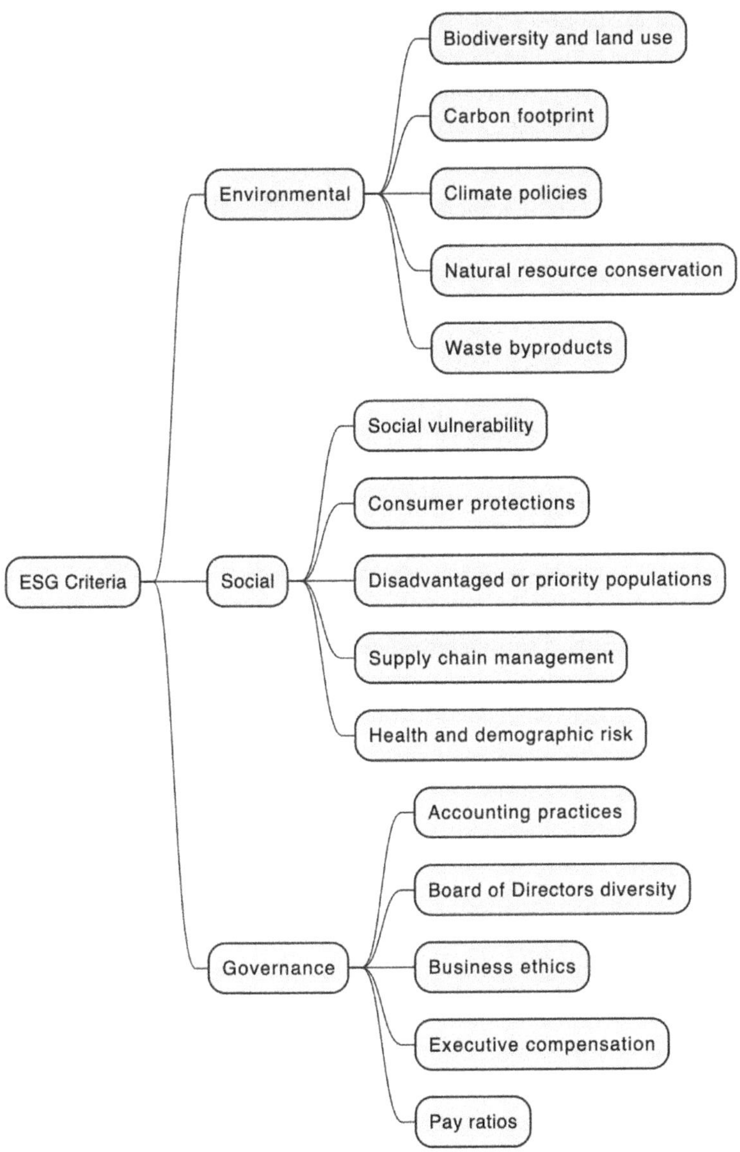

Figure 3.23: An example of ESG criteria that fall under each category. (SOURCE: UN, 2022).

Figure 3.23 depicts a few examples of criteria that fall under each category. While these examples are outlined into categories, these criteria are often intertwined. For instance, a poor executive leadership decision could lead to waste byproducts that impact the health and safety of a community. The complex, interconnected nature of ESG criteria is what makes ESG scoring such a challenge. These intersections are often pivotal to interpreting ESG scores, and the overlap between variables makes it difficult to determine where resources should be allocated. But at the same time, companies that can analyze these intersections effectively can make a faster, more significant, and more positive ESG impact.

Companies often turn to third-party software for a more holistic picture of their present and future ESG achievements. This way, companies can improve faster with fewer resources. While discrepancies exist within the ESG scoring framework, all ESG scores are calculated using the same scale of 0–100, as illustrated in Figure 3.24, with specific ranges representing excellent, good, average, or poor scores.

The following is a breakdown of these scores:

- Excellent – Excellent ESG scores are at or above 70. These companies have demonstrated outstanding efforts to evangelize ESG throughout their organization, follow ESG best practices, and have proven their dedication through their performance. Organizations with excellent ESG scores have little to no negative impact on people or the environment.
- Good – A good ESG score is between 60 and 69. Companies that obtain an excellent ESG rating follow most ESG best practices, and their work does little to harm the environment or society.
- Average – Average ESG scores are between 50 and 59. The company is not implementing most ESG best practices, is not actively working toward ESG goals, and has adverse environmental, social, or governance effects.
- Poor – A score of 50 or less is considered a poor ESG score. Companies with poor ESG ratings have not adhered to ESG best practices. They currently have a demonstrably negative environmental impact and do not treat their employees well.

While a low or high ESG score may give investors high-level insight into a company's ESG performance, it does not tell the whole story. For instance, despite the notoriety of the oil and gas sector on the environment, companies within this sector could spearhead initiatives to employ low-income or otherwise disadvantaged workers to offset their low environmental score. This means that an ESG score should not be the only metric by which companies evaluate potential investments. Many companies are turning to third-party ESG providers for a comprehensive view of the complex interplay between data points.

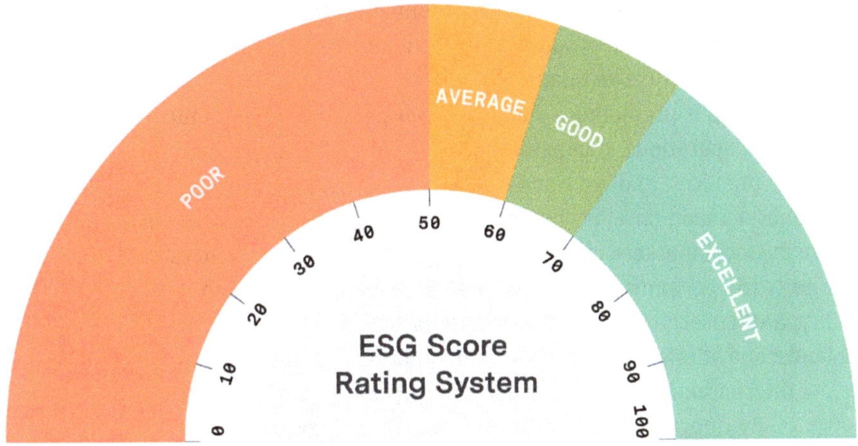

Figure 3.24: ESG scores are calculated from 0–100.

ESG and Legal Landscapes

The legal frameworks surrounding international trade and intellectual property are also evolving under the influence of ESG criteria. Environmental and social considerations are becoming embedded in international intellectual property (IP) agreements. For instance, the push for greater transparency in the pharmaceuticals sector, driven by social components of ESG, influences global IP laws, advocating for more equitable access to medical innovations. This shift is evident in debates around patent waivers for COVID-19 vaccines, where global public health considerations are challenging traditional IP protections, arguing for a balance between rewarding innovation and addressing global emergencies.

Social considerations, part of the ESG framework, reshape labor laws and standards within trade agreements. Modern trade agreements now often include chapters on labor standards influenced by the social criteria of ESG. These provisions aim to improve working conditions, prohibit child labor, and ensure fair wages. The enforcement of such standards is increasingly tied to trade benefits, with non-compliance risking tariffs or restrictions, demonstrating how deeply ESG considerations are woven into international trade's legal fabric.

ESG and Cultural Shifts in International Business

ESG criteria also foster cultural shifts within international businesses, influencing leadership styles, corporate culture, and stakeholder relationships. There is a growing emphasis on corporate responsibility and ethics, driven by the social and governance aspects of ESG. This shift impacts international business practices by promoting a culture of inclusivity and diversity, ethical leadership, and stakeholder engagement. Companies are not only expected to perform economically but are also judged on their impact on communities and the environment. This cultural shift is redefining corporate success in the global marketplace, where reputation and ethical standing are increasingly as critical as financial metrics.

Moreover, ESG is promoting a culture of transparency and accountability in international business operations. Companies are now more forthcoming about their supply chains, labor practices, and environmental impacts, driven by regulatory requirements and consumer demand for ethical practices. This transparency is becoming a competitive advantage in global markets, influencing purchasing decisions and investment flows.

As the world continues to grapple with global challenges such as climate change, inequality, and governance issues, ESG criteria will play a pivotal role in defining the future landscape of international trade and intellectual property rights. ESG criteria are reshaping international business's geopolitical dynamics, legal landscapes, and cultural frameworks. By integrating environmental, social, and governance considerations into every aspect of business operations, from compliance and risk assessment to corporate culture and stakeholder engagement, businesses are enhancing their competitive edge and contributing to more sustainable and equitable global trade practices.

Discussion Questions

1. **How do geopolitical dynamics influence the legal frameworks of international trade, and what impact does this have on global business operations?**

2. **What is the main reason for a government to engage in the nationalization of businesses?**
   A) To reduce foreign dominance in the domestic economy.
   B) To increase the import of goods.
   C) To deregulate the market.
   D) To reduce transparency and increase corruption.

3. **Which type of patent is usually granted for 14 years?**
   A) Utility patent
   B) Design patent
   C) Plant patent
   D) Trade secret

4. **Privatization always reduces government intervention in the economy. True or False?**

5. **Copyrights protect the physical expression of ideas, not the ideas themselves. True or False?**

Recommended Readings

Gammeltoft, P., & Panibratov, A. (2024). Emerging market multinationals and the politics of internationalization. *International Business Review*, 33(3), 102278.

Ghauri, P. N., Oxelheim, L., & Randøy, T. (2024). The changed geopolitical map: implications for international business policy in a sustainable finance perspective. In *Handbook of International Business Policy* (pp. 170–189). Edward Elgar Publishing, Cheltenham, UK.

Katelouzou, Dionysia and Zumbansen, Peer C., Transnational Corporate Governance: The State of the Art and Twenty-First Century Challenges (February 11, 2020). TLI Think! Paper 06/2020, Available at SSRN: https://ssrn.com/abstract=3536488 or http://dx.doi.org/10.2139/ssrn.3536488. TLI Think.

Teece, D. J., Gupta, K., & Rosenberg, D. (2023). New Priorities of Corporate Directors: Geopolitical and Technological Disruptions. *International In-house Counsel Journal*, 16, 1–9.

Yeoh, P. (2022). Environmental, social and governance (ESG) laws, regulations and practices in the digital era.

Casanova, L., & Miroux, A. (2022). Emerging Markets Report 2022: Reinventing Global Value Chains.

Sandul, M. (2023). Transformational Factors in the Development of Global Supply Chains. *International Economic Policy*, (38), 77–100.

Chapter 4
Global Dynamics: Economic, Socioeconomic, and Financial Forces Shaping the International Monetary System

Learning Objectives

- Understand the purpose of international economic analysis
- Compare various levels of economic development across the globe
- Discuss the social economic dimensions and its relevance for international business
- Describe the international monetary system
- Understand the present floating currency exchange rate system and IMF currency arrangements
- Explain the significance of the balance of payments to international business decisions

Overview

The first half of this chapter is a captivating exploration of the economic and socioeconomic forces that shape international business and trade. International economics analysis grapples with issues that arise from economic interaction among sovereign nations. These analyses are not just important. They are vital for international trade, financial flows, aid, and when providing technical assistance for emerging economies. Economic analysis is also critical when examining international migration and exchange rate systems, as these often pose significant global economic challenges. Various quantitative and qualitative measurements are necessary for each economic factor to examine the issues and evaluate the solutions thoroughly. Social measurement is particularly crucial in specific fields of international economics, such as international business, trade, and finance.

The second part of this chapter delves into the intricate workings of the international monetary system and the complex financial forces at play. The international monetary system, in its essence, is a sophisticated set of rules that countries agree to abide by when conducting business with each other. It plays a crucial role in determining the value of one country's currency relative to another's and how money can be transferred between nations. As a set of internationally agreed-upon rules and conventions, the international monetary system, with the backing of other international institutions, facilitates international trade, cross-border investment, and the general redistribution of capital between states with different currencies.

https://doi.org/10.1515/9783111510286-004

International Economic Analysis

An international economic analysis deals with those economic principles that govern the international exchange of goods and services between sovereign nations, particularly policy issues that typically arise. Figure 4.1 depicts the importance of global economic analysis in assessing the economic factors affecting international business operations.

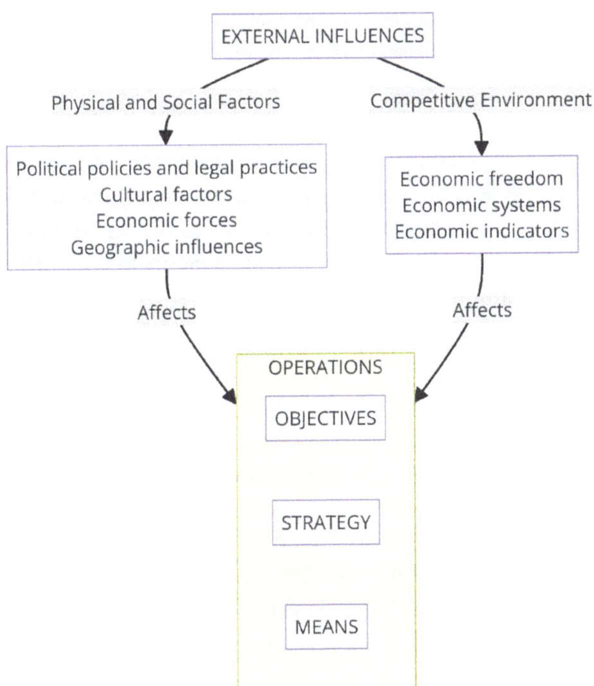

Figure 4.1: The importance of international economic analysis in assessing the economic factors affecting international business operations.

Economic and market forces, such as those depicted in Figure 4.2, are among the most significant uncontrollable forces in the external environment business phase. How can leaders and business analysts keep current with the latest developments and prepare for the future? For many years, enterprises have been estimating and forecasting economic conditions at the national and international levels. Analysts typically rely on data published by governments and international organizations such as the World Bank (WB) and the International Monetary Fund (IMF). While such data may not be as timely or accurate as analysts would like, much of it is available.

International economics analysis is crucial for international business and trade because of the rapid integration of global economic markets. Increasingly, interna-

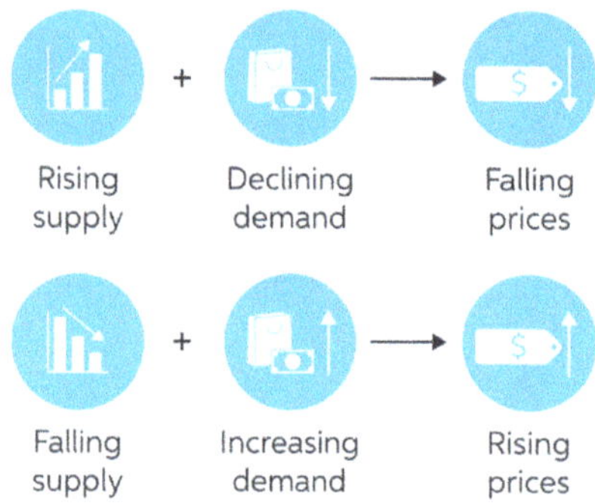

Figure 4.2: Economic and market forces are among the most significant uncontrollable forces in the external environment business phase.

tional companies, global consumers, and governments across the globe realize that their lives are impacted not only by what happens in their local and domestic markets but also by what is happening worldwide. Shoppers can walk into local stores today, tap into e-commerce via the internet without leaving their homes or offices, and purchase goods and services worldwide. While local businesses must compete with these foreign offerings, primarily via the ubiquitous and pervasive digital shopping platforms, many of these businesses also have new prospects to expand their markets to internationalize and sell their products and services to many consumers across the globe. The advance in integrated communications technologies (ICT) and telecommunications is also rapidly lowering the cost of providing services internationally. At the same time, the internet continues to change the nature of many products and services as it expands markets even further.

An international economic analysis aims to assess the overall outlook for the economy and the impact of economic chains on the firm. For instance, Figure 4.3 shows the result of an international economic analysis related to the initial effects of the COVID-19 pandemic on the GDP of various economies across the globe, enabling international business managers and investors to assess the impact of the pandemic on their business. In another example, suppose an increase in employment is forecasted in a particular market. It would cause most marketing managers to revise their sales forecast upward, which requires the production managers to increase production. They might add a new work shift, but new machinery will be needed if the plant operates 24 hours a day. Either situation may require more workers and raw materials, resulting in extra workloads for human resources and purchasing managers.

When an enterprise enters overseas markets, economic analysis becomes more complex because managers must now operate in two new environments: foreign and international. The foreign environment includes all the uncontrollable forces outside the home country that surround and influence the firm. There are many economies instead of one, and they can be very different. The international environment includes the interactions between domestic and foreign environmental forces or between sets of foreign environmental forces when an affiliate in another country does business with

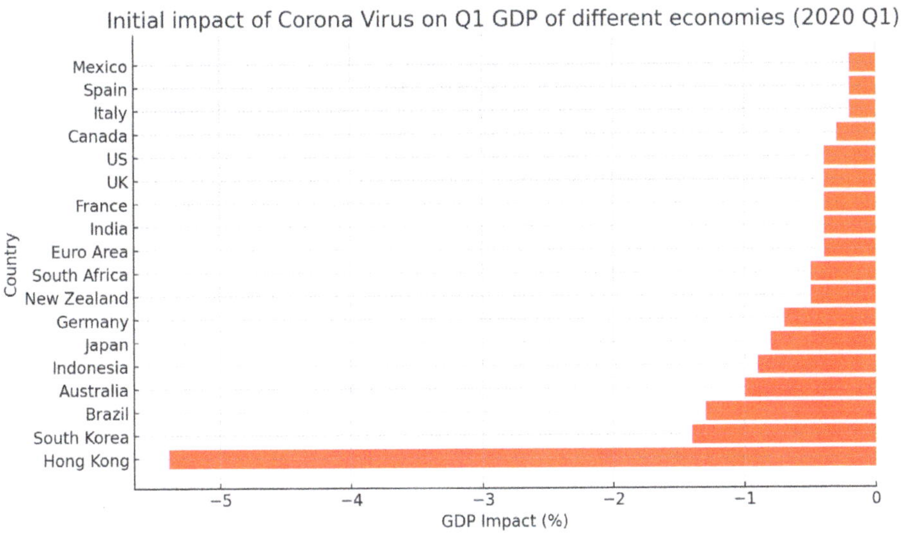

Figure 4.3: The result of an international economic analysis related to the initial impact of the COVID-19 pandemic on the GDP of various economies across the globe, enabling international business managers and investors to assess the effects of the pandemic on their business. (SOURCE: BCCL, 2020).

customers in yet another country. As you can see from this brief portrayal, expanding into overseas markets greatly complicates the enterprise's management.

Policies developed for economic conditions in one market may be inappropriate for conditions in another. For instance, the central office may instruct its subsidiaries to maintain the lowest possible inventory. The chief financial officer (CFO) may permit only foreign currency-denominated loans based on favorable interest rates. These policies usually work well for countries with low annual inflation rates (0–15%). However, for countries such as Zimbabwe, with peak inflation reaching 98% per day in November of 2008, it is a very different scenario. Another example is Venezuela, battling an inflation rate close to 20,000% in 2018, according to the IMF. In such a least desirable scenario, subsidiaries in such countries would have to hold cash or foreign currency-denominated loans, so the policy for markets with high inflation rates will be just the reverse of what it is for the countries with low inflation rates.

A straightforward way to recognize the importance of international economic analysis is to glance at the development of exports in the world during the past sixty or more years. Figure 4.4 provides data on trends in the global export value of trade in goods from 1950 to 2020 (in billions of U.S. dollars). Note the pick in global trade through 2008, when the global financial crisis hit, causing a significant drop in trade, which quickly recovered by 2011 but dropped again by 2016 due to a currency war caused by the global financial crisis. The global market recovered again by 2018 and dropped again in 2019 due to the global COVID-19 pandemic. Even more data insights are gained by analyzing one country's exports versus another's imports, and interna-

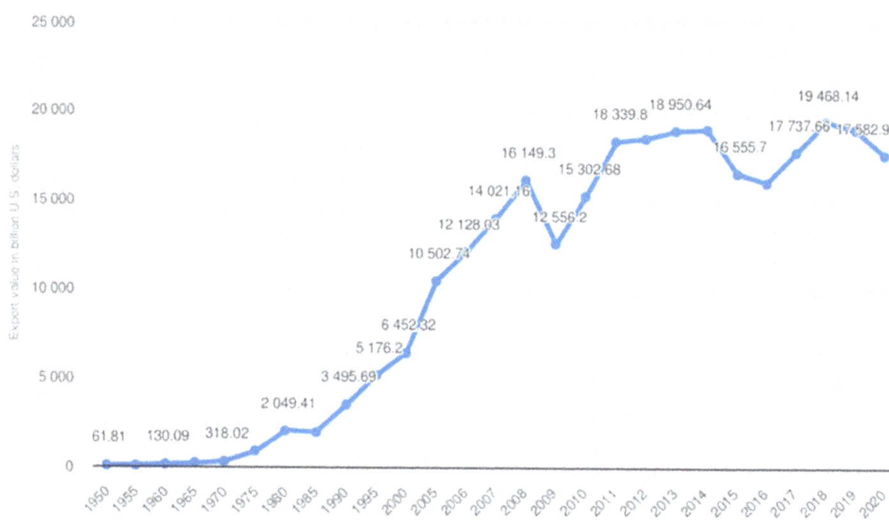

Figure 4.4: Trends in the global export value of trade in goods from 1950 to 2020 in billions of U.S. dollars. (SOURCE: UNCTAD, Statista, 2021).

tional business professionals can assess the exponential growth in outflows and inflows opportunities in a global market.

Nonetheless, a rapid increase in the value of exports does not necessarily mean that international trade is becoming more substantial. A better international economic analysis approach is to look at the percentage of traded goods as a percentage of the size of the global economy. Figure 4.5 shows the exports of goods by selected countries between 2010 and 2020, broken down by share of global exports. China's exports grew from 13.1 to 18.6 percent during those ten years, while the U.S. exports dropped from 10.6 to 10.3 percent.

International trade and investment growth have been stimulated partly by the ongoing decline of trade barriers since the Great Depression of the 1930s. After World War II, the General Agreement on Tariffs and Trade (GATT) initiated ongoing negotiations among members to reciprocate tariffs on imported goods. During these regular negotiations, nations pledged to reduce their import taxes in exchange for concessions, or tariff reductions, by other GATT members. When the Uruguay Round was finalized in 1994, the member countries expanded the agreement to include liberalization commitments in a much greater sphere of influence. Nations would reduce tariffs on goods traded and liberalize the agriculture and services markets. These nations also agreed to eliminate the many quota systems from previous decades and to adhere to specific minimum standards to protect intellectual property (IP) rights such as patents, trademarks, and copyrights. The World Trade Organization (WTO) was created to manage this system of new agreements, to offer a forum for regular dialogue

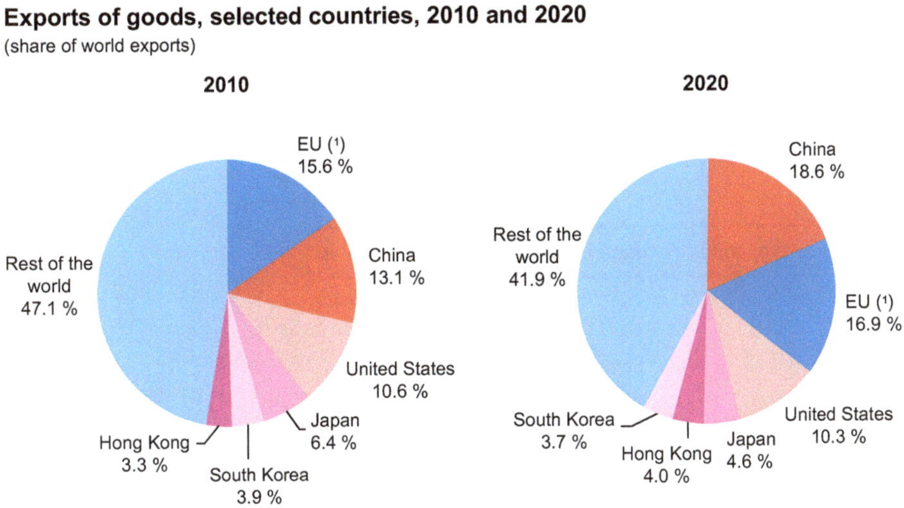

Figure 4.5: shows exports of goods by selected countries between 2010 and 2020, broken down by share of global exports. (SOURCE: Eurostat, UN, and IMF, 2021).

on trade matters, and to execute a well-defined procedure for settling trade disputes that could arise among these member nations.

Levels of Economic Development

A country's level of economic development affects all aspects of business conducted there, and international managers encounter markets with widely different levels of development. Figure 4.6 depicts the main factors of economic growth, including but not limited to political stability, macroeconomic stability, levels of infrastructure development, natural resources, educational standards, savings rates and foreign aid, and trade barriers.

Gross Domestic Product

Another measure frequently used by economists and international business managers is gross domestic product (GDP), a metric measuring the production level of a nation's local economy, commonly described as the total annual value of all goods and services produced in that country. GDP is a well-known economic indicator widely used by investors and market analysts. It is intended to gauge an economy's overall size in terms of productive output and current growth rate. Also important to assess is the GDP per capita of a nation, which shows a country's GDP divided by its total population, which should not be confused with Purchasing Power Parity (PPP) per capita, as PPP takes into account the relative cost of living, rather than using only exchange

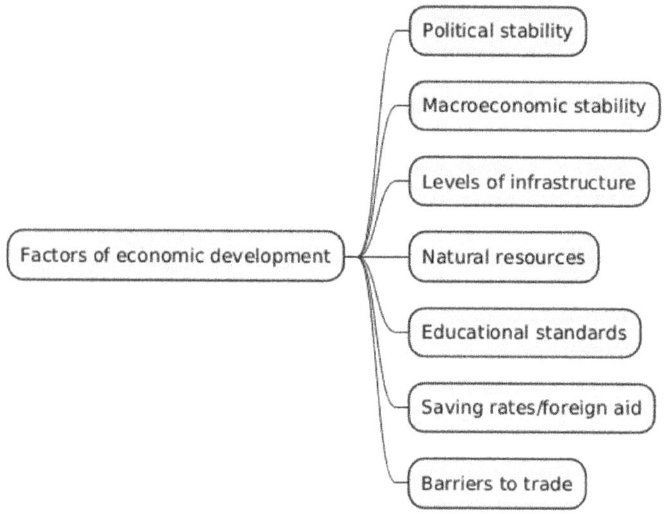

Figure 4.6: The main factors of economic development.

rates, therefore providing a more accurate picture of the real differences in income. Figure 4.7 provides a brief differentiation between GDP and GDP per capita.

Central banks rely on GDP measurements to assess how well the domestic economy functions. They also depend on GDP to determine how susceptible the economy is to inflationary or recessionary pressures. Economists, relying on GDP and other economic metrics, make decisions regarding taxes, government spending, and monetary and fiscal policies that can significantly impact a nation's economy for years. Despite its widespread use, the GDP measure has several potential shortcomings. One major shortcoming is the measure's inability to correctly attribute economic ups or downs to fundamental economic health shifts or temporary, seasonal, cyclical fluctuations. Although it measures the overall economic output of a nation, GDP does not adequately account for flows of foreign income and investments into and out of a country. Another possible weakness of GDP is that it sometimes leads to overcorrections by government authorities. For instance, when the U.S. Federal Reserve creates situations where monetary policy is tightened to reduce inflationary pressures, which leads to a threat of recession.

For instance, in GDP terms, as of 2021, the U.S. and China occupy the first two places in GDP ranking. The U.S. and China's margins were reduced in nominal ranking as China's GDP growth rate in 2021 (8.02%) was higher than the U.S.'s 5.97%. On a nominal basis, the U.S. was ahead of China by $6 trillion in 2021. On a Purchasing Power Parity (PPP) basis, China has overtaken the U.S. since 2017, is ahead by $4 trillion, and the gap is increasing. According to data from the IMF, China will remain the world's largest economy on a PPP basis over the next few decades as 2nd ranked U.S. growth is slow, and 3rd-ranked India is way behind. In the nominal GDP list, among the top 20 largest countries, Iran has overtaken the Netherlands, and Saudi Arabia is overtak-

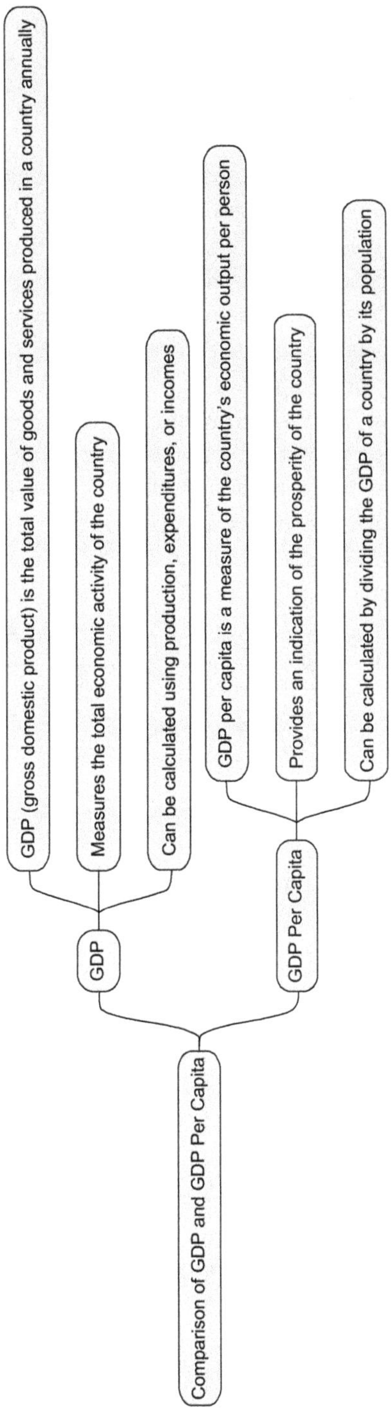

Figure 4.7: A brief differentiation between GDP and GDP per capita.

ing Turkey and Switzerland. Among the top 50, the Economic rank of South Africa would move up by eight positions, while Egypt would lose four places.

Gross National Income

Although GDP is among the most popular economic indicators, gross national income (GNI) is potentially a much better metric for a country whose economy includes substantial foreign investments. Both GNI and GDP may vary significantly because they are measured differently. GNI accounts for an economy's total income, regardless of the origin of the income, whether earned domestically by nationals within the country's borders or from investments in foreign business or trade. Compared with GNI, GDP also fails to consider incomes earned outside the nation.

Economists often prefer to use GNI every day to assess economic development. GNI represents the total value of all income generated by a nation's residents, including the domestic production of goods and services and income from abroad, as well as subtracting income paid to entities outside the nation. For example, the World Bank categorizes countries based on their level of GNI per person, usually called GNI per capita, using the following data for 2022, as depicted in Figure 4.8.

Group	July 1, 2022 for FY23 (new)	July 1, 2021 for FY22 (previous)
Low income	< 1,085	< 1,045
Lower-middle income	1,086 – 4,255	1,046 – 4,095
Upper-middle income	4,256 – 13,205	4,096 – 12,695
High income	> 13,205	> 12,695

Figure 4.8: The new thresholds for Atlas GNI per capita 2022. (SOURCE: World Bank, July 2022).

The World Bank assigns the world's economies to four income groups: low, lower-middle, upper-middle, and high. These classifications are updated each July 1 based on the GNI per capita from the previous year. GNI measures are expressed in United States dollars (USD) and determined using the conversion factors of the Atlas method.

Classifications can change for two reasons:

1. Changes to Atlas GNI per capita: In each country, economic growth, inflation, exchange rates, and population growth influence Atlas GNI per capita. Revisions to improve national account estimates and methods can also impact this.
2. Changes to classification thresholds: To keep income classification thresholds fixed in real terms, they are adjusted annually for inflation using the IMF's Special Drawing Rights (SDR) deflator, a weighted average of the GDP deflators of China, Japan, the United Kingdom, the United States, and the euro area.

Figure 4.9 illustrates the various GNI per capita from nations across the globe.

Region	High Income	Upper Middle Income	Lower Middle Income	Low Income	Not Classified
East Asia & Pacific	5	15	10	5	0
Europe & Central Asia	40	10	5	0	0
Latin America & Caribbean	5	20	10	0	0
Middle East & North Africa	5	15	10	5	0
North America	3	0	0	0	0
South Asia	0	5	5	5	0
Sub-Saharan Africa	0	5	20	25	0

Figure 4.9: shows GNI per capita for nations worldwide. (SOURCE: World Bank, July 2023).

Gross National Income and Gross National Product Considerations

GNI is, in essence, the total dollar value of all items produced or generated by all of a nation's residents, plus the income received by the nation's residents, which may include employee compensation and property income. The primary relevance of GNI versus GDP as an economic metric is that it recognizes all revenue that enters a national economy, regardless of whether it was earned within or abroad. There is not much difference between GNI and gross national product (GNP), another alternative metric to GDP. The GNP calculates a country's total productive output from all its citizens and companies, including domestically generated production and production generated by its citizens or businesses in other countries. GNI is a helpful metric to consider because it provides an alternative perspective to GDP and can, therefore, aid analysts in obtaining a better picture of total economic activity.

Developed Versus Developing Economies or Advanced Versus Emerging Economies

Another classification of economic development differentiates between *developed* and *developing* economies, with low- and middle-income economies referred to as developing economies. However, developed economies, also known as *advanced*, are frequently characterized as those industrialized or postindustrial, service-based nations that are economically advanced, with established infrastructures, such as roads, bridges, utilities, power supplies, communications, and other structural elements needed for the smooth operation of a society.

There is no universally agreed-upon criterion to differentiate between developed and developing economies. Indeed, the United Nations statistics division states that they utilize terminology such as developed and developing only for statistical convenience. These designations do not necessarily suggest a judgment regarding the state reached by any particular nation or area in the development process. Countries in the U.S. Central Intelligence Agency, the IMF, and other economically developed nations include the Western European nations, Israel, Japan, Australia, New Zealand, Singapore, Taiwan, South Korea, Canada, and the United States. Figure 4.10 offers the main characteristics of developed versus developing economies.

Developed Economies	Developing Economies
Per capita gross national income above $12,375 (World Bank criterion). A high material standard of living, high quality of life index, and a substantial middle class.	Per capita gross national income of $12,375 or less (World Bank criterion). A moderate to low material standard of living and quality of life index, regional dualism reflecting a high productivity and incomes in some regions and little economic development in others, unequal distribution of income with a very small middle class.
Frequent application of the most advanced production techniques and equipment.	Technological dualism, meaning the presence of a mix of firms employing the latest technology and companies using very primitive methods.
A large base of productive capital, sophisticated financial markets and banking systems, and vigorous international trade in a range of sectors.	Low savings rates, inadequate banking facilities, and high dependence on a few products for export, generally agricultural products or minerals.
A very small share of total output coming from agriculture and a declining share for manufacturing.	A relatively unproductive agricultural sector that provides a living for most of the population.
Well-established governmental and legal systems.	Political instability and deficient governmental and legal systems.
Plentiful educational opportunities and low illiteracy.	High illiteracy rate and few educational facilities.
Relatively low levels of unemployment or underemployment.	Disguised unemployment or underemployment (two people do a job one person could do).
Adequate or high levels of nutrition and access to health care.	Widespread malnutrition and a wide range of health problems.
	Inhospitable topography, such as deserts, mountains, and tropical forests.

Figure 4.10: Characteristics of Developed and Developing Economies. (SOURCE: World Bank, 2023).

Social Economic Dimensions and Relevance for International Business

Selecting a foreign market is crucially relevant for enterprises in their internationalization process. Choosing an international target market is a fundamental decision that needs to be made. Such a decision requires various levels of information. International business leaders need to decide about the potential destination markets and their conditions, such as government policies and regulations, transaction-specific factors, global strategic variables, and the dynamics and nature of market variables, and the valuing of this information is going to largely determine the degree of success or failure in the international market.

Numerous relevant analyses exist about choosing attractive target markets. Still, the great majority agree that social, political, and cultural indicators, among others, must be considered to establish the potential attractiveness of foreign markets. Various internationalization frameworks exist; some are already discussed here, and others will be discussed in more detail in future chapters. They all propose phases of internationalization in the chosen markets, the methods to use in this process, and the indicators that must be employed to value the appeal of an international market.

Most criteria for choosing international target markets are influenced by socioeconomic dimensions such as total population, age distribution, discretionary income, population density and distribution, rural-to-urban shift, and many other indicators such as the size of the product's or service-specific markets and its growth potential, the availability and potential costs of the production factors, the rate of economic development, the country's environment, the psychic distance, and the market's competition and knowledge. However, other frameworks are much more comprehensive, with some listing 200 indicators. Figure 4.11 lists leading socioeconomic indicators when selecting a foreign market, mainly the market's potential, the country's risk, and the cultural distance.

Understanding the socioeconomic factors affecting international business can help companies make better decisions about the future and direction of their internationalization process and business abroad. One must appreciate external and environmental factors and how their interplay affects internationalization.

The first step to understanding socioeconomic factors is to understand social economics, a specialized branch of economics that studies the relationship between economics and social behavior. Ethics, social norms, and distinct social principles impact how consumers behave in an economy and the eventual shape of the economy. Socioeconomic elements are the social and economic factors that shape and determine the dynamics a society will experience. These factors affect a particular group's behavior, also known as socioeconomic class. The most noteworthy behavior of a socioeconomic class is their behavior as consumers. Distinct socioeconomic classes will generally have different priorities, affecting how they spend their money.

Environmental Analysis

Environmental analysis is a unique term that refers to external socioeconomic concerns in a business, domestic or international. It is considered a subsection of general business analysis. It can assist business leaders in growing their organization, increasing revenue streams, and getting ahead of competitors. As discussed in Chapter 3, a subset of environmental analysis is the PESTEL analysis, used for analyzing the macro-environmental factors (political, economic, social, technological, environmental, and legal) that can impact an organization's strategic planning and decision-making.

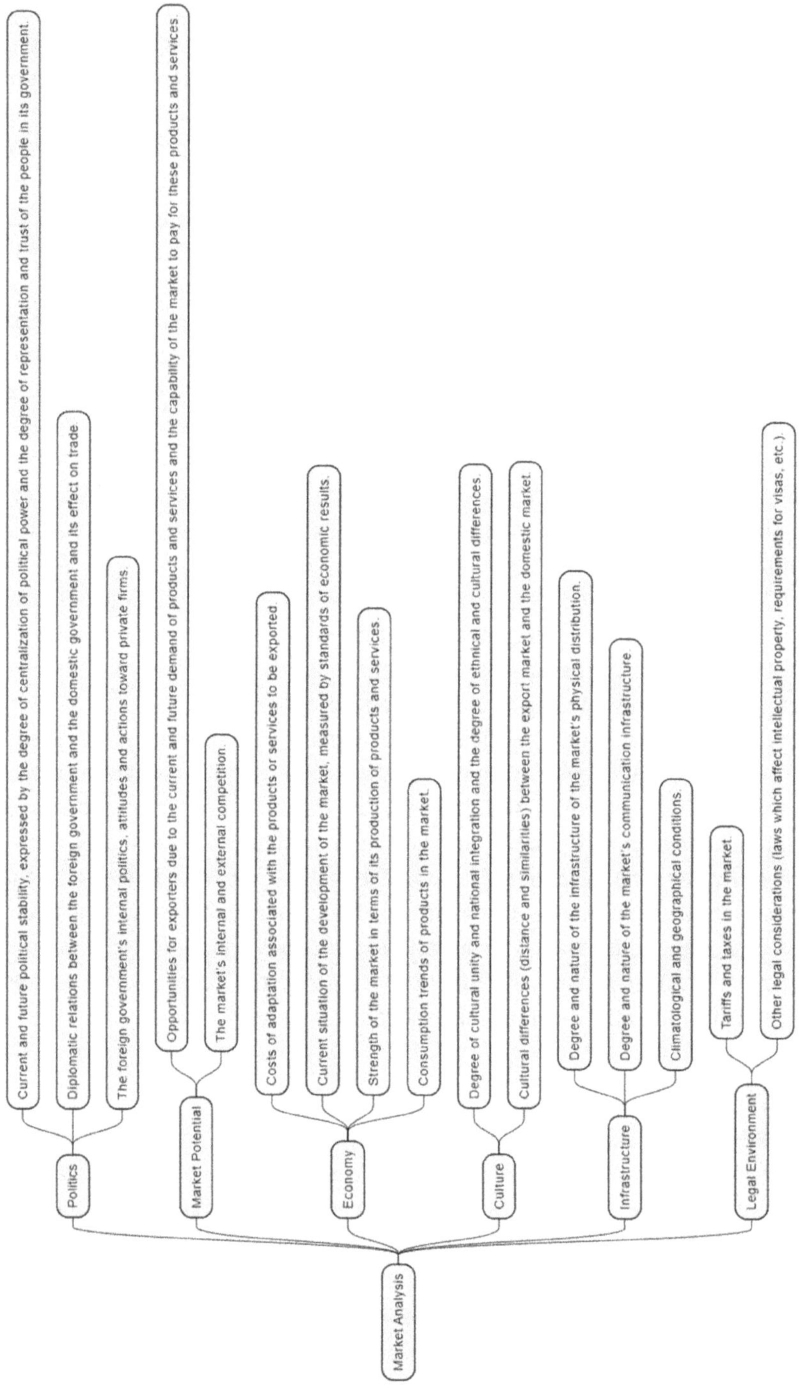

Figure 4.11: List of leading socioeconomic indicators when selecting a foreign market.

Economic Factors

Economic factors are crucial in all aspects of business analysis. They are the primary factors considered when a company makes financial decisions. The local or global economy will be a determining factor in the firm's operation domestically and abroad. Some of these factors may include the value of its assets, consumer demand, and even taxes. Other factors may include interest rates, exchange rates, inflation, recession, taxation, and supply and demand, to name a few. Such factors are related to money, goods, and services. These factors affect businesses on a micro and macro level. The following are three main factors and their connection to businesses:

- **Interest Rates** – Many different institutions impose interest rates. Banking institutions rely on the status of interest rates as they determine their lending policies and practices. Such interest rates also offer vital information for firms that depend on debt capital to finance their projects.
- **Exchange Rates** – These are essential factors for any business importing and exporting several goods and services. As these rates fluctuate, they affect the ability of a company to pay its international suppliers satisfactorily. They can also affect the profit margin of the company, as well as the amount of resources it needs to stay afloat.
- **Recession** – Whenever an economy faces a recession, it can change consumers' attitudes toward purchasing decisions, forcing companies to drop prices to stay afloat.

Socioeconomic Factors May Affect Health

People's health, in general, is primarily determined by the environment and circumstances. Many factors come together to affect the health of an individual and an entire community. These include a person's education level, genetic composition, the environment they are inserted into, geographic factors, relationships with friends and family, and so on. These factors have an even more significant effect on health than access to healthcare services.

Three significant factors affect the health of society:

- Socioeconomic environment
- Physical environment
- Individual behaviors and characteristics

A person cannot be entirely blamed for poor health; for the most part, such a person is the product of the environment. In other words, a socioeconomic context is the most significant determinant of health. Determinants may include:

- **Social Status and Income** – A high social status and an above-average income predispose an individual to better health. Studies show that as the gap between the rich and the poor increases, the same goes for the gap between their health levels.
- **Education Level** – Education is also commonly observed to be directly correlated to health. Communities characterized by low educational levels tend to have

lower health. A low education level is linked to lower self-confidence and more stress.
- **Physical Environment** – Safe homes, healthy workplaces, safe drinking water, clean air, healthy communities, and better infrastructure are essential for a healthy society. The mere fact of being employed predisposes an individual to better health. Also, the more control individuals have over their working conditions, the better their health.
- **Social Support Network** – When individuals have lots of support from family, friends, and the community, they are predisposed to enhanced health. Greater support factors may include, but are not limited to, the community's culture, traditions, rituals, beliefs, faith, and customs. Improving all these factors may lead to advancing the community's health.
- **Genetics** – Genetics plays a significant role in people's health, lifespan, and probability of contracting certain diseases. Other personal factors impacting health include people's coping skills and behavior. Examples include the level of physical activity, whether they are smokers or not, whether they are alcohol drinkers, and how they manage stress. All of these factors have a significant impact on an individual's health.
- **Access to Health Services** – People's ability to access and use quality health facilities affects their health. Their access to preventive medicine and procedures that protect them from certain diseases is critical.

Business owners are responsible for raising the socioeconomic status of their employees and those in their community, even as they seek to grow their own. They can do this by improving workplace conditions, offering better work benefits to their employees to care for families' health and education, and participating in corporate social responsibility (CSR) projects to improve their community. Doing so can pave the way for ESG and DEI criteria alignment and a more sustainable future.

The International Monetary System

An international monetary system comprises internationally agreed-upon regulations, conventions, and supporting institutions that facilitate international trade, cross-border investment, and generally the reallocation of capital between states with different currencies. It refers to the financial environment's operating system, consisting of financial institutions, multinational companies, and investors. The system supplies the institutional framework for defining the rules and procedures for international payments, determination of exchange rates, and movement of capital. The evolution of the international monetary system can be classified into the following phases, as depicted in Figure 4.12: the gold standard, Bretton Woods, the Smithsonian Agreement, and the managed float.

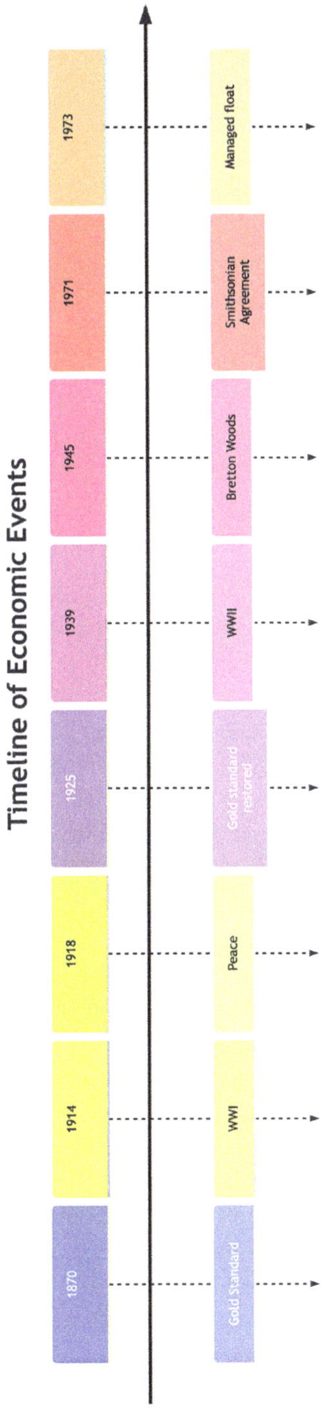

Figure 4.12: The evolution of the international monetary system.

The Bimetallism Era

Before 1870, the international monetary system consisted of bimetallism, which was used in the United States as early as 1791 but abandoned in the early 1800s. The system reemerged in the mid-to-late 1800s, and the government began purchasing silver for its reserves through the Bland-Allison Act and the Sherman Silver Purchase Act. Gold and silver coins were adopted as the leading international form of payment, and exchange rates between currencies were determined by the amount of gold or silver they contained. Some nations were either on a silver or gold standard.

Supporters of the system thought that bimetallism would help the economy by causing inflation. This would help farmers and others who had too much debt. Those in the movement wanted money backed by silver to be added to the money supply backed by gold. Adding to the money supply would have ended the deflation and created the possibility of inflation. A significant problem in the international use of bimetallism was that, with each nation independently setting its exchange rate between the two metals, the resulting rates often differed widely from country to country.

The Gold Standard

In the gold standard system, only gold alone was guaranteed unobstructed coinage. However, in an exchange, there was two-way convertibility between gold and any national currency at a steady ratio. However, no restraints were imposed on the import or export of gold – the gold content defined the exchange rate between any two currencies. The international gold standard existed between 1875–1914. As depicted in Figure 4.13, under the gold standard, if governments wanted to add more money to their economies, they had to add more gold to back it up. Such a system offered advantages to the economy, its people, and foreign trade, as it promoted long-term price stability, making it difficult for governments to inflate prices. It also fostered fixed international exchange rates between trading nations and reduced uncertainties. However, it also had disadvantages, especially for countries that did not produce gold. Other constraints included the limitations it brought to economic growth, and according to many economists, the gold standard prolonged economic recessions, as the government could not inject liquidity onto its markets (print money at will). Hence, standards also limited the central bank's ability to respond to an economic crisis.

1914, during World War I, the gold standard ceased to exist. Great Britain, Germany, France, and several other nations imposed sanctions on gold exports and discontinued the redemption of bank notes in gold. During the interwar period between World Wars I and II (1915–1944), the United States replaced Britain as the world's dominant financial power. In 1919, it decided to return to the gold standard. During this intermittent period, many countries sterilized gold by matching gold inflows and outflows with domestic money and credit changes.

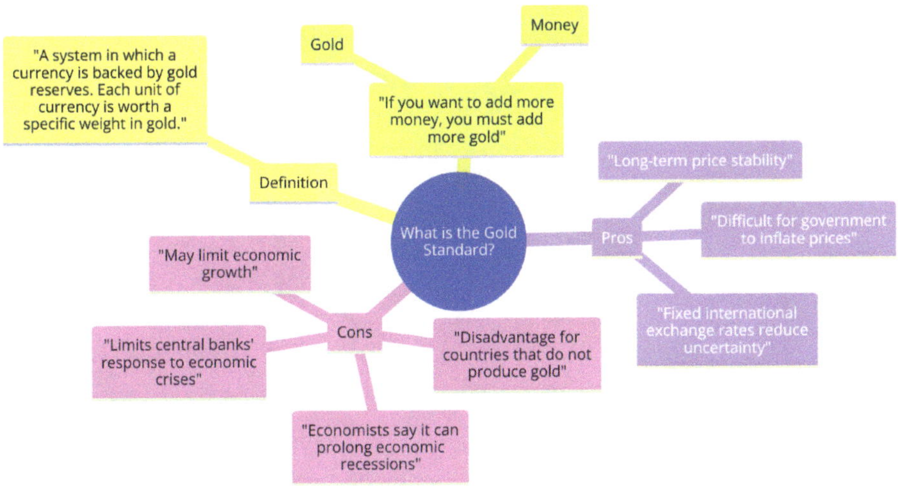

Figure 4.13: According to many economists, the gold standard's main pros and cons.

A Gold Exchange Standard

The Bretton Woods System was founded in 1945, right after World War II, and lasted through 1972. It resulted from 44 representatives of world nations who met at Bretton Woods in New Hampshire, tasked to design a new international monetary system, which endorsed adopting an exchange standard that included foreign exchanges and gold. This new monetary system called for each nation to establish a par value correlation to the U.S. dollar, pegged at the time, to gold at an exchange rate of $35 per ounce. Figure 4.14 outlines the main differences between the gold and gold exchange standards developed at Bretton Woods. This new system also called for the nation's reserve currency to aim at running a balance of payments (BOPs) deficit to supply reserves. If such debts ended out to be too large, the reserve currency would then witness a crisis. Such phenomenon was coined *the Triffin paradox. E*ventually, in the early 1970s, under President Nixon, the gold exchange system collapsed precisely for these reasons.

How did it happen, you may ask? The U.S. started facing trade deficit problems after 1950. With the development of the euro markets, there was a massive outflow of dollars. The U.S. government took several dollar defense measures, including the Interest Equalization Tax (IET) imposition on U.S. purchases of foreign stocks to prevent unprecedented outflows of U.S. dollars. During that time, the IMF issued a new reserve asset dubbed special drawing rights (SDRs) to alleviate the pressure on the U.-S. dollar, the main reserve currency. Initially, the SDR was modeled as a weighted basket of 16 international currencies of nations whose global export share was greater than 1%. In 1981, however, the SDR was restructured to constitute only five major currencies: the U.S. dollar, German mark, Japanese yen, British pound, and French franc.

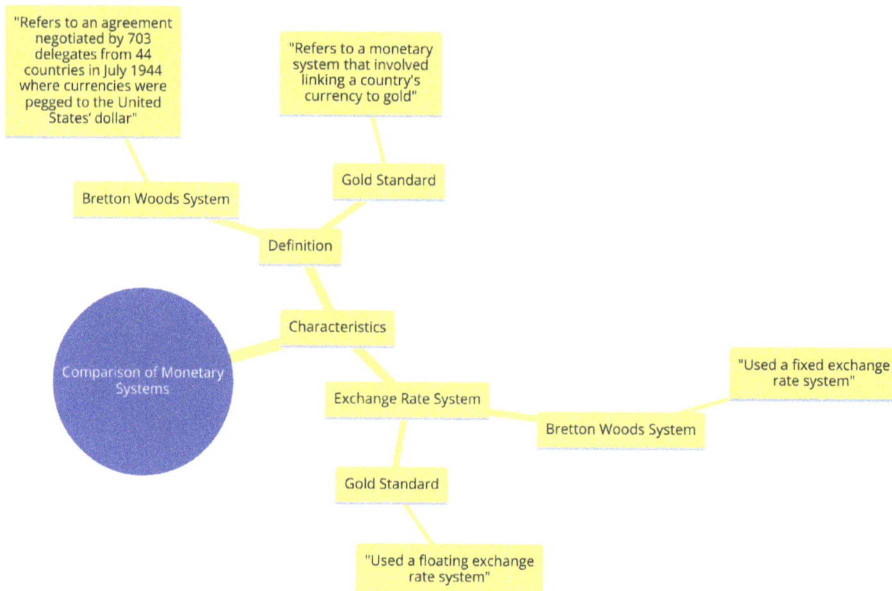

Figure 4.14: Differences between the gold and Bretton Woods gold exchange standards.

The SDR was also being used as a denomination currency for international transactions. However, the dollar-based gold exchange standard could not be sustained due to rising inflation and monetary expansion. In 1971, the signing of the Smithsonian Agreement by the Group of Ten Major Nations changed the gold exchange standard. The price of gold increased to $38 per ounce while other countries revalued their national currencies by up to 10%. The Smithsonian agreement likewise proved inefficient, and the Bretton Woods System finally collapsed.

The Floating Currency Exchange Rate System

A floating exchange rate, as illustrated in Figure 4.15, is a system where the currency price of a nation is set by the foreign exchange (forex) market based on *supply* and *demand* relative to other foreign currencies, in contrast to a fixed exchange rate, in which the government entirely or predominantly determines the rate. Unlike those with fixed exchange rates, currencies with floating exchange rates can be traded without restrictions. Floating exchange rates mean that currencies change in relative value all the time. For instance, at the time of this writing (summer 2022), one U.S. dollar could buy one euro after the latter experienced a drop in value, but that was not the case in the spring of 2022, as the dollar was worth about 0.97 euros, depending on the day.

Figure 4.15: In a floating exchange rate system, the foreign exchange market sets a nation's currency price based on *supply* and *demand* relative to other foreign currencies.

In 1973, Japanese and European currencies evolved into free-floating currencies. The IMF members ratified this flexible currency exchange rate system in 1976 through the Jamaica Agreement, which stipulated that respective countries' central banks could intervene in the exchange markets to safeguard against unwarranted fluctuations. In 1985, the Plaza Accord envisaged the depreciation of the U.S. dollar against most major international currencies to solve the U.S. trade deficit issues. Around the same time, gold was officially abandoned as a global reserve asset.

As pointed out thus far, various flexible currency exchange rate systems exist. In an independent-floating or free-floating currency, its exchange rate is defined by the global market, with foreign exchange interventions by central banks occurring only in rare situations to prevent undue fluctuations. For instance, Australia, the United Kingdom, the Eurozone, the United States, and Japan have free-floating currencies. But in a *managed-floating system*, the central monetary authority of a country, typically a central bank (the Federal Reserve in the U.S.), influences the movement of the exchange rate through active interventions in the foreign exchange (forex) markets with no preannounced pathway for the exchange rate. Some examples include countries such as the U.S., China, India, Russia, and Singapore. In a fixed-peg arrangement, the country pegs its currency to a major currency or a basket of currencies at a fixed rate. For example, many Gulf Cooperation Countries (GCC), such as the United Arab Emirates and Saudi Arabia, have pegged their national currencies to the U.S. dollar.

Global Economies at Currency War

More than a decade has passed since the global financial crisis of 2008, which traversed the global economy swiftly, confirming how interconnected the world had already become in ideas, information, capital, and new technologies, which had streamed across borders with increasing ease over the past decades. Nevertheless, the lack of sustained financial crisis response has made it clear how fractured the international political landscape has become, as advanced and emerging economies' diverging interests made global economic stabilization coordination ever more complex. Hence, despite sustained globalization, and in some cases because of it, we are seeing a growing vacuum of global leadership and traditional geopolitical risks, which are on the rise.

This section addresses tomorrow's critical global issues that, in my opinion, demand our attention today. As James Rickards argued in his book *Currency Wars: The Making of the Next Global Crisis* (2011), the world is amidst a full-blown currency war. Assuming he is right, as he provides factual data to support his claim, several undercurrents between advanced economies and emerging markets must be assessed and analyzed. In addition, the world, more than ever, is constantly changing, and international business professionals must seek guidance in understanding some of the key players in the evolving global game. Essential topics include the U.S.-China dynamics, the relations between China and the Russian Federation, and the rest of Asia more broadly.

Such trends have gained momentum in shaping global trade, especially among advanced economies and emerging markets. This has led to new challenges for policymakers worldwide, international traders, and multinational enterprises. In a world where the international agenda is cracking, local and shorter-term challenges take precedence for policymakers and global business leaders.

Economies at War

For the past decade, at least since 2010, government officials from the G7 economies have been very concerned with the potential escalation of a global economic war, a currency war. Finance ministers and central bankers from advanced economies worry that their peers in the G20, including several emerging economies, may continue to devalue their currencies to boost exports and grow their economies at their neighbors' expense.

Brazil led the charge, the first emerging economy to accuse the U.S. of instigating a currency war in 2010 when the U.S. Federal Reserve bought piles of bonds with newly created money. From a Chinese perspective, with the world's largest holdings of U.S. dollar reserves, a U.S.-led currency war based on dollar debasement is an American act of default to its foreign creditors, no matter how you disguise it. So far, the Chinese have been more diplomatic, but global headlines suggest their patience is wearing thin.

Quantitative easing (QE) made investors flood emerging markets with hot money for better returns, which lifted their exchange rates. These two countries are not alone. Several other emerging markets, such as Saudi Arabia, Korea, Russia, Turkey, and Taiwan, have also been impacted by a weak dollar. Japan continues to face charges that it is trying to lower the value of its currency, the yen, to stimulate its economy and get the edge over other countries. The government is trying to reignite Japan's economy, which has been in recession after two decades of stagnant growth and deflation. The government pushed the Bank of Japan to accept a higher inflation target, which has triggered speculation the bank may create more money. As the yen falls, its exports become cheaper, and those of Asian neighbors South Korea and Taiwan and those further afield in Europe become relatively more expensive.

The critical issues in the U.S., China, and Japan stem from minimally blatantly ineffective public policy but insist on a failed and destructive economic policy. Common sense should prevail, ending the dangerous game of beggar (and blame) thy neighbor. After all, the International Monetary Fund was created to prevent such races to the bottom and should try to broker a truce among foreign exchange competitors. So far, Europe has felt the impact of the falling yen the most. At the height of the Eurozone's financial crisis in 2012, the euro was worth US$1.21, potentially benefiting big exporters like BMW, Audi, Mercedes, or Airbus.

Most advanced economies have over-consumed in the past decade and beyond. It has too much debt. But rather than dealing with those debts – living a life of austerity, accepting a period of relative stagnation – these economies want to shift the burden of adjustment onto their creditors, even when they are relatively emerging nations with low per capita incomes. During the Asian crisis in 1997–98, Western countries, under the auspices of the IMF, insisted that Asian nations, having borrowed too much, should now tighten their belts. However, many advanced economies did not seem to think they should abide by the same rules. It is far better to use the exchange rate to pass the burden on to someone else than to swallow the bitter pill of austerity.

Meanwhile, European policymakers, fearful that their countries' exports were caught in this currency war crossfire, have entertained unwise ideas such as directly managing the euro's value. While generating money out of thin air may not be available to emerging economies, where inflation tends to remain a problem, limited capital controls may be a sensible short-term defense against destabilizing inflows of hot money.

Currency War May Cause Damage to the Global Economy

As more countries try to weaken their currencies for economic gain, there may come a point where the fragile global economic recovery could be derailed, and the international financial system will be thrown into chaos. In September of 2011, Switzerland took action to arrest the rise of its currency, the Swiss franc, when investors, looking for somewhere safe to store their cash from the debt crisis afflicting the 17-country

Eurozone, saw it as the traditional instrument to fulfill that role. The Swiss intervention was viewed as an attempt to protect the country's exporters.

Policymakers are focusing on the wrong issue. Rather than focus on currency manipulation, all sides would be better served to zero in on structural reforms. The effects of that would be far more beneficial in the long run than unilateral U.S., China, or Japanese currency action and more sustainable. The G20 should focus on a comprehensive package of structural reforms in all countries, advanced economies, and emerging markets. Exchange rates should be an essential part of that package, no doubt. For instance, Americans must save more to reduce the U.S. current account deficits. Continuing to devalue the dollar will not be sufficient for that purpose. Likewise, China's current account surpluses were caused by a broad set of domestic economic distortions, from state-allocated credit to artificially low interest rates. Correcting China's external imbalances requires eliminating all of these distortions as well.

As long as policymakers focus on currency exchange issues, the volatility in the currency markets will continue to escalate. It has become so problematic that the G7 advanced economies have warned that volatile movements in exchange rates could adversely hit the global economy. These currency moves have shocked Brazil, Russia, India, China, South Africa (BRICS), and other emerging-market economies, including Thailand. The G20 is divided between the advanced economies – the UK, the U.S., Japan, France, Canada, Italy, and Germany – and emerging countries such as Russia, China, South Korea, India, Brazil, Argentina, Indonesia, and the like. Top leaders of Russia, South Korea, Germany, Brazil, and China have all expressed concern over the currency moves, which drive up their currencies' value and undermine their exports' competitiveness. If they decide to enter the game, the world would be plunged into competitive devaluations, leading to runaway inflation or hyperinflation. Nobody wins in these currency wars.

The international monetary system may destabilize and collapse if policymakers do not change course. There will be so much money printing by so many central banks that people's confidence in paper money will wane, and inflation will rise sharply. If policymakers genuinely want to stage off this currency war, then it is a matter of doing what was done in 1985 with the Plaza Accord. This time, however, we will need a different version, as it will not be about the U.S. and the G5 of the time. It will have to be an Asian Plaza Accord under the support and auspices of the G20. It must be about the Asia export-led and mercantilist leadership agreeing among them. The chances of this happening, of advanced economies seeing the requirement for it, or these economies relinquishing their powers in any measurable fashion are not at all possible under the current political gamesmanship presently being played.

The perspective presented here is focused on international trade and currency exchange, specifically its impact on international trade rather than geopolitical and economic aspects. Currency wars are approached not from theoretical or simulation models conducted behind a desk but from the standpoint of practitioners engaged in international business and foreign trade on the ground in four different countries.

Balance of Payments

The balance of payments (BoP), also dubbed the balance of international payments, is a statement of all transactions made between entities in one nation and the rest of the world over a specified period, such as a quarter or a year. It outlines all transactions of a nation's individuals, businesses, and government bodies transacted with individuals, businesses, and government bodies outside the home country.

A nation's BoP and net international investment position constitute its international account positions. The BoP transactions consist of imports and exports of goods, services, and capital and transfer payments, such as foreign aid and remittances. As illustrated in Figure 4.16, the BoP subdivides transactions into a current and a capital account. A current account contains goods, services, transfers, and investment income transactions. Such an account is also dubbed the financial account, with a different, usually minimal, capital account listed separately.

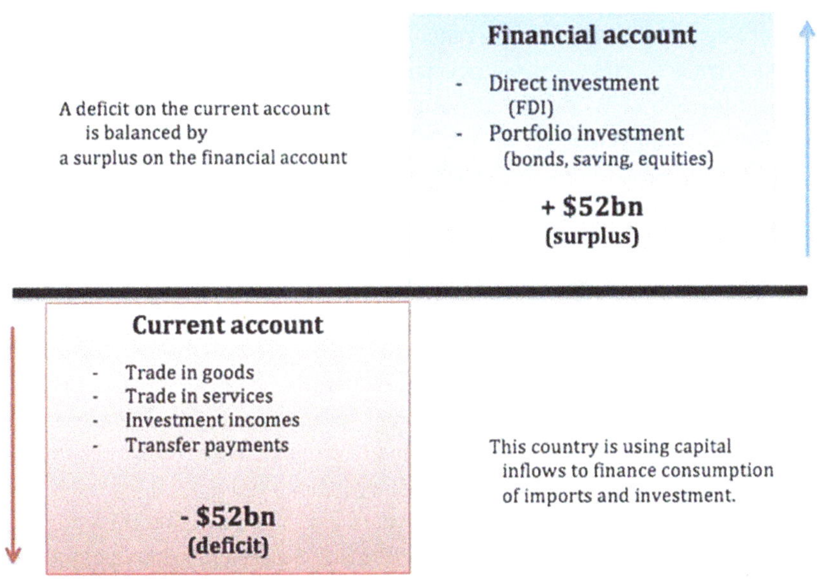

Figure 4.16: shows an example of the balance of payments in equilibrium.

The capital account includes trades in financial instruments and central bank reserves. Narrowly described, it only contains transactions made through financial instruments. While the current account is incorporated in calculations of national output, the capital account is not. If a country exports an item, it effectively imports foreign capital when paid for (a capital account transaction). Suppose a nation cannot finance its imports via exports of capital. In that case, it will need to tap into its reserves, a situation known as the BoP deficit, using the narrow definition of the capital account that excludes central bank reserves. In reality, however, the broadly depicted BoP must add up to zero by definition. In practice, statistical differences arise due to the hardship of accurately calculating every single transaction between a country and the rest of the world, including all the discrepancies caused by foreign currency exchanges.

History of BoP

National economies were not well integrated. As discussed earlier in this chapter, before the 19th century, international transactions were denominated in gold, furnishing little flexibility for nations experiencing trade deficits. During this period, growth rates were generally low, and maintaining a trade surplus was the primary method for strengthening a nation's financial position. While steep trade imbalances did not commonly trigger crises at that time, the onset of the Industrial Revolution marked a significant increase in international economic integration, leading to a more frequent balance of payments crises.

The Great Depression led nations to renounce the gold standard and compete with their national currencies' competitive depreciation. Still, the Bretton Woods system that prevailed from the end of World War II until the 1970s presented a gold-convertible dollar with fixed currency exchange rates to other international currencies.

During the Great Recession, several nations ventured into competitive devaluation of their currencies to boost their exports into currency wars, as discussed in the section earlier. This led to many other countries' currencies, particularly in emerging markets, appreciating their currency against the U.S. dollar and other major currencies. Many of these countries reacted by further loosening the controls on their monetary policy to support their exports, especially those nations whose exports were under severe pressure from a stagnant global demand during the Great Recession. The world's major central banks had to respond to this enormous financial crisis, which I believe we are still dealing with. Still, many economists argue it has subsided in response to dramatically expansionary monetary policy.

International investment position and BoP data are vital in formulating national and foreign economic policy. Certain aspects of the BoP data, such as payment imbalances and FDI, are important issues that a country's policymakers attempt to address. Although a country's BoP necessarily zeroes out the current and capital accounts, imbalances can and do appear in different nations' current accounts. Figure 4.17 illustrates the current global BoP in U.S. billions of dollars as of 2021, with the United States accounting among the countries with the largest debts (light blue) and China with trade surplus (dark blue).

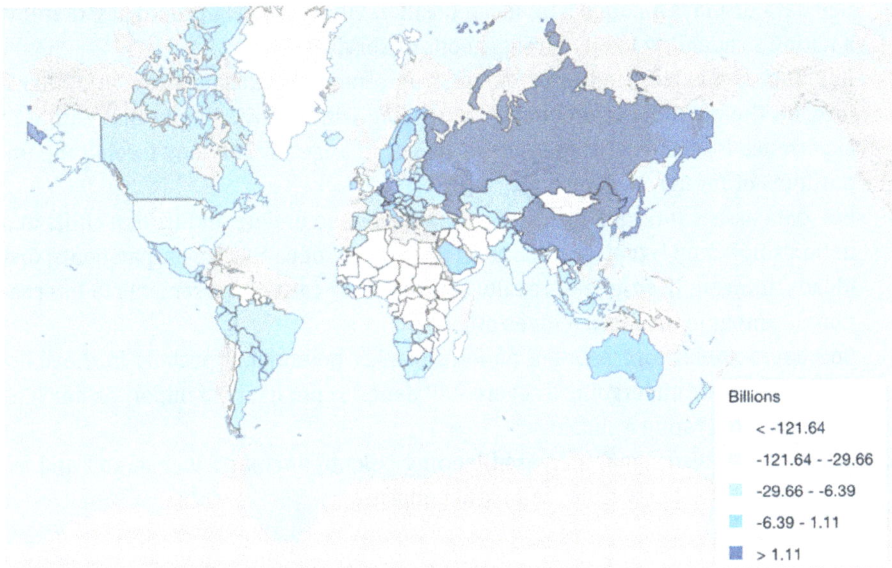

Figure 4.17: The current global BoP in the U.S. is billions of dollars as of 2022. (SOURCE: World Bank, IMF, 2023).

The Importance of BoP Data for International Business Managers

The BoP is an essential indicator of pressure on a nation's exchange rate and, therefore, on the potential of a company trading with or investing in that nation to incur foreign exchange gains or losses. Changes in BoP may foretell the imposition of foreign exchange controls. The BoP is an important indicator of the financial health of any nation's business as it mirrors its international trade and investment performance.

The BoP data of a home nation and the host country is of vital significance to government officials, foreign investors, international business managers, and overall consumers, as this data influences and tends to be influenced by other key macroeconomic variables such as GDP, GNI, interest rates, unemployment rates, price levels, currency exchange rates. Therefore, BoP can be used to indicate economic and political stability. For instance, a nation with a consistently positive BoP may suggest a significant presence of FDI inflows. However, it may also indicate that the country does not export much of its currency.

Monetary and fiscal policy development must consider the BoP at the national level. Multinational enterprises utilize various BoP measures to assess the growth and health of specific trade or financial transactions by nation and global regions compared to their home country. International business managers need BoP data to predict shifts in the host nation's economic policies driven by BoP activities and events. Therefore, BoP data may be necessary for the following reasons:

1. BoP data displays a nation's financial position vis-a-vis foreign countries, thereby, a nation's capability to buy foreign goods or services.
2. BoP data is a critical indicator of stress on a nation's exchange rate and, therefore, on the potential of an enterprise trading with or investing in that nation to experience foreign exchange gains or losses. Changes in BoP may foretell the impositions of foreign exchange measures.
3. BoP data assists international business managers in understanding that shifts in a nation's BoP may signal an imposition or removal of controls over payments, dividends, interest, license fees, royalty fees, or other cash disbursements to international companies or foreign investors.
4. BoP data enables forecasting a nation's market potential, especially in the short term. A country undergoing a severe BoP deficit is not likely to import as much as it would if operating a surplus.
5. BoP data can also signal increased lending risks to any particular nation and assist in developing new trade and fiscal policies.

ESG Impact on Economic, Socioeconomic, and Financial Forces Shaping the International Monetary System

ESG factors, with their significant influence on global business, economy, and society, are shaping and improving economic evaluation, impacting the international financial system, and influencing social and economic aspects. With the growing focus on sustainability, social equity, and good governance among companies and policymakers, ESG criteria are set to play a crucial role in steering the future of global dynamics toward a more sustainable and equitable path. Incorporating ESG into business strategies and policy frameworks is essential and promising for securing sustainable economic growth, societal welfare, and environmental preservation in the long run.

ESG factors play a pivotal role in shaping economic policies on a global scale. Understanding these factors is crucial for conducting international economic analysis, as they significantly impact market dynamics, investment decisions, and economic policies. For instance, the increasing emphasis on sustainability has led to a surge in investments in renewable energy and green technologies, thereby transforming the global economic environment. Economic analysts are now considering environmental risks, such as climate change, for their potential to disrupt supply chains and affect economic stability. Social factors, such as labor rights and community impacts, are crucial in shaping consumer behavior and corporate reputation. Concerns about governance, such as transparency and ethical behavior, impact investor trust and regulatory landscapes.

ESG and the Global Monetary System

ESG factors substantially influence the intricate regulations and traditions of the global financial system. The rise of sustainable finance, a notable trend, underscores the importance of integrating ESG criteria into investment choices and financial activities. This shift is evident in the proliferation of green bonds and sustainable investment funds designed to support eco-friendly and socially responsible initiatives.

Central banks and financial institutions increasingly recognize the significance of ESG for maintaining economic stability. An example is how the European Central Bank (ECB) has included climate risk in its monetary policy framework. These actions guarantee that the financial system can withstand environmental shocks and encourage sustainable economic development. Furthermore, changes in governance within the global monetary system are motivated by the desire for increased transparency and accountability. The IMF and WB push for more robust governance standards to fight corruption and improve economic governance, showing a rise in the impact of ESG principles.

ESG in Socioeconomic Aspects

Socioeconomic factors heavily influence businesses' internationalization process. ESG criteria, by emphasizing the significance of social equality, growth within communities, and ethical conduct in business operations, are not just influencing but also championing these crucial values. Businesses are now required to positively impact the communities they are located in, going beyond just making money, and this shift is a testament to the growing importance of these values in the global business landscape. Environmental sustainability is an important factor in socioeconomics. Companies are implementing strategies to lessen their environmental impact, including cutting back on waste, lowering carbon emissions, and opting for sustainable resources. These initiatives help safeguard the environment and appeal to consumers and investors who care about sustainability.

ESG criteria profoundly impact the establishment of a solid corporate image and the fostering of customer loyalty. Companies that prioritize fair labor practices, safe work environments, and community growth are more likely to earn the trust and support of the public. This emphasis on ESG contributes to societal welfare and enhances the business's reputation and customer base. Governance is crucial in determining socioeconomic results. Maintaining investor confidence and regulatory compliance relies on essential good governance practices, such as transparency, accountability, and ethical conduct. Firms with solid governance frameworks are better positioned to navigate global markets and reduce risks.

ESG and Effects on Culture

Culture is crucial in global business, and ESG factors significantly impact cultural interactions. Companies need to navigate varied cultural environments while sticking to ESG principles. For instance, a multinational corporation must adhere to local traditions and behaviors while promoting environmental sustainability and social responsibility. Global evidence indicates cultural changes toward sustainability and social responsibility are happening worldwide. Consumers are increasingly aware of their purchases' environmental and social effects, resulting in a higher requirement for sustainable products and ethical business behaviors. This culture change motivates companies to incorporate ESG criteria into their operations and marketing strategies. Moreover, businesses need to adjust their practices to align with local cultures while also upholding international standards due to variations in governance practices. Developing knowledge and acknowledging cultural differences is essential for successfully implementing ESG measures across various areas.

Discussion Questions

1. **Discuss how changes in the international monetary system can influence global trade and investment patterns. Provide examples based on the historical shifts described in the chapter.**

Multiple-Choice Questions

2. **What was the primary goal of the Bretton Woods System established after World War II?**
   A) To reintroduce the gold standard as the global economic policy.
   B) To stabilize national currencies and provide a predictable monetary environment.
   C) To eliminate the use of gold in international economic transactions.
   D) To encourage countries to adopt floating exchange rates.

3. **According to the chapter, what is one significant effect of adopting the floating currency exchange rate system in the 1970s?**
   A) It restricted the ability of central banks to intervene in currency markets.
   B) It led to more stable and less volatile currency values.
   C) It allowed currencies to be valued based on supply and demand market forces.
   D) It mandated that all international transactions be conducted in U.S. dollars.

4. **The Bretton Woods System was primarily based on a gold exchange standard, in which currencies were pegged to the U.S. dollar and convertible into gold. True or False?**

5. **The gold standard system allowed governments unlimited freedom to print money as needed without economic repercussions. True or False?**

Recommended Readings

Alami, I., Alves, C., Bonizzi, B., Kaltenbrunner, A., Koddenbrock, K., Kvangraven, I., & Powell, J. (2023). International financial subordination: a critical research agenda. *Review of International Political Economy*, 30(4), 1360–1386.

Casanova, L., & Miroux, A. (2022). Emerging Market Multinationals Report 2021: Building the Future on ESG Excellence, Cornell SC Johnson College of Business, Emerging Markets Institute, https://ecommons.cornell.edu/bitstream/1813/110935/2/EMR%202021%20-%20Building%20the%20Future%20on%20ESG%20Excellence.pdf, last accessed on March 27, 2024.

Haberly, D., & Wójcik, D. (2022). *Sticky power: Global financial networks in the world economy* (p. 400). Oxford University Press, Oxford, UK.

Lorenzi, A. (2023). Sustainable Investments and ESG Financial Framework, Università Ca' Foscari Venezia, Italy, http://hdl.handle.net/10579/23333, last accessed on May 3, 2024.

Mooneeapen, O., Abhayawansa, S., & Mamode Khan, N. (2022). The influence of the country governance environment on corporate environmental, social and governance (ESG) performance. *Sustainability Accounting, Management and Policy Journal*, 13(4), 953–985.

Murau, S., & van't Klooster, J. (2023). Rethinking monetary sovereignty: the global credit money system and the state. *Perspectives on Politics*, 21(4), 1319–1336.

Norrlof, C., Poast, P., Cohen, B. J., Croteau, S., Khanna, A., McDowell, D., . . . & Winecoff, W. K. (2020). Global monetary order and the liberal order debate. *International Studies Perspectives*, 21(2), 109–153.

Oatley, T., & Petrova, B. (2022). The global deregulation hypothesis. *Socio-Economic Review*, 20(2), 611–633.

Petare, P. A., Josyula, H. P., Landge, S. R., Gatala, S. K. K., & Gunturu, S. R. (2024). Central Bank Digital Currencies: Exploring The Future Of Money And Banking. *Migration Letters*, 21(S7), 640–51.

Semet, R. (2020). The Social Issue of ESG Analysis. Available at SSRN 3838372.

Svartzman, R., Bolton, P., Despres, M., Pereira Da Silva, L. A., & Samama, F. (2021). Central banks, financial stability and policy coordination in the age of climate uncertainty: A three-layered analytical and operational framework. *Climate Policy*, 21(4), 563–580.

Chapter 5
International Competitive Strategy

Learning Objectives

- Differentiate the role of main international institutions
- Understand the development of an international competitive strategy
- Explain the process of global strategic planning
- Assess the types of international strategic planning

Overview

This chapter discusses the importance of an international competitive strategy. It focuses on an international strategy and why it is essential. It also addresses the importance of planning for internationalization, covering the global strategic planning process, its features and implementations, and its facilitators. This chapter provides theoretical knowledge and equips you with the practical skills to apply global strategic planning in real-world scenarios. Finally, this chapter reviews some of the main different types of strategic planning, giving you a comprehensive understanding of the subject.

International Institutions

An international institution, also known as an intergovernmental or international organization, is a stable set of norms, rules, and regulations meant to govern the behavior of states and other actors in the international system. Understanding these institutions is crucial as they draw membership from at least three countries, have activities in several countries (states), and have a formal agreement with member countries. Over the years, international institutions of various types and conventions, including treaties, organizations, and regimes, have significantly grown in numbers and importance, making them a key area of study for anyone in international business or strategic management.

The Union of International Associations (UIA), a coordinating entity, provides a comprehensive overview of the complex and diverse landscape of international strategic planning. It distinguishes between the 250+ international governmental organizations (IGOs) established by intergovernmental agreements and those whose members are countries, and then about 6,000 nongovernmental organizations (NGOs) members who are individuals or associations. These IGOs range from three members to more than 185, and their geographic representation varies from one world region to all regions. Their organizational structures differ from simple to highly complex, depending

https://doi.org/10.1515/9783111510286-005

on their size and tasks, with some IGOs designed to achieve a sole purpose and others tasked with multiple tasks. This complexity and diversity make international strategic planning a fascinating and challenging field to study and understand.

International institutions may be established by a treaty or be instruments governed by international law and possess their legal personalities, such as the United Nations (UN), the World Health Organization (WHO), and the North Atlantic Treaty Organization (NATO). As mentioned above, international institutions are composed primarily of member states but may include other entities, such as international organizations. Additionally, entities and countries may hold observer status. The following is a list of some of the most notable international institutions, but by all means, not an all-inclusive one.

United Nations

The United Nations (UN) is an intergovernmental organization with the primary purposes of preserving international peace and security across the globe, developing friendly relations among nations, achieving international cooperation, and being a center for harmonizing the actions of nations' governments. It is the world's largest and most well-known global organization. The UN is headquartered on international territory in New York City, with other main offices in Geneva, Nairobi, Vienna, and The Hague, where the International Court of Justice is based.

The UN was founded after World War II to avert future wars, succeeding the League of Nations, characterized as inadequate. In 1945, 50 international governments met in San Francisco to draft the UN Charter, which was adopted and taken into effect later that year when the UN began operations. According to the UN Charter, the organization's objectives include:

- Supporting global peace and security.
- Protecting human rights.
- Delivering humanitarian aid.
- Promoting sustainable development.
- Upholding global law.

The UN membership grew significantly following widespread decolonization beginning in the 1960s. As illustrated in Figure 5.1, the UN had 51 members at its founding. With the addition of South Sudan in 2011, membership is now 193, representing almost all of the world's sovereign states.

The UN has six principal organs: the General Assembly, the International Court of Justice, the Security Council, the Trusteeship Council, the Economic and Social Council (ECOSOC), and the UN Secretariat. The UN System includes many specialized agencies, funds, and programs such as the World Bank Group, the World Health Organization, the World Food Programme, UNESCO, and UNICEF.

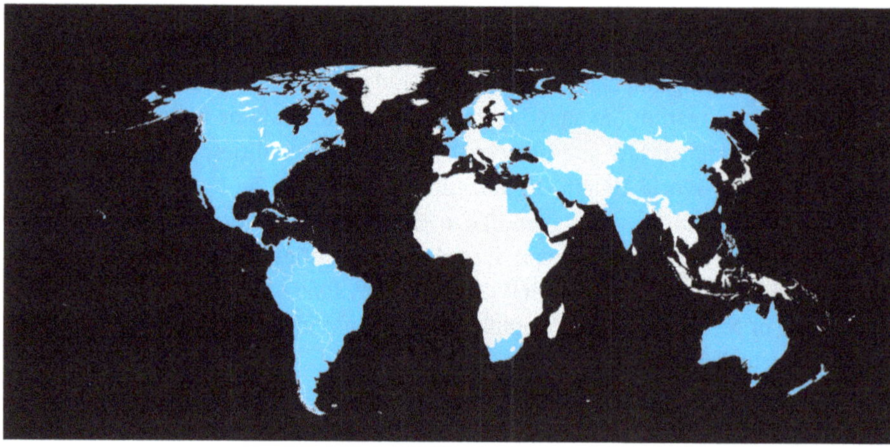

Figure 5.1: UN 51 founding members in 1945. (Source: UNEP).

The UN's chief administrative officer is the secretary-general, Portuguese politician, and diplomat António Guterres, who began his first five-year term on January 1, 2017, and was re-elected on June 8, 2021. The organization is financed by assessed and voluntary contributions from its member states. The UN, its officers, and its agencies have won many Nobel Peace Prizes, though other evaluations of its effectiveness have been mixed. Some commentators believe the organization is vital for peace and human development, while others have called it ineffective, biased, or corrupt.

The World Bank Group

The World Bank Group, or World Bank (WB) for short, is affiliated with the UN and instituted to finance projects that improve the economic development of member countries. The WB is the largest source of financial assistance to developing (emerging) nations, offering technical assistance and policy advisory services and supervising the implementation of free-market reforms on behalf of international creditors. In cooperation with the IMF and the WTO, the WB plays a central role in overseeing economic policy, reforming public institutions in developing countries, and defining the global macroeconomic agenda. The WB is headquartered in Washington, DC.

The WB was founded in 1944 at the UN Monetary and Financial Conference, commonly known as the Bretton Woods Conference, and began operating in June 1946, with the first loans geared toward the postwar reconstruction of Western Europe. Starting in the mid-1950s, it significantly financed investments in infrastructural projects in emerging nations, including hydroelectric dams, roads, water and sewage facilities, and ports, including maritime and airports. As illustrated in Figure 5.2, the World Bank Group comprises five constituent institutions, two of them making up the "World Bank:"

- **International Bank for Reconstruction and Development (IBRD)** – provides loans at market rates of interest to middle-income developing countries and creditworthy lower-income countries.
- **International Development Association (IDA)** – provides long-term interest-free loans and policy advice to low-income developing countries in areas such as technical assistance, education, rural development, and health.
- **International Finance Corporation (IFC)** – operating in partnership with private investors, provides loans, guarantees, and equity financing to business undertakings in developing countries.
- **Multilateral Investment Guarantee Agency (MIGA)** – provides loan guarantees and insurance to foreign investors against losses caused by noncommercial risks in emerging nations.
- **International Centre for Settlement of Investment Disputes (ICSID)** – operates independently of the IBRD and is responsible for the settlement by reconciliation or arbitration of investment disputes between international investors and their host developing countries.

Figure 5.2: The World Bank Group. (Source: The World Bank; http://www.worldbank.org/en/about).

Although the WB is related to the UN, it is not accountable to the General Assembly or the Security Council. Each bank's more than 180 member states are represented on the board of governors, which meets annually. Although the board of governors has some influence on IBRD policies, actual decision-making power is mainly wielded by the bank's 25 executive directors. Five major countries, including the US, Japan, Germany, the UK, and France, are responsible for appointing their executive directors. The other nations are grouped into regions, each electing one executive director.

The WB is the world's largest multilateral creditor institution, and many of the world's poorest (frontier) economies owe the Bank large quantities of money. Indeed, for several of the most heavily indebted emerging countries, most of their external debt, in some cases constituting more than 50 percent, is owed to the WB and the multilateral regional development banks. The burden of these debts, which, according to the bank's regulations, cannot be canceled or rescheduled, has perpetuated economic stagnation throughout the global emerging and frontier economies.

The International Monetary Fund

The International Monetary Fund (IMF), a UN-specialized agency, was founded at the 1944 Bretton Woods Conference to secure international monetary cooperation, expand global liquidity or access to hard currencies, and stabilize currency exchange rates.

In the early 20th century, we witnessed two major destructive forces: the two world wars, which caused enormous physical and economic destruction in Europe, and the Great Depression, which wrought economic devastation in Europe and the US. Both events kindled a world desire to create a new international monetary system that could stabilize currency exchange rates without backing currencies entirely with gold. There was also a need to reduce the frequency and severity of balance-of-payments deficits and to remove destructive mercantilist trade policies, such as competitive devaluations and foreign exchange restrictions.

In 1944, multilateral discussions by delegates representing 44 countries at Bretton Woods in New Hampshire, US, drafted the Articles of Agreement for the recommended International Monetary Fund that could oversee the new international monetary system. This new Bretton Woods financial system hoped to foster global trade, investments, and economic growth by keeping convertible currencies at stable exchange rates. Nations with temporary, mild balance-of-payments deficits could finance their deficits by borrowing foreign currencies directly from the IMF instead of attempting to impose exchange controls, devaluations, or deflationary economic policies that could spread their economic problems to other nations.

Figure 5.3 depicts a board of governors directing the IMF, each representing one of the organization's approximately 180 member states. The governors, typically their nations' central bank directors or finance ministers, attend the meetings on IMF issues annually. The fund's day-to-day operations are managed by an executive board of 24 executive directors who meet at least thrice weekly. Eight directors represent individual countries, including China, France, Germany, Japan, Russia, Saudi Arabia, the United Kingdom, and the United States. World regions group the 16 other remaining members. Since the IMF executive board makes most decisions by consensus, it rarely conducts formal voting.

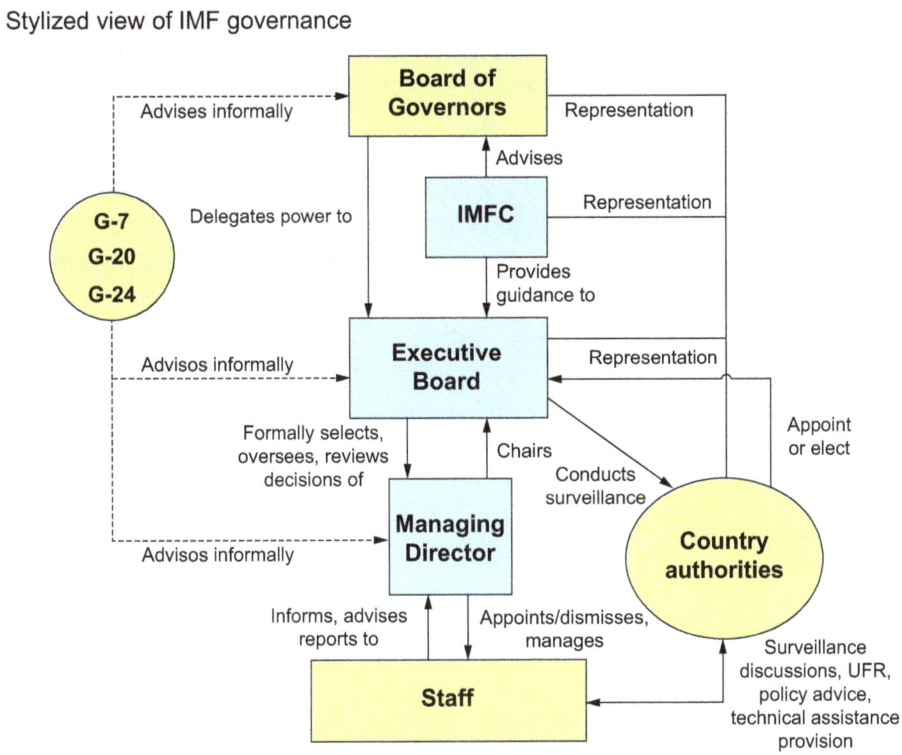

Figure 5.3: A board of governors directs the IMF, each representing one of the organization's approximately 180 member states. (Source: IMF, 2022).

Each member nation contributes a sum of money called a quota subscription. The quotas constitute a pool of loanable funds and determine how much each member nation can borrow and how much voting power they can have. Quotas are reviewed every five years based on each country's wealth and economic performance, with the wealthier nations contributing a larger quota. For instance, the U.S.'s approximately $83 billion contribution is the most of any IMF member, accounting for roughly 17 percent of total quotas. Therefore, the US receives about 17 percent of the votes on the board of governors and the executive committee. The G7 (Group of seven industrialized nations), including Canada, France, Germany, Italy, Japan, the UK, and the US, became the G8 in 1998 when Russia, which had held guest status since 1994, was officially added to the group. However, the G8 process was suspended in 2014 because Russia violated Ukraine's sovereignty and territorial integrity. The G7 controls nearly 50 percent of the fund's total votes.

Member nations with a balance-of-payments deficit may borrow money in foreign currencies, which they must repay with interest by purchasing the foreign currencies held by the IMF with their currencies. Each member nation may borrow up to

25 percent of its quota. The funds available for purchase are denominated in the IMF's currency, the Special Drawing Rights (SDRs), which are international reserve assets devised by the IMF in 1969 to supplement member nations' existing reserve assets of foreign currencies and gold. The value of the SDR is calculated daily as a weighted average of four currencies: the US dollar, the Japanese yen, the euro, and the British pound sterling. Countries use the SDRs allocated to them by the IMF to settle international debts. Figure 5.4 depicts the currency weighting in IMF's SDR basket from 2000 to 2022.

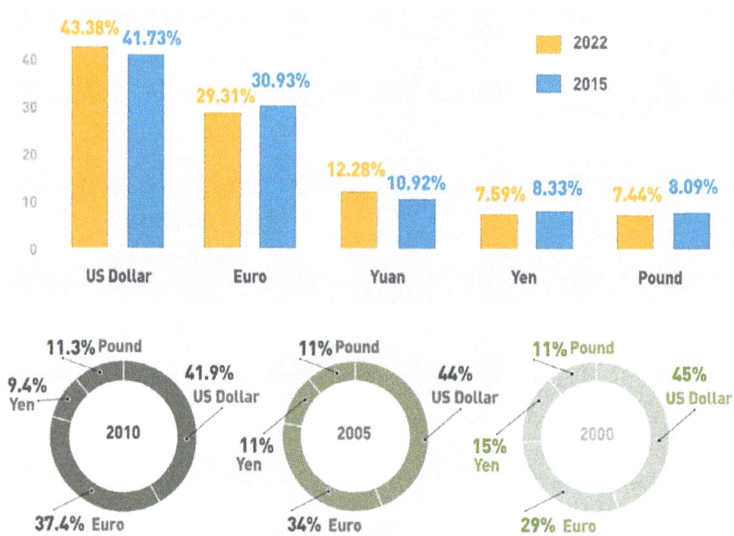

Figure 5.4: shows the currency weighting in the IMF's SDR basket from 2000 to 2022. (Source: IMF, 2022; Graphic: Lu Ting/GT).

The IMF adopts the SDR as its unit of account for all transactions. SDRs are not included in the quota subscriptions supplied by member nations. Therefore, they are not part of the general asset pool for member loans. Drawing on the IMF by a country raises the fund's holdings of that nation's currency, but concurrently, it lowers its holdings of another nation's currency. Hence, while the composition of the fund's resources changes, the total resources, as measured in SDRs, do not. Borrowing countries repay their loans over a specified period, usually three to five years, using the member nation's currencies acceptable to the IMF to repurchase their national currency. About 20 currencies are borrowed throughout a typical year, with most country borrowers exchanging their currency for highly convertible currencies such as the U.S. dollar, the Japanese yen, the euro, and the British pound sterling. Countries with currencies borrowed by other member governments receive remuneration, typically 4 percent of the amount borrowed.

Bank for International Settlements

The Bank for International Settlements (BIS), an international financial institution owned by central banks across the globe, has as a charter the fostering of international monetary and economic cooperation and serves as a bank for central banks. The BIS is based in Basel, Switzerland, with representative offices in Hong Kong and Mexico City. The BIS conducts its work through its meetings, programs, and the Basel Process, hosting international groups seeking global financial stability and facilitating this interaction. It also provides banking services only to central banks and other international organizations.

The BIS was founded in 1930 by an intergovernmental agreement between Germany, Belgium, France, the United Kingdom, Italy, Japan, the U.S., and Switzerland. It was initially developed to facilitate and support reparations imposed by the Treaty of Versailles on Germany post World War I and to act as the trustee for the German Government International Loan floated in 1930. The charter for the BIS was proposed at the International Bankers Conference at Baden-Baden and adopted at the second conference in The Hague in January of 1930. The charter allowed for shares in the bank to be held by individuals and nongovernmental entities. However, voting rights and representation at the Bank's General Meeting were exercised exclusively by the countries' central banks where shares were issued.

As an apolitical organization, the BIS could not prevent transactions reflecting contemporaneous geopolitical realities despite being regarded as immoral. As a result of the UK and France's appeasement policy of Nazi Germany, in 1939, the BIS had to transfer 23 tons of gold it was holding in storage on behalf of Czechoslovakia to the German Reichsbank after the German annexation of Czechoslovakia. After World War II, the BIS retained a distinct European status. It acted as an Agent for the European Payments Union, an intra-European clearing arrangement designed to help the European countries restore currency convertibility and free, multilateral trade. During the 1960s, the BIS played an essential role in transatlantic monetary cooperation through the Bretton Woods fixed exchange rate system. It coordinated the central banks' Gold Pool and many currency support operations.

As the bankers' bank, the BIS today serves the financial needs of its member central banks by providing them with gold and foreign exchange transactions and holding central bank reserves. The BIS is also a banker and fund manager for other international financial institutions.

World Trade Organization

The World Trade Organization (WTO) was established to oversee and liberalize global trade. The WTO superseded the General Agreement on Tariffs and Trade (GATT), created in 1947 with the assumption that it would be replaced by a specialized agency of the UN to be named the International Trade Organization (ITO). Although the ITO never came to fruition, the GATT proved highly successful in liberalizing global trade over the following decades. In the late 1980s, there were calls for a more robust multilateral organization to monitor trade and resolve trade disputes. After the Uruguay Round of multilateral trade negotiations, the WTO began operations in early 1995. As of the summer of 2022, the WTO has 164 members.

The WTO has six key objectives:

- Set and enforce rules for international trade
- Foster a forum for negotiating and monitoring further trade liberalization
- Resolve trade disputes
- Increase the transparency of decision-making processes
- Develop cooperation with major international economic institutions involved in global economic management
- Assist emerging economies in fully benefiting from the global trading system

The rules and regulations embedded in both the GATT and the WTO serve at least three purposes:

To protect the interests of small and weak nations against discriminatory trade practices from larger and powerful countries. The WTO's most favored nation and national treatment articles dictate that each member nation must grant equal access to their market to all other members and that domestic and international suppliers must be treated equally. The rules require member nations to restrict trade only through tariffs and provide market access that is less beneficial than those specified in their schedules, such as commitments agreed upon when granted WTO membership. The rules are formulated to assist governments in resisting lobbying efforts by domestic interest groups seeking special favors. Although some exceptions were made, its presence and duplication in the core WTO agreements are intended to prevent the worst excesses, providing greater certainty and predictability to international markets. The goal was for the WTO to improve economic welfare and lessen political tensions.

The GATT offered an avenue for settling trade disputes, a role strengthened substantially under the WTO. Procedures for dispute resolutions under the GATT have been automated and significantly streamlined, and the timetable has been tightened. Members commit not to engage in unilateral actions or decisions against other member nations. They are expected to seek recourse through the WTO's dispute-settlement system and abide by its rules and findings.

The WTO also seeks to enhance awareness of the dimensions, extent, and impacts of trade-distorting policies, which it achieves through annual information requirements and a policy review system. Communication of all changes in members' trade and trade-related policies must be disseminated and made available to all trading partners. This requirement was a significant step toward more transparent governance for many developing countries and countries whose economies were formerly centrally planned. The WTO revises the trade policies of the world's four most prominent traders, which include the EU, the U.S., China, and Japan, once every two years. It also reviews the policies of the following 16 largest trading nations (determined by their total trade volumes, including imports and exports combined) once every four years, and lastly, the policies of all other trading nations at least once every six years. As of summer of 2024, the 16 largest trading nations after the EU, the U.S., China, and Japan are Germany, United Kingdom, France, Netherlands, Hong Kong, South Korea, Italy, Canada, Belgium, India, Mexico, Singapore, Spain, Taiwan, Switzerland, and Australia. After extensive consultations with the member nations that are subject to review, the WTO Secretariat publishes its review and a comprehensive report by the nation's government. Therefore, such a process monitors the extent to which members meet their commitments and agreements and provides data on newly opened markets. The WTO offers a robust platform for subsequent trade negotiations and agreements and for resolving trade disputes.

Organization for Economic Co-operation and Development

The Organization for Economic Co-operation and Development (OECD) is a forum constituted by governments of 38 democracies (Costa Rica recently joined in May 2021) with market-based economies. The OECD's 38 country members are Austria, Australia, Belgium, Canada, Chile, Colombia, Costa Rica, the Czech Republic, Denmark, Estonia, Finland, France, Germany, Greece, Hungary, Iceland, Ireland, Israel, Italy, Japan, Korea, Latvia, Lithuania, Luxembourg, Mexico, the Netherlands, New Zealand, Norway, Poland, Portugal, the Slovak Republic, Slovenia, Spain, Sweden, Switzerland, Turkey, the United Kingdom, and the United States.

The Forum collaborates on developing policy standards for sustainable and responsible economic growth. The OECD offers a setting where governments can compare experiences, seek answers to everyday challenges, identify good practices, and develop high standards for monetary policy. The OECD has been a reliable source of evidence-based policy analysis and economic data for over five decades. The U.S. consistently works with other members to reinforce transparency, accountability, budget discipline, and responsiveness to member priorities at the OECD.

Along with its two sister agencies, the International Energy Agency (IEA) and the Nuclear Energy Agency (NEA), the OECD assists the U.S. and its partners in reaping the benefits and confronting the challenges of a global economy. It promotes sound economic policies, more accessible markets, more efficient use of resources, and better innovation through science and technology. Today, OECD member nations account for more than 60 percent of global GDP, 75 percent of world trade, over 90 percent of worldwide official development assistance, 50 percent of the world's energy consumption, and 18 percent of the globe's population.

The OECD Guidelines for Multinational Enterprises

In 1976, the OECD established a set of Guidelines for Multinational Enterprises. These Guidelines encompass a comprehensive set of government recommendations for multinational enterprises (MNEs) to voluntarily adopt to minimize and resolve impacts arising from operations in international jurisdictions and to promote positive contributions to social, economic, and environmental development. These guidelines cover human rights, environment, labor, anti-bribery, corporate governance, disclosure, supply chain management, and taxation issues; they have received broad international support. They are the only multilaterally approved and comprehensive code of responsible business conduct that governments across the globe have agreed to promote. MNEs' compliance with laws and regulations within foreign markets is an essential principle of the OECD's Guidelines, which are not intended to override any local law or restrictions or expose MNEs to conflicting expectations.

World Intellectual Property Organization

The World Intellectual Property Organization (WIPO) is an international body designed to facilitate the worldwide protection of intellectual properties (IP), such as inventions, trademarks, and designs, and other copyrighted materials such as literary, musical, photographic, and other artistic work. The organization, headquartered in Geneva, was founded by a convention signed in Stockholm in 1967, started operating in 1970, and became a specialized UN agency four years later.

WIPO's origins date back to 1883 when 14 nations signed the Paris Convention for the Protection of Industrial Property (known as the Paris Convention for short), which developed intellectual property protections for inventions, trademarks, and industrial designs. The Paris Convention supported inventors in protecting their original work outside their home nation. In 1886, the Berne Convention mandated member nations to supply automatic protection for original works developed in other countries. These two organizations, which had developed separate secretariats to implement their respective treaties, merged in 1893 with a base in Bern, Switzerland, becoming a new entity dubbed the United International Bureau for the Protection of Intellectual Property (BIRPI).

The main objectives of WIPO can be broken up into two folds. First, through foreign cooperation, to promote the protection of IP. WIPO now manages more than 20 IP treaties. Second, WIPO oversees administrative collaboration between Paris, Bern, and other IP unions related agreements on copyrights, patents, and trademarks. WIPO's role in enforcing IP protections was enhanced in the mid-1990s when it signed a cooperation agreement with the WTO. As e-commerce grows through the advancements of the internet, WIPO was commissioned to help resolve any disputes over the use of internet domain names. WIPO's membership is comprised of more than 180 nations. Its primary policy-making body is the General Assembly, which convenes every two years.

World Health Organization

The World Health Organization (WHO), headquartered in Geneva, Switzerland, is a specialized UN agency responsible for international public health. It has six regional offices and about 150 field offices worldwide. The WHO Constitution states its primary objective as "the attainment by all peoples of the highest possible level of health."

The WHO was established in 1948 by incorporating assets, personnel, and general duties from the League of Nations' Health Organization and the Office International d'Hygiène Publique, which included the International Classification of Diseases (ICD). Its mandate seeks to work worldwide to promote health, keep the world safe, and serve the vulnerable. The WHO advocates that a billion more people across the globe should:

- Access to universal health care coverage.
- Active engagement with the monitoring of public health risks.
- Coordinated responses to health emergencies.
- Benefit from the promotion of health and well-being.

The WHO offers technical assistance to nations, sets international health standards, and collects data on global health issues. A publication, the World Health Report, provides assessments of worldwide health topics. The organization also functions as a forum for discussions of health issues. It plays a leading role in several public health achievements, most notably the eradication of smallpox, the near eradication of polio, and the development of an Ebola vaccine. Its current priorities include infectious diseases, particularly HIV/AIDS, Ebola, COVID-19, malaria, and tuberculosis; non-communicable diseases such as heart disease and cancer; healthy diet, nutrition, and food security; occupational health; and substance abuse. Its World Health Assembly, the agency's decision-making body, elects and advises an executive board of 34 health specialists. It selects the director-general, sets goals and priorities, and approves the budget and activities.

North Atlantic Treaty Organization

The North Atlantic Treaty Organization (NATO), headquartered in Brussels, Belgium (its military headquarters are near Mons), is an intergovernmental military alliance between 30 member nations, including 28 European countries and two North American. Under the coalition, all of its independent member nations agree to defend and protect one another against attacks by third parties. NATO operated as a risk assessment of the perceived threat posed by the Soviet Union during the Cold War–a term commonly used to refer to a period of geopolitical tension between the US and the Soviet Union and their respective allies, the Western Bloc and the Eastern Bloc. The NATO alliance was kept in place after the Soviet Union was dissolved and continues to be involved in military missions in the Balkans, South Asia, the Middle East, and Africa.

The alliance has targeted its NATO Response Force deployments across Eastern Europe, including a combined military of all NATO members, around 3.5 million soldiers, and personnel. The alliance's combined military spending as of 2020 constituted over 57 percent of the global nominal total. Members have agreed to reach or maintain a target defense budget spending of no less than two percent of their GDP by 2024.

Although NATO was established with twelve founding members, it has been adding new members eight times, with the most recent application coming from North Macedonia, which joined the alliance in March 2020. After accepting their membership applications in June 2022, Finland and Sweden will likely become the 31st and 32nd members. NATO currently recognizes Bosnia, Herzegovina, Georgia, and Ukraine as aspiring potential members.

International Competitive Strategies

Enterprises implementing an international competitive strategy can gain a competitive advantage, further enhancing their competitive position by creating barriers to entry and enabling them to adapt to their competitive perspective in response to market changes. A competitive strategy consists of a company's business approaches and initiatives to attract customers and deliver superior value by fulfilling its expectations and strengthening its market position.

In this process, there are two main factors to consider. First, enterprises should have a set of distinctive competencies and activities that they do better than their competitors but require superior skills and resources. Unique competencies can create barriers to imitation and help sustain competitive advantage. Exceptional skills and resources improve the enterprise's position, as it may enable it to lower costs through economies of scale or capacity utilization or create value for customers. Tangible assets such as technology, the distribution network, superior resources, and access to supplies and raw materials can also enhance the position. The organization's structure is another element of distinctive competence. A well-planned organizational structure enables a company to adapt more responsively to foreign markets and market changes.

Secondly, the strategic fit is relevant to dynamic competitiveness in internal and external conditions. Enterprises can achieve higher levels of competitiveness solely when management accurately determines the skills and resources corresponding to strategic options, including goals, the target market, the entry mode, and the quality of tactics and execution. Some enterprises may invest in unprofitable projects to establish a position in a potentially attractive market or technology and then attempt a move into that market later. It is typical regarding new technologies, where the initial investment often provides experience and valuable information for further investments. A first-mover strategy offers a competitive advantage, mainly when ambiguity and non-recoverable costs are associated with the market entry. Levels of uncertainty also influence the strategic fitness of the firm. In the case of a volatile market, for instance, due to changing technology, political risk, or economic uncertainty, a first-mover bears the risk and high cost of pioneering since new products can often be replaced quickly. This unstable condition requires a quick response. Changes in demand and competitive conditions in the host market also affect a firm's strategic flexibility.

Four Types of Competitive Strategy: Michael Porter's Four Generic Strategies

Michael Porter has identified four types of competitive strategies that can be applied in any business organization irrespective of the size and nature of products. Because of their susceptibility to everyday use by all business enterprises, they are labeled *generic strategies*, as depicted in Figure 5.5. These are, in fact, basic types of competitive strategy.

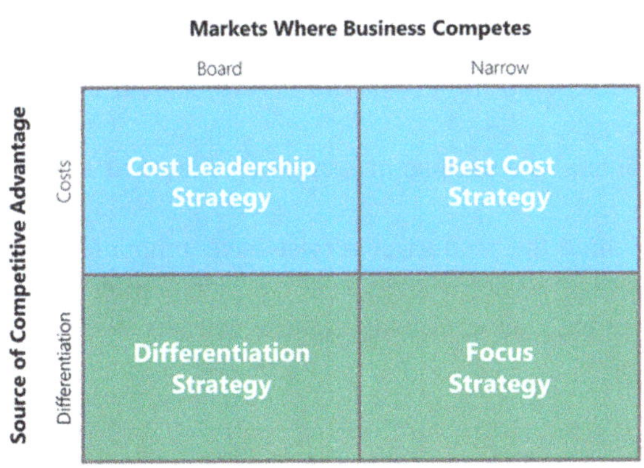

Figure 5.5: Michal Porter's Four Types of Competitive Strategies.

In addition to these, there are also other strategies that an enterprise can employ when deemed necessary, such as strategic alliance, collaborative partnerships, mergers, acquisitions, vertical integration, outsourcing strategies, etc. An enterprise's success relies on its ability to reshape strategies in response to changing global environments and markets. An effective competitive strategy also depends on product and market characteristics, and the types of products influence the degree of standardization. High-technology companies tend to use international diversification strategies, as cultural factors and preferences less restrict their products and services, and only aspects of product design need to be customized. Expansion or switching strategies fit into a time horizon and affect competitiveness.

A Brief Overview of Theories of Competitive Strategies

An international competitive strategy is an action plan designed to allocate resources and functions to address a foreign environment while achieving a competitive advantage and attaining the organization's goals. Competitive advantage sets the enterprise apart from others and provides it with a distinctive edge for meeting customer needs in the marketplace. The choice to make the organization different is the essence of formulating a strategy. To remain competitive, enterprises must focus on core competencies, developing synergy, and creating value for prospective consumers.

A competitive advantage strategy is an enterprise's ability to perform in various strategies that impose barriers to entry to its competitors. It refers to factors that allow an enterprise to produce goods and services better or at a lower cost than its rivals. As depicted in Figure 5.6, Michael Porter proposed that once the potential for profitability in a market has been established, the next step toward gaining a competitive advantage is to decide whether to use a *low-cost or differentiation approach.* Once this too has been chosen, the third element that he calls *focus* needs to be decided; this part of the framework identifies who the product or service should be marketed to:

- **Cost leadership strategy** – Should the product or service be offered at a lower price than the competitors?
- **Differentiation strategy** – Should the product or service have unique features or benefits so appealing that customers are willing to pay a premium price?
- **Focus strategy** – Should the product or service target niche markets overlooked or underserved by competitors?

		Competitive advantage	
		Lower costs	Differentiation
Competitive scope	Broad target	Cost leadership	Differentiation
	Narrow target	Cost focus	Differentiation focus

Figure 5.6: Porter's competitive advantage strategy framework.

Porter looked at competitive strategies from a long-term, sustainable angle and maintained that creating a sustainable competitive advantage helps boost a company's image in the marketplace and affects valuation and the potential for future earnings. These factors allow the productive entity to generate more sales or superior margins than its market rivals. A competitive advantage is sustainable when it can edge rival companies from competing markets and favor customers. Although sustainability is crucial in competitive advantages, most are leverageable so that an enterprise can adopt them as catalysts for new strategies. Any competitive advantages a company develops will likely fail if customers do not value them as necessary. Thus, enterprises must focus on building customer advantages.

Porter argues that competitive advantage results from an organization's ability to execute the necessary activities and functions at a collectively lower cost than its rivals. Or perform some actions in unique ways that create buyer value, enabling the organization to command a premium price for the goods it sells. The following are some of the main distinct theories of competitive advantage.

The SCP Framework

In the Structure Conduct Performance (SCP) framework, as depicted in Figure 5.7, the organization's acts are determined by external forces in the industry (market or industrial structure). This school of thought argues that the structure of the industry will evaluate the strategies (or conduct) and that this, in turn, will determine performance:

- Market structure: the degree of market concentration, product differentiation, barriers to entry and exit, vertical integration, and diversification.
- Conduct: goals of the organizations, strategies, anti-competitive practices, research, innovation, advertising, etc.
- Performance: several performance indicators, such as output growth, sales revenue growth, profitability, technical progress, employment, efficiency, added shareholder value, and added economic value.

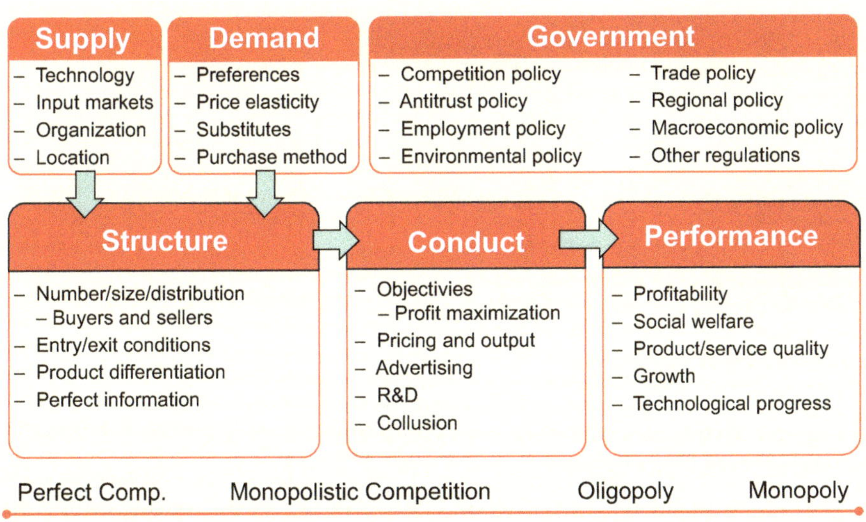

Figure 5.7: Structure Conduct Performance framework, the organization's acts are determined by external forces in the industry.

Not all strategies are appropriate for all sectors. Successful strategies may fail (not produce the intended outcome) if applied as-is in a different environment. Therefore, the industry's structure is crucial in forming a strategy. However, this linear paradigm proves itself too deterministic. When strategic managers apply this approach, they consider the industrial structure a given. In this way, they respond to external forces and plan their strategies automatically by analyzing the competitive environment. However, in many industries, the environment follows turbulence change. Strategists tend to change the environment by designing strategies that will shape it to their needs and advantage instead of spectators to the change. In these cases, the strategy shapes the industry structure, not vice versa, as the SCP paradigm argues.

Porter's Five Forces and Generic Strategies

Michael Porter's work is organizationally rooted in the SCP paradigm. According to his approach, two factors underlie the choice of competitive strategy: Industry attractiveness and the factors that determine it, as well as the determinants of relative competitive position within an industry. Porter developed the Five Forces model to analyze the industry attractiveness, as illustrated in Figure 5.8. According to the model, in any industry, competition is mutually influenced by five forces:

- The bargaining power of buyers
- The bargaining power of suppliers
- The entry of new competitors
- The rivalry among the competitors
- The threat of substitutes

Figure 5.8: Porter's Five Force Model.

Although the Five Forces model is rooted within the SCP approach, Porter differentiates in arguing that an organization is not a prisoner of its industry structure. Organizations can shape the industry through their strategies by influencing competitive forces. For example, industry leaders can influence buyers, suppliers, and competitors and shape the underlying industry structure. Through positioning, organizations can possess two basic types of competitive advantage: low cost and differentiation. These competitive advantages result from the ability to cope with the industrial forces better than the competitors. The specific relative position within the industry also influences competitive strategy. Porter introduces three 'generic competitive strategies' for achieving above-average performance in an industry. Cost leadership is when the organization tries to become the low-cost producer or operator of the industry.

Risks associated with cost leadership include:
- Changes in technology allow new entrants to become themselves the cost leaders. This risk is minimized by constant research and development, but such investments require rising costs.
- Margins fall when costs rise (due to internal or external factors). In such scenarios, the differentiation advantage may overcome the cost leadership advantage.
- Differentiation occurs when an organization seeks to be unique within the industry along some dimensions valued by buyers (higher quality, more functions, etc.). If it succeeds, it is rewarded for its uniqueness with a premium price. However, when choosing to differentiate, companies should seek appropriate ways that lead to a price premium greater than the determining cost.

Risks related to this strategy include:
- Consumers may choose another differentiated product they value more or their needs change over time.
- Consumers may choose low-cost products, especially when the price difference tends to be high.
- Other competitors may imitate the chosen differentiation.
- The focus rests on choosing a narrow competitive scope within an industry and optimizing the strategy for the target segment. An organization seeks a cost advantage in the target segment regarding cost focus. In terms of differentiation focus, the organization seeks differentiation in the narrow segment.

Risks associated with focus may include:
- The focus strategy is imitated. For this to be avoided, entry barriers are required (e.g., assets valued by the customers such as customer care services, reputation, etc.).
- The target segment becomes unattractive.
- Broadly targeted competitors dominate the segment. Again, entry barriers will sustain the competitive advantage experienced.

Organizations that try to position on multiple generic strategies but fail to achieve any of them are *stuck in the middle*. Not only do they not possess a competitive advantage, but they are in a disadvantageous situation since the cost-leader, the differentiators, or the focusers are already better positioned. Although Porter's positioning framework has been an industry standard for over twenty years, Mintzberg argued that it constrains creative thought. Strategists do not think outside the box, and the given options (cost leadership, differentiation, and focus) tend to minimize the strategic thinking process.

Resource Based View (RBV)

According to Barney, the environmental models of competitive advantage have assumed that organizations within an industry are identical regarding the resources they control and the strategy they pursue. Further, they think that if resource heterogeneity develops within an industry, it will not last long since strategic resources are highly mobile (they can be bought and sold). His proposed resource-based view substitutes these assumptions. As illustrated in Figure 5.9, the resource-based view model assumes that strategic resources can be heterogeneous and that these resources may not be perfectly mobile. An organization's resources include all assets, capabilities, processes, attributes, information, knowledge, etc., controlled by an organization that enables it to implement strategies that promote efficiency.

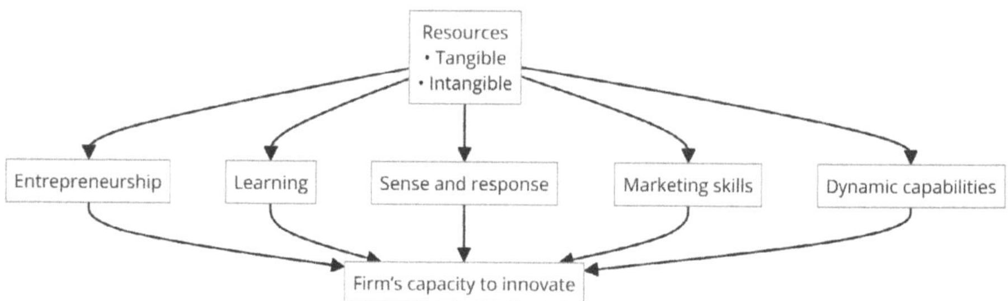

Figure 5.9: The resource-based view model assumes that strategic resources can be heterogeneous and may not be perfectly mobile.

For a resource to hold the potential of sustained competitive advantage, it must have four attributes:

- It must be valuable for exploiting opportunities and neutralizing threats.
- It must be rare among existing and potential competitors. A valuable resource cannot be considered a source of competitive advantage if it is shared among many organizations because all organizations can exploit it, leading to a common strategy.
- It must be imperfectly imitable. Valuable and rare resources can only be sources of sustained competitive advantage if competitors that do not possess them cannot obtain them.
- It cannot be strategically equivalent to substitutes. Organizational resources are strategically equivalent when they can be exploited separately to implement the same strategy. That is, an organization may be able to substitute a similar resource that enables it to conceive and implement the same strategy. Further, very different resources may also be strategic substitutes.

The proposed resource-based view framework reasons that resource heterogeneity and immobility within an industry allow organization resources to be valuable, rare, imperfectly imitable, and not easily substitutable. Such resources will lead to exploiting opportunities and neutralizing threats for sustained competitive advantage. It should be noted that a distinction is drawn in the literature between resources (tangible) and capabilities (less tangible). Barney's framework unites both resources and capabilities under the umbrella of "resources."

Core Competences

Some capabilities are much less visible, making them more difficult to imitate and establish a competitive advantage. These are referred to as core competencies. Prahalad and Hamel took the resource-based approach one step further through the notion of core competencies. They argue that in the long run, competitive advantage depends on the ability to build core competencies at lower cost and more speedily. Management should consolidate corporate-wide technologies and production skills into competencies that empower individual businesses to adapt promptly to environmental changes.

Three criteria are being used to categorize capabilities as core competence:

- Provide potential access to various markets.
- Significantly contribute to the customer's perceived end-product benefits.
- Be difficult for competitors to imitate.

Examples of core competencies include Apple's ability to innovate and create from scratch and Sony's ability to miniaturize. According to this framework, a company's common mistake is outsourcing manufacturing, as they tend to lose their core competencies. Another common mistake is that companies often miss opportunities to establish evolving competencies in an existing business. At the strategic business unit level, core competencies are frequently sabotaged by under-investment and improper allocation, which may result in atrophy and missing opportunities.

Global Strategy Planning

As illustrated in Figure 5.10, global strategy planning assesses a multinational organization's internal and external environments to develop its strategic plan. The business can leverage its strengths and overcome weaknesses by looking at the internal environment. In evaluating its external environment, the company should assess the political, social, environmental, and technological factors that could provide opportunities or raise potential risks and threats. Multinational firms that bypass a global strategic plan process are increasingly at risk of facing unexpected challenges and threats and are ill-prepared to compete with rivals in new international markets.

Any business must research international markets before entering them. One significant aspect of global strategic planning is conducting an internal audit to determine the business's strengths and weaknesses. This internal audit includes a company's human capital, technology, structure, communication methods, and policies. While this may

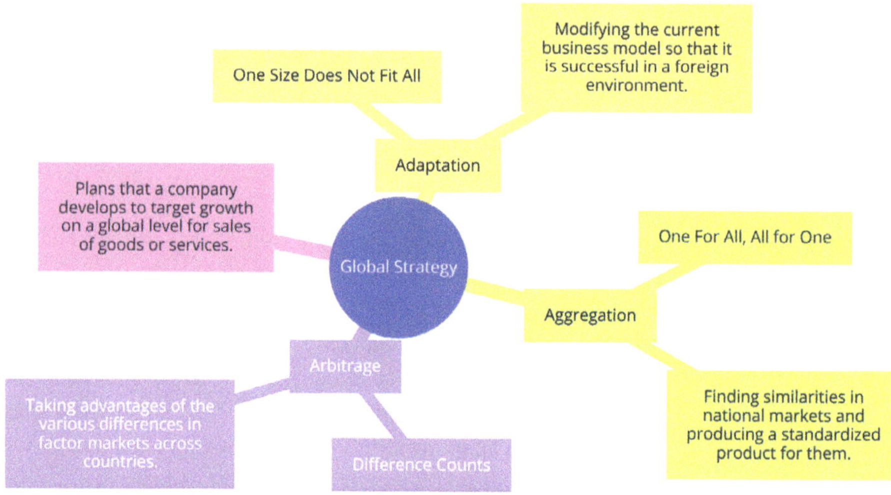

Figure 5.10: Factors determining global strategic planning.

seem unnecessary, a company may find that it does not have the structure or technology to support its efforts to compete in foreign markets. It may demand the creation of new departments, hiring a more internationalized human resource, or even investing in new digital technologies. The company may gain a fresh perspective on its internationalization strategy by hiring an unbiased organization to analyze its current business processes.

MNCs and MNEs may realize that new international markets bring political, social, environmental, and technological challenges and risks they have never faced before. For example, political instability can result in a loss of currency value, social norms may cause locals to reject the product, technical support may not be readily available within the country, and environmental policies may require changing a product design. Any of these factors may result in business failure if a proper strategic plan is not in place. Global strategic planning must also consider transportation and logistics costs, such as international shipping regulations and transportation costs. External audits are another significant aspect of global strategic planning and are especially vital for competitive advantage development in foreign markets.

Postponing a global strategic planning process can be catastrophic for MNEs since they will likely be ill-prepared to address any obstacles or challenges. A business must research international markets before entering them to compete efficiently against host-country competitors while being aware of their rules, regulations, and social customs. For instance, local consumers in a foreign market may not be willing to purchase from a foreign company because they may believe the opportunity may take away jobs from their neighbors and take money out of their nation. Such reactions should be mitigated by hiring local marketing professionals and producing marketing campaigns about the company's corporate social responsibility (CSR) commitments and how it will invest a portion of its profits in the local community.

Global strategic planning is a process, not a business event. It is designed to be a dynamic document and not something prepared once a year, and then it remains in a file referred to by no one. The plan should be reviewed often and updated along the way. If not, something is usually wrong since the world is fluid, and so is a business plan. A global strategic planning development is a must. It should map the demands by examining the company's current sales, distribution strategy, manufacturing costs, and available alternatives. Before venturing abroad, a general needs assessment of the company's SWOT (and PESTLE) is needed, as illustrated in Figure 5.11. MNEs planning to internationalize should look at their readiness for a changing global market, including cultural needs, currency, etc. A Strengths, Weaknesses, Opportunities, and Threats (SWOT) analysis, or a PESTEL (or PESTLE), can help see gaps and determine possible scenarios.

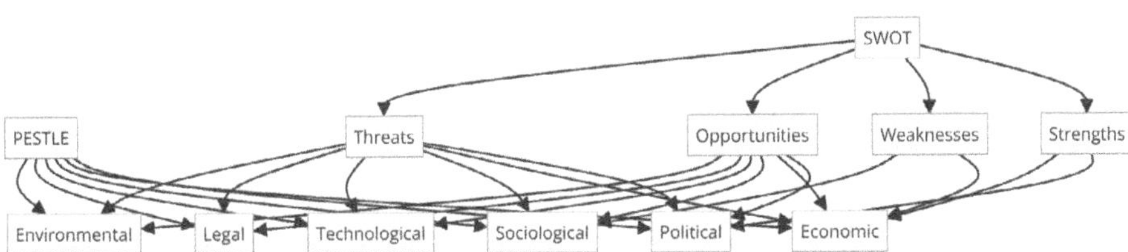

Figure 5.11: Assessing a firm's SWOT and PESTLE factors.

Assumptions Considerations

Companies should not assume their current business model can be replicated or exported. When they first began to expand globally, Harley Davidson made a huge mistake that we can all learn from. They assumed that brand recognition would carry them worldwide into new markets. The company quickly learned about the Japanese Kaizen practice (ways to reduce waste) and its designed novelty products that focused on value vs. the brand alone and realized they had to strategize their market entry approach. The company was able to enter the market successfully.

On the flip side, companies should never underestimate the value and power of their brand. Playboy's global expansion saved the company when its revenue in the U.S. domestic market was deteriorating. Considering their brand was the 3rd most recognized worldwide, Playboy springboarded globally with new product offerings. Swensen's, a top-rated, San Francisco-based ice cream company in the 1970s, virtually disappeared from the U.S. while flourishing in the Asian markets. A company's leverage and understanding of its products and services are critical when identifying target markets that may be shrinking while others expand. Such considerations should also be part of global strategic planning.

Mergers and Acquisitions Considerations

An internationalization plan may be accomplished more cost-effectively through acquisitions rather than internal expansion. Companies planning to internationalize should study their competition locally and look abroad. By way of FDI, an acquisition could jumpstart global growth and quickly broaden the company's sales if done right. VingCard Elsafe expanded by observing customer needs. The company found that customers often desired to recharge their electronic devices when using a safe in a hotel room. The company identified a power outlet firm and purchased them so they could add the much sought-after feature. Paying close attention to customer needs can be a driving force for growth.

Quality and consumer service standards are another critical factor to be considered and must be maintained to avoid eroding the brand's standards. Occasionally, international expansion can be driven by the fate of a passionate executive officer of the company who is willing to take a risk. But, In-N-Out Burger had a very different opportunity to expand into Singapore. The company was approached by a high-net-worth individual investor who believed the brand would be accepted and successful in that part of Asia. The strategy did not cost the company money, yet it could expand into a new international region.

It is imperative not to rush global planning and expansion. Several components come into play and must be well thought out. Factors such as employee development, market tests, supply chain partners, and thorough analysis are just the tip of the iceberg. If done correctly, the process can pay off by reducing the risk of the immediate investment and by allowing the company to refine and learn about its progress in its internationalization process. Take Alcatel-Lucent as an example, which spent over a billion dollars on a fixed cellular network technology that proved less effective and efficient than a standard cellular network. It all happened because the company took the path of least resistance, as they had already built the technology and had all the staff in place. The company, however, neglected to test the product on the market in the rural areas in which it was intended to be used, and it did not have the necessary government relationships to ensure the contracts. Therefore, cellular contracts were more rapidly signed and built out, causing that business unit to be closed and a billion-dollar write-off absorbed.

Xerox Corporation had a disciplined process when expanding into frontier (least developed countries, or LDCs) markets. The company turned to local host-country high-potential people to develop a plan over 12–18 months. The team identified the necessary talent at the local Xerox branch levels. Along with seasoned professionals from advanced countries, Xerox built an organization ready to deploy a sophisticated operation that would be successful from the start with pride in its brand and positive revenues within the first year of operation.

Types of International Strategic Planning

Any enterprise with business operations in more than one nation is known as a multinational corporation (MNC). The largest MNCs are influential actors in the global markets. Walmart is a good example, as its annual global sales, in dollar terms, are more significant than the whole economies of Norway, Austria, and Saudi Arabia. Despite the fact that the company is viewed as a U.S. retailer, the company earns more than 35% of its total revenues outside the U.S. Walmart owns several stores in Brazil, Argentina, Chile, Central America, Mexico, Canada, the UK, Botswana, and joint ventures in India and China. Even modestly sized MNCs tend to be mighty. For instance, If Kia were a nation, its current gross sales revenue of about $24 billion would place it among the top 100 worldwide.

Four leading global strategies – domestic exporter, multinational, franchiser, and transnational – form the basis for international enterprises' organizational structure. These strategies are developed with a particular business organizational structure, as depicted in Figure 5.12.

Business Function	Domestic Exporter	Multinational	Franchiser	Transnational
Production	Centralized	Dispersed	Coordinated	Coordinated
Finance/Accounting	Centralized	Centralized	Centralized	Coordinated
Sales/Marketing	Mixed	Dispersed	Coordinated	Coordinated
Human Resources	Centralized	Centralized	Coordinated	Coordinated
Strategic Management	Centralized	Centralized	Centralized	Coordinated

Figure 5.12: Types of international strategies.

Each strategy involves a distinct approach to being sensitive to costs and efficiencies and responsive to variations in customer preferences and market conditions worldwide. A company's ability to respond or not to these pressures of cost and local cultural conditions determines which of the four strategies it may pursue.

Typically, there are three types of governance or organizational structure:

- Centralized in the home country
- Decentralized to local foreign units, and
- Coordinated, in which all branches participate equally.

Other types of organizational structure design exist, such as those with authoritarian dominance by one division or a confederacy of equals. Others are characterized as federal structures that balance power among strategic units.

A *domestic exporter* or *international* strategy is characterized by solid centralization of the company's activities in the home country. Almost all international enterprises internationalize this way, except for born-globals and new international ventures (NIVs). Still, even with these, some aspects of the internationalization process are permanently based in the home country. Once the internalization process starts, some enterprises often adopt other forms of governance. Typically, except with born-globals/NIVs, finance, accounting, human resources, production, marketing, sales, and strategic management functions tend to be set in the home country to optimize local resources. International sales, however, tend to be dispersed through agency agreements or subsidiaries, although global marketing relies on a domestic home base. Caterpillar Corporation, for instance, and many other heavy capital-equipment manufacturers follow this enterprise category.

Enterprises devising an international strategy are not concerned with costs or adapting to local culture. They try to mass produce and sell their goods globally with minor or no changes. For instance, when Harley Davidson sells its motorcycles abroad, it does not need to reduce prices or adapt the bike to meet local motorcycle standards. Consumers in international markets buy motorcycles because they differ from those available in their local markets; they desire the American design, power, and distinct sound of a Harley-Davidson motorcycle and are willing to pay for such differentiation. Similarly, Belgian chocolate exporters do not lower prices when they export goods to the U.S. when competing with Hershey's American brand. They do not try to adapt the product to the U.S. market's taste. The strategy is international. Rolex and Starbucks are yet another example of companies pursuing a global approach.

A *multinational* or *multi-domestic strategy* focuses on financial management and controls abroad, away from the home country, decentralizing production, marketing, and sales functions to its branches abroad. The products and services in distinct foreign markets are adapted or co-located to suit local market conditions. In such a case, the enterprise becomes a far-flung confederation of production and marketing facilities in its countries. Such an internationalization strategy includes several financial service companies and manufacturers such as CITI, Chase, General Motors, Chrysler, and Intel.

An enterprise using a multinational strategy does not focus on cost or efficiency but emphasizes responsiveness to local requirements within each market. For instance, Netflix does not try to force American-made shows and films on other viewers across the globe. They customize their programming offerings to dozens of countries, including New Zealand, Portugal, Brazil, Pakistan, Spain, and India. Similarly, food company H.J. Heinz adapts its products to local preferences. For instance, some Indian consumers will not eat garlic and onion. Hence, Heinz offers a version of its ketchup without these two ingredients. Another example is Outback Steakhouse, which adopted a multi-domestic strategy in multiple international markets, adapting its offerings to local eating costumes and preferences but not significantly reducing prices.

A *franchiser* is a mix of an old and new strategy. The product or service is designed, developed, financed, and initially produced in the home country. However, due to product-specific needs, it must rely heavily on international personnel for further glocalization (the launching and cultural adaptation of a product or service to be accepted among local customers), production, marketing, and human resources. Food franchises like Mrs. Fields Cookies, McDonald's, and KFC fit this pattern. For instance, while McDonald's developed a fast-food chain in the U.S., the company still relies mainly on the U.S. for inspiration for new products, financing, and strategic management. However, since its perishable products must be produced locally, extensive coordination and dispersal of production, local marketing, and local personnel recruitment are still required.

Generally, international franchisees tend to be cloned to the franchisor in the home country. Still, a fully coordinated global production optimizing the factors of production is impossible. For example, beef and potatoes could be bought from the cheapest source in the world markets, but their short shelf life requires them to be produced reasonably near the consumption area.

Transnational enterprises are stateless, fully globally managed, and may represent a more significant part of international business in the future. Transnational firms have no national headquarters but many regional branches and sometimes a global headquarters. In this strategy, almost all the value-adding functions are managed from an international perspective without considering international borders. The main objective is to optimize all sources of supply and demand as they present themselves and take advantage of local competitive advantages whenever possible. Transnational enterprises look at the global markets, not the domestic ones, as a frame of reference for their management strategy. The governance of these enterprises has been likened to a federal structure in which there is a robust central management core of decision making but considerable dispersal of power and financial muscle throughout the global divisions. Not many MNCs have achieved transnational status, but Sony, Citicorp, Ford, and others are attempting such a transition.

An enterprise using a transnational strategy seeks a middle ground between a multi-domestic and global strategy. These enterprises try to balance lower costs and efficiencies by adjusting to local market preferences within the various markets. For instance, fast-food chains such as McDonald's and KFC rely on brand names and core menu items worldwide. These companies make concessions to local tastes as well. For instance, in France, customers can buy wine at McDonald's since wine is a central element of French diets. Similarly, McDonald's serves a McArabia Chicken sandwich in Saudi Arabia, and its breakfast menu features no pork products like ham, bacon, or sausage.

An enterprise using a global strategy sacrifices responsiveness to local requirements within each market to emphasize lowering costs and improving efficiency. A global strategy emphasizes the necessity to achieve low costs and develop economies of scale by selling the same goods in all their markets. Such a global strategy is very different from a multi-domestic strategy, as some minor adjustments and modifications to product offerings and services may be adopted in many international markets. For example, Microsoft offers the same software suite (M.S. Office or 365) worldwide, adjusting the package only to co-locate the language to the markets in which it operates. Likewise, Procter & Gamble, an American consumer goods manufacturer, seeks efficiency by creating global brands as much as possible. Global strategies can be highly effective for enterprises whose goods are mostly hidden from the international customer's purview. Examples include Intel and Lenovo. For these companies, the variance in local preferences is not as significant as pricing.

The Influence of ESG on Global Competitive Strategy

Factors related to the environment, society, and corporate governance are now more critical than ever in influencing the strategies of global companies. These criteria not only affect the way companies function but also impact how stakeholders view them. Understanding the significant influence of ESG on international competitive strategy involves studying its effects on business operations, economic performance, and cultural integration worldwide. ESG factors are more than just a checkbox; they offer a competitive edge when creating and executing a global competitive strategy. By integrating ESG criteria into their strategic planning, businesses can obtain a competitive advantage, improve their position in the market, and develop more robust connections with community stakeholders. In the global market, ethical imperatives and strategic advantages are found in environmental sustainability, social responsibility, and strong governance practices. While companies operate globally, ESG factors will remain crucial in influencing their achievements.

ESG in International Institutions

International institutions such as the UN, the WB, and the IMF significantly influence global business practices, particularly by advocating ESG standards. These institutions have crafted frameworks and guidelines encouraging companies to embrace sustainable and responsible practices, setting the stage for a more environmentally and socially conscious business environment.

For instance, the UN's Sustainable Development Goals (SDGs) provide a comprehensive blueprint for achieving a better and more sustainable future. These goals cover various aspects of ESG, including climate action, quality education, gender equality, and decent work and economic growth. Companies that align their strategies with the SDGs can gain a competitive advantage by demonstrating their commitment to sustainability and social responsibility.

The WB and IMF also emphasize the importance of ESG criteria in their lending practices and policy recommendations. By incorporating ESG factors into their operations, companies can enhance their eligibility for funding and support from these institutions, strengthening their competitive position in the international market.

ESG in the Development of International Competitive Strategy

Integrating ESG criteria into international competitive strategy is not just a suggestion but a necessity for companies vying for a competitive edge in the global market. ESG considerations permeate various aspects of strategic planning, including market entry, product development, and risk management. By incorporating these factors into their strategies, companies can meet regulatory requirements, enhance their brand image, attract investors, and build stronger relationships with local communities.

Market Entry and Expansion

When entering new markets, companies must consider the host country's environmental and social regulations. Adopting ESG principles can help businesses navigate these regulatory landscapes more effectively. For example, a company that prioritizes sustainable practices may find it easier to gain approval for new projects and operations in countries with stringent environmental regulations.

Companies that engage in responsible social practices, such as fair labor conditions and community development, can also build strong relationships with local stakeholders. This can facilitate smoother market entry and expansion, as local communities and governments are more likely to support businesses that contribute positively to their well-being.

Product Development and Innovation

ESG factors also drive innovation in product development. Companies that prioritize sustainability invest in green technologies and develop eco-friendly products. This helps reduce their environmental footprint and meets the growing consumer demand for sustainable products. For instance, the automotive industry has significantly shifted towards electric vehicles (EVs) as companies respond to environmental concerns and regulatory pressures. By investing in EV technology, companies like Tesla and Toyota have positioned themselves as leaders in the sustainable automotive market, gaining a competitive advantage over traditional car manufacturers.

Risk Management and Resilience

Incorporating ESG criteria into strategic planning is not just a trend but a necessity for enhancing a company's ability to manage risks and improve resilience. Environmental hazards like climate change and resource scarcity can significantly impact business operations. However, companies adopting sustainable practices can mitigate these risks and ensure long-term viability, providing security in an uncertain world.

Social and governance factors also play a crucial role in risk management. Companies that uphold high corporate governance and social responsibility standards are better equipped to handle crises and maintain stakeholder trust. For example, businesses prioritizing transparency and ethical conduct are less likely to face legal issues and reputational damage.

ESG and Cultural Integration

Cultural integration is a critical aspect of international competitive strategy. Companies must navigate diverse cultural landscapes and adapt their practices to align with local norms and values. ESG criteria can facilitate this process by promoting respect for cultural differences and fostering positive community relations.

Environmental sustainability is closely linked to cultural integration. Companies that adopt sustainable practices demonstrate respect for local environments and communities. This can lead to stronger community support and collaboration, essential for successful market entry and operations. For example, mining companies implementing robust environmental management practices and engaging with local communities can minimize conflicts and gain a social license to operate. This not only enhances their competitive position but also ensures long-term operational success.

Social responsibility involves understanding and addressing the needs and concerns of local communities. Companies that engage in socially responsible practices, such as supporting education, healthcare, and economic development, can build positive relationships with local stakeholders.

Cultural sensitivity is also crucial. Businesses that respect local customs, traditions, and values are more likely to be accepted by local communities. This can facilitate smoother integration and reduce the risk of cultural conflicts. For instance, multinational corporations operating in diverse markets often adapt their marketing strategies to reflect local cultural nuances, enhancing their brand image and customer loyalty.

Strong governance and ethical practices are fundamental to building trust and credibility in international markets. Companies that adhere to high standards of corporate governance are perceived as reliable and trustworthy, which can enhance their competitive position. For example, businesses prioritizing transparency, accountability, and ethical conduct are more likely to attract investors and customers who value these principles. This can lead to increased market share and financial performance.

Discussion Questions

1. **How does the role of international institutions like the UN or WTO influence the strategic planning of multinational corporations?**

2. **What is the primary purpose of the World Bank?**
   A) To resolve international trade disputes
   B) To provide financial assistance for healthcare
   C) To offer financial assistance and policy advice for economic development
   D) To enforce international law

3. **Which strategy is characterized by centralizing corporate activities in the home country?**
   A) Multinational strategy
   B) Domestic exporter strategy
   C) Transnational strategy
   D) Franchiser strategy

4. **The International Monetary Fund (IMF) was established to promote international monetary cooperation and stabilize currency exchange rates. True or False?**

5. **A multinational strategy focuses primarily on minimizing costs and maximizing efficiency without adapting products to local markets.**

Recommended Readings

Chouaibi, S., & Affes, H. (2021). The effect of social and ethical practices on environmental disclosure: evidence from an international ESG data. *Corporate Governance: The International Journal of Business in Society*, 21(7), 1293–1317.

Daugaard, D., & Ding, A. (2022). Global drivers for ESG performance: The body of knowledge. *Sustainability*, 14(4), 2322.

Gündoğdu, H. G., Aytekin, A., Toptancı, Ş., Korucuk, S., & Karamaşa, Ç. (2023). Environmental, social, and governance risks and environmentally sensitive competitive strategies: A case study of a multinational logistics company. *Business Strategy and the Environment*, 32(7), 4874–4906.

Iliescu, E. M., & Voicu, M. C. (2021). The integration of ESG factors in business strategies–competitive advantage. *Challenges of the Knowledge Society*, 838–843.

Liang, Y., Lee, M. J., & Jung, J. S. (2022). Dynamic capabilities and an ESG strategy for sustainable management performance. *Frontiers in psychology*, 13, 887776.

Martins, H. C. (2022). Competition and ESG practices in emerging markets: Evidence from a difference-in-differences model. *Finance Research Letters*, 46, 102371.

Muhmad, S. N., Ariff, A. M., Majid, N. A., & Kamarudin, K. A. (2021). Product market competition, corporate governance and ESG. *Asian Academy of Management Journal of Accounting & Finance*, 17(1).

Shaikh, I. (2022). Environmental, social, and governance (ESG) practice and firm performance: international evidence. *Journal of Business Economics and Management*, 23(1), 218–237.

Chapter 6
International Organizational Design and Control

Learning Objectives

- Describe why the design of the organizational structure is essential to international companies
- Specify the many organizational dimensions management must consider when choosing organizational structures
- Explain how decision-making is distributed between parent and wholly owned subsidiaries in an international enterprise
- Examine how international enterprises can retain control of a joint venture or a business of which it owns less than 50 percent of the voting stock
- List the type of information and international company units worldwide that need to report to the parent company

Overview

Small and medium enterprises (SMEs) and early-stage MNEs do not have to worry much about how to organize a few dozen people they may have worldwide. Multinational companies, however, are in very distinct circumstances and have several alternatives when determining how best to structure their operations abroad. The structure these MNCs adopt can determine, in large part, how they can respond to the international environment's opportunities and threats. How these MNCs structure themselves can influence:
- Communications
- Degree of collaboration between country subsidiaries
- Leadership and management styles
- Strategies that country management can employ

As introduced in Chapter 5, ensuring that the organizational structure is congruent with its objectives is crucial to the enterprise's competitive advantage.

Organizational Design and Controls Affect International Companies

An enterprise's international organizational structure and controls ensure the top management's attention toward developing a holistic and unified approach to global operations. Such a structure facilitates cross-product and cross-geographic coordination and

https://doi.org/10.1515/9783111510286-006

reduces resource duplication. An organizational structure is how an organization formally arranges its domestic and international units and activities and the various relationships among its divisions or branches. Enterprises need to organize in a way that allows them to integrate their worldwide business activities efficiently and effectively.

In general, enterprises tend to follow a broad path when internationalizing. As discussed in earlier chapters, many enterprises begin their internationalization by exporting. Later, they expand abroad through overseas sales divisions and international manufacturing facilities. As enterprises go through these phases, their organizational designs will also change. So, as enterprises start to export, they usually develop an international division responsible for all non-home country activities; at this stage, the international division is at the same level as the domestic division. Only after the enterprise's international sales relative to domestic sales have been established does the company shift to an innovative design, which is discussed in more detail later in this section. Figure 6.1 illustrates the evolution of an enterprise's organizational structure.

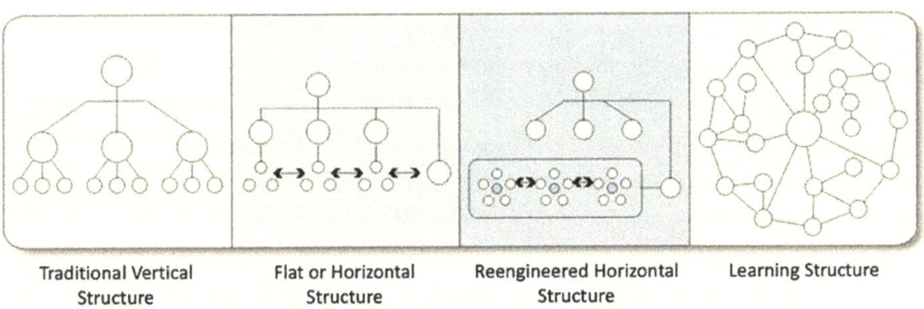

Figure 6.1: The evolution of an enterprise's organizational structure.

Traditional Vertical Organizational Structure

As depicted in Figure 6.2, traditional enterprises are usually vertical organizations with a well-defined leadership structure, typically by functions, at the top. Their influence flows downstream to middle management roles and department heads. In turn, middle managers delegate tasks to workers within their divisions. When an employee finishes a task, it is submitted back up the hierarchy until a leader with sufficient authority approves or rejects the outcome. The approved task is then pushed out of the originating division and to other enterprise areas for further testing or production.

A significant challenge of vertical organizational structure is linked to the global economy transitioning to a knowledge economy in the early 2000s, as early-stage enterprises began to outperform organizations that utilize command and control project management. Innovation rivaled production capability as a critical competitive advantage, enabling newcomers with a flatter, more horizontal organization to compete against veteran companies with vertical organizations directly. In response, vertically

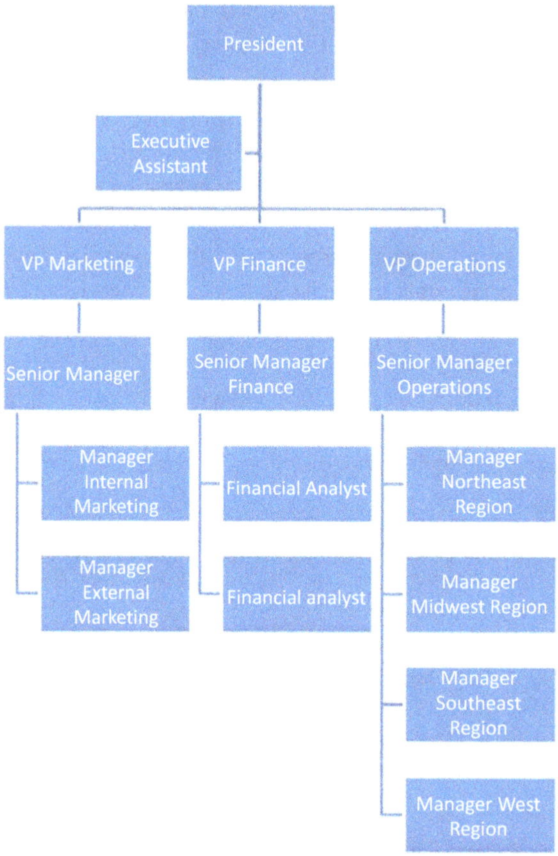

Figure 6.2: Traditional vertical organizational structure.

structured organizations evolved and pursued a waterfall methodology, where tasks flow through different divisions until they reach an endpoint. Activities began to occur sequentially, and jobs depended on prerequisites to be completed first. It has more room for deviation but enables limited collaboration between different workers.

Flat or Horizontal Organizational Structure

As depicted in Figure 6.3, flat or horizontal organizational structures focus on skill mastery instead of management hierarchy. Fewer departments exist between executives in upper management positions and the workers. A CEO with industry experience might work directly with a software development team in smaller enterprises. However, they usually defer technical questions and situations to the senior software engineer. Horizontal organizations are seen in startups, prioritizing the delivery of project tasks instead of traditional management approaches. All workers throughout the enterprise are given the same trust, responsibilities, and opportunities for input into project management decisions. Productivity and achievement of goals are more significant concerns, so the ability to solve problems creatively is encouraged.

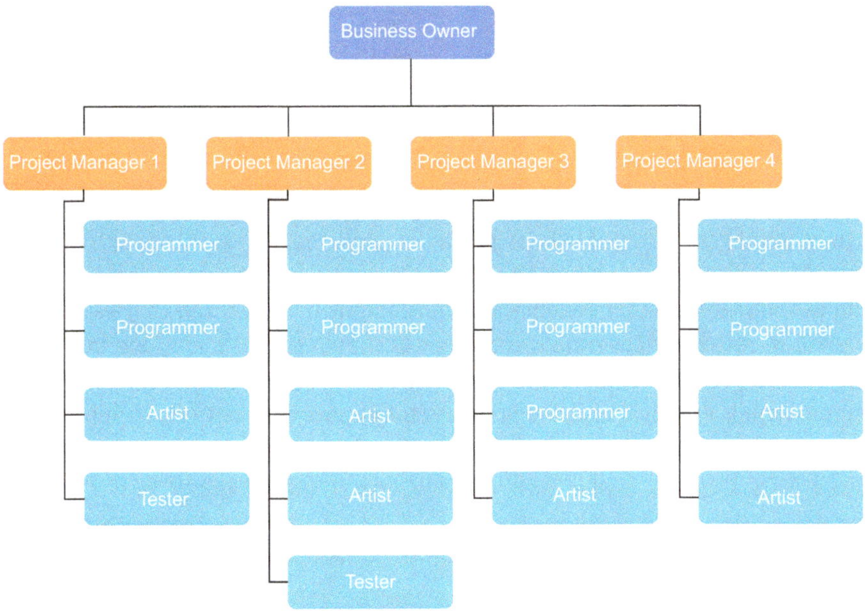

Figure 6.3: Horizontal organizational structure.

A horizontal organizational structure is an employee-centered process in which workers play a big part. They get more satisfaction due to greater freedom and autonomy. Its cross-functional design allows for optimum utilization of resources across different teams, with significant cost savings since money is saved from hiring middle management. Lastly, the structure is quite flexible; business managers could easily adjust the priorities based on different tasks.

There may be contradictions between departments because the responsibilities are interdependent, hindering productivity. It can also lead to a feeling that employees working in a small, flat organization lack professional skills in their career path because their effort is diluted. It does not promote innovation and creativity because of the breaking up of specialized lines of business. Everyone is becoming a jack of all trades, a master of none.

Another significant drawback of flat organizational structures is the scaling process. Scaling magnifies any dysfunction present at the team level. In such a structure, especially in the age of agile project management, it is difficult for a flat organizational structure to scale up when international business demands it. As the enterprise teams grow and get bigger, decision making becomes more complex and slower since every staff across the organization can offer inputs concerning the tasks at hand. A significant number of teams will have more complicated cross-team dependencies, which are difficult to track and visualize. Integration of work also becomes more challenging.

Reengineered Horizontal Structure

As depicted in Figure 6.4, enterprise business process reengineering is a process-oriented business transformation in which the organizational structure is based on the processes leading to customers' needs. The organization must change radically to improve quality, speed, costs, and services. Reengineering is commonly described as a re-design of the organization's business processes, including all associated systems and organizational structures, to attain a robust improvement in business performance.

In the service sector, for instance, notwithstanding the speed and courtesy companies place in managing customers, consumer hostility endures due to the incapacity of the service provider to sustain consistency in delivery and service. Another frequent problem is a delay due to the failure of the service worker to make appropriate and satisfactory decisions when handling an impatient consumer, which is very typical in banking, customer support calls, and fast-food restaurants.

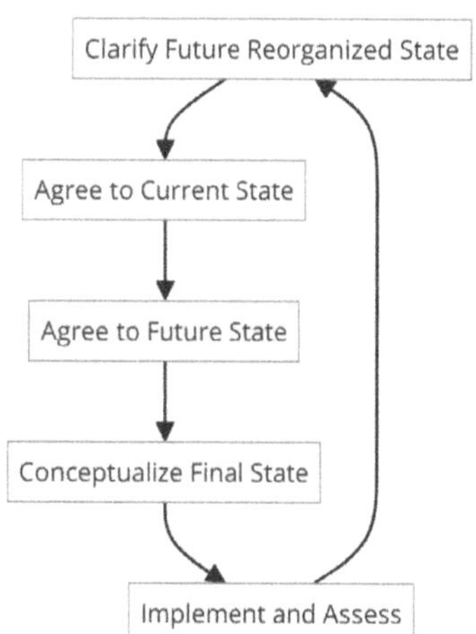

Figure 6.4: An enterprise business process: reengineering – stages of an organization's re-design.

Although some enterprises that start anew tend to best satisfy their consumers in the early stages of operations, they become sluggish due to their size increase and becoming increasingly intense and complex. Work habits evolve into unacceptable performance levels, further complicating their problems. To remain competitive today, service enterprises must focus on customer satisfaction and real-time consumer needs, wants, and expectations. Enterprises must operate according to their customer's standards, not their own.

The concept of reengineering offers a significant opportunity for the domestic and international service industry, which may include the following main features:

1. **Use the consumer as the starting point for change, identifying what** customers want and then creating the kinds of jobs and organizational structures that can satisfy those expectations.
2. **Design work processes considering organizational goals** – to become more focused on the customer. Enterprises that reengineer tend to change current job positions significantly by incorporating work processes or activities and empowering workers with more authority and responsibility.
3. **Restructure to support front-line performance** – Every aspect of the enterprise strives to foster the highest degree of service to its consumers, particularly those who directly connect with them. Consequently, enterprises undertaking reengineering projects must develop work teams to support their customer service representatives or create workstation professionals who can perform front- and back-office activities.

Reengineering represents a significant advance for improvement over traditional organizational management strategies. As an integrated process, it affects three dimensions of a service organization:

1. **The human** – to achieve a more robust customer-driven focus, workers across the organization's structure must realign their thinking and recognize that customer satisfaction is the ultimate goal. Some enterprises accomplish this by rewriting their mission statement to reflect the importance of their customers or by fostering a new organization's vision to reinforce customer satisfaction's prominent role. Some enterprises train to help workers become better listeners, probe customer issues more efficiently, or creatively satisfy customer wants and needs. The motive for reengineering an organization's structure, especially when internationalizing, is to enable the organization to be more motivated to deliver exceptional services and be proficient at doing it.
2. **The work process** focuses on work processes that must be designed based on how well they satisfy customer needs, not according to any internal logic or external description of the organization's efficiency. It sometimes requires substantial structural changes in an enterprise that does more than revamp job descriptions. It may necessitate the setup of work teams to perform all necessary functions once these are split among several divisions or converging several individual assignments to form one *customer service multi-skilled professional.*
3. **New** digital technologies should be introduced because they are more advanced and genuinely support the organization's drive in an era of digital business transformations to attain higher customer satisfaction. Such technological innovations should focus on automating the various secondary activity functions, allowing service workers time to focus on more critical issues such as fulfilling customer needs and cracking business problems.

Learning Organizations

In 1990, Peter Senge, author of *The Fifth Discipline: The Art & Practice of The Learning Organization*, coined the term *learning organization*. This definition begins with a simple truth: innovative ideas are essential if learning occurs. As depicted in Figure 6.5, a learning organization is skilled at creating, acquiring, transferring knowledge, and modifying its behavior to reflect new knowledge and insights. Five pillars comprise this structure of building a learning organization: systems thinking, personal proficiency, mental models, shared vision, and team learning. These pillars can also be broken up as follows:

- Collaborative Learning Culture (Systems Thinking)
- "Lifelong Learning" Mindset (Personal Mastery)
- Room for Innovation (Mental Models)
- Forward-Thinking Leadership (Shared Vision)
- Knowledge Sharing (Team Learning)

Figure 6.5: The enterprise organizational learning framework. (SOURCE: AMS Consulting, 2021).

One main challenge KM faces today concerns organizational and behavioral changes. These are the most difficult tasks when implementing anything, particularly developing a learning organization. Implementing technology and buying software is the least complex variable of the equation. Thus, today's knowledge workers must be aware of these challenges. In the past, behavioral, and functional changes inside the organization were not taken so much into consideration. Decisions were made from the top down (vertical or functional organizations), and all the divisions beneath just adapted to it. Today, organizations are much more decentralized, and the global economy and shorter business cycles allow for options workers didn't have before. No longer are professionals looking at positions within their enterprises as permanent. Typically, professionals move around within two to three years. Whatever can be done to minimize turnovers becomes very important, as long as the knowledge of those leaving before they do so is captured.

It is not the scope of the chapter to focus too much on learning organizations. Still, many examples of enterprises have been genuine learning organizations for many years, if not decades. Their long-term success is testimony to the value of continuous learning. Some examples include but are not limited to:

- **Apple**: Apple perceives unrecognized marketplace needs and creates new products.
- **General Electric**: Its Croton Ville learning center drives continuous learning by managers and other leaders as they return to Croton Ville to learn and teach at critical career transitions.
- **Goldman Sachs**: Its Pine Street learning center provides ongoing essential learning to a large segment of its managerial population.
- **Honeywell**: By applying the Six Sigma approach, quality is constantly improved while costs are simultaneously decreased.
- **Johnson & Johnson**: Driven by its famous credo, Johnson & Johnson constantly improves products and invents new ones, with the user at the center of its focus.
- **Microsoft**: Microsoft successfully shifted the mindset from desktop to the internet when its marketplace changed.
- **Pizza Hut**: constantly invents and implements innovative technology, and it treats its customers as long-term assets by recognizing their lifetime value.
- **Toyota Motor Co.**: uses lean manufacturing and continuous improvement to make minor but never-ending improvements (known as Kaizen) in products and processes.
- ***USA Today***: It invented and kept reinventing publishing technology to move information colorfully and electronically and manage distribution.

Any learning organization should have a defined learning plan and a clear picture of the knowledge management (KM) requirements to strive for and succeed. In building and maintaining a learning organization, management must look for traits, nurture some of them, and eliminate others so they can bridge the knowledge gap in the organization to allow a successful knowledge transfer into action from know-how to how-to. The following are some factors to attend to:

- Does the organization know what it needs to know, regardless of the industry, competition, market capitalization, technology trends, customer profiling and services, production processes, knowledge collaboration, or information gathering?
- Is the organization pursuing these knowledge goals with multiple approaches? Once the organization can identify its needs for knowledge, it must follow up with several methods, which should not be reduced to training and education alone. These methods should include experimental research studies via analyst firms or in-house resources, simulations, customer surveys, appropriate benchmarking, etc.

Learning organizations should be open to dissonant and incongruent information and disruptive knowledge to foster innovation. Learning organizations must simultaneously become effective and efficient in their actions to bridge the knowledge gap that stops organizations from acting on what they know or need to know. However, this requires a higher level of continuous learning among the leaders who drive the organization, including knowledge workers and executive C-level management, the staff delivering the organization's products or services, and the organization's customers. A learning organization must be viewed as a complex adaptive human system, trying to become a generative system, more than just mindless machines or merely structured systems. A learning organization breathes and lives out of the paradox of dissonant information. Management must strive and guide the organization in doing the same when facing contradictions such as these:

- **The organization may be losing when winning** – When a product is a success or organizational processes are working, the tendency is to let it be, not to fix what is not broken. However, if you look back at all the successful stories, those businesses disappeared or were replaced because they failed to respond to a new challenge. The American automobile industry went through it with the Japanese. Apple Computers committed the same mistake with its Apple and Macintosh lines of computers. What happened to excellent software applications such as WordPerfect, dBase II, III, IV, and Lotus SmartSuite? What happened to Netscape, or better yet, Mosaic? Organizations and their products will die if they cannot keep up with the rate of changes in their industry, and trying to play the new game with the old rules is a recipe for disaster. Due to disruptive innovation, several organizations fail to make sense of pseudo-chaotic, though not as chaotic as one might think. In other words, when information and feedback come in from a tumultuous global market, trying to react with obsolete tactics wastes capital, people, time, and eventually, the eagerness to fight on. Management must realize that learning organizations must compete and cooperate with their competitors in today's business. The either-or solutions no longer will hold.
- **Choices as a cause** – If an organization is not adopting a generative learning system, it relies on adaptive learning systems. Such systems show patterns that can never be predicted in advance, regardless of management's familiarity with the inputs, because they rely on a reactive system. Thus, the outcomes result from random choices from staff members or organizations. The intention here is synonymous with chance, and chance is the one driving the outcome.
- **Being reasonable can be limiting** – In today's business front, being rational is not necessarily business savvy. Most entrepreneurs use a significant amount of intuition in their everyday business decisions. Leaders with tremendous business acumen often feel the advantages their structural positioning in the business network offers them and learn how to exploit the stream of opportunities their position allows for flowing in their direction. A key factor here is that professionals must learn to identify these opportunities and use intuition in association with the busi-

ness's structures and themselves. For too many CEOs and other senior staff, relying on intuition and feelings and trying to tie these insights to business structures is too intimidating. Most executives are convergent thinkers, data-rational, reductionist managers who accept such paradoxical management challenges. That is why business plans have a provision for *an exit strategy*, which I call the moment when the ostrich puts its head on the sand and does not even know where the kick came from. Instead, learning organizations should adopt a more *Hellenic* posture to business, armed with a breastplate. Still, an unprotected back, just in case management feels tempted to give their back to business challenges.

- **Organizations are not simply structures** – Organizations are much more than simple structures, as they suffer the influence of human process energies, both negative and positive. People are the ones driving the organization. If people are energized, the organization will also be energized. Changing the behavior of such organizations is challenging, and many give up in the process. That is one of the main reasons the big four consulting firms repeatedly return to the same organizations and tell them through reports and best practices the same things, which challenges their status quo and calls for changes in those areas. A proper learning organization will not avoid discussing sensitive issues and make necessary changes in areas such as dissension in ranks, unhappy customers, pre-emptive moves by the competition, and issues with disruptive and innovative technologies. Typically, information gathered in these areas is filtered, and there is resistance to dealing with them, especially among those at the senior level, who tend to avoid being confronted with ideas that may change their status quo or require them to change or leave their comfort zone.

Generally, an enterprise's organizational structure and systems should be consistent with each other and the environmental context. When choosing a corporate or organizational design, enterprises must consider their size and business activities. A structure must be able to evolve to respond to change and reconfigure to integrate its competencies and resources. When international sales are only a smaller portion of overall sales, the existence of an international division is very typical, as shown in Figure 6.6. Only when international sales begin to grow will enterprises shift to alternative

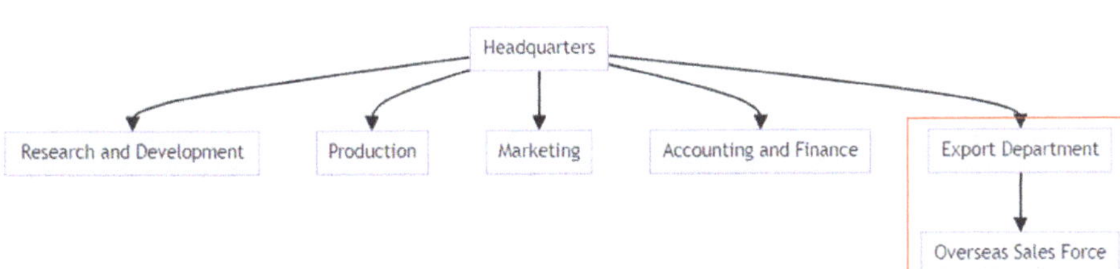

Figure 6.6: Sample organizational structure with a separate and distinct export department.

structures. For instance, exports are often managed by an enterprise's marketing or sales department in the initial stages when export sales volume is low. However, with increased exports, an independent export department is often set up apart from domestic marketing.

A company's home-based office controls export activities through a designated head of the export department, such as a vice president (VP), director, or country or region manager of exports. The human resources (HR) department mainly plans and recruits the staff for exports, training, professional development, and personnel compensation. Often, a few HR activities, such as recruiting the international sales force or agency personnel, are carried out by the exports or marketing department with or without consultation with the HR department.

Organizational Control

Organization structure refers to the role-responsibility relationships of distinct workers and their pre-defined interchange patterns. It eases the flow of information both horizontally and vertically in an enterprise. The structural dimensions of organizational design are broken down into:

- formalization
- specialization
- the hierarchy of authority
- centralization
- professionalism, and
- personnel ratios.

An organization should be structured in such a way as to go beyond maximizing performance levels and effectiveness of operations. It should encourage participation and innovation throughout the organization. Some contextual dimensions of organization design are organization size, technology, and the environment in which it operates. The organizational structures include functional, divisional, matrix, horizontal, and hybrid. The functional structure is characterized by grouping people based on their expertise and skills. In the divisional structure, the divisions are formed based on an organization's product range, the specific markets it caters to, or the geographic locations in which it operates. The matrix organization tries to integrate the desired features of both the functional and divisional structures. In this structure, an employee reports simultaneously to two different supervisors. One of these supervisors represents a functional division, and the other represents the department, product, market, geography, or project. The horizontal structure prevents rigidity and departmentalization in a vertical system by grouping the managers and employees into synergistic teams for problem-solving. When organizations combine structures (say, functional and divisional or functional and horizontal), the resulting structure is called a hybrid structure. It combines the strengths of the structures being merged.

A responsibility structure is a collection of responsibility centers. A responsibility center is an organization's function, division, or unit under a specified authority with a specified responsibility. Responsibility accounting can be defined as a system of management accounting under which accountability is determined according to the responsibility allotted to various levels of management. In an organizational setting, the performance measurement systems must be fair. Two significant aspects being considered are controllability and goal congruence. The controllability principle says managers should be assessed and rewarded only for the factors under their control. Goal unity is achieved when managers and workers work toward their best self-interest as perceived and make successful decisions in attaining the organization's overall goals. It happens when their objectives are aligned with the organizational goals. Transfer pricing is a tool used in responsibility accounting to assign monetary values to transactions between two or more responsibility centers.

According to monetary inputs and outputs, responsibility centers can be classified into four types: cost centers, revenue centers, profit centers, and investment centers. Cost centers are further divided into standard cost centers and discretionary expense centers.

As discussed earlier, corporate decisions can be made at the headquarters, subsidiary, or a combination. Where a corporate decision-making process takes place often depends on various factors. In addition, it is essential to consider how long the enterprise has been involved in the international business environment. Crucial factors may include:
- the enterprise's access to information systems and technologies
- the size of the enterprise
- the subsidiaries' managers' level of competencies

The enterprise's product and equipment can influence where decisions are made. Decisions are typically made at the headquarters when products are standardized, and global policies are in place. Subsidiaries that can successfully make a case for a product to be adapted to the local market may gain decision-making power. Another factor influencing decisions is the degree to which headquarters relies on subsidiary manager input, which may depend on how well executives know one another. Some enterprises have a policy that moves executives from country to country so managers get to know each other and the conditions in foreign markets. The geographic distance can also play a role – distant subsidiaries may have more decision-making power since headquarters are less likely to know the local market situation.

The controllability of a subsidiary's results moves from high to low as it evolves from a multi-domestic to an international, then a global, and finally a transnational strategy. At the same time, the interdependencies and control costs go from low to high. For multi-domestic and international strategies, results controls are hence more appropriate. For global and transnational strategy, action and personnel/cultural controls are more appropriate.

Management control of non-profit organizations is distinguishable from for-profit organizations because of the inherent difference concerning the source of funds, service features, the strategies for selling the service, the mode of delivering the services, reward systems for employees, etc. According to Hofstede, four criteria that help in better management control of non-profit organizations are clear objectives, quantifiable results, predictable interfaces, and repeatable activities. For distinct combinations of the four criteria, the enterprise can embrace diverse types of controls, such as routine, expert, trial and error, intuitive, judgmental, and political controls.

Management must identify strategies to motivate workers to be innovative and creative and to have the initiative to implement process improvements while still retaining enough control to ensure that workers' innovative ideas benefit the enterprise. Robert Simons' concept of levers of control, including diagnostic control, beliefs, boundaries, and interactive control systems, is very relevant. Diagnostic control systems rely on quantitative data and statistical and variance analyses to scan for anything distinctive that might suggest a potential concern. Diagnostic processes work well if the objectives are suitable and feasible. Belief systems are utilized to convey the principles of corporate culture to all employees. Boundary systems have a foundation on the principle that in an age of empowered workers, it is easier and more efficient to set regulations regarding what is improper rather than what is proper. Such a thinking process enables workers to innovate and determine new alternatives, solutions, and methods within specified conditions. Interactive control systems are forward-looking and futuristic, involving regular communication between top management, allowing enterprises to position themselves strategically in this rapidly changing global market.

International Organizational Structures

There are two main design concerns confronting international enterprises: first, identifying the most effective way to departmentalize to take advantage of efficiencies gained from the specialization of labor, and second, coordinating the activities of those departments so that the firm can meet its overall objectives.

The international organizational structure assures the top management's awareness of the need to forge a holistic and unified process for international operations. Such a structure enables cross-product and cross-geographic coordination and lessens resource duplication. Organizational structure is critical because it calls the enterprise to provide value to a market. The enterprise's value chain is a series of high-level functions representing the core value-creating process, converting a competitive strategy into business activities.

The pressure to adjust to an organizational structure that enables enterprises to react more quickly, reduce costs, and enhance quality is substantial. Such forces often require reengineering and restructuring the enterprise or part of its operations, especially by exploiting information technology solutions. Enterprises that reengineer hope to reduce middle management levels, restructure work processes, reduce fragmentation across departments, improve strategy execution speed and quality, empower employees, communicate instantly, and transmit information more swiftly. Virtual enterprises and horizontal structuring are two organizational designs that attract a lot of attention.

Virtual enterprises coordinate economic activity to deliver value to customers using resources outside the organization's traditional boundaries, often relying on digital technologies, especially considering the digital business transformations accelerated since the COVID-19 pandemic broke out in 2019 worldwide. Dell Computer and Nike are good examples of such companies. The main advantages of these types of organizations are the greater business processes' flexibility they provide, the network of dynamic relationships they involve, and how they take advantage of other organizations' competencies. However, a significant challenge such as the virtualization of enterprises brings is that it can potentially reduce management's control over the corporation's activities.

Horizontally structured enterprises are characterized by lateral decision processes, horizontal networks, and corporate-wide solid business philosophy. Such a flat organizational structure creates, builds, and markets products through cultivated interrelationships rather than conventional ones. This type of structure is used by firms in the high-tech industry like 3M and DuPont that need to respond to technological advances and be product innovators.

Organizational structures enable enterprises to ensure that all the functions required for profitable operations are allocated to the proper personnel. They direct workers, from staff members to senior executives, to comprehend their roles and responsibilities in the enterprise, their reporting structure (to whom they report), and whom they supervise. How to select an appropriate organizational structure:
1. Examine the various organizational structures.
2. Define the enterprise's strategy.
3. Evaluate the business environment, size, and demographics.
4. Review the available information.
5. Develop a visual organizational chart and then decide.

Six Primary Organizational Structures

While there are many different spin-offs, there are seven primary recognized structures for the multinational environment, including:
1. Global Functional Structure
2. International Division Structure
3. Global Organizational Structure
4. Transnational Network Structure
5. Area or Regional Division Structure
6. Matrix Structure
7. Hybrid Structure

Each structure reflects differences in organizational approaches to production, sales, and marketing and defines the communication channels between the company's headquarters and foreign affiliates. In most cases, the organizational structure must adapt as foreign involvement increases. Note that no preferred organizational structure exists for all enterprises in all contexts. Management needs to look at the enterprise's situation at a particular time.

Global Functional Structure

Enterprises often adopt a global functional structure, as depicted in Figure 6.7, with a minimal product or service scope. Upper management must oversee multiple business functions that are essential to business operations. In this case, the upper management team, the CEO, acts as the common denominator between these functions. Since the product mix is limited, the CEO can coordinate the functions' activities and bring each resource to bear on the product line.

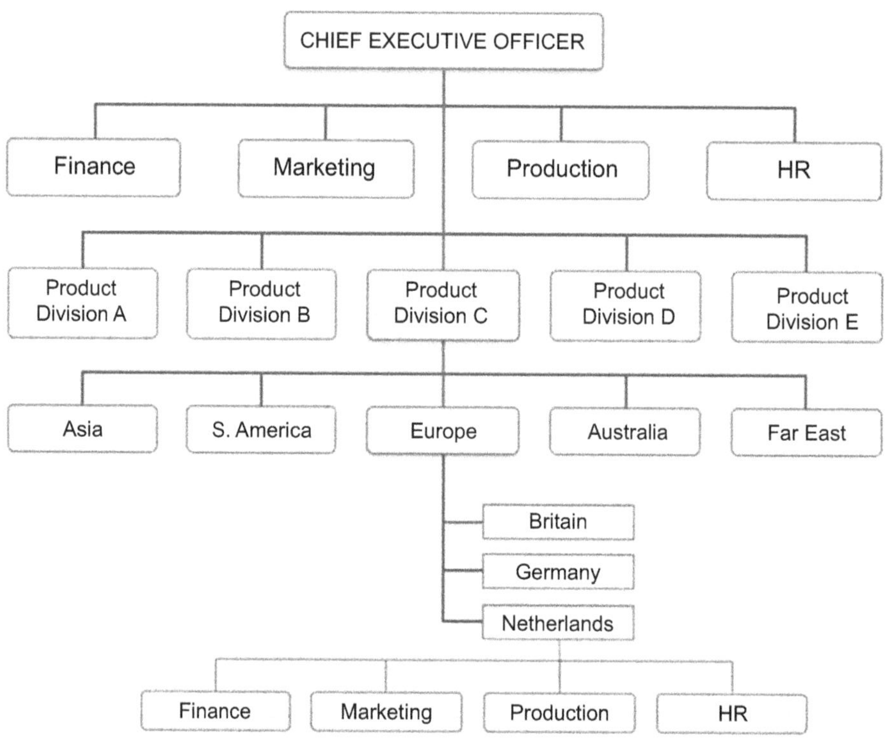

Figure 6.7: An example of an organization's global functional structure.

Since the primary sources of expertise in a global functional structure are functionally based, an advantage of this organizational structure is the economies of scale it can achieve through grouping these resources by function. For instance, in the case of HR, a centralized function can be a consultant to all other enterprise divisions on issues such as pay and performance evaluation. It eliminates redundancy when multiple divisions of the enterprise attempt to devise similar programs. A functional organization also enables the organization to standardize policies, practices, and procedures that can be carried out throughout the organization.

A disadvantage of this organizational structure is that its primary focus on functional business activity often distracts enterprises from specific product requirements, customer needs, and geographic idiosyncrasies. With the organization's top management serving as the common denominator and judge between the functions, strategies may not reflect realities on the ground. Decisions are made without the benefit of close interaction with customers and a deep understanding of local circumstances.

International Division Structure

As an enterprise's international operations grow, management often realizes overseas growth opportunities and sets up an independent international division to handle them, as illustrated in Figure 6.8. The head of the international division directly reports to the chief executive officer (CEO) and coordinates and monitors all foreign activities.

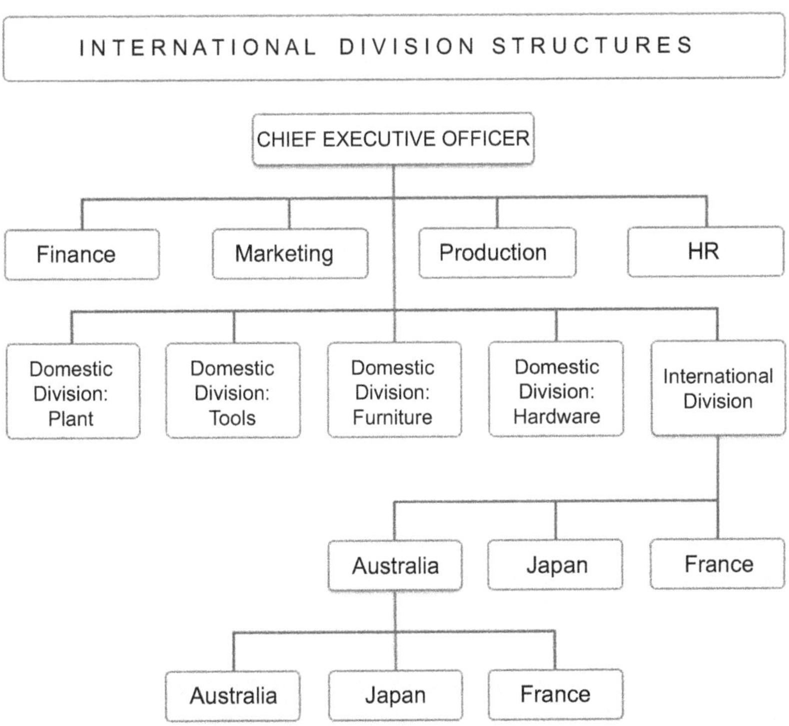

Figure 6.8: An example of an organization's international division structure.

Whoever oversees subsidiaries reports to the head of the international division, and some parallel but less formal reporting occurs to various functional authorities at the enterprise's headquarters. The enterprise's HR department is responsible for coordinating and implementing staffing needs. Such needs may include expatriate management, training, and development at the enterprise level for all international activities. In addition, it also interfaces with the HR divisions of all subsidiaries abroad.

The international structure design assures the awareness of the top management towards devising a holistic and unified procedure for international operations. Such a structure facilitates cross-product and cross-geographic coordination and prevents HR resource duplications. Although an international structure offers much greater independence in decision making, it is usually used during the initial stages of the internationalization process, with a relatively low ratio of international to domestic sales, limited international product and service offerings, and geographic diversity.

Global Organizational Structure

A global organization structure is similar to a global function strategy. In a global functional structure, the organization's reporting relationships are bifurcated according to their *functional areas*. In contrast, in a global organizational structure, the organizational functions are categorized into divisions per product, service lines, markets, etc., which is what is known as *divisional structures*.

The rise in an enterprise's overseas business operations requires the integration of all firm's activities throughout the world and the development of a global organizational structure. Through the conceptualization process of a global organizational structure, the internationalizing enterprise has to often deal with the following clashing factors:

1. The dimension or type of control exercised by the parent headquarters over the subsidiaries.
2. The degree of independence in critical decision making is to be decided by the parent headquarters versus the subsidiaries, in other words, rather than centralization or decentralizing the decision-making process.

Such dilemmas lead to re-organizations and often an amalgamation of previously fragmented enterprise interests into a globally incorporated organizational structure based on functional, geographic, or product-based divisions. Depending upon the enterprise strategy and the needs of the external business environment, the organizational strategy may move on to a global matrix or even a transnational structure.

As illustrated in Figure 6.9, the global product structure efficiently and effectively controls diversified product lines. Such a structure is highly effective in product modifications to meet fast-changing consumer demands in a diversified global market. Given the distinctions in product life cycles in these markets, it allows for closer coordination between the technological and marketing elements of diverse needs across the globe, for instance, in the case of consumer electronics, such as smartphones, laptop computers, flatscreen TVs, music players, etc.

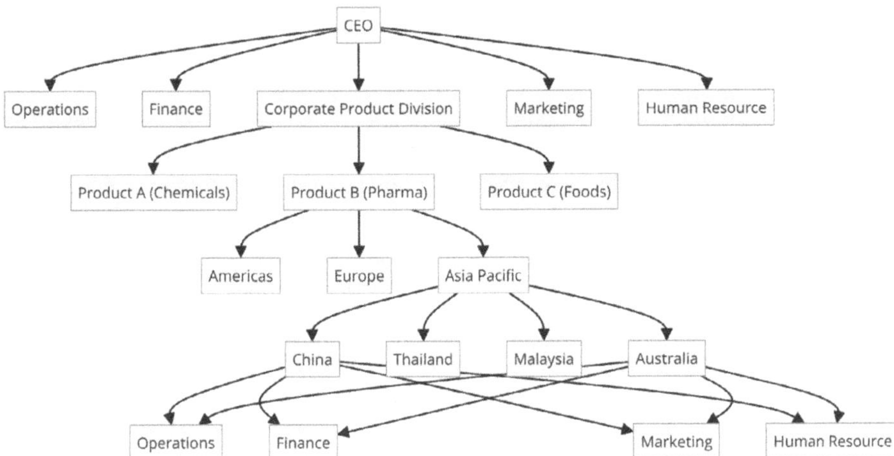

Figure 6.9: An example of an organization's global product organizational structure.

However, creating exclusive product divisions replicates various functional activities and staff diversity. Besides, not much attention is given to global market demand and strategy. Product managers often pursue attractive markets, neglecting those with better long-term potential. Lack of cooperation among different product lines may also result in sales loss.

Under the global geographic structure, as depicted in Figure 6.10, an enterprise's international operations are structured based on global geographic regions. It is commonly utilized by enterprises with mature businesses and limited product lines. It enables independent country managers of various geographical subsidiaries to concentrate on their local market needs, watch for environmental shifts, and react fast and effectively. The business headquarters is accountable for moving surplus resources from one country to another when needed. The corporate HR division coordinates and supplies synergy to achieve the enterprise's overall strategic goals between all subsidiaries in different markets.

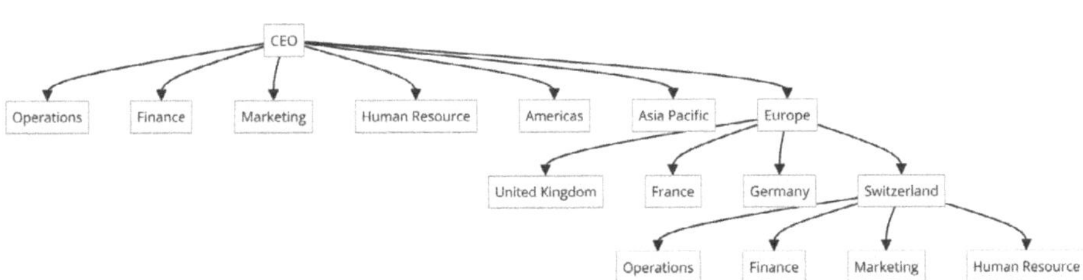

Figure 6.10: An example of an organization's global geographic organizational structure.

As depicted in Figure 6.11, the global geographic structure is effective when the product lines are not too diverse, and resources can be shared. Under such an organizational structure, subsidiaries in each market are significantly entrenched with nationalistic biases that may prohibit them from collaborating.

The global matrix structure is an integrated organizational structure superimposing on each other more than one dimension. It may consist of many product divisions intersecting with dispersed geographical regions or functional divisions. Unlike functional, geographical, and product division organizational structures, this structure shares joint control over the enterprise's various functional activities. Such an integrated organizational structure facilitates a more significant flow of information and interactivity throughout the enterprise. It tends to balance the MNE's perspective since this structure has a built-in concept of interaction between intersecting perspectives when considering the cross-functional aspects. It also enables access to technology transfer to international operations and innovative products to diverse markets, leading to higher economies of scale and outstanding international sales performance. Large MNCs such as Royal Dutch Shell and Dow Chemical have successfully used a matrix organizational structure.

The matrix structure may lead to conflicting situations as it tries to reconcile divergent perspectives within the organization. It inhibits an enterprise's ability to respond quickly to environmental changes if an effective conflict resolution mechanism is not in place. Since the structure requires most managers to report to more than one boss, often multiple ones, the fundamental principle of unity of command is violated (Fayol's). Conflicting directives from various authorities may compel workers to compromise with sub-optimal choices to evade conflict, which may not be the most suitable strategy for an organization.

Transnational Network Structure

The transnational network structure, in many ways, is a subset of a global organizational structure such as the ones listed above. It encompasses function, product, and geographic design elements while relying upon a network arrangement to link worldwide subsidiaries, as depicted in Figure 6.12. This organizational structure is not defined by its formal structure but by how its processes are connected. It may be characterized by an overall integrated system of various interrelated sub-systems. However, this globally integrated structure deserves its own subsection for representing the ultimate structure for a global-spanning enterprise, eliminating the meaning of two or three matrix dimensions.

This organizational structure is designed around *nodes*, which are the units responsible for coordinating with the product, functional, and geographic aspects of an MNE across the globe. Thus, transnational network structures build up multi-dimensional, fully networked organizations.

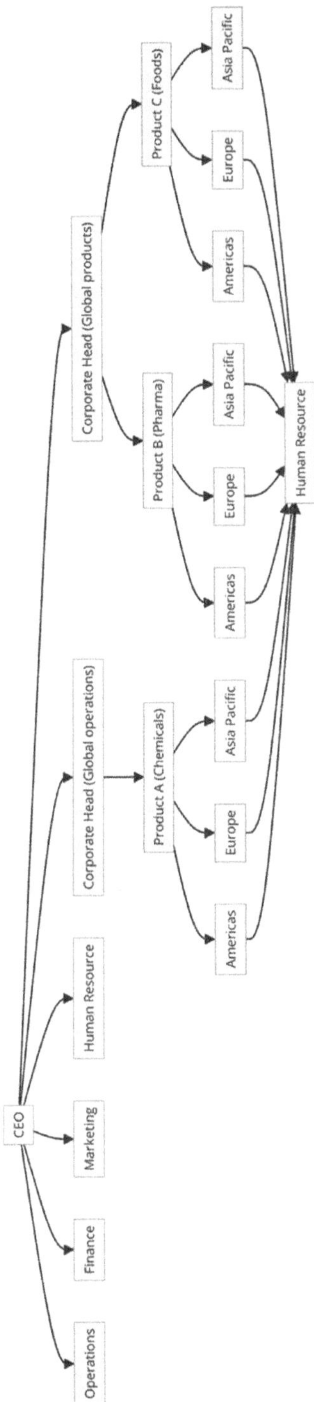

Figure 6.11: An example of an organization's global matrix organizational structure.

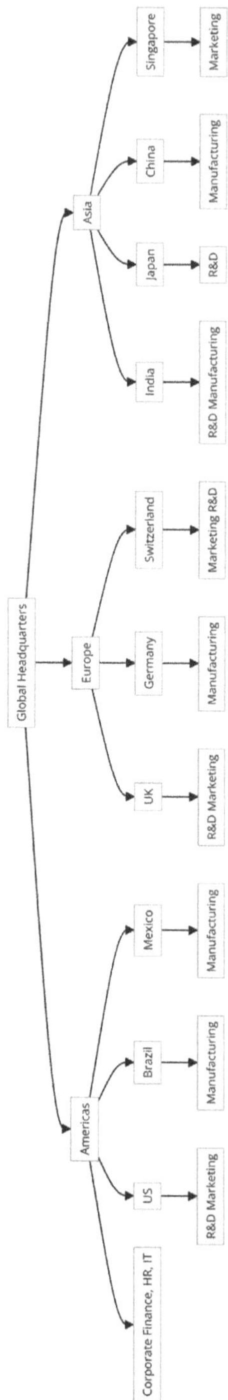

Figure 6.12: An example of an organization's transnational network structure.

Area or Regional Division Structure

A global area (or regional) division organizational structure is used for operations controlled on a geographic rather than a product basis. Enterprises with mature businesses and select product lines tend to use it, with their international and domestic operations remaining at the same level. In a divisional organizational structure, people are grouped based on the product or service they provide, not their work. For instance, a large corporation such as General Electric has electronics, transportation, and aviation divisions across the globe, each with its team of accountants, marketers, etc.

A divisional organizational structure arranges the activities of a business around geographical, market, or product and service groups. Thus, an enterprise organized on divisional lines could have operating groups for the U.S. or Europe, commercial customers, or any particular (even secret) product or service lines. Each of such divisions may contain a complete set of functions. Thus, a secret product development division would handle its accounting activities, sales, marketing, engineering, production, etc.

This approach is very functional when decision making should be clustered at the division level to react more quickly to local conditions. The divisional structure is instrumental when a company has many regions, markets, or products. However, it can cause higher total costs, which may result in several small quarreling battles within an enterprise that do not necessarily work together for the good of the entire entity.

The regional, divisional structure adopted by PepsiCo, as illustrated in Figure 6.13, is another of the best organizational structure examples. PepsiCo's regional divisions include North America Beverages (NAB), Latin America (LA), Europe, Sub-Saharan Africa (ESSA), Quaker Foods North America, and Asia, Middle East & North Africa (AMENA).

Matrix Structure

In its most basic form, a matrix organizational structure comprises two chains of command, one person reporting to two supervisors. In other words, a matrix organizational structure combines two or more frameworks, such as functional management and project management. The relationships in an organizational chart are shown as solid or dotted lines. Employees may have more than one line showing that they report to multiple leaders. The vertical lines represent the reporting structure within a hierarchy, such as a functional department. For instance, a market research analyst may report to the marketing manager and an executive director.

A matrix organization structure combines two or more different organizational structures. Thus, in a global matrix organization structure, a foreign subsidiary reports to more than one group, namely product/project, functional or geographic. Figure 6.14 illustrates the matrix structure of a multinational enterprise. Matrix structures work by fostering cross-team collaboration and shared resource planning across projects. Simply put, a matrix organization structure reorganizes companies to maximize their productivity and uses two chains of command to make them more dynamic.

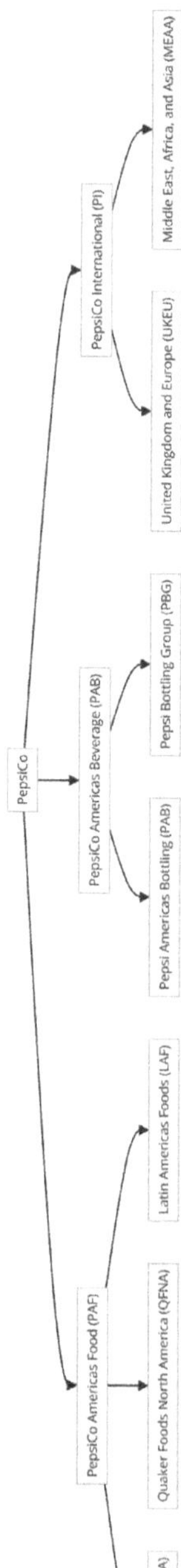

Figure 6.13: Organization of PepsiCo's division, with operations broken down into six main divisions. (SOURCE: PepsiCo's Investor's Relations, 2022).

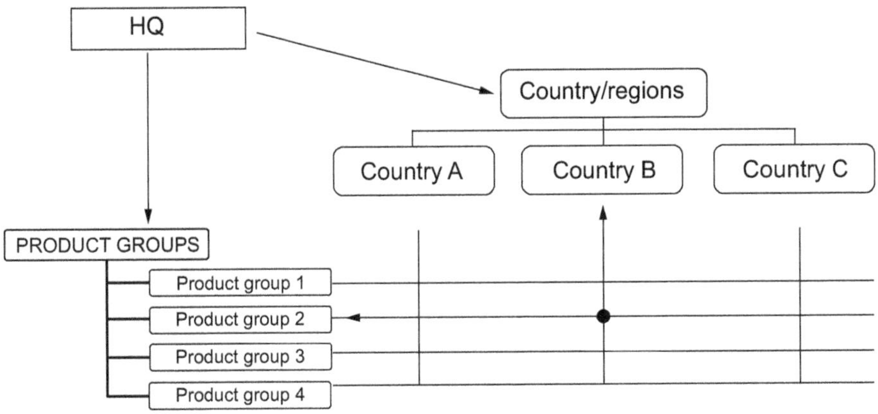

Figure 6.14: A sample matrix organizational structure of a multinational enterprise.

Besides an organizational structure's functional or vertical lines, a country manager may manage teams from various divisions. The horizontal lines on the organizational chart represent the additional reporting structure. A country manager may use resources from multiple departments, such as marketing, administration, and human resources, to work together. The functional department manager and the country manager use the same resources within the enterprise. For instance, an employee may primarily report to the enterprise's marketing manager and a country manager for a new product launch.

An enterprise may use a matrix structure to use resources and employees across multiple global locations. This organizational structure also spreads skills and abilities among various departments or divisions when needed. It allows an international enterprise to maximize its pool of talent, strengths, and expertise, which is its most valuable asset: its personnel spread across the globe.

There are three types of matrix organizational structures:

1. **Weak matrix structure** – A weak matrix structure resembles a traditional hierarchically structured workplace. A functional manager is the dominant decision-maker and oversees all aspects of a project. The project manager is in a position of authority but ultimately reports to the functional manager. An employee in this structure will work under the functional and country managers' guidance and direction. However, the main direction comes from the functional manager.
2. **Balanced matrix structure** – A balanced matrix structure gives more authority to the country manager than a weak matrix structure. Both the functional and country managers hold power. An employee in this structure will work under the guidance and direction of both managers, while the the functional manager is the primary contact. However, the employee still reports to the country manager.
3. **Strong matrix structure** – A strong matrix structure gives the country manager equal or greater authority than a functional manager. The country manager has

primary control over resources and the distribution of tasks. An employee in this structure will receive primary direction and guidance from the country manager, with secondary direction from the functional manager.

An excellent example of a matrix organization is Phillips, which was established in 1970. All managers report to both the product division and global geographical managers. Other examples include Caterpillar and Texas Instruments, which have all used the matrix structure at some point.

Hybrid Structure

As depicted in Figure 6.15, hybrid organizational structures adopt multiple reporting structures. For instance, a hybrid organization combines functional and product structures. It blends elements, value systems, a line of command, and action logic, such as international market growth and profit generation initiatives.

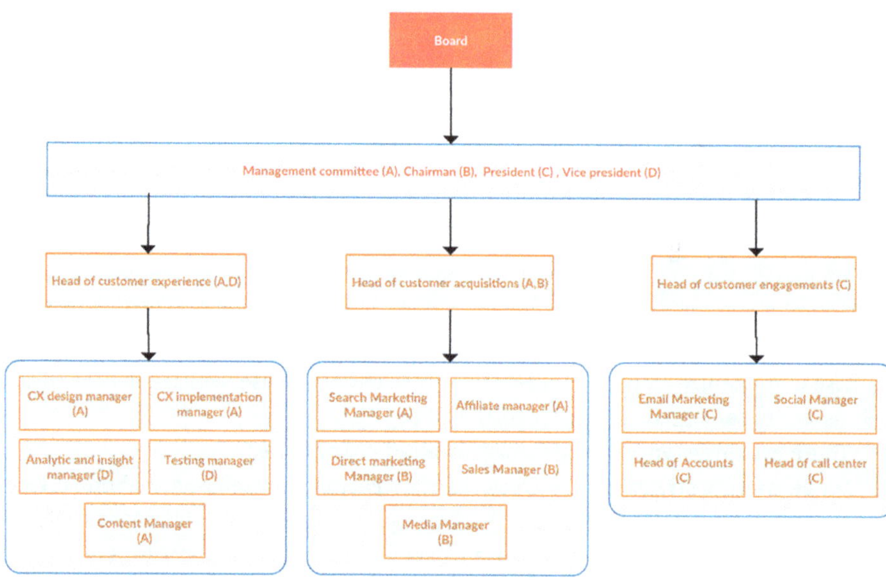

Figure 6.15: A sample hybrid organizational structure of a multinational enterprise.

Organizations under a hybrid organizational structure have the following features:

1. Shared ownership
2. Goal incongruence and different institutional logic in the same organization
3. Various sources of finance
4. Differentiated methods of resource controls

Under a hybrid organizational structure, workers must work on many projects and report to multiple managers. In an ideal world, for instance, international marketing professionals working on a project should report to their project manager. In the hybrid management structure, however, professionals from one project may be recruited to contribute to another project if required, resulting in a situation in which they report to both project managers.

As hybrid organizations combine diverse stakeholder groups, the potential for conflict within them might be more significant, challenging stakeholders and sponsor management. Such constraint is typically emphasized from the agency theory perspective. The alleged *numerous crucial issues* are tied to specific aggregated activities that can potentially occur in such a hybridity setting. For instance, duplication of efforts or controlling mechanisms, workers' free-riding, and the need for more monitoring tools and methodologies can significantly raise management costs. Vagueness in task requests or preferential priorities to a task associated with one project versus another by an individual contributor (employee) can cause wastefulness of resources (e.g., time, money, personnel, etc.). Such constraints can have positive and negative economic, cultural, execution-related, and administration-related impacts on the enterprise, its standards, and its customers.

The hybrid organization comprises four major organizational elements:

1. **Core structure or backbone** – secures the enterprise's overall strategy, governance, and synergies.
2. **Functional units** – assure the operational excellence, protection, and further development of the company's key capabilities, skills, and competencies.
3. **Agile units** – operate close to or with the customer and the market. They execute the operational business, especially in volatile environments.
4. **Shared services** – represent the interface between the agile and the functional units.

The following are some hybrid business examples:
- International institutions and hospitals (in the European setting)
- State-owned enterprises that compete in the global markets
- Franchises, joint ventures, and business groups
- Trade associations often combine impact-oriented operations through a wholly owned subsidiary

Starbucks is an example of a hybrid organizational structure. The company implements three organizational structures: functional, geographical, and product-based. Starbucks has functional departments in finance, marketing, and human resources.

Some of the advantages of a hybrid organizational structure include:

1. **Increased efficiency** – The significant advantage of a hybrid organizational structure is increased efficiency. This structure ensures that the correct number of activities is distributed at the right time to the right staff, thus ensuring the

optimum utilization of the organization's resources and avoiding waste. A hybrid organizational structure works very well even when the resources are scarce. As the specialized staff is readily available, projects are launched quickly, thus increasing the efficiency of the organization.
2. **Development of cross-functional skills** – In hybrid organizational structures, groups are formed considering specializations and services. Thus, employees with different skills are mingled, allowing for learning and developing various skills from many other participants. The main advantage of a hybrid structure regarding employees' personal growth is that the organization can utilize it later, minimizing project costs since resources can be shared.
3. **Flexibility** – The hybrid business structure is more flexible than divisional and functional structures. A healthy relationship exists between senior managers and junior employees, which helps address all employee problems efficiently, thus increasing the employees' effective output.

Some of the disadvantages of a hybrid organizational structure include:
1. **Conflicts** – The primary disadvantage of a hybrid structure is the chance of having conflicts between corporate departments and divisions. There could be dilemmas among project and department managers regarding deadlines and resources, as many employees may become confused about the line of authority. There can also be confusion regarding the roles and responsibilities of each employee.
2. **Too much administration overhead** – Hybrid organizational structures can lead to time and effort waste. Meetings to resolve conflicts among corporate divisions can be a waste of time and effort. Meetings are also required to better utilize and coordinate staff in the case of two or three concurrent projects.

Wholly Owned Subsidiaries Considerations

An enterprise can evolve from equity investment to a partly owned subsidiary into a wholly owned subsidiary through a parent company's 100 percent acquisition, as depicted in Figure 6.16. A wholly owned subsidiary (WOS) is an enterprise whose common stock is 100 percent owned by another company. A majority-owned subsidiary is an enterprise whose common stock is 51 to 99 percent owned by a parent company. When lower costs and risks are desirable or unattainable to obtain complete or majority control, the parent company might introduce an affiliate, associate, or associate company with a minority stake.

A WOS can assist the parent corporation in maintaining operations in diverse global geographic areas, markets, or distinct industries. These factors help hedge against shifts in the market or geopolitical trade practices and industry declines. Because the parent company owns all the shares of a WOS, it does not have any minority shareholders operating under the auspices of the parent company, with or without any

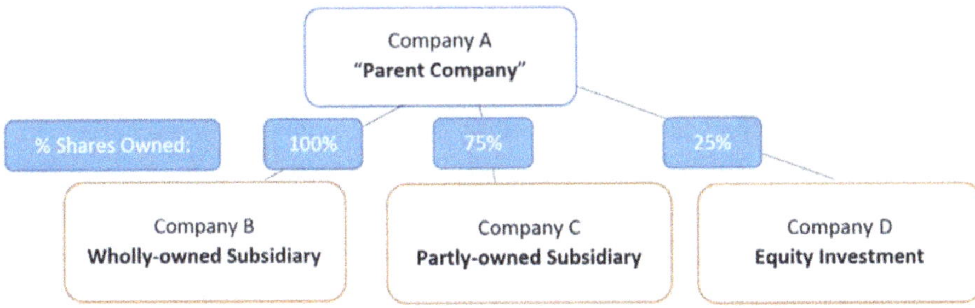

Figure 6.16: An enterprise can evolve from equity investment to a partly owned subsidiary into a wholly owned subsidiary through a parent company's 100 percent acquisition.

direct input to the subsidiary's operations and management, making it an unconsolidated subsidiary. A WOS may also preserve its management structure, clients, and corporate culture despite being owned by another entity. When a firm is acquired, its staff may worry about layoffs or restructuring.

From an accounting perspective, a WOS is still a separate company. It must keep its financial records and bank account transactions tracking all its assets and liabilities. All transactions between the parent company and the subsidiary must also be recorded. If the parent company is public, typically, the General Accepted Accounting Principles (GAAP) and the International Financial Reporting Standards (IFRS) require MNCs and MNEs to report the financial data of all their subsidiaries. Although parent companies have operational and strategic control over their WOS, the overall control usually is less for any acquired subsidiary with a solid operating history overseas. When a company hires the staff to manage its subsidiaries, forming standard operating procedures (SOP) is much less complicated than taking over a company with an already established leadership.

A parent company manages how its WOS assets are invested. In addition, the parent company may apply for its data access and security directives for the subsidiary to reduce the risk of losing IP to other competing companies. Likewise, adopting similar financial systems, sharing administrative services, and developing similar international marketing campaigns can help lower costs for both companies. Acquiring a WOS may result in the parent company paying a high price for its assets, mainly if competing companies bid on the same opportunity. Furthermore, developing relationships with suppliers, vendors, and local consumers and clients invariably takes time, which may impact the company's operations. Cultural differences can also become a concern when recruiting staff for subsidiaries placed in different markets overseas. Finally, the parent company must bear all the inherited risks of owning a subsidiary, which could increase when local laws and regulations vary significantly from those in the parent company's country.

There are tax advantages for WOS that can be lost if a parent company absorbs all the assets of an acquired subsidiary. When a parent company receives a subsidiary by purchasing that company's stock, such acquisition is deemed a qualified stock purchase for tax purposes. Furthermore, any losses incurred by the subsidiary can be utilized to offset the parent company's profits, which might result in lower tax liability for the parent company. Sometimes, a subsidiary can behave in ways a parent company is not allowed to. For instance, a non-profit entity can create a for-profit subsidiary to raise revenues and be subject to federal income taxes, but not the parent company, which would be exempt. Figure 6.17 outlines some of the main pros and cons of WOS.

Pros and Cons of Wholly Owned Subsidiaries	Pros	Cons
	• Tax-exempt organizations can have for-profit subsidiaries • Parent companies can use losses from one subsidiary to offset profits from another. • The parent company inherits the acquired company's clients and good-will, which would be hard to recreate from scratch.	• Running a subsidiary can be difficult if the acquired company has a different management culture. • Acquiring another company can be expensive, especially if other companies are also seeking to acquire them. • Risks may be higher if the subsidiary is located in a different jurisdiction than the parent company.

Figure 6.17: Pros and cons of wholly owned subsidiaries.

Volkswagen AG is a well-known example of adopting the WOS system, which wholly owns Volkswagen Group of America, Inc., and its prominent brands, including Audi, Bentley, Bugatti, Volkswagen, and Lamborghini Audi AG wholly owns. Other examples include Marvel Entertainment and Lucasfilm, the WOS of The Walt Disney Company, and Starbucks Japan, a WOS of the U.S.'s Starbucks Corp.

It is important not to confuse a subsidiary with a WOS. The former is a company whose stock is more than 50 percent owned by a parent company (or holding company), allowing the parent company to control interest in the subsidiary's generated profits and decisions. A WOS is 100 percent owned by a parent company without any minority shareholders. *Subsidiary detriment* refers to a situation in which a slight loss for a subsidiary results in a more significant gain for the total firm. For instance, an enterprise may move production from one location to another because of critical factors such as cost, labor, taxes, and political stability. Such a decision may help the enterprise but would undoubtedly be detrimental to the subsidiary.

When deciding which subsidiary will fill an order, enterprises might also consider other factors, such as transportation costs (logistics), production costs, tariffs, currency restrictions, and order backlogs. Taxes, currency controls, labor relations, political climate, and social unrest may be considered when deciding which subsidiary will declare profits. When countries use a multicountry production strategy to gain economies of scale, decisions usually require centralized control and coordination. The level of subsidiary frustration is a critical factor in determining where decisions are made. Enterprises want subsidiary managers to be motivated and loyal since if headquarters makes all the decisions, the subsidiary managers may lose their incentive to work, prestige, and face with their employees. In this situation, subsidiary managers could become hostile and disloyal.

Joint Ventures: Considerations

An international joint venture can be defined as a corporate entity between two or more companies that are both foreign to the country where the joint venture is located. While joint ventures offer many benefits, such as shared costs and risks, they also imply a loss of freedom and flexibility. Shareholders can bring both legal pressures and political pressures to take specific actions. For instance, a joint venture partner can block efforts to move production or fill an order from another subsidiary. To maintain control, enterprises can use a management contract, take control of the joint ventures' finances or technology, and place people from the company in critical executive positions within the joint venture.

An international enterprise interested in exploring international trade without taking on the full accountabilities of cross-border business dealings can form a joint venture with an international partner. An international joint venture (IJV) is established when two businesses develop a partnership in two or more nations. International investors engaging in a joint venture reduce the risk of outright acquiring a company. In international business development, due diligence on the foreign markets and the partner limits the risks involved in such a business transaction.

International joint ventures are perceived as a suitable vehicle for knowledge and technology transfers, from MNC's expertise to local partnering enterprises. Such transfers can contribute to the performance improvement of local enterprises. IJVs also assist enterprises in developing strategic alliances, which allow them to gain a competitive advantage by accessing a venture partner's resources, including technologies, markets, people, and capital. Within IJVs, one or more of the partners are typically located where the business operations of the IJV take place and involve a local and foreign company.

Many motivations lead to the formation of a joint venture (JV). They include:

- **Acquisition** – Companies interested in acquiring other strategic companies but cannot due to cost, size, geographical restrictions, or legal barriers may team up with a venture partner as an attractive option. This arrangement enables the purchaser to reduce the costs of complete acquisition until the market is proven profitable, at which point a total acquisition can be executed. Usually, many IJVs end up in mergers or acquisitions.
- **Economies of scale** – In markets with elevated fixed costs, an IJV with a more prominent MNC may offer the economies of scale needed for global competitive advantage, as these two enterprises can pool resources and reach critical mass in targeted markets.
- **Funding constraints** – When confronted with elevated up-front development costs, international companies can benefit from finding a compatible venture partner that can offer the necessary financing and credibility in the target market and third parties.
- **Geographical reason** – There are many attractive business opportunities across international markets. Partnering with a local company appeals to a global enterprise when penetrating a foreign market. However, it can be challenging due to a lack of experience in such needs and regional barriers to internationally owned enterprises.
- **Market access** – For enterprises lacking a fundamental understanding of customers' services, the relationships, and the necessary infrastructure to develop a supply and distribution chain, developing an IJV with the right venture partner may enable instant access to establish efficient and effective distribution channels up and downstream and an eager customer base.
- **Risk sharing** is a common reason to form an IJV, particularly in highly capital-intensive industries and industries with high product development costs or elevated likelihood of a product or service offering.

For decades, China has been an attractive market for IJV. International companies unfamiliar with the local market and culture can benefit from joint ventures in the country. However, China's regional businesses are becoming increasingly internationalized, and IJV has been falling out of practice. It has become challenging to select the proper venture partner, management, technology transfer, profit sharing, etc.

Two common types of IJV found in China and many other international markets are: *equity joint ventures* and *cooperative joint ventures.*

An equity joint venture (EJV) is a partnership between an overseas and a Chinese individual, enterprise, or financial organization approved by the Chinese government. An equity joint venture company shares mutual rewards, risks, and losses according to the investment ratio. The international partners and no minimum investment for the Chinese partners must contribute at least 25 percent of the initial capital. The IJV is free to hire Chinese nationals without interference from government employment industries by abiding by Chinese labor law, purchasing land, building buildings, and preventing privileges from restricted to representative offices.

Cooperative joint ventures (CJVs) are an unevenly regulated form of IJV between Chinese and foreign-based companies. They are usually found in both technology-based ventures and have a substantial requirement for fixed assets, such as infrastructure and volume manufacturing. No minimum international investments are required to start the cooperative ventures. All contributions international investors make are not necessarily expressed in a monetary value. These contributions, such as labor, resources, and services, can be excluded from the equity joint venture process. Greater flexibility in structuring a cooperative venture is also permissible, including the organization's structure, management, and assets.

Reporting in an International Business Setting

An international enterprise's annual report has been a cornerstone of financial reporting for over a century. During that time, many things have changed. The economy's structure has moved from an industrial base to one driven more by technology and information. Social expectations have changed, particularly regarding environmental, social, and governance (ESG) and diversity, equity, and inclusion (DEI). What might have been considered acceptable 50 years ago is simply unacceptable today. Technology has changed, too, as the internet and social media have revolutionized how information is shared.

A company's ability to access and process data has been transformed, and international business managers should expect other disruptive technologies to emerge, such as cybersecurity, blockchain, and digital currencies, to name a few. Despite those changes, periodic corporate reports summarizing the business will continue to be a cornerstone of corporate reporting to stakeholders, government compliance agencies, shareholders, investors, and customers. These actors will continue to want and need international business managers to provide a periodic overview of their business operations and results. Such reporting activity is upper management's opportunity to tell their story, but it must be developed within a widely accepted high-quality standards framework. What information should be included in which report and how it should be presented or delivered must evolve and adapt to the ever-changing global landscape. All interested parties listed earlier need information on a broader range of matters. They want to access the report on various, primarily electronic, platforms and reshape the data using analytical tools.

In summary, corporate reporting links a company and all its internal and external constituents, which use such information to assist them in assessing whether they trust an organization enough to put their capital at risk by investing in it, purchasing the products or services the company offers, or evaluate the company's corporate social responsibility (CSR). A company can enhance or damage its reputation value through how it behaves and reports.

Financial Reporting

Financial reporting is essential for international companies and investors, as it provides vital information that provides financial performance over a period, usually annual quarters. Government and private regulatory agencies and institutions also monitor these financial reports to ensure fair trade, compensation, and financial activities. Typically, enterprises record financial activities on several critical statements, which interested parties (e.g., government agencies, investors, consumers, etc.) can use for review. This sub-section discusses financial reporting, why it is essential for domestic and international companies, joint financial statements, and who uses and monitors these documents.

Financial reporting documents and communicates financial activities and performance over specific periods, typically quarterly or yearly. Enterprises develop financial reports to organize accounting data and report their financial situation. These reports are essential in forecasting future industry position, growth, and profitability, as many of these financial reports are available for public review and required for publicly traded companies. There are many primary financial statements to adopt when reporting results. The information included in these reports satisfies several key objectives of financial reporting, including:

- Tracking cash flow
- Evaluating assets and liabilities
- Analyzing shareholder equity
- Measuring profitability

Financial reporting is an essential practice as it provides critical information necessary to:

- **Monitor income and expenses** – Monitoring income and costs is a crucial process supported by financial reporting. Tracking financial reports is critical for effective debt management and budget allocation and provides insight into critical areas of spending. Monitoring income and expenses ensures enterprises can track debts and credits periodically to remain transparent in domestic and internationally competitive markets. Thus, financial reports provide a methodology to keep track of liabilities and assets and accurately assess essential metrics such as debt-to-asset ratios, which investors rely on to evaluate how effectively a company is paying down debts and generating revenues.
- **Ensure compliance** – Financial reporting encompasses companies' specific processes for complying with mandatory accounting rules and regulations. Several financial regulatory institutions review these reports used to assess financial activities.
- **Communicate essential data** – All shareholders, shareholders, executives, investors, creditors, and business professionals rely on financial reports to plan budgets, monitor the company's performance, and make decisions. They count on

the information communicated in financial statements to evaluate risk, profitability, and potential future returns.
- **Support financial analysis and decision making** – Financial reporting is also crucial for performing analysis to support business decisions. Financial reports, particularly a balance sheet and income statement, offer real-time data that can be used to monitor historical business performance, identify critical areas of spending, and develop forecasts more accurately. Better-developed data models and detailed financial analysis enable financial reporting to assess current business activities, forecast future outlooks, and make decisions for future growth. The use of financial reporting enhances corporate accountability and provides support for the analysis of vital business financial data.

Most companies document financial data on three critical statements but sometimes include the shareholder equity in separate reports. The following is a set of essential reports used by companies to monitor their financial activities:

1. A balance sheet records the enterprise's total assets, liabilities, and equity. A quick balance sheet overview can describe and assess a company's total assets minus its equity and liabilities. Typically, businesses track balance sheets quarterly and include balance sheet data when developing annual reports. Typically, balance sheets depict the following items:
   - Liquid assets include cash, short-term securities, certificates of deposit, treasury bills, etc.
   - Current assets include accounts receivable, fixed assets, inventory, and prepaid expenses.
   - Current liabilities include short-term and long-term debt, accounts payable, payable wages and dividends, tax expenses, and client prepayments
   - Shareholder and owner equity values, such as retained income, capital gains, receivable dividends, and stocks
2. **Income statement** – While a balance sheet reviews current activities, the income sheet tracks these processes over a more extended period. Some companies track income statements quarterly and rely on these reports to monitor financial processes. The income statement provides the company's performance for total revenues, net income, total expenses, and earnings per share (EPS) if publicly traded. There are several critical elements in this report:
   - Operating revenue is an account of all products or services sold
   - Net and gross revenues, which include the total sales revenue and the remaining revenue after subtracting the costs
   - Nonoperating revenue from any accrued interest, investment returns, royalty payments, capital gains
   - Primary expenses include the cost of goods sold (COGS), and the depreciation and selling, general and administrative costs (SG&A)
   - Secondary expenses, such as debt or loan interest, asset loss, and capital loss

3. **A cash flow statement** – is an essential report for assessing the efficiency with which the enterprise generates cash to pay its debts. Such a report can give investors and stakeholders a valuable understanding of whether a business offers a higher investment risk. Cash flow statements also inform how well the company funds operations and investments, provides all the ongoing business operations, generates revenues to support expenses, and turns a profit. A cash flow statement typically provides three important financial factors:
   - Operational activities, which include accounts receivable and payable, wages, inventories, income tax, and cash receipts
   - Primary investment activities include developing and using investment earnings, issued loans or credit, asset sales, and payments disbursed for mergers or acquisitions
   - Secondary investment activities include office space or property and fixed-asset purchases for equipment.
   - Financing activities include stock repurchases, debt repayments and issuance, payable dividends, cash from investors, and cash payments to shareholders
4. **Statement of shareholder equity** – Shareholders' equity is usually shown on balance sheets. Still, larger enterprises may report these activities on separate statements, such as the statement of shareholder equity, which also includes the amounts key stakeholders and owners have invested in the business, such as company stocks and securities, which pay dividends at specific periods. Other items found in the statement of shareholder equity include:
   - A list of common and preferred stock sales and repurchases
   - Purchased treasury stock after subtracting any reissued treasuries in the report's period
   - Any retained earnings minus losses and dividends
   - Accrued income, including those from unrealized capital gains, minus capital losses

Financial reporting is a necessary process across all industries. Businesses and corporations depend on analyzing and reviewing these reports when making decisions and gaining financial support. Financial institutions rely on such statements to assess the company's compliance, profitability, and performance and issue credit. The following is a list of potential groups and professionals who tend to rely on financial reports:

- **Investors, shareholders, and creditors** – These groups typically own company stocks and are interested in reviewing their financial reports to monitor companies' profit generation. Creditors, for instance, use information from these reports to understand how effectively companies are paying off their debts and investing their credits to foster business growth.
- **Executive managers** – These executives rely on financial reporting to assess their company's performance and evaluate all the documentation. It also assists them in making decisions when setting or reviewing goals and divisions' objectives.

- **Regulatory institutions** – These entities often gather and inspect business financial data from such reports. Several government entities, such as the Securities Exchange Commission (SEC) and the Internal Revenue Service (IRS), monitor the compliance of financial reporting activities of enterprises.
- **Industry consumers** – Financial reports are essential for educating consumers about their company's activities and fostering market transparency. Open communication regarding corporate earnings, investment activities, and charitable donations informs customers and drives additional sales.
- **Unions and employees** – These organizations monitor financial reports to ensure their members receive fair salaries and treatment at the workplace.

Several regulatory entities regulate financial reporting and compliance, including the Financial Accounting Standards Board (FASB), the International Financial Reporting Standards (IFRS), the IRS, and the SEC, which set standards that delineate protocols and required best practices relating to financial activities and reporting. The SEC, for instance, oversees capital markets and sets up regulations for investment activities in the stock markets. The FASB, a private regulatory entity, sets up and monitors the Generally Accepted Accounting Principles (GAAP), which provides a framework for financial processes supporting efficiency in reporting and ensuring regulatory compliance with other standards.

The IFRS is a set of accounting standards by the IFRS Foundation and the International Accounting Standards Board (IASB). Both institutions constitute a standardized way of reporting a company's financial performance and position so that a company's financial statements can be understood and compared across international borders. These standards are essential for MNCs and MNEs traded in public stock exchanges across the globe. The IFRS has replaced many other national accounting standards worldwide but has not replaced the different accounting standards in the US, where GAAP is adopted.

Nonetheless, the IFRS Standards are a requirement in more than 140 countries and allowed in several parts of the globe, including South Korea, the European Union, Brazil, India, Australia, Hong Kong, Malaysia, GCC countries, Pakistan, Russia, Philippines, Chile, Kenya, Singapore, South Africa, Turkey, and Israel. To evaluate progress toward a single global accounting standard, the IFRS Foundation has produced and posted several profiles regarding using its IFRS Standards in individual countries. Due to the difficulties of keeping up-to-date information on respective jurisdictions, three sources of information on current worldwide IFRS adoption are recommended:
- IFRS Foundation profiles website
- The World Bank
- International Federation of Accountants

Market Opportunities Reporting

A market opportunity report (MOR) carefully analyzes various market conditions that determine the potential for a new international opportunity. A MOR provides upper management, stakeholders, investors, and clients with information and insight into the possible business model that aligns with the corporate mission and its definition of success. It may include local and international markets' demographics and socioeconomics, spending habits and discretionary income, GDP per capita, cultural information, government rules and regulations, regional competitors, and specific industry factors. International marketing opportunities are the tactics and methods used to market products and services in multiple countries. They may assume the form of import/export, franchising, licensing, and online sales.

When analyzing market opportunities reports, upper management must:

1. Identify potentially aligned opportunities
2. Understand the prospective customer profile
3. Research the competitors
4. Identify and assess external factors.
5. Be aware of internal forces.

International Sustainability Reporting

By establishing goals, measuring performance, and managing change, upper management can make their enterprise operations more sustainable. The first step is to choose which reporting framework to follow. Sustainability reporting frameworks mainly aim to turn theoretical issues into concrete actions. Sustainability reporting can help international enterprises set priorities to reach environmental and social impact goals by exposing both positive and negative impacts on the planet, society, and the economy. The UN Sustainable Development Goals should now be familiar to international business professionals. The following are other standards and frameworks to assist in sustainability reporting:

- **Global Reporting Initiative (GRI)** – The GRI is an independent international organization that has pioneered sustainability reporting since 1997. The GRI Sustainability Reporting Standards (GRI Standards) are a reporting framework for organizations across the globe to disclose both positive and negative impacts on the environment, society, and the economy. GRI Standards are designed to be universally applicable to all organizations of all types and sectors, large and small, worldwide.
- **International Organization for Standardization (ISO)** – ISO is an independent, non-governmental organization with 164 national standards bodies as members. One of its most essential standards is ISO 14001, which specifies requirements for an effective environmental management system. It provides a framework that an organization can follow rather than establishing environmental performance requirements.

- **Principles for Responsible Investment (PRI)** – Supported by the United Nations, the PRI is the world's leading proponent of responsible investment. It works to understand the investment implications of ESG factors and supports its international network of investor signatories in incorporating them into their investment and ownership decisions. The PRI actively encourages investors to use responsible investment to enhance returns and manage risks but does not profit.
- **Sustainability Accounting Standards Board (SASB)** – Founded in 2011, SASB focuses on developing standards for sustainability information aimed at investors: data that could affect their financial decisions about a company. It connects businesses and investors to the financial impacts of sustainability. With GRI, SASB is one of the most important frameworks for sustainability reporting. At the end of 2020, SASB and GRI announced a collaboration to create better transparency and trust among reporting companies.
- **United Nations Global Compact** – The UN Global Compact is a voluntary initiative for companies willing to change their business operations so that the UN Global Compact and its Ten Principles become part of their strategy, culture, and day-to-day operations. Since July 2000, the UN Global Compact has received more than 62,000 public reports from over 9,000 companies in 159 countries.

The Impact of ESG on International Organizational Design and Control

The design and control of international organizations are pivotal in determining how multinational enterprises (MNEs) and global companies navigate the complex landscape of international business. With the increasing importance of ESG criteria, these factors are crucial in shaping organizational structures and control mechanisms. ESG considerations are integral to the design and control of international organizations. Environmental sustainability, social responsibility, and good governance shape organizational structures and control mechanisms, influencing decision-making processes and cultural integration. By adopting flexible, transparent, and inclusive structures, companies can enhance their ESG performance and achieve long-term success in the global market. Integrating ESG criteria into organizational design and control is an ethical imperative and a strategic advantage in today's competitive business environment.

ESG and Organizational Structure

Environmental sustainability is a significant driver in the evolution of organizational structures. Companies increasingly adopt structures that facilitate sustainable practices and reduce their environmental footprint. For instance, many organizations are transitioning from traditional vertical structures to more flexible, flat, or horizontal structures that promote collaboration and innovation in sustainability.

Environmental Considerations

A flat or horizontal organizational structure enables faster decision making and greater employee involvement in sustainability initiatives. This structure fosters a culture of innovation, where employees at all levels can contribute ideas for reducing waste, improving energy efficiency, and developing sustainable products. Companies like Tesla and Unilever have adopted such structures to enhance their environmental performance and achieve sustainability goals.

Social Responsibility

Social responsibility, another critical aspect of ESG, influences organizational design by emphasizing the need for ethical labor practices, diversity, and community engagement. Companies are restructuring their organizations to ensure fair treatment of employees, promote diversity and inclusion, and engage with local communities.

For example, multinational corporations are adopting reengineered horizontal structures to integrate social responsibility into their operations. This structure focuses on cross-functional teams that address specific social issues, such as labor rights and community development. By doing so, companies can better respond to social challenges and build stronger relationships with stakeholders.

Governance and Ethical Practices

Good governance is fundamental to organizational control and design. It involves implementing transparent, accountable, and ethical practices that enhance stakeholder trust and compliance with regulations. ESG considerations have led companies to adopt more decentralized and transparent governance structures, ensuring that decision-making processes are ethical and inclusive.

A notable trend is the adoption of matrix and hybrid organizational structures, which combine functional, product, and geographic divisions. These structures allow for better oversight and coordination across different regions and business units, ensuring that governance standards are maintained globally. Companies like Royal Dutch Shell and Dow Chemical have successfully implemented matrix structures to enhance their governance and control mechanisms.

ESG in Decision-Making and Control Mechanisms

Environmental Impact on Decision-Making

Environmental considerations significantly impact decision-making processes in international organizations. Companies are integrating environmental criteria into their strategic planning and operational decisions. This includes assessing the environmental impact of their activities, investing in green technologies, and setting ambitious sustainability targets.

For instance, companies are using diagnostic control systems to monitor their environmental performance. These systems use quantitative data to track emissions, resource consumption, and waste generation. By analyzing this data, companies can identify areas for improvement and make informed decisions to enhance their environmental sustainability.

Social Factors and Control Systems

Social factors, such as labor practices, human rights, and community engagement, are critical in shaping control systems within international organizations. Companies are adopting interactive control systems that involve regular communication and feedback between top management and employees. These systems ensure that social issues are addressed promptly and effectively.

For example, companies implement belief systems that communicate the importance of social responsibility and ethical conduct. By embedding these values into the corporate culture, companies can foster a more inclusive and responsible work environment. Additionally, boundary systems set clear guidelines on acceptable behaviors, ensuring that employees adhere to ethical standards.

Governance and Organizational Control

Good governance is essential for maintaining effective control mechanisms in international organizations. Companies are adopting more robust control systems to ensure compliance with ESG standards and enhance transparency and accountability. One practical approach uses transnational network structures, which link various subsidiaries and business units through a network arrangement. This structure facilitates better coordination and control, allowing companies to implement governance practices consistently across different regions. For instance, companies like Nike and Dell have adopted virtual enterprises and transnational network structures to enhance their governance and control mechanisms.

ESG and Cultural Integration

Environmental sustainability plays a crucial role in cultural integration. Companies must respect local environmental regulations and engage with communities to promote sustainable practices. This involves collaborating with local stakeholders, investing in community development projects, and reducing the environmental impact of their operations.

For instance, mining companies that adopt sustainable practices can gain the support of local communities and reduce conflicts. By implementing robust environmental management systems and engaging with stakeholders, these companies can build trust and ensure the long-term success of their operations.

Social responsibility is essential for navigating diverse cultural landscapes. Companies must understand and respect local customs, traditions, and values while ensuring ethical labor practices and community engagement. This requires adapting their organizational structures and control mechanisms to align with local cultural norms. For instance, multinational corporations often adopt regional or area division structures more responsive to local market conditions and cultural preferences. By empowering local managers and teams, companies can ensure their operations are culturally sensitive and socially responsible.

Strong governance and ethical practices are crucial for building trust and credibility in international markets. Companies must adapt their governance structures to meet local regulatory requirements and cultural expectations. This involves implementing transparent and accountable control systems that ensure ethical conduct and compliance with regulations. For example, companies operating in regions with different governance standards may adopt hybrid structures that combine global and local governance practices. This approach ensures that companies maintain high governance standards while respecting local customs and regulations.

Discussion Questions

1. **How does the choice of organizational structure impact multinational corporations' ability to implement effective global strategies and control their operations internationally?**

2. **What is the primary challenge associated with a flat organizational structure in a multinational corporation?**
   A) Too much centralization of decision making
   B) High degree of bureaucracy and formalization
   C) Difficulty in scaling operations internationally
   D) Lack of clear accountability

3. **Which organizational structure is characterized by product division and geographic region reporting lines?**
   A) Functional structure
   B) Divisional structure
   C) Matrix structure
   D) Hybrid structure

4. **In a hybrid organizational structure, conflicts between different departments are more likely due to overlapping authorities. True or False?**

5. **A wholly owned subsidiary (WOS) is less controlled by the parent company than a joint venture. True or False?**

Recommended Readings

Daugaard, D., & Ding, A. (2022). Global drivers for ESG performance: The body of knowledge. *Sustainability*, 14(4), 2322.

Harasheh, M., & Provasi, R. (2023). A need for assurance: Do internal control systems integrate environmental, social, and governance factors? *Corporate Social Responsibility and Environmental Management*, 30(1), 384–401.

Khoruzhy, L. I., Katkov, Y. N., Romanova, A. A., Katkova, E. A., & Dzhikiya, M. K. (2022). Adaptive management reporting system in inter-organizational relations of agricultural enterprises according to ESG principles. *Journal of Infrastructure, Policy and Development*, 6(2), 1649.

Pinheiro, A. B., dos Santos, J. I. A. S., Cherobim, A. P. M. S., & Segatto, A. P. (2024). What drives environmental, social and governance (ESG) performance? The role of institutional quality. *Management of Environmental Quality: An International Journal*, 35(2), 427–444.

Szóka, K. (2022). The importance of Green Controlling–The connection of the Sustainability Balanced Scorecard and the ESG. In 38th EBES Conference-Warsaw: Proceedings (Vol. 1, pp. 866–880).

Xia, J. (2022). A systematic review: How does organisational learning enable ESG performance (from 2001 to 2021)? *Sustainability*, 14(24), 16962.

Yeh, T. T., Xiao, Y., & Daniel, S. J. (2024). Stakeholder influences on management control systems for ESG governance and reporting in the global automotive industry. *Journal of Corporate Accounting & Finance*, 35(2), 103–120.

Zhang, Y., Zhang, C., Zhang, S., Yang, Y., & Lan, K. (2024). Insight into the risk-resistant function of ESG performance: An organizational management perspective. *Chinese Management Studies*, 18(3), 818–846.

Chapter 7
Global Leadership Issues and Practices

Learning Objectives

- Examine the importance of developing a company's global mindset
- Explain what distinguishes the practice of global leadership from domestic leadership
- Determine the competencies required for effective global leadership
- Discern the approach for selecting and developing influential global leaders
- Define international team leadership skills
- Recognize some of the challenges of leading global change

Overview

As illustrated in Figure 7.1, leadership theory has been a study and research topic for many years. What works for one company in one sector may not work for another, but there are some universal characteristics that all influential leaders demonstrate. Leadership qualities prevalent 100 years ago are no longer relevant today, and leadership techniques have changed over time. In earlier days, autocratic leaders who controlled a strict hierarchy while leading from the top were more prevalent, whereas current leaders demonstrated a more empowering and empathetic approach.

Leadership can form the collective culture and influence the organizational climate, creating the moral and ethical norms that guide behavior from the top down. Great global leaders have been a constant point of interest and study throughout human history. Leadership is an amorphous idea that intrigues CEOs, military members, and business professionals alike, all in the pursuit of an answer to a simple question: what does effective leadership look like? Modern leadership theory attempts to answer this question universally and divest from the traditional "heroic" view of leadership. The idea of leadership that devolves all aspects down to the individual is not practical within the global business setting. This section delves into some of the most popularized theories, analyzes their merits, and brings up considerations international firms must have when installing, improving, and evaluating leadership.

Global leadership can be broken down into relationship versus task complexities. As illustrated in Figure 7.2, four distinct dimensions exist to describe and categorize each leadership type's roles and behaviors, including authenticity, resilience, humility, and curiosity. For instance, a senior executive of a global multi-unit firm would be considered an integrative leader with high relationship-task complexity. In contrast, an export director in an enterprise that operates internationally through licensing would be

https://doi.org/10.1515/9783111510286-007

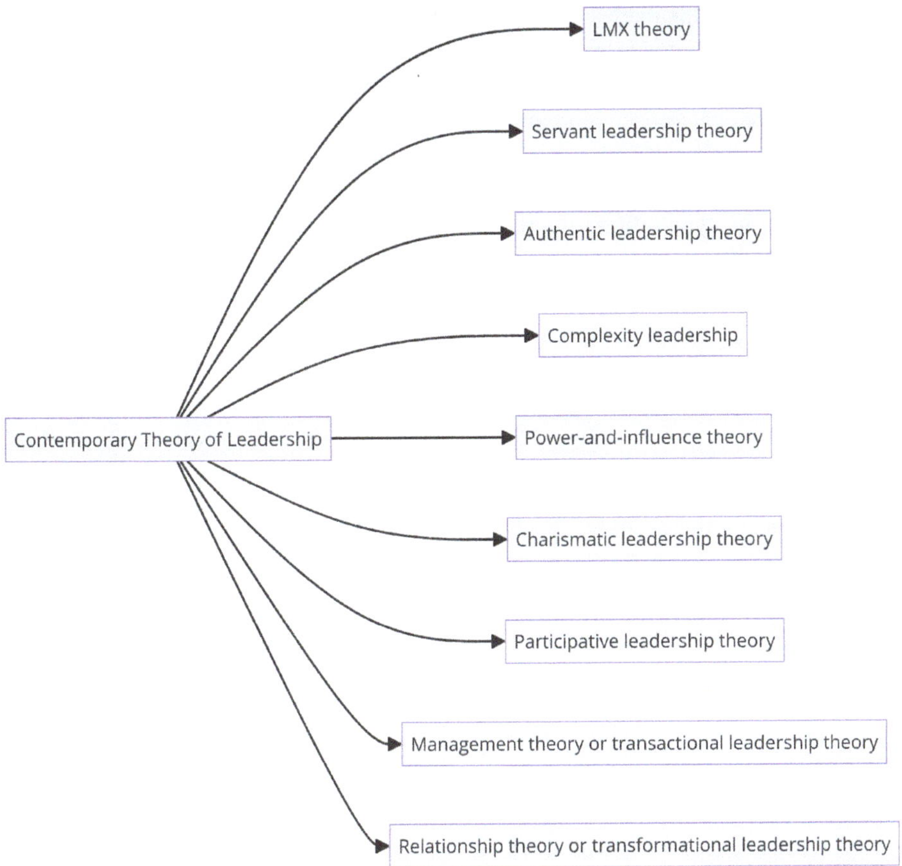

Figure 7.1: Contemporary theories of leadership.

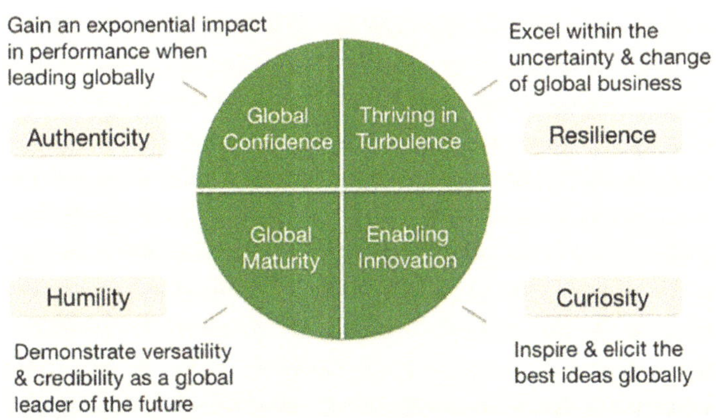

Figure 7.2: One of the main global leadership frameworks.

viewed as an incremental leader with lower relationship-task complexity. While these frameworks can categorize leadership types, there are fundamental elements, including business units, competitors, customers, regulatory regimes, languages, and religions, that internal assignees encounter and need to deal with in their environment. In other words, so many different influences contribute toward impacting leadership.

Global leaders up and down the hierarchy face the same challenge: how to adapt their leadership style to fit local circumstances to achieve corporate objectives. Much of what we think we know about leadership is flawed because it is mainly based on the view of Western beliefs and values that don't necessarily apply to organizations in other cultures.

Nonetheless, when considering global leadership, there are three approaches:

- **Contingency** – This is the belief that there is not one right way to be a leader. For instance, a successful leader in New York is not necessarily a successful leader in Japan or France.
- **Normative** – The normative approach suggests that leaders with certain traits like curiosity and humility will succeed.
- **Universal** – The universal approach assumes that leadership traits are constant across all cultures.

Global leadership is still underdeveloped and ill-defined.

Global Leadership Issues and Practice

There are many different styles of leadership. Two styles that have been at the forefront recently are transformational and transactional. Each style has its merits, and each has a place and time in which it could and should be implemented. When properly implemented, these leadership styles can be catalysts in developing a global mindset, which can positively impact organizational commitment.

Two Leading Leadership Theories

As Mendenhall et al. (2012) have already argued, when referring to global leadership, there are as many definitions of leadership as there are people who attempt to define the concept. It has been proven repeatedly, and many of these definitions have evolved into leadership theories. In recent years, two approaches have been at the forefront of global leadership research: transformational and transactional leadership.

Transformational Leadership

Transformational leadership, as illustrated in Figure 7.3, has been a topic of much research as of late. It is defined in many ways, but the consensus is that it is a style that looks to transform employees in ways that inspire them to think of "we" rather than the "I" or the organization rather than self-serving interests. Such a goal is typically achieved by encouraging a vision with morale-boosting values that portray an image of what a company can be. Working as a cohesive unit is the way of achieving this organizational goal. There are five dimensions of transformational leadership:

1. **Vision – Transformational leadership is based on the idea that a leader can illustrate to their employees what it is based on organizational values and an** idyllic future.
2. **Inspiration** – Inspirational communication can appeal to the employees' emotions, resulting in additional motivation.
3. **Support** – A supportive leader shows concern for the individual employees and tends to their specific needs. Showing concern for the welfare of their employees can create a supportive and morale-boosting environment.
4. **Stimulation** – A leader who can intellectually stimulate their employees may be able to achieve new levels of success by inspiring the employees to think in new and creative ways. Doing this will create innovative solutions to problems facing the company and team.
5. **Personal Recognition** – Finally, recognizing the individual achievements of employees can help show their value to the company and inspire new levels of motivation. Recognition is based more on praise and acknowledgment.

Figure 7.3: Transformational leadership model.

Transactional Leadership

Transactional leadership, as opposed to transformational leadership, is based on a system of interactions, exchanges, and rewards. There are three categories of rewards:

- **Contingent rewards** – This style instills a reward-based performance system in which employees are rewarded for a job well done. Think of it as a Pavlovian style of leadership in which employees can be conditioned to achieve their goals for such rewards.
- **Management-by-exception passive** – refers to a method by which corrective action is taken when the employee's performance is not at the level needed and expected by the leader. An example would be a salesperson failing to meet a quarterly quota and being reprimanded with a written warning. To take an extreme example, it could potentially lead to termination if a continuous failure to perform.
- **Management-by-exception active** – An active method of management-by-exception is when the leader actively monitors their employees closely and steps in to mitigate any issues as they see them develop rather than waiting for a problem to occur. Using the previous scenario from the passive management-by-exception, however, in an active method, the leader would step in before the warning or termination. While monitoring the employee's performance and observing a trend that would fail to meet a goal, the leader would provide coaching and an opportunity for the employee to correct their course.

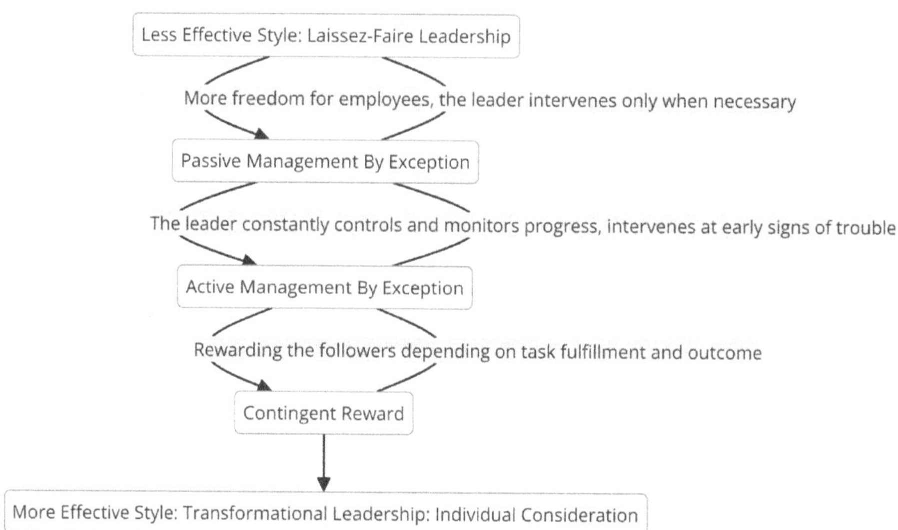

Figure 7.4: Transactional leadership model. (SOURCE: leadershipahoy.com).

Organizational Commitment

One critical mission of leadership development is to gain organizational commitment through transformational or transactional leadership or one of the several other leadership styles. The development of a corporate commitment can be defined through three crucial factors:

- A belief and acceptance of corporate values
- The willingness to work hard for the organization and
- An aspiration to remain a part of the organization

In other words, leaders want to develop their employees' commitment to the organization by motivating them to remain and work to the best of their abilities. Organizational commitment can be viewed as a dimensional construct in three different components, as depicted in Figure 7.5:

- **Affective commitment** – can be viewed as an emotional attachment to the organization. An emotional tie to an organization provides a deepened commitment in ways the following two commitments cannot.
- **Normative commitment** – a feeling of obligation to remain with an organization instead of an affective commitment that stays with the organization due to an emotional connection.
- **Continuance commitment** – can be compared to the affective commitment as well. This type of commitment is viewed through the lens of cost. Those with a continuance commitment may consider leaving an organization too costly. The cost could be monetary, time value, or emotional/mental strain.

Figure 7.5: Types of organizational commitment.

Implementation of Leadership Styles and the Impact on Organizational Commitment

A transactional leadership method can negatively affect value-based leadership and follower outcomes. Conversely, transformational leadership has a more substantial impact on follower outcomes. Affective organizational commitment is less likely to be impacted by economic or societal forces. The most likely effect on affective organizational commitment is the leadership style. However, with all of the positive studies on transformational leadership, there are some drawbacks and negative impacts. Transformational leadership can result in unethical behavior from employees. It can influence employees to have blind obedience and group thinking. It can also result in pro-organizational yet unethical behavior due to an employee's enhanced identification or affective organizational commitment to the company. Such behavior can ultimately lead to adverse outcomes for the company, such as damaged reputation, customer distrust, and potential loss of business. Leaders with a transactional style may not inspire such a solid affective organizational commitment, which could be seen as positive since employees may be less likely to act unethically for the greater good.

As individuals, we are inspired in different ways and by various factors. Other leadership styles may need to be considered based on the company's personnel, cultural traits, and organizational structure. It is also essential to consider leadership styles within the cultural context in which the company is inserted. Distinct cultures perceive leadership styles in different frames. For instance, power distance and hierarchical differences under a transformational leadership style, which encourages employee feedback and inclusion in decision making, can often be viewed as a sign of weakness. In cultures with higher power distance, employees may need firm direction and look to the leaders to make the decisions. If a leader asks for the employee's feedback on making a decision, this could impact the employee's trust in the leader. As such, cultures with a higher power distance would benefit more from a transactional style of leadership, which would result in more organizational commitment.

Various leadership styles are needed for different individuals and other cultures. The need to understand these differences increases in an organization that is or wants to be multinational. Global leaders operate in a world of heightened, nonstop ambiguity to a greater degree than domestic leaders. One aspect of ambiguity is how to lead individuals and cultures. Selecting a leadership style is a challenging task that must be made cautiously based on the organization's and its employees' needs. Choosing a style of leadership is not a one-size-fits-all. Instead, leaders may need to take aspects of transformation, transactional, and other theories to lead their employees effectively.

Developing a Leader's Global Mindset

Leadership, defined broadly, is the use of social influence that maximizes the efforts of others toward the achievement of a common goal, which can be challenging to quantify. For instance, the military provides a controlled environment for analyzing leadership. Military operations have specific objectives of a binary nature, mission accomplishment or mission failure, and the leader's job is clearly defined: to accomplish the mission while minimizing cost. These objectives are specific and have a well-documented chain of events that isolate the root causes of problems and determine if they stem from poor leadership decisions or lackluster execution. Leadership within international enterprises does not share the luxury of such clarity; therefore, a different approach must be considered.

Nowadays, however, business success relies on the cognition, understanding, and capacity to steer through various traditions and cultural dissimilarities, global economic and political climates, international workforce conditions and expectations, rules and regulations, domestic and international consumers, and global competition– a global mindset. But what does a global mindset mean? As illustrated in Figure 7.6, the following are some definitions:

- A set of characteristics and competencies that support existing and prospective global leaders in working more effectively with people, groups, and international organizations like themselves.
- It is the capacity to comprehend the similitudes and dissimilarities among cultures and their rationales.
- The proficiency to bypass the simplification of presuming that all cultures are identical and concurrently not be paralyzed by the complexity of the dissimilarities.
- Being satisfied with being uncomfortable in awkward environments.

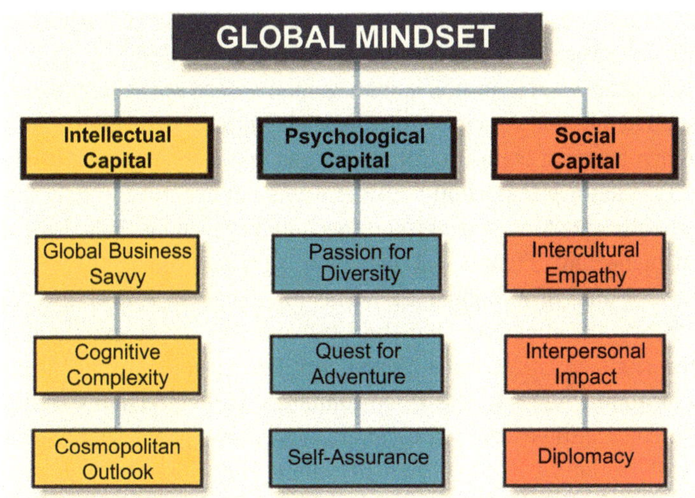

Figure 7.6: Characteristics of developing a global mindset.

Leadership has traditionally been viewed through the so-called *heroic leadership*. Heroic leadership constrains its scope on the specific qualities and actions of the individual leader and how these attributes and qualities affect success. This determinist approach is not without fruit but alone is inadequate in the context of business. It does not account for the internal and external forces that come to bear on a CEO or leadership team. In business, specific leader actions are much less critical than the interdependent forces that inform and determine how much success leaders will have. Analyzing organizational effectiveness through CEO and board decisions illuminates how the factors interact. These factors can be divided broadly into two categories: power and discretion.

Power is essentially the origin and amount of persuasiveness a leader has. It can be derived from insider knowledge, subject-matter expertise, shared ownership, and position. Discretion is the ability of a leader to use that power to create and pursue changes within the organization and the market. There is no formula for a CEO's specific types of power that relate to organizational success. However, there is a strong trend between specific "power bundles" and the amount of discretion a CEO has that can predict organizational effectiveness. In businesses in more volatile markets where innovation and responsiveness are essential, consolidation in a singular leader with higher power and discretion to make more sweeping decisions has a more significant impact on the success or failure of an enterprise. Inversely, leaders with limited power and discretion can influence an enterprise in a well-established market where movement within the market is relatively stagnant. Leadership in these firms is more effective by being distributed rather than monolithic. Essentially, how well an enterprise understands its internal organizational structure and the market it exists in will dictate how effective its leadership and organization are. Therefore, it is far more critical for an enterprise to understand the nature and strength of factors acting to address leadership.

While leadership is concentrated in upper management, there are seldom examples where it is consolidated in one person. Often, the leadership burden within enterprises is shared with management teams, referred to as the upper management teams (UMT). Power and discretion are important considerations but are not the only factors. Personality traits also must be considered, especially concerning UMT. That is because, by numbers, management teams will have more significant interpersonal interaction with employees than any singular CEO. This phenomenon is described as the upper echelon theory and theorizes that the UMT and executives' personality traits impact an enterprise's organizational effectiveness. Conscientiousness is highly correlated with organizational effectiveness when combined with emotional stability. UMTs who show high conscientiousness can be effective as they tend to be more determined and aware of the implications of their decisions. The UMT can create and disseminate a clear and unified vision for the rest of the organization to follow. Essentially, a leadership team is only as effective as its ability to communicate its vision and receive feedback from the subordinates within the company. It is typical within large MNCs because top-down communication takes longer as they get larger. An enterprise leveraging a UMT that can concisely and efficiently communicate will be successful. It ties directly into the opening points that leadership within an enterprise must stem from an intimate understanding of the business to ensure that leadership is implemented correctly. Communications become more critical as the business grows and spreads into international markets. More factors will inevitably arise that need to be considered by the management team.

In international joint ventures (IJV), several factors tend to create roadblocks to such ventures, including but not limited to branches of culture and history that are not shared between the enterprises. For instance, Chinese work tempo and education are very different from those of Western nations and, therefore, put a higher premium on age and experience than formal training. The factors are exacerbated by the difference in loyalties between the joint venture and the individual parent companies within the joint venture, which creates stress on both enterprises and splits loyalties between the two trying to do business between the parent firms and the IJV management team. To combat this, when doing business outside of one's home country, an enterprise should put a premium on having a diverse management team to encourage a diversity of views so that the sum parts of the team will make up for any deficiencies within one member, including the team leader. Because it is implausible that one individual alone can understand all the cultural nuances and practices of another, it is essential from the start of negotiations to go in with a team mindset instead of the individual. In this same vein, enterprises should avoid putting all the decision-making power into one person when dealing with a joint venture and encourage cooperation and team problem-solving.

Finally, observing the role of organizations and business leaders in a globalizing world is essential. As the world increasingly integrates, one business or organization's actions have far-reaching consequences. Since the financial crisis of 2008, the role of an organizational leader has changed from the traditional view of profit maximization to a macro-level view that considers stakeholders' concerns. In this context, stakeholders differ from shareholders in that stakeholders are not individually invested in the company but are affected by the company's actions. This effect could range from individual towns dealing with industrial pollution to countries dealing with the economic fall-out of foreign direct investment (FDI). Leaders in a global business should seek to improve on both the macro and micro levels, ensuring that all stakeholder considerations are addressed and that individual employees within the company operate ethically. The leader should ensure these values are taught within the organization and to the extent possible effects on the employees.

Ethical leadership has become a modern-day struggle businesses face. Ethical leadership differs dramatically from traditional leadership, where instead of only being concerned about the company's well-being, leaders and leadership teams need to be aware of the actions being taken by employees and the perceptions surrounding those actions. Ethical leadership has been shown to increase buy-in from employees down the ladder and increase organizational effectiveness. It also has the added benefit of making regulations more accessible and providing regulations on itself, which, in theory, increases public trust and profits in a business.

There is no comprehensive leadership theory. However, the nature of leadership points in the same direction: as business globalizes, leadership must adjust from a traditional view or "heroic" theory to a top-down organizational structure that reflects the change of concerns in a globalizing market. There is no one-size-fits-all approach to leadership, and information will inform the best strategy for an enterprise. The driving factor behind making appropriate leadership decisions is information. An enterprise requires intimate knowledge of itself and the international market in which it exists to understand what leadership is best and whether preserving the status quo or responsiveness is desirable. This berth of information only increases depending on the forces acting on the firm, whether the presence of a foreign partner whose culture must be considered or operations in foreign nations with different regulatory and ethical values. These differences in values need to be considered to maximize the effectiveness of businesses abroad. Understanding that information is widely available is also essential, so ethics concerns are even more critical. It can affect the organizations if they decide to operate non-ethically and subsequently lose business. Businesses should begin with their leadership and ensure that ethical practices are followed, allowing that to permeate throughout the rest of the organization.

Leadership is not consolidated top-down to the actions of one single individual. It is the amalgamation of several interdependent and connected forces within an enterprise. It concerns itself not only with the actions of a few at the top but also with how those actions affect and filter down through the rest of the organization. Picking the proper form of ethical leadership for the correct organization will increase overall organizational effectiveness.

Some Challenges in Developing a Global Mindset

There are several challenges when leading global teams and international organizations and developing a global mindset. A few of them are listed in Figure 7.7. Global leaders must manage people across barriers of distance and cultural differences, working through technology, across time zones, and in a highly complex matrix and international organization structures. Five significant barriers to global leadership exist that need to be overcome:

- **Distance:** Human beings have evolved from operating face-to-face, especially with the sweeping digital business transformations that continue to develop worldwide. The lack of communication bandwidth, the ability to monitor non-verbal messages and having substantial face-to-face time together have significant implications for trust, collaboration, and communication. Many of our team's individual contributors and employees may no longer be face-to-face with colleagues they work with, which is probably the most intractable barrier. There is a need to develop the necessary skill set to remain in contact with international subsidiaries and virtual teams through digital communication technologies and to create new collaborative ways to work without the same depth of relationships so common in the past.
- **Culture:** When enterprises internationalize and staff is moved abroad, culture is usually the first barrier they notice, as its differences can be frustrating and generate several misunderstandings. The ability to work across a multicultural environment is vital for global leaders. The ability to interact with other cultures alone is not enough. Leaders must also understand their culture's impact on other distinct

ones and how it may impact work and communication. Thus, a good knowledge of culture in target markets should infuse everything a global leader does. When leading global teams, leaders need to be able to present to an international audience, negotiate with people who have different negotiating styles, and communicate with people who get their points across in different ways. A true global leader should be flexible in leading people from other cultures and have a level of authenticity that allows them to be credible globally. Because cultural traits are so explicit, global leaders often develop the capability to deal with the most apparent differences quite quickly. Working across cultures has been customary for decades in many MNCs, and they have developed the skills to overcome such barriers.

- **Technology**: It may be surprising to consider technology a barrier, as it is often perceived as a bridge. However, technologies can be a barrier if they are absent or a critical enabler if carefully chosen when leading internationally. It would be hard to imagine leading an international team without communication technologies. However, communicating through technology can cause misunderstandings. Although technology does not force us to communicate ineffectively, it can make it easy for leaders and staff to miscommunicate. An obvious example is the mass of poor-quality emails people routinely receive. Focusing on technology can also cause leaders to underestimate the need for participation and involvement. If leaders run a boring staff meeting, they likely will not realize if participants were engaged or distracted by other things. With the high volume of emails, we receive daily, much of it just clutter or spam, not to mention instant messaging systems and other tools, a global leader must learn to control communication technologies. Otherwise, they may start to manage them.
- **Complexity:** Large MNCs are very complex places, and decisions have implications beyond the immediately obvious, in particular, complex organizational structures such as a matrix or when the need to engage virtual networks is required to get things done. Such complexities demand global leaders to develop new skills of influence without authority, manage competing priorities, and create diverse networks and alliances. It can be frustrating for leaders who have been used to getting things done through position or hierarchical power.
- **Time zones:** Time zone differences are a permanent feature of global working; they will not disappear. Global leaders need to organize their work schedules and habits to reflect them. The inability to master working schedules across global time zones may lead to delays, confusion, dysfunction, and frustration. Learning such necessary skills is paramount for global leaders to overcome and turn these barriers into advantages. International teams bring diverse perspectives and enable leaders to take advantage of global scale and local skills. For instance, leaders can use time zones to generate 24-hour working schedules on critical issues and problems and learn from worldwide to improve our products and processes.

Figure 7.7: Challenges in developing a global mindset.

Leading with Cultural Intelligence

In his book, *The World is Flat*, Thomas Friedman depicts forces that flatten the world and converge many systems into one. These forces include spreading information technology (IT), online collaborative communities of practice, and outsourcing, including offshoring and outsourcing. These elements are transforming our global businesses and social and political environments and redefining how international businesses and consumers interact with each other. Globalization has changed lifestyles worldwide, from Argentina to Iceland, Nepal to South Africa, and around the globe. Traveling worldwide is no longer necessary to experience national cultural shifts; they come to us, regardless of where we are.

In an age of global social transformation, cultural intelligence (CI), as depicted in Figure 7.8, has become a topic of urgency for international organizational leaders. Environmental, political, and technological factors are fast pivoting the manners in which we function and interrelate with each other. Cultural transformations are occurring faster than international organizations are prepared for and capable of managing, thus developing cognitive and emotional havoc in managing and leading across the globe through cultural shifts. In many cases, the result is a tighter hold on the invisible aspects of culture and a stronger emphasis on *the 'right' way to do the work.*

International enterprise managers increasingly need tools and information to assist them in carrying through their intercultural and cross-cultural interactions when leading abroad and developing a global mindset. Many methodologies and tools exist to assist international leaders; a cultural intelligence framework can improve the management and leadership of cultural interactions. But no matter what methods or tools are used, the leader's personality, who they are, and how they use such tools or techniques are the most significant parts of the equation.

The responsibilities of a global leader have a certain level that is very different from the complexities faced by domestic and or regional leaders. The leap from being a successful upper manager in a domestic setting to a global leader is enormous. To

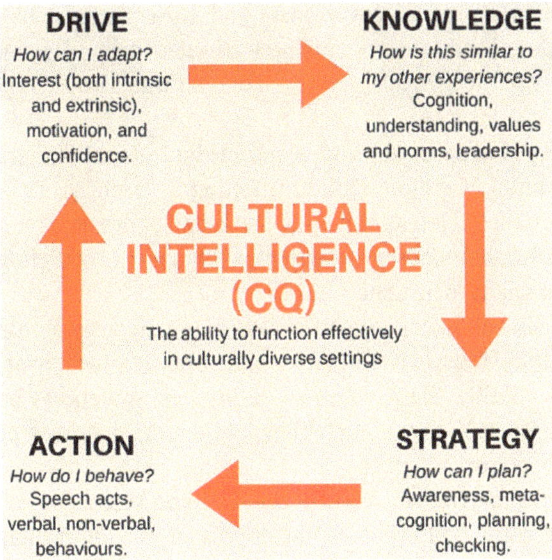

Figure 7.8: The four circular stages of developing cultural intelligence.

be an effective global leader and be able to lead multicultural teams across multiple international locations with cultural intelligence, leaders must be able to operate amid myriad challenges. Previously successful strategies and preferred leadership methods might not transition smoothly into a globalized setting as the rules of engagement change. What was generally understood by one division, group, or culture may not be easily understood or relevant to another international market. In addition, leading remote and virtual divisions and teams can be highly challenging, as it creates multiple complexities.

Common Cultural Intelligence Challenges Faced by Global Leaders

The following are the six most common cultural intelligence challenges global leaders frequently face when working in international business environments:

1. **Adapting organization behavior.** Cultural assumptions and behaviors also play a role in a leader's identity. Global leaders must be highly aware of the potential influence of culture on their thinking process, work ethics, and operations. Such leaders cannot limit their preferences and activities to reflect only their culture or social identity group. Leaders must be skilled at accurately reading people and situations and adapting behaviors according to the local culture and customs.
2. **Communicating across barriers.** Communication can be challenging in any setting, especially a global one, due to the high level of complexity and the need to communicate more effectively in virtual spaces since most of the collaboration will be with virtual team members and staff placed overseas, often in different

time zones, and dealing with technological, government and infrastructure challenges. Influential global leaders need to overcome these barriers, primarily cultural and language, to make sure their virtual presence communicates effectively and efficiently.
3. **Creating and implementing shared goals and work ethics.** Global leaders must develop ways to find common ground while respecting differences. They must instill trust in their international teams and understand and appreciate multicultural perspectives while simultaneously developing alignment surrounding the mission and the work that needs to be done.
4. **Handling culture conflicts.** Global leaders often operate simultaneously across multiple geographic regions and cultural groups, facing situations in which priorities and value systems often conflict. These cultural conflicts can sometimes be glaring, with subtle differences, and easy to miss. Thus, developing a culture of respect can help manage these cultural conflicts.
5. **Handling external forces.** Business abroad requires leaders to be abreast of foreign governmental, legal, historical, and economic factors that may impact their business activity in any target market. These external forces can impact MNEs' operations. Global leaders must understand when they can exert influence on these challenges and accept that some of these factors may be outside their control. But to be effective in foreign and unfamiliar environments, leaders must think and act innovatively and maintain sensitivity to cultural differences.
6. **Managing global versus local tensions.** A significant challenge for global leaders is understanding and managing the tensions between global headquarters and regional or local offices. When do local organizations' needs, customs, regulations, practices, or markets drive decisions, and how do organization-level expectations get infused locally?

One of the most challenging aspects of global leadership is to manage tensions between the need to be globally consistent while considering local differentiation. Global and regional leaders must develop strategies to balance the uncertainty inherent in their positions. Global leaders can do this in three ways.

1. **Leaders should think and act *globally*** – *A global mindset is required, especially when consistency globally* is crucial. For instance, when the enterprise is crafting universal business policies and procedures, seeking economies, or efficiencies, of scale, and integrating decision-making processes across international boundaries.
2. **Leaders should think and act *locally*** – *Global enterprises must attempt to meet local demands and maximize their regional level of adaptation. For instance, the HR function could take a more local approach to establishing healthcare benefits and policies. Each country could be determined and managed at the hosting country level to include staff's* cultural variables and demands.
3. **Leaders should think and act *glocally*** – It means attempting to operate locally and globally simultaneously since an *either/or* approach to such decision making

is often faulty. Frequently, both global *and* local viewpoints must be considered simultaneously. For instance, HR might decide on a "glocal" approach to devise the enterprise's hiring strategy and processes, then integrate global and local efforts by recruiting, selecting, and utilizing the best talent.

Optimum balance results from knowing when to act globally, or locally, or when a new, yet-to-be-invented "glocal" approach is required. By considering these approaches, international leaders can more easily understand the implications for worldwide leadership, determine when to let go of an issue or decide that work must be done to deal with the complexities of developing a "glocal" approach.

To improve their CI, global leaders should try to:

- **Bond over similarities** – Many global leaders think the most helpful way to tackle diversity in their organizations and develop a global mindset is by instantly highlighting everyone's differences. Taking the opposite approach, focusing on what teams across the globe have in common versus what makes them different, is the right approach. Developing associations and recognizing similarities will lead to attitudes and behaviors that capitalize on human distinctions for international organizational success. When staff from multiple cultures bond over similarities, they will likely accept each other's differences, which enables CI to thrive.
- **Challenge stereotypes** – Stereotypes should be dealt with as soon as they arise. It is crucial to challenge stereotypes and avoid allowing them to seize every business association. Question attitudes and decisions that involve cultural diversity, equity, and inclusion.
- **Diversify hiring methods** – To develop a global mindset with a staff ready to foster cultural intelligence, the hiring process must include talent from various criteria. The hiring practice must be diverse.
- **Improve communication skills** – How the staff communicates with each other directly affects how they feel about the global organization. Some employees feel uncomfortable being singled out for distinction or praise in front of the entire team, which is typical in the U.S. In other cultures, workers do not trust communication from their upper managers or leaders. They would prefer to receive information from their immediate boss or supervisor. To improve CI and a global mindset, leaders must enhance their communication skills and understand that distinct cultures communicate and prefer to be addressed and receive information differently. A slight change of attitude such as these may appear trivial but concentrating on appealing to the complexities of individual cultures can take global leaders far.

Leading with Emotional Intelligence

Emotional intelligence (EQ) in global leadership comprises empathy, social skills, self-awareness, self-regulation, and motivation, as depicted in Figure 7.9. These are all teachable soft skills. With the rise of artificial intelligence (AI) in HR, it has become more critical for global leaders to display EQ. In the context of international business and HR, EQ is the ability to recognize and manage emotions and the feelings of other people in the workplace across the globe, which must consider the cultural variances from one country to another in which the enterprise operates.

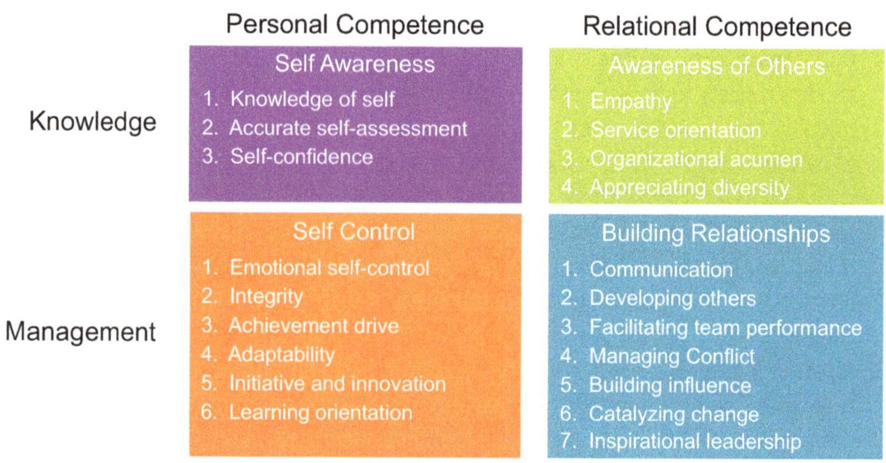

Figure 7.9: Qualities of an emotionally intelligent global leader. (SOURCE: adapted from Britt Andretta, 2020).

Emotional intelligence is critical to global leaders and managers. These professionals must be able to address issues in the organization when conflicts due to diversity factors (e.g., in culture, language, religion, political views, etc.) erupt or negative sentiments steam below the surface, forming a toxic working environment. A global leader with high EQ can help promote a workplace culture that does not become unhealthy. Global leaders with high EQ should be able to strive and praise team equilibrium and diversity, inspire and influence the staff across borders, make decisions utilizing critical thinking, and positively impact the international business strategy.

According to Daniel Goleman, an American psychologist, author, and science journalist, as illustrated in Figure 7.10, EQ consists of five traits:

- **Self-awareness:** Self-aware global leaders should know how they feel. They should be able to recognize how their emotions impact those around them. Their self-awareness should not just be restricted to emotions. They acknowledge their ego and are aware of both their strengths and weaknesses. They aim to ensure their ego and personal attributes function for the benefit of the staff and the international organization. Hence, such leaders should not react to circumstances instantly. They should ensure their reactions are calculated and fitting, not flawed by emotional responses in the heat of the moment.

- **Self-regulation**: Leaders should be able to keep control of their emotions. They should not react or lash out and do not compromise their organization's ethics. When leaders are calm, people around them are reassured and encouraged to take positive action. They hold themselves accountable for their actions. When they hold themselves responsible and behave accordingly, they uphold the organization's code of ethics and lead their staff by example. When leaders invariably respond calmly to pressure, it creates a broad sense of enhanced well-being in the organization. Emotional literacy, the ability to express emotions and feelings using speech and other forms of communication, is crucial to this process and the mental well-being at the workplace, particularly in international business settings.
- **Motivation**: Motivation stems partly from understanding WHAT leaders want to do and WHY they want to do it. Understanding the *why* often requires a certain degree of self-reflection, which is where high EQ can assist. Motivated global leaders have high professional standards and invariably work towards their goals. Leaders with high EQ also comprehend what motivates their staff and colleagues, incentivizing them to find their reasons for working to the best of their ability. To strengthen this trait, leaders should view optimism as an effective response to stress. Optimism does not just mean thinking joyful thoughts, though, but being aware of the benefits of circumstances and utilizing that constructive optimism to support their dedication to succeed.
- **Empathy:** When global leaders have empathy, they can place themselves in anyone's shoes. They can challenge stereotypes and unjust premises, provide critical feedback wisely, and be a great listener when their team requires somebody to guide them through challenging situations. Such ability can help them develop their staff members domestically and abroad. An empathetic global leader creates a positive international work environment supported by team loyalty and mutual respect.
- **Social skills:** Leaders are typically identified as having excellent social skills or the art of making an emotional connection through communication. Global leaders with excellent social skills can communicate a piece of bad news and commemorate good news in ways that cause people to feel endless actionable possibilities for improvement exist. Leaders with high communication talents are also proficient at conflict resolution and managing change diplomatically. When decisions impact individuals' lives, leaders with high EQ demonstrate respect for them, including their fears and hopes.

Regarding global leadership, EQ is not a soft skills option, as it can be the key to global leaders' professional success. Once leaders understand workplace emotions, including their own, they can lead teams to increased mindfulness and productivity across the organization.

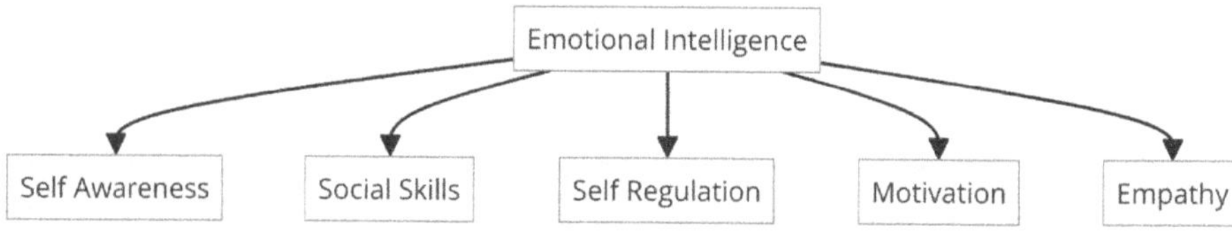

Figure 7.10: Emotional intelligence's five traits. (SOURCE: Adapted from Goleman, 2021).

Leading Global Teams

Leadership theories explain why and how some individuals become leaders. This theory concentrates on the behaviors and talents that individuals must imbibe to increase their leadership skills. Leadership promotes a higher level of performance in a team. Leaders are good at articulating a vision, which is a starting point for creating change in organizations. The vision is a source of goals that motivate effort toward the future. A strong leader with a great vision encourages employees for the long term. Leaders cannot just ask the employees to be more proactive and expect them to follow suit. Simply proclaiming "adapt well to change" to a job description is unlikely to promote greater adaptivity. The ability of a leader to connect with the team and establish a trusting and supportive relationship between them is crucial. Leaders should create a unique relationship with each of their followers, and that leader-employee relationship is based on the social exchanges between parties.

Interpersonal relationships are more important than a leader's behavior. Leaders need to train themselves as a coach. Coaching the team encourages better individual performance. For instance, managerial coaching is positively connected to job satisfaction which several studies in turn link to better performance at work. Good quality leadership predicts good performance in organizations. Research indicates that a leader's active coaching behavior facilitates employees to reach their goals and perform well at work. Leaders are usually experts in their domain, with specfic knowledge and skills acquired through experience and practice. At the individual leader level, allocating time to update their skills and perform challenging tasks, as well as developing a sense of humility and being aware of their limitations, will help experts be more flexible and, thus, more effective at work. Empathizing with others' experiences and rediscovering the experience of being inexperienced could also help experts become more humble.

Many studies show that professionals benefit from working cooperatively. However, rarely published in the literature are guidelines to help team builders effectively develop teams in the organization. There are a lot of *how-tos* and team-building activity books, but not many discuss the fundamentals of team-building. In my consulting experience, I always explain to our clients how to create a positive learning experience by explaining team dynamics and using team contracts and team-building activities. We also share templates for evaluating team projects. I believe any team leader can benefit from such a strategy.

Team builders should view themselves as professionals and subject matter experts in their particular fields and as educators. Their job is to prepare professionals for excellence with the task at hand, collaboration among their peers, and business success. These varied professional paths require that team members have training in communication and interpersonal skills, team planning, team decision-making processes, and leadership skills. In my 30 years of experience in this area, professional training in understanding team planning, decision making, and team dynamics is rudimentary compared to the explicit business (making money!) instructions professionals receive throughout their academic formation. Many organizations have a slew of courses available and promoted by human resources (Motorola has its university) systems built into their curriculum to help people develop communication skills, which is crucial in any successful team interaction.

Professionals working in teams (or aspiring to build one!) need to know how to work effectively in teams. Still, the skills and processes required for effective teamwork, typical in business and communication courses, are usually not part of the science curriculum. How do they use the diverse skills of different team members brought to a project? What level of planning is necessary at the outset, and how much communication among team members is needed to keep a project running smoothly? We use teamwork in our organizations because the benefits of cooperative work are numerous and varied, including an increased understanding of content, improved ability to explain concepts to peers, and improved business effectiveness.

Most team development approaches tend to be reactive rather than proactive, especially in more technical fields; engineers like us focus on what we do best and like to do well. We tend to place professionals in teams and then leave them on their own without instructions as to what they could expect from each other, what normal team behavior might resemble, or how to work through challenging team dynamics. Oh, and we tend to call this team of people teams! When peers would talk to us about problems with team members, our response typically tended to be little more than "work it out among yourselves." However, our subsequent professional development activities showed us that this response is ineffective in building teams. In particular, engineering-oriented projects tend to be technical, with little room for team-building activities (unless HR demands it!). So, what is involved in building teams? This section focuses on the fundamentals of team building and the logistics team leaders face when team members work together on a project.

Leaders must foster a culture open to multiculturalism, learning, encouraging risk-taking, and learning from mistakes. In a globally changing environment, a leader should be able to respond quickly to changing environments and according to the different types of teams being led, which can vary, as depicted in Figure 7.11, by national or global teams, often being virtually based. The solution sometimes may be counterintuitive: one must unlearn what one has learned, refrain from doing what has been successful, and keep in perspective what one has achieved. Having a piece of the humble pie and the mindset to learn new practices continually can help knowledge experts go further and be more resilient in today's uncertain world.

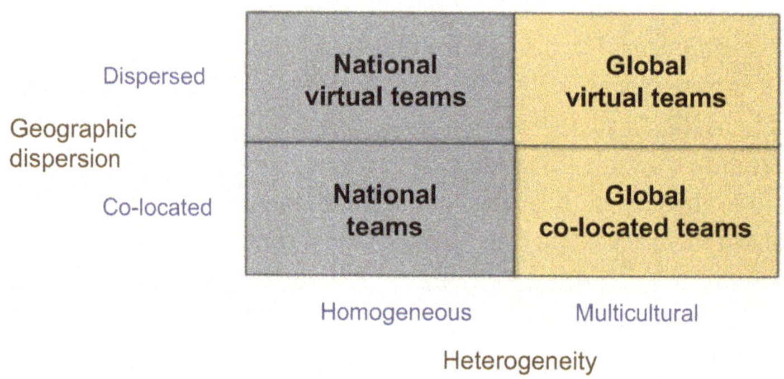

Figure 7.11: Leading different types of teams.

In today's world, being a leader is not enough; one needs to work as an Innovation leader. They have to come up with ways to execute the same job effectively. For that, leaders need to perform as innovation leaders by:

1. Developing the proper group norms
2. Designing teams strategically
3. Managing interactions with those outside the team
4. Showing support as a leader
5. Displaying organizational support and
6. Using performance management effectively.

Innovation leaders build norms that encourage politeness and the respectful sharing of ideas. Leaders encourage employees to promote knowledge sharing with members of other teams; innovation leaders encourage employees to demonstrate trust in their interactions. Innovation leaders try to avoid making constant changes in team composition; the longer a couple has been exchanging information, the higher that team's level of cohesiveness and the more likely members are to share knowledge. Leaders need to be trained in mindfulness to motivate the team and not get burned out. A mindful leader embodies the four C's: concentration, clarity, creativity, and compassion in the service of others.

Mindful leadership provides dual benefits; it encourages leaders to strengthen their ability to connect to themselves and strengthen their ability to initiate change skillfully. Leaders notice the impact of mindfulness training on their work lives and leadership ability. Mindfulness training also increases the resilience of leaders. Mindfulness interventions are effective in improving several health-related conditions, including depression, pain, and addiction in a clinical setting and stress and burnout in workplace settings. Organizations consider mindfulness as a differentiating skill for influential leaders and managers. Mindful training allows leaders in this high-paced and demanding world to be more accepting of changing situations, which fosters a more profound understanding that change happens and that it is not helpful to get worked up about it.

The Four Team-Building Development Phases

No business leader can do it alone! Building and maintaining teams in a domestic, and even more so international, workplace is crucial to any job. Developing teams and individual team members is key to helping professionals develop the necessary skills and abilities to motivate staff management and problem-solving effectively. Building a team may be viewed in five distinct phases, as depicted in Figure 7.12:

1. **Forming**, the team is still a collection of individuals (a group) dealing with procedural issues, and the atmosphere is often artificially polite. Enthusiasm for and commitment to the new team but competence is low.
2. **Storming**, team members begin to experiment and flex their muscles. Relationships become stormier between members and between the team and other groups, and members question outside influences such as set procedures. As the team struggles to find the best way to work together, members may experience a temporary lapse in commitment.

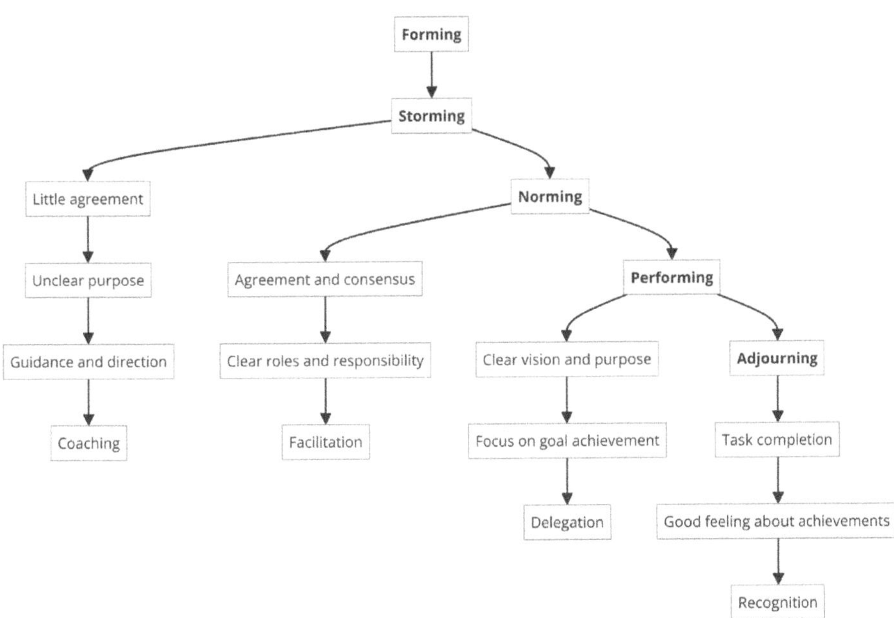

Figure 7.12: The five phases of team-building development.

3. **Norming**, the team is beginning to achieve its potential. It has developed its way of working that is producing results.
4. **Performing**, the team is fully mature and practical. It deals with change openly and flexibly, constantly challenges itself but avoids damaging conflicts. The development of team members is a high priority.
5. **Adjourning**, when the team is dispersed. Too often, this phase is excluded from the set, but this is a crucial phase, as team members should share lessons learned, be reassigned, and have a chance to synthesize their experience while in the team.

Teams are unlikely to develop their potential without a struggle. They can get stuck in the early stages of members being too polite and unprepared to challenge the status quo. Teams may also become complacent after they reach an acceptable level of performance. If teams stagnate or encounter problems they cannot overcome with their resources, they will need help from management. It may include clarifying objectives, providing additional resources, training, and team-building exercises.

More on Forming a Team

There are three common ways of determining team composition: random, professional, or function-directed, and team leader-directed. Many organizations use arbitrary and function-directed team determination but have not tried the couple leader-directed method. Many organizations randomly assign professionals to teams because it reflects real-life situations; you do not often get to pick whom you work with on committees or assignments. They have ensured randomness by having professionals draw playing cards or numbers from a hat. Random team formation also avoids the perception that team leaders treat team members unequally. Although team members often express apprehension about this form of team determination, these teams often work out very well; I have had team members who first met working on a chemical lab project become inseparable friends for the rest of the project and beyond.

Occasionally, team leaders allow team members to self-select team members. Most team members seem to prefer this method, saying they know whom they can or cannot work with, may have similar professional backgrounds, and know how seriously they are taking the project. One drawback in this process is that these teams are more likely to support a “free rider,” a friend let off the hook without contributing to the team. Another drawback is that team members who do not know anyone on the team can feel left out. It is helpful for team building to occur within the very early stage of a project, allowing the team to begin functioning during the team-building activities and to work together on all aspects of the project:

- Creating a team contract
- Forming workgroups
- Reviewing project scope and specifications

- Collecting data
- Analyzing and presenting the results

Team Members' Self-Regulation

Team members' self-regulation is necessary if teamwork is to be achieved. Teams will always be subject to management direction to some degree, and the boundaries of their authority must be understood from the early stages. Nevertheless, research indicates that self-regulation tends to be lacking in teams that do not perform to their full potential. However, it is essential to remember that self-regulation will not happen automatically but must be developed. The task of team leaders when building their teams is to oversee the development of teams and provide the necessary support and training. Team leaders must also accept that mistakes will be made as teams are given more responsibility. The emphasis should be on learning from mistakes rather than establishing blame. Unless teams are prepared to take reasonable risks, they are unlikely to develop independence and the ability to innovate.

Self-regulation often begins within the team as members decide how tasks should be tackled and their distribution among members. As teams develop, they can take on more responsibility for the quality, production methods, hours and times of work, and the selection of, or discipline of, team members. Mature teams may also manage their relationships with other teams and take on responsibility for dealing with the broader organization in such matters as the provision of finance and resources. Three cyclical phases seem to emerge in the acquisition of self-regulation skills, as depicted in Figure 7.13:

1. **Phase 1, forethought/pre-action** – This phase precedes the actual performance, sets the stage for action, maps out the tasks to minimize the unknown, and helps to develop a positive mindset. Realistic expectations can make the task more appealing. Goals must be set as specific outcomes, from short-term to long-term. We have to ask team members to consider the following:
   - When will they start?
   - Where will they do the work?
   - How will they get started?
   - What conditions will help or hinder their activities during this phase?
2. **Phase 2, performance control** – This phase involves processes during learning and the active attempt to utilize specific strategies to help team members become more successful. Team leaders should ask team members the following:
   - Are the team members accomplishing what they hoped to do?
   - Are they being distracted?
   - Is the project taking more time than they thought?
   - Under what conditions do they achieve the most?
   - What questions can they ask themselves while they are working?
   - How can team members encourage themselves to keep working (including self-talk, such as: *come on, get your work done so you can take some time off!*)?

3. **Phase 3, self-reflection** – This phase involves reflection after the performance and self-evaluation of outcomes compared to goals. Team leaders must ask team members to consider the following:
   - Did they accomplish what they planned to do?
   - Were they distracted, and how did they get back to work?
   - Did they plan enough time or need more time than they thought?
   - Under what conditions did they accomplish the most work?

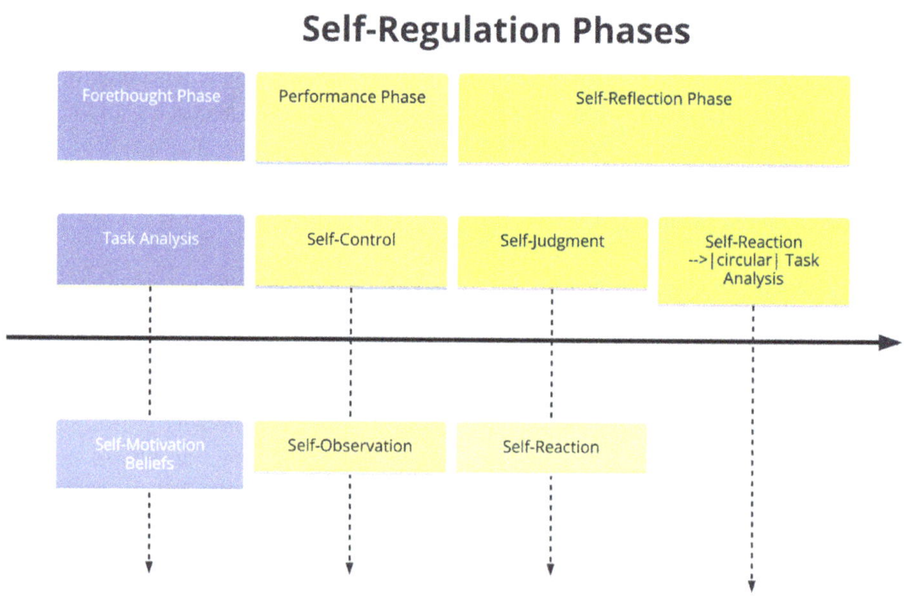

Figure 7.13: The three cyclical phases in the team members' acquisition of self-regulation skills.

The development of good self-regulation usually involves the following:

A. **Self-observation** – systematically monitoring one's own performance; keeping records is a big part of this.

B. **Self-judgment** – systematically comparing performance with a standard or goal (e.g., re-examining answers, checking procedures, rating answers concerning answer sheet, another person)

C. **Self-reaction** – engage in personal processes such as:
   - Goal setting (e.g., meta-cognitive planning, behavioral outcomes);
   - Self-administering praise or criticism
   - Rehearsing, memorizing
   - Proximal goal setting

- Structuring environment (e.g., changing the project task's difficulty, changing the project setting, the immediate physical environment, creating a working area), and
- Asking for help, etc.

Work organization theorists have described developmental models for teams. These should not be used as prescriptions but can aid understanding, particularly if a team is not developing.

Team Contracts

Team leaders should conduct a team-building activity before discussing the team's contract. In creating a contract, you should ask team members to list all the tasks they think will be associated with the project. Each team creates an agreement that addresses the tasks, how important (on a scale of 1–10) each task is, and what deadline should be set for each task. As the team lists the tasks, team members choose which tasks to handle.

The team contract also decides how conflicts are managed. Would all team members be part of the conversation? Would the conversation be face-to-face? Having team members think through how they will handle conflict before it occurs is a powerful way for teams to learn about conflict resolution. Figure 7.14 illustrates a conflict resolution model.

Team-Building Activities

In its early stages, team builders must try to pit teams against each other on small projects, using simple activities that take less than 15 minutes to complete. The objective is to build team spirit. Team leaders can use a variety of activities to capitalize on multiple intelligences and to help teams work through problems. If they know teams are experiencing conflict in their project, they can choose an activity to help diffuse conflict among team members (usually something silly). If they notice that a specific team member has taken on a more aggressive role, they can choose an activity that evens out individual contributions to the team score. If one team member is excluded from team conversations, they can choose an activity that gives individual members different information.

The communication and coordination of all that information are critical to successfully completing the task. Team leaders can, for example, get their team to play Pictionary and complete mind puzzles. They can give math problems and have team members compete physically, throwing tennis balls into targets at varying points in the landscape. They can also play a version of the newlywed game, asking questions like, "How many pets will your team members say they have?"

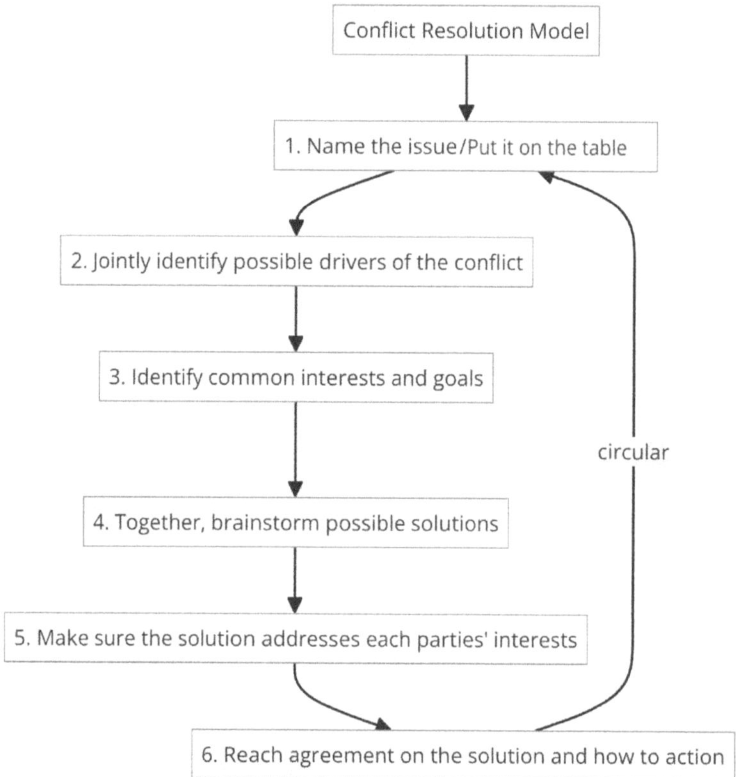

Figure 7.14: Conflict resolution model.

The Challenge of Leading Global Change Management Programs

As argued by Goncalves in his book *Change Management Concepts and Practice*, change management (CM) has always been characterized as the process through which organizations generate value from their change process and business realignment. Developing value from such assets globally involves sharing it among employees, departments, and other companies to devise the best international CM practices. Since CM is a business practice and not a technology-based concept, CM programs should be led by the global leadership, the CEO, or whoever is the *change agent* and not the more technical professionals, such as a chief information officer (CIO) or technology officer (CTO). Of course, CIOs might be the most indicated professionals if the CM implementation is contained within the IT department, with concrete deliverables and expectations. Although it may appear that CM programs should be led by CEOs/change agents, many companies have dedicated CM staff headed by CIOs, CTOs, and other high-profile executives.

The concern with using CIOs and CTOs to lead CM projects is that these professionals typically approach CM programs from the technology point of view, relying on IT. However, such reliance on promoting corporate competitive advantage no longer guarantees successful results. International business has become so volatile that the same change process in a particular global region and context can be irrelevant, if not incorrect, in another region of the globe and context. Thus, one of the main challenges in leading CM programs concerns the value of implementing the change process, as not all change is valuable. Change management processes tend to be *explicit* or *implicit*, as found in knowledge management (KM). Explicit change, the type that is documented, required, and codified, though laborious, is generally manageable. But a more complex concept is the tacit change, which occurs in people's heads. The challenge inherent in tacit change is figuring out how to recognize, generate, share, and manage it. While IT in the form of email, groupware, instant messaging, social media, and related digital technologies can help facilitate the dissemination of tacit change, identifying such changes in the first place is very often a significant challenge.

In addition, global change agents must be able to bring every department and every individual on board with the CM program across all its international branches and subsidiaries. Global leaders and other high-level staff and decision-makers must be sold on the program, so a list of very tangible and quantifiable benefits and results CM will bring to the organization is necessary. Global leaders should map out the increase in revenues the company can expect from an improved CM process. One alternative is to outsource the task. Hiring a consulting firm to spend time educating, setting expectations, and listening to concerns expressed by the company's employees before the CM system goes live is advisable. Then it would be best if global leaders got ready to persuade the rest of the organization. By explaining how the new CM system would make their job more straightforward and less complex, they increase the chances of receiving full support from the company, which will be vital for the project's success.

Once leaders have convinced employees that CM is good for business, it is time to retrain them: change begins. CM systems change the way people work. Unless upper management educates them about the impact and how to use and take advantage of the new system, the project may go awry, and people will not support it. Best practices indicate that for every dollar spent on CM systems, leaders must spend at least another dollar and a half on awareness and training programs. Leaders should also be prepared to face resistance, as people tend to be very uneasy about sharing their knowledge and best practices instead of changing for fear of becoming a dispensable commodity inside the organization.

The Challenge of Managing Change

Change management is a business strategy, and as such, it has the potential to change any organization's behavior fundamentally. CM is so fundamental that it requires calibrated strategy and tactics in every core business function. Thus, one of the main challenges in managing change is to gain full support from the executive staff. Suppose the global leader (e.g., the CEO, principal, country manager, etc.) and the executive management team do not support the CM strategy. In that case, there is no chance that CM can significantly transform the organization. As international organizations increasingly rely on CM programs, CM professionals must realize that mere policies and procedures cannot hope to provide all levels of change today's organizations require. Any fundamental change within the organization requires generating and effectively deploying a culture that embraces change and the need for change. Knowledge such as how to penetrate and dominate global and new markets, enhancement of employee recruitment and retention, and better and more rapid development of products and services must be cataloged, aggregated, and managed to aid change processes.

To be effective, especially in globally challenging times like ours, change management must encompass a structured system with processes and technologies that inspire people to share what they know and use what they learn. This process should involve:

- Aiding and abetting collaboration, knowledge sharing, and continual learning
- Capturing the patterns recognized in human experience and insight (knowledge) and making them available to and reusable by others
- Improving decision-making processes and quality
- Making it easy to find and reuse this knowledge, either as explicit knowledge that has been recorded in physical form or as timely access to a human expert's tacit, intuitive knowledge

Measuring Results

At the core of the success of any CM, the initiative is a premise that every professional serious about their career should have. Instead of buying into the concept that global leaders should know what they know and profit from it, they should strive to obsolete themselves daily. What they get to know before others obsolete it, and they profit by creating the challenges and opportunities others have not considered. Such a premise may go against the leading business strategist authors and consultants out there, but I know that it works, and you need only ask any successful foreign immigrant in this country, or any other, to confirm it. When I arrived in this country in 1986, I strived to obsolete myself as a burger maker at Burger King. With the grace of the almighty, working at the core of the city of Boston on Summer St., I tried hard to obsolete myself, and I figured out a way to make 12 burgers in less than one minute. By doing so, I was also observing my peer's way of doing burgers. In the process, I set a new standard for making burgers, got a medal and diploma from Burger King University, and advanced myself to kitchen manager in less than three months on the job (and barely speaking any English). Another example is Ram Charan (an Indian-American business consultant, speaker, and writer), who, from his childhood in India, where he worked in his family's shoe shop, was able to break the rules by obsolescing and innovating.

While attending Harvard Business School, he reversed business rules and instituted the universal laws of business success, all based on common sense.

To remain globally competitive in the 21st century, MNEs and MNCs must employ all the knowledge they can master to promote specific and timely change. Such companies retain a unique advantage by not sharing this knowledge with other corporations. However, unshared knowledge does not equal success if the knowledge is not shared within the organization and effectively quantified. Global leaders should be aware that intellectual property rights cannot do much to protect corporate knowledge. Only learning creates new knowledge, provides the primary competitive advantage, and radically impacts the organization. As global leaders think about how to measure the success of your CM implementation, consider the following indicators and then plan and execute a clear strategy to address these problems at their source:

- What change management aspects need to be managed in the organization? Attention should be concentrated on real business needs, such as reducing asset intensity and improving revenue collection.
- What are the high-transaction and short-cycle processes that need to be concentrated on? Some key processes should be concentrated on, including accounts payable, customer service, or inside sales, where the impact of efforts will quickly be exposed.
- How important is it to include a review of current business practices? Global leaders should watch for operations in which an ability to capture and reuse knowledge will improve efficiency, lower costs, and boost profits.
- Are there any knowledge gaps, and if so, does the leadership know why? Leaders should identify any knowledge gaps and their origins and try to determine if they are related to systems (IT), processes (management), or people (organization). Knowledge gaps tend to be present in the unstructured nature of essential decisions and diversity of managerial roles and often cause complexity in decision making. Figure 7.15 depicts the relationships between information systems components.
- Is the CM implementation working accordingly? In such a cognitive model, knowledge exists in a context, making it difficult to measure success or failure, especially across different global regions and cultures, as results are not tangible but indirect. Therefore, leaders should be able to identify the results by measuring the impact of new tools and practices on their business and benchmarking its performance before and after changes are implemented.
- How can management consistently improve knowledge sharing? Whether intended or not, most organizations reward those who hoard knowledge. Every knowledge-based organization has resident experts who revel in the status their knowledge brings them. Unfortunately, knowledge hoarding leads to reinventing the wheel. In addition, it often causes ill-informed decisions to be made and incur unnecessary costs and revenue loss. Thus, leaders should implement incentives that encourage employees to share knowledge and discourage hoarding. The challenge is transforming tacit knowledge into explicit, transitioning from know-how to how-to. Figure 7.16 provides an outline of a typical knowledge-based organization.

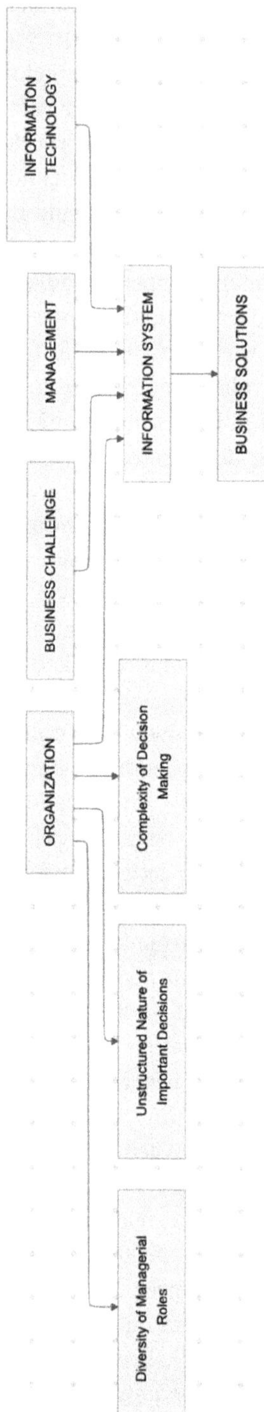

Figure 7.15: Process flow of information system models.

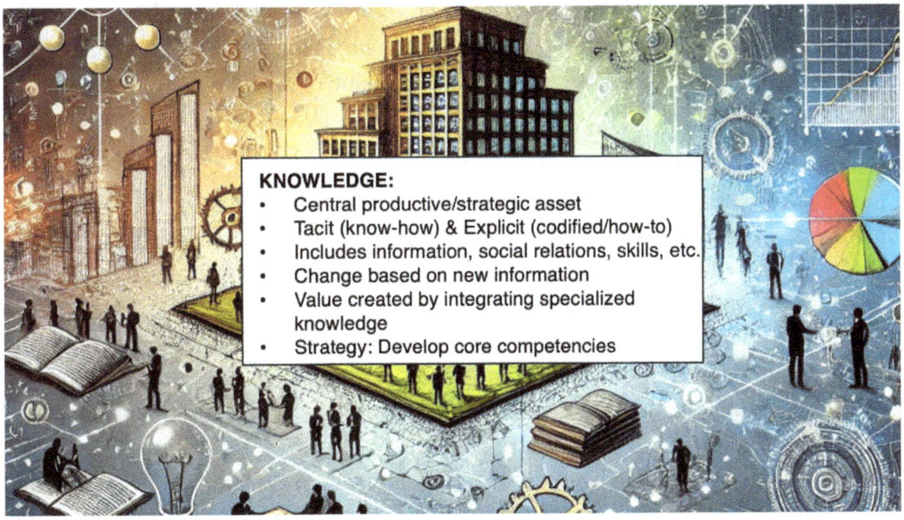

Figure 7.16: Knowledge-based view of the firm.

CM should be able to provide everyone within the organization, across the globe, with the tools that will enable them to obsolete themselves daily, a sort of Japanese Kaizen. CM tools should also empower global workers to renew themselves daily as well. Measuring results is critical in this process, as productive knowledge work should be very tangible. It is all about how each other's time and attention are used as the people in the organization try to get their job done. Remember that when it comes to CM, your worst challenge is day-to-day confusion or lack of clear key result areas. Thus, to survive and succeed, global CM initiatives should bring about very tangible results, which should at least include:

- Reduction of product development times – Roche Holding AG products are sent to the U.S. Food and Drug Administration (FDA) for approval six months faster through CM programs.
- Creation of more opportunities for innovation – CM enabled Dow Chemical to save $40 million a year by reusing patents.
- Improvement of customer relationships – Ford Motor Co. saved more than $600 million over three years.
- Ability to make decisions faster and closer to the point of action – Royal/Dutch Shell's deployment of a best-practice sharing methodology from Ford Motor Co. in two pilot communities of practice realized cost avoidance and savings of more than $5 million in four months.

While many scholars, specialized publications, and corporate executives point out the failures of CM, the facts above show that a well-defined CM project can save an organization millions of dollars, dramatically impacting the bottom line. Thus, today's change agents must be aware of the diversity of perspectives from which one can comprehend the concept of knowledge. In addition, be aware of problems with the generally known understandings and notions of management (in CM) that have filled many mainstream business texts concerning the value of CM.

Addressing the Challenges

Change management is undoubtedly an oxymoron that explains the difficulty in reconciling the soft issues around it, such as innovation and creativity, with complex issues, such as performance benchmarks, measurement, and assessment. There is an opposing assumption about the definition of, and nature between, change and management. Although CEOs and change agents tend to understand that management and control are not synonymous, this is not typically so for CTOs or CIOs, which rely on controlling systems as management. The gap is based on the fact that the job descriptions of CIOs and CTOs, although a relatively new breed of professionals have their roots in contemporary management theories, typically developed between 1930 and 1962. Management focused on individual and collective behavior during this period, driven by social psychologists, organizational behaviorists, and sociologists. As discussed earlier, most of today's CEOs and change agents came from that era or were influenced by it. Many of them were former CIOs or CTOs or adopted that management theory.

However, today's CEOs and change agents must fundament themselves in a post-modern management theory, which began to gain ground after 1965. Today's CEOs and change agents must transcend this post-modern management model to one that considers the fast-changing business landscape and the roaming nature of professionals. I would call this new management theory a post-internet one. As a result of this super-fast-paced international business landscape, CM initiatives are often disappointing, as there is a lack of user uptake and a failure to integrate CM into everyday working practices. However, such outcomes can be avoided, which is what this section addresses. Global leaders should focus on these best business practices:

- Make sure to tighten CM efforts to a high-priority business objective – As they would not fish on a pond with a bazooka, they should not invest in CM just for CM's sake. To be successful, change and learning goals must be articulated at the same level as an organization's business objectives. It is the only way learning and knowledge sharing can become culturally embedded in the organization.
- If leaders want CM to succeed, they must integrate their people with the organization's business process and the tools they will be using. CM should always be a work-in-progress, never a finite project. Its never-ending integrated process should consistently implement a competitive strategy recognizing that learning and sharing knowledge are equally important.
- When considering starting a CM implementation, the best tools are the cheapest in the process: pencil and paper. The knowledge strategy must be aligned with the organization's business strategy before considering any technology tool. The strategy should define all key CM processes:

a. Creation of strategies
b. Identification of goals
c. Development of the process
d. Implementation mapping
e. Knowledge sharing, application, and reuse of it

The Impact of ESG on Global Leadership Issues and Practices

The rise of ESG criteria has not just influenced but transformed global leadership. As businesses expand and operate internationally, leaders are now navigating a landscape where sustainability, social responsibility, and ethical governance are critical and the foundation of success.

ESG considerations are not just integral but are the essence of global leadership, shaping how leaders develop a global mindset, competencies, and cultural integration strategies. Environmental sustainability, social responsibility, and good governance are strategic advantages and ethical imperatives in the worldwide market. By incorporating ESG criteria into their leadership practices, global leaders are not just driving long-term success, but they are building strong stakeholder relationships, and they are navigating the complexities of international business with a moral compass. As the world continues to evolve, ESG will not just remain a critical factor but will be the defining factor in effective global leadership and sustainable growth.

ESG and Developing a Global Mindset

Global leaders today are encouraged and compelled to incorporate environmental sustainability into their strategic thinking and operations. A global mindset now demands recognizing the interconnectedness of business practices and their impact on the planet. Leaders must develop and master competencies in managing resources sustainably, reducing carbon footprints, and fostering innovation in green technologies. This shift is not just in line with global environmental goals but positions companies competitively as consumers and investors increasingly prioritize sustainability.

Leaders with a robust global mindset understand that environmental sustainability is not merely a regulatory requirement but a strategic advantage. Companies like Patagonia and IKEA have effectively integrated sustainability into their core business strategies, earning consumer trust and loyalty. By championing sustainable practices, leaders can steer their organizations towards long-term profitability and resilience, ensuring their entities thrive in an eco-conscious global market.

Social responsibility is another critical component of a global mindset. Leaders must be adept at addressing social issues such as labor rights, diversity and inclusion, and community engagement. These aspects are essential for building a positive corporate image and fostering solid stakeholder relationships. A global mindset requires leaders to be culturally aware and sensitive to the social dynamics in different regions. This involves understanding local customs, addressing social inequalities, and contributing to community development. Companies like Unilever and Microsoft have demonstrated leadership in social responsibility by implementing inclusive policies, supporting local communities, and ensuring ethical labor practices across their global operations.

Good governance is fundamental to developing a global mindset. Leaders must establish transparent, accountable, and ethical practices that build trust with stakeholders and ensure compliance with international regulations. This involves implementing robust governance frameworks that promote ethical decision making and responsible business conduct. Leaders with a global mindset recognize that ethical governance is crucial for mitigating risks and enhancing organizational reputation. Companies like Johnson & Johnson and Nestlé have set high standards for corporate governance, emphasizing integrity, transparency, and stakeholder engagement. By prioritizing ethical leadership, global leaders can navigate the complexities of international markets and foster sustainable growth.

ESG and Transformational Leadership

Transformational leadership is a style that inspires and motivates employees to achieve collective goals. ESG criteria are integral to transformational leadership, emphasizing the importance of vision, inspiration, support, stimulation, and personal recognition. Transformational leaders can drive ESG initiatives by articulating a compelling sustainability and social responsibility vision. They inspire employees to think beyond individual interests and work towards a common goal of creating positive environmental and social impact. Transformational leaders also provide employees with the necessary support and resources to innovate and implement ESG strategies.

For instance, Paul Polman, former CEO of Unilever, exemplified transformational leadership by embedding sustainability into the company's core strategy. His vision and commitment to ESG principles inspired employees and stakeholders, significantly improving Unilever's environmental and social performance.

ESG and Transactional Leadership

While transformational leadership focuses on inspiring change, transactional leadership is based on rewards and penalties. ESG considerations can enhance transactional leadership by integrating ESG metrics into performance evaluations and reward systems. Leaders can use contingent rewards to incentivize employees to achieve ESG goals. This involves setting clear targets for sustainability, social responsibility, and governance and rewarding employees for meeting these objectives. By linking rewards to ESG performance, leaders can align individual motivations with organizational goals.

For example, companies like Salesforce and Danone have implemented incentive programs that reward employees for contributing to sustainability and social initiatives. These programs drive ESG performance and enhance employee engagement and commitment to the company's values.

ESG and Cultural Integration

Environmental sustainability and cultural sensitivity are closely linked in the context of global leadership. Leaders must navigate diverse cultural landscapes while implementing sustainable practices that respect local environments and communities. A global mindset necessitates understanding the cultural implications of environmental initiatives and active engagement with local stakeholders to garner support. This demands that leaders be adaptable and culturally sensitive, ensuring that sustainability strategies are relevant and effective in diverse regions.

For example, Starbucks has integrated environmental sustainability into its operations while respecting local cultures. The company collaborates with local farmers to promote sustainable coffee farming practices, ensuring that its ecological initiatives align with the needs and values of local communities.

Social Responsibility and Cultural Awareness

Social responsibility requires leaders to be culturally aware and responsive to the social dynamics in different regions. This involves addressing social inequalities, supporting community development, and promoting diversity and inclusion. Leaders with cultural awareness can effectively engage with local communities and address their specific needs and concerns. This enhances the company's social impact and builds strong relationships with stakeholders.

For instance, Coca-Cola's "5by20" initiative launched in 2010 aimed to empower millions of women entrepreneurs by 2020. The initiative was a significant program aimed at empowering five million women entrepreneurs across Coca-Cola's global value chain by 2020, which they successfully exceeded. By understanding women's unique challenges in different cultures, Coca-Cola has tailored its programs to provide the necessary support and resources, enhancing its social responsibility efforts globally.

Good governance and ethical conduct are essential for building trust and credibility in international markets. Leaders must navigate diverse regulatory environments and cultural norms while maintaining high standards of governance and ethics. A global mindset involves understanding and respecting local governance practices while ensuring the company's operations adhere to international standards. This requires leaders to be adaptable and culturally sensitive, balancing global and regional governance requirements.

For example, Siemens has implemented a comprehensive compliance program that addresses governance and ethical conduct across its global operations. By understanding and respecting local regulatory environments, Siemens has built a reputation for integrity and transparency, enhancing its competitive position in international markets.

Discussion Questions

1. **How can global leaders effectively manage the challenges of leading across different cultures and business environments to ensure organizational success?**

2. **Which leadership style is focused on building relationships and inspiring employees towards a collective vision?**
   A) Transactional leadership
   B) Autocratic leadership
   C) Transformational leadership
   D) Laissez-faire leadership

3. **According to the chapter, what is a critical aspect of developing a global mindset among leaders?**
   A) Prioritizing profit over people
   B) Focusing solely on domestic strategies
   C) Understanding and integrating into local cultures
   D) Avoiding risks at all costs

3. **Transactional leadership is primarily based on rewarding employees for their performance and compliance. True or False?**

5. **To maintain consistency, global leaders should apply the same leadership style regardless of cultural differences. True or False?**

Recommended Readings

Cardoso, M. D. O., Fernandes, G. A. D. A. L., & Teixeira, M. A. C. (2023). Women leaders and ESG performance: Exploring gender equality in global south companies. *Cosmopolitan Civil Societies: An Interdisciplinary Journal*, 15(2), 64–83.

Chouaibi, S., & Affes, H. (2021). The effect of social and ethical practices on environmental disclosure: evidence from an international ESG data. *Corporate Governance: The International Journal of Business in Society*, 21(7), 1293–1317.

Chung, R. K., Margolin, A. M., & Vyakina, I. V. (2023). Theory and Practice of ESG Transformation of Management Systems. *Экономическая политика*, 18(2), 80–103.

Esteves-Miranda, V., Liao, W., Abington-Prejean, E., & Parker, C. (2020). Incorporating ESG Strategy in DEI for Leadership Roles in Higher Education. *American International Journal of Business Management*, 4(09), 75–82.

Krambia-Kapardis, M., Stylianou, I., & Savva, C. S. (2023). Ethical leadership as a prerequisite for sustainable development, sustainable finance, and ESG reporting. In *Sustainable Finance and Financial Crime* (pp. 107–126). Cham: Springer International Publishing.

Niu, S., Park, B. I., & Jung, J. S. (2022). The effects of digital leadership and ESG management on organizational innovation and sustainability. *Sustainability*, 14(23), 15639.

Sandretto, D., Esposito, G., & Rizzi, A. (2023). Gender corporate leadership and ESG performance: global insights. In NA (pp. 35–35). World Finance and Banking Symposium, Vilnius, Lithuania, December 13–15, 2023, https://iris.unito.it/bitstream/2318/1954250/1/bf8a0d3d95a167ce61a071de98a133ae.pdf, last accessed on February 6, 2024.

Chapter 8
International Markets: Assessment and Entry Mode

Learning Objectives

- Examine the steps of market screening and techniques for environmental analysis
- Depict some of the problems market researchers encounter in foreign markets
- Describe international market entry methods
- Discuss the value of trade missions and trade fairs

Overview

To make informed decisions, qualitative and quantitative information gathering or market research, both primary and secondary, is required to identify market needs, opportunities, and threats. It is the minimum necessary to maximize the probability of success and minimize risks. The type of information required would depend on the stakeholder's specific needs. For example, an automotive company from a developed country interested in establishing its business presence in an emerging country might like the research for information, such as the country's demand projection, growth prospects, competitors' profile, import policy, and tariffs, competitive price points, buying pattern, and business nuances. Its initial interest may be to shortlist a few countries out of a list of probable countries with business potential and a high probability of success.

Assessing New Markets

International business enterprises aim to grow market share, revenues, and profits. SMEs and MNEs frequently accomplish these objectives by penetrating new global markets or introducing innovative products into markets with a presence. An enterprise's capability to enter a new market effectively hinges on developing a thorough understanding of a given geographical or product market, including but not limited to its culture, laws, language, and customers. To successfully grow its market share, revenue, and profits, enterprises must typically pursue three steps:

1. Consider alternative international markets
2. Assess the respective costs, benefits, and risks of penetrating each of them, and
3. Choose those new markets that have the most possibility for entry or development.

https://doi.org/10.1515/9783111510286-008

Assessing Alternative Foreign Markets

In assessing alternative international markets, an enterprise must consider a myriad of factors, including the existing and likely sizes of the target markets, the levels of competition, the legal and political environment, and socio-cultural factors that may affect the performance of its operations. Data on these factors is relatively objective and easy to obtain and should cover:

- **Market potential**: Assessing the target market potential should be the first step. May international institutions such as the WB, the IMF, the OECD, the UN, and others offer data about population, GDP, per capita GDP, public infrastructure, and ownership of such goods as automobiles and televisions. The decisions an enterprise makes from this data often rely upon the positioning of its products or services relative to its competitors. An enterprise delivering high-quality products at premium prices will find a more affluent market conducive but may experience difficulties entering a poorer market. Conversely, an enterprise specializing in low-priced, lower-quality goods may see the needs with lower discretionary income as even more lucrative than those in more affluent markets with higher ones.
- **Competitiveness levels:** When selecting an international target market, the enterprise must consider the level of competition in the market, as well as both the current status and future forecasts. To analyze the host-country competitive landscape, it should determine the size of the needs and competition, their relative market share, pricing and distribution strategy, and their relative SWOT.
- **Legal and political environment**: An enterprise considering entry into a foreign market must also comprehend the host nation's international trade policies and legal and political environment. An enterprise may forgo exporting its goods to a market with high tariffs, quotas, and many other trading restrictions in favor of exporting to markets with fewer barriers. As discussed in Chapter 3, government stability is also critical in the target market review and selection.
- **Socio-cultural influences**: Enterprises considering international new markets should feel the socio-cultural effects of those target markets, which can be challenging to understand due to their subjective nature. To minimize uncertainties related to these factors, enterprises should consider their initial internationalization in markets culturally similar to their home markets.

Accessing Costs, Benefits, and Risk Exposure

A careful evaluation of the costs, benefits, and risks exposure associated with the expansion of an MNE into a new foreign market should include, but not be limited to:

- **Costs:** Both direct and opportunity costs should be considered. Direct prices should include those directly included when entering a new international market. These may include expenses associated with starting up operations in the country, hiring and transferring, relocating managers and remaining personnel to the new branch, shipping equipment, other necessary corporate assets, and any products, merchan-

dise, and initial inventory. The enterprise also needs to assess the opportunity costs it may incur since resources are always limited. Investing in one venture may limit the investment in others; cost/benefit analysis is paramount.
- **Benefits:** Among the most apparent potential benefits are the expected market sales and profits. Other benefits may include lower acquisition and manufacturing costs, foreclosing needs to competitive advantage, competitors, new technologies, and the opportunity to develop synergies with other co-operations.
- **Risks:** Enterprises are exposed to a wide array of potential risks when expanding abroad, including, but not limited to, exchange rate fluctuation, additional operating complexity, direct financial losses due to poor or inaccurate market assessment, government confiscation or nationalization of property, civil unrest, etc.

Market Research Methods

To select the country or countries, the company would invariably need information, such as the country's market size, GDP, per capita income growth rates, demography, import-export trade, currency rate, and economic and political stability. The required information is customized to the stakeholder's needs, and the information gathered is country and timeframe specific. After deciding which country to expand to, the company may shift its focus to select potential partners, necessitating operational, financial, and legalese, requiring extensive detailed data gathering and information analysis. After establishing a presence, the company might research brand acceptance, customer satisfaction, market share, and new product prospects. On the other hand, a developed country's automotive industry association, wanting to estimate the business potential of its members, might require more broad-based market research to gather information, such as the current status of the industry, demand patterns, and growth potential for compact cars, trucks, sport utility vehicles, and sedans in selected countries. Numerous global organizations, such as the World Bank and the OECD, and leading consulting firms, such as McKinsey and Boston Consulting Group, develop research and survey reports that provide:
- Data and qualitative information about the global economy
- Industry
- Topics relating to advanced and emerging countries

In addition, various agencies release at regular intervals information relating to the relative position of countries by metrics, such as ease of doing business, global competitiveness index, nominal GDP, GDP growth rate, per capita income, export and import trade, demography, current account deficit, global innovation index. The stakeholders, such as the business corporations, nation states, consultants and analyst firms, economic development and research organizations interested in global economic growth and in ensuring the future stability of the financial system, and institutional and private equity investors, not only macro-level data and basic information; they need it in granular detail. With the help of analytics and business intelligence tools, they can generate actionable information that helps them make informed investments and decisions. Business intelligence tools could also help them to perform what-if analyses under changing economic scenarios. Succeeding in business, formulating a country's growth strategies, making the right investment decisions, developing and introducing the right product, and advising clients about business transformation are complex and require real-time information gathering and analysis with powerful algorithms.

If, instead of an automotive company, a durable consumer manufacturer from a developed country wanted to explore the feasibility of entering an emerging market, the research requirements would be very different. A durable consumer manufacturer typically offers a broad portfolio of products ranging from simple generic models to feature-rich high-end products. Therefore, the company may need information that would facilitate decision making on sales channels, which products to offer initially, branding strategy, distribution logistics, and the best location of the company's production facility.

On the other hand, if a developing country wants to draw up its industrial roadmap, it will probably start by researching its developmental needs and priorities, its industry's capacity to absorb the technology, and skills availability. The need for research-based data and information gathering and business intelligence and analytics to analyze and generate actionable information and track the efficacy of the actions is all the more significant in a world on the threshold of entering a new economic order. The lingering perception is that organizations and institutions operating in a real economy often resort to a research-based, analytical approach rather than those in the financial-economic fraternity.

The capture of accurate qualitative and quantitative information is essential. Stakeholders must also clearly define the purpose of the exercise upfront, as that will decide the research methodology and the information to be gathered and analyzed. They must stipulate what data and information they need, why they need them, and how they intend to use them. The answers to these questions would determine the type, either primary or secondary, and in the case of primary, the questionnaire design, mode of data and information collection, and the responsible agency. In the case of secondary research, the sources, their time relevance, and their reliability would be necessary. Market research requires that it be both systematic and objective to serve the intended purpose. Before analyzing the data and information, it is necessary to validate them.

Selecting and appointing the firm to conduct market research is crucial to a project's success. This process involves evaluating the market research firm's past performance and whether it has the necessary resources, such as the required field staff, domain knowledge, and expertise. It is essential for the stakeholder commissioning the market research to be involved entirely during each market research phase, such as formulating the questionnaire, the data, and the information gathering methodology.

As depicted in Figure 8.1 below, market research is a critical component when launching a product in a new international market, improving existing products or services in such foreign markets, or developing a competitive advantage when looking to be ahead of foreign and domestic competition. It can provide all the essential information needed for a better business decision.

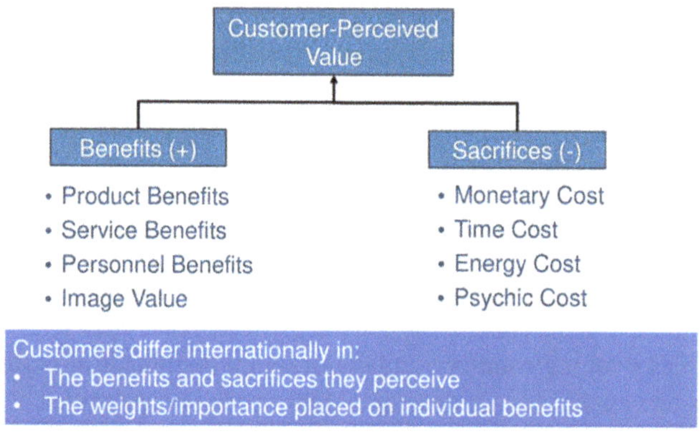

Figure 8.1: The importance of international market research.

The Importance of International Market Research

Among the many advantages market research may offer, below are five essential ones to aid in product development and business growth for domestic and global markets. Market research enables you or a company to:

1. **Better understand local or international markets or customers, depending on your objectives** – Questions such as: Who would buy your product or service? What are the ideal target customers and segments? How often would customers buy the product/service? What do they need? What do they want or expect? The more information you gather about specific markets, the more information and answers you have, and the more understanding about such a market you will acquire, which can result directly in meeting the customer's needs better than your competitors.

2. **Map out the complete profile of an ideal market or customer** – Knowledge of current or prospective customers can assist in solving management decision problems (MDP), which we'll address in more detail later. It can help determine many market variables, such as the market size that triggers customers to buy, market demand, barriers, competitive forces, etc. Market research enables you to gain valuable insights, such as customer demographics (i.e., age, location, gender, and income). It can also help you develop practical market solutions for your MDPs and objectively tailor market strategies and customer mix, including product/service features, promotions, pricing, and more.

3. **Gather knowledge about the competition and their approach to the market** – To be more competitive and drive an edge on the competition, a better understanding of the competitive forces in a particular market is critical, as these forces differ from market to market, especially on international markets. Market and economic research and analysis can help assess these very diverse (and global) markets to determine both key players and those on rising. Furthermore, it can help a company gain leverage over the competition by identifying the weaknesses in its market approach. These gaps can be utilized to gain a competitive advantage and expand your company's customer base. Such market and economic analysis can help you respond to an MDP and give you insight into what strategies worked well for the competition. It can also prompt you, in turn, to be able to think more creatively while modeling your new strategy. Knowing as much as possible regarding your customers or competition is always pivotal to the success of your business and the decision-making process.

4. **Test your product/service or strategy before launching it** – Testing is essential to learning what works before jumping into the implementation of any strategy. All business decision-making processes must be tested before fully being executed on the target market. Testing a market with your product, service, or idea will save the company a lot of extra costs and, most importantly, from delivering a bad product/service to the marketplace. Since you can never be 100% sure that your market or economic strategy will be successful with your target market or potential customer, by conducting market research, you can find what approach you should take when marketing a product or service or addressing a business problem.

5. **Prevent poor business decision making** – We live in a digitally interconnected world, where digital markets abound through a diverse digital market platform. Darwin's famous "survival of the fittest" comes to mind here. However, while he uses the phrase in chapter four of *On the Origin of Species* to describe the process of natural selection, he borrowed it from English philosopher Herbert Spencer. The latter first talked about the survival of the fittest in his *Principles of Sociology*. In any event, his words are insightful and still echo today in possibly the most innovative era in the history of humankind. We have all witnessed large brands such as Blockbuster (now bankrupt) and Nokia, not to mention DEC, AOL, Compaq, and many others, ceasing to exist or still struggling to survive due to their inability to remain relevant in the markets and customers' lives. By contrast, companies such as Netflix and Apple have done their market research before competitors and utilized every open gap in the market to their competitive edge. To stay in business and relevant, companies (and you!) must not only attempt to anticipate change but also be able to predict change. That is when market research comes into play and how good it needs to be!

6. **Foster business growth** – Market research helps companies address their problems and best comprehend customers' demands. It can also assist in detecting more business opportunities, planning the perfect marketing campaign, minimizing losses,

and keeping track of the competition, to name a few. It allows companies to classify their objectives while following the current trends and take advantage of reaching out to their target audience. Identifying business problems before they happen is crucial to the success of any company. Active market research can not only assist in predicting potential business pitfalls that may occur, but it can also save a lot of corporate resources (i.e., time, money, personnel, etc.). A corporate solution may look like a proper market fit, but the company may be in big trouble if not.

Market research provides valuable information to help identify and analyze the needs and opportunities of markets, customers, and competitors. The market research development process is designed to reduce the risk and make the marketing strategy cost-effective for your business. When considering entering new markets abroad, international market research becomes a vital step in the process, as it assists in assessing the many variables that exist when internationalizing. There are many market research techniques to adopt, depending on the data type necessary for decision making and whether data already exists or needs to be freshly gathered. Good and flawed market research can distinguish between the success and failure of an enterprise's products, products, and services in a new market, which is even more true when launching in international markets.

All the challenges and barriers of international market entry are compounded when an enterprise enters a new market with distinct cultures, rules and regulations, customs, languages, geography, and infrastructure than what it has been used to dealing with in a domestic market. Without rigorous research, international enterprises with plans to expand abroad may risk being ill-prepared for a challenging internationalization process. This section looks at some effective methodologies for international market research and the factors to consider compared to domestic research.

Before exploring research methods, it is crucial to determine what type of data is needed so the enterprise can select the best way to gather it:

- **Secondary data** – refers to data not explicitly gathered for the research needs, unlike primary data. These are typically data about the research objective but are not precise. They already exist and can often be provided by government records, business reports, non-government organizations (NGO) data, and several scientific publications available at international institutions such as the WB, IMF, WEF, OECD, UN, specialized market research firms, and others. Secondary data is often much easier to gather and offers a good starting point, an overview, of the research topic, often known as a management decision problem (MDP). An essential factor to remember when conducting research in a foreign market is the linguistic distinctions and the fact that detailed data are not as accessible due to political reasons.
- **Primary data** – refers to new, first-hand data (fresh) collected by the research team themselves; unlike secondary data, which was compiled by someone else, it

did not exist beforehand. Various methods are available, including surveys, experiments, observations, personal interviews, questionnaires, etc.

- **Survey data** – refers to a general process of collecting data by interacting with individuals in a target market. Data can be gathered in various surveys, including electronic methods such as email, telephone interviews, social media, online questionnaires, face-to-face surveys and interviews, and many other methods. Surveys can be efficient when assessing international markets, as they can provide direct engagement with the target customers in the target market. Still, many challenges include language and cultural differences, infrastructure, legal environment, and more.
- **Experimental data** – refers to data collected through an experiment, which can take many formats. For instance, the enterprise may break up the research populations into sub-groups (and a control group) and offer some incentive to a group, then compare how each group reacts. This data type can be a valuable instrument when researching international target markets. It tends to yield real-time findings, allowing the enterprise to assess and draw concrete insights regarding how its product may be received.

The Basic Components of Market Research

The essential components of market research may vary, depending on how granular and detailed the researcher may be when developing a research plan or requirements from funding organizations. In general, as depicted in Figure 8.2, it includes the following phases:

- **Definition of research objectives** – What is the objective for the research, and the problem or critical questions that need to be answered in the market research? It should address the research expectations, what is hoped to be learned from the market research, and what results should enable it to fulfill by answering the research question or providing information for decision making.
- **Development of research design, plans, and methods, or approach** – What research method or approach best addresses the research problem or questions? Should the research be quantitative, qualitative, based on secondary data, primary, or both? In this phase, the researcher designs the research process, selecting the best method or approach to gather and analyze datasets to answer the research question or business problem. The researcher should develop a plan for the data collection analysis and reporting results based on the method/approach selected and qualitative or quantitative (or both) analytical tools to be used, according to specific requirements. For example, if the research is quantitative, there will be a need to test the statistical significance of the results by selecting the most appropriate inferential statistical tool. How will the results be coded and presented if the data is qualitative?

- **Fieldwork, collection of information** (data gathering) – This is the phase where researchers gather data from secondary and primary sources, such as focus groups, surveys, or interviews. Still, many other data sources are available on the internet, such as big data farms, social media, blogs, digitized content, and libraries, such as journals, books, magazines, etc.
- **Data analysis** – Once data is gathered, it is time to analyze it using various instruments, depending on the nature of the data, whether quantitative, qualitative, or, in many cases, mixed methods. Descriptive and inferential statistical analyses may be necessary to test the statistical significance of the results; the hypothesis may be tested if necessary.
- **Reporting and presenting findings** – In this phase, the researcher provides the analysis and reporting of the market research. Communicating the results is essential, giving readers a mental/visual picture of the presented data. This section would include reports such as an executive summary, recommendations, an infographic, an appendix of question-by-question results, etc. Contingent to the complexities of the project, the information should also include some advanced analytics such as TURF, regression, correlation, or any other inferential statistics and non-traditional forms of analysis and reporting.

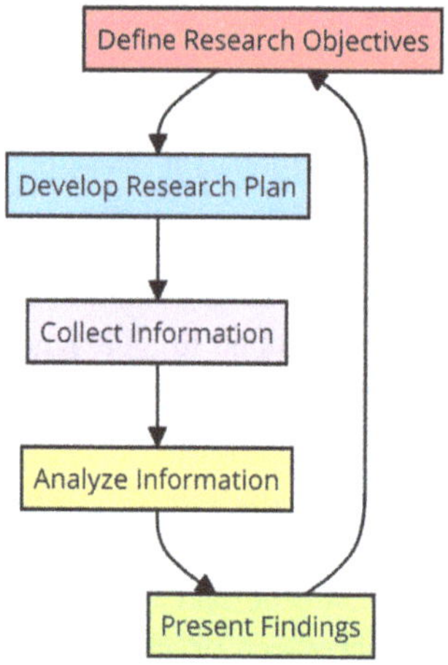

Figure 8.2: Market research process phases.

The Four Basic Concepts of Market Research

Although market research is a vast discipline with various sub-disciplines, four basic concepts remain common, regardless of the field or industry:

A. Methodology
B. Type of data, which can be quantitative or qualitative
C. Sources of data, which can be primary or secondary (and even tertiary), and
D. Sampling methods.

A. Methodology

In research, the methodology is the process the researcher will follow to investigate that is *accurate* and *valuable*. A researcher must see that the research goals are established in any research method. Additionally, researchers must ensure that the population sample (size) can be determined and that the data-gathering method aligns with the selected methodology. More importantly, the mode of analysis must also be appropriate, and conclusions and recommendations must be well-formulated, as well as the actionable insights that must be considered.

To determine which methodology to use, the researcher must first define the research problem or questions and any hypothesis he wants to test. In market research, the MDPs typically concentrate on business challenges, problems that require decisions, and decisions that need more information before making decisions. It is not always easy, therefore, to be able to assess the type of data being required or where and how to collect it. The research objectives and questions must guide the entire research process. In other words, based on the MDP and MRP, the researcher needs to decide on the methodology, data collection, and interpretation of such data, as well as conclusions and recommendations for answering these research questions. Again, the research question(s) will determine the data collection method needed.

B. Type of Data

Qualitative – Qualitative research is exploratory. In a market research project, it is adopted in situations where qualitative data is sought, such as best understanding prospective consumers' opinions about a given topic, product, or service. In addition, this type of data assists in identifying potential new theories, as opposed to quantitative data, which tends to focus on testing hypotheses through hard numbers. Figure 8.3 offers an overview of the main qualitative research methods used.

Quantitative – Quantitative research uses numerical data to draw statistically significant conclusions. Quantitative and qualitative data can be gathered from various sources, as illustrated in Figure 8.4. The internet, for example, is a vast source of secondary data that can be gathered through data mining tools that tap into large and small data repositories, discussion forums, and social media. You can also use the internet to collect primary data via online surveys, focus groups, or interviews (both structured and semi-structured).

C. Source of Data

Secondary Research and Data

Researchers may choose to gather primary or secondary data or both. Secondary research is often crucial in identifying potential issues with the research question that may require primary research to be examined. Secondary data, as illustrated in Figure 8.5, refers to the existing, published data that may be utilized as a source of data and informa-

Figure 8.3: An overview of qualitative research methods.

Figure 8.4: Some of the main quantitative research methods.

tion for market research. Such data is more cost-effective and probably time-saving than gathering primary research data because the information already exists and can often be accessed via the internet. Still, it is also available in hard copy at libraries in books, magazines, and journals that have not been digitized as of yet.

There are many advantages to relying on secondary data, including, but not limited to, its readily available sources and often cheap acquisition. Unfortunately, such types of data can often be outdated. Also, it does not always fit the specific research question or directly answer the research question, as the data would have been collected originally to solve business problems other than the one at hand, lacking sufficient details.

Note that secondary research and data analysis should always take precedence over primary research and data analysis. Secondary research allows for a review of

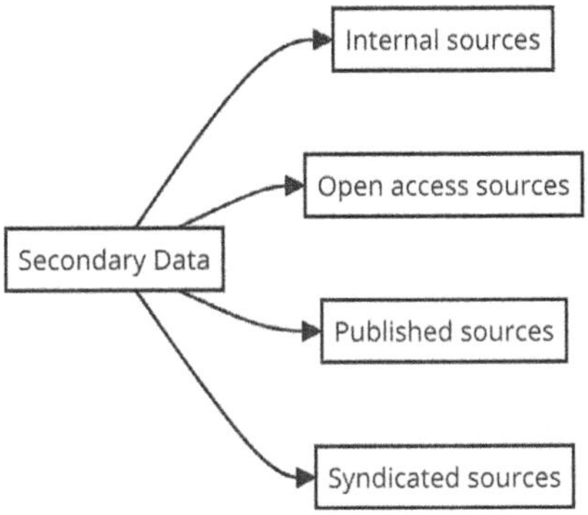

Figure 8.5: Main types of secondary data.

the related literature and existing data, which should assist the market researcher in setting the context and parameters for the primary research.

Digital Research Data

Many companies engaged in market research have been taking advantage of web analytics recorded digitally as an excellent data source. However, remember that it is typically not feasible for researchers to access web analytics data from their competitors. This method, however, can provide a company with information about its customers or clients. Another strategy to adopt when it comes to digital data is the available communications and interactions with customers via customer relationship management (CRM) resources, which can provide a good source of data about their opinions related to products and services, as well as the market and competitors. Committed customers who complain, comment, or compliment products and services provide primary information that can lay the foundation for customer satisfaction research.

Social Network Research Data

Researchers can gather data from social networks such as Twitter (now X), Facebook, LinkedIn, Pinterest, Instagram, etc. Blogs and vlogs like those on YouTube, TikTok, and the like are also good customer and market data sources. The internet can help researchers during primary or secondary (or both!) data research and with many free research tools, such as population sample size calculators, including confidence levels, the margin of error, etc. One example that comes to mind is Creative Research Systems, which provides such services for free. Social media can also be an excellent channel to reach large numbers of survey respondents or subjects at a very affordable cost. It offers a variety of ways to assess data on consumer and client sentiments or behavior patterns, which can be tracked, monitored, and analyzed. This sort of data can significantly enhance secondary research.

D. Sampling Methods

Market research sampling methods are techniques used to select a group of respondents from a larger population to estimate the characteristics or opinions of the entire population. Here is a quick summary of the primary methods:

- Random Sampling: This method, where every member of the population has an equal chance of being selected, is a beacon of fairness in market research. It effectively reduces selection bias and is best used when the population is well-defined and accessible.
- Stratified Sampling: The population is divided into smaller groups or strata, subsets that share a common characteristic. A random sample is then taken from each stratum. This method ensures representation from each stratum and is useful when researchers need to compare specific subgroups within the population.
- Cluster Sampling: The population is divided into clusters (often geographically), and these clusters are randomly selected. Further samples can be drawn within each selected cluster, making it a cost-effective choice for large-scale surveys, mainly when the population is spread out geographically.
- Systematic Sampling: A sample is drawn by randomly selecting a starting point and picking every nth element in the population list. This method simplifies and streamlines the sampling process, making it a straightforward choice for many researchers.
- Convenience Sampling: Respondents are chosen based on ease of access. It's the least expensive and most straightforward method but is prone to significant bias, making it less reliable for generalizing results to the entire population.
- Quota Sampling: Researchers fill quotas from specific subgroups like stratified sampling but without random selection. It ensures representation from each subgroup but lacks the randomness of stratified or cluster sampling, potentially leading to bias.
- Snowball Sampling: Existing study subjects recruit future subjects from among their acquaintances. This approach is beneficial for reaching populations difficult for researchers to access.

Each method has its strengths and limitations, and the choice depends on the research objectives, the nature of the population, the resources available, and the desired accuracy of the results.

Taking Advantage of Search Engines' Advanced Features

Although the internet can be a potent data source, quality can be compromised due to the sheer number of data collected through data mining and web scraping tools, such as Python, and the large array of inferior quality or fake data available. Finding credible sources can be very daunting. An alternative to improving the odds of getting credible data is to tap on advanced search engine features.

For example, Google, today's leading search engine, offers advanced search options and many other digital research features, such as Google News Archives, Google Book Search, and Google Scholar. Another alternative is to resort to several online publications, some of which are free, although some require payment.

Internal Search Data

Although web analytics packages are not a valuable source of data, they can offer significant help in using data when searching for topics or URL referrals. It can also be useful for internal data search, providing qualitative data on consumer behaviors when visiting the company's website. But then, such a resource is not only restricted to qualitative data. It can assist in quantitative data collection and research provided the data is at least observable and accurate. Examples are impressions and click-through rates left by prospective or actual customers when visiting a website. It should be noted that quantitative and qualitative data can be either primary or secondary data.

Primary Research and Data

Primary research is original research. The primary research process involves collecting primary (original) data that has never been gathered. Markets and many other investigations can be carried out through this approach, leading to the development of new theories or even research questions that may require further research and analysis. Primary research data can be quantitative or qualitative. Figure 8.6 lists the main sources of primary and secondary research data.

Primary Market Research	Secondary Market Research
Interviews	Sales reports
Questionnaires (online, phone, in person, by mail, intercepts)	Trade associations
Mystery shopping	Census data
Focus groups	Websites
Product tests	Previous market research
Diaries	Sales force input Competitive intelligence

Figure 8.6: Main sources of primary and secondary market research data.

The most common method of primary research is a survey. Primary research is conducted for a specific product or hypothesis. The data is typically gathered after secondary research has already been gathered to collect additional information that could not be gleaned. Advantages include that primary research can be tailored to answer a specific research question and focus on an appropriate target market. Disadvantages include that it can take more time to collect, and there are often higher costs involved.

Market Screening

The international market selection process requires segmentation and market target strategies. It divides the international market into distinct subsets (segments) of consumers with common needs. Segmentation varies according to various criteria, in line with the business' internationalization strategy, which can be based on demographic, psychographic, geographic, and benefit segmentation. The purpose of the screening process is not to select foreign markets but to allow the international firm to quickly focus efforts on the most promising markets by developing a group of markets that merit further research.

The International Marketing Entry Evaluation Process is a five-stage process, as depicted in Figure 8.7. It aims to gauge which international markets offer the best opportunities for our products or services to succeed. This section outlines how an organization should select which foreign to enter. The five steps are:

1. **Country Identification:** When internationalizing, enterprises have a wide selection of new markets to expand abroad. Identifying the market, country, or choice means undertaking a broad overview of all potential opportunities. While there may be a simple choice, for instance, countries with similar heritage, such as Australia and the United Kingdom, or similar languages, such as the U.S. and Australia, or even comparable cultures, political ideology, or religion, such as Cuba and China. At this stage, such selection tends to be more straightforward – for instance, a country with geographic proximity, such as Canada and the U.S. – alternatively, export markets in the same trading zone, such as the European Union or the eurozone. Again, at this stage, potential markets could be included or discarded for many reasons.
2. **Preliminary Screening:** At this second stage, the enterprise makes a more detailed analysis of those markets that were preselected after the initial screening. At this point, it is essential to start ranking the possible choices, weighing and ranking them based on macroeconomic factors such as GDP, GDP per capita, GNI, currency stability, inflation, exchange rates, level of domestic consumption, etc. Such data provide the basis for computing the market entry costs and cost-benefit analysis. A few countries, such as China, demand that a fraction of the enterprise entering their market is owned by a national, which may need to be considered. Other countries may be going through political turmoil or instability, which could significantly increase the risk of any company entering a new market. By now, at the end of this stage, a short list of potential countries should be completed before the in-depth screening begins.

3. **In-Depth Screening:** All countries making it to this point should be considered feasible for market entry. Therefore, detailed data on these potential target markets must be gathered to make the decision-making process more accurate. At this point, microeconomic factors and market research concerning the marketing mix (the 4 Ps or 7 Ps) should be considered.
4. **Final Selection:** The final shortlist of potential countries should be decided at this stage. Upper management should reflect upon their strategic goals and align them with the best alternative among the countries that made the final list. Management should also consider the competition in the market or any similar domestic companies that could impose a barrier to entry into the new market. All the data should be ranked, and a final scoring should be weighted among the potential markets based on the selected criteria, aligning with the enterprise's mission and goals. Upper management, at this stage, should try to visit *finalists* few nations remaining on the shortlist.
5. **Direct Experience:** Personal experience is essential. Upper management should travel to the finalist's nation(s) and experience the market's culture, business environment, and practices firsthand. Management needs to be flexible and experimental in these new countries and avoid being judgmental. Remember to be cognitive of self-reference criteria (SCR), as the impressions one may have are based on their professional life, mainly from their nation, and their expectations will be based on what they already know.

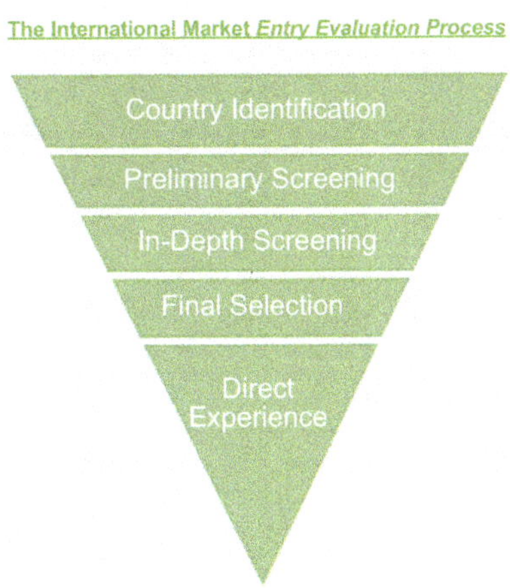

Figure 8.7: International Marketing Entry Evaluation Process. (SOURCE: Adapted from Johansson, 2000).

Internationalization Modes of Entry

Due to the intricacy of the processes involved in the internationalization of MNEs, scholars have proposed several theories to enable a smoother internationalization entry into foreign markets. Among the many approaches and their unique features, as depicted in Figure 8.8, internationalization theories can be divided into four primary schools of thought, subdivided into based and non-based FDI, and focused on how MNEs can gain and sustain competitive advantages through their operations in foreign markets.

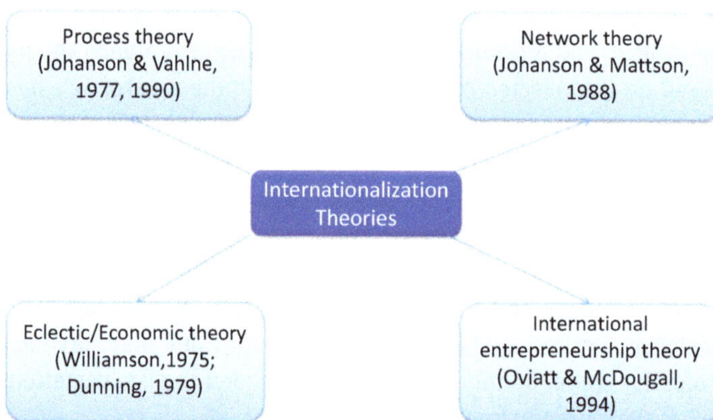

Figure 8.8: Main internationalization process theories.

Table 8.1 provides an overview of these main paradigms, theories, and approaches. These can be broken up into nine major internationalization theories, which share various constructs and explain enterprises' strategic decision making to remain successful in international markets.

Table 8.1: Theories of the internationalization process and market selection entry mode.

Paradigm	Theory	Explanation of the Choice of Entry	Founder
Market Imperfection Paradigm	Monopolistic Advantage Theory	If market imperfection is high, FDI will be preferred. Otherwise, licensing is adopted.	Hymer (1960)
Market Imperfection Paradigm	International Product Life Cycle Theory	In the early stage of product life cycle, exporting is preferred. In later stages, FDI is adopted.	Vernon (1966)
Behavioural Paradigm	Internationalization Theory	Due to market uncertainty, firms use sequential stages entry modes from indirect exporting to direct exporting and full ownership.	Johanson & Wiedersheim-Paul

Table 8.1 (continued)

Paradigm	Theory	Explanation of the Choice of Entry	Founder
Behavioural Paradigm	Networks Theory	If network relations provide strong competitive advantages, FDI is preferred. Otherwise, low control modes are adopted.	Håkansson (1987)
Market Failure Paradigm	Internalization Theory	If firms face a high market failure, FDI is preferred. Otherwise, licensing is adopted.	Buckley & Casson (1976)
Market Failure Paradigm	Eclectic Theory (OLI Model)	If home market has (L), exporting is preferred. If (L) resides in the host market, high (I) will result in FDI. Otherwise, licensing is adopted.	Dunning (1977)
Market Failure Paradigm	Transaction Cost Theory (TC)	If transaction-specificity of an asset is high, firms prefer high control modes. Otherwise, low control modes are adopted.	Anderson & Gatignon (1986)
Current Approaches	Resource-based View (RVB)	Firms with strong firm-specific resources prefer high control modes. Otherwise, low control modes are adopted.	Wernerfelt (1984)
Current Approaches	Contingency Theory	Choice of entry mode depends on the internal and external environmental factors. Intrapreneurial service firms prefer franchising or WOS.	Okoroafo (1990)

Theories of Internationalization Process and Mode of Entry

Over the past decade, the academic and economic importance of MNEs from emerging and frontier economies has grown in importance, with numerous scholars attempting to document and explain the internationalization processes of those enterprises. Starting with Hymer in 1960, several researchers have tried to document their mode of entry and market selection when internationalizing, including but not limited to Dunning (1981), Rugman (1981), Whitelock (2002), Zhou and Wu (2007), Zucchella et al. (2007), and others.

International business research initially relied on economic theories from the 1930s. Researchers then introduced the early theories of internationalization in the 1960s and 1970s. Sharma and Erramilli, back in 2004, had grouped these theories into three paradigms: market imperfection, behavioral, and market failure. The first theories aiding the understanding of the internationalization of enterprises had a microeconomic scope when trying to explain the reasons for an enterprise to internationalize.

The Market Imperfection Paradigm

An imperfect international market is any economic market that does not meet the rigorous standards of a hypothetical perfectly competitive market partial equilibrium framework. It arises whenever individual buyers and sellers influence prices and production or when perfect data is unknown to all market actors.

There are two internationalization theories derived from this line of thought. First is Hymer's monopolistic advantage theory developed in 1960, which argues that an MNE will only enter a foreign market if market imperfections are high. FDI is preferred; otherwise, licensing is adopted. Second is Vernon's international product lifecycle theory, developed in 1966, which contends that an MNE will select export as a choice of entry during the early stages of the product life cycle. The MNE would adopt FDI in later stages.

The market imperfection paradigm originated from the industrial-organizational theory of the enterprise in which industries operating in imperfect international markets with fewer competition forces and more significant entry mode barriers are prone to offer higher returns on investment (ROI). International market imperfections might exist in production marketplaces (i.e., product/service differentiation, branding, and international marketing skills) and factor markets (i.e., proprietary technology and managerial skills). These imperfections may also include competitive imperfections brought by government regulations and policies, other types of restrictions (i.e., tariffs), and imperfect competition due to economies of scale.

Some scholars have argued that in an imperfect market, the certainty of the competitive environment is higher, and an enterprise obtains more market power, controls products and prices, and gains higher profits. Such an enterprise can control the number of existing and potential rivals differently. Others, however, argued that enterprises try to restrict markets in their home country and aim to control foreign markets. Based on the industrial-organizational theory, an international operation is costlier than doing business in the home country. Therefore, MNEs must have some advantages to operate in foreign markets and bear the consequent costs. The international market imperfection paradigm includes the monopolistic advantage theory and the international product life cycle (IPLC) theory.

The Monopolistic Advantage Theory

The monopolistic advantage theory attempts to explain international business and why enterprises can compete in foreign settings against indigenous competitors). It is often linked to the seminal contribution of Stephen Hymer. Before Hymer's doctoral thesis, theories did not sufficiently explain why enterprises invested in expansions abroad. Hymer started his research by analyzing the motivations behind the international investment of US MNCs in foreign markets. Neoclassical theories, mainstream at the time, explained foreign direct investments as capital movements across borders based on perceived benefits from interest rates in different markets; there was no need to separate them from any other kind of investment.

Hymer argued that producing overseas was costly for the enterprise due to the significant uncertainty regarding this operation, such as exchange rate fluctuations, more attention needed to switching costs, and lower market knowledge. Hymer started his research in 1976 by analyzing the motivations behind FDI outflows of U.S. corporations in other foreign markets. The neoclassical theories of Hymer's time explained FDI as capital movements across borders based on perceived benefits from interest rates in different markets. There was no need to separate them from any other kind of investment. Hymer effectively differentiated FDI and portfolio investments by including the notion of control of foreign enterprises in FDI theory, which implied control of the operation. In contrast, foreign investment portfolios bestow a share of ownership but not control. He focused on and considered FDI and MNE as part of the enterprise theory.

Given these reasons, any local enterprise would have some intrinsic advantages against any MNE trying to produce locally. Accordingly, Hymer suggested that an MNE assess market and product imperfections overseas via an owned competitive advantage correlated to all its intangible business assets. This imperfection may refer to local producers' inefficiency in providing the market or existing unexplored opportunities. The competitive advantage for enterprises exploring foreign markets directly correlates with product diversification or knowledge acquired through research and development.

After Hymer, many other approaches have contributed to the argument about the development of MNEs. Hymer considered FDI levels and MNE's structure as part of the enterprise theory. Still, he effectively differentiated FDI and portfolio investments by including the notion of control of foreign enterprises in FDI Theory. Such theory implied that control of the operation, although within portfolio foreign investment, confers an ownership share but not control. He also ignored the premise that FDIs are driven by the search for low costs in foreign countries. He emphasized that local enterprises cannot compete effectively against MNE, even though they must face foreign barriers such as cultural, political, linguistic, etc., to enter the market. He suggested enterprises invest in foreign markets to maximize their specific business advantages in imperfect markets. In other words, markets where the flow of information is uneven allow enterprises to benefit from a competitive advantage over the local competition.

Hymer also suggested removing conflicts as a second element for enterprises engaging in foreign operations. A dispute arises when competing MNEs are operating in a foreign market or are willing to enter one. An MNE can share or take complete control of foreign production through FDI, effectively removing conflict. Such a process can increase market power for the specific MNE, increasing imperfections in the market.

A final determinant for MNEs engaging in FDI is the distribution of risk through diversification. By choosing different markets and production locations, the danger inherent in foreign operations is spread and reduced. These incentives for FDI are all built based on market imperfections and conflict. An enterprise engaging in FDI could reduce competition, eliminate conflicts, and exploit its business-specific advantages, capacitating it to succeed in a foreign market.

Critique of the Monopolistic Advantage Theory

At Hymer's time, about thirty years earlier, the dominant business activities of MNEs were monopolies and oligopolies. In other words, giant multinational corporations were heavily involved in internationalization, often with the support of oligopolies.

Such a trend affected his interpretations, while the nature of international business and trade, the origin of MNEs, and their business strategies have changed over recent decades. If host governments follow Hymer and restrict FDI flows and the activities of MNEs, they would lose their access to the capabilities.

The main problem with Hymer's theory was that he had no realistic welfare criteria to assess MNEs. He considered *flawless competition* his benchmark, which is rarely attainable in a domestic market, much less globally. Further, Hymer's views were shaped based on his experiences in third-world countries with poor agriculture-based economies at the end of the colonial era. Therefore, his theory cannot understand international business strategies and activities in a global market landscape. In 1985, however, Dunning maintained that the aggressive approach of the governments of emerging economies toward private enterprises influenced Hymer's ideas about MNEs.

In contrast, nowadays, the relationship between MNEs and host governments is friendlier, especially considering that MNEs often supply host countries with resources they cannot obtain quickly or should buy at a higher cost. The monopolistic advantage theory has overlooked the role of government in shaping institutions and its responsibility for setting effective policies to support MNEs and participate in international economic development. Hymer ignored the part of small enterprises in the world economy. He kept pushing for central planning by governments in line with the Marxist ideology, which subsequently failed in most socialist nations.

International Product Life Cycle Theory

Raymond Vernon developed the international product life cycle (IPLC) theory back in 1966, with some improved revisions in 1974, as a reaction to the inability of the Heckscher-Ohlin model to explain the observed pattern of international trade. Per Vernon, each product has a specific life cycle that begins with its development and ends with its decline. The theory proposes that early in a product's lifecycle, all parts and labor related to the product originated from the areas in which it was invented. Once products are adopted and on-demand in the international markets, production gradually moves away from the point of origin. In some situations, the product becomes an item imported by its original country of the invention. In other words, as illustrated in Figure 8.9, products would enter a market and gradually disappear again.

This model applies to labor-saving and capital-using products that, at least at first, cater to high-income groups. The model shows an active comparative advantage. The country with the comparative advantage in manufacturing the product changes from innovative countries to emerging or frontier countries. According to this theory, there are four steps in a product's life cycle: a. introduction; b. growth; c. maturity; and d. decline. The duration of each of these stages may vary according to different products. One phase of the product life cycle may last some weeks, while others could last even decades. The lifespan of a product and how fast it goes through the entire process depends on the market demand and how marketing tools are used, as illustrated in Figure 8.10.

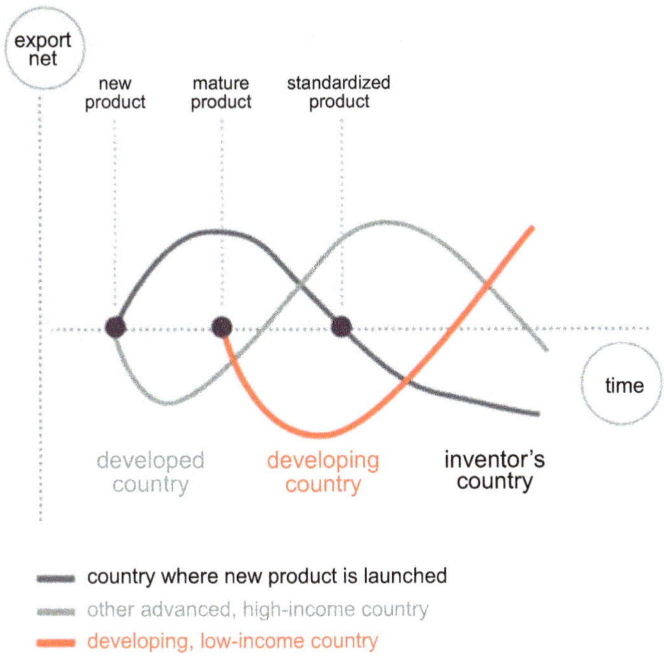

Figure 8.9: International product life cycle theory. (SOURCE: Vernon, 1974).

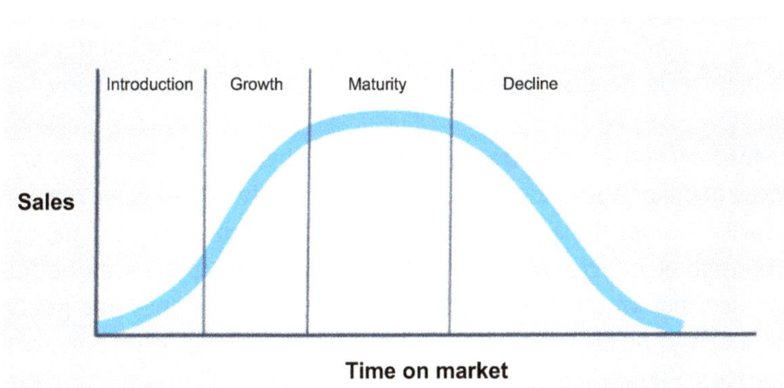

Figure 8.10: Vernon's international product life cycle. (SOURCE: Vernon, 1966).

Critiques of International Product Life Cycle

Although the IPLC model considers the enterprise level, it focuses on the country level of trade. By concentrating on the location advantage of the host country, this theory elucidates why enterprises make different FDI decisions in various target markets. In 1993, the first two stages of the IPLC model merged, and a third stage was established, incorporating three steps: a new product stage, a maturity stage, and a standardization stage. Later, in 2003, other scholars altered this three-stage IPLC model again, arguing that enterprises with innovation capability could benefit from the main comparative advantage that MNEs in the U.S. enjoyed.

The IPLC model was also criticized as too wide-ranging to describe the globalization patterns of all enterprises., especially considering that the entry mode choice in the globalization stage is more discerning and strategic. Also, the model disregards products not traded throughout all the steps of the IPLC because of technological improvements or market deregulations.

The IPLC theory's main limitation is its attempt to explain a time-dependent process and deterministic evolutionary path. In addition, the IPLC model does not sufficiently describe the products with a short life cycle. If an enterprise has previous experience in international markets, this model cannot accurately explain its new products' internationalization process. Such a model tends to be more viable for manufacturing enterprises than service ones. The IPLC theory does not explain the different forms of exporting and joint ventures.

Behavioral Paradigm

The behavioral paradigm originated from the behavioral theories of Cyert and March in 1963, later enhanced by Aharoni in 1966. The theory viewed internationalization as a reactive and progressive learning process where collective knowledge prompted enterprises to enter international markets. The theory proposes that the market knowledge of an enterprise grows progressively over time because acquiring information has a high cost, and managers have limited rationality. In an imperfect market, an enterprise seeks short-term benefits, avoids risk, and favors contentment instead of maximizing profit.

Several decades later, other scholars argued that the behavioral paradigm proposed that an investment in a foreign market increases slowly. MNEs are driven to evade inter-enterprise relationships as they demand a high resource commitment in the long term. Yet another internationalization theory was developed based on this method, which argued that an internationalization process occurs slowly and gradually. This process is driven by an enterprise's experiential knowledge gained by market activity in international markets.

The Uppsala Model

After analyzing the existing internationalization theories up to that time and the internationalization of four Swedish enterprises, Johanson and Wiedersheim-Paul introduced a new theory in 1975. They contended that enterprises needed an *international attitude* that led them to venture abroad and that this attitude was affected by experiences that enterprises gained from their international activities. When enterprises decide to enter global markets, they face countless difficulties and risks. They need to acquire knowledge of these foreign markets to decrease investment risks. In their view, the gradual internationalization process is when enterprises expand their operations into foreign markets through a series of steps. These steps included four sequential and successive stages representing higher international involvement and resource commitment degrees.

As a theory, the Uppsala model explains how enterprises gradually intensify their activities in foreign markets. This framework has been one of the most discussed dynamic theories in the Nordic Schools and international business research, as it has affected many studies that explain the internationalization process of MNEs. These Swedish researchers from Uppsala University criticized the current theories of that time explaining international involvement. They held that most theories of that time did not consider much of the problems caused by cultural differences and ignored the internal foundations needed so that companies could handle international activities.

As shown in Figure 8.11, the Uppsala model is based on four central concepts:

1. *Market knowledge* is the enterprise's knowledge about the targeted foreign market and operations. It is subdivided into general knowledge about marketing methods, customer tastes, and market-specific knowledge about the business environment, market structure, and cultural patterns.
2. *Market commitment* refers to the quantum of resources committed to the targeted foreign market or the size of the investment, which may include marketing, organization, personnel, and other areas.
3. *Current activities* relate to the current business operations of enterprises that help them acquire experience, identify opportunities abroad, achieve desired outcomes, and start a new business more efficiently.
4. *Commitment* decisions may include decisions taken to formalize resources with operations overseas.

These decisions are often made in response to market opportunities and threats.

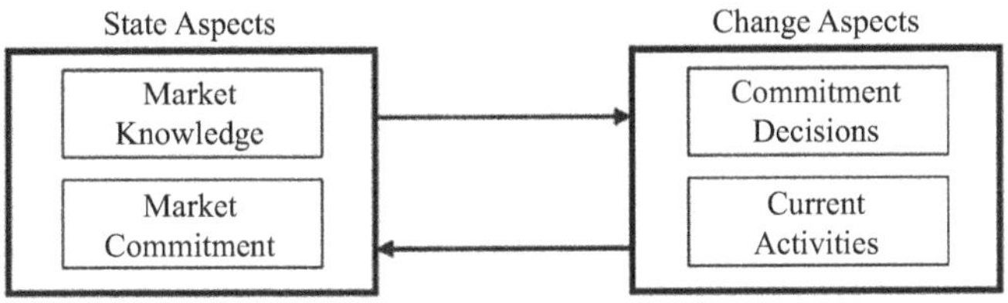

Figure 8.11: The basic mechanism of internationalization.

As depicted in Figure 8.12, enterprises operate in the domestic market in the first stage and have no ordinary export activities. In the second stage, enterprises export their products through agents or intermediaries in host countries. Then, in the third stage, MNEs establish an overseas sales subsidiary. In the last step, enterprises locate their overseas production line or manufacturing units. In other words, enterprises initially enter an international market using indirect exporting as a low-control entry mode. Then, they switch to direct exporting and wholly owned subsidiaries as high control modes. In such a process, enterprises gradually increase their involvement and resource commitment.

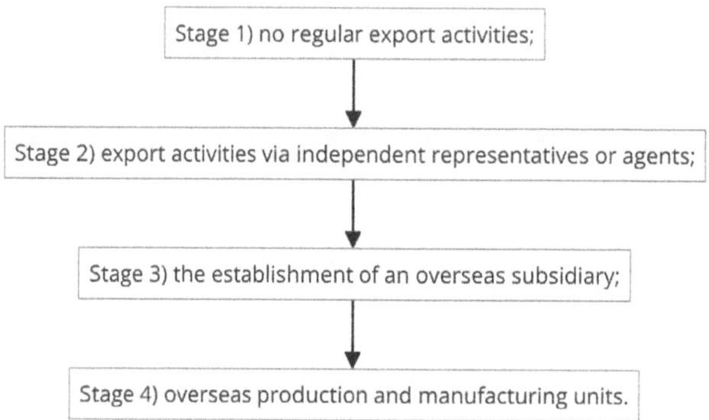

Figure 8.12: Internationalization through decreasing psychic distance.

Another essential theme argued by Johanson and Vahlne is the concept of *psychic distance,* which could offer insights into how challenging it would be to enter a new market. It includes language, education, culture, business practices, and industrial development differences, potentially hindering information flow from and to the markets and raising uncertainty. To minimize market uncertainty and exploit market opportunities, enterprises should obtain experiential knowledge through personal experience in the specific market. Such experiential understanding enables them to bear the risk of higher resource commitment, allowing them to enter the markets with higher psychic and greater geographical distance.

The Uppsala internationalization model distinguishes four different steps of entering an international market, which cannot be viewed independently of a company's situation, market, or knowledge. A more detailed depiction of these four steps is shown in Figure 8.13, which includes: 1. No regular export activities (sporadic export); 2. Export via an independent representative (export mode); 3. Establishment of a foreign sales subsidiary; and 4. Foreign production/manufacturing.

Critiques of the Uppsala Model

The Uppsala model has been criticized for using an experimental survey method approach that was not explained in detail. Consequently, making a logical connection between the empirical study and the theoretical concept is challenging. The model assumes experiential knowledge is achieved through seeking and learning. It also argues that enterprises usually prevent risk. Nevertheless, such postulations have been questioned.

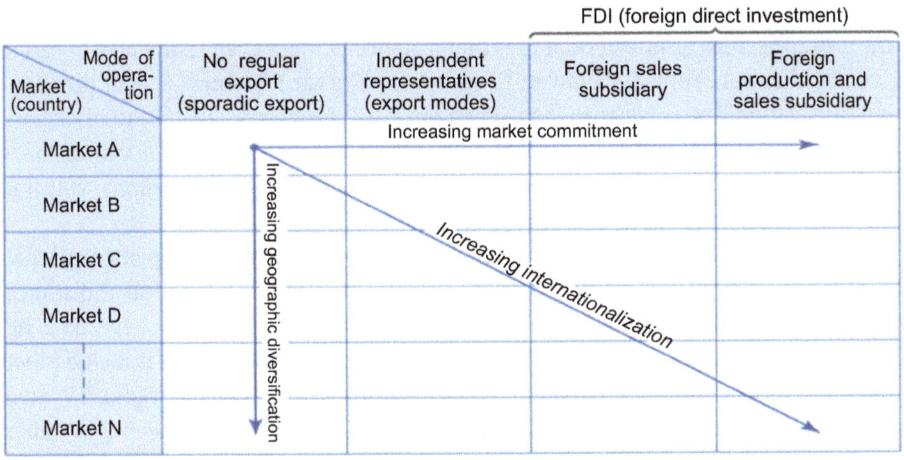

Figure 8.13: Uppsala's incremental approach to internationalization.

In 2009, Johanson and Vahlne made some modifications to their model. Then, in 2011, two other IB scholars, Santangelo and Meyer, argued that gaining experiential knowledge through the learning process helps enterprises assess their strategies and make necessary changes. But this establishment chain is deterministic. It cannot be stopped once an internationalization process starts. This claim ignored essential elements, such as the influence of key decision-makers, which can end an internationalization process through opportunistic behavior, power games, or even corrupted behavior, which tends to be frequent in emerging and frontier economies. Furthermore, the basic settings of the U-model are changed during the internationalization process, which means that the model's variables may turn into constants.

Another issue with the U-model is that it was based on research in manufacturing industries only and neglected the services sector. It focused on individual enterprises, excluding the effects of networks, supply chains, and distribution channels. Hence, the model cannot be used to develop forecasts as it only provides a limited explanation since it excludes essential aspects of the internationalization process. Some of the most critical processes include technology, enterprise size, strategic considerations, economies of scale, and many other economic variables that may affect internationalization.

Subsequently, within the next two decades, Johanson and Vahlne introduced and enhanced the Uppsala internationalization stages model. This model is also known as the *U-model,* in which an enterprise applies high control modes when its knowledge of international markets is low and when it achieves more experience and maturity. This method inspired other IB scholars in the early 1990s and 2000s to develop *innovation-related models of internationalization* or *I-models.*

CAGE Distance Framework

The CAGE Distance Framework argues that distance matters even in the face of extensive globalization. Pankaj Megawatt Ghemawat, a Harvard Business School professor and international strategy guru, developed the CAGE framework in 2001 to offer businesses a way to evaluate countries regarding their distance. He argues that distance between two countries can manifest itself along four primary dimensions: cultural, administrative, geographic, and economic distance (CAGE).

He argued that MNEs would always face complex challenges during internationalization due to enduring distance between people through CAGE. Cultural distance, concerning different ethnicities, religions, languages, and social values, can be a significant barrier when internationalizing. Industries most impacted by it include food and those having linguistic content (i.e., printed or electronic media, radio, TV, etc.). Size is also a cultural factor (Americans prefer big cars, while Japanese and Brazilian small ones). In the Americas, a strong demand exists for small trucks, while this does not happen in Europe.

As illustrated in Figure 8.14, MNEs considering internationalization into a new market must first consider the distance factors that separate the two countries. An international market selection should be made by evaluating the market potential versus the distance factor that exists among them.

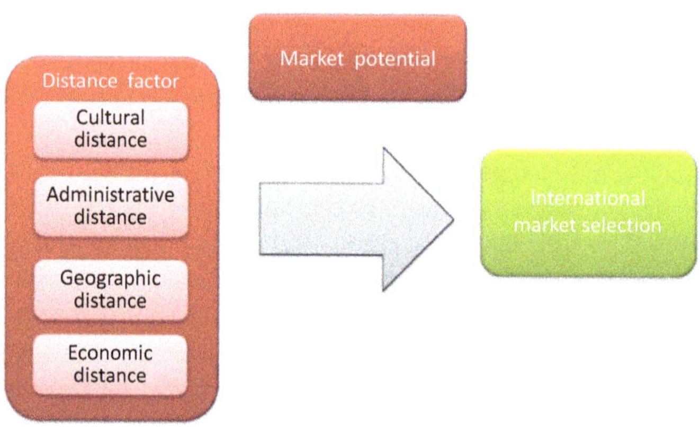

Figure 8.14: CAGE distance framework.

These studies' results reveal an incremental behavior feature for their internationalization. Such differences may include religious beliefs, attitudes toward time, relationships with the environment, social norms, and language. In addition, psychic distance tends to affect the market selection process, although it is not considered a determinant factor when considering expansion abroad or the foreign direct investment (FDI) destination.

One of the main differences between the CAGE framework and other nation analysis frameworks is its inclusion of bilateral and unilateral factors. CAGE's distances and differences have been demonstrated quantitatively via gravity models. These models resemble Newton's law of gravitation in linking interactions between countries to the product of their sizes. Usually, gross domestic product (GDP) is divided by some composite measure of distance. Table 8.2 provides more details on each CAGE subcategory and how it may manifest depending on whether one compares a pair of countries as internationalization targets or looks at anyone in isolation.

He developed the CAGE framework, depicted in Figure 8.15, to assist businesses in gauging the distance between a target country and the firm's home country on four distinct dimensions. The greater the distance between two countries, the greater the risks and the lesser the opportunities for success.

The following is a brief description of these four distance dimensions:

- **Cultural** – refers to cultural distinctions between the target and home countries. The history of affinities between countries explains the similarities or distance (differences) between these cultures. For example, numerous nations underwent colonialism and domination of many imperial rules in the past, which centuries later still impacted their contemporary culture and influenced national relationships. For example, despite being a former British colony, there is a smaller cultural distance between Americans and the British than between the Americans and the French. Nonetheless, it has not always been the case. Similarly, Western European nations have a substantial cultural distance from many Asian nations despite colonizing numerous countries.

  So, history alone only offers a partial understanding of such cultural distances. Other factors to help best understand such distances include societal traditions and customs, as well as values and moral traits. Language must be considered, as such differences can significantly increase or decrease cultural distance. Take the example of the U.S. and India, which, at a glance, would suggest a considerable cultural distance. Such distance is significantly reduced as businesses in India and the U.S. are conducted similarly, and both nations were British colonies in the past.
- **Administrative** – refers to the influence of the government of a country and its legal and political systems compared to the MNC's/MNE's home country. In nations where the political systems are very distinct, for instance, democracy versus theocracy or communism, there is a more significant distance and uncertainty. Different laws and regulations between nations can cause compliance and the business process between the two countries more challenging. For example, some governments do not enforce contracts or agreements compliance laws. In other nations, if a customer fails to make payment for goods or services, the vendor may sue, but it likely will take years before a tribunal even has a chance to hear the case. Labor legislation can be distinct among countries across the globe. In the Dominican Republic and Brazil (and many other countries in Latin America), for example, firms are mandated to compensate workers for an extra month in

Table 8.2: CAGE categories and how they can manifest themselves depending on whether one compares a pair of countries or examines one in isolation.

	Cultural Distance	Administrative Distance	Geographic Distance	Economic Distance
Country Pairs (Bilateral)	– Different languages – Different ethnicities; lack of connective ethnic or social networks – Different religions – Lack of trust – Different values, norms, and dispositions	– Lack of colonial ties – Lack of shared regional trading bloc – Lack of common currency – Political hostility	– Physical distance – Lack of land border – Differences in time zones – Differences in climates/disease environments	– Rich/poor differences – Other differences in the cost or quality of natural resources, financial resources, human resources, infrastructure, information, or knowledge
Countries (Unilateral/ Multilateral)	– Insularity – Traditionalism	– Nonmarket/closed economy (home bias vs. foreign bias) – Lack of membership in international organizations – Weak institutions, corruption	– Landlockedness – Lack of internal navigability – Geographic size – Geographic remoteness – Weak transportation or communication links	– Economic size – Low per capita income

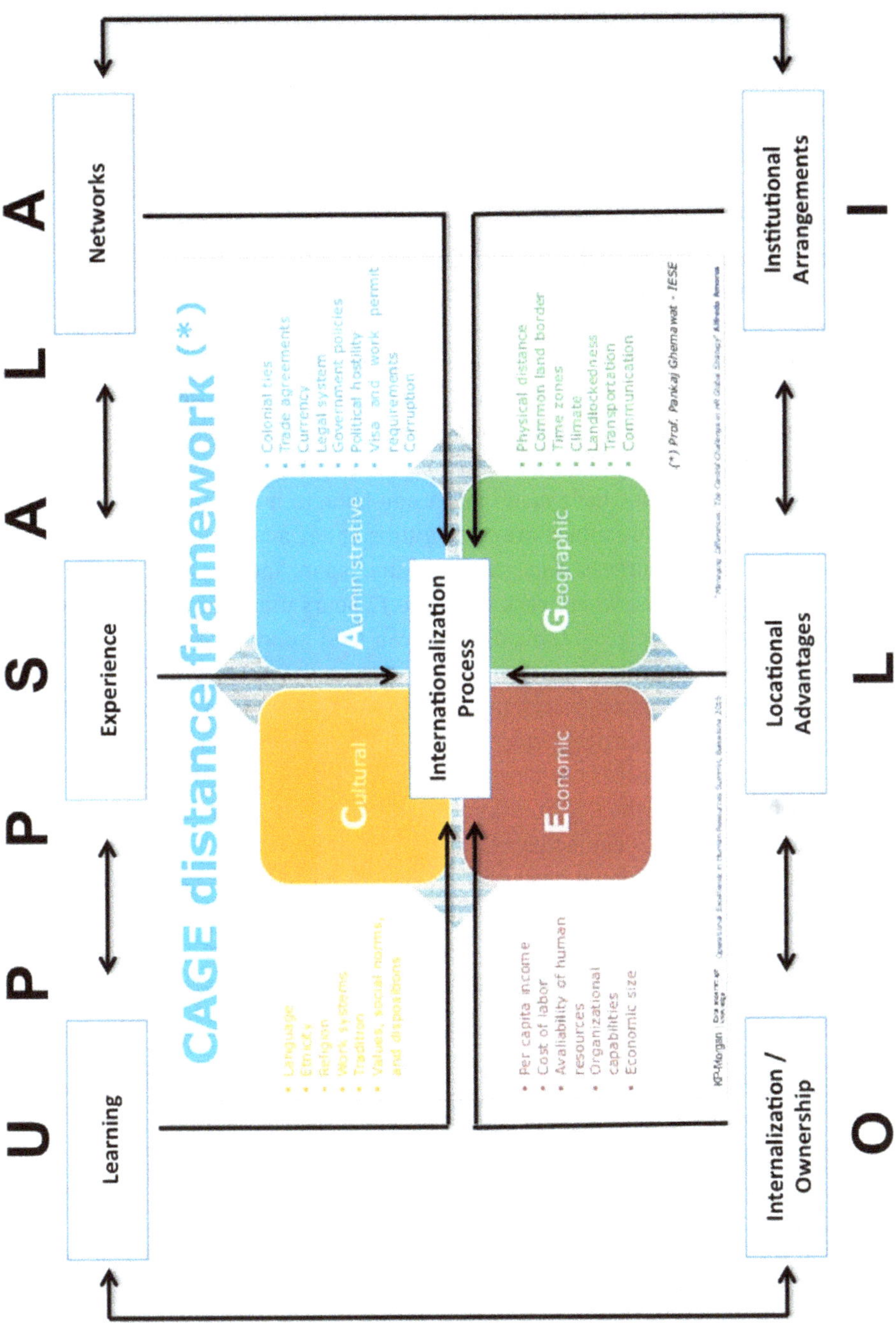

Figure 8.15: The CAGE distance framework.

the year, known as the thirteenth month of salary, as a bonus. Other countries have more robust protection of the civil rights of individuals who fall within considered vulnerable categories. For instance, in the U.S., under diversity, equity, and inclusion (DEI), some examples are workers' age, race, sex, class, gender, sexual orientation, etc. In many other countries, it may not. Such differences, or distances, can raise especially problematic issues for international firms, who must abide by their home country's laws but adapt to those in a target country.

- **Geographic** – refers to the physical distance between the home country and the target nation. The more miles or kilometers separating it from the target nations, the more expensive it will be to reach that market and export or import products. But the physical distance is not the only concerning factor. Communication between nations is essential, especially when countries are spread far apart. Advances in integrated communication technologies (ICT), such as telephone, the internet, social media, and community of practice platforms such as LinkedIn, Instagram, and the like, have made this a non-issue in most countries, but not all. However, when two nations are twelve time zones apart, such as the U.S., and many nations in Southeast Asia, such as China, Japan, and Singapore, communication can be hindered when work plans are 12 hours uncoordinated. Another factor impacted by the geographic distance can be a nation's other infrastructures besides telecommunications, such as access to roads, seaports, airports, railroad grids, electrical grids, water systems, etc. For instance, Brazil is physically close to the U.S. but lacks good deep-water seaports, making loading and unloading heavy ships difficult and time-consuming. Haiti is another example as, despite its even closer proximity to the U.S., it lacks adequate port facilities, making it a poor target for outsourcing manufacturing.
- **Economic** – International business between two nations can be impacted by the economic differences. The more significant the discrepancies between the two nations, the more challenging it is for a foreign firm to be successful there. If a target country's purchasing power and disposable income are too different from the home country, working in the target country will be more challenging.

Let us assume Chipotle thinks there are excellent opportunities to go international. The CAGE framework can help management devise an internationalization strategy and make decisions. These four dimensions for each nation can be measured on a 10-point scale, with the higher values indicating more significant distance and challenges. Upper management has narrowed the target nations to two: Canada, for being close and similar to the U.S., and Spain, for its more than 10 million extra inhabitants than Canada, with a more geographically concentrated market, and the fact Spaniards may be more attracted to the company's Mexican cuisine menu. Thus, the nation with the lower score should be more suitable. Table 8.3 illustrates the process.

Table 8.3: Using the CAGE framework to assess Canada vs. Spain for Chipotle's expansion.

	Cultural (C)	Administrative (A)	Geographic (G)	Economic (E)	Total
Canada	3 Oh, there is the French-speaking part of Canada	2 Parliamentarian with Prime Minister vs. US	2 Very close, but cities very spread out	2 About the same except for currency	9
Spain	7 Language difference, and they don't eat much Mexican food	5 Member of EU, similar to US, some laws different	5 Easy 6 hour plane flight, 6 hour time difference	6 US GDP per capita twice Spain's.	23

Networks Theory

The networks theory was developed in the late 1980s. It was based on organizational sociology postulating that network relationships enable enterprises to expand internationally much faster than traditional models of internationalization, as business activities are collaborative, especially in service industries. Organizational and industrial sociological theoreticians have contended that management actions are entrenched in social network relationships. A social network may be described as a set of nodes (e.g., persons, organizations) linked by a set of social relationships (e.g., friendship, transfer of funds, overlapping memberships) of a specified type. Think about LinkedIn.com, Instagram, etc.

Considering this view, management researchers have argued that the social capital exemplified in developing managerial social networks and ties with external entities, a micro-level concept, affects an enterprise's competitive advantage and performance as a macro-level concept. Most empirical studies testing the micro-macro linkage have focused on the impact of social capital developed from the networking relationships with only the upper management of other enterprises (i.e., providers, buyers, and contenders) on organizational activities.

A model of networks developed by IB scholars Håkansson and Johanson back in 1992 presents the basic structure of the industrial network as a combination of three variables: activities, actors, and resources. These elements are linked together to describe the dimensions of industrial networks. An actor can be anyone in the network who controls activities or resources. Activities occur when an actor combines, uses, develops, creates, or exchanges resources in a way that makes value, and finally, resources are anything that the actor controls. In a network, it is typical that the relationships between actors are invisible and fluid, and they cannot be seen from the outside, so one, such as a potential competitor, cannot gain a clear idea of the network structure. Consequently, preparing pre-entry checklists to enter the new market will be less beneficial for an outsider.

Critiques of the Network Model

Aside from its empirical arguments, several scholars have criticized the network theory. Some have argued that the theory does not offer a predictive model and that the network relations it outlines are intuitively ad hoc and unintentional. Also, other researchers have argued that the qualitative methodology used by this model could not be verified. The theory does not explain the internationalization process of enterprises without network relationships or demonstrate the mechanism by which such MNEs can identify network contacts. Network relationships are assumed to be a semi-permanent system based on structured interdependence, although, in some industries, these relations only survive for a few exchanges. In addition, other scholars have argued that relationships in business networks are not always constant and that if an enterprise enters turbulent or conflictive business networks, it will deal with all sorts of ambiguities and changes, especially when attempting to access reliable information, which could be problematic. The networks theory also neglects the fundamental power relations dominating the business relationships of service enterprises.

Market Failure Paradigm

The market failure paradigm (MFP), proposed by Coase in 1937, is grounded in the theory of an enterprise's nature. He alleged that an enterprise selects between international markets and hierarchies by considering relative efficiency. According to MFP, when foreign market competition is perfect, low control modes, such as exporting or licensing, are very effective. If this market fails, however, an enterprise will prefer FDI and internalize its operations. This paradigm has been a primary paradigm when studying internationalization entry modes since the late 1970s.

Internalization Theory

Internalization theory is a branch of economics used to analyze international business behavior. It focuses on imperfections in intermediate product markets. Buckley and Casson first developed the theory in 1976 to explain the progression of American MNEs after World War II. The internalization theory has roots in the theory of the nature of the enterprise offered by Coase earlier in 1937, which argued that the internalization of external transactions might affect the nature, survival, and growth of enterprises. He suggested that the existence of enterprises is related to the transaction costs of using the price mechanism. Enterprises must pay such fees to determine their property rights and negotiate, monitor, and enforce business contracts.

The internalization theory is the most effective application of transaction cost economics (TCE). Therefore, some IB researchers use the terms interchangeably. Based on the internalization theory, markets are naturally imperfect. In host markets, MNEs avoid market imperfections by internalizing their operations regarding tacit knowledge, raw materials, intermediate products, and perishable goods. Nevertheless, internalization may reduce economies of scale and result in host government restrictions or difficulty in cross-border communication. As illustrated in Figure 8.16, when transaction costs in the markets for the intermediate inputs of technology and knowledge are high, FDI or hierarchical integration will be more efficient. MNEs are formed when markets are internalized across national borders to disseminate them among different product categories and international target markets. Through this drive to reduce costs, enterprises would attempt to select the best structures possible based on evaluating the costs related to each production phase.

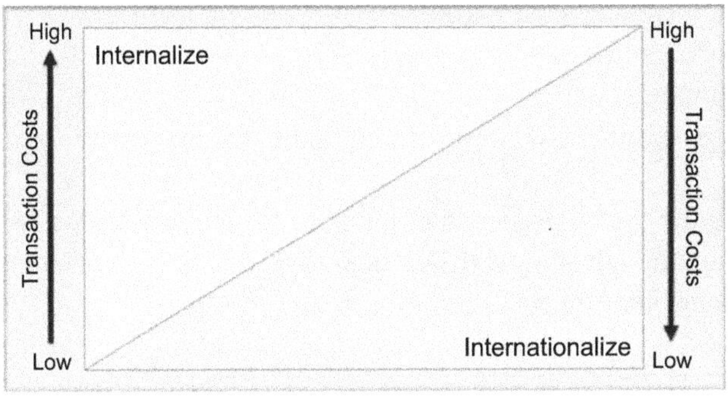

Figure 8.16: Internalization theory.

The internalization theory focuses on the relative costs and benefits of collaboration concerning the type of knowledge that partners exchange.

Critique of Internationalization Theory

The internalization theory has been criticized for some of its limitations. One main criticism argues that the theory does not show the effect of location advantages on the entry mode choice. Other critics point out that the theory assumes that competition in foreign markets and host countries involves a monopolistic enterprise with inferior technology that is inactive in dealing with the entrant. In today's markets, the nature of competition is dissimilar and dynamic.

Critics argue that this theory only addresses the situation in which enterprises enter international markets to seek new opportunities or to gain access to a niche market. In addition, critics point out that the theory's focus on cost minimization is quite restrictive, as it does not include enterprises' motivation to enter a foreign market and enhance their capabilities. In addition, the internalization theory cannot compare FDI with exporting, as it assumes conditions that result in FDI. This theory does not explain the ambiguities caused by the behavior of local partners in a joint venture or major problems regarding mergers and acquisitions. The approach also disregards network actors' impact on enterprises' internationalization process.

Eclectic Paradigm Theory – The OLI Model

As a theory in economics, the eclectic paradigm, also known as the OLI model or OLI framework, developed by Dunning in 1979, is a further development of the internalization theory, which is based on the transaction cost theory. The premise of this theory is that transactions are made within an enterprise if the transaction costs on a free market are higher than the internal costs, known as internalization. Integrating perspectives from these disciplines, Dunning proposed a comprehensive framework, which postulated that three types of determinant factors influence the choice of an internationalization entry mode into a target market:

- **O**wnership advantages of an enterprise
- **L**ocation advantages of a market and
- **I**nternalization advantages of integrating transactions within the enterprise.

As illustrated in Figure 8.17, the model argues that, for FDI to occur, an MNE must possess firm-specific or ownership advantages (FSAs) such as trademarks, economies of scale, and technology, among other things.

Source: Dunning (1981)		Categories of advantages		
		Ownership advantages	Internalization advantages	Locational advantages
Form of market entry	Licensing	Yes	No	No
	Export	Yes	Yes	No
	FDI	Yes	Yes	Yes

Figure 8.17: The eclectic paradigm model.

Various empirical research has attempted to use the Dunning framework directly or indirectly in explaining the choice between a joint venture and solo venture, licensing and solo venture, and the acquisition ratio to total subsidiaries. Three factors determine the international activities of multinational enterprises (MNEs), as depicted in Figure 8.18.

The OLI paradigm explains outward foreign direct investment (FDI), suggesting that MNEs develop competitive O advantages domestically and transfer these overseas to specific markets (depending on L advantages) through FDI, which allows the MNE to internalize the "O" advantages. In contrast to the eclectic paradigm, internalization theory mainly explains the entry mode choice. For instance, "I" advantages surpass the externality of knowledge as a public utility, such that FDI is the best choice for licensing,

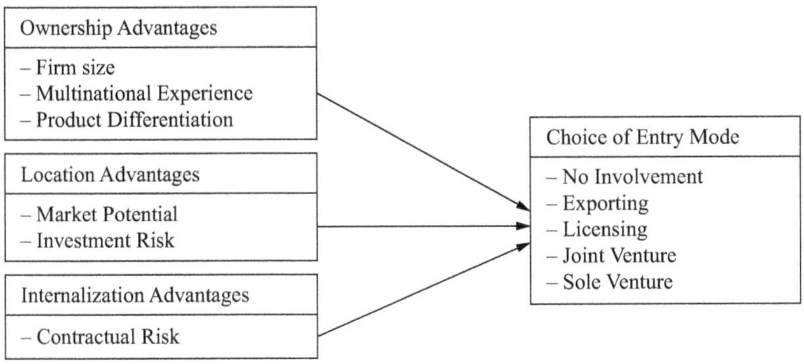

Figure 8.18: An eclectic model of entry strategy.

joint ventures, or alliances. Using Dunning's arguments, there is a close connection between "O" and "I" advantages in that a knowledge-type "O" advantage must attract "I" advantages. This process is best understood by transaction cost analysis at the enterprise level. In contrast, country-level analysis can fully explain " L " advantages.

Critique of the Eclectic Paradigm Theory

Various IB researchers point out that one of the problems with Dunning's eclectic paradigm is that it is too eclectic, as, in many ways, each of the three motives for FDI is over-determined, especially for "O" advantages. Per Dunning, these include the enterprise's intangible assets, such as branding, knowledge, formal organizational structures, management skills, natural factor endowments, workforce, capital, the cultural, legal, and institutional environment, and industry market structure. Dunning, however, argues that such foreign market factors could somehow be converted to "O" advantages. He argued that "O" advantages elucidate MNEs' ability to develop alliances by benefiting from common governance structures across borders. Relational assets allow enterprises to access resources controlled by partners. OLI also ignores the effect of home country factors, the nature of products, enterprise-specific resources, transportation costs, and currency exchange rates on the entry mode choice.

Transaction Cost Theory

Transaction cost theory (TCT) is a cost incurred in creating economic trading (the cost of participating in a foreign market, economies of scale, and transportation costs). It involves all the costs incurred from the start of a transaction to the end. It is the summation of all the expenses involved in establishing a new market in a foreign country. It consists of explicit and implicit costs and affects the service provider and the customer. Usually, it is advantageous to have the external transaction costs be more than the internal transaction costs. It will ensure the firm's growth, but since internal transaction costs are often more than external transaction costs, it may well lead the firm to a downscale by outsourcing.

As illustrated in Figure 8.19, the TC model further extends the internalization theory. Due to their common ideas concerning the role of transaction costs in internalizing business activities, these two views are sometimes considered one approach.

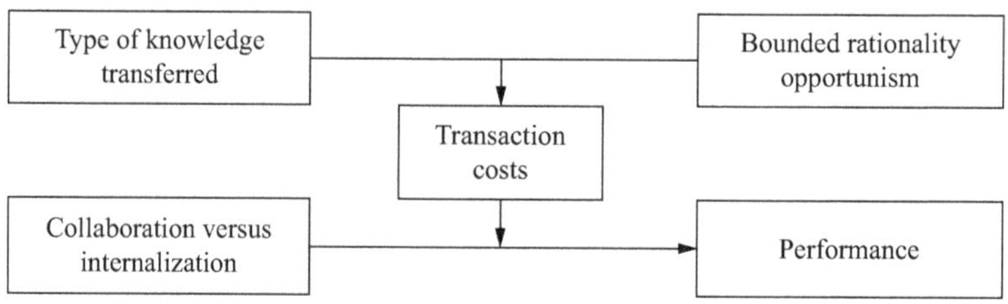

Figure 8.19: The effects of transaction costs on collaboration performance.

Critiques of Transaction Cost Theory

Critics argue that the TCT ignores the role of location advantages and the costs related to location factors related to market potential and investment risks. For instance, IB scholars Brouthers and Nakos identified the effect of nationality as a home-country factor that influences entry mode choice. At the same time, Taylor, Shaoming, and Osland believed that TCT is only applicable in Western developed countries because it neglects the effect of institutional structure on transaction costs and partnerships.

Some other IB scholars have added institutional factors to the model. Still, TCT ignores the role of strategic concern in motivating enterprises to use collaborative entry modes. The theory does not reflect the decision-makers' position in the internationalization process and overlooks the effect of entry mode choice on creating a competitive advantage for enterprises.

Other Recent Approaches to Internationalization

The internalization, eclectic, and transaction cost theories provide different perspectives on the internationalization mode of entry. Since the 1980s, researchers who criticized the existing static models of internationalization have tried to offer innovative ideas to draw a better decision-making framework.

International New Ventures, Born-Global

In the early 1990s, McDougall and Oviatt drew attention to a different type of MNE, those *newly created* enterprises that *were international from the very beginning,* dubbed *international new ventures (INVs),* which they defined as enterprises that, from inception, seek to derive significant competitive advantage from the use of resources and the sales of outputs in several countries. For this type of MNE, international market conditions, technological developments (i.e., the internet, telecommunications, and social media), the skill set and competencies of the managerial team and entrepreneurs, and their international network connections are essential to assisting these enterprises in becoming international from inception. Also critical to creating INVs is the global awareness the managerial team and international entrepreneurs have about international business opportunities and their ability to link up resources from other international markets to meet the demand of inherently international markets.

In such instances, enterprises with innovative products or services, having a competitive advantage over other enterprises, provide competitive advantages to MNEs to gain internationalization from inception. It occurs when the international target market needs that innovative product or service. Often INVs are defined as *born global*, as argued by IB scholars Knight and Cavusgil in 1996. These small enterprises attempt to achieve a competitive advantage based primarily on technology and operate purposely in various foreign markets from the earliest days of their foundation.

To cope with the ever-changing international market landscape, INVs must have flexible operating procedures to adapt and react promptly to the changing environments of global markets. Such a level of nimbleness often requires senior management to make business decisions. Such a management dynamic is usually inappropriate for most enterprises, huge MNCs, as international market commitments are less inclined to be persuaded by organizational policies and procedures and internal politics. Born-global, or INV, MNEs are known to be enterprises whose competitive advantage is often their superior knowledge and technological know-how. Such advantages, combined with management and experience in the international markets, can enable these MNEs to internationalize more easily.

Criticism of Born-Global and INV Theory

Despite claims within the literature, born-global/INVs are not unique to the 1990s, having been identified in large and small economies since 1947. Chetty and Campbell-Hunt argued in 2004 that born-global/INVs were a new concept based on a rehash of an old phenomenon. The born-global/INV concept does not consider incremental efforts made by traditional exporters when sending products to overseas agents, attending international trade fairs, establishing international networks, and then finally shipping products to a foreign country. Instead, if the focal point begins when the first export product sells, there is no difference between a traditional and a born-global exporter.

Ignoring the considerable time and effort spent establishing networks, arranging finance, contacting manufacturers, arranging production, and deliberately beginning to categorize a born-global/INV exporter only when they declare their business open is not a valid proposition. Different standards are being applied to the definition of the term. Furthermore, most born-global/NIVs studies were conducted within hi-tech and information and communication technology (ICT) industries that frequently require significant research and development (R&D) before launching the venture and that need to capture short windows of opportunity within global markets. It risks making the findings of these studies tautological and potentially unreliable.

Resource-Based View

Wernerfelt and Barney proposed the resource-based view (RBV) in the late 1990s based on the fundamental ideas of another IB scholar from 1959, Penrose, and his theory of the enterprise's growth. They also influenced Rubin's (1973) theory of the expansion of enterprises. The RBV theory argues that if an enterprise has abundant resources and can use them successfully, it will be able to compete in international markets and attain its long-term goals. Figure 8.20 provides a resource-based model of sustainable competitive advantage.

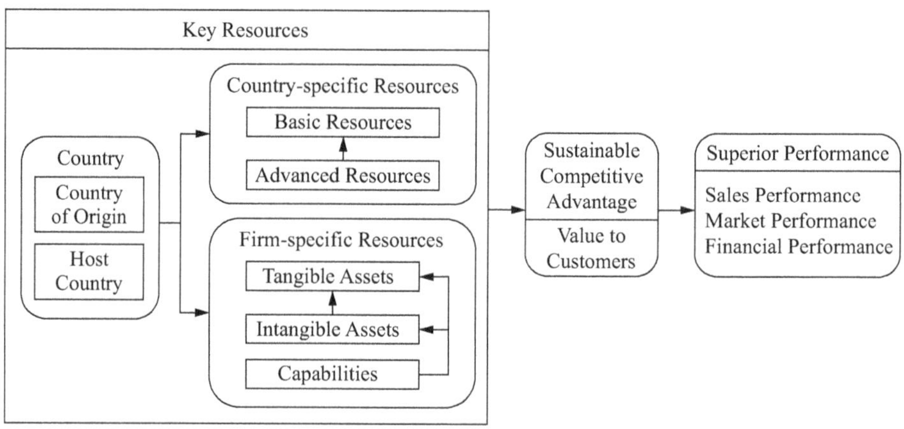

Figure 8.20: A resource-based model of sustainable competitive advantage.

Internationalizations occurs using resources, knowledge, and capabilities. Each enterprise has unique assets known as enterprise-specific resources. These resources are not distributed across business enterprises within an industry. Therefore, enterprises may benefit from the Ricardian rents, which are the economic rents caused by limited resources.

An enterprise owns various interrelated tangible and intangible assets that generate organizational capabilities. Such core competencies explain the enterprise's ability to carry out a specific task and increase the efficiency of its operations and customer value. Capabilities help the enterprise to transform its resources into products or services. They are intangible but differ from intangible resources because they require tacit or implicit knowledge and skills, whereas resources comprise explicit knowledge. In addition, resources are independent of the individuals and enterprises that possess them, while capabilities are related to capable individuals and enterprises. Furthermore, intangible resources are typically under legal protection, whereas it is difficult to protect capabilities.

An enterprise can gain a sustainable competitive advantage if it owns an advanced, unique combination of internal resources compared to its rivals, which may develop superior capabilities and better competencies. Such resources should be valuable, durable, unique, and complicated, and other enterprises cannot quickly transfer or duplicate them. Resources may differ, however, in asset specificity, opacity, complexity, and tacitness. To make a competitive advantage sustainable, enterprises should have dynamic capabilities to adjust and rearrange their resources and capabilities to identify market opportunities and respond quickly to environmental changes. Based on the RBV, innovation can help the enterprise to accomplish and maintain a competitive advantage. In addition, enterprises need an interaction between systemic knowledge, innovation, and external information networks.

In the RBV theory, FDI in wholly owned subsidiaries is considered the default mode of entry preferred by enterprises in normal conditions. In contrast, in the transaction cost theory, shared-control modes are the default entry mode. An enterprise with valuable resources and capabilities does not need to collaborate with local enterprises. Instead, it favors full ownership in foreign markets. They may also adopt joint ventures as the second preferred mode. Figure 8.21 illustrates a modified resource-based framework.

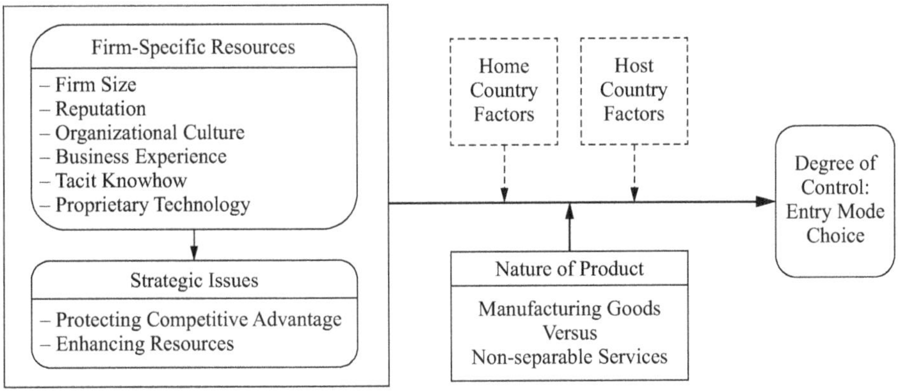

Figure 8.21: A modified resource-based framework.

Enterprises participate in alliances to obtain knowledge, resources, and complementary assets. They also aim to minimize costs or increase efficiency and effectiveness. However, alliances decrease an enterprise's level of control and autonomy.

Criticism of the RBV Theory

Researchers have criticized the resource-based view because it is static and does not explain how a specific resource can create a sustainable competitive advantage. In contrast, enterprises do not have enough knowledge about the productivity of each asset. In addition, the concept of enterprise-specific resources is ambiguous, and it is not easy to operationalize measurement items for them.

According to the critics, the RBV is only helpful if it can recognize resources that can create a competitive advantage in the future. In contrast, many valuable resources develop during foreign operations. The RBV focuses on the role of resources in creating competitive advantage but does not show the relationship between resources and capabilities. An enterprise may have some superior capabilities while it lags in other capacities. Such disadvantages may neutralize the effect of an enterprise's competitive advantage. In such a case, the enterprise should reconfigure its resources to fill the gap between its capabilities and weaknesses. It requires a long-term investment in resources, which is not always possible. Therefore, enterprises should aim to improve their core competencies and minimize their inferior capabilities related to production, marketing, or R&D activities.

Contingency Theory

Contingency theory refers to any of several management theories. Numerous contingency approaches have been developed since the 1960s. These theories suggested that previous theories, such as Weber's bureaucracy and Frederick Winslow Taylor's scientific management, had failed because they neglected that management style and organizational structure were influenced by various aspects inherited from the environment: the contingency factors. Hence, there could not be one best way for leadership or an enterprise. As an organizational theory, contingency theory states that no best alternative exists to organize, lead, or make decisions for an enterprise. Instead, the optimal course of action is contingent (dependent) upon the internal and external situation. The literature on internationalization has offered different models for the entry mode choice. Nevertheless, these models were content-oriented and ignored the role of decision-makers. In the early 1990s, researchers developed a contingency theory, also known as a business strategy approach.

The business strategy approach is a pragmatic view in which enterprises adapt their expansion strategies by trade-offs between market attractiveness, enterprise-specific resources, and management attitudes. This theory originated in Fiedler's contingency model (1967), which suggested that leadership styles depend on various situational factors, including leader-member relationships, task structure, and leader position power. In contingency theory, managers seek an excellent choice, not an optimal one. They make decisions under organizational and environmental constraints. Enterprises do not necessarily follow the stage models of internationalization. Still, due to the limited domestic market, they may need to expand their activities into foreign markets early in their operations. Consequently, decision-makers choose the appropriate entry mode based on the enterprise's market position.

There are three strategic views about decision making, as depicted in Figure 8.22: first, the situation-specific view, in which the enterprise's decisions are related to the unique situations it deals with; second, the universal view, in which the universal strategic laws apply to all enterprises and in all cases; and third, the contingency view, in which there is no universal optimal choice for all enterprises and situations, but the optimal choice depends on a set of organizational and environmental conditions.

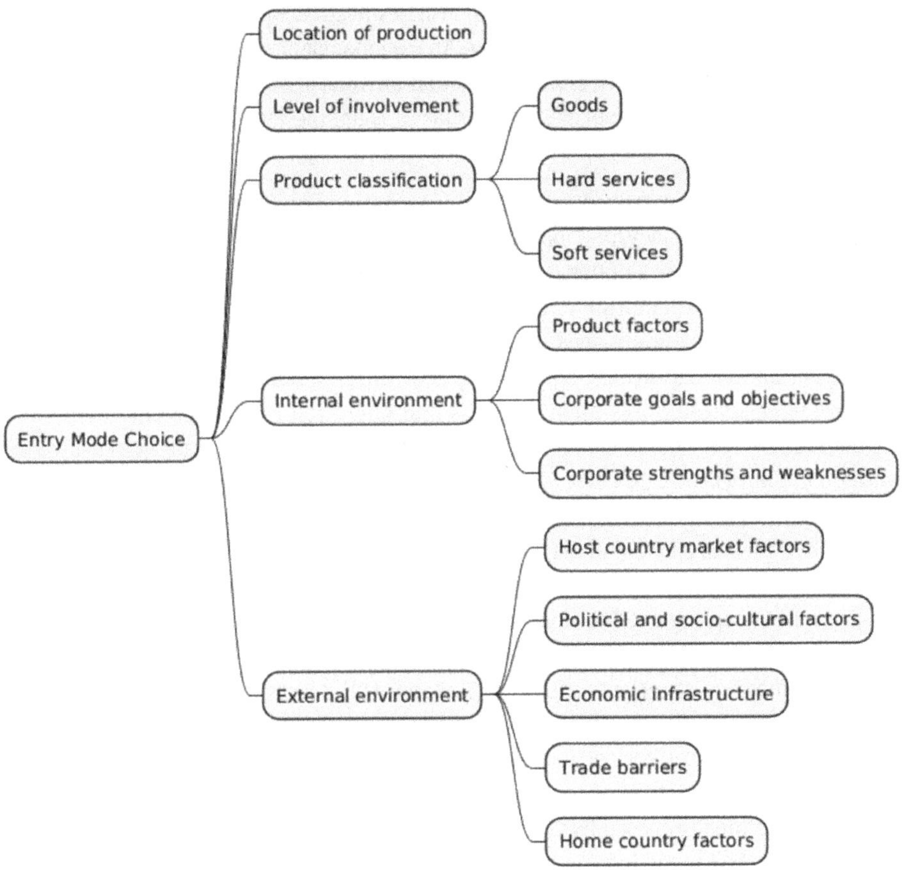

Figure 8.22: A contingency model of entry mode. (SOURCE: Ekeledo & Sivakumar [1998]).

In the contingency theory, the unit of analysis is the decision-maker, which refers to the top managers of an enterprise who decide on expansion and the choice of entry mode. They simplify the decision task, only consider a few variables, use a hierarchical process, and decompose the problem into stable sub-systems and the environment into constant sub-systems. Some IB researchers argue that market and entry mode choices are interdependent strategic decisions. Market selection is influenced by market opportunities and risks, while the choice of entry mode results from enterprise resources and market characteristics. In addition, the nature, depth, and types of interaction between supplier and client influence the entry mode choice.

Criticism of Contingency Theory

As contingency theory is a novel approach, critics argue it needs to be better examined and supported by further empirical studies. However, there are some main criticisms regarding the contingency models because there is no clear definition for the contingency variables and their operational measurements. Some of these factors conflict and their net effect is not explained. In addition, enterprises need adequate information concerning the contingency factors when deciding. An essential element that the contingency approach ignores is the network relationships that an enterprise needs for its international expansion. However, the importance of this factor is not the same for all enterprises.

A Proposed Reconceptualized Integrated Internationalization Approach Method

The inability of any given internationalization framework to wholly explain the internationalization process implies that existing frameworks may not consider the challenging realities of attempting to build competencies or select an ideal partner. Those competence-building challenges, by comparison, diverge from one SME to another, contingent on distinct factors, particularly how internationalization drivers manifest, as more experienced SMEs have business and operation capabilities not evident in earlier-stage SMEs. That is true locally and abroad, not to mention the increasing reliance on the internet, ICTs, CoPs, SM, and other business digitalization tools.

Several IB scholars have proposed inclusive or more cohesive models to explain the rationale influencing SMEs' internationalization process to overcome some of the gaps in current internationalization theories. Not much progress has been attained thus far, however. In the spring of 2022, Goncalves introduced a reconceptualized and more integrated approach, as depicted in Figure 8.23. The model is focused on Lusophone African small and medium enterprises (LASMEs), which still necessitates examining existing internationalization frameworks and how adaptable these are to Lusophone African economies' geopolitical, socioeconomic, and entrepreneurial contexts.

To accomplish such a task would require considerable effort. This new theory of internationalization proposed by Goncalves is merely a first step, a work in progress, and a collaboration call to the international business research community for more extensive theoretical analysis and empirical investigations. The framework proposes a more holistic approach that relies on an integrated internationalization approach (*IIAM).* The framework integrates some of the main internationalization frameworks discussed earlier in this chapter. An essential distinctive consideration LASMEs face when developing an internationalization path. These are important considerations when analyzing the internationalization process taken by LASMEs, including but not limited to the enterprise's organizational and market environment factors, both endogenous and exogenous.

The IIAM framework might be suitable for LASMEs and SMEs across Africa as a viable lens to understand the internationalization process best when considering similar environmental scanning. Each construct in the proposed framework consists of presets from four internationalization frameworks – OLI, U-model, network, and

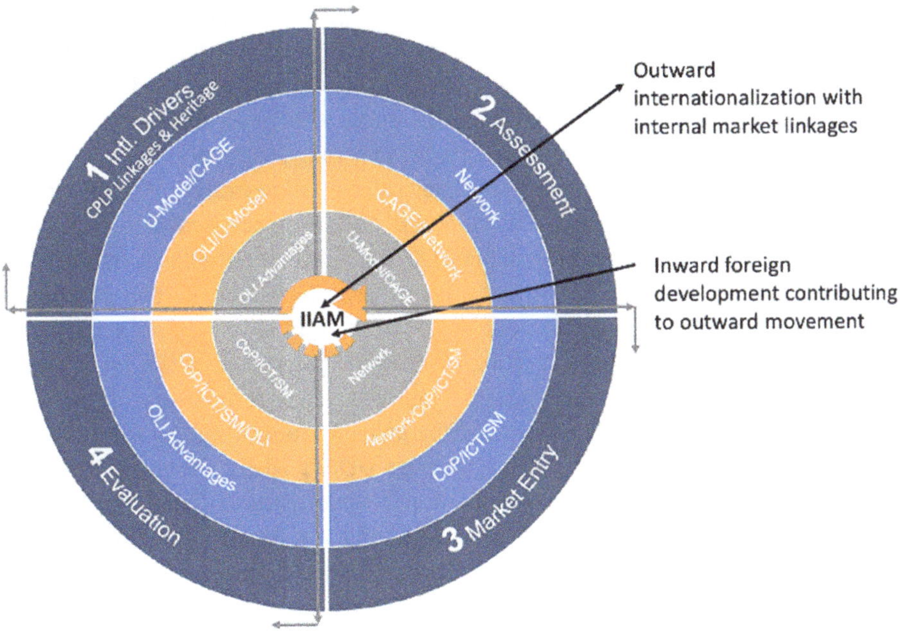

Figure 8.23: A proposed integrated internationalization approach method (IIAM).

CAGE – and the adoption of a business digitalization strategy through the internet and the convergence of ICTs, CoPs, and SM, all of which takes into consideration variables and various dimensions.

In the first quadrant, the *international driver's phase*, internal factors are considered potential internationalization drivers, including more specific resources required by LASMEs, such as market expansion among the Community of Portuguese Language Countries (CPLP) as a historical link and common language heritage, internationalization strategy development and products or service's attributes. Among enterprise-specific resources, examples of tangible assets include LASME's maturity level and size, competitive intelligence, and overall financial health and profitability. Models of intangible assets could be incorporated into LASME's organizational culture, standing reputation, and brand awareness. The LASME's competencies may comprise knowledge of targeted international markets, global business acumen, digital literacy, tacit know-how of international operations management, and potentially privately owned technology and other forms of intellectual property. These internationalization drivers are developed through an outward process with internal market linkages.

During the earlier stages of the *internationalization drivers' phase* (while in the domestic market position), in an outward effort to internationalize, all 29 LASMEs studied by Goncalves in Angola and Mozambique considered OLI advantages but relied on the U-model as a way of evaluating potential drivers in this process, from exporting and licensing to FDI. During this initial phase, the historical links and common language heritage of the CPLP group and the CAGE framework also become fundamental in providing early-stage knowledge about the foreign market. Both assist in determining the psych distance, as common language tends to reduce such distances, and related factors to be weighed before stepping into the second, subsequent IIAM phase: *assessment*. A more mature and experienced SME would have a broader range of options than earlier and less experienced ones in developing their internationalization strategy. As predicted by the U-model, SMEs can best recognize and utilize OLI advantages and consider a more gradual internationalization process in line with its ability to support the strategy.

Indeed, most of the LASMEs investigated by Goncalves internationalized through joint ventures abroad, which in its nature required an intense two-way relationship with the partnering enterprises, creating between the parent enterprise. Twenty-three of the 29 LASMEs could not assess potential joint venture opportunities and commit to such a relationship until they understood the potential foreign market (through OLI) and their partners. Its business contexts (through OLI/U-model) assess capabilities and reputation and build enough trust to evaluate such opportunities (U-model/CAGE). Tacit knowledge is necessary, however, which could be obtained through experience or feedback from online CoPs and a network of expert professionals in areas being sought out. This knowledge could provide preliminary and ongoing information, including the role of language in the internationalization of these SMEs. Although globalization has led to a convergence of practices, LASMEs' responses have diverged due to local conditions, a process described as glocalization. That is to say, the success of the entrepreneurial attitude might be found abroad, and to remain relevant and active, the local language is of primary importance. When internationalizing, LASMEs are confronted with a dilemma to either transform and adapt to the language spoken in the target market or keep the local language as the primary language of communication and instruction. This first step, broken up into a three-stage process (first quadrant), is vastly more integrated than other internationalization frameworks have depicted.

In the second quadrant, the *assessment phase*, the relative relevance of this phase varies with the degree of access LASMEs have to information concerning a potential internationalization process gathered in the first stage of *internationalization drivers* (through U-model/CAGE). This phase assesses external factors such as industry and local and international market factors. CAGE enabled these 29 LASMEs in MZ and AO to determine their psychic distance level concerning target markets, especially ones associated with dissimilarities among the local and international target markets relative to the culture (e.g., linguistic dissimilarities, religion, customs), administrative (e.g., government policies, taxes, tariffs), geographic (e.g., infrastructure, accessibility), and economics. SMEs typically can assess business processes and practices that could influence their selection. Indeed, diligence at this phase is paramount, as CAGE offers valuable support. Local or international government restraints, political unpredictability, and corruption, the ineffective legal system, and tariffs can potentially increase risks for the internationalization strategy and quickly turn the investment inviable.

During this phase, industry-specific factors are assessed, including considerations regarding the industry and market size, current demands, and potential growth projections. More specifically, such factors are correlated to the industry's existing structure, including capital-intensive versus labor-intensive requirements and the level of competitiveness in the targeted industry. Such elements are essential, as the degree and speed of internationalization might influence the entry mode selection. For all 29 LASMEs investigated by Goncalves, network relations were crucial to assessing such industry-specific variables for the inception of the enterprise structure abroad, its memberships in CoPs, and engagement with SM and networks. LASMEs followed prospective and current customers within the African continent and overseas markets. LASMEs sought to offer their unique products and services abroad and sought other resources complementary to theirs.

In the third quadrant, the *market entry* phase, the reliance of the LASMEs pertains to networking, both CoPs and SM, expanded, as they helped the investigated LASMEs to enter international markets in several ways. Developing relationships with foreign partners remained challenging due to insufficient financial resources, local government incentives, and infrastructure. Once present in a foreign market, LASMEs continued to rely on the internet, CoPs, and SM as an affordable and versatile way to cope with challenges. Meetings were conducted predominantly over the internet via Zoom, Skype, WhatsApp, Signal, Telegram, WeChat, and Line. Products and services were showcased and traded via platforms over the internet, such as eBay, Taobao, Alibaba, Facebook, Sina Weibo, Renren, Youku, Tudou, Instagram, Wish, and many others. Web scraping tools such as Python and Octoparse were used to gather market and customer data over the internet and feed big-data systems, accurately identifying niche markets, customers, and opportunities using data analytics.

These digital technologies and the digitalization of business could significantly accelerate knowledge accumulation and sharing very inexpensively, including gathering limited intelligence specific to target markets abroad. Without a reliable reference about the quality of data collected over the internet, however, at this third stage, these investigated LASMEs mainly relied on a reputable and well-established network of international business professionals familiar with foreign markets and the internationalization process. All 29 LASMEs collected business intelligence from various global markets, empowering them to assess market opportunities independently. In this phase, these LASMEs expanded their knowledge-gathering beyond U-model/CAGE to rely more heavily on networks and CoPs. Access to the internet, SM, and CoPs became a significant competitive advantage at this stage. Professionals with international business experience can offer newly internationalized firms potential benefits from networks they have formed to evaluate potential partnerships and the development of relationships able to foster a mutually profitable joint venture.

The fourth quadrant, the *evaluation* phase, is a critical stage in the IIAM framework, as scholars have already argued that SMEs tend to experience a reduction in performance during internationalization. However, other studies suggest the opposite, a positive impact, especially for banks or other financial institutions. No extant internationalization framework offers an explicit phase where SMEs can evaluate their international strategy. All 29 LASMEs studied observed that the internationalization process's impacts were broad and diverse across performance measures and variables. Although internationalization may result in a positive return on assets (ROA), earnings before provision and tax margins (EBPTM), and net profit margin (NPM) across financial institutions, on average, the net effect of internationalization can be detrimental, resulting in a net burden on operations and costs. Therefore, LASME's internationalization process must be evaluated, relying not only on technical and quantitative data, such as financial reports, profit and loss statements, and revenue forecasts, but also on substantial amounts of information, both quantitative and qualitative, and tacit knowledge available through CoPs, social networks and think tanks. Goncalves also observed that more mature LASMEs had mechanisms and business processes to evaluate the results effectively, but most did not. While such information may not be scientific, it can signal early warnings that a particular data set from vetted venues may not be accurate. LASMEs can access such CoPs and industry-specific SM to explore information further to understand the international market opportunities and subsequently seek scientific evidence.

Trade Missions and Fairs

National or provincial governments usually organize trade missions. They explore potential international business opportunities and can help create networks of buyers, agents, suppliers, and critical government contacts in a specific country or region. A trade mission is an international trip where business executives travel together as a delegation to overseas destinations and, occasionally, are accompanied by government officials. Its aim is that trade mission members will meet potential buyers or agents and participate in site visits and any networking receptions. In a trade mission, government officials and businesspeople from one country travel to another to promote trade between the two.

An initial step to discovering the opportunities for a company's product or service in the global environment is participating in international trade shows or visiting your potential business partners directly. Indeed, several ways to reach potential business partners are now available through the development of the internet and digital technologies. Nevertheless, holding a personal meeting with the hosting company at a trade show is still one of the most efficient ways to win the confidence of international business counterparts, understand their needs, and gauge their interest in the company's products or services. Not to forget are the differences that can arise due to the contrast of business cultures.

Trade Shows

Attending trade shows is frequently a marketing activity that is postponed during the development of the year's plan due to costs and uncertain ROI. Independent of the industry business targets, trade shows are often repetitive and standardized, making it difficult to fully take advantage of your visit, optimize your time, reach your potential business partners, or make it worth investing in placing a stand.

ESG Considerations in International Market Evaluation and Entry Strategies

Environmental, social, and governance (ESG) criteria have evolved into strategic tools for businesses assessing new markets and determining their entry modes. ESG considerations are integral to assessing international markets and selecting entry modes. Environmental sustainability, social responsibility, and good governance shape market assessment, entry mode selection, and cultural integration strategies. By incorporating ESG criteria into their internationalization strategies, companies can gain a competitive edge, enhance their market position, and build strong relationships with local stakeholders. Integrating ESG into market assessment and entry mode selection is an ethical imperative and a strategic advantage in today's global business environment. As companies expand internationally, they encounter a complex landscape where sustainability, social responsibility, and ethical governance are not just buzzwords but essential for long-term success.

ESG in Market Assessment

Environmental sustainability is a crucial factor in assessing new markets. Companies must consider the environmental regulations and sustainability practices of potential markets. This involves evaluating the target market's commitment to reducing carbon emissions, conserving natural resources, and promoting renewable energy. Markets with strong environmental policies can offer opportunities for businesses that prioritize sustainability as they align with global ecological goals and consumer preferences. For instance, a company eyeing expansion into the European Union (EU) must grapple with the EU's rigorous environmental regulations and unwavering commitment to sustainability. The EU's Green Deal, a comprehensive plan to make Europe the world's first climate-neutral continent by 2050, presents a unique opportunity for businesses championing sustainable products and services. By aligning with these ambitious goals, companies can gain a competitive edge and underscore their dedication to environmental sustainability.

Social responsibility is another critical aspect of ESG that impacts market assessment. Companies must evaluate the social dynamics of potential markets, including labor practices, community engagement, and human rights. Understanding these factors helps businesses determine the suitability of a market for their operations and ensures that they can operate ethically and responsibly. For example, companies expanding into developing countries must assess the local labor market and provide fair wages, safe working conditions, and respect for workers' rights. Businesses prioritizing social responsibility can build positive relationships with local communities and enhance their reputation, leading to greater market acceptance and customer loyalty.

Governance and the regulatory environment play a significant role in market assessment. Companies must evaluate potential markets' legal and political stability, including trade policies, regulatory frameworks, and governance standards. Markets with transparent and stable governance structures are more attractive to businesses as they reduce risks and uncertainties associated with regulatory compliance. For instance, a company considering expansion into the Asia-Pacific region must assess each target market's governance and regulatory environment. Countries like Singapore and Japan, known for their strong governance and regulatory frameworks, offer a favorable environment for businesses. In contrast, markets with weak governance and high levels of corruption pose significant risks and may deter investment.

ESG in Entry Mode Selection

Companies must consider their operations' environmental impact when selecting an entry mode. Entry modes such as joint ventures, strategic alliances, and greenfield investments allow businesses to implement sustainable practices and reduce their environmental footprint. These modes enable companies to collaborate with local partners, leverage existing infrastructure, and adopt environmentally friendly technologies. For example, a renewable energy company venturing into a new market might opt for a joint venture with a local partner to develop and operate a solar power plant. This entry mode allows the company to tap into local expertise and navigate regulatory requirements. It enables the implementation of sustainable practices, thereby reducing its environmental footprint and enhancing its reputation in the long run.

Social factors and local engagement are critical in determining the appropriate entry mode. Companies must consider how their chosen entry mode will impact local communities and contribute to social development. Entry modes that involve significant local engagement, such as joint ventures and strategic alliances, can foster positive relationships with local stakeholders and enhance social responsibility. For instance, a consumer goods company entering a new market may choose a strategic alliance with a local distributor. This entry mode enables the company to engage with local communities, understand their needs and preferences, and ensure that its products and services align with local social norms and values and contribute to their social development. By prioritizing social responsibility, the company can build a strong regional presence and gain customer loyalty while positively impacting the local community.

Governance and compliance are essential considerations when selecting an entry mode. Companies must ensure their chosen entry mode aligns with the target market's governance and regulatory requirements. Entry modes that provide greater control, such as wholly owned subsidiaries, can help businesses ensure compliance with local laws and regulations. For example, a pharmaceutical company entering a new market may opt for a wholly owned subsidiary to maintain strict control over its operations and ensure compliance with local regulatory standards. This entry mode allows the company to implement its governance practices, maintain high standards of quality and safety, and mitigate risks associated with regulatory compliance.

ESG and Cultural Integration

Environmental sustainability and cultural sensitivity are intricately intertwined in the context of international market entry. Companies must implement sustainable business practices and respect and uphold local ecological and cultural norms. This involves understanding the cultural implications of environmental initiatives and engaging with local stakeholders to gain their support, fostering respect and consideration for the local culture. For example, a food and beverage company entering a new market may adopt sustainable sourcing practices that respect local agricultural traditions and environmental standards. By collaborating with local farmers and suppliers, the company can promote sustainable practices, enhance cultural sensitivity, and build strong relationships with local communities.

Social responsibility requires businesses to be culturally aware and responsive to the social dynamics of new markets. Companies must respect local customs, traditions, and values while ensuring ethical labor practices and community engagement. This involves adapting business practices to align with local cultural norms and addressing social inequalities. For instance, a technology company entering a new market may implement diversity and inclusion initiatives that reflect local cultural values. By promoting equal opportunities and supporting local communities, the company can enhance its social responsibility and build a positive corporate image.

Good governance and ethical conduct are essential for building trust and credibility in international markets. Companies must navigate diverse regulatory environments and cultural norms while maintaining high standards of governance and ethics. This requires adapting governance structures to meet local expectations and ensuring business practices align with global ethical standards. For example, a financial services company entering a new market may establish a local advisory board to ensure its governance practices align with local regulations and cultural norms. The company can build trust with local stakeholders and enhance its reputation by fostering transparency and accountability.

Discussion Questions

1. **What are the most critical factors to consider when conducting market screening for international expansion, and why are they important for successful market entry?**

2. **Which method is not typically used for gathering primary data in international market research?**
   A) Surveys
   B) Government economic reports
   C) Observations
   D) Personal interviews

3. **What is the primary benefit of using trade fairs for market entry?**
   A) They provide legal advice on market entry.
   B) They offer a platform for direct consumer feedback.
   C) They help assess the competition and establish business contacts.
   D) They are mainly used to advertise new products locally.

4. **Secondary data in international market research is collected for specific research needs. True or False?**

5. **Trade missions are valuable for firms because they allow them to directly experience a foreign market's business environment. True or False?**

Recommended Readings

Amer, E. (2023). Internationalization, institutional pressures in foreign markets, and environmental sustainability. *Journal of International Management*, 29(1), 100974.

Appadu, N., & Morico, A. *Revisiting the Assessing Market Attractiveness for Mergers and Acquisitions Index Score: The effect of Geopolitics and ESG.*

Chang, W., & Yim, H. R. (2023). The Influence of Political Risk and Cross-national Distance on Overseas Enterprise Performance. *Asia-Pacific Journal of Convergent Research Interchange*, 9(5), 197–206.

Gammeltoft, P., & Panibratov, A. (2024). Emerging market multinationals and the politics of internationalization. *International Business Review*, 33(3), 102278.

Han, G. R., & Lee, J. E. (2024). The Moderating Effect of ESG Level in the Relationship between Digital Transformation Capability and Financial Performance: Evidence from Foreign Subsidiaries of Korean Firms. *Sustainability*, 16(9), 3764.

Li, X., & Wangui, M. (2023). The Impact of ESG on Foreign Direct Inuestments in Deueloping and Emerging Markets (Master's thesis, Handelshøyskolen BI).

Tang, R. W., & Yang, J. Y. G. (2024). Diversity in foreign direct investment and environmental innovation of emerging market firms: The effect of ownership-conveyed institutional logics. *Journal of Business Research*, 172, 114405.

Wang, X., Ren, K., Li, L., Qiao, Y., & Wu, B. (2024). How does ESG performance impact corporate outward foreign direct investment? *Journal of International Financial Management & Accounting*, 35(2), 534–583.

Chapter 9
Marketing Internationally

Learning Objectives

- Differentiate domestic versus international marketing
- Discuss why international marketing managers may wish to standardize the marketing mix
- Distinguish among the total product, the physical product, and the brand name
- Compare the traditional 4 Ps marketing mix versus the 7 Ps
- Understand some of the effects the internet may have on international marketing
- Explain *glocalization* as an advertising strategy
- Define pricing and distribution strategies

Overview

As illustrated in Figure 9.1, global marketing strategies aim to meet the demands of global customers, which encompass various facets. International marketing is the exchange of goods and services across national borders to meet customers' requirements. It includes customer analysis in foreign countries and identifying the target market. It refers to any marketing activity that occurs across borders. Types of international marketing include export, licensing, franchising, joint ventures, and foreign direct investment.

A global marketing strategy involves comprehensive planning and execution to promote products or services in international markets successfully. The critical ideas highlighted in Figure 9.1 are essential for navigating the complexities of global markets and ensuring effective marketing. Here's a summary of their importance and interconnections:

- **Market Research**: The fundamental steps are understanding target markets, analyzing local competition, and recognizing cultural differences. Thorough market research helps companies identify opportunities, tailor strategies to local preferences, and anticipate challenges.
- **Product Adaptation**: It is crucial to adapt products to meet local tastes and ensure they comply with regulatory requirements. This ensures that products resonate with consumers and meet legal standards, increasing their chances of success in diverse markets.
- **Pricing Strategy**: This component is designed for your target market, the consumer. Setting competitive prices while considering local purchasing power ensures our products are attractive and affordable. Effective pricing strategies can drive sales and establish a strong market presence.

https://doi.org/10.1515/9783111510286-009

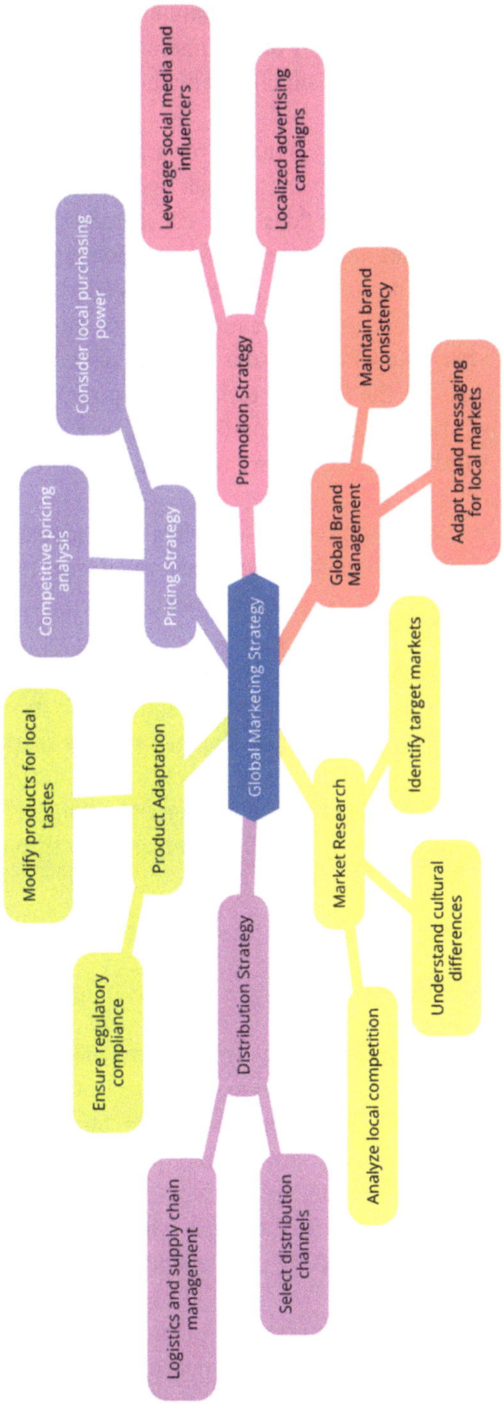

Figure 9.1: The various facets of a global marketing strategy.

- **Distribution Strategy**: Selecting the proper distribution channels and managing logistics efficiently are vital for getting products to customers. Effective distribution strategies ensure timely delivery and availability, enhancing customer satisfaction.
- **Promotion Strategy**: Imagine you're a marketing manager for a global fashion brand. You've just launched a new collection and want to reach your target audience in different countries. How would you do it? Consider localized advertising campaigns and leveraging social media and influencers to help achieve and engage the target audience. Tailored promotion strategies, as demonstrated by Zara, a fast-fashion retailer that sells clothing, accessories, beauty products, and perfumes, ensure marketing messages resonate with local consumers, driving brand awareness and loyalty. The subsidiary of the Spanish fashion group Inditex is known for quickly developing new products and getting them to stores within two weeks. They were among the first fashion retailers to introduce the fast-fashion concept to the global market.
- **Global Brand Management**: Maintaining brand consistency while adapting messaging for local markets balances global brand identity with local relevance. This builds a strong, cohesive brand image that can appeal to diverse audiences.

These ideas are interconnected as each element supports and reinforces the others. Effective international market research informs product adaptation and pricing strategies, while a well-planned distribution strategy ensures that adapted products reach the market. Promotion strategies enhance brand visibility, and global brand management ensures that all efforts align with the overall brand vision. These elements create a cohesive and effective global marketing strategy, enabling companies to thrive in international markets.

Defining an International Marketing Strategy

As depicted in Figure 9.2, an international marketing strategy is an overall marketing strategy to expand a business into global markets. It is a reference for localized international marketing plans to reach various regions abroad and new foreign markets.

An international marketing strategy does not only cover selling products across borders. As illustrated in Figure 9.3, it includes layering the marketing mix, or the 4 Ps of marketing, including product, pricing, promotions, and place, with many other marketing procedures such as analysis, planning, tracking results, and gathering social proof.

International marketing requires adapting an enterprise's primary marketing strategy and branding to international cultures and conditions in each market or region. The strategy should aim to increase global brand awareness, gain a competitive advantage, and position the company as a valuable solution for its customers. It

Figure 9.2: Global marketing strategy framework.

Figure 9.3: The marketing mix, the 4 Ps framework.

should also highlight the company's relationships with their communities and how they give back, including corporate social responsibility (CSR) or environmental, sustainability, and governance (ESG) initiatives.

International marketing enables forecasting and analyzing the market situation beyond national borders to ensure more advantageous conditions for selling products or services. It involves the practical implementation in international markets of the activities of a particular enterprise on initiatives that may incorporate main components, including:

- Research and development (R&D)
- Development and sales of products and services
- Advertising support of products or service offerings
- Implementation of after-sales service to international consumers

To obtain the intended outcomes at the international level, an enterprise must choose the right international marketing strategy to promote its goods and services and ex-

tend its life cycle. The essence of international marketing motivates enterprises focused on operating across national borders to accomplish these main tasks:
- Assess the entire global market as a potential target market
- Analyze the characteristics of the international target customers and assess their interest in the company's products and services
- Satisfy their international customer's needs

Entering an international market is typically driven by a company's internal motivations. But, before making such a decision, companies should assess the feasibility and prospects of such activities and identify the desired outcomes. The unique essence and idiosyncrasies of international markets enable companies to achieve several goals, including:
- Development of a positive image of the company outside the country
- Increase in sales volume
- Winning strategic positions
- Making production cheaper and standardization of products
- Gaining experience to promote products and services in other markets further
- Saving money by increasing the scale of operations and the volume of products sold

The international marketing strategy, as depicted in Figure 9.4, also involves a set of quantitative and qualitative indicators of the company's activities in the foreign market and decisions that direct specific marketing activities toward implementing the company's development strategy as a whole. The following are the main strategies usually adopted by enterprises when developing a global marketing strategy:
- **Export activities** involve producing goods and services in a company's primary domestic marketplace (or internationally) and selling these goods in the international target market. There are three possible directions of export activity: direct, indirect, and joint export. For example, if a company chooses the export method to enter a new market, it must decide which functions to adopt to promote its products and services. It must determine which functions to retain and those to delegate to intermediaries in the international markets. The delegation level of these many functions will determine the company's degree of responsibility and risks. Still, this choice's main advantage is the reduced risks and costs that the company incurs through implementing this access method in international markets. The primary disadvantage is the company's low control over the chosen trade intermediaries in the international target market.
- **Licensing:** a type of cooperation agreement whereby an enterprise transfers the right to another company in a foreign market to adopt its proprietary production processes, trademarks, patents, technological innovations, and any other valuable business process or skills for an agreed-upon fee. Licensing authorizes the enterprise to establish strict conditions and controls for compliance with the business

processes, international marketing strategies, and company policies. Such licensing agreements are convenient for organizing local operations and production in global target markets without incurring high capital investments. The main advantage of such an approach is the low cost of managing, supporting, and controlling international activities for the company. However, one of the main challenges in licensing agreements is the loss of uniqueness over the company's products and services and the difficulty of controlling the operations abroad via a third party.

- **Franchising:** Franchising is a business license in which the enterprise franchisor transfers a permit to operate under its trademark to its intermediary (the franchisee company). The company can transfer either the ability to use the company's trademark and products or an entire business process, for example, in the case of McDonald's or KFC operations abroad. A franchise arrangement differs from a licensing one by incorporating more stringent requirements for the third-party company, the franchisee and the existence of a narrower scope of application. For instance, a franchising agreement is created to make another branch out of an intermediary third party and incorporate it into the company's (franchisor) business processes by imposing its own rules of operation.
- **Joint venture:** under such agreement, separate enterprises, two or more, join forces and share responsibilities and risks in the operations of the international venture. An enterprise may create a joint venture with one of the players in a target external market to gain access to resources, knowledge, contacts, or technology. In such cases, the company shares risks and the potential revenue from activities in the foreign market with its partner(s). The primary advantage of joint ventures is gaining access to specific knowledge and technologies of the target market, such as the partner's distribution channels, understanding of the local market specifics, production base, trademarks, patents, and technological innovations. The main disadvantages of such a strategy may include higher costs (compared with other methods) and the risk of management contentions due to different priorities of the company and its partner's preferences.

Before the internet, only larger companies such as MNCs would need global marketing strategies. But, with the digitalization of business processes since the mid-1990s, internationalization went digital. Digitalization also is reducing costs and increasing its reach into international markets substantially. Several examples today of enterprises that are born *global*, also known as *INV*, as discussed in Chapter 8. The internet allows companies to quickly develop a digital business presence by having a one-page website or engaging in e-commerce, e-business, platform, and social media marketing. With reasonable budgets, companies can develop innovative digital marketing techniques, develop international marketing strategies, and draw more customers worldwide, often without a dedicated international marketing team. Hence, creating a deliberate global marketing strategy before executing global marketing campaigns is

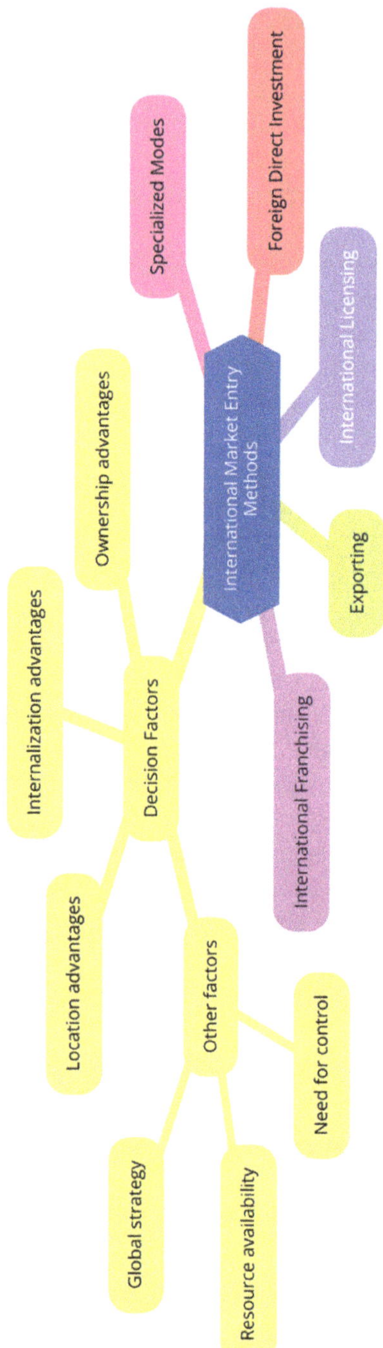

Figure 9.4: Entering international markets.

essential. A solid international marketing strategy can increase a company's chances of connecting with its target market and converting prospects into customers.

Planning an International Marketing Strategy

Planning an international marketing strategy, as depicted in Figure 9.5, is essential to the success of any company abroad. This section summarizes such a strategy, as our focus is not on marketing but international business. Also, it is essential to realize that digital is a significant part of international marketing strategy today. It is primarily divided into owned, paid, and earned marketing channels. The enterprise's market demographic and location determine where it spends most of its budget and effort. Hence, global marketing managers must ensure their global marketing strategy is consistent with a uniform brand name, similar products, identical packaging, aligned messages, comparable pricing, and synchronized product launches. They must attempt to group similar countries to form a geographical segment and streamline their marketing efforts. Some critical questions to be asked when developing a global marketing strategy may include:

1. What is the company trying to achieve in the international market?
2. Is the company developing a new market or tapping into an existing one?
3. Which nations or markets support the company's business most?
4. What is the prevalence demographic in the target market?
5. Why do customers love the company's products or services?
6. Where are the company's competitors most active?
7. What is the company's competitive advantage in potential markets?
8. How can the company improve and scale what works best?
9. What are the peculiarities of the potential target markets?
10. Should the company have a single brand story or different messaging for different target markets?

The answers to these questions will set the company on the right path to creating a well-rounded international marketing strategy. The following steps are essential in helping the company plan a robust international marketing strategy:

- **Market research:** Understanding and assessing a potential target market abroad is crucial. Companies should study the prospective customer's cultures and behaviors. What channels are most appropriate for marketing? Where do they meet online and offline? Companies should also assess the existing market segments and consider all factors contributing to converting prospects into customers. Global managers should select regions where they have the most significant business opportunity. Conducting thorough market research protects companies from making avoidable, costly mistakes abroad.
- **Assemble a team:** Market research should determine which regions work best for the product or service offerings and enterprise. Next, the talent and the team

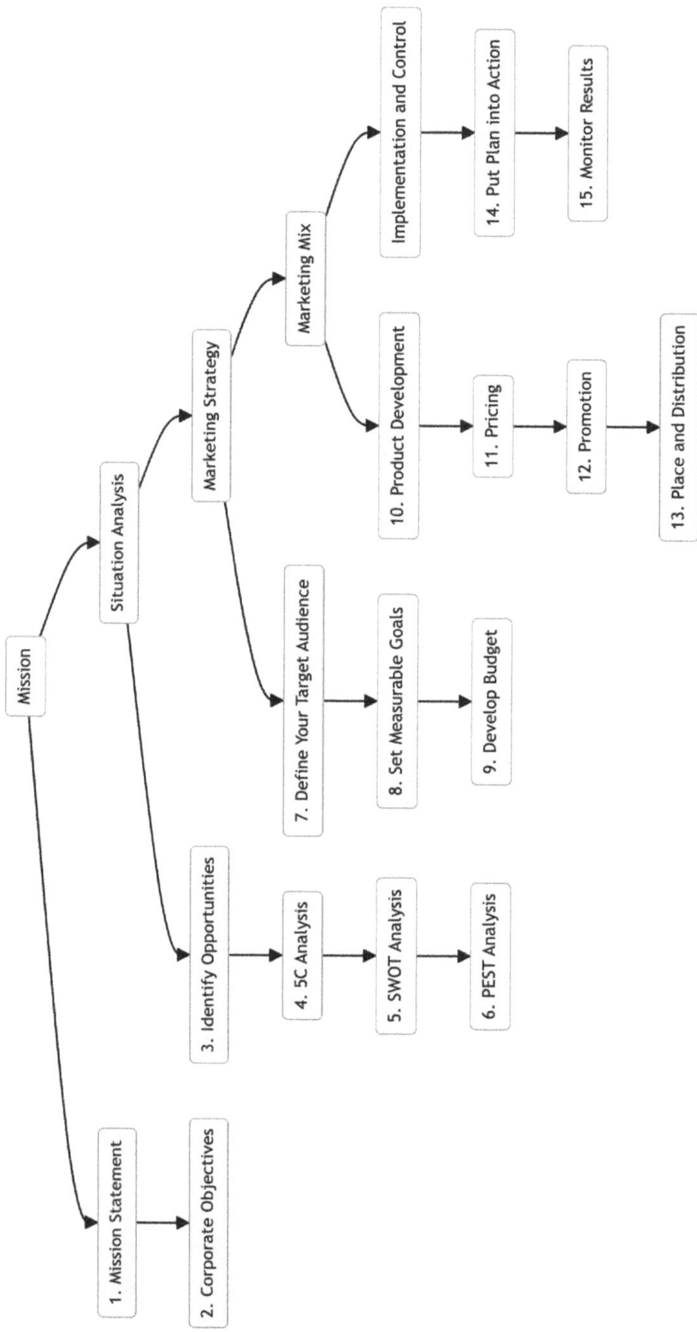

Figure 9.5: International marketing planning process.

must be gathered to execute the marketing strategy. Having some team members with experience and expertise living or working in target market areas is essential. Depending on budgetary positions and logistics, a company may hire local freelancers or a marketing agency. Inviting the team into the company's digital workspace is also crucial, giving each of them appropriate permissions, access, and visibility.

- **Create a marketing plan:** Once the target market is selected and the marketing team is formed, it is time to develop the international marketing strategy. The first step should be for the company to identify and fit the goals into the potential target market landscape. The company must study the marketing personas and communicate the value of its products and services in its marketing message. They must consider their competitors' positioning and outline a marketing plan emphasizing their strengths. Their product's value proposition may change in different markets, so they must adapt accordingly. Uber, for instance, promotes cash over cards in developing markets where cash payments are predominant.
- **Localize the company's brand message:** It is inaccurate and a marketing mistake to assume that every target market shares the same characteristics and challenging points. What works in one foreign market may not work in another. A company must localize its international marketing strategy and adopt prevailing marketing practices to delight its new market with a tailored-to-fit experience. Companies should focus on connecting with their customers when developing ads and media assets. Companies must familiarize themselves with the market's desires and make their message clear and personalized, so there is no confusion regarding whom they are selling to. Learning about popular cultural references, events, and holidays is paramount to creating a genuinely global, local experience.
- **Fine-tune and improve:** An international marketing strategy is never a one-and-done task. Global marketing management software like Wrike, Trello, and many others can assist in executing marketing campaigns, extracting insights, collaborating with internal and external teams, and re-creating what works. Global marketing managers must split test elements, track marketing analytics, and improve their marketing message to get the best results.

Benefits and challenges abound when developing an international marketing strategy. The following are a few of them:

- **Advantages over competitors:** Conducting business worldwide gives a company the upper hand over local competitors who cannot or do not have an international marketing strategy. It also enables them to adapt quickly to customer demands or market trends.
- **Improved product quality:** The knowledge a company gains from expanding into new international markets enables it to fine-tune its products and processes, creating more value for its customers.

- **Increased brand awareness:** What brand would not want McDonald's or Starbucks's name recognition and customer base? A global marketing strategy allows a company to place its product in markets it could not reach otherwise.
- **Lower costs:** Customers worldwide should be able to find the company online and engage in e-commerce or e-business, which typically lowers marketing and promotion costs.

Some of the potential international marketing strategy challenges, as summarized in Figure 9.6, may include:

1. **Adapting to new markets:** Adapting the marketing strategy to fit recent international geographical locations is critical. For instance, Starbucks is not as ubiquitous in Australia or Italy as in the rest of the world. Despite being inspired by Italian culture, the Starbucks model probably would not fly in Italy. The coffee experience for Italians is much more personal and intimate than what any Starbucks store would be able to offer. It is about "slow food" instead of American "fast food." Similarly, in Australia, as local coffee is essential in the Australian coffee market, people find Starbucks' coffee too expensive. Therefore, localizing the strategy is crucial to a company's international marketing success abroad.
2. **Compliance issues:** Different markets in the EU have different data protection and security rules, such as the California Consumer Privacy Act (CCPA) and the General Data Protection Regulation (GDPR). Management must ensure the company follows the rules when doing business in other countries.
3. **Language barriers:** Whenever language barriers exist, companies need to be extra diligent. A local translation agency can proofread all translation materials to prevent misunderstandings and embarrassment. For instance, when Pepsi launched the slogan *Pepsi Brings You Back to Life* in the Chinese market, it mistakenly translated it as *Pepsi Brings You Back from the Grave*. Another example is BMW, the German car manufacturer, which improperly used the United Arab Emirates (UAE) national anthem in one of its car commercials. The company displayed the Al Ain Football Club singing the anthem and then quickly running toward several BMW cars as soon as they heard the sound of the engines. BMW was trying to create an intense emotion towards their vehicles. Still, instead, it caused rage, as Emiratis were offended by the suggestion that a car was more important than their national anthem.

There's no one-size-fits-all approach to international marketing. There are many examples when looking at the brands dominating their respective industries. The following are a few examples of successful international marketing strategies:

- **Airbnb** – embraces the power of social media. Their *#OneLessStranger* campaign engaged three million people worldwide in three weeks.
- **Domino's** uses a different set of toppings based on each international market it has a presence in. Its pizzas are sold to reflect each market's preferred tastes. The

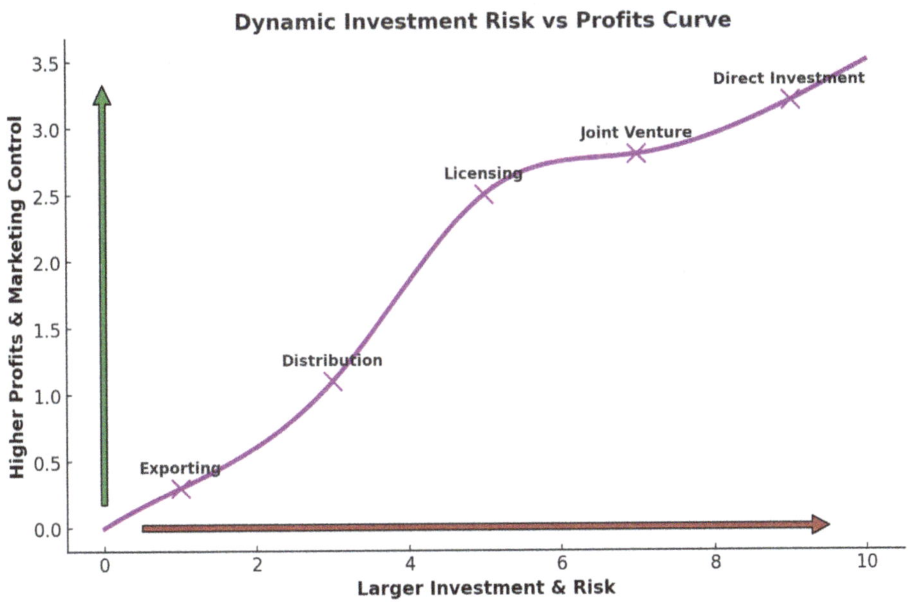

Figure 9.6: International marketing opportunities and challenges.

basic pizza dough recipe is the same for all markets, but the toppings vary and deliver local appeal.

- **Lay's** – adapts flavor offerings to accommodate local customers' tastes and adopts distinct brand names, such as Lay's in the U.S., Walkers in the U.K., and Smith's in Australia. This strategy is based on maintaining consumer connections with the brand they already know.
- **Netflix** – commissions local productions within a global infrastructure. The company's massive international marketing highlights the value of linguistic and cultural connections.
- **Nike** – captures international attention by carefully selecting international sponsors. The demand often rises seasonally due to triggers such as world championships and tournaments.
- **Shopify** – develops websites with localized content and language. Customers are driven to a fully localized website section for each international region. This localized marketing content helps the company grow massively globally.
- **Starbucks** – taps into what makes local audiences tick, providing localized menus, such as Dragon Dumplings in Hong Kong.
- **Uber** – strives to adapt fluidly to international local spending habits and customs as it offers customized solutions for each target market context. For instance, in some foreign locations where cash is preferred to credit card payments, the company adapted its service offerings and marketing message to suit.

International Marketing Segmentation

As summarized in Figure 9.7, international marketing segmentation subdivides the foreign target market into sub-groups with specific requirements and characteristics to identify particular groups within the target market and deliver a more targeted, niche-focused message, products, and services. The following are the four main types of international marketing segmentation:

- **Behavioral** – Behavioral market segmentation categorizes the market based on their previous behavior with the brand, such as purchase patterns, business awareness, previous purchases, and product rating.
- **Demographic** – Demographic market segmentation focuses on who the customer is. The traits in this segment depend on whether to run a business-to-business (B2B) business-to-consumer (B2C), or even consumer-to-consumer (C2C) business. B2B companies include industry type, company size, years of practice, and revenue range. Traits in a B2C and C2C company would consist of age, education, gender, occupation, family status, and income.
- **Geographic** – market segmentation allows the split of a market audience based on location, which can sometimes be a helpful purchase decision factor.
- **Psychographic** – Psychographic market segmentation divides markets based on their *personalities,* such as lifestyle, values, attitudes, and interests.

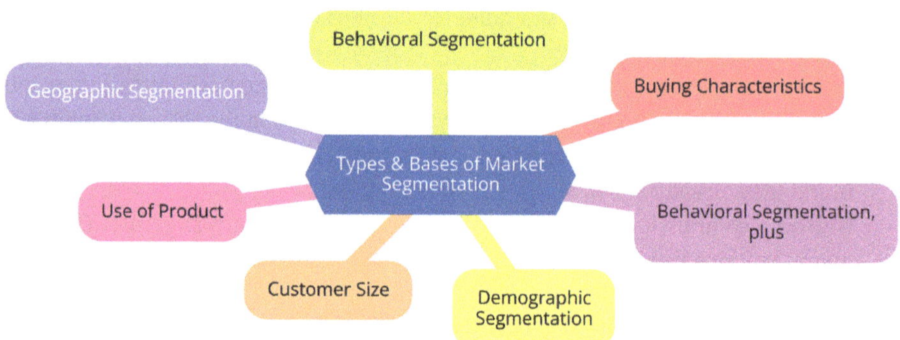

Figure 9.7: International marketing segmentation.

Effective marketing communication is among the best ways to differentiate a business offer when entering a new international market. International market segmentation assists in pinpointing the messages that may drive the customers to make a purchase, helping develop better marketing communications. When marketing campaigns are targeted to specific customer subsets, management gets an improved response rate, better than a marketing campaign that adopts only generic descriptors that apply to anyone but appeal to no one.

Domestic vs. International Marketing

As discussed earlier, marketing is a company's activity to satisfy customers through value addition to enhance its brand value proposition. It determines and converts needs into products and services to meet the customers' wishes and wants. Two kinds of marketing strategies exist, namely, domestic and international marketing. Figure 9.8 provides a brief comparison between the two strategies. Operating in a domestic market is quite distinct from expanding overseas into a foreign market. Growing into a new global market comes with various challenges requiring a strategic approach with empirical methods.

Domestic marketing refers to marketing within the nation's geographical boundaries when the commercialization of goods and services is only limited to the home country. It refers to carrying out marketing activities within national borders. It relates

BASIS FOR COMPARISON	DOMESTIC MARKETING	INTERNATIONAL MARKETING
Meaning	Domestic marketing refers to marketing within the geographical boundaries of the nation	International marketing means the activities of production, promotion, distribution, advertisement and selling are extended over the geographical limits of the country
Area served	Small	Large
Government interference	Less	Comparatively high
Business operation	In a single country	More than one country
Use of technology	Limited	Sharing and use of latest technology
Risk factor	Low	Very high
Capital requirement	Less	Huge
Nature of customers	Almost same	Variation in customer tastes and preferences
Research	Required but not to a very high level.	Deep research of the market is required because of less knowledge about the foreign markets

Figure 9.8: Comparison table between domestic and international marketing.

to marketing in the local market, and its scope is limited. It demands less investment compared to international marketing. There is one nation with the same language and culture, as opposed to many countries, languages, and cultures. In domestic marketing, only one currency is used, and companies can have the same policies and strategies.

Domestic marketing also refers to the marketing activities employed on a national scale, where marketing strategies are carried out to cater to domestic customers in a small segment or area, typically within the border limits of a nation. It offers services and influences the customers of a specific country only. Domestic marketing enjoys many privileges like easy-to-access data, fewer communication barriers, deep knowledge about consumer demand, preferences, and taste, market trends, less competition, one set of economic, social, and political issues, etc. However, due to the limited market size, growth is also limited.

International marketing, however, as the name suggests, is the type of marketing stretched across several countries worldwide, such as the marketing of products and services done globally. International marketing refers to carrying out marketing activities outside the national boundaries, and it relates to doing marketing in the global market, and its scope is broad. It requires more investment as compared to domestic marketing. Different currencies are used in international marketing, and companies need different strategies to promote their product.

Usually, the companies start their business in their home country. After achieving success, they took their business to another level and became a transnational company, seeking to enter several countries' markets. So, the company must know about that country's rules and regulations. International marketing has no boundaries, focusing on worldwide target markets and customers. Nonetheless, some disadvantages exist, such as the challenges of expansion and globalization. Some of these are sociocultural differences, changes in foreign currency, language barriers, differences in customers' buying habits, setting and international prices for the product, and so on.

The Market Mix

The marketing mix, also called the 4 Ps, is a set of critical considerations that must be thoughtfully considered and wisely implemented to successfully market a company's goods, including the product, price, place, and promotion. The 4 Ps encompass a range of factors that are considered when marketing a product. Factors may include consumers' needs and wants, how products or services meet or fail to meet consumers' expectations, how products or services are perceived in global markets, how these offerings stand out and compare with those offered by the competition, and how the enterprise that gives them interacts with its customers.

Neil Borden, an advertising professor at Harvard, developed the marketing mix concept and popularized it as the 4 Ps in the 1950s. A few decades later, Borden's concepts are still popular and adopted by companies to advertise their goods and services. When the idea was introduced, it helped companies breach the physical barriers that could hamper widespread product adoption. Today, the internet has allowed businesses to overcome some of these barriers. People, processes, and physical evidence are extensions of the original 4 Ps, also known as the 7 Ps, and are relevant to current trends in marketing. The marketing mix a company develops should not be static. It should evolve, be adjusted, and refined as product offerings grow and the customer base changes.

The 4 Ps of Marketing

The 4 Ps of marketing, as depicted in Figure 9.9, provide a framework for building a marketing strategy. Think through each factor. And don't worry when the elements overlap, which is common and unavoidable. The first step is to analyze the *product* the company wants to market, its characteristics, and what makes it appealing to consumers, not forgetting to consider other similar products already offered. Determine the attributes that make the product appealing to the target consumer markets. The product may be more challenging, easier to use, longer-lasting, unique, or attractive. Its features might be eco-friendly or naturally sourced. Then, *price* and the appropriate pricing strategy must be given special attention. It is not only the cost of production plus a profit margin that needs to be considered but also the premium or luxury product or a bare-bones lower-priced alternative. *Placement* involves identifying the online and off-store that may carry competing products. *Promotion* should only be assessed in the context of the target consumer. The product might appeal to a hip, younger crowd, upscale professionals, or bargain hunters. The media strategy needs to reach the right audience with the right message.

Figure 9.9: The 4 Ps of the marketing mix.

These are the 4 Ps of marketing:

– **Product:** Developing a marketing campaign starts with understanding the company's product offerings. Who needs or wants it, and why? Is there a demand for it? How does it differentiate from a competitor's product line, and how it differs? Are there any unique features compared to the competition?

The marketer's job is to describe the product offerings, qualities, and uniqueness and then introduce it to the global market and its consumers. Defining the product's characteristics is also crucial to its effective distribution, or the fourth P, for *Placement*. International marketing managers must understand the product's life cycle and plan to deal with developments at every life cycle stage. The product type also dictates how much it will cost, where it should be offered (placed), and its promotion. The most successful products are often the first to be launched in their category.

– **Price:** Price is the amount consumers, the market, are willing to pay for the product or service. Marketers must connect the product's price to a real and perceived value while considering its development costs and other indirect costs such as seasonal discounts, retail markups, competitors' pricing strategies, etc. Occasionally, management may raise prices to convey the appearance of a luxury item or exclusivity. But they may also choose to lower the price to ramp up more extensive sales and give a chance to consumers to try the product.

Marketing teams must also decide when and if rebates or discounts are appropriate and will be offered, as these strategies may draw a higher influx of new customers. However, it may give an impression that the product is less desirable than before. For instance, UNIQLO, headquartered in Japan, is a global casual wear manufacturer. Like Zara and Gap, UNIQLO manufactures fashion-forward and low-priced apparel for younger customers. UNIQLO's offerings are unique due to its innovative and high-quality product line. They purchase fabrics in large volumes, always searching for the lowest-cost and highest-quality materials globally, negotiating directly with its manufacturers, and building strategic partnerships with innovative Japanese manufacturers.

– **Place:** Place considers where the product should be available, in brick-and-mortar stores and online, and how it will be displayed. Think of luxury cosmetic manufacturers who want to show their products in Sephora and Neiman Marcus instead of Walmart or Family Dollar. Global marketing managers' goal is always to place their products in front of consumers who are the most likely to buy them. Such a decision is critical.

Placement also involves advertising strategies for the product in the most suitable media to get consumers' attention, placing product ads only in certain stores and displaying them to the best advantage. For instance, the James Bond movie *GoldenEye* was the first, after 17 previous films, not to feature an Aston Martin, with actor Pierce Brosnan getting into a BMW Z3. Even though the car was released only months after the film had already left the theatres, BMW received 9,000 orders for it in the month after the movie opened.

– **Promotion:** The main objective of promotion is to convey to the market the consumers' need for this new product and that the price is appropriate to what they are receiving. Promotion strategies may include advertising campaigns, public relations, and the overall media strategy for introducing a product. Global marketing managers combine promotion and placement to reach their core audiences. For instance, as the world gets more digitalized, and consumers spend much time in front of screens connected to the internet, the *place* and *promotion* factors can be as offline as online. In particular, where products appear on a company's web page or social media and the types of searching functions can trigger targeted ads for the product.

For instance, the Swedish vodka brand Absolut sold only 10,000 cases in 1980, but by 2000, it had sold more than 4.5 million cases, partly due to an iconic advertising campaign it had released on the markets. It featured images of Absolut's brand's signature bottles styled in a range of surreal images, such as bottles with a halo, bottles in the shape of trees standing on a ski slope, or bottles made of stone.

Product Strategies

A product strategy is a high-level strategic plan, as depicted in Figure 9.10, defining what a company intends to accomplish with its product or services and how it plans to do so. The strategy should answer critical market-oriented questions such as who will be served by the product or service, how the offering will benefit target markets and prospective customers, and the company's goals for the product throughout its life cycle.

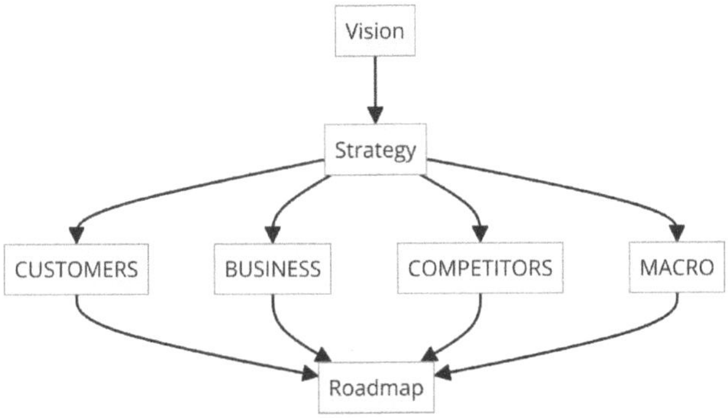

Figure 9.10: A product strategy roadmap.

Main Components of a Product Strategy

A product should contain the following essential factors:

1. A market and the specific gaps or demands it will address.
2. The key differentiators or unique selling offerings.
3. Management's business goals for the product.

Building a product strategy before beginning development is necessary because it serves three valuable business purposes:

- **A product strategy clarifies the company's goals** – The team will be better positioned to deliver their best work when a strategy is in place and communicated clearly. New product developers can best understand how the parts of their product contribute to the company's overarching strategic goals. They can often feel caught up in all the details and lose sight of the overriding purpose behind their work. A product strategy clarifies that for them. Marketing and sales teams can articulate the product's benefits and unique selling proposition. However, generating anticipation and sales becomes difficult without a defined strategy behind a product.
- **It assists in prioritizing the product roadmap**. After management earns stakeholders' agreement for the new product, it will be time to translate that strategy into a high-level action plan and build a compelling product roadmap. When management starts with a plan, it has a clearer picture of what it hopes to accomplish with the product and translates it into a more strategically sound product roadmap. Unfortunately, several product development teams tend to bypass the strategy-drafting phase and dive right into listing features and war stories on their product roadmap. However, without a product strategy to orient the decision-making process, the team might prioritize the wrong factor or quality and misuse the limited time and resources.
- **A product strategy improves the team's tactical decisions** – Companies cannot deliver a product to the market following a plan drafted in the early stages of development. Priorities, resources, and other market, product, or company factors will change. Product managers must be prepared to adjust their strategies and priorities to deal with those changes. When management and the marketing team have a clear product strategy as a reference point, they can make smarter strategic decisions about adjusting the plans, especially if they lose resources or change their estimated timetables.

The following is a typical template commonly used following the three-step process discussed above:

- **Define the vision:** Add bullets to describe each outer circle illustrated in Figure 9.11, such as competitors, buyer personas, marketspace, etc. Through such a process, marketing teams should be able to draw a picture of the issues they hope to solve for the market and the niche they plan to fill. This process should help them develop a vision for the product.

- **Establish product goals**: Product goals should be defined, deciding, for each purpose, on quantifiable ways to track its success and set a deadline.
- **Product initiatives**: At this stage, product goals are translated into high-level themes that can be added to a product roadmap. Once they are on the roadmap, a cross-functional team should review these themes, break them into detailed tasks, and begin working on them.

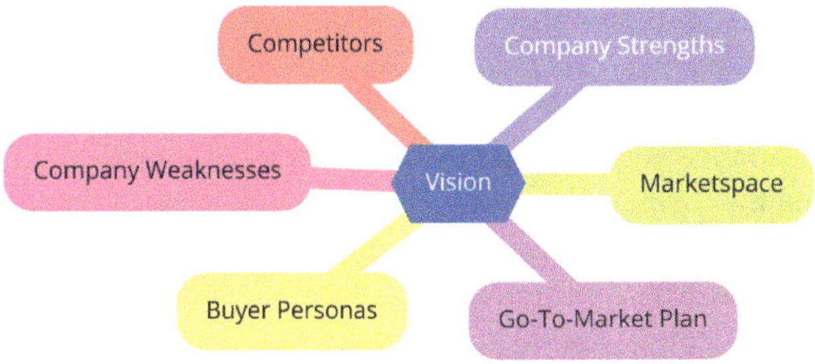

Figure 9.11: Common template for developing a product strategy roadmap.

Another way to understand this is to remember that a product strategy should include the following three components:

1. **Product vision** – As discussed earlier, a product vision depicts the product's or service's long-term mission. It is usually written in concise and descriptive statements to define what the company expects the product to achieve. For instance, Google's early vision for its search engine was to *organize the world's information and make it universally accessible and helpful.*
2. **Goals** – The product's vision should convey high-level strategic goals, influencing the management team's priorities and the product's roadmap. The following are examples of product goals, which could include:
   - Generate $4MM in revenue within 18 months
   - Improve the average customer satisfaction rating by one star on major product review sites
   - Increase free-trial downloads by 60% in the next six months

   The best approach for a product strategy is to use SMART (specific, measurable, achievable, relevant, and time-bound) goals.
3. **Initiatives** are strategic themes derived from the product goals and placed in the roadmap. They tend to be essential to the strategy, containing complex objectives the team must be able to break down into actionable tasks. The following are some examples:
   - Add customer delight
   - Break into new industries or geographical areas
   - Improve customer satisfaction

- Increase lifetime customer value
- Increase mobile adoption
- Reduce churn
- Sustain product features
- Upsell new services

The following are additional examples of effective models for product strategies.

a. **Product-led growth (PLG)** – PLG approaches enable a focus on the development of products, a marketing strategy, and forming a sales team. Like Dropbox and Spotify, it often means making the product accessible to a specific market for free and charging users for upgraded and advanced features and services on demand. Since customers may find the basic service useful, they tend to share information about the product with their social network, coworkers, family, and friends, who may end up signing up for the service or product. Companies may rely on the network effect to succeed with their product-led growth in other cases. Slack and Zoom are great examples, as they have benefited from such a model. For instance, Zoom decided to refocus its strategy early in the COVID-19 pandemic in 2019 to offer a more user-friendly platform for many new businesses and individual users who wanted to connect with work, friends, and family while in quarantine. Zoom also developed features for new customers, particularly schools, who have unique needs.

b. **Product segmentation** – An effective product strategy adopted by many companies, including Zoom, is to develop distinct versions of their product or service to meet unique demands for different markets or clusters of users. For instance, if a company develops apps for cybersecurity, it may consider creating a single-user or consumer version instead of only a corporate one. The main selling feature of the application could be that it would run entirely in the background, protecting individual users' data and devices. The team may decide to develop an enterprise version targeted at IT professionals, but the features and selling points are distinct.

c. **The lean product differentiator** – In the early days of the web, Yahoo! held the dominant position in online search. But the company's homepage was cluttered with links, buttons, and ads. Then Google came with a home page with almost no connections, not a single ad, and almost entirely white space. The only explicit following action on the Google homepage was to type in a search request. We know who won that competition.

Price Strategies

The main objective of any management team is to maximize profits and the return on investment (ROI) by effectively getting the products off the shelf; let us define and explain this better. As depicted in Figure 9.12, a price strategy is an approach to determining a competitive price for a product or service. This strategy is combined with the other: the 4 Ps strategy (products, price, place, and promotion), economic patterns, competition, market demand, and product features. It is typically one of the most significant factors in the product mix, focusing on producing and increasing the company's total revenues and profits. Having a good grasp of the market conditions and demands and identifying the gaps and unmet demands of the market is paramount to the success of this strategy. Along with the price consumers would be willing to pay is the opportunity to develop a pricing strategy successfully. Remember, the goal of a company is to maximize profit by being in competition and sustaining the competitive market. However, to maximize profits and retain consumers, management must choose the right pricing strategy, as it will help the company attain its objectives.

The pricing of any product is highly complex and intense as it results from several calculations, including insights from research work, risk assessment and mitigation, and understanding of the overall target market and consumers. Management must consider all these variables before identifying a product's optimum price structure. It includes the product segment, the consumer's ability to pay for it, market conditions, competitors' actions, production, and raw material cost. In other words, the cost of manufacturing and the profit margins. As a strategy, it is used to set prices

Figure 9.12: Examples of pricing strategies.

according to current prices in the market for the same or comparable products or services. It allows businesses to charge higher prices initially before matching market prices to stay competitive while still growing return on investment.

Aside from developing a pricing strategy based on distinct market segments, there are several factors to consider when implementing a market-based pricing strategy:

- **Expenses** – A company cannot simply charge what it costs to produce a product; it also needs to factor in enough money to support its overhead (building costs, admin costs, etc.).
- **Capital and cash flow** – If the company has a significant amount of cash in reserve, it may have more flexibility in dealing with operating and development costs than if it were cash-strapped and needed financing. The pressure to increase the customer base is lower if the company can introduce a product at a higher price than it may otherwise. Think of luxury products that sell for very high prices and are typically under limited editions.
- **Competitors' prices** – If the company has several competitors and their prices are all similar, its prices will probably be similar, too, unless it is chasing a budget or prestige market and wants to use price as a critical differentiator.
- **Demand vs. market saturation** – If there is a high demand for a service, but very few people are offering it in the area, the company can charge higher prices. Conversely, if demand is low or the company has many competitors, it may have to adjust its price accordingly.
- **Differentiation** – Although price is often the most significant factor influencing purchase decisions, other factors are involved. That is why we usually see multiple brands in the same market with very different, unique selling points. If the company offers something none of its competitors have, it can use that to attract a market share. And it will not necessarily have to rely on low introductory rates to gain traction.
- **Market average pricing** – If the company is in an established industry with set prices, it will probably price its product accordingly. A price that is too low can cause customers to equate the offering with an inferior product; an inexplicably high price may turn customers away.
- **Positioning** – Understanding how the company positions itself in the market will affect the product's price and can help develop a stable pricing strategy, as market pricing and positioning often intersect. The following are typical areas in which they intersect:
  - **Product lifecycle** – Products with a short life, such as smartphones, tablets, and other high-tech devices, undergo a gradual price reduction the further they are in their lifecycle.
  - **Production costs** include materials, manufacturing costs, shipping, packaging, and employee hours, regardless of whether the company produces a product or service. If it is selling a service, it consists of any equipment and supplies, employee hours, and operational costs.

- **Business maturation** – If the company just started on the market and is looking to build a client base, it may want to start with a lower price and increase its worth as it becomes more established.

In each of the above factors, the average market price is not necessarily the right choice for that business. As a strategy, market pricing depends on the industry, customer, and company-specific information – it is essential to consider all that data.

Placement or Distribution Strategies

Figure 9.13 depicts the distribution strategy as the approach adopted to deliver products, goods, and services to a market. Companies often acquire repeat clients by certifying an easy and effective way to get their products and services to their customers, contingent on the article and its distribution requirement. Companies ponder which distribution approach is most cost-effective and how to increase the firm's profitability. Management can adopt multiple or overlapping distribution approaches to reach their target markets and meet the company's sales targets and objectives. For instance, a product may sell better online (e.g., e-commerce or e-business) to one market demographic and via a mail-to-order catalog in another target market.

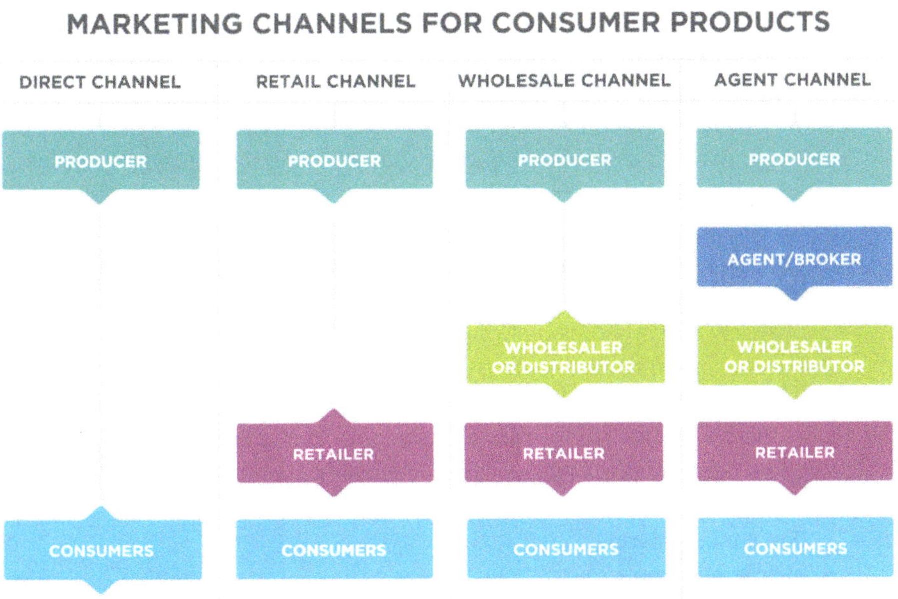

Figure 9.13: Examples of marketing channels for consumer products.

The item is often vital in determining the right distribution strategy, type, and channel. Companies should consider choosing distribution channels based on their primary market and customers. They should also consider where and how they procure their products and what can be done to make purchasing their goods or services more accessible to their customer base. For instance, if the company's product is a high-end designer line of home furniture, procuring such items directly from the manufacturer might be worth the customer's effort and time. If the product is a routine, everyday item like a bottle of juice, beer, or water, buying it through convenience stores and nearby shops can appeal more to the customer.

When planning a distribution strategy, there are several factors to consider, including:

- **Product type** – The distribution strategy may vary depending on the product or service. For instance, the distribution strategy of a paper towel manufacturer is very different from that of a luxury car brand. Notwithstanding the type of product being sold, most consumer purchases are categorized into three groups:
  - **Extensive**: Customers often consider expensive items before buying, such as automobiles, houses (real estate), high-end jewelry, college educations, etc.
  - **Limited**: a moderately priced item customers spend more time considering and selecting than a less expensive, routine purchase, such as home appliances (e.g., refrigerators, stoves, dishwashers), furniture, or high-tech consumer electronics products such as computers, smartphones, tablets, smart speakers, augmented reality devices, etc.
  - **Routine**: typically, a low-cost item or service customers select quickly, such as candy, chocolates, gum, beverages, paper goods, etc.
- **Customer base** – Another factor to consider is the user or customer base. Depending on where customers typically shop, distribution strategy varies, and often, technological advances influence distribution, too. For instance, if the target customer base for paper towel products is a middle-aged woman buying at a grocery store, the company may distribute through several brick-and-mortar storefronts, such as supermarkets, grocery store chains, convenience stores, wholesale clubs, warehouses, etc. So, if the ideal customer base for customizable furniture is an affluent, wealthy customer who is savvy on digital technologies and used to digital purchases over the internet, distribution from the manufacturer's warehouse via online sales directly to the customer might be the best alternative. Some of the leading sales channels preferred by consumers may include:
  - Direct mail ordering
  - Door-to-door sales
  - E-commerce or e-business websites
  - Storefronts, booths, and shops
- **Warehouse and transportation logistics** – Another important consideration when developing a distribution strategy is the abilities and costs of operating a

warehouse and distribution logistics. For instance, managing warehouses, vehicles such as trucks and vans, and personnel to run the warehouse and deliver the products is a significant financial investment. Depending on the company's product or service's storage and delivery needs, selecting another distribution approach might lead to increased cost savings and revenue, such as relying on third-party shipping companies like DHL, FedEx, UPS, etc.

Main Distribution Strategies

Distribution strategies provide distinct benefits and cost reductions depending on the company's goods. There are mainly two types of distribution strategies:

- **Direct**: when manufacturers interact directly with their customer base, selling and shipping products directly to them without relying on third parties. Typically, such a strategy will require a warehouse to store the inventory and a shipping process to get the products to customers.
- **Indirect**: manufacturers rely on intermediaries to provide logistical support to get their customers' products. Such a strategy is typical when large amounts of routine products need to be shipped, which saves the company on shipping costs.

Within these two main types of distribution strategies, there are a few other relevant ones worth mentioning:

- **Dual**: It combines direct and selective strategies to grow market influence and maintain direct customer sales.
- **Exclusive**: It is more appropriate for manufacturers to pick a few sales outlets to develop exclusivity for a particular brand or product, such as luxury goods and other exotic items.
- **Intensive**: This strategy is typical when manufacturers need access to markets to sell their goods in mass through as many outlets as possible. It is common for affordable routine items such as household products, candy bars, and drinking products.
- **Reverse**: not as expected, is a term adopted for merchandise returns from the customer to the company. It happens when the product is defective and under warranty for recycling or refurbishing purposes.
- **Selective**: a mix of exclusive and intensive strategies, offering more expansive locations and opportunities to sell a product without being too fussy about which stores to sell within. A good example would be a high-end rug manufacturer retaining a particular retail department store to reach a broader customer base.

Distribution Channels

A distribution channel is the path through which services or products flow until they reach customers. An appropriate distribution channel relies on the product's characteristics, who it serves, and where it goes. For example, a product could flow from a factory to a warehouse and consumer. However, it may flow from a factory to the wholesaler and then to a retailer before reaching consumers. Such a chain of events comprises the many distribution channels a product may flow through. The following are four primary distribution channels:

- **Distributor** – A distributor gets and transports items from manufacturers to retailers and other locations. This method is appropriate to save on shipping costs, staff, and logistics. Distributors also may benefit by having several clients overlapping, allowing for the creation of comprehensive product groupings that generate more sales. For instance, a distributor working with the separate rug, furniture, and lighting manufacturers could set up an all-in-one combo offering comprised of a living room package deal that could include a sofa, rug, chairs, coffee table, end tables, and two lamps.
- **Franchisor** – a unique approach for the distribution of products and services. For instance, a third-party company (franchisee) may be willing to pay to use the company's (franchisor) branding to enhance its sales through specific royalty fees agreed upon. Companies and manufacturers with brand recognition may collaborate, establish joint ventures, and offer their customers their goods. Customers can benefit from such collaboration and enhanced distribution channels without the everyday responsibilities of managing each location. Some common franchise distribution channels are well-known fast-food restaurants, real estate offices, and healthcare companies. Franchising often centers on these three types:
  - Business format franchising
  - Product distribution franchising
  - Social franchising
- **Retail** – A retail distributor is often where an item ends before being sold to a customer. In this case, retailers purchase products from wholesalers or manufacturers, marking up the costs to earn a profit. Although retailers are often correlated to storefronts, such as department stores, supermarkets, bike shops, etc., with the advances of the internet and other digital technologies, retailers also have a presence online through websites, catalogs, or even phone-order businesses.
- **Wholesale** – The wholesale distribution channel entails the purchase of products in bulk from a manufacturer and then reselling these to retailers. Substantial savings are realized when products are purchased in bulk and the economy of scale. Wholesalers exploit these opportunities by buying large quantities and storing, selling, and delivering these goods to retailers. Wholesalers rarely interact directly with the customer.

Promotion Strategies

Companies use a promotional strategy to advertise, promote, and sell their goods, choosing their promotional strategy based on product characteristics, marketing budgets, target markets, etc. An effective promotional strategy yields more significant revenue than marketing spending. Promotion of any product or service is essential for any company. This is because only through promotion would people know about the product after learning about the product they are considering purchasing. Since many companies and brands compete to sell their products to the same customers, advertising, and promotion are essential to ensure that each brand is differentiated and identified.

Types of Promotional Strategies

As illustrated in Figure 9.14, promotional strategies can be classified under two categories – push and pull.

1. **Push strategy** – In a push strategy, promotional activities are done for the distributors, wholesalers, and retailers to push the product to the consumers. Trade fairs, wholesaler discounts, bonuses, and the related actions that benefit distributors are examples of such push strategies: the demand is pushed in the distribution chan-

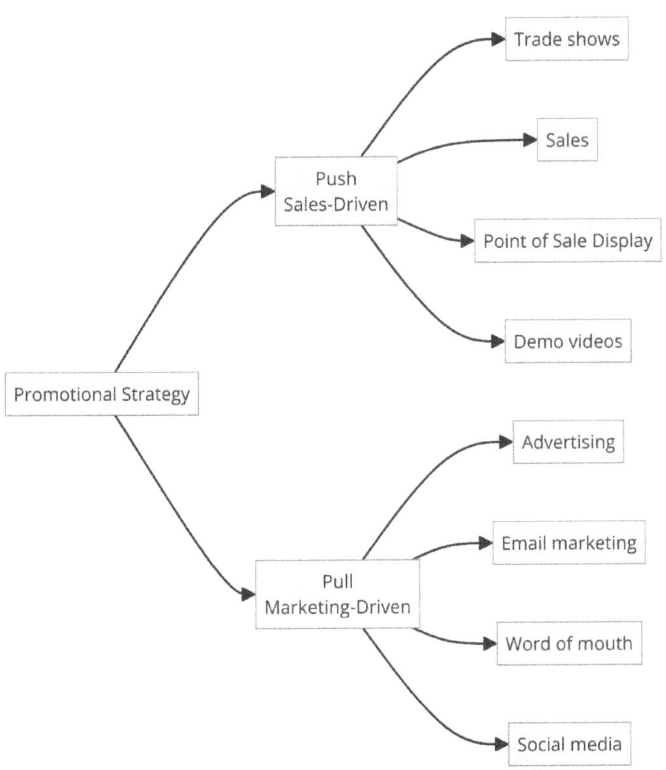

Figure 9.14: Two types of promotional strategy.

nel. Therefore, these activities are not visible to consumers and are typically unknown. For instance, if a customer goes to a mobile phone store to acquire a new smartphone, and the store clerk insists and demonstrates only iPhones, this is push marketing. The store and the clerk are getting a better margin or commissions on the sale of the iPhone, which is better for them than any other brand.

2. **Pull strategy** – In the pull strategy, promotional campaigns are designed for the target markets and their consumers, including advertising and digital campaigns, discounts in stores (e.g., coupons, BOGO free incentives), etc. The demand is initiated by the consumers, who are motivated to acquire a particular product or service they may have no intention to at the moment, and in turn, go to the retail stores or e-commerce websites to buy these products. These activities are visible to all the customers.

A pull strategy occurs when a customer approaches the market with a specific brand and product in mind, even though the customer already knows what they want.

Steps to Execute a Promotional Strategy

The process for driving promotion for any product or service is as follows:

1. **Identify the promotion objectives** – These should be quantifiable regarding revenue, unit sales, increased brand awareness, etc.
2. **Evaluate promotional channels** – This involves evaluating the marketing channels required for promotion, such as TV, social media, radio, events, trade fairs, etc.
3. **Formulate a marketing budget** – The investment required to drive a promotional strategy should be allocated channel-wise, which can help you keep track of assets.
4. **Execute promotional activities** – This involves creating advertising campaigns, scheduling advertisements, and ensuring that promotions occur without disruptions.
5. **Monitor, measure, and evaluate** – All promotional activities must be monitored for effectiveness and evaluated for further improvement.

Publicizing the Promotion

There are many venues to publicize the promotion strategy; the following are the main ones:

- **Email marketing** – may have a decades-long history, but it has not lost clout. Promotions make emails even more attractive to consumers. One research study from 2019 showed that for every dollar spent, email campaigns could get up to an average $42 return on investment.
- **Social media** – Social media ads and organic posts can publicize a promotion campaign to new or existing customers, targeting existing markets and customers and finding new customers with similar interests. Customers are on social media,

so management should ensure they do not miss a sales opportunity to highlight their offers.

- **Retargeting** – In the age of automation, it is easy to set up messages to retarget customers who have gone astray. A customer may have added items to a shopping cart but decided against the purchase, browsed away from the site without concluding the purchase, or changed their mind. Promotions may get many potential or current customers back on board and compel them to complete the purchase.
- **Postcards** – Postcards can make a big impression in today's digital world. Postcards have some advantages, as they typically will not get lost, as emails tend to be in a customer's email inbox. In addition, the sensory engagement factor might allow shoppers to feel special.
- **Tagging new customers** – The more a company knows about its new customers, the better it can personalize a message for them in the future. Management should make sure to tag all of the new customers who visit their corporate site during a promotion.
- **Welcome emails** – Such emails are a great way to build relationships.
- **Ongoing communication** – new customers should keep hearing from the company after the promotion. Management should use the tags for those customers to send personalized product recommendations.

The 7 Ps' Considerations

Once management has developed its 7 P framework (product, price, promotion, place, packaging, positioning, and people), as depicted in Figure 9.15, it should constantly be monitored. As products, markets, customers, and needs often change rapidly, management must continually revisit these seven Ps to ensure they are on track and achieving the maximum results possible for you in today's marketplace. The following is a brief set of considerations regarding these factors:

- **Product** – management should develop the habit of looking at products as though they were an outside marketing consultant brought in to help the company decide whether it is in the right business at this time. Critical questions should be asked, such as: Is the current offering or a mix of them appropriat*e for today's market and customers?*
- **Prices** – I recommend continually examining and reexamining the prices of the products and services sold to ensure they are still suitable for the present market. Sometimes, prices need to be lowered or increased.
- **Place** – Develop the practice of revising and reflecting upon the exact location where the customer meets the sales staff. Often, a change in place can lead to a speedy increase in sales. Companies can sell a product in numerous distinct areas. Companies typically adopt direct selling, sending their salespeople to meet

and talk with the prospect personally. Others sell through telemarketing, catalogs, mail orders, trade shows, retail establishments, joint ventures, or even manufacturers' salespeople or distributors. Many companies use a combination of one or more of these methods.

- **Promotion** – Management should always consider promotion. Promotion includes telling customers about the company's products or services and how to market and sell them. Slight changes in how to promote and sell products can lead to dramatic changes in results. Even minor changes in advertising can immediately lead to higher sales.
- **People** – Develop the habit of thinking about the people inside and outside the business responsible for every element of sales, marketing strategies, and activities. Outstanding customer service tends to convert to sales and can increase the customer base through referrals. Acquiring these referrals from customers who love the brand can also testify to how marketing efforts can support the sales process.
- **Process** – Develop the habit of standing back and looking at every visual element in the packaging of the goods sold through critical prospects' eyes. Remember, first impressions are formed within 30 seconds of seeing some aspect of the firm, product, or salespeople. Minor enhancements in the packing or external appearance of the product or service can often lead to entirely different customer reactions. Packaging refers to the way the product or service appears from the outside. It also includes the store, offices, ambiance, waiting rooms, marketing collaterals, brochures, logos and trademarks, correspondence, and virtually every single visual element of the company. Packaging also refers to the company's people and how they dress and groom.
- **Physical evidence** – Management should develop the habit of continually thinking about how they are positioned in the hearts and minds of their customers. How do people think and talk about them when they are not present? How do people think and talk about the company? What positioning does management have in their marketing, and what specific words and expressions do customers use when describing the company or products it sells?

Figure 9.15: The marketing mix 7 Ps.

How ESG Shapes International Marketing Strategies

With the expansion of globalization, the role of environmental, social, and governance (ESG) criteria in shaping international marketing strategies has become increasingly significant. ESG considerations encompass regulatory compliance, alignment with global sustainability goals, and meeting consumer demands for ethical business practices, which are now at the forefront of strategic decision making. ESG considerations are integral to marketing internationally. Environmental sustainability, social responsibility, and good governance shape market research, product adaptation, pricing, distribution, promotion, and brand management strategies. By incorporating ESG criteria into their international marketing strategies, companies can gain a competitive edge, enhance their market position, and build strong relationships with local stakeholders. Integrating ESG into international marketing is an ethical imperative and a strategic advantage in today's global business environment.

ESG in Market Research and Product Adaptation

Environmental sustainability is not just a buzzword but a crucial factor in market research. Companies must explore consumers' environmental regulations, climate policies, and market sustainability preferences. This understanding is informative and instrumental in identifying international markets where sustainable products are likely well-received and can influence product adaptation strategies. For instance, in markets like the European Union, which has stringent environmental regulations and a strong consumer preference for sustainable products, companies must adapt their products to meet these standards. This could involve using eco-friendly materials, reducing carbon footprints, and ensuring that products are recyclable or biodegradable. Such adaptations comply with regulations and appeal to environmentally conscious consumers, enhancing market acceptance and brand loyalty.

Social responsibility is a crucial aspect of product adaptation. It involves ensuring that products are designed and marketed in a way that respects local cultures, supports fair labor practices, and contributes positively to communities. Companies must consider local social norms and values when developing marketing strategies to tailor their products. This responsibility is a duty and an opportunity to impact society positively. For example, a company entering an emerging market might focus on community engagement by supporting local education and healthcare initiatives. This builds trust and goodwill, making consumers more likely to support the company's products. Additionally, ensuring fair labor practices in the supply chain can prevent negative publicity and enhance the company's reputation.

Good governance and ethical practices are essential for product development and marketing. Companies must ensure that their products are safe, reliable, and ethically produced. This includes transparency in sourcing materials, fair trade practices, and ethical marketing strategies that do not exploit consumers. Companies like Patagonia and Ben & Jerry's have successfully integrated ESG into their product strategies and reaped significant benefits. Patagonia's emphasis on environmental sustainability in its product design and Ben & Jerry's focus on social justice and fair trade practices have enhanced their brand reputation and fostered consumer loyalty. This success story demonstrates that by integrating ESG, companies can meet global sustainability goals, gain a competitive edge, and build strong consumer relationships.

ESG in Pricing and Distribution Strategies

The integration of environmental considerations into pricing strategies can yield significant benefits. While companies that invest in sustainable practices often face higher production costs, they can leverage these practices to justify premium pricing. Consumers are increasingly willing to pay higher prices for environmentally friendly and ethically produced products, enhancing the company's profitability and sustainability. For example, Tesla's electric vehicles are priced higher than conventional cars, but its commitment to sustainability and innovation allows it to command a premium price. Consumers perceive the higher cost as a worthwhile investment in sustainability and cutting-edge technology.

Distribution strategies must consider the social impact on local communities. Companies should minimize their environmental footprint through efficient logistics and support local economies by partnering with local businesses. This can involve using local suppliers, reducing transportation emissions, and ensuring fair labor practices throughout the distribution chain. For instance, Starbucks sources coffee beans from local farmers in various countries, supporting local economies and ensuring fair trade practices. This helps build strong relationships with suppliers and appeals to consumers who value ethical sourcing.

Good governance ensures that distribution practices are transparent and ethical. Companies must provide clear information about their supply chains, sourcing practices, and environmental impact. Transparency builds trust with consumers and stakeholders, enhancing the company's reputation and competitiveness. For example, Apple provides detailed information about its supply chain practices, including labor conditions and environmental impact. This transparency helps build trust with consumers and stakeholders, reinforcing Apple's commitment to ethical business practices.

ESG in Promotion and Brand Management

Promotion strategies must highlight a company's commitment to environmental sustainability. Companies can use advertising campaigns to educate consumers about their sustainable practices and the environmental benefits of their products. This not only enhances brand image but also drives consumer engagement and loyalty. For instance, The Body Shop's promotional campaigns often focus on its commitment to cruelty-free and environmentally friendly products. By emphasizing sustainability in its promotions, The Body Shop attracts environmentally conscious consumers and differentiates itself from competitors.

Social responsibility should be a core component of brand messaging. Companies must communicate their commitment to social causes, community engagement, and ethical practices through storytelling, social media campaigns, and partnerships with local organizations. For example, Nike's *Equality* campaign highlights the company's commitment to diversity and inclusion. By aligning its brand with social justice issues, Nike resonates with consumers who value these principles and builds a strong, socially responsible brand image.

Ethical advertising practices are crucial for maintaining consumer trust. Companies must ensure their marketing messages are honest and transparent and not exploit consumers. This involves avoiding misleading claims, respecting consumer privacy, and promoting products responsibly. For example, Dove's Real Beauty campaign encourages body positivity and challenges unrealistic beauty standards. Dove builds consumer trust and enhances its brand reputation by adopting ethical advertising practices.

ESG and Cultural Integration

Cultural sensitivity is essential when implementing environmental sustainability initiatives in different markets. Companies must understand local environmental challenges and priorities to tailor their sustainability strategies accordingly. This involves engaging with local communities, respecting cultural norms, and addressing specific environmental issues. For example, Coca-Cola's *World Without Waste* initiative collaborates with local communities to improve recycling and waste management practices. By addressing local environmental challenges and respecting cultural norms, Coca-Cola enhances its sustainability efforts and builds stronger relationships with local stakeholders.

Social responsibility requires cultural awareness and responsiveness to local social dynamics. Companies must respect local customs, traditions, and values while ensuring ethical business practices. This involves adapting marketing strategies to align with local social norms and addressing community needs. For instance, McDonald's adapts its menu and marketing strategies to reflect local tastes and cultural preferences in different markets. By showing cultural awareness and respect, McDonald's enhances its social responsibility and builds a positive brand image.

Good governance and ethical conduct are essential for building trust and credibility in international markets. Companies must navigate diverse regulatory environments and cultural norms while maintaining high standards of governance and ethics. This requires adapting governance structures to meet local expectations and ensuring business practices align with global ethical standards. For example, Nestlé's *Creating Shared Value* initiative addresses social and environmental issues in its communities. By aligning its governance practices with local cultural norms and global ethical standards, Nestlé builds trust with local stakeholders and enhances its reputation.

Discussion Questions

1. **How can companies balance the need for global brand consistency with localizing their marketing efforts to different cultural and regional preferences? Provide examples from the chapter.**

2. **What is the primary benefit of adapting products to local markets?**
   A) It reduces production costs significantly.
   B) It ensures compliance with local regulatory requirements.
   C) It eliminates the need for market research.
   D) It allows for a uniform global product offering.

3. **Which of the following is NOT a component of the 4 Ps of marketing?**
   A) Product
   B) Price
   C) Promotion
   D) Positioning

4. **The primary goal of international marketing is to standardize the marketing mix across all global markets to ensure consistency. True or False?**

5. **Digitalization has made it easier for small and medium-sized enterprises (SMEs) to enter international markets. True or False?**

Recommended Readings

Bae, G. K., Lee, S. M., & Luan, B. K. (2023). The impact of ESG on brand trust and word of mouth in food and beverage companies: Focusing on jeju island tourists. *Sustainability*, 15(3), 2348.

Cheng, L. T., Sharma, P., & Broadstock, D. C. (2023). Interactive effects of brand reputation and ESG on green bond issues: A sustainable development perspective. *Business strategy and the environment*, 32(1), 570–586.

Chusniyah, T., Pambudi, K. S., Zahra, G. A., & I'tisham, M. R. (2023). How the ESGs Affect Company Branding and Stakeholder Psychology. *KnE Social Sciences*, 373–384.

Farmaki, A., Hadjielias, E., Olya, H., Taheri, B., & Hadjielia Drotarova, M. (2023). CSR communication and international marketing: Insights from the COVID-19 pandemic. *International Marketing Review*, 40(5), 1071–1111.

Ferrell, O. C. (2021). Addressing socio-ecological issues in marketing: environmental, social and governance (ESG). *AMS review*, 11(1), 140–144.

Ferrell, O. C., & Ferrell, L. (2021). New directions for marketing ethics and social responsibility research. *Journal of Marketing Theory and Practice*, 29(1), 13–22.

Hu, W., Sun, J., Lin, Y. E., & Hu, J. (2023). ESG and Investment Efficiency: The Role of Marketing Capability. *Sustainability*, 15(24), 16676.

Paolone, F., Cucari, N., Wu, J., & Tiscini, R. (2022). How do ESG pillars impact firms' marketing performance? A configurational analysis in the pharmaceutical sector. *Journal of Business & Industrial Marketing*, 37(8), 1594–1606.

Pinheiro, A. B., dos Santos, J. I. A. S., Cherobim, A. P. M. S., & Segatto, A. P. (2024). What drives environmental, social, and governance (ESG) performance? The role of institutional quality. *Management of Environmental Quality: An International Journal*, 35(2), 427–444.

Tripopsakul, S., & Puriwat, W. (2022). Understanding the impact of ESG on brand trust and customer engagement. *Journal of Human, Earth, and Future*, 3(4), 430–440.

Chapter 10
Managing Human Resources in an International Context

Learning Objectives

- Determine several significant factors that may affect a nation's quantity and quality of labor
- Describe the relationship between competitive strategies – such as international, multi-domestic, and global – and transnational and international human resource management approaches, such as ethnocentric, polycentric, region-centric, and global
- As international company executives, compare recruitment and selection considerations for nationals of home countries, host countries, and third countries
- Differentiate among the training and development considerations for home dash country, host dash country, and third dash country nationals as international company executives
- Specify some of the challenges and opportunities of an expatriate position
- Explain some of the complications of the compensation package for expatriate executives

Overview

As discussed in previous chapters, internationalization is critical for the survival of enterprises. The internationalization of an enterprise requires the internationalization of all of its functional areas. International human resource management (IHRM) is vital in this process, and a strategic approach, as depicted in Figure 10.1, must be developed. Managers must decide what human resource practices best suit the firm's international operations globally. Knowing the differences between domestic and international human resource management is essential for global managers when establishing operational mechanisms to deal with differences in industrial labor, culture, and firm practices in different countries. After reading the textbook module and these chapters, you should be able to understand various aspects of this process, such as adaptation versus standardization of human resource (HR) practices, international staffing, and relevant issues regarding compensation, training, expatriation, and repatriation.

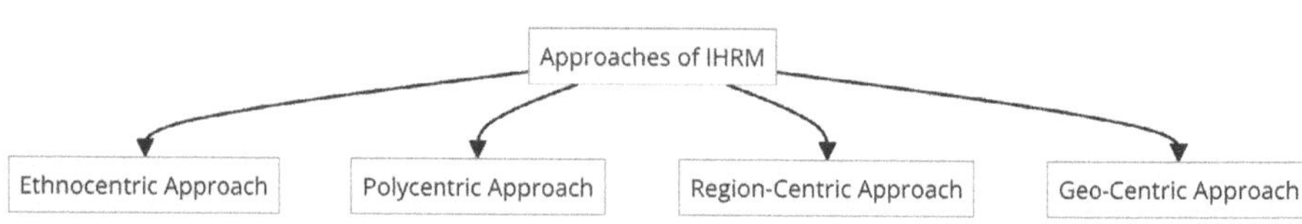

Figure 10.1: The strategic approaches to IHRM.

https://doi.org/10.1515/9783111510286-010

Due to expanded globalization, easy mobility, and communications between international markets, companies are operating at the international level even more. An essential function for organizations working across international borders is to manage the different pressures of the drive for integration and differentiation. international human resource management (IHRM) is a unit of international management studies that explores the design and effects of organizational human resource management (HRM) practices in cross-cultural contexts. It is influential in the nexus of international business, human resources (HR), and organizational behavior. Several theoretical studies explain that IHRM is the interplay between three dimensions:
- HR activities
- The types of workers employed in an organization
- The countries in which organizations operate

Complexities caused by these dimensions differentiate IHRM from domestic HRM, as the HR activities are relatively alike. In a broader sense, the IHRM process, as depicted in Figure 10.2, has the same activities as Domestic HRM, such as planning and staffing. However, domestic HRM operates in one nation, while IHRM activities are performed in many countries.

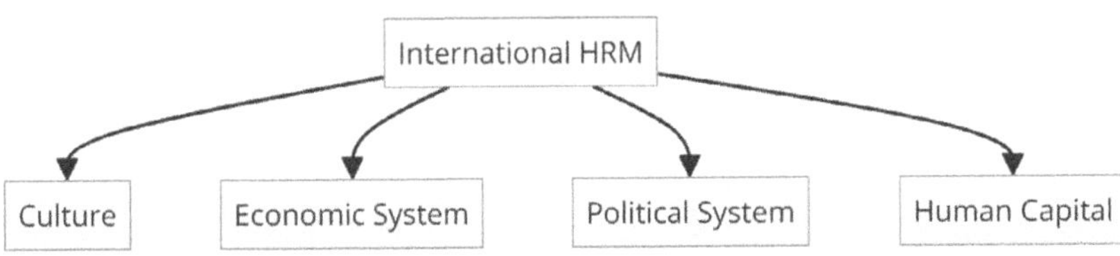

Figure 10.2: International human resource management processes.

IHRM has five functional areas: recruitment and selection, development and training, performance evaluation, remuneration, and labor relations. The enterprise employs newly talented prospects for international operations in the first function of IHRM, recruitment, and selection. Selection requires picking from a pool of candidates whose qualifications closely fit the job requirements. Staffing can be a complex function of IHRM, as, in an international company, the managing and staffing strategy strongly impacts the employees the company selects. For instance, parent country nationals usually staff important positions at headquarters and subsidiaries in a company with an ethnocentric approach. In recruitment and selection methods, companies consider both their headquarters' practices and those widespread in the countries where they have subsidiaries. Local culture also greatly influences recruitment and selection methods; local laws may mandate a specific hiring approach. Balancing internal corporate consistency and sensitivity to local labor practices is essential in choosing an appropriate candidate.

Global Labor Conditions

As depicted in Figure 10.3, employment rates across the globe have declined significantly. To respond to such significant challenges in business, International HR executives are forced to formulate strategies and practices that will make their organizations successful. At the macro level, strategic global HRM ensures that HR policies, procedures, and practices support the organization's overarching values, objectives, and goals. In the middle class, HR executives are mainly concerned with issues relating to unions in the host country. At the micro level, HR executives are attempting to foster a global mindset among the workforce by developing HR competencies and business-related skills necessary for navigating the complex international landscape.

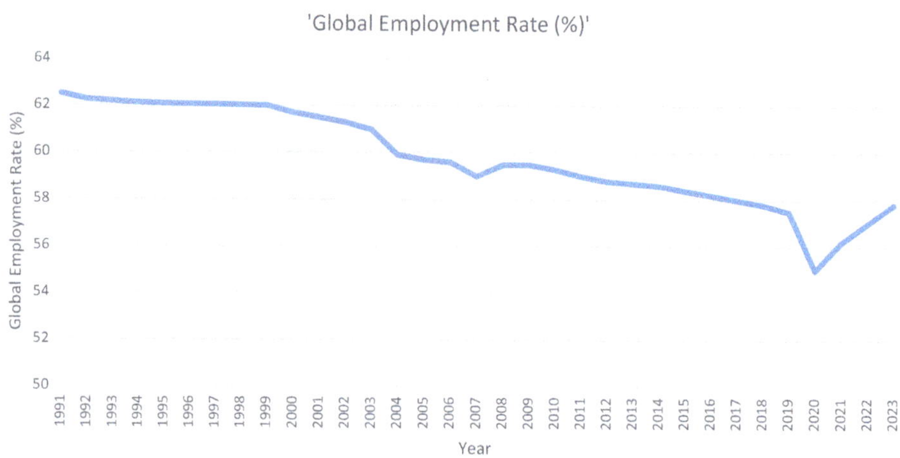

Figure 10.3: Global employment rates from 1991–2023 (projected). (SOURCE: ILO, 2023).

While implementing an IHR strategy, the management team must ascertain the current and intended nature of international operations in the organization, such as whether it is a multi-domestic, international, global, or transnational, so they can determine the extent to which HR policies and practices should be standardized or localized according to the organizational strategy. Management must assess how local cultural, social, political, economic, and legal factors impede any attempts to apply standard HR policies. This is essential if integration is a critical factor in the organizational strategy. It is also crucial to ensure a computerized database of global human resources is used to assist in the desired integration. In formulating the IHRM strategy, upper management must identify the necessary competencies to attain the global organizational objectives. It is also recommended that national HR and line managers work with national HR to formulate international HR (IHR) policies and practices in the critical sourcing, development, and reward areas, which will embed a global mindset. Keep in mind that government agencies regulate labor relations practices in many countries.

The international approach to human resource management requires numerous steps. First, there is the need for explicit recognition by the parent organization that its specific standard operating procedures (SOPs) in managing HR reflect some of the assumptions and values of its home culture. Secondly, a clear recognition by the parent organization that its specific SOPs are not universally better or worse than others but are different and likely to exhibit strengths and weaknesses, particularly abroad. The third is the explicit acknowledgment by the parent organization that its international subsidiaries might prefer alternative ways of managing their talent that are neither inherently better nor worse but could be more effective locally. Fourth is the headquarters' preparedness to acknowledge cultural differences and take action to make them discussable and, therefore, useable. The last step is developing genuine belief by all parties that more creative and effective ways of managing people could be developed due to cross-cultural learning.

Some people consider IHRM similar to expatriate management. Still, the former is more critical and includes more activities than managing expatriates, as it involves international staff management. Although IHR managers assume the same actions as their domestically-based counterparts, the scope and complexity of these tasks often depend on the extent of the organization's internationalization. Moving into the global economy, organizations must adjust their traditional policies of managing their employees. The human factor is increasingly more recognized as critical to organizational success. In the past, scholars feared that machines might one day eliminate the need for people at work. Just the opposite has been occurring. Talented people are more critical than in earlier times.

In fast-growing economies, it is easier to access money and technology than talented people. The competitive advantage is companies that know how to attract, select, deploy, and develop talent. In multinational companies, a significant objective of the IHRM function is to ensure the most effective use of its human resources. To accomplish this, HR professionals undertake various activities related to sourcing, development, reward and performance management, HR planning, employee involvement, and communications. These activities will support and inform organizational strategy if the organization has a strategic HR function. HR professionals are also used extensively in organizational change and development initiatives. As illustrated in Figure 10.4, for international organizations, these HR activities need to be coordinated across both the home-country and diverse national subsidiaries and to take into consideration the requirements of parent-country nationals (PCNs), host-country nationals (HCNs), and third-country nationals (TCNs).

The role of an IHR manager often differs and depends on the organization's international orientation. Managers must be able to interpret global organizational strategy and devise IHR policies and procedures supporting. The IHR manager, as a strategic partner, must counsel senior management on any mismatch between stated organization internationalization goals and actual IHR practice. To enhance the firm's competitive advantage, IHR professionals must focus on their international competencies and learn about the basics of global business.

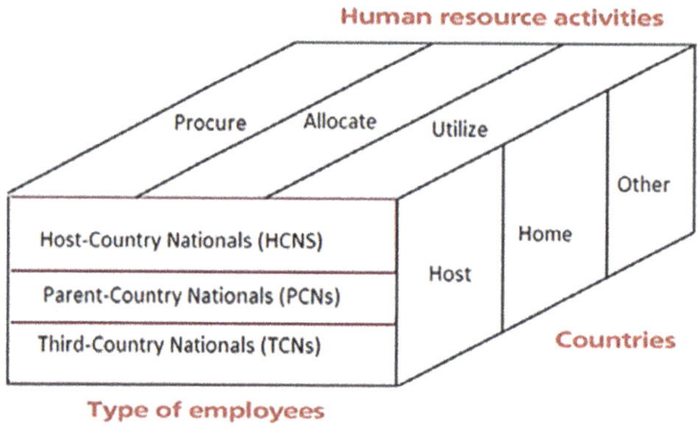

Figure 10.4: IHRM model.

International Human Resource Management Challenges

International enterprises today are a part of a global village with evolving technology. There is a vast paradigm shift in how we work, interact, and perceive. It pushes the IHR division to broaden its horizons to obtain the best professional talent. It is challenging to manage an international workforce. Developing an IHRM strategic plan to address such talent, mobility, and cultural diversity is essential since, as per the World Economic Forum (WEF), we are entering an era of unparalleled talent scarcity. Enterprises operating abroad need to recruit, sustain, motivate, and retain professional talent and have the flexibility to search for the best talent where they may be available and at the best price. Hence, IHRM presents many challenges, as illustrated in Figure 10.5.

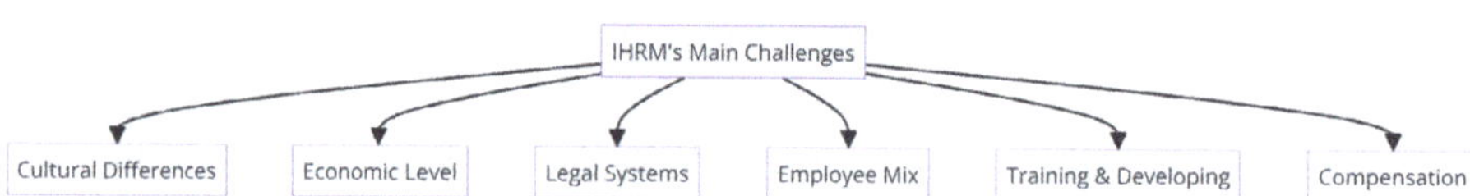

Figure 10.5: IHRM main challenges.

The following are the main challenges international companies are facing with a global workforce:

- **Abiding by Local Laws** – Legal implications may harm an organization's brand image and generate high costs if ignored, as several labor laws tend to vary beyond states' or countries' borders. The firm must comply with local laws, rules, and regulations. Otherwise, the firm may be required to stop operations in that market.
- **Conflicts of Interest** – Integrating different markets will be challenging when your organization has a global presence. The local host market is also subject to changes and will often differ from one to another. Regarding the world market,

resources belonging to other nations will have their interest that impacts your business goals.

- **Effective Communication** – It is challenging to work closely within a team when they are spread across the globe. Handling a virtual workforce can be quite complex as it relies on digital technologies that may not be available in all markets, and staff may not be familiar with them. There is an enormous difference between managing in a physical office and a virtual one. Teams must put extra effort into maintaining professional relationships through a virtual environment and ensuring effective communication.
- **Managing Talent Diversity** – When organizations have a presence in diverse locations across the globe, the culture in these locations will also likely differ. Globalization has produced a diversified and globally distributed workforce. Hence, HR managers face a challenging environment when providing services to a heterogeneous and geographically spread team. A diverse workforce brings various complexities to management, as they must understand the idiosyncrasies of the local and remote offices, especially considering human resources.
- **Decisions** – Decisions must implement SOPs that foster unity and enhance creativity, productivity, and efficiency among the staff across the various divisions and subsidiaries. Managing the global team effectively will require HR software applications that promote transparency, enhanced communications, and a positive work culture.
- **Talent Gaps** – One of the HR department's biggest challenges is attracting, hiring, developing, and retaining employees with the skill set to execute a skilled job. Another challenge is finding someone experienced and knowledgeable about the local and international markets. The HR teams must also know immigration laws when recruiting talent abroad.

Challenges for IHR Managers

Operating HR across geographic and cultural boundaries can be challenging for companies internationalizing and their HR managers. Nonetheless, IHR issues are essential to grasping global HR issues with the widespread use of technology, the ability to communicate with anyone worldwide, and access to new and varied markets. The following are some of the main challenges IHR managers face.

- **Adapting to Change** – Organizations are adapting to the transformation of the global village. Technology is also evolving, and adapting and implementing change is challenging. The whole workforce must also be acquainted with the changes.
- **Maintaining a Low Attrition Rate** – Organizations often invest time and money in recruiting and training for globalization, which has fostered many opportunities in foreign markets. As human resources from various cultures and backgrounds interact, attrition can become an issue. Keeping a low attrition rate is a big challenge for IHR managers.

- **Needed Organization Restructures** – The world is rushing, pushing organizations to adapt to swift changes and restructuring the workforce to function effectively. It is a challenge for managers to restructure these processes.
- **Setting up the Right Ethics and Values** – Ethics and values play a fundamental role in business success. A diverse workforce brings people from different backgrounds together. Aligning the workforce with organizational goals is challenging. The best way to achieve this is by developing best practices to increase sustainability and staff longevity.
- **Stress and Conflict** – Globalization has fueled competitiveness and accelerated business processes. It has also increased the number of working hours, business targets, and competition. In this case, the HR department is responsible for reducing stress and solving conflicts when they arise. It is challenging for IHR managers to keep the tension and conflicts between the teams to a minimum.
- **Work Culture and Environment** – When businesses internationalize and expand, they interact with and merge with different people, governments, and businesses. Setting up a high work culture and sustaining a positive work environment is challenging during this phase.
- **Work-Life Balance** – A balance in workers' professional and personal lives is crucial for their work satisfaction and stability. IHR managers are responsible for creating a sustainable balance between work and staff's personal lives. Such balance helps boost productivity and retention rates.

Overcoming IHR Challenges for a Global Workforce

To accomplish such a balancing act, firms must integrate and concentrate their international activities and distinguish and adopt local activities that include being able to determine core and non-core business activities, achieving consistency while allowing flexibility, building global brand equity while honoring local customs, obtaining leverage while gaining focus, sharing learning and creating new knowledge and engendering an international perspective while ensuring local accountability.

The following are some initiatives IHR managers may engage in to foster a tighter integration of global resource management:

- **Analysis of Results** – An IHR manager must regularly assess business processes and activities related to payroll, professional development, and work environment, to name a few. Evaluating and analyzing HR-related strategies and initiatives is essential to understanding their sustainability and development. It is helpful to understand the changes required in the work process, such as roles and responsibilities, revision of job descriptions, etc.
- **Develop Mentoring and Coaching Programs** – Mentoring and coaching programs are among the most effective ways to manage a diverse workforce. Business leaders can select managers from various divisions for such programs to train and provide feedback to employees from different backgrounds.

- **Devise Monetary Benefit Strategy** – Such benefits motivate workers to strive for excellence in their roles and responsibilities. Organizations should consider devising such appreciation programs to reward top performers with gifts, bonuses, incentives, perks, vouchers, and even international travel to other subsidiary offices to immerse and educate them in those foreign environments.
- **Motivate the Global Workforce** – This is essential to success as it can inspire the staff to achieve higher business results. If the staff is content, they tend to be more motivated to excel in their tasks and responsibilities.
- **Talent's Strategic Global Deployment** – International business and trade continue to grow, propelling more organizations to internationalize and increasing the demand for strategic deployments of a more diverse workforce to assess, operate, and succeed in such markets. International firms must carefully distribute such talents across all divisions in-country and abroad.

A crucial challenge for international enterprises is the demand to devise and achieve market targets, including but not limited to the competing demands of international integration of human resources and coordination of these initiatives locally and abroad. Some of these primary challenges in IHRM include:
- High rates of failure in the expatriation and repatriation process
- Staff development and deployment
- Developing, recruiting, and retaining the appropriate mix of skills independent of the geographical locations
- The dissemination of knowledge and innovative initiatives
- Knowledge management strategy development
- Speed in which information flows up and downstream across the organization and global subsidiaries
- Talent identification and development
- Recruitment of talented staff who can function effectively
- Barriers to diversity, equity, and inclusion (DEI), in particular for women
- International business ethics
- Language skills, including spoken, written, and non-verbal.
- Cultural intelligence development
- Emotional intelligence development

Other challenges in managing international assignments may include:
- Different labor laws
- Distinct political climates
- Diverse stages of technological advancement
- Diversity, equity, and inclusion, especially in value systems, attitudes, time management, risk-taking, and the roles of religion
- Educational level attained

- Social organizations, including social institutions, authority structures, interest groups, and status systems
- Employee and family adjustment
- Selection of the proper professional for international tasks
- Cultural and communication barriers

Recruitment and Selection of Employees

Three main staffing strategies exist when companies must recruit and select new employees while expanding into a new international market. Each of these strategies has its advantages and disadvantages, and the option of one versus another will depend on the company's internationalization strategy and its HR needs. The first, a *home-country national strategy,* is adopted when employees from the home country are asked to travel abroad, live, and work in the host country; these professionals are known as expatriates. The second, a *host-country national strategy,* is selected when the company hires employees born in the host country. Lastly, a *third-country national strategy* is chosen when employees from an entirely different country are hired from home and host countries. Table 10.1 summarizes the advantages and disadvantages of these strategies.

Table 10.1: Advantages and Disadvantages of the Three Staffing Strategies.

	Home-Country National	Host-Country National	Third-Country National
Advantages	Greater control of the organization	No language barrier exists	Such staff may be the best option to bring an international perspective to the business
	Managers gain experience in local markets	A possible better understanding of local rules and laws	Costs associated with hiring, such as visas, may be less expensive than with home-country nationals
	Possible greater understanding and implementation of business strategy	Hiring costs such as visas are eliminated	
	Cultural understanding		
	Morale builder for employees of the host country		

Table 10.1 (continued)

	Home-Country National	Host-Country National	Third-Country National
Disadvantages	Adapting to a foreign environment may be difficult for managers and families, resulting in less productivity	Host-country managers may not understand business objectives as well without proper training	Must consider traditional national hostilities
	Expatriates may not have cultural sensitivity	It may create a perception of "us" versus "them"	The host government and local businesses may resent hiring a third-country national
	Language barriers		Can affect the motivation of local workers
	Cost of visa and hiring factors		

International Recruitment

As depicted in Figure 10.6, companies may opt among four distinct approaches to international recruitment: ethnocentric, polycentric, geocentric, and regiocentric. The following is a description of each of these recruitment approaches and how and when companies typically adopt them:

- **Ethnocentric** – In an ethnocentric approach, the company hires professionals from its parent country to fill positions worldwide. For instance, if the company wants to fill an executive role in a foreign country, we could:
  - Relocate one of their existing employees, a permanent resident of their parent country.
  - Hire a person from their parent country who lives or wants to live in the host country.

  The ethnocentric method is adopted when opening new branches abroad in new markets or countries. It tends to be easier for the company's policies and procedures to be transferred from the parent country to the new branches. Typically, expatriates from a parent company comprise less than 20% of an international subsidiary to reduce the costs of hiring the staff and avoid changing the subsidiary's local culture.
- **Polycentric** – In a polycentric approach, the company hires local professionals to fill positions in a host country. For instance, they could advertise on local job boards or create a contract with a local recruitment agency. Companies adopt a polycentric approach when they need the skills of local professionals in the markets they operate to conduct their business. For instance, if they need to expand their clientele to a specific new country or market, they would hire a local professional who knows the market and can coordinate their marketing sales operations.

- **Regiocentric** – In a regiocentric approach, the company hires or transfers professionals within the same region, such as European, Asian, or Latin American countries, to fill open positions. For instance, the company may transfer employees within the EU or South East Asia countries. So, if they were to hire someone in Mexico (a host country), they could transfer one of their employees from Chile or Peru, a host country in the same region. The regiocentric approach is used when the costs of moving a company's staff from a host country are less than transferring them from the parent country. When using this approach, management must consider language and cultural barriers.
- **Geocentric** – In a geocentric approach, the company hires the best professionals to fill positions regardless of where they come from or live. The company may:
  - **Hire a remote employee** – This approach is used when the company wants to hire talent from a location where they don't have an office or presence. For instance, if the company needs a customer support representative in another time zone to support their customers there.
  - **Relocate employees** – This approach may include bringing foreign talent into the parent. company's country and relocating professionals to a new host country. This approach may be used when staff needs to be physically placed at a specific subsidiary location, and the best professional for the job lives elsewhere.

    Note, however, that to use a geocentric approach, the company needs to have a global outlook on recruitment. For instance, whenever a position opens in a host country or parent country, the hiring team may:
  - Advertise on global job boards before using local job boards, mentioning the location of the job. Also, advertise on job boards that focus on remote work when possible.
  - Ask for referrals from existing employees, as they may have someone in their network who could fit this position and be willing to relocate.
  - Ask recruiters to suggest candidates they met at international career fairs or events.

Ethnocentric	Regiocentric	Polycentric	Geocentric
The subsidiary must comply with the default policies and procedures of headquarters.	Regiocentric orientation is the belief that countries existing in the same geographic region have economic, social, cultural, or political similarities.	With a polycentric orientation, marketing strategies are based on the economic, political, or cultural disparities of the countries where subsidiaries are located.	Geocentric orientation means the company sees the whole world as a potential market.

Figure 10.6: Four approaches for recruitment of workers for international assignments.

- Check a global employee database to find internal candidates who may wish to relocate.
- Source candidates online without looking at their current location.

Training and Development of International Employees

Another critical function of IHRM is the training and development of its staff, as depicted in Figure 10.7, which is directed to provide adequate training to personnel in an enterprise and allow them to fulfill their goals and objectives, as well as foster better performance and growth in their activities and responsibilities. At the international level, human resource development professionals must be accountable for training and developing workers worldwide, offering specialized training to equip expatriates for appointments abroad, and creating a distinct group of managers with a global mindset.

Figure 10.7: Importance of training and development of international staff.

These programs may be done in two ways: centralized and decentralized. Training originates at the headquarters in a *centralized* process, and corporate trainers travel to subsidiaries abroad, often adapting to local situations. A *geocentric* approach is also centralized, and trainers and coaches may be sent from various positions in the headquarters or subsidiaries to any other location in the enterprise. It fits the ethnocentric model. In a *decentralized* approach, training is given locally, following a polycentric model. When training is decentralized, the cultural backgrounds of the trainers and trainees are usually comparable. Local qualified professionals produce training materials and techniques for their area and discipline and deliver the training programs.

Medium- to high-intensity training typically comprises one to two months. Such programs provide practical learning, detailed information about the country, city, and local people, and cultural immersion. Medium, less intensive training typically involves intercultural experience delivered through workshops, including cultural simulations, skits, role plays, and case study analysis. Such skill development programs can cover culture-general topics and be more culture-specific. Lastly, companies may select high-intensity programs, which are more appropriate for internationally inexperienced expatriates without foreign working experience, who are not multi-culturally aware, or when the host country requires specific skills (e.g., less common languages, the rule of law, customs, traditions, geographic challenges, etc.). Working in a distinct culture often requires sensitivity training, including communication workshops and field exercises concentrating on self-awareness, listening skills, open-mindedness, risk and ambiguity tolerance, and communication skills.

Expatriates

An expatriate is a worker sent by their employer to operate in a foreign country. Figure 10.8 lists the top countries for expatriates to work in as of 2022. In such an environment, the enterprise is referred to as a parent company, whereas the engagement country is the host country. For instance, if General Motors, the parent company, sends one of its U.S. directors to supervise a new development in Brazil, the director would be an expatriate, and Brazil would be the host country. Equally, if a worker from Brazil is sent to the U.S. or someone from Germany is sent to China, they would also be expatriates.

1. Canada
2. United Arab Emirates
3. Taiwan
4. Mexico
5. Vietnam
6. Portugal
7. Malaysia
8. Thailand
9. Costa Rica
10 Ecuador
11. Colombia
12. Czech Republic
13. Spain
14. Bahrain
15. Singapore
16. US
17. France
18. Philippines
19. Ukraine
20. UK

Figure 10.8: Best countries for expats, 2022. (SOURCE: CEOWORLD Magazine Research, 2022).

Several companies send expatriates to their overseas operations. Expatriates may be a response to the high demand for internationally competent managers, which is predicted to rise as global competition continues to increase. Organizations need to comprehend the dynamic relationships between adding staff and increasing productivity. Expatriates supply several benefits for companies, including greater parent company control and distinct expertise. International experience also nourishes opportunities for personal and professional development and career advancement. However, expatriates tend to be expensive, which can deter their extensive use. In addition, many companies tend to experience relatively high failure rates, primarily due to their families' inability to adapt.

Expatriate success and job performance are closely related to their intercultural adjustment level and their families. Hence, companies must employ a strict selection process to determine which employees would potentially succeed as expatriates, including consideration of the family. Surprisingly, given the high cost and failure rates, many companies continue to make these expensive investments and commitments with little preparation, if any, due to their need for cross-cultural transitions.

Several characteristics distinguish an expatriate's predicted level of success, including but not limited to job, language, and relationship skills, motivational state, multicultural awareness, and family situation. Technical competency is frequently considered a selection criterion for expatriates, but that is seldom the most appropriate selection approach. The expatriate's technical skills are necessary, but many other skills can be critical. For instance, expatriates are likely to make more progress overseas if they have practical skills, management competencies, and solid connections and relationships with the host country and headquarters operations. Conflict resolution skills are also essential, and expatriates must firmly believe their work will succeed and advance their careers.

To succeed, expatriates must be committed to learning new behavioral patterns and the host-country's local attitudes. Motivation is probably the highest factor when considering whether a candidate is suitable for an overseas position. Successful expatriates often enjoy the opportunity and challenges to forge their way through a new environment and are very comfortable when networking and developing new social contacts. Such attributes are critical for the expatriates' families as well. Therefore, training for expatriates and their families is often necessary.

Management should select expatriates with excellent cultural and emotional intelligence and relationship skills to diminish any premature termination of an international assignment. Some attributes and skills are essential for the success of expatriates, including but not limited to behavioral flexibility, tolerance for ambiguity, strong interpersonal and communication skills, and a nonjudgmental disposition. Ethnocentric expatriates tend to have more significant challenges adjusting to a new culture and environment, and the local community will likely perceive them negatively. The expatriates must have some working knowledge of the host language and be familiar with standard nonverbal communications and protocols in the new culture.

Most expatriates take their families to a foreign country. The family transition must be taken very seriously, as the family situation is one of the most critical factors in completing an overseas assignment. Expatriates should feel comfortable at their level, as something seemingly trivial can generate significant stress for the whole family, such as transporting a family cat. In addition, expatriates' spouses must be highly willing to live abroad and be supportive and adaptive to new situations and environments. Many companies end up having expatriates' assignments terminated early due to their spouse's unwillingness or inability to implement necessary adjustments to the host country.

Predeparture training for the expatriate dramatically increases the likelihood of success. The training an employee needs before being assigned abroad may depend on various variables, such as previous overseas experience, the time available before they depart, and how unique or novel the new country they are assigned to. Cross-cultural training is essential for expatriates and their families. Training programs should, at the minimum, inform the expatriate about the new host country and immerse expatriates into a new culture. Low-intensity and interaction training focuses on information distribution through chapters, audio and video materials, and reading assignments. These materials should include general area studies and a company operational overview. A low-intensity training would be appropriate for someone familiar with the host country or who has been on an expatriate assignment before. Unfortunately, this is often the only training most expatriates receive, whether they have previous experience. This lack of training programs is usually due to last-minute selection or lack of training budget.

Expatriates Allowances

The following are some typical allowances usually offered to expatriates:

- **Car and Driver Allowances** – Most companies offer expatriate managers a car allowance. The expatriate can buy, rent, or lease a car in the host country. In some cases, expatriates are given funds to hire a chauffeur.
- **Club Membership Allowances** – In some countries, the only way an expatriate can access recreational facilities, such as tennis courts, country clubs, and swimming pools, is by joining clubs. These facilities are also essential to meeting or conducting new business contacts in many cultures. Such an allowance is typically made on a case-by-case basis.
- **Cost of Living Allowances** – Cost of living allowances (COLAs) allows expatriates to keep up with their accustomed living standard. COLAs are typically given when expatriates are assigned to locations where the cost of living is higher than that of the home country. Figure 10.9 illustrates an example of an expatriate assignment from the U.S. to the U.K. regarding how multiple variables may affect COLA.

	Home Currency	USD				
	Host Currency	GBP				
Changes to Index and COLA United States to UK	Spendable (A) USD	Index (B)	COLA (C)= ((B-100)/100)*A	Host Spendable USD (B + C)	Exchange Rate (D)	Host Spendable GBP
January 1	100,000	135.5376	35,538	135,538	0.6356	86,148
October 1	100,600	129.5685	29,746	130,346	0.6829	89,009
	-0.6%	-4.4%	-16.3%	-3.8%	7.4%	3.3%

Figure 10.9: How multiple variables may affect COLA in an international assignment.

- **Education Allowances** – Most expatriates send their children to private schools overseas. Companies often pay the total cost of tuition, books, and supplies.

- **Foreign Service Premiums** – This allowance rewards the willingness to move the family abroad to a foreign country. The total amount is usually a percentage of the expatriate's base salary, often around 10 to 25 percent.
- **Furnishing Allowances** – Often, the parent company ships all of the expatriate's personal belongings and furnishings to the new location overseas, with some restrictions, typically 5,000 pounds in a shipping container, for example. Another approach is to provide an allowance for expatriates' lease or purchase of overseas furnishings. A third is to give the expatriate a fixed sum, often around $10,000 to $15,000, to buy those necessary items.
- **Hardship Allowance** – The hardship is another foreign premium allowance typically added to the original one, based on expatriates' difficulty in certain parts of the world. Hardship allowances are most significant when expatriates are sent to locations with poor living conditions, vastly different cultures, safety issues, poor access to reasonable health care, etc. Relocating expatriates from the United States to the United Kingdom differs significantly from Angola or Afghanistan.
- **Home Leave Allowances** – Expatriates and their families typically receive allowances for round-trip, business-class airfare to visit their home country and families at least once a year.
- **Housing Allowances** – The cost of housing in various parts of the world is higher than in the United States. For instance, large apartments in Tokyo or Hong Kong can cost upwards of $12,000 a month. Such allowances compensate expatriates for these much higher costs.
- **Medical Allowances** – Companies usually pay for all medical expenses. In countries with hardship, inadequate medical facilities include emergency trips to other countries for medical care.
- **Relocation Allowances** – The allowance compensates for any mistakes made in other assistance for unforeseen complications. Expatriates receive about one month's salary.
- **Taxes** – Often, companies reimburse expatriates for taxes they may need to pay more than they would have typically paid in their home country if they had remained there.
- **Utility Allowances** – Some companies give expatriates a fixed sum above their base salary to pay their utility bills. In contrast, others try to compensate for the difference between their home and host countries.

Women expatriates and male spouses represent a different challenge that must be considered. There are currently relatively few women expatriates, but their numbers will likely increase. Also, other factors such as religion, race, disabilities, political convictions, or sexual orientation may make it difficult for expatriates to succeed in a particular location. Since expatriates are expensive, ensuring the assignment succeeds is in a firm's interest. Proper expatriate selection, training, and attention to the family's needs can be a productive investment.

Repatriation

Repatriation is assisting expatriates in their transition back to their home country. It is the last phase of a cycle that starts with the expatriation of the employee, as depicted in Figure 10.10. Upon returning home, many expatriates experience reverse culture shock – a psychological phenomenon that can lead to fear, helplessness, irritability, and disorientation. All these factors can cause expatriates to leave the organization soon after returning from an assignment and take their knowledge with them. One problem with repatriation is that expatriates and their families have assumed things stayed the same at home, while work colleagues may have changed or moved, or new managers and employees may have been hired.

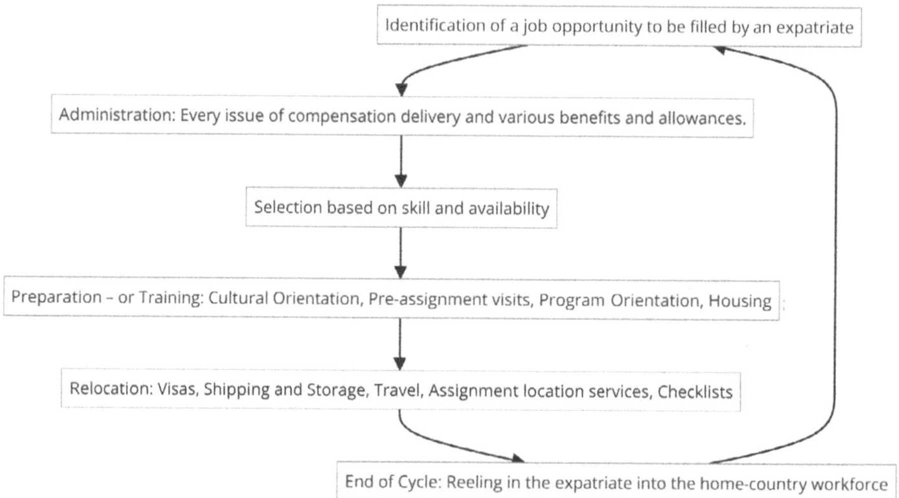

Figure 10.10: Phases of expatriation and repatriation of employees.

Although managers may be on the same level as other managers when they return, they may have less informal authority and clout than others working in the particular office for some time. An effective repatriation program can be expensive, costing $10 to 20 thousand dollars per family. Still, the investment is worth it, given the critical skills the managers will have gained and can share with the organization. Repatriation planning must happen before the employees leave their home country for a foreign assignment, and it should be a continuous process throughout the project and upon their return. The method may include the following initiatives:

- Training and counseling on overseas assignments before leaving
- A clear understanding of goals before leaving gives the expatriate a sense of what new skills and knowledge they will bring back home
- Job guarantees upon return
- Identifying and assigning expatriates with mentors, ideally former expatriates

- Keeping communication from the home country wide open through newsletters, regular virtual meetings, special in-person events (e.g., quarterly report meetings, holiday celebration parties, etc.), and special announcements
- Allowance for periodic return trips home to visit family and friends
- Counseling
- Promoting virtual brown bag lunches, where expatriates can present and discuss their learning while on assignment abroad

The same information on training applied to expatriates is also used for third-country nationals. Training programs vary according to the type of business, the skills necessary, and the country where it takes place. Different training considerations might occur if it is decided that host-country citizens will be hired. For instance, are they required to train at the parent company headquarters, learn the business traits, and then apply the new skills in their home country? Sometimes, sending a domestic manager abroad to train host-country managers and staff may make more sense. As discussed earlier in this chapter, understanding the host-country's cultural factors is essential to implementing training programs that can be utilized in any country.

A sample list of the likelihood that an assignment will succeed depends on the attributes listed in Table 10.2. Five categories determine expatriate success: job factors, relational dimensions, motivational state, family situation, and language skills.

Table 10.2: Categories of Expatriate Success Predictors with Examples.

Job Factors	Relational Dimensions	Motivational State	Family Situation	Language Skills
Technical skills	Tolerance for ambiguity	Belief in the mission	The willingness of the spouse to live abroad	Host-country language
Familiarity with the host country and headquarters operations	Behavioral flexibility	Congruence with a career path	An adaptive and supportive spouse	Nonverbal communication
Managerial skills	No judgmentalism	Interest in overseas experience	Stable marriage	
Administrative competence	Cultural empathy and low ethnocentrism	Interest in specific host-country culture		
	Interpersonal skills	Willingness to acquire new patterns of behavior and attitudes		

Some other important factors to consider are family stress, cultural inflexibility, emotional immaturity, too much responsibility, and long working hours. These factors can draw the expatriate away from family, who could also be experiencing culture shock, which are reasons for expatriate failure. The appropriate selection process and training program can prevent some of these failings.

Figure 10.11 illustrates that most expatriates undergo four adjustment phases when moving abroad for any assignment. These adjustments include elation/honeymoon first, then resistance, followed by adaption, and eventually, biculturalism. During the elation phase, expatriates are excited about the novelty of the experience and the new surroundings, finding the new culture different, interesting, exotic, or stimulating. But in the resistance phase, expatriates typically start comparing what they have at home and what they now have in the host country, which may include working conditions, feeling of safety, food, foreign language, etc. These comparisons can be favorable but often tend to be negative. Increased frustration may ensue due to everyday living conditions, such as cultural and typical food differences and language. At the adaptation stage, expatriates gain better language skills, integrate better into the community and society, and adjust to life overseas. Sometimes, during this phase, expatriates may even begin to reject their own culture, at which point they embrace life abroad. In the last step, biculturalism, expatriates fully embrace the new environment and culture and begin to appreciate their old life at home equally as much as their new life abroad. Many problems associated with expatriates' failures, such as family life and cultural stress, have been greatly diminished at this stage.

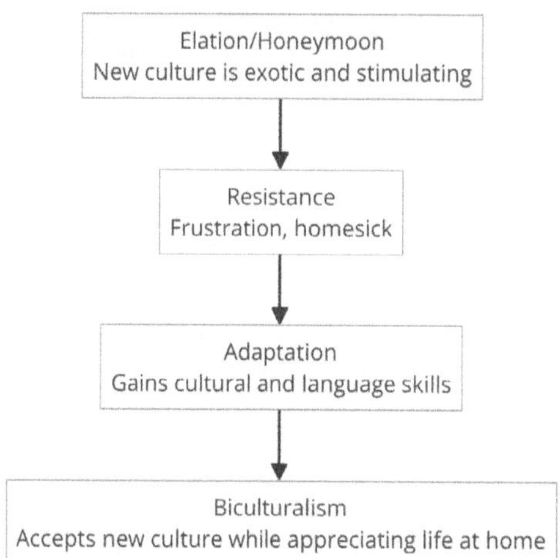

Figure 10.11: Expatriates four adjustment phases.

Compensation for International Assignments

Remuneration and benefits are other functional approaches of IHRM. The remuneration of employees plays a vital role in hiring new employees because employment compensation is one of the primary sources of income for people across the globe. Firms have two primary concerns in developing an international compensation and employee benefits system: comparability and costs. Regarding comparability, a sound compensation system disperses salaries to internally equivalent and competitive employees within the marketplace. The international company must also consider the wages of workers who may transfer from other locations. Companies struggle to reduce costs, and payroll is one of the most significant costs incurred by any business.

An international assignment compensation system must balance adequately rewarding and motivating expatriates while controlling corporate headquarters' costs. Because of the enormous investment, developing a comprehensive global compensation system for expatriates is one of the most critical challenges facing global human resource management.

Compensation Strategies

Companies with multinational operations must develop employee compensation plans that align with their global business strategy. Companies that articulate a clear global pay philosophy and develop corresponding compensation programs are best positioned to execute their strategy effectively. An effective global compensation strategy creates consistency in pay management and facilitates global employee mobility. Establishing guidelines and practices with consistent communication of key messages is vital to the success of the compensation program. Although multinational employers strive to globalize their compensation practices, local and regional approaches to international pay are still the most common.

International assignment compensation has many moving parts and is difficult to standardize, as illustrated in Figure 10.12. Many factors affect the settlement of a particular expatriate, including assignment type and length, location, family needs (if applicable), and benefits. The main compensation items for expatriates involve base pay, cost-of-living adjustments, housing allowances, home leave, education assistance for dependents, and premium pay. The U.S. Department of State indexes the living costs abroad, quarters allowances, hardship differentials, and hazard pay allowances. The information, published quarterly, is used by many organizations to assist in establishing private compensation systems. While the U.S. Fair Labor Standards Act does not apply to employees outside the U.S., employers must be familiar with the host country's labor laws.

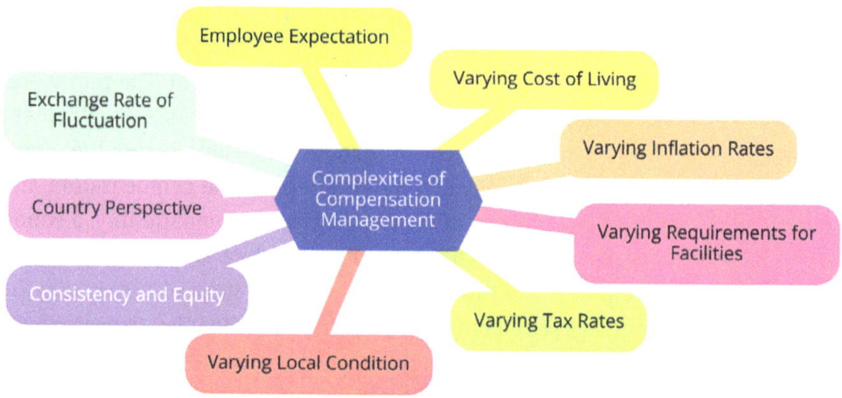

Figure 10.12: Complexities of international compensation management.

An international compensation plan includes elements typical of any rewards strategy and a few extra incentives and allowances, depending on the host country, as summarized below:

- **Base salary** – When an employee accepts an international assignment, it is up to the employer to determine the base pay rate. The base salary is usually related to paying ranges in the home country, which may be adjusted based on local variances (i.e., economic fluctuations). Companies typically adopt one of the following approaches to establish base salaries for expatriates:
  - **The home-country-based** – A home-based compensation program aims to equalize the employee to a standard of living enjoyed in their home country. This approach divides the expatriate's base salary into four general categories: taxes, housing, goods and services, and discretionary income.
  - **The host-country-based** – With this approach, the employee's compensation is based on local and national rates. Several companies continue to cover the employee in their defined contribution or defined benefit pension schemes and provide housing allowances.
  - **The headquarters-based** – This approach assumes that all assignees, regardless of location, are in one country (i.e., a U.S. company pays all assignees a U.S.-based salary, regardless of geography).
  - **Balance sheet** – In this scenario, the compensation is calculated using the home-country-based approach with all allowances, deductions, and reimbursements. After the net salary is determined, it is converted to the host country's currency. As one of the main objectives of an international compensation management program is to maintain the expatriate's current standard of living, developing an equitable and functional compensation plan that combines balance and flexibility is highly challenging for multinational companies. To this end, many companies adopt a balance sheet approach. This approach guarantees

that employees in international assignments maintain the same standard of living they enjoyed in their home country. A worksheet lists the costs of significant expenses in the home and host countries, and any differences are used to increase or decrease the compensation to keep it in balance.

Some companies also allow expatriates to split payments of their salaries between the host countries and the home country's currencies. The expatriate receives money in the host country's currency for expenses but keeps a percentage in the home country's currency to safeguard against wild currency fluctuations in either country.

- **Variable or incentive compensation** – The globalization of business has increased the use of variable and incentive pay worldwide. However, some cultures do not readily accept linking pay to individual or group performance. Other roadblocks to paying for performance include financial (insufficient funding from the pool), target setting (defining performance parameters), and pay equity. Yet when it is done right, pay for performance effectively allocates limited rewards and retains top performers. Variable pay has become an increasingly important compensation element in many countries. Variable pay plans generally fall into one of two categories:
  - **Short-term incentive** plans are usually annual plans that link awards based on meeting individual or group performance criteria and objectives. Unlike long-term plans, these incentive plans provide a payout to be awarded yearly.
  - **Long-term incentive plans** can vary from three to five years. These plans typically include equity-based incentives, such as stock options and restricted share grants, and equity-based programs, like phantom stocks or stock appreciation rights. Awards are closely linked to achieving company goals and objectives over three to five years.

    Participation and eligibility for each type of plan, as well as the level of incentives and average payouts, vary significantly among companies, industries, and countries worldwide.
- **Premium and allowances** – Premiums and allowances are added to the base salary so that expatriate employees can maintain their standard of living. Those add-ons are removed when the employee repatriates. Some types of premiums and allowances are as follows:
  - **Hardship, hazard, and danger pay** – Employers sometimes need to send employees on assignments to host countries where conditions are difficult or hazardous (i.e., remote locations or countries with high rates of violence). As a result, a hardship allowance may be granted as an additional incentive to compensate employees for accepting assignments in less-than-desirable countries. Premiums typically range from 10 percent to 50 percent of base pay, depending on the severity of the hardship. For assignments in developing countries with a history of violence or experiencing political unrest, expatri-

ates often receive hazard pay, such as an additional 25 percent of their base salary.

- **Cost-of-living adjustments** – A cost-of-living adjustment is an increase or decrease in an expatriate employee's pay in response to economic fluctuations, such as inflation or deflation. Companies often raise the employees' base salary to prevent the attrition of global employees' purchasing power and keep up with inflation. When price levels drop, companies may also decrease the base wage accordingly.
- **Educational assistance** – Educational assistance for dependents of expatriate employees varies based on conditions in the host country. Aid is usually not provided if local educational institutions are deemed adequate. When the educational system of the host country is substandard, employers may use a variety of benefits, such as employers operating a school in the foreign country, paying for dependents' educational expenses, including room and board, to attend schools in the United States; or providing an allowance for attendance at private schools in either the United States or the host country. Other employers may pay employees a specified amount (stipend) necessary for schooling at the nearest suitable school. The employees make no difference in sending their dependents to an institution they choose.
- **Housing assistance** – Housing assistance is usually provided either in the form of free company-owned housing or via a housing allowance that is typically equal to the difference in housing costs between the home and host countries or based on a specified percentage of an employee's base salary. Housing allowance rates are usually calculated based on a single-person or two-person household. Employers may provide an additional supplement for employees with larger families living with them, typically ranging from 15 to 30 percent of the two-person allowance.
- **Home leave** – Home leave policies aim to allow the assignee and their family to maintain personal and business relationships and remain abreast of any economic, political, social, or cultural changes in the home country. Although home leave policies vary among multinational corporations, most policies grant leave based on the employee's level within the organizational structure. Executives, managers, and more senior-level professionals are often granted home leave once or every other year for up to four weeks. Lower-level employees may be allowed only a single visit during their assignment. Companies that provide home leave allowances generally purchase or reimburse the employee for travel-related expenses, such as airline tickets for the employee, spouse, or partner and any dependent children younger than college age.

Compensating Third-Country Nationals

Third-country nationals (TCNs) are employees who are not from the home country or the host country. TCNs are traditionally technical or professional employees hired for short-term employment and are often considered international freelance. In the case of TCNs, multinational companies have one of three options regarding compensation:

- Pay the TCNs as if they were local nationals
- Treat them as any other U.S. citizen would be treated
- Establish an arrangement based primarily on the third country's pay ranges

Integrating ESG into Global Human Resource Management

Environmental, social, and governance (ESG) criteria have become fundamental in shaping the strategies and practices of international human resource management (IHRM). As organizations expand globally, they face the challenge of managing diverse workforces while adhering to sustainability and ethical standards. ESG considerations are not just integral to managing human resources internationally. They are an ethical imperative. They shape recruitment, training, performance evaluation, compensation, and cultural integration strategies. By incorporating ESG criteria into their HR practices, companies demonstrate their commitment to ethical business practices, enhancing their global operations, building strong relationships with local stakeholders, and achieving long-term success.

ESG in Recruitment and Selection

Environmental sustainability significantly influences recruitment and selection processes. Companies aiming to reduce their environmental impact seek individuals who are knowledgeable about and committed to sustainable practices. This includes hiring professionals with expertise in energy efficiency, waste reduction, and sustainable resource management. For example, businesses need to align their recruitment strategies with local sustainability standards in regions with stringent environmental regulations, like the European Union. This often involves prioritizing candidates with a proven track record in implementing eco-friendly initiatives, ensuring that the organization meets regulatory requirements and fulfills its environmental commitments.

Social Responsibility in Recruitment

Social responsibility is crucial in recruitment and selection, emphasizing fair labor practices, diversity, and inclusion. Companies must ensure their recruitment strategies promote equal opportunities and respect local cultures and communities. This means adhering to local labor laws, supporting gender equality, and recruiting underrepresented groups. For instance, multinational corporations such as Unilever and Microsoft implement inclusive hiring practices to build diverse workforces. These companies actively seek candidates from various demographic groups, ensuring equal opportunities and fostering a culture of inclusivity, which enhances the company's reputation and employee engagement.

Governance and Ethical Recruitment Practices

Good governance in recruitment involves transparency, fairness, and adherence to ethical standards. Companies must ensure their recruitment processes are free from discrimination and bias, adhering to international labor standards. This includes clear communication about job requirements, fair selection processes, and ethical treatment of all candidates. For example, implementing standardized assessment tools can help ensure fair candidate evaluations, regardless of their background. By maintaining high governance standards, companies build trust with potential employees and stakeholders, enhancing their reputation and attractiveness as employers.

ESG in Training and Development

Integrating environmental sustainability into training programs is essential for fostering a culture of sustainability within organizations. Companies should offer training on sustainable practices, such as energy conservation, waste management, and resource efficiency, empowering employees to contribute to the company's environmental goals. For instance, companies like Google and Siemens provide sustainability training that covers topics like renewable energy and environmental regulations. These programs improve the company's environmental performance and align employee actions with the company's sustainability objectives.

Social Responsibility in Employee Development

Employee development programs should emphasize social responsibility by promoting diversity, equity, inclusion, and ethical behavior. This involves offering training on cultural sensitivity, anti-discrimination, and ethical decision making to ensure a supportive and respectful workplace. For example, cross-cultural training programs help employees understand and respect cultural norms and values, improving communication and cooperation among diverse teams. This is crucial for multinational companies operating in varied cultural contexts.

Governance and Ethical Development Practices

Governance in training and development involves ensuring transparency and fairness when providing training opportunities. Companies must ensure that all employees have equal access to development programs and that they are conducted ethically. For instance, companies like Johnson & Johnson and Nestlé ensure their training programs are accessible to all employees and align with ethical standards. Transparent communication about training objectives and fair employee performance evaluation is vital to maintaining high governance standards.

ESG in Performance Evaluation and Compensation

Incorporating environmental sustainability into performance evaluations encourages employees to contribute to the company's environmental goals. Setting clear sustainability targets and metrics allows companies to assess employee performance based on their contributions to these objectives. For example, companies like Patagonia assess employees' efforts to promote sustainable practices and achieve environmental goals. This alignment between individual performance and company sustainability objectives encourages employees to prioritize environmental considerations in their roles.

Social Responsibility in Compensation

Ensuring fair and equitable compensation is a crucial aspect of social responsibility. Companies must address pay equity, provide benefits that support work-life balance, and ensure non-discriminatory compensation practices. For example, companies like Salesforce and Danone have implemented pay equity programs to ensure all employees receive fair compensation, regardless of gender or ethnicity. Regular pay audits and adjustments are part of these programs, promoting social justice and enhancing employee satisfaction.

Good governance in compensation involves maintaining transparency and fairness in salary and benefits administration. This includes clear communication about pay structures, performance-based incentives, and ensuring consistent application of compensation policies. For instance, companies like Apple and Intel maintain transparency in their compensation policies, informing employees about how salaries are determined and what benefits are available. This builds trust and enhances employee motivation.

Discussion Questions

1. **What are the main challenges international human resource managers face when managing expatriates, and how can these challenges be effectively addressed?**

2. **What is the primary advantage of using a polycentric approach in international staffing?**
   A) Greater control from the parent company
   B) No language barriers and a better understanding of local markets
   C) Lower costs associated with hiring
   D) Easier to transfer policies and procedures from the parent country

3. **Which of the following is NOT typically included in an expatriate's compensation package?**
   A) Cost of living allowances
   B) Hardship allowances
   C) Long-term stock options
   D) Club membership allowances

4. **The ethnocentric staffing approach involves hiring employees from the host country to manage the subsidiaries. True or False?**

5. **Effective repatriation programs include pre-departure training and maintaining open communication between expatriates and the home office. True or False?**

Recommended Readings

Aust, I., Cooke, F. L., Muller-Camen, M., & Wood, G. (2024). Achieving sustainable development goals through common-good HRM: Context, approach and practice. *German Journal of Human Resource Management*, 38(2), 93–110.

Jorgji, S., Teta, J., Mousa, S., Ponkratov, V., Elyakova, I., Vatutina, L., . . . & Kosov, M. (2024). Sustainable Human Capital Management, ESG, and Firm Performance: Moderating Role of ESG Disclosure. *Journal of Human, Earth, and Future*, 5(2), 260–278.

Kuznetsova, S. N., Kuznetsov, V. P., Smirnova, Z. V., Andryashina, N. S., & Romanovskaya, E. V. (2024). Corporate Governance in the ESG Context: A New Understanding of Sustainability. In *Ecological Footprint of the Modern Economy and the Ways to Reduce It: The Role of Leading Technologies and Responsible Innovations* (pp. 53–57). Cham: Springer Nature Switzerland.

Lazareva, E. I., Rivza, B. A., & Gavrilova, J. V. (2022). The Sustainability Formula: A Human-Centred Strategy for Managing Economic Trends in the Context of ESG-Transformation. In *Innovative Trends in International Business and Sustainable Management* (pp. 3–12). Singapore: Springer Nature Singapore.

Maslak, O., Pochtovyuk, A., Yakovenko, Y., Maslak, M., Grishko, N., & Marchenko, V. (2022). Innovative Approaches to Staff Motivation Based on ESG Business Principles and Intellectualisation: International Experience. *Biblioteka Regionalisty, Regional Journal*, (22), DOI: 10.15611/br.2022.1.05.

Nekhili, M., Boukadhaba, A., Nagati, H., & Chtioui, T. (2021). ESG performance and market value: The moderating role of employee board representation. *The International Journal of Human Resource Management*, 32(14), 3061–3087.

Vinnikova, I. S., Prokhorova, M. P., Krylova, T. V., Shkunova, A. A., & Zhulkova, J. N. (2024). Human Resource Management Tools for Companies Based on ESG Guidelines. In *Sustainable Development of the Agrarian Economy Based on Digital Technologies and Smart Innovations* (pp. 191–197). Cham: Springer Nature Switzerland.

Chapter 11
International Accounting and Financial Management

Learning Objectives

- Summarize the significant accounting issues international firms face when operating in foreign currencies
- Outline the benefits and limitations of triple-bottom-line accounting
- Compare the capital structure choices open to international firms and their significance
- Define why international companies move funds and the utility of an international finance center
- Recognize foreign exchange risks that international companies face and ways to address them
- Depict taxation as an international financial force

Overview

International managers regularly face financial challenges in their daily operations. These include fluctuating currency values, exchange controls, taxation, and inflation and interest rates. Global managers must also follow the accounting practices of the host government and those of the United States if they work for a U.S.-based company. This section looks at international managers' methods to deal with challenging forces, some imaginative and elegant, and all legal.

International finance can be complex, but an advanced background in accounting or finance is not needed to understand that financial issues are at the core of how companies work and often make the difference between moderate and outstanding results. We begin with accounting because it is a fundamental financial management tool and because accounting practices and standards change across national borders. First, we look at the differences in how countries record stored value, which is the essence of accounting. Fortunately, there is a strong movement toward converging accounting standards, making the process much easier for international companies (IC). Figure 11.1 illustrates some main tasks involved in international accounting and finance management.

https://doi.org/10.1515/9783111510286-011

Figure 11.1: The main tasks involved in international accounting and finance management.

Accounting and Foreign Currency Exchange

As the economy becomes increasingly global, so do the activities of companies and lenders, also increasing the need for an internationally accepted framework where financial records and reports are consistent, comparable, reliable, and transparent at international and domestic levels. The need and the purpose of international standards in accounting rise from the ever-increasing volume of capital flowing across international borders. It calls for international standards with high levels of quality and is testable across the board. The main goal of such standards is to ensure that global financial centers, now more interconnected than ever, can adopt an internationally accepted financial reporting framework that provides adequate financial market regulations. Such standards enable capital markets in various jurisdictions to develop more efficient capital flows that benefit regulators, organizations, and the market.

Accounting Standards Considerations

The International Accounting Standards (IAS) was developed and issued by the Board of the International Accounting Standards Committee (IASC) to advise international companies on reporting financial events in their financial statements. In 2001, a new set of criteria was developed by the International Accounting Standards Board (IASB): the International Financial Reporting Standards (IFRS). However, the IFRS has no authority over whether a company adopts its standards or not. Nonetheless, several countries have financial rules and regulations requiring publicly traded companies to produce financial statements in compliance with the IAS to protect investors, stakeholders, and creditors. The United States, for instance, does not adopt the IFRS, which has led to criticism. Figure 11.2 depicts the main stages of effective financial reporting.

International Auditing Governance

The terminology of international auditing governance can come across as pretentious, especially when there are better venues to express the need to regulate the auditing principles of more developed and industrial nations. Universal finance may come to mind, but governance is the operative word as an enforcing characteristic. In addition, to be ubiquitous would mean all countries agree to adopt such auditing standards, which is not the case. Before international standards were developed, companies developed their financial statements using the principles, rules, and regulations of the countries where they were located. It worked well in a less internationalized world, where most trades were carried out within that country's boundaries or the region.

As economies grew and industry became more extensive and complicated, issues arose in financial reporting focused on expanding business domains, especially related to cultural and linguistic differences and even the types of currencies involved in international trade. In the U.S., for example, corporations such as U.S. Steel and Standard Oil have made accounting principles obsolete just by the amount of capital required in producing and selling their products and by the large number of individuals and firms investing in them. Several investors who were often part of an organization, insiders, used to invest and realize massive profits via insider trading, stock manipulation, and many other schemes, which at the time may or may not have been legal. Then came Black Friday in 1929, when the stock market crashed, workers lost their jobs, people ended their lives in desperation, and faith in the financial institutions was lost. At this point, there was a massive motivation for financial reporting reform. The U.S. Securities Exchange Commission (SEC) was created and given the authority to govern accounting principles and enforce the newly developed financial laws, but not make them, which was left to the private sector. In 1971, a commission was created, the Wheat Commission, which issued several documents. One of these was the generally accepted accounting principles (GAAP), which is still used in the U.S., although most other countries adopt the IAS.

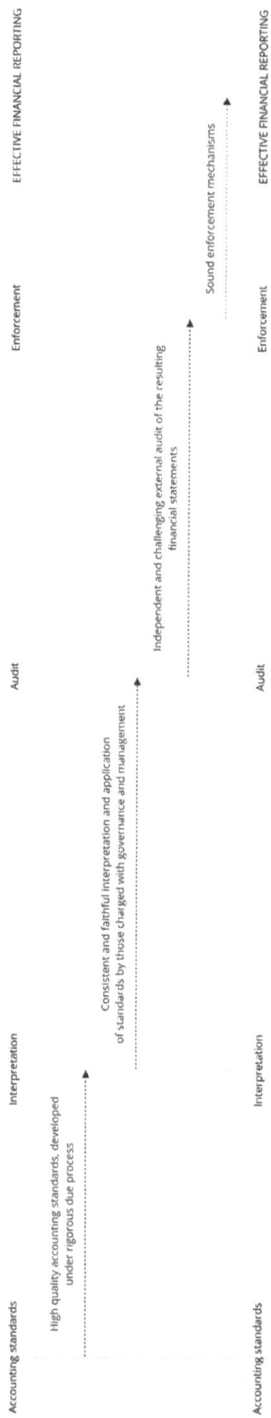

Figure 11.2: Required stages for financial standard compliance.

Today, companies are internationalizing and establishing a global presence, with large amounts of capital being exchanged to support international supply chains and market expansions. In addition, innovative forms of exchange, such as fintech, blockchain, and digital currencies, have added much complexity to the issue of ever-changing and volatile monetary systems.

Auditing and financial reporting depict a company's financial position and health. Investors can use that portrayal to compare companies and opportunities and evaluate corporations' economic well-being. Still, such portraits can be altered, frauds perpetrated through loopholes, inadequacies in financial laws, or even misrepresentations in financial statements. The effect of such deceitfulness on a global economy is immense, as what may have been proper and legal today may not be tomorrow. Figure 11.3 depicts the relationship between corporate governance, audit committee, and internal audit performance.

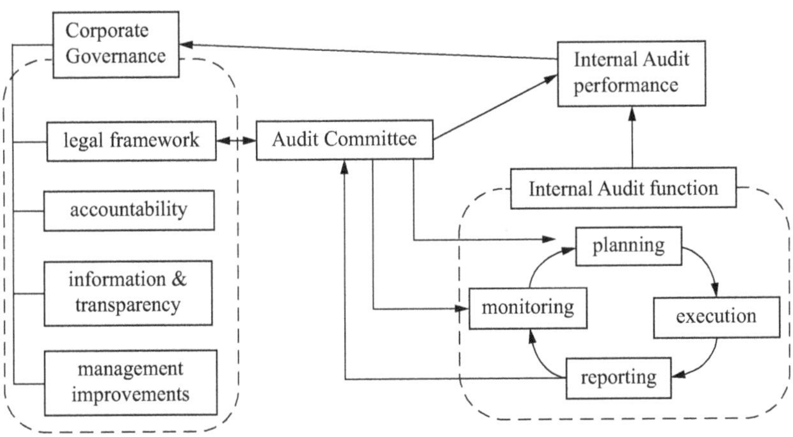

Figure 11.3: Relationship between corporate governance, audit committee, and internal audit performance. (SOURCE: Adapted from World Bank, 2011).

Even though accounting standards are not only to detect fraud, transparency also such standards seek to employ helps detect such discrepancies. Most countries, therefore, either require the adoption of the IFRS or recommend corporations to adopt it, although the U.S. chose not to. According to several experts in the industry, there are some caveats in applying these principles and guides to global financial reporting:

- Contributions from member countries fund the IFRS. That makes it subject to political manipulation.
- The American Financial Accounting Board would be weakened by ceding power to the IFRS. Some believe the U.S. should maintain control because American equity accounts for almost half of the global capitalization.

- The GAPP is more detailed and principles-based. Accountants must make value judgments, which means company incentives may influence an accountant. The IFRS is open to interpretation.
- Several issues have significant differences in wording. For example, IFRS is unclear about whether certain expenses should be listed and how much to account for.
- Transitions to the system are costly. According to some sources, the estimate for the U.S. to convert is at least $9 billion for the entire U.S. economy as of 2021, although a one-time transition cost for a small enterprise would be around $420 thousand.

Many advocates believe that the main reason for this conflict is political, that the U.S. is protecting American investor interests, with the SEC stating that the U.S. does not believe that high-quality standards should be compromised for uniformity. Most advocates, however, consent that a universal financial language would benefit the global economy, including a healthier global economy with greater levels of efficiency in the market and potentially much less expensive operating costs. Not all countries would benefit equally, especially frontier economies, as these cannot become global economic leaders without adopting strong accounting standards. No investor would take any risk in industries that are not secure, not transparent, and where they cannot quantify investments and returns because of discrepancies in currencies and best practices. Therefore, countries invested in the IFRS must enforce the rules and allow the administration of consequences for any infringement. As of fall 2022, more than 100 nations agreed to adopt the IFRS, although the U.S. remains reluctant to sign on.

While attaining a universal set of accounting practices has slowed, globalization has not. That may obstruct the process of financial unification. That is because technology has not restricted either. With new methods and greater access to more significant data, IT may outpace the initiative by making some not-yet-accepted principles outdated. Plus, if – as some have said – a universal financial language is unobtainable, the world will spin its wheels for a long time trying to devise an alternative to the International Accounting Standards.

It is essential to have international standards that every country can adopt and use globally. The worldwide adoption of the IFRS will make the reading and analysis of financial statements much more accessible for all investors and make the framework more reliable and consistent. While the U.S. currently adopts the GAAP standards that the Federal Accounting Standards Board created, some companies that operate on a multinational level have adopted international standards. While all listed and unlisted companies do not use international accounting standards, more countries prioritize adoption.

Foreign Currency Exchange Considerations

A foreign currency transaction occurs when a company enters into a transaction denominated in a foreign currency other than the one it uses functionally. A company's functional currency is the currency it uses in the primary economic environment in which it operates. Typically, transactions may include buying or selling goods or services across international borders with related accounts payable and receivables and lending and borrowing money. Any foreign exchange gains or losses resulting from such transactions can be treated differently for tax purposes based on the company's financial statements.

When an international company conducts transactions in more than one currency, preparing financial statements in a single currency requires recognizing and measuring changes in the relationship between different currency units. Figure 11.4 depicts the terminology used when companies report foreign transactions involving foreign currencies. Two distinct processes express all the company's dealings in a single reporting currency.

- **Foreign currency measurement** is the process by which a company expresses transactions whose terms are denominated in a foreign currency in its functional currency. Changes in functional currency amounts that result from the measurement process are called transaction gains or losses; transaction gains and losses are included in net income.
- **Foreign currency translation** expresses a foreign company's functional financial statements in the reporting currency. Changes in reporting currency amounts that result from the translation process are called translation adjustments; translation adjustments are included in the cumulative translation adjustment (CTA) account, which is a component of other comprehensive income.

Term	Definition
Reporting currency	The currency in which a reporting entity prepares its financial statements
Foreign currency	Any currency other than the functional currency of the referenced distinct and separable operation
Foreign entity	A distinct and separable operation whose financial statements are prepared in a currency other than the reporting currency, and that is consolidated, combined, or accounted for on the equity method. A reporting entity must identify its foreign entities to determine which financial statements have to be translated. Distinct and separable operations whose financial statements are prepared in the reporting currency are domestic entities which, by definition, do not need to be translated.
Distinct and separable operation	An operation that can be clearly distinguished, operationally and for financial reporting purposes, from the rest of the reporting entity for which a meaningful set of financial statements are routinely prepared
Functional currency	The currency of the primary economic environment in which a distinct and separable operation operates

Figure 11.4: Terminology used when companies report foreign transactions involving foreign currencies.

Foreign exchange accounting involves recording transactions in currencies other than the company's functional currency, which it typically operates with. For instance, in a transaction, a company may be paid by an international customer in a foreign currency or a supplier in a foreign currency. On the execution date of these transactions, the accounting team records the transaction in the company's functional currency, according to the exchange rate. If it is impossible to determine the currency exchange rate on the transaction date, the accounting team adopts the available exchange rate.

If the currency exchange rate between the functional currency of the company and the currency in which a transaction is denominated changes, then the team will record a gain or loss of earnings in that period according to the exchange rate changes. Such a transaction may result in a series of gains or losses over several accounting periods if the settlement date of the transaction is delayed for long periods.

There are two situations in which the accountant should not recognize a gain or loss on a foreign currency transaction, including:

- When the purpose of the foreign currency transaction was an economic hedge for an investment in a foreign entity or
- There is no expectation for a transaction settlement between companies to be consolidated.

Foreign Exchange Accounting Examples

A foreign currency transaction is recorded in a company's books at the date a foreign currency transaction occurs. Each type of transaction, such as assets, liabilities, revenues, expenses, gains, or losses arising from the trade, should be recorded in the functional currency of the recording company using the exchange rate in effect at that date. If using the exchange rate at the trade date is not practical or possible, then a weighted average rate may be used. Transaction gains or losses may arise due to changes in the exchange rate in the following:

- Transaction date and the settlement date,
- Transaction date and a subsequent balance-sheet date, or
- The following balance sheet date and settlement date are needed.

For example, XYZ Corp. sold products to a company in France, to be paid in euros and valued at the booking date of $150,000. XYZ Corp records this transaction with the following journal entry:

	Debit	Credit
Accounts receivable	150,000	
Sales		150,000

Later, when the customer pays XYZ Corp, the exchange rate changes, resulting in a payment in euros that translates to a $144,000 sale. Thus, the foreign exchange rate change related to the transaction has created a $6,000 loss for XYZ Corp, which it records with the following entry:

	Debit	Credit
Cash	144,000	
Foreign Currency Exchange Loss	6,000	
Accounts Receivable		150,000

The following table shows the impact of transaction exposure on different scenarios.

	Import Goods	Export Goods
Home currency weakens	Loss	Gain
Home currency strengthens	Gain	Loss

Triple-Bottom-Line Accounting

The triple-bottom-line (TBL or 3BL), as illustrated in Figure 11.5, is an accounting system composed of three pillars: social, economic, and environmental. It differs from traditional reporting frameworks as it includes environmental) and social measures that can be difficult to assign appropriate measurements. The TBL also has three dimensions, known as the 3 Ps: people, planet, and profits. Many international organizations have adopted TBL to evaluate their corporate social responsibility (CSR) and environmental, social, and governance (ESG) performance from a broader perspective to create more excellent business value.

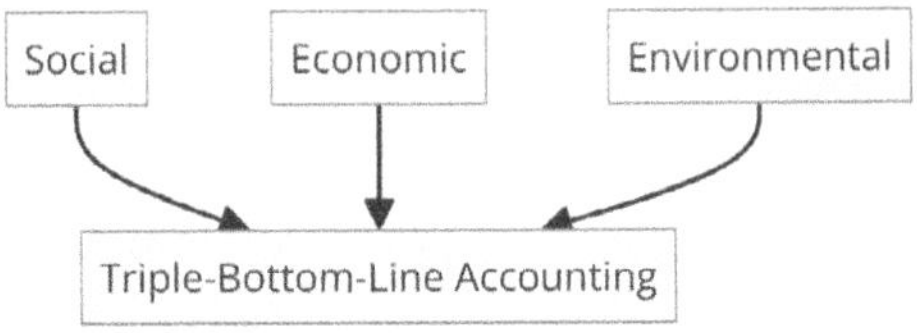

Figure 11.5: The triple-bottom-line accounting system comprises social, economic, and environmental pillars.

Traditionally, in business accounting, the bottom line refers to profit or loss, which is usually recorded at the bottom line of a financial report, such as revenue and expenses or profit and loss statements. Over the past five decades, environmentalists and social justice advocates have struggled to bring a broader definition of the bottom line into public consciousness by introducing full-cost accounting. For instance, if a corporation shows a monetary profit, but their coal mine causes thousands of deaths from pneumoconioses (dusty lung), their silica mines pollute a river and cause silicosis and the government may need to spend taxpayer money on health care and river clean-up, how do we perform a complete societal cost-benefit analysis? Adopting TBL adds two more bottom lines: social and environmental concerns.

With the ratification of the United Nations (UN) and the International Council for Local Environmental Initiatives (ICLEI), the TBL standard for urban and community accounting in early 2007 became the dominant approach to public sector full-cost accounting, similar to the UN standards applied to natural and human capital measurements to assist in assessments required by TBL, such as the EcoBudget standard for reporting ecological footprint. For instance, a social enterprise company would be an excellent example of an organization seeking a TBL. The company could operate as a non-profit but earn income by offering opportunities for disabled people labeled unemployable to make a living through recycling jobs. The company would earn a profit and then invest a portion of it back into the local community, generating social benefits, such as offering meaningful recycling jobs for disadvantaged citizens, reducing society's welfare, disability costs, or both. The environment would benefit as well from the recycling efforts.

In the private sector, a pledge to CSR indicates an obligation to publicly report the business's substantial impact on improving the environment and people's lives; TBL is one framework for reporting such a CSR and ESG impact. In addition, the TBL has also been extended to contain four fundamental pillars, the quadruple bottom line (QBL), which conveys a future-oriented approach, such as in future generations and intergenerational equity. A long-term outlook fosters sustainable development in sustainability issues aside from existing ESG considerations.

Implementing TBL into practice can be challenging, mostly related to measuring social and ecological categories. Despite this, the TBL framework enables organizations to take a longer-term perspective and thus evaluate the future consequences of decisions. The challenge is not so much in defining TBL but in measuring it.

Measuring TBL through 3 Ps

Profits are measured in dollars, but how can we measure social capital and environmental or ecological health? The 3 Ps do not have a fixed standard unit of measurement, so finding one can be challenging. Some support monetizing all the dimensions of the TBL, including social welfare or environmental damage. However, that would benefit a standard unit, such as dollars, euros, or any other major currency, many objects to putting a monetary value on marshlands or endangered species on strictly philosophical grounds. Others question the process of finding the right price for lost marshes or endangered species.

Another answer would be to assess the TBL in terms of an index, eliminating any incompatible elements and, as long as there is a universally accepted accounting method, allowing for comparisons between entities. For instance, by comparing the performance of companies' CSR or ESG efforts, cities, development projects, or any other benchmark. An example of such an index is the Indiana Business Research Center's Innovation Index, which compares a county to a nation's performance for various components. Still, some subjectivity remains even when using an index. For instance, how do you calculate the elements of an index? Should each of the 3 Ps have equal weighting? If not, who decided it?

Despite these controversies, no universal method for calculating the TBL is available. Neither is a universally accepted standard for the measures comprising the three TBL categories. In some ways, such ambiguity can be perceived as a strength as it enables flexibility in TBL's framework. A business and local government agency might gauge environmental sustainability. Similarly, as depicted in Figure 11.6, reducing the amount of solid waste dumped in the trash yard. Still, a regional mass transit authority might count success regarding passenger miles, while a for-profit bus or taxi business may measure success in earnings per share. The TBL can accommodate these differences. Some factors that can be measured may include:

- **Economic** – Such variables ought to be variables that deal with the bottom line and the flow of money. It could consider income, expenditures, taxes, business climate, employment, diversity, equity, and inclusion (DEI) factors. Some examples may include:
  - Employment demand and distribution by sector
  - Human resources churn
  - Job growth indexes
  - Organization's sizes
  - Percentage of companies in each sector
  - Personal income
  - Realized revenue by sector
  - Underemployment costs
- **Environmental** – These variables could characterize measures of natural resources, their preservation, and global climate change and reflect possible effects on their viability. It could include water and air quality, natural resources, energy consumption, land use/land cover, and solid and toxic waste, to name a few. Ideally, having long-range trends available for each environmental variable could assist companies in identifying the level of impact a project or policy can have on the area. Some specific examples might include:
  - Change in land use/land cover
  - Electricity consumption
  - Excessive nutrients levels
  - Fossil fuel consumption
  - Hazardous waste management

  - Levels of nitrogen oxides concentration
  - Levels of sulfur dioxide concentration
  - Set priority pollutants
  - Solid waste management
- **Social** – These variables refer to the social dimensions of a community or region. They could contain measures of schooling, DEI and access to social resources, healthiness and well-being, quality of life, and social capital. The instances listed below are a small sample of potential variables:
  - Average commute time
  - Health-adjusted life expectancy
  - Median household income
  - Percentage of inhabitants with a post-secondary degree or certificate
  - Rates of female labor force participation

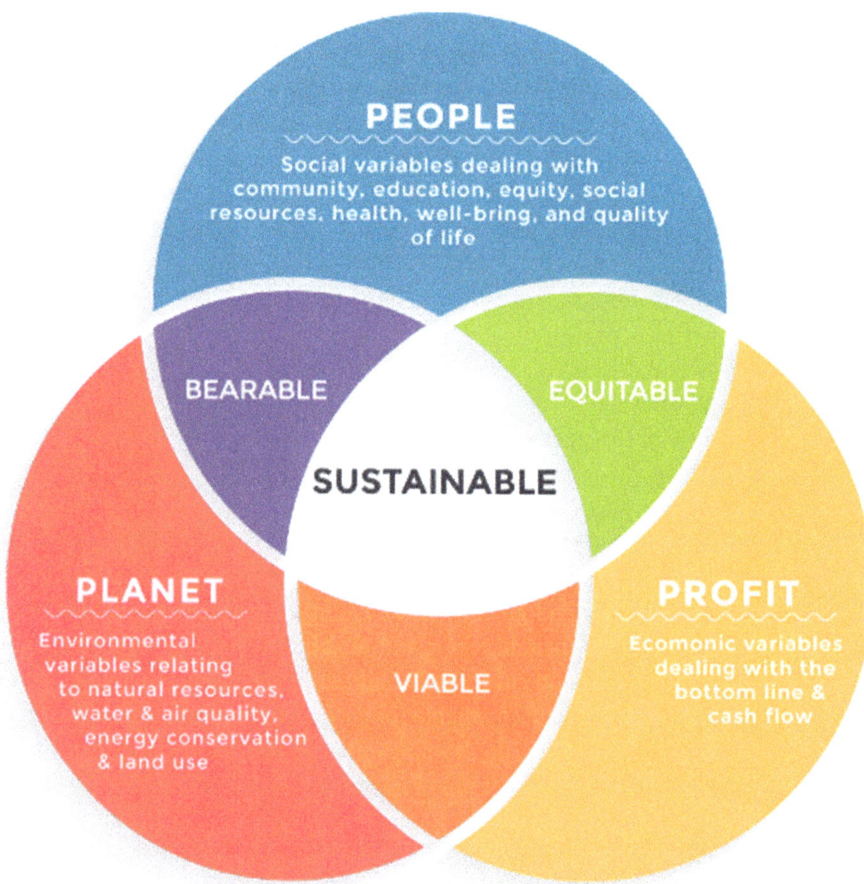

Figure 11.6: Measuring TBL through 3 Ps.

  - Relative poverty rates
  - Unemployment rate
  - Violent crimes per capita

Data for many of these measurements are available and can be gathered at the state and national levels as well as at the local or community levels. Many are suitable for a society to use when constructing a TBL. Nevertheless, as the geographic dimensions and the nature of the project narrow, the set of appropriate measurements may change. For instance, at a local or community-based project, the TBL measurements of success are best determined locally.

Several comparable procedures ensure stakeholder engagement and input in developing the TBL framework. For instance, companies can create a decision matrix to include public preferences in project planning and decision making. A *narrative format* can be designed to request shareholder participation and extensive project evaluation and have stakeholders rank and weigh components of a sustainability framework according to community priorities. For instance, a neighborhood may consider an essential measurement of success for an entrepreneurial development program to be the number of woman-owned enterprises started over five years. The organization will produce a final set of measures applicable to the task.

Businesses' TBL Adoptions

Businesses, for-profits, nonprofits, and government entities can use the TBL. The TBL and its core value of ESG/DEI have become persuasive in the business world due to accumulating anecdotal evidence of greater long-term profitability. For instance, when companies reduce waste from packaging, they also reduce costs. Noteworthy companies adopting TBL's approaches include Unilever, General Electric (GM), 3M, Proctor and Gamble, and Cascade Engineering. Although these corporations do not own an index-based TBL, it is not difficult to realize how they measure sustainability. Cascade Engineering, for instance, although a private company and exempt from filing detailed financial reports as public companies must, has identified the following variables for its TBL scorecard:

- **Economic**
  - Amount of taxes being paid
- **Social**
  - Average hours of training/employee
  - Charitable contributions
  - From welfare to career retention
- **Environmental**
  - Amount of waste to landfill
  - Greenhouse gas emissions
  - Lost/restricted workday rate

- Safety incident rate
- Sales dollars per kilowatt hours
- Use of post-consumer and industrial recycled material
- Water consumption

Corporations realize that aligning with nonprofit organizations makes good business sense, especially those with economic prosperity, social well-being, and environmental protection goals. Numerous nonprofit firms have adopted the TBL, and some have partnered with private companies to address comprehensive sustainability matters that impact mutual stakeholders. The Ford Foundation, for instance, has subsidized studies that used variations of the TBL to estimate the outcomes of programs to increase prosperity in dozens of rural regions across the U.S.

State, regional, and local governments increasingly embrace the TBL and similar sustainability appraisal frameworks as performance monitoring and decision-making tools. Maryland, Vermont, Minnesota, Utah, Northeast Ohio, and the San Francisco Bay Area have performed studies utilizing the TBL or a comparable sustainability framework. Policymakers use these frameworks to determine activities they should take to foster a more sustainable society.

Internationally, the EU utilizes integrated assessment to determine the favorable and unfavorable effects of proposed policy measures. This allows informed political decisions regarding the proposal and identifies trade-offs in achieving competing objectives.

International Financial Management and Capital Structure

As depicted in Figure 11.7, international financial management, also dubbed international finance, is finance management in an international business setting where trading and revenue generation depend on foreign currency exchange. International financial activities enable companies to develop international business with overseas business partners, customers, suppliers, distributors, lenders, etc. Government institutions and non-profit organizations also utilize it.

After World War II, as discussed earlier, the GATT was established to enhance international trade. It withdrew the international trade barriers substantially over the years, resulting in a robust increase in international trade. It started when various countries started liberalizing international trade, as many countries consented to open their doors to each other and trade. The trader's importers and exporters' financial participation and the international transactions flowed smoothly. The advancement of information systems and technology (and later the internet and the web) and such trade liberalization resulted in the idea of financial management both domestically and internationally.

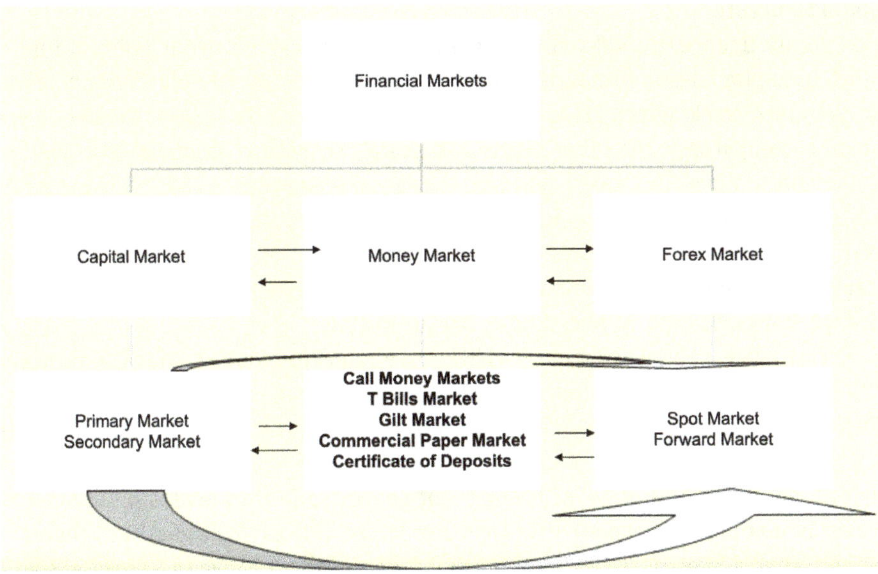

Figure 11.7: International financial management, capital structures, and interlinks.

Domestic vs. International Financial Management

Financial systems may be categorized as domestic or international, closed or open. Thus, a domestic financial system is inherent to a country. The U.S.'s financial system is international from the EU's perspective. The mean and intent of both financial management systems remain the same. Still, the dimensions and dynamics widen drastically due to variables such as foreign currency exchange, international market imperfections, enhanced opportunities, and political risks.

The goal of international financial management (IFM) is not only restricted to the maximization of shareholders but also stakeholders. International markets have various shapes and analytics than domestic financial markets. Appropriate management of international finances can assist the company in achieving the same efficiency and effectiveness in all global markets. Hence, without IFM, remaining sustainable in the global market can be challenging.

Companies may be compelled to invest capital abroad for several reasons. The following are some of them:

- Access to essential raw materials
- Broadening of markets and diversification
- Earning higher returns
- Efficient manufacturing/development of products and services in foreign markets than domestically
- Foreign investment

Capital Structure

In corporate finance, capital structure is the mix of various forms of external funds, known as capital, used to finance a business. It comprises shareholders' equity, debt, and preferred stock, which are detailed in its balance sheet. The larger the debt component is compared to the other sources of capital, the greater financial leverage the firm is said to have. Too much debt can increase the company's risk, reducing its financial flexibility. At some point, these significant debt levels may worry investors, resulting in a greater cost of capital. Upper management is responsible for developing a capital structure for the company that allows for optimal utilization of its financial leverage and holds the cost of capital as low as possible.

For instance, capital structure is critical in establishing rates charged to consumers by regulated utility companies in the U.S. These companies have the right to determine any capital structure they deem appropriate. Still, government regulators decide on a proper capital structure and cost of capital for rate-making purposes. Financial analysts closely monitor various leverage (or gearing) ratios to evaluate the amount of debt in a company's capital structure. The Miller and Modigliani (M&M) theorem contends that a company's market value is unaffected by a change in its capital structure. This school of thought is typically viewed as a purely theoretical result since it considers a perfect market, disregarding other elements such as business fluctuations and uncertain market situations in financing a company. In academia, much consideration has been extended to arguing and softening the assumptions made by M&M to explain why a company's capital structure is relevant to its value in the real world.

Leverage and EPS

To a certain point, incurring debts, such as bonds or bank loans, in a company's capital structure is advantageous. When debt is a portion of a company's capital structure, it permits the company to achieve greater earnings per share (EPS) than would be attainable by issuing equity. However, the interest on the debt needs to be paid regardless of the company's operating income level, or bankruptcy may result, but these are tax-deductible. Paying fewer taxes allows a company to increase its operating income to flow to investors. That related increase in EPS is known as financial leverage or gearing in the U.K. and Australia. Financial leverage can be advantageous when the company is expanding and profitable, but it is dangerous when it enters a market or business contraction phase. If the company does not prosper and profits do not meet management's targets, too much debt (or leverage) can increase the risk of its inability to pay its creditors. Eventually, investors may become apprehensive, expanding the company's borrowing cost or issuing new equity.

Optimal Capital Structure

A company's management must acknowledge the intrinsic risk of assuming debt and strive to maintain an optimal capital structure with a proper balance between equity and debt, consistently minimizing the cost of debt and equity financing and maximizing the firm's value. Internal policy decisions regarding capital structure and debt ratios must be tempered by realizing how outsiders view the strength of the company's financial health. Key concerns include sustaining the company's credit rating at a level where it can entice new sources of external funds with reasonable terms and keeping a stable dividend policy and good earnings record.

Once upper management has determined how much debt should be employed in the capital structure, determinations must be made concerning the proper mix of short and long-term debt. Raising the percentage of short-term debt can improve a company's financial flexibility since the borrower's adherence to paying interest is typically shorter. Nonetheless, short-term debt also exposes the company to greater refinancing risk. Consequently, as the allocation of short-term debt in a company's capital structure increases, equity holders will expect greater returns on equity (ROE) to compensate for the increased risk.

The Seniority of Capital Structure

Should a company face bankruptcy, the seniority of the capital structure is considered. Usually, a company has the following seniority structure, which is outlined from the most senior to the least. Still, in practice, the capital structure may be more complex and include other sources of capital.:

- **Senior debt** includes mortgage bonds secured by expressly pledged property,
- **Subordinated (or junior) debt** may include debenture bonds dependent upon the overall credit and financial strength of the company,
- **Preferred stock** is those whose holders are privileged to have their claims met before those of common stockholders and
- **Equity**, which may include common stock and retained earnings.

Foreign Exchange Risk Management

Foreign exchange risks are financial risks that exist when financial transactions are denominated in a currency other than the company's domestic currency. The exchange risk arises from an unfavorable change in the exchange rate between the domestic and the foreign currency before the date the transaction is completed. Similar risks also exist when the foreign subsidiary of a company keeps financial statements in a currency other than the domestic currency of the consolidated entity. Investors, companies exporting or importing goods and services, and foreign investors also are exposed to foreign exchange rate risks. Taking steps to mitigate such risks is paramount.

Foreign Exchange Risks

The currency crises between the 1990s and 2000s, such as the Mexican peso crisis, the Asian currency crisis, the Russian financial crisis, and the Argentine peso crisis, led to substantial losses from foreign exchange and companies to pay closer attention to their foreign exchange risk. Many companies were indifferent and did not manage foreign exchange risks under the international Bretton Woods system. Only when floating exchange rates began, after the Bretton Woods system collapsed, did companies become exposed mainly to an ever-increasing risk of exchange rate fluctuations. To mitigate these risks, companies began trading an increasing volume of financial derivatives by hedging their exposure.

Economic Risks

A company has an economic risk to the degree that its market value is influenced by unexpected exchange-rate fluctuations, which can severely affect its market share concerning its competitors, future cash flows, and the company's value. Economic risks, such as a shift in exchange rates that impacts the demand for goods sold in a foreign market or the possibility that macroeconomic conditions may affect investments in a foreign country, can affect the present value of future cash flows of a company.

Risks associated with macroeconomic conditions may include exchange rate fluctuations, new government policies and regulations, or political instability. When planning expansions into new foreign markets and financing new investments or projects abroad, companies' operating costs, levels of debt obligations, and their ability to predict economically unsustainable circumstances should be thoroughly analyzed to prevent unforeseeable risks and to generate adequate revenues to cover such economic risks. For instance, when a company in one country invests in a manufacturing plant in another, the hosting country's government may institute changes that negatively impact the investing company's ability to operate the plant. Such modifications may include:

- New laws
- Nationalizations
- Seizing the manufacturing plant
- Imposing barriers makes operating in the country difficult or moving profits out

Therefore, any risks that outweigh an investment's profits and outcomes must be carefully analyzed, and mitigation strategies must be developed before engaging in such investments, especially if incurring FDI. Other potential economic risks are steep market downturns, geopolitical tensions, unforeseeable cost overruns, or low market demand for goods.

Foreign investments are associated with significantly higher economic risk levels than domestic investments. In international companies, economic risk heavily affects bondholders, investors, and shareholders, especially when negotiating purchases and sales of foreign government bonds. Nonetheless, such economic risk could generate investment opportunities and profits across the globe, as investors may be able to profit from foreign exchange fluctuations and interest rates. Still, investors should be aware of possible changes imposed by international regulatory agencies and authorities. Any changes in the laws, policies, and regulations concerning bonds' purchase specifics, such as amounts, timing, types, disclosures, and credit quality, can immediately affect such investments in foreign markets. For instance, if a central bank of a foreign nation decides to raise interest rates or institute legislation to increase taxes, such transactions' return on investment (ROI) can be substantially impacted. Such economic risks may be diminished by relying on analytical and predictive approaches considering time, exchange rates, and economic development diversifications in markets offering distinct currencies, instruments, conditions, industries, and sub-sectors.

Contingent Risk

Companies are exposed to contingent risk abroad when bidding on foreign projects, negotiating contracts, or handling foreign direct investments (FDI). These risks often arise from the potential of companies to suddenly face international or foreign exchange risks related to negotiations or agreements. For instance, companies may be in situations where they need to wait for the results of a project bidding, whereas, if accepted, it could result in an immediate receivable. Still, while waiting for the bidding results, companies face contingent risk from the uncertainty of whether or not the potential receivable may be realized and the impact of external forces, such as currency exchange, may impact it.

Transaction Risks

International companies are often involved in transactions involving more than one currency. To meet the legal and accounting standards for processing these transactions, companies must convert (exchange) foreign currencies into their domestic currency. Eventually, companies must exchange or translate these foreign currencies into domestic ones. Companies incur transaction risks whenever they are exposed to contractual cash flows. Examples include receivables and payables, in which values are subject to unexpected exchange rates due to negotiated contracts in foreign currencies.

Businesses aim to make all monetary transactions profitable, and the currency markets must thus be carefully observed. When companies negotiate contracts with set fixed prices and delivery dates, they face higher foreign exchange volatility, as rates may constantly fluctuate during the initiation of a transaction and its eventual settlement or payment, which imposes significant risks of revenue losses.

Currency Conversion, or Translation, Risks

All international companies must prepare consolidated financial reports. The financial consolidation process for these companies comprises the translation of all foreign assets and liabilities, including the financial statements of their foreign subsidiaries, from the foreign currency they operate to their domestic currency. Such companies' translation risks are the extent to which their financial reporting is affected by exchange rate fluctuation in global markets. While translation risk may not involve a company's cash flows, it could significantly impact their reporting earnings and, consequently, the value of their stock.

Translation risks also deal with the risks to companies' equities, assets, liabilities, or income, which are subject to changes in value due to foreign exchange rate fluctuations when a portion of it is denominated in a foreign currency. As foreign exchange rates fluctuate up and down, appreciating or depreciating, it becomes difficult to predict any adjustments in the value of the foreign currency. A company operating in foreign markets will eventually have to exchange its host country's currency for its domestic currency. For instance, international U.S. companies must convert dollars into euros, the British pound, yuan, yen, etc., and vice versa.

A whole-subsidiary company conducting business in a host country must adhere to that country's prescribed foreign exchange translation method, which may vary depending on the subsidiary's business operations. Subsidiaries can be characterized as either integrated or self-sustaining foreign entities. An integrated foreign subsidiary operates as an extension of the parent company, with cash flows and highly interrelated business operations. A self-sustaining foreign subsidiary, however, operates in its local economic environment, independent of the parent company. Both integrated and self-sustaining foreign entities use functional currency, the currency of the primary economic environment where the subsidiary operates and transacts day-to-day operations.

There are three currency conversion methods, as illustrated in Figure 11.8:

- **Current rate** – in this method, all financial statement line items are translated at the *current* exchange rate.
- **Temporal** – in this method, specific assets and liabilities are translated at exchange rates consistent with the timing of the item's creation.
- **The U.S. translation procedures** – this method differentiates foreign subsidiaries by functional currency, not subsidiary characterization.

If companies translate by the temporal method, a condition of zero net exposed position is called fiscal balance. The condition cannot be achieved by the current-rate method because total assets must be matched by an equal amount of debt.

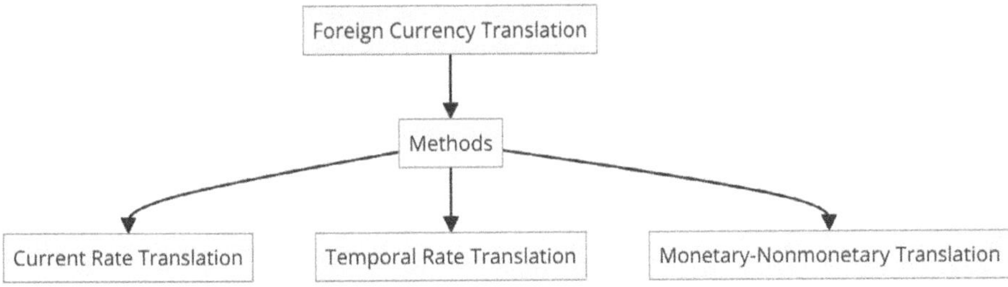

Figure 11.8: Foreign currency translation methods.

Managing Risk

Companies exposed to foreign exchange risk may use several hedging strategies to reduce that risk.

Transaction Hedging

Transaction exposure can be reduced by various means, including foreign exchange derivatives (e.g., forward contracts, futures contracts, options, and swaps), money markets, or operational techniques, including currency invoicing, exposure netting, and leading and lagging of receipts and payments. Each of these hedging strategies has benefits that may make one more suitable than another, based on the nature of the business and the risks being faced.

For instance, forward and futures contracts allow transactions that occur in the future for a specified price at a specified rate to offset otherwise adverse exchange fluctuations. To some extent, forward contracts are more flexible because they are customizable to specific transactions. In contrast, futures come in standard amounts based on distinct amounts of commodities or assets, such as other currencies. However, since futures are only available for certain currencies and prescribed periods, they do not fully mitigate risks, as there are always risks that the exchange rates change up or down.

Companies engaged in international trade can also use two other popular and inexpensive methods to minimize potential losses, such as hedging with forward contracts and options. If companies decide to take out a forward contract, they will set a specific currency rate for a future date. When buying options, companies can put their rate at the worst scenario possible for the transaction. If and when the option expires, companies can process the transactions in the open market at favorable rates.

Another transaction hedging is currency invoicing, which refers to invoicing transactions in the currency that benefit the company. Although this approach does not eliminate foreign exchange risks, it moves most of the risks from one party to another. For instance, companies can issue an invoice for imports from another country in their home currency, shifting the risks to the exporter company and away from themselves. If both the importer and exporter wish not to use their own currencies, the two companies may conduct the exchange by adopting a third, more stable currency.

Leading and lagging involve the movement of cash inflows or outflows forward or backward in time. A company must exercise extreme caution if it looks to lead and lag as a hedge. For instance, if companies need to pay a large amount of money in a few months but are also expecting to receive similar amounts from another order within that same timeframe, the companies may move the date of receipt of the sum to coincide with the payment or lagging. If the receipt date were pushed sooner, this would lead to the payment.

Natural hedging, or netting foreign exchange exposures, is another way to reduce exposure risks. Companies operating abroad and dealing with large inflows and outflows in the same foreign currency may experience efficiencies and reductions in risk exposure by assessing the net of the inflows and outflows and using foreign currency account balances that can be used to pay in part for some or all of the exposure. To enforce the netting, there is a need for a systematic approach, an ability to assess the exposure in real-time, and a platform to initiate the process.

Translation Hedging

Translation exposure largely depends on the translation methods required by the home country's accounting standards. For instance, the U.S. Federal Accounting Standards Board specifies when and where to use specific strategies. Companies engaged in international trade can manage translation exposure by conducting a balance sheet hedge since translation exposures originate from gaps between net assets and net liabilities exclusively from exchange rate discrepancies. Thus, a company may acquire the necessary amount of exposed assets or liabilities it needs to balance any outstanding differences.

Balance sheet hedging is yet another common approach to hedging translation risks. It requires companies to speculate on the forward markets, hoping that a cash profit may be realized to offset a non-cash loss from a translation. This approach requires equal amounts of exposed foreign currency assets and liabilities on the company's consolidated balance sheet. The net translation exposure can be zero if each foreign currency is attained. However, a change in the exchange rates can alter the value of exposed liabilities to an equal degree but opposite to the difference in the value of exposed assets.

Other Strategies

International companies may adopt strategies other than financial hedging to manage their economic or operating exposure. For instance, they may carefully select production sites with the intent of lowering costs of labor or materials, adopting a policy of flexible sourcing in its supply chain management, diversifying their export market across a more significant number of countries, or implementing intense market research and development (R&D) activities and differentiating its products through innovation, in pursuit of less foreign exchange risk exposure.

International Taxation

International taxation determines how much tax a person or business is subject to base on the taxation laws of different nations or the international characteristics of a person's nation's tax laws. Governments typically limit the scope of their income tax laws or provide offsets to taxation relating to extraterritorial income. The limitation is generally based on territory, country or residence status, or some exclusionary approach. Some governments have tried to mitigate these differing limitations found in these three broad approaches by enacting a hybrid system.

Many governments tax individuals and/or enterprises on income. However, such taxation systems vary widely, and no general guidelines or rules exist. Such variations tend to cause the potential for double taxation when distinct countries tax the same income. Others may cause a situation where there is no taxation, with governments not requiring taxes on income. For countries with income tax systems, such taxes are imposed on local income only or even income generated across the globe. Where worldwide income is taxed, taxation reductions or foreign credits are typically provided for taxes paid to other jurisdictions. Limits are almost universally imposed on such credits. Multinational corporations usually employ international tax specialists, a specialty of lawyers and accountants, to decrease their worldwide tax liabilities.

With any taxation system, it is possible to shift or recharacterize income to reduce tax. Jurisdictions often impose rules relating to moving income among commonly controlled parties, often referred to as transfer pricing rules. Residency-based systems are subject to taxpayer attempts to defer income recognition through the use of related parties. A few jurisdictions impose restrictions limiting such deferral ("anti-deferral" regimes). Deferral is also authorized explicitly by some governments for particular social purposes or other grounds. Agreements among governments (treaties) often determine who should be entitled to tax what. Most tax treaties provide at least a skeleton mechanism for resolving disputes between the parties.

Taxation Systems

Nations that tax income typically employ one of two systems: territorial or residence-based. In the territorial system, local income is taxed from a source inside the country. In the residence-based system, residents of the nation are taxed on all their income, locally and from across the globe; nonresidents are taxed only on their local income. In addition, some governments also tax the international revenue of their nonresident citizens in some cases. Nations with a residence-based taxation system usually permit deductions or credits for the tax residents already paid to other nations. In corporate income tax cases, some governments allow exclusion or deferment of particular items of foreign income from the base of taxation. Many governments also sign tax treaties to eliminate or reduce double taxation.

Residency-Based Taxation

Most jurisdictions tax income on a residency basis. They need to define residents and represent the income of nonresidents. Such depictions vary by nation and type of taxpayer. Usually, these implicate the location of the individual's principal home and the days the individual is physically present in the nation, such as, for example:

- The U.S taxes its citizens as residents and provides lengthy, detailed rules for individual residency of foreigners, covering:
  - periods establishing residency
  - start and end date of residency
  - exceptions for transitory visits, medical conditions, etc.
- The U.K., before 2013, designated three categories: nonresident, resident, and resident but not ordinarily resident. Since 2013, the categories of residents have been restricted to nonresidents and residents. Residency is designated by applying the tests in a test known as the Statutory Residency Test.
- Switzerland residency may be appointed by having a permit to be employed in Switzerland for the person who is employed.

Territorial systems usually tax local income regardless of the residence of the taxpayer. This has led nations to enact hybrid systems to recover lost revenue. The critical problem argued for this type of system is the ability to avoid taxation on portable income by moving it outside the country. Figure 11.9 depicts individual taxation systems across the globe.

Transfer Pricing

The number of related party charges is generally referred to as transfer pricing. Many jurisdictions have become sensitive to the possibility of shifting profits with transfer pricing and have embraced rules regulating the setting or testing of prices, allowance of certain deductions, or inclusion of income for other related party transactions. Many jurisdictions have implemented broadly similar transfer pricing rules. The OECD has adopted fairly comprehensive guidelines, subject to specific country reservations. These guidelines have been embraced with slight adaptation by many countries. Notably, the U.S. and Canada have implemented rules that sometimes depart in specific criteria from OECD guidelines, generally by providing more detailed rules.

Country/Region	Taxation System
No income tax on individuals	
Bahamas	No income tax on individuals
Bermuda	No income tax on individuals
Cayman Islands	No income tax on individuals
Saudi Arabia	No income tax on individuals
United Arab Emirates	No income tax on individuals
Territorial	
Hong Kong	Territorial
Malaysia	Territorial
Panama	Territorial
Singapore	Territorial
Paraguay	Territorial
Residence-based	
Most of Europe	Residence-based
Australia	Residence-based
Canada	Residence-based
China	Residence-based
India	Residence-based
South Africa	Residence-based
Japan	Residence-based
Citizenship-based	
United States	Citizenship-based
Eritrea	Citizenship-based

Figure 11.9: Individual taxation systems across the globe.

A crucial concept of most transfer pricing rules, known as the arm's length principle, works by having prices charged between related companies be those that could be charged among unrelated counterparts dealing at arm's length. Most of these rules prescribe procedures for testing whether prices charged should be considered to meet this standard. Such rules generally involve comparing related party transactions to similar transactions of unrelated parties. Several surrogates for these types of transactions may be permitted. Most guidelines permit some methods for testing prices, including the following:

- Comparable uncontrolled transaction prices
- Resale prices based on similar markups
- Cost plus a markup
- Enterprise profitability method

Tax Avoidance

Tax avoidance techniques may take advantage of low – or no-income tax nations known as tax havens. Companies may move their headquarters to a nation with more favorable tax environments. In nations where the movement has been restricted by legislation, reincorporation into a low-tax enterprise might be required by reversing a merger with a foreign corporation. Furthermore, transfer pricing may allow for earnings stripping as profits are attributed to subsidiaries in low-tax nations.

For individuals, tax avoidance has become an important issue for governments worldwide since the 2008 recession. These tax directives began when the U.S. introduced the Foreign Account Tax Compliance Act (FATCA) in 2010. It was subsequently substantially expanded by the Organization for Economic Co-operation and Development (OECD), which introduced a novel international system for automatic tax information exchange known as the Common Reporting Standard (CRS). Such a system has aroused concerns about privacy and data breaches due to the volume of information exchanged. Around 100 nations have already committed to it, but for some taxpayers, the CRS is already operational, while for others, it will be coming live soon.

Integrating ESG Principles in Global Accounting and Financial Strategies

Integrating environmental, social, and governance (ESG) factors into accounting and financial management is not just a trend but a global shift reshaping how companies operate and report across borders. Such integration is not just about compliance; it is a strategic approach that enhances corporate responsibility and financial performance across global markets. As international businesses increasingly operate across diverse environments, the ability to manage and report on ESG factors becomes crucial in navigating the complex landscape of global finance. This shift supports sustainable business practices and aligns financial strategies with broader global goals such as the United Nations' Sustainable Development Goals (SDGs), thereby contributing to a more sustainable and equitable global economy.

Environmental Considerations

The environmental aspect of ESG focuses on a company's ecological impact. Internationally, companies are increasingly held accountable for their environmental footprint, which includes carbon emissions, waste management, and resource conservation. This accountability is reflected in their financial reporting and management practices. For instance, the triple-bottom-line (TBL) accounting framework mentioned in this chapter extends traditional financial reporting to include environmental and social measures. This framework allows companies to report on financial outcomes and how their operations impact the planet.

Adopting TBL and similar ESG-oriented frameworks internationally requires companies to adapt their accounting standards and practices. Companies operating in multiple countries must navigate varying environmental regulations and reporting requirements. For example, the European Union's stringent environmental policies may necessitate more detailed disclosures about emissions and energy usage than other regions. These differences underscore the importance of adaptable and transparent accounting practices that can accommodate diverse environmental standards while ensuring the comparability and reliability of financial statements globally.

Social Impact

The social component of ESG emphasizes the impact of business operations on human capital – both within the organization and in the broader community. This includes labor practices, human rights, community engagement, and customer satisfaction. International businesses must consider local cultural norms and labor laws, which can vary significantly from one region to another.

Social considerations in financial management involve assessing and reporting on workforce diversity, employee engagement, and community impact. For example, a multinational corporation operating in South Africa might report on its initiatives to support local employment and anti-apartheid labor practices. These initiatives affect the company's social standing and influence its financial health through brand reputation and consumer loyalty.

Governance Structures

Governance in ESG refers to the policies and procedures that ensure a company's accountability to its stakeholders. This includes leadership structure, executive pay, audits, internal controls, and shareholder rights. Internationally, governance standards can significantly influence financial management and reporting. For instance, companies listed in the United States might adhere to the Sarbanes-Oxley Act, which mandates strict auditing and financial transparency requirements to protect investors from fraudulent activities.

In international finance, governance also involves compliance with international standards like the International Financial Reporting Standards (IFRS), which aim to harmonize accounting practices worldwide. However, as discussed in this chapter, not all countries have adopted these standards uniformly. The U.S., for example, continues to use Generally Accepted Accounting Principles (GAAP), leading to significant differences in financial reporting and complicating international financial comparisons and investments.

ESG's Economic Influence

Integrating ESG into financial management and accounting is not just a matter of corporate responsibility; it can also be a strategic move leading to better investment decisions, enhanced market reputation, and economic sustainability. Companies that proactively adopt ESG standards stand to gain increased investor confidence and access to capital, particularly as global awareness and regulations around sustainability continue to grow. Financial markets increasingly recognize ESG metrics as crucial indicators of a company's long-term viability and resilience, further underscoring the economic benefits of ESG integration.

Moreover, ESG considerations can lead to cost savings and operational efficiencies. Environmental efficiencies in energy use and waste management can reduce operational costs, while robust governance structures can mitigate financial and legal risks.

Cultural Context and ESG

Culturally, ESG integration helps businesses align more closely with local norms and expectations, enhancing their international license. For instance, a company that invests in community development and adheres to ethical labor practices in a foreign country may see an improvement in its local business environment and relationships.

Discussion Questions

1. **Discuss the challenges and strategies for managing foreign exchange risk in international companies. Why is it important for companies to hedge against foreign exchange risk, and what methods can they use?**

2. **What is the primary purpose of the International Financial Reporting Standards (IFRS)?**
   A) To establish tax rates for international companies
   B) To provide a consistent and transparent framework for financial reporting across countries
   C) To manage foreign currency exchange rates
   D) To regulate the transfer pricing among multinational corporations

3. **Which of the following is NOT a component of the triple-bottom-line (TBL) accounting system?**
   A) Social
   B) Economic
   C) Environmental
   D) Technological

4. **All countries universally accept and use GAAP standards for financial reporting. True or False?**

5. **A company's functional currency is the currency it primarily uses in its economic environment. True or False?**

Recommended Readings

Adeneye, Y. B., Fasihi, S., Kammoun, I., & Albitar, K. (2024). Does earnings management constrain ESG performance? The role of corporate governance. *International Journal of Disclosure and Governance*, 21(1), 69–92.

Budiasih, Y. (2024). Integration of Environmental, Social and Governance (ESG) Factors in Financial Reporting: A Global Perspective. *Management Studies and Business Journal (Productivity)*, 1(3), 261–269.

Kumar, P., & Firoz, M. (2022). Does Accounting-based Financial Performance Value Environmental, Social and Governance (ESG) Disclosures? A detailed note on a corporate sustainability perspective. *Australasian Accounting, Business and Finance Journal*, 16(1), 41–72.

Murgolo, M., Tettamanzi, P., & Minutiello, V. (2024). Accounting, ESG dynamics and the pandemic: when the quality of disclosure becomes crucial to sustainable success. *Corporate Governance: The International Journal of Business in Society*, 24(3), 509–540.

Raghavan, K. (2022). ESG reporting impact on accounting, finance. *Journal of Global Awareness*, 3(1), 9.

Şeker, Y., & Şengür, E. D. (2021). The impact of Environmental, Social, and Governance (ESG) performance on financial reporting quality: International evidence. *Ekonomika*, 100(2), 190–212.

Simmons, V., Serafin, A., Stampone, A., & Rayeski, L. A. (2024). Integrating ESG into the Accounting Curriculum: Insights from Accounting Educators. *Issues in Accounting Education*, 39(2), 85–106.

Tettamanzi, P., Venturini, G., & Murgolo, M. (2022). Sustainability and financial accounting: A critical review on the ESG dynamics. *Environmental Science and Pollution Research*, 29(11), 16758–16761.

Wang, X., Ren, K., Li, L., Qiao, Y., & Wu, B. (2024). How does ESG performance impact corporate outward foreign direct investment? *Journal of International Financial Management & Accounting*, 35(2), 534–583.

Chapter 12
Export, Import Practices, and Global Operations and Supply Chain Management

Learning Objectives

- Describe the concept of supply chain management
- Distinguish between supply chain management and international supply chain management
- Discuss the relationship between design and supply chain management
- Described the reasons for sourcing globally and the benefits and challenges of global sourcing
- Explain why manufacturing systems and logistical elements may vary within the same company
- The role of e-business in international supply chain management

Overview

As companies continue to enter international markets, global competition increases. It forces the upper management of international and domestic companies to search for ways to lower costs while improving the products or services to remain competitive. Sometimes, the desired results are obtained through improvements within existing operations. Other times, improved competitiveness is pursued by having the company open new or transfer existing operations abroad or find alternative sources for labor, raw materials, or the inputs currently sourced from inside the company. Another option is outsourcing, which is hiring others outside the company to perform noncore activities and decision making in a company's value chain rather than having the company and employees continue to perform those activities.

As illustrated in Figure 12.1, companies face four significant global supply chain challenges: data and application silos, lack of know-how, tools, and technologies to generate valuable insights, lack of predictive and prescriptive capabilities, and lack of off-the-shelve solutions. Coordinating and integrating the flow of materials, information, finances, and services within and among companies in the value chain, from suppliers to the ultimate consumer, is often referred to as supply chain management. In this Chapter, we discussed the topics of international supply chain management and the critical issues in managing global operations, including global sourcing, manufacturing systems, productivity, and performance of international manufacturing operations.

https://doi.org/10.1515/9783111510286-012

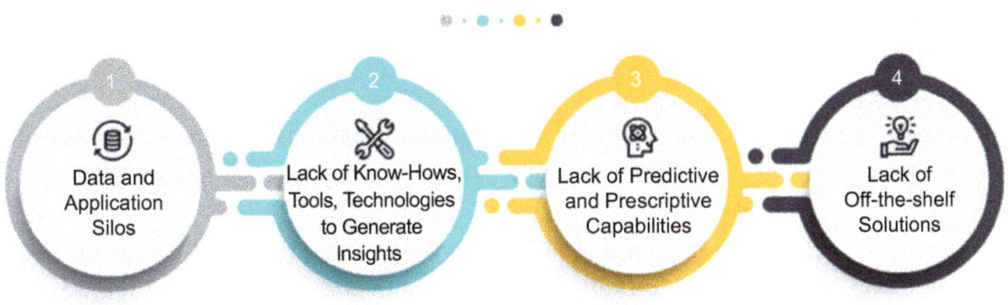

Figure 12.1: The main tasks involved in international accounting and finance management.

Sources of Export Information

Exporting is transporting merchandise to a foreign country for trade or sale. International business is potentially lucrative for many companies, but the exporters should know that establishing themselves in an international market can be complex and time-consuming. Still, most successful enterprises did not enter the world of international trade until they had thoroughly researched their exporting capabilities and various business conditions in the target market(s) abroad. There are several factors to consider when exporters assess their readiness to expand beyond their national borders, including but not limited to exporting readiness, product distribution, potential international markets' perspectives, legal factors, financing resources, operating costs, profit margins, and exporting alternatives including joint ventures, or offshore manufacturing.

Exporting is often seen as a practice that is essentially carried out by large businesses, MNEs, and MNCs, but exporting can also be helpful to a small business in various ways. Any small and medium enterprise (SME) establishing its products in the international marketplace can tap into multiple opportunities. Some of them may include the following:

- The increase in sales and profit
- Enhancement of its domestic reputation
- Reduction of its dependence on domestic markets
- The reinvigoration of the sales potential of existing products and services
- The stabilization of seasonal market fluctuations
- The sale of excess production capacity, and
- The increasing awareness of possible foreign competitors.

Exporting, however, is not a risk-free venture. Expanding an SME's operations into international markets may require strategies that could include new business process developments and assumptions, such as:

- The development of new promotional materials, potentially in other, or many, languages

- The need to increase short-term debt as a result of new operational and administrative costs
- Likely re-assignment of personnel
- Product functionality and appearance adaptation and adjustments to meet the commercial and social standards of the new targeted foreign market environment

As discussed throughout this course and the previous chapter, as the lines between domestic and international markets continue to blur, SMEs that remain ignorant of exporting do so at their peril.

Preparing for Exporting

As illustrated in Figure 12.2, international management consulting firms will walk exporters through the necessary steps. They advise clients to undertake a stringent regimen of research and self-analysis before committing time and resources to internationalization strategies into new markets. They stress that SMEs should be able to answer the following questions affirmatively before considering expanding their business to include exporting:
- Is the company currently successful in its domestic operations?
- Does the upper management team understand the types and amounts of investments, such as time, capital, and personnel, they must make to establish the business's offerings in the targeted foreign market?
- Is the company sensitive to the cultural implications of doing business in the targeted foreign market?
- Is the company willing to commit needed resources to make the exporting effort work?

To respond to the questions above, international management consultants typically recommend that companies with an eye on international markets invest enough time in developing an international business plan, highlighting any potential trouble spots and business areas that need further research. Several exporting factors must be assessed regarding the potential targeted foreign markets when developing an international business plan, including:
- Identification of such markets
- Their demographics and political environment
- Their economic status
- The social and cultural background
- Analysis of potential threats or challenges, including but not limited to research on tariffs, quotas, and any other possible trade barriers, treaties, trade regulations, patent, and trademark protection
- Product or service demand
- Levels of potential competition within those markets
- Possible distribution channels available

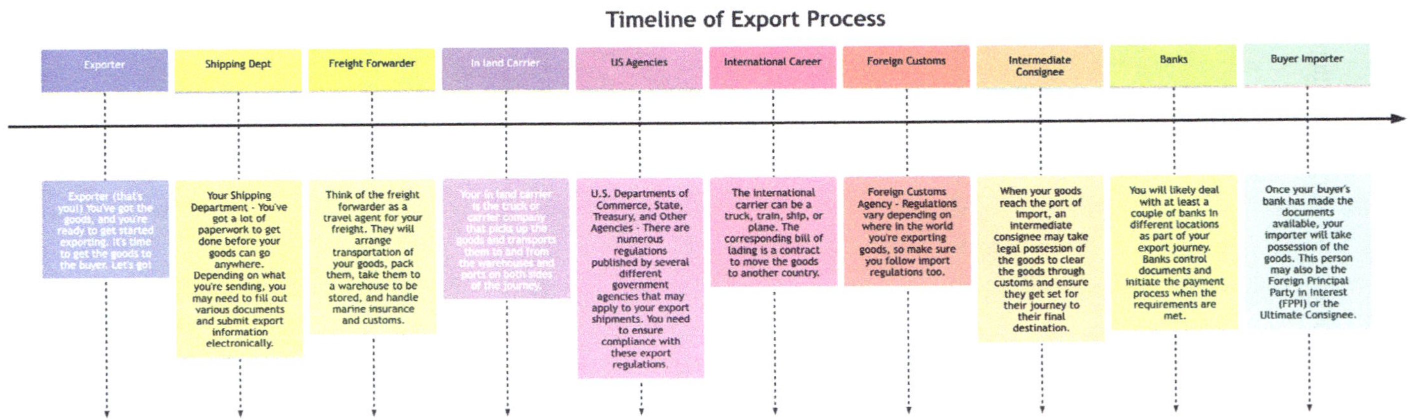

Figure 12.2: Steps in the exporting process. (SOURCE: Shipping Solutions, 2022).

- Availability of local distribution and production environment
- Exporting procedure requirements
- Any necessary adjustments or adaptations to products, services, or packaging
- International marketing strategy
- Cost of exporting operations
- Pricing strategies
- Projected sales forecasts
- Projected added revenues to domestic operations

Sources of Exporting Information

A wide range of sources is available to help SMEs research the issues and concerns when considering exporting strategies. Trade and exporters' associations, state or federal government agencies, and foreign governments are all potential sources of valuable information.

Relevant trade associations include:

- The Small Business Exporter's Association.
- The American Association of Exporters and Importers.
- The National Association of Export Companies (NEXCO)
- The National Federation of Export Associations (NFEA)
- The International Trade Association (ITA)
- National Federation of International Trade Associations (FITA)

In addition, the U.S. has more than 6,000 professional and trade organizations offering a wide array of industry expertise and specializations, many of which actively promote exporting among their members. In addition, the U.S. federal government maintains many agencies that can be tremendously helpful to companies considering expansion into international markets, including:

- The United States and Foreign Commercial Service (US&FCS),
- The Small Business Administration (SBA) and many of its programs and services, such as the Service Corps of Retired Executives (SCORE), the Small Business Development Centers (SBDCs), the Small Business Institute (SBI), and
- The U.S. Department of Commerce (DOC) houses the ITA (listed above) and has critical available resources, including international trade specialists and District Export Councils (DECs). Many DECs are scattered around the country and comprise thousands of executives with experience in international trade who have volunteered their time to help SMEs.

Lastly, the U.S. government supports several databases to supply exporters with essential data on various exporting factors, including:

- Automated Trade Locator Assistance System (SBAtlas), which provides current market information to SBA clients on world markets suitable for their products and services
- National Trade Data Bank (NTDB), maintained by the DOC, includes thousands of government documents on various aspects of export promotion and international economics
- Foreign Trade Report FT 925 provides users with vital information on foreign trade and a breakdown of imports and exports by its Standard Industrial Trade Classification (SITC) number for each country monthly

Adjusting Products for International Markets

Before entering an international market, exporters must ensure that the products they sell suit the target market. Only minor changes may be required to successfully market these products, often involving changes such as the product's color, the package's design, and the product's size, all of which may need adjustment. When entering an international market, companies should consider the tastes and preferences in each global market as part of their international marketing strategies. Figure 12.3 illustrates an example of McDonald's adjustment of its grilled chicken sandwich offering for the Arab market: McArabia.

Figure 12.3: An example of McDonald's adaptation of its offerings to the Arab market.

Many disastrous stories abound of exporters that have launched products in international markets, only to belatedly realize that their product's name had a negative connotation in the target market's local language, demanding the product's name be changed. Frequently, however, exporters find it necessary to make product labeling changes, such as changing size measurements from an imperial to a metric system or vice-versa or providing instructions in three languages, as required when selling products within the European Union.

New exporters might have to change their products to meet the standards of their foreign target market in which they hope to enter and establish. Many countries, for instance, have different electrical power systems. An exporter that neglects to outfit its electrical-powered products with plugs that will fit into the target market's electrical outlets is doomed to fail. To avert such disastrous scenarios, exporters should familiarize themselves with the International Organization of Standardization (ISO) guidelines, which issue policies on selecting and implementing appropriate quality management programs for international business operations. These ISO standards are checked every five years to keep up-to-date with ever-changing international regulations and standards. Figure 12.4 depicts the ISO standards.

Standard	Description
BS ISO/IEC 15504	The concepts of process assessment and its use in process improvement and process capability determination
ISO/IEC TS 17021-4:2013	Conformity assessment - Requirements for bodies providing audit and certification of management systems
ISO 19011:2011	Guidelines for auditing management systems
ISO/IEC 17065	Conformity assessment — Requirements for bodies certifying products, processes, and services
ISO 10006:2006	Quality management systems - Guidelines for quality management in projects
ISO 14000 Series	
ISO 14001	Environmental Management Systems
ISO 14004	EMS General Guidelines
ISO 14010	Guidelines for Auditing of an EMS
ISO 14012	Auditing - Qualification Criteria
ISO 20121:2012	Specifies requirements for an event sustainability management system for any type of event or event-related activity and provides guidance on conforming to those requirements
ISO 21500:2012	Guidance on Project Management
ISO 9000 Series	
ISO 9001:2008	Sets out the requirements of a quality management system
ISO 9000:2005	Covers the basic concepts and language
ISO 9004:2009	Focuses on how to make a quality management system more efficient and effective
ISO 19011:2011	Sets out guidance on internal and external audits of quality management systems

Figure 12.4: ISO standards. (SOURCE: ISO, 2022).

Exporters should not move too quickly in the exporting process. Instead, they should submit their product offerings to a *test drive* on one or two selected international markets. By conducting such testing, exporters can uncover unanticipated factors hindering a product's acceptance in any international market. Indeed, testing potential target markets allows exporters to check on the viability of much of their business forecasting and strategy.

Exporting Methods

Exporters have several options to choose from when entering international markets. One standard method is to enter into a joint venture (JV) with a company based in the foreign targeted market. However, most exporting companies introduce products or services to international markets via various exporting arrangements. These arrangements often take the form of licensing agreements, wherein exporters assign the rights to offer, distribute, or even manufacture their products to the foreign company, or off-shore production, where a business establishes its facility or contracts with an off-shore facility operator to manufacture the product. Figure 12.5 offers a list of the various exporting methods. Although there are many nuances and options associated with exporting, these multiple practices are commonly divided into two areas:

- **Direct Exporting** – typically requires a more significant initial outlay of funds, personnel, and other resources and is generally considered riskier than the indirect exporting alternatives. Direct exporting, however, can be an extremely profitable practice. It requires companies to find an international buyer for their products and make all arrangements to deliver those goods to the buyer. There are four methods of direct exporting, each of which entails doing business with a different element of the international business world. The first and simplest option is to export products directly to the end users, such as foreign governments, major corporations, distributors, or consumers. The second is for exporters to sell goods directly to international retailers by hiring sales representatives to work in the target market or introducing themselves and their products to retailers via direct mail campaigns or the internet through innovative digital marketing techniques. This approach is less expensive, eliminating commission fees and travel expenses associated with maintaining a sales force. Still, it also curtails opportunities for one-on-one communication with potentially valuable clients. The third approach is to secure the services of a sales representative or agent who conducts business in the target market on a commission basis to assure buyers of the exported product. Still, a drawback is that these agents often handle other non-competing products, although they are usually authorized to execute legal commitments on behalf of the client's companies. The fourth and most commonly employed method is to rely on distributors, who purchase goods from companies across the globe and re-sell them for profit in the international markets. A list of distributors can be found through the DOC's Agent/Distributor Service program, trade associations, and the U.S. and foreign chambers of commerce located in targeted international markets or at the International Chamber of Commerce (ICC).

- **Indirect Exporting** – many options involve intermediaries, such as commissioned agents or brokers, who serve companies by linking their products or services with international purchasers. A second alternative is to rely on export management companies (EMCs), firms representing the interests of a range of other companies, acting as representatives for their client companies, and soliciting and transacting business with prospective international buyers. EMCs are not responsible for ensuring that international buyers meet their payment obligations once a transaction has been made. Some of the services offered by EMCs may include conducting market research, assessing the viability of various distribution channels, arranging finance, handling export logistics such as preparing invoices and arranging insurance while providing legal advice on trade matters, and even assistance in negotiating export contracts and after-sales support. A third alternative is the export trading companies (ETCs), similar to EMCs in many functional respects but with a more neutral standing, as these act as agents between buyers and sellers, directly paying manufacturers for goods they sell to purchasers. Since companies do not have to rely on the end purchaser to receive compensation under this arrangement, an ETC can be seen as a relatively risk-free indirect exporting option.

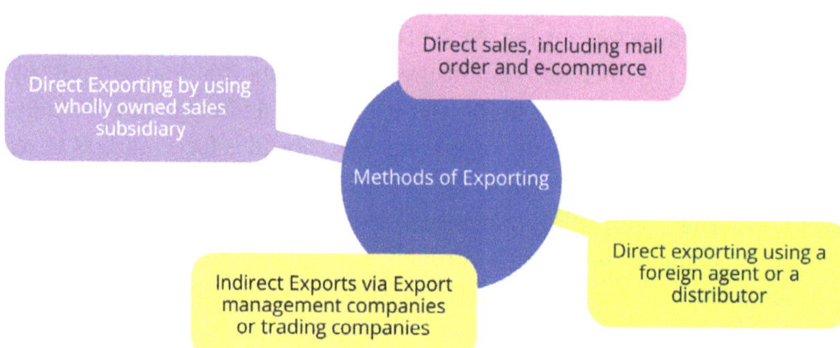

Figure 12.5: Methods of exporting.

Finally, exporters that choose not to enter into any of the above agreements may still engage in exporting through agreements with export merchants or via a practice commonly known as *piggyback exporting*, where a company with an already-established export distribution system sells its products and those of others that are not yet ready for exporting by themselves. Export merchants or agents are businesspeople who purchase and repackage products for export. These companies assume all risks associated with selling the goods. Still, arrangements can also compromise a company's control over the pricing and marketing of its products in key markets.

Exporting options such as EMCs and ETCs are sensible alternatives because they provide businesses with more excellent financial protection than direct exporting avenues. Moreover, these indirect exporting options still allow exporters to publicize their products in international markets relatively inexpensively. Finally, they offer an opportunity for exporters to gain knowledge from well-connected outfits and experience various nuances of international trade.

Incoterms, Pricing, Terms of Sale, and Payments

Freight incoterms, or international commercial terms, are the standard terms adopted in international sales agreements for importing and exporting goods. They are used to determine responsibility and liability for goods throughout a shipment. They spell out when responsibility for the goods transfers from the supplier to the buyer. They also define who pays which costs for the goods and their transport. Figure 12.6 illustrates how these incoterms differentiate.

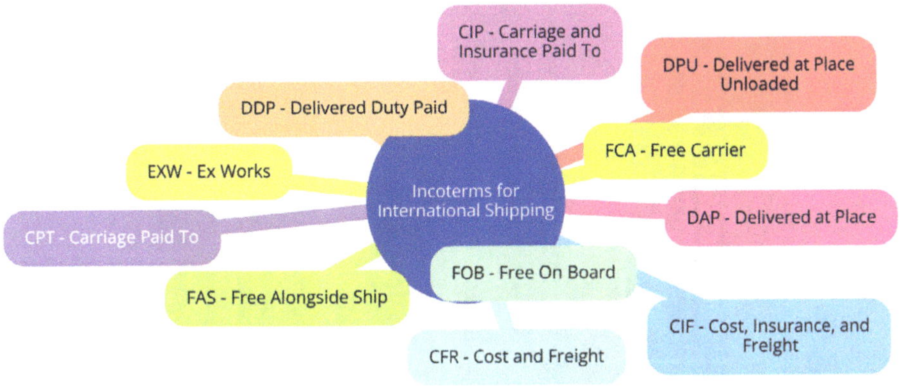

Figure 12.6: Differentiation of various incoterm available during contract negotiation.

Incoterms impact international shipping costs and are essential when calculating or quoting freight fees as they clarify the underlying international commercial transaction. As itemized in Figure 12.7, incoterms inform the sales contract by defining the obligations, charges, and risks of delivering goods from sellers to buyers. Incoterms rules are grouped into four categories:

- **The "E" term**: **EXW is the only incoterm where the sellers/exporters make the goods** available to the buyers/importers at their premises.
- **The "F" terms FCA, FAS,** and **FOB** are used where sellers/exporters are responsible for delivering the goods to a carrier determined by buyers.
- **The "C" terms**: **CFR, CIF, CPT**, and **CIP**, incoterms are used when sellers/exporters/manufacturers are responsible for contracting and paying for carriage of the goods but not responsible for additional costs or risk of loss or damage to the goods once they have been shipped.

Types of Transport	Any Mode or Modes of Transport		Sea and Inland Waterway Only				Any Mode or Modes of Transport				
INCOTERMS 2020	EXW	FCA	FAS	FOB	CFR	CIF	CPT	CIP	DAP	DPU	DDP
	Ex Works (place)	Free Carrier (place)	Free Alongside Ship (port)	Free On Board (port)	Cost & Freight (port)	Cost, Insurance & Freight (port)	Carriage Paid To (place)	Carriage & Insurance Paid to (place)	Delivered At Place (place)	Delivered At Place Unloaded (place)	Delivered Duty Paid (place)
Transfer of Risk	At Buyer's Disposal	On Buyer's Transport	Alongside Ship	On Board Vessel	On Board Vessel	On Board Vessel	At Carrier	At Carrier	At Named Place	At Named Place Unloaded	At Named Place
Responsibilities & Charges											
Export Packaging	SELLER	SELLER	SELLER	SELLER	SELLER	SELLER	SELLER	SELLER	SELLER	SELLER	SELLER
Loading Charges	BUYER	SELLER	SELLER	SELLER	SELLER	SELLER	SELLER	SELLER	SELLER	SELLER	SELLER
Delivery to Port/Place	BUYER	SELLER	SELLER	SELLER	SELLER	SELLER	SELLER	SELLER	SELLER	SELLER	SELLER
Export Duty, Taxes & Customs Clearance	BUYER	SELLER	SELLER	SELLER	SELLER	SELLER	SELLER	SELLER	SELLER	SELLER	SELLER
Origin Terminal Handling Charges	BUYER	BUYER	SELLER	SELLER	SELLER	SELLER	SELLER	SELLER	SELLER	SELLER	SELLER
Loading on Carriage	BUYER	BUYER	BUYER	SELLER	SELLER	SELLER	SELLER	SELLER	SELLER	SELLER	SELLER
Freight Charges	BUYER	BUYER	BUYER	BUYER	SELLER	SELLER	SELLER	SELLER	SELLER	SELLER	SELLER
Insurance	*Negotiable*	*Negotiable*	*Negotiable*	*Negotiable*	*Negotiable*	SELLER	*Negotiable*	SELLER	*Negotiable*	*Negotiable*	*Negotiable*
Destination Terminal Handling Charges	BUYER	BUYER	BUYER	BUYER	BUYER	BUYER	SELLER	SELLER	SELLER	SELLER	SELLER
Delivery to Destination	BUYER	BUYER	BUYER	BUYER	BUYER	BUYER	BUYER	BUYER	SELLER	SELLER	SELLER
Unloading at Destination	BUYER	BUYER	BUYER	BUYER	BUYER	BUYER	BUYER	BUYER	BUYER	SELLER	BUYER
Import Duty, Taxes & Customs Clearance	BUYER	BUYER	BUYER	BUYER	BUYER	BUYER	BUYER	BUYER	BUYER	BUYER	SELLER

Figure 12.7: Incoterms table from 2020. (SOURCE: Guided Imports, 2020).

- **The "D" terms, DAF, DES, DEQ, DDU**, and **DDP**, incoterms, are used when sellers/exporters/manufacturers are responsible for all costs and risks associated with bringing the goods to the named place of destination.

Exporters must calculate freight costs before final negotiations to decide how different incoterms may affect the freight cost of their goods being shipped abroad. *Ex Works (EXW), Free on Board (FOB),* and *free carrier (FCA)* are the most commonly used incoterms that determine the buyer's and seller's responsibilities, including who is required to cover all expenses and logistics arrangements connected to the shipping of goods.

When exporters ship EXW, they deliver (the product is considered delivered) when they place the goods at the buyer's disposal at the exporters' premises or another named place agreed upon, such as a corporate office, a manufacturing facility, or a warehouse. In such a case, the exporters do not need to load or clear goods for export. The buyers are responsible for the added cost of getting the goods from the exporters to the seaport or airport. To calculate EXW freight charges, buyers choose a container, box, or pallet shipping, enter their dimensions and weight, and get an instant estimate of freight shipping costs.

Conversely, with FOB, exporters (sellers) must load the products using the buyer's preferred method of transport at the shipping point (seaport or airport). They may also be responsible for these products sold throughout the journey and their final destination. Still, typically, exporters retain ownership and responsibility for the products sold until these are loaded (or "on board") on a shipping vessel. At this time, all liabilities are transferred to the buyer.

When using a free carrier (FCA), exporters accept responsibility and costs once the goods are loaded onto a form of transportation or delivered to any specified location agreed upon by buyers and exporters, typically a seaport or airport. This incoterm is adopted for all shipping modes. With FCA, exporters are responsible for packaging and transport at the origin, meaning they have more responsibility than EXW. However, the buyer still assumes costs and responsibilities earlier than when using FOB.

It is important to note that contracts concerning international transportation often contain abbreviated trade terms that describe conditions such as the time and place of delivery, payments, and when the risk of losses shifts from the exporter to the buyer. For instance, agreements should determine who pays freight costs and insurance considerations. The ICC publishes these incoterms rules, but exporters shipping goods in the U.S. must also observe the Uniform Commercial Code (UCC), a comprehensive set of laws governing all commercial transactions in the U.S. The UCC is not federal but a *uniformly* adopted state law essential for interstate business transactions. Because the UCC has been universally adopted, exporters can confidently engage in contracts as the terms will be executed in the same way by the courts of every American jurisdiction. The resultant assurance of business relationships enables businesses to grow and the American economy to thrive. For this reason, the UCC has been called *the backbone of American commerce*. Due to more than one set of rules, the parties in a contract must specify which governing laws they used for a shipment.

Buyers and sellers adopt many other individual incoterms depending on specific situations in their contracts. The following list of the most common ones are EXW, FCA, FAS, FOB, CPT, CIP, CFR, CIF, DPU, DAP, and DDP. Figure 12.8 illustrates the 2022 leading Incoterms Guide in International Trade. Figure 12.8 illustrates the 2024 leading Incoterms Guide in International Trade.

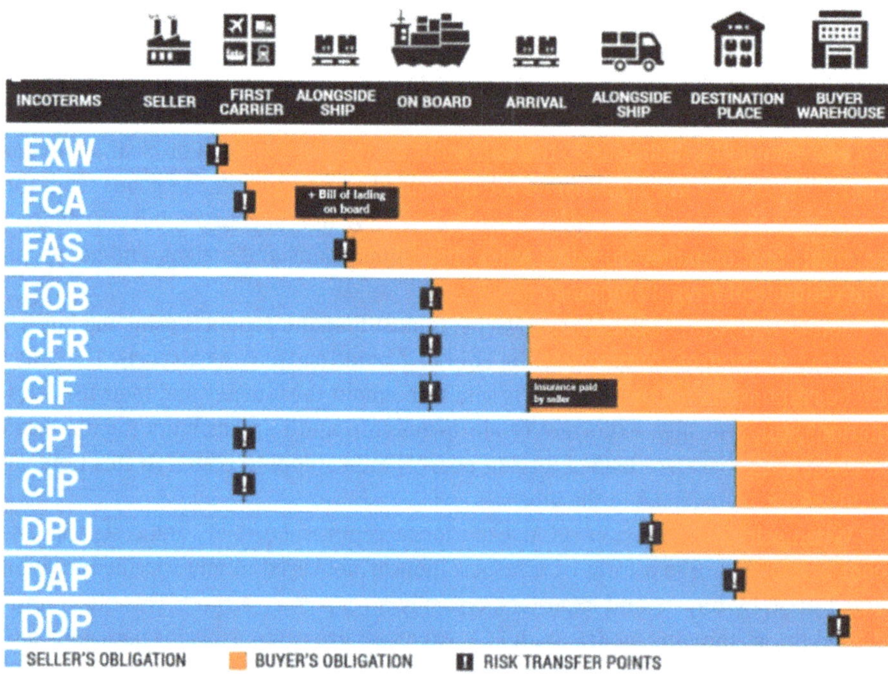

Figure 12.8: 2022 Main Incoterms Guide in International Trade. (SOURCE: Union Source, 2022).

Export Financing

Figure 12.9 provides an overview of the various steps in export financing, often required to cover the gap between when exporters can turn inventory and trade receivables into cash and when they must pay on their trade payables. Export financing is a cash-flow solution for exporters that facilitates the commerce of goods internationally. It allows exporters to access working capital before their clients pay for purchased products. Usually, in international trade, exporters agree to the payment terms of international buyers. Then exporters ship the goods abroad, while payments are received later, once the deal is concluded and depending on the incoterms adopted, which often creates a cash flow issue.

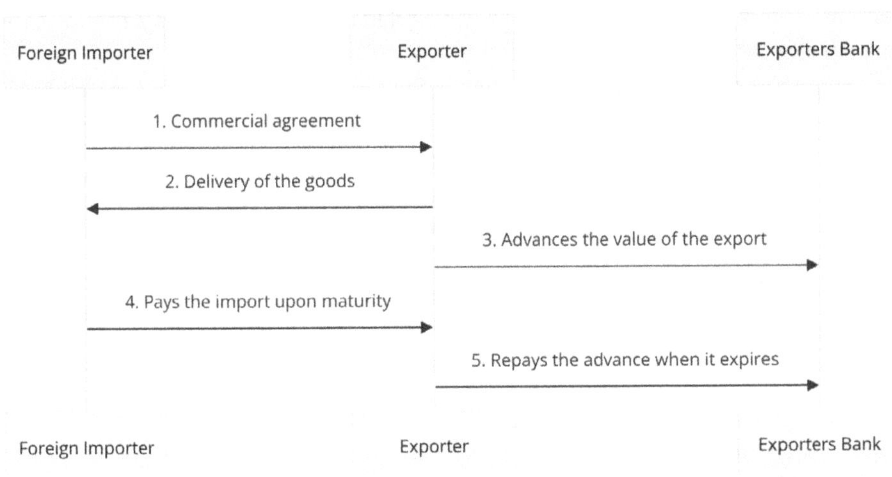

Figure 12.9: An overview of the various steps in export financing.

When buyers or importers purchase orders from exporters, both parties must agree on payment terms. Export financing facilitates this process by offering finance payment terms, usually between 60 and 90 days, but payment terms can be as short as 30 days or as long as 120 days, and at times, even longer, but this is not common. Once the terms are set, exporters bill importers with extended payment agreed to the date. Then, they ship the products sold, which tends to create a gap in the revenues for exporters. Even though they have already sold and shipped the products, they will not receive the payment until the invoice is due. That is when export finance comes into play, usually through the following steps:

1. Exporters transfer the sale invoice(s) to export finance service companies or financiers.
2. Export finance providers exchange the invoice(s) with funds.
3. Financiers deduct their finance fees to advance the revenue and give exporters a substantial percentage of the total purchase, but not all of it.
4. Financiers then receive the payments once due and may even collect them.
5. Importers are responsible for paying the financiers directly instead of the exporters.
6. Financiers can then deduct any administrative fees and control payment flows, allowing them to estimate better the risk involved in these transactions.
7. Finally, financiers transfer the remaining balance to exporters.

Estimating the export finance costs is complex because it assumes several variables. Some are quantifiable and easier to compare and contrast. For instance, the invoice amount, payment terms, and Incoterms, to mention a few. Other variables analyzed are qualitative, assessing business relationships between exporters and importers, going beyond volumes and growth. Some financiers use Export Credit Agencies (ECAs) for a more accurate risk assessment, providing detailed information on a case-by-case examination.

In practice, ECAs can be helpful when doing credit checks, due diligence, and risk assessment, allowing financiers to check the creditworthiness of the parties involved. The more data is available for input, the better the risk assessment in each transaction becomes. Better risk assessment permits financiers to offer better rates. Nonetheless, given the increasing default stories in trade finance, credit insurance companies are reluctant to cover certain export finance products. For this reason, traditional lenders cannot finance capital for export activities. Therefore, many exporters sometimes do not have access to trade finance products. For instance, SMEs are less likely to access financing than larger MNEs and MNCs.

Export Financing Programs

When needing export financing, exporters tend first to contact their commercial bank. The U.S. federal government has many export financing programs available through the Export-Import Bank of the United States, the U.S. Small Business Administration, and the U.S. Department of Agriculture. The following are some of the primary sources of export financing programs:

SBA Export Financing Programs

The SBA offers two types of export services: the Export Express Program and the Export Working Capital Program.

– Export Express Program

Even if a business hasn't started exporting yet, they are eligible for a loan if they have been in operation for at least 12 months. They need to demonstrate that the loan will support export activity. So, if you're a business just getting into exports, this would be an excellent way to finance that expansion. The main characteristics of these loans include the following:

- Maximum loan size of $500,000
- Revolving lines of credit may not exceed seven years
- The lender and borrower can negotiate an interest rate but may not exceed the SBA maximum interest rate limit
- Application forms include lender's forms, SBA Form 1919, and Borrower Information
- The credit decision is made by the lender, with the response from SBA within 24 hours
- SBA will guarantee up to 90% for loans of $350,000 or less and 75% of loans over $350,000

– Export Working Capital Program

The Export Working Capital Loan program is designed for businesses that have already begun exporting and need capital to support those export sales. The main characteristics of these loans include the following:

- Maximum loan size of $5 million
- Revolving lines of credit have terms of 12 months or less
- The lender and borrower can negotiate the interest rate; however, there is no SBA maximum interest rate limit
- Application forms include SBA Form 1920
- The credit decision is made by the SBA, with a response between 5–10 business days
- SBA will guarantee up to 90% of the loan

EXIM Bank's Working Capital Loan Guarantee Program

The EXIM Bank offers the Working Capital Loan Guarantee Program, which allows exporters to borrow more funds with the same amount of collateral. However, the bank does not provide loans; instead, it works with qualified lenders to guarantee up to 90% of the loan. For instance, inventory is typically financed at 50% of its value. Still, under the Working Capital Guarantee Program, it can be funded for up to 75% of the value, which includes raw materials and work-in-process goods. Foreign accounts receivables that do not have credit insurance are typically completely excluded by banks. Still, under the program, banks can finance uninsured accounts receivables for up to 90% of their value.

However, since the program aims to support U.S. businesses and jobs through export, there are some eligibility requirements and restrictions a company must meet:

- Must have been in business for at least one year
- Have at least one full-time employee
- Positive net worth
- Be exporting products with more than 50% U.S. content, based on all direct and indirect costs
- Must be exported from the U.S.
- It must be non-military use
- Cannot export to restricted countries
- The EXIM Bank does not support early-stage startups, grants, crude oil, direct investments, personal loans, or land purchases

Export Credit Insurance

Although the EXIM Bank does not require an exporter to ensure its receivables to get a loan, businesses should still look into export credit insurance to protect themselves from risk, especially if they don't plan to go through one of the SBA or EXIM Bank programs.

The EXIM Bank offers several export credit insurance products, depending on a business's needs. However, all insurance products must have their claims filed 3 to 8 months after the due date, cover 12 months, and offer report shipments monthly.

- **Multi-buyer standard**

This was designed for experienced U.S. exporters to protect against non-payment by foreign buyers. It covers the exporter from the commercial risk of insolvency or protracted default of the foreign buyer just not paying, as well as against political risks, such as currency and convertibility, expropriation, naturalization, war, cancellation of import/export licenses, or anything that has a political orientation.

Terms:

- 95% base coverage
- A deductible based on the U.S. company's export experience and risk portfolio
- Discretionary credit limit
- A portfolio tailored rate with discounts for exporting to low-risk country concentration and many buyers
- Refundable $500 minimum policy issuance fee

- **Small business multi-buyer**

This is designed for businesses that meet the SBA's small business definition and whose three-year annual average of export credit sales is $10 million or less

Terms:

- 95% base coverage
- No deductible
- Discretionary credit limit based on the company's experience
- A premium rate per $100 for private sector buyers of:
  - $0.55 for 1–60 days
  - $0.90 for 61–120 days
  - $1.15 for 121–180 days
- Refundable $500 minimum policy issuance fee

- **Express**

Express insurance is made for small businesses new to exporting, with $10 million or less in export credit sales, ten or fewer buyers, and no more than five years of export credit experience.

Terms:

- 95% base coverage (but not all accounts must be covered)
- No deductible
- No discretionary credit limit (EXIM Bank must approve all buyers)
- A premium rate per $100 for private sector buyers of:

  - $0.65 for 1–60 days
  - $1.06 for 61–120 days
  - $1.35 for 121–180 days
- Refundable $500 minimum policy issuance fee

– **Single buyer**

Single-buyer insurance can be purchased by any exporter looking to insure just one buyer.

Terms:
- 90% base coverage
- There is no discretionary credit limit, but EXIM Bank must approve the single buyer.
- No deductible
- Premium rates will vary depending on the buyer's country and the length of the payment terms
- A minimum $500 policy issuance fee is waived for renewals and repeat small business customers; it will also be refunded if the premium paid exceeds the cost

Sources for Imports Information

There are several sources for import information: WITS supplies access to information on external trade (imports) from the UN COMTRADE Data Base, the United Nations Conference on Trade and Development (UNCTAD) TRAINS database, and the World Trade Organization (WTO) IDB and CTS Data Bases. The statistical offices of each country report the data to relevant international organizations. No trade information for any given product indicates a non-traded product according to the reporting country. As a rule, missing country/period data means the reporting country had not reported data for that specific year.

UN COMTRADE:
- Offers the most extensive country/period coverage of all three databases (from 1962 and virtually all countries).
- Records not only imports but also exports and re-exports.
- However, information is not as detailed as in the other databases (HS or SITC nomenclatures for UN COMTRADE, national tariff line level for TRAINS and IDB).
- UN COMTRADE is better fitted for cross-country analysis since the information from all countries shares standard international nomenclatures.

TRAINS:
- It contains information at the national tariff level, meaning more details than UN COMTRADE.

- Country/period coverage (from 1988, less than 100 countries) is smaller than in UN COMTRADE.
- Contains only imported flows.
- TRAINS are best fitted for detailed country or sector analysis with links to market access information.

IDB:
- It contains information at the national tariff level, which means more details than UN COMTRADE.
- Country/period coverage (from 1996, less than 100 countries) is smaller than in UN COMTRADE.
- Contains only imported flows.
- IDB is best fitted for detailed country or sector analysis with links to market access information.

International Supply Chain Management

No other sector of business functions involves the complexity, depth, and breadth of logistics geography. Across the globe, around the clock, logistics are concerned with bringing products and services where they are required at the precise time desired, often just-in-time (JIT). Figure 12.10 offers an overview of an international supply chain management framework. Attempting to envision any international marketing strategy, global manufacturing, or international business and trade without logistics is nearly impossible. Consider the scenario where the U.S. car manufacturer General Motors procures parts from global suppliers and assembles cars in factories worldwide. Think about just one car model and the thousands of components used to make that car. Now, think about the locations where these car parts came from. This example focuses on only one car and does not include other models or categories such as trucks, vans, and other vehicles. Much like in an orchestra, there is a need for a conductor who can keep all the various instruments in synchrony, in tune, participating at the right moment, without interruptions. The same is true for the GM example, with its logistics, where someone must manage all the flows of raw materials and shipments of all the necessary parts and vehicles so that they are delivered at the right location and when needed.

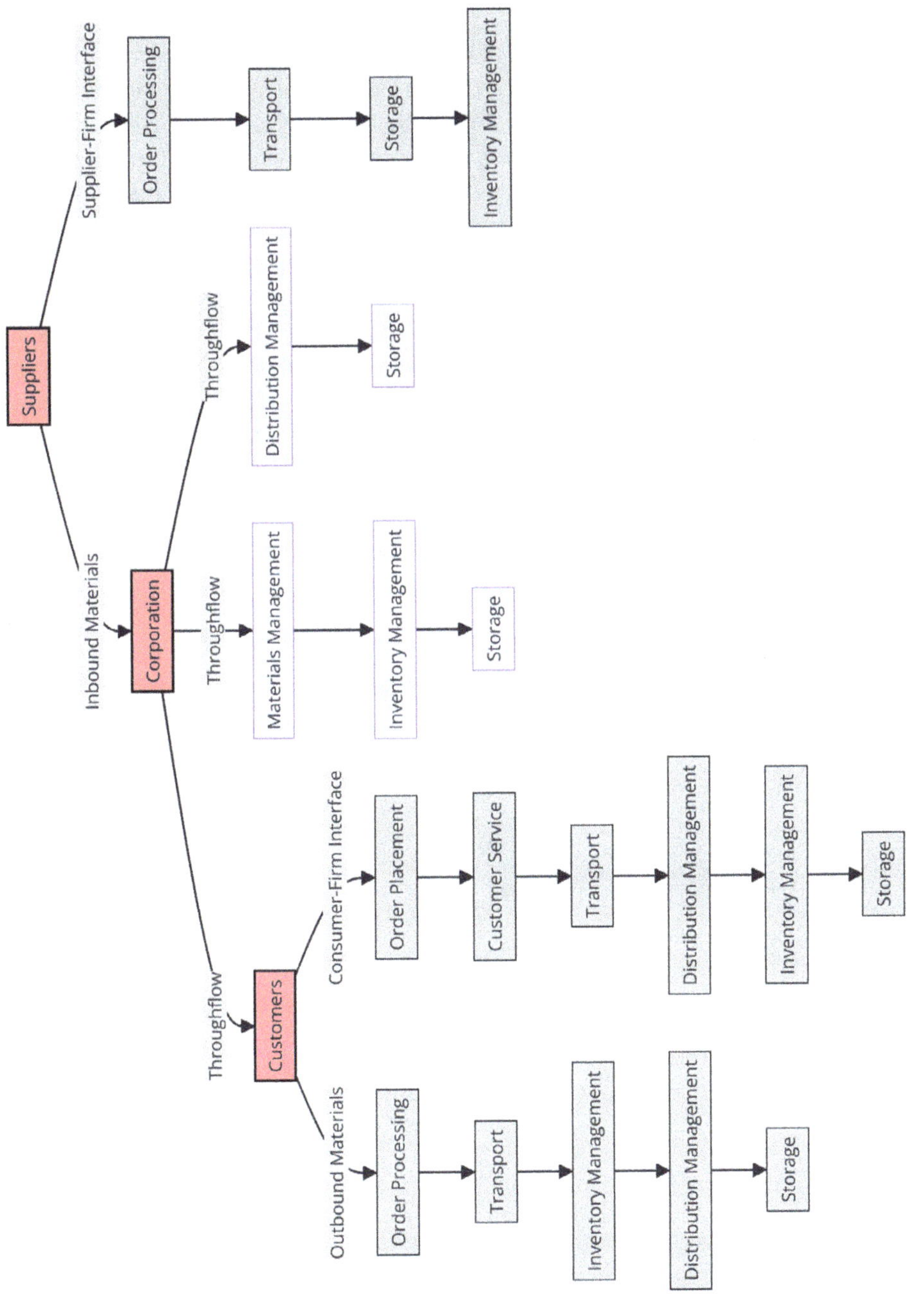

Figure 12.10: An overview of an international supply chain management framework.

A Word About Logistics

Figure 12.11 offers a broad definition of the concept of logistics. The word logistics is derived from the Greek term logistikos and the Latin term logisticus, denoting the science of computing and calculating. In ancient times, the term was adopted to refer to the art of driving armies and supplies to the war front. This term can be traced to the 17th century when the French military presumably first utilized it. During WWII, logistics acquired significance in army operations, supporting the flow of supplies, men, and equipment across the border. Today, logistics has gained a broader meaning. Philip Kotler defined logistics as planning, implementing, and controlling the physical flow of materials and finished goods from the point of origin to the point of use to meet the customer's needs at a profit. However, the American Council of Logistics Management (ACLM) defines it slightly differently, as the process of planning, implementing, and controlling the efficient, cost-effective flow and storage of raw materials, in-process inventory, finished goods, and related information from the point of origin to the point of consumption to conform to customer requirement.

Figure 12.11: A broad definition of the concept of logistics.

Logistics is at the heart of the supply chain, and both must be managed. Supply chain management (SCM) denotes an effort by suppliers to develop and execute supply chains that are as efficient and economical as possible. Supply chains cover all related processes up and down the stream, from gathering raw materials and added-value production to product development and the critical information systems and technologies (IS&T) to direct these undertakings.

A Brief Overview of Supply Chain Management

Supply chain management (SCM) typically tries to centrally control or link supply chains to a product's production, shipment, and distribution channels. That is done by controlling internal inventories, production, distribution, sales, and vendors' inventories. By managing the supply chain, businesses can reduce costs and deliver products to consumers faster. SCM is founded on the idea that almost every product that arrives on the market results from the actions of numerous organizations that make up a supply chain. Although supply chains have existed for quite some time, most businesses have only recently paid attention to them as a value-add to their operations.

Lowering barriers worldwide to facilitate the easy flow of goods and services has been one of the most significant trends in promoting globalization and international business. Regardless of their sizes, nearly all businesses are motivated to expand their operations internationally. When a company decides to internationalize, transforming itself successively from a local into an international and then a global one, it begins to rely on the global supply chain network. It will need to import raw materials, manufacture its products, store its inventories and sales on many international markets, and adjust the supply and demand according to international market forces.

Such initiatives will almost invariably require purchasing raw materials from international suppliers, assembling products using various parts manufactured in multiple other countries, and ultimately selling such products or services to customers in different international markets.

International Supply Chain Management

Figure 12.12 illustrates an example of an international supply chain management process (ISCM), which manages the flow of goods, services, or people between various countries. In ISCM, business logistics expands beyond the home country's frontier into different countries. It manages the company's supply chain concerning the flow of resources across at least one international border. As globalization increases, ISCM has become one of the essential disciplines in 21st-century business as the science of planning how goods and services can be distributed across the globe, from manufacturers to consumers. A supply chain comprises interconnected functions, suppliers and distribution channels, and consumers. It starts upstream, with those who produce and supply raw materials or components to manufacturers. It continues downstream with the logistics companies that move finished goods to warehouses and distribution centers and concludes with the hand-off to wholesalers and retailers.

Consider the importance of a well-managed ISCM. As of fall 2022, Taiwan makes 65% of the world's semiconductors and about 90% of the advanced chips, while China produces about 5% and the U.S. 10%. If there were to be any break or disruption in the flow of such resources from Taiwan, the manufacturing of computers, smartphones, electronics, cars, and other advanced systems would halt. In today's interlinked global economy, businesses and people's lives rely on the fast, efficient, and

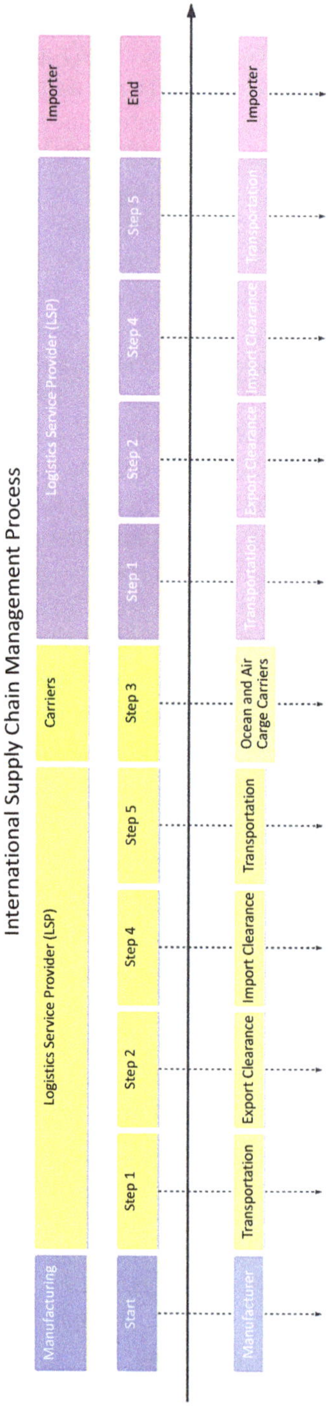

Figure 12.12: International supply chain management process. (SOURCE: Wang & Yang, 2007).

safe flow of a high volume of materials, components, and finished products across the globe. According to the WTO, world trade was about $22.3 trillion in 2021. Supply chains can only operate if interconnected systems work harmoniously: air and sea shipping and transportation modes, information systems and international business and trade management, global security, and infrastructure constructions. Within these integrated systems, there is little room for error. If the cocoa supply from Guinea is disrupted, a factory in Pennsylvania cannot produce chocolate bars. If a single paint supplier in Japan cannot ship goods for a week, car production in Michigan may temporarily cease.

To illustrate the dynamics of ISCM, take another example of a large jewelry firm based in New York City. The firm has an extensive international supply chain for crafting a diamond bracelet. A source in South Africa may supply the diamond, the gold from another source in China, and the jewelry, which may be assembled in Switzerland. The firm's ISCM team manages the international supply chain from beginning to end. It must oversee all functional steps, from producing a resource through its value-added transformations (making a gold bracelet and adding diamonds to it, then packaging it appropriately) into a finished product until the final product is sold to a customer. Such ISCM endeavor may include the following functional steps that require management and control:

1. Business process oversight of diamond purchases from South Africa and gold from China to fulfill the production demands.
2. Provide temporary warehousing of the purchased diamonds and gold at local storage facilities.
3. Provide for the international shipping of the gold stored in China to a subsidiary in a small Eastern European country, where the gold will be refined and prepared for the jewelers in Geneva.
4. Arrange for the international shipping of the diamonds stored in South Africa to the company's facilities in Geneva for cutting and polishing.
5. Arrange for the international shipping of the refined gold to the company's Geneva facility to create rings and settings.
6. Once the rings are finished, arrange for warehousing at the company's central warehouse until needed to fill orders, keep meticulous computerized inventory records, and ensure adequate security to safeguard such valuable items.
7. Arrange for the shipment of an order of diamond rings to the company's flagship Manhattan retail store.
8. Monitor the inventory at the retail store until the product is sold to a customer.

ISCM, like SCM, encompasses materials management, sourcing, and physical distribution. However, unlike SCM, ISCM can be better defined as the design and management of a system that supervises and monitors the flow of materials into and out of the company across international borders to attain its corporate objectives at the lowest cost. In other words, it is a global manufacturing and material-sourcing network. It is a business practice where companies source materials from one or more nations, manufacture products in another, and sell these finished products in many countries. These are complex networks, however, as various actors from several nations are part of this network. Hence, ISCM involves cross-border, inter-organizational connections among suppliers, government institutions, business intermediaries, local and international traders, and customers across the globe. Indeed, MNEs and MNCs are notable examples of ISCM that combine their production systems with the value-added complexity of a global supply chain management to link several countries with different currencies, import tariffs or quotas, and fiscal systems. Hence, one of the essential activities of ISCM is global sourcing and outsourcing.

Distinctions Between Domestic and International Supply Chain Management

Although the principles and functions that govern domestic and international supply chain management are very similar, they are different, with the international component adding to the complexity of ISCM. The following are some of the main differences:

- **Distance** – In the international landscape, the flow and transportation of materials concerns tend to monopolize the thinking and problem-solving of logistics managers. The distances to be managed in ISCM are much broader and more complex, often traversing the globe, unlike domestic SCM. Hence, managing such international distances is usually the primary factor when developing ISCM systems. Transportation issues frequently highlight the importance of a full-service, flexible, and reliable transportation system for ISCM excellence. A lengthier distance suggests higher direct transportation costs, import/export insurance for damages, transportation incidents caused by sea piracy, deterioration of products, pilferage in transit, and higher indirect costs of insurance, warehousing, and inventory. The breakdown of the system, as it happened during and after the global COVID-19 pandemic, can be very detrimental to ISCM, especially considering sourcing imbalances, such as the advanced chip manufacturing in Taiwan or energy supply from Russia, as experienced in 2022.
- **Transportation** – Domestic SCM can rely on various alternatives to move goods, typically via road or rail. For ISCM, transportation options are limited, mostly requiring air or sea, unless in adjacent markets where road and rail are available. Whereas SCM tends to rely only on one form of transportation, ISCM may depend on multiple alternatives. Products may be transported by truck or rail within domestic regions, by air or sea for the international portion, and then back to truck or rail for local distribution at targeted markets. This multimodal transportation and improved IS&T have helped ISCM and SCM professionals cope with global sourcing and manufacturing demands.
- **Exchange rate fluctuation** – While domestic SCM relies on one currency and is not impacted by currency exchange rate fluctuations, ISCM professionals do, as they must adjust their planning and forecasting to include the existence of cur-

rency exchange rate fluctuations. In a domestic market, SCM relies on using a single domestic currency, whereas, in an ISCM environment, different currencies and exchange rates may be adopted.

- **Regulations** – Domestic SCM professionals deal with one national law on customs procedures, documentation, packaging, and labeling requirements. ISCM professionals must cope with different host-country rules and various intermediary actors in the distribution channels, such as customs brokers, shipping forwarders, financial institutions, insurance companies, etc.
- **Management** – Typically, domestic SCM teams have a single manager with supervisory and management responsibilities overseeing the team, or division, in all aspects of the planning and execution concerning the flow of goods across the country. On the other hand, ISCM is typically composed of a corporate manager coordinating international supply chain activities with other managers, often located across the globe, requiring complexity. However, clear plans for the execution and distribution processes usually lead to challenges in the decision-making process.
- **Costs** – In domestic SCM and ISCM, managers must consider the costs of store facilities, transportation, workers, and technology. Nevertheless, in ISCM, additional charges need to be considered, including international shipping costs, tariffs, quotas, government taxes, import/export fees, and currency exchange rate fluctuations.
- **Supply chain relationships** – To build relationships between businesses or between a company and customers, trust is a vital factor in deciding the quality of the business relationship. Developing trustworthy relationships domestically rather than internationally in various countries, regulations, geography, and economic environments is much easier.
- **Culture** – In ISCM, sourcing processes such as supplier selection, supplier assessment, supplier involvement, and so on need to consider more sophisticated factors such as language and culture, which may be insignificant in domestic supply chain management. Unfamiliarity with the supplier's language and culture increases the risk of communication challenges, misunderstandings, and uncomfortable encounters.

Driving Forces

Globalization and technology are the two most significant drivers of transformations in the ISCM arena. The globalization of markets has developed prospects for conducting business abroad. As companies continue to internationalize, attention has increasingly shifted to ISCM operations. The swiftness and efficiency in the flow of goods across international borders rely on the available forms of transportation, available capability, and capacity, as well as inter-modal facilities for moving, storing, packaging, handling, and shipping where the buyer, sellers, and carriers are located. Cargo movement must be done physically, utilizing any available means of transportation. Globalization has increased trade, necessitating an efficient and cost-effective logistics services network. It has led to transformations in the overall structure of the ISCM, including third- and fourth-party logistics and outsourcing logistics services.

The swift advancements in information and communication technologies (ICT), particularly the digital transformation of business processes, changed how the world does business. The internet has made it easier to conduct business electronically (e-business and e-commerce) in any part, from anywhere in the world. Digital technologies have also provided faster and more accurate supply chain services and monitoring. Two significant effects of these transformations are the advancements in containerization of cargo shipping and the use of wide-bodied aircraft. These shifts, in particular, have, on the whole, allowed large turnover volumes of goods, time, and cost efficiency. Furthermore, mass communication, especially digital marketing techniques, and IS&T resources exposes international consumers to foreign products and services, thus stimulating global needs and preferences and promoting even more global marketing and logistics.

The Role of E-Business

E-commerce allows an organization to enhance its competitiveness, as illustrated in Figure 12.13, through its integration with the supply chain. It traverses geographic borders and saves time and cost. E-commerce has many positive effects on multiple areas and business management domains, such as international marketing, finance, economics, accounting, decision making, production, supply chain, project management, and operation management.

Online transactions through e-commerce permit customers to analyze and purchase goods and services without leaving their homes or offices, boosting access and convenience. Utilizing online sales, businesses can scale efficiently and reach customers in new markets, both domestically and internationally, particularly small and mid-sized enterprises (SMEs) strapped for resources for international expansions. Although some online purchases substitute what may have been in-store transactions, other purchases are new sales. The global COVID-19 pandemic in 2019 led to a boom in online sales as lockdowns temporarily shut stores and consumer spending diverted from services to goods. According to the U.S. Department of Commerce (DOC), in the second quarter of 2020, business-to-consumer (B2C or retail) e-commerce rose to 16% of all U.S. retail sales, up from less than 11% in the second quarter of 2019. COVID-19 hastened online sales growth, and many analysts anticipate continued growth in online shopping as pandemic restrictions and concerns ameliorate. In 2021, 79% of the U.S. population engaged in e-commerce, with clothing as the top category of online purchases.

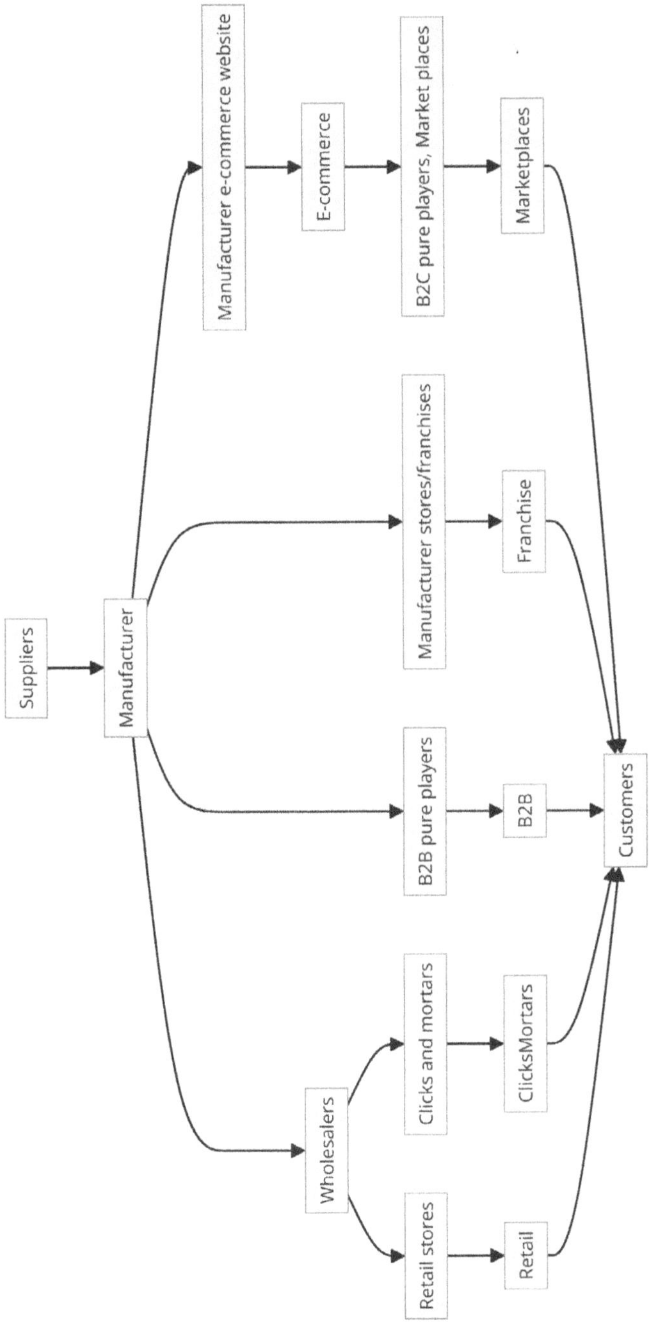

Figure 12.13: Global supply chain and e-business integration. (SOURCE: Zair, 2018).

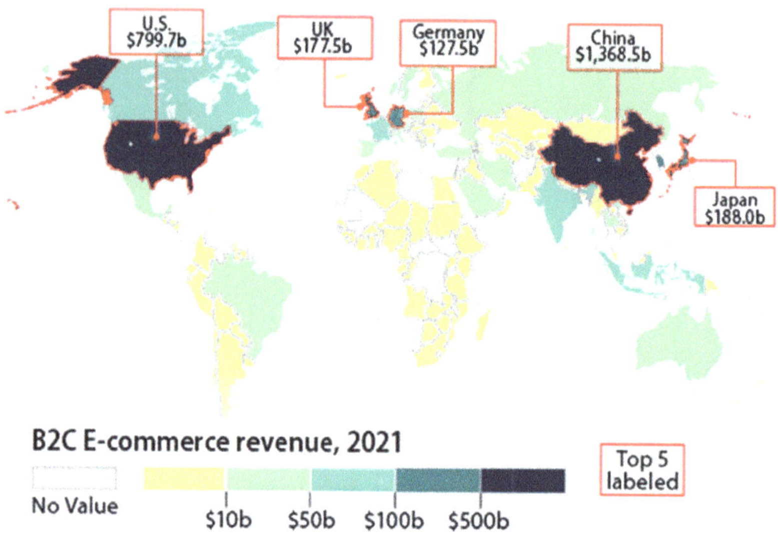

Figure 12.14: Global B2C e-commerce revenue forecast, 2021 ($ in billions). (SOURCE: CRS, Statista.com, 2021).

As depicted in Figure 12.14, Statista projects that the global B2C e-commerce market will grow to $4.1 billion in 2022. Agileintel Research estimates that the larger global business-to-business (B2B) e-commerce market was $15 billion in 2020 and will grow to over $35 trillion by 2025. Such trends raised concerns that specific foreign trade policies, friction in international shipping and border processes, poor infrastructure, and the lack of enforceable multilateral trade rules may impede U.S. companies' access to overseas markets and hinder further e-commerce growth.

E-commerce platforms allow SMEs to flourish by supplying access to a broader consumer base, domestically and internationally. Platforms provide online services to match shoppers to suppliers, facilitate orders, accept payments, and coordinate goods' physical logistics and delivery. Data Catalyst (2021) found that almost 70% of U.S. SMEs use third-party online marketplaces or their web store, with most companies opting to use multiple online markets. Many of these platforms and online marketplaces are household names in the U.S., including Amazon, Shopify, Facebook, PayPal, and Etsy, not to mention others that specialize in niche markets. Competition from foreign platforms is also growing. As illustrated in Figure 12.15, according to Forbes magazine, in 2020, 44% of all global e-commerce transactions were owned by four Chinese Companies: Taobao, TMall.com, JD.com, and Pinduoduo. While eBay captures only 3% of this market, 96% of the exports of U.S. companies on the platform reach an average of 17 different foreign countries.

China's e-commerce market is presently the world's largest in terms of transactions and potential consumers, outperforming those of the U.S., the U.K., Japan, and Germany combined. According to commerce data, China is home to around 710 million e-commerce customers. In 2020, Alibaba's Taobao sales dwarfed those of Amazon for

E-Commerce Player	Percentage of Global Online GMV
Taobao	15%
Amazon	14%
JD.COM	13%
Pinduoduo	9%
eBay	4%
Rakuten	3%
Walmart	2%
Vip.com	2%
Shopee	1%
Rest of the Web	37%

Figure 12.15: Four Chinese companies own 44% of all global e-commerce transactions. (SOURCE: Forbes, 2020).

B2C e-commerce, with the former having sales of $1.1 trillion, compared to Amazon's $269 billion, according to eMarketer (2021).

Potential Barriers to Growth

Because e-commerce in goods involves the online and offline worlds, trade obstacles span both spheres. Various policy restrictions on e-commerce exist in many countries across the globe. Trade barriers, inadequate infrastructure, and discriminatory trade practices regarding international e-commerce may emerge at multiple points, restricting businesses' capability to sell or customers' ability to purchase online or receive goods. Likewise, limitations or restrictions on what goods a company may sell or technical regulations on how it must label specific products, such as medicines, may vary by jurisdiction. For example, India restricts foreign investment in e-commerce.

Market access barriers require companies to have a physical presence, local internet domain name, or local representative in a country, adding costs to online selling to customers abroad. For example, Indonesia's regulation requires e-commerce companies to obtain licenses and promote local products, while South Korea needs a local presence to process won-denominated transactions.

Data localization is another concern. Restricting data flow beyond a nation's boundaries may restrain what websites and platforms are available, how they can function, and what goods and services, such as online payments or shipment tracking, can be offered online. Consumer privacy rules may restrict how e-commerce firms process customer data, often limiting companies from sending the data across borders. For instance, China greatly restricts cross-border data transfer. The EU imposes extensive data protection requirements for all entities that process or offer goods or services online to individuals in the EU.

Regarding counterfeits, the growth of e-commerce platforms has helped fuel the growth of counterfeit and pirated goods. The USTR's annual Notorious Markets List (2021) reports online markets facilitating trade in these goods. For instance, Mercado Libre is a leading e-commerce operator in Latin America, and many U.S. intellectual property owners report high volumes of counterfeit products for sale on the site. President Biden has ordered the Department of Homeland Security to strengthen customs enforcement to help prevent counterfeit items being imported online.

Tariffs, Duties, and Digital Taxes

Tariffs or customs duties on international shipments raise prices for customers, as do taxes on online purchases, though the latter may apply to domestic and foreign purchases. Some countries establish a de minimis level, and shipments below that value do not pay duties. For instance, some countries, such as Brazil, set a low de minimis, effectively broadening the scope of traded products and e-commerce goods subject to duties. In the U.S., Congress established the U.S. de minimis at $800.

Inefficient customs procedures or delayed clearance of goods, especially for express or perishable deliveries, may also deter buyers and sellers. Shipments below a de minimis level may be eligible for less stringent customs procedures. For instance, U.S. express delivery companies say China applies overly burdensome rules, such as inspections, for domestic package delivery. Argentina does not allow the use of electronically produced documents, hindering the customs processing of e-commerce delivery.

Integrating ESG into Global Supply Chain Operations: Impacts on Export and Import Practices

As businesses expand across international markets, the complexity of their operations increases significantly, especially in export and import practices and global operations in supply chain management. Environmental, social, and governance (ESG) considerations are now critical in shaping these functions within international business, economics, and culture. Companies that proactively integrate ESG principles into their international strategies comply with regulatory requirements and gain competitive advantages through improved efficiencies, better risk management, and enhanced reputational value. This integration is a regulatory necessity and a strategic move that can lead to sustainable and profitable international operations as global markets evolve.

Environmental Impacts and Supply Chain Management

The environmental component of ESG focuses on companies' sustainability practices, particularly in relation to their global supply chains. As discussed in this chapter, companies must adapt their operations and sourcing strategies internationally, where environmental standards vary significantly. Integrating ESG into supply chain management involves adopting practices that reduce carbon footprints, enhance energy efficiency, and manage waste more effectively. For instance, a company looking to export or import goods must consider the environmental regulations of the target market. These regulations, which can affect everything from packaging materials to the emissions standards of transported goods, are not just red tape but a crucial part of the business environment that companies must navigate. Moreover, companies are increasingly held accountable by consumers and regulators for their supply chain's environmental impact, a trend that underscores the necessity of sourcing from suppliers who uphold high environmental standards.

Environmental considerations significantly impact global supply chains. Companies involved in international trade are increasingly held accountable for their carbon footprint, from production to distribution. For example, a firm exporting goods may adopt greener logistics solutions, such as utilizing electric or hybrid freight options or optimizing route planning to reduce fuel consumption and emissions. Similarly, import practices can be aligned with environmental sustainability by taking specific actions, such as prioritizing goods that meet specific eco-friendly standards or rejecting suppliers who fail to comply with environmental regulations. These measures contribute to environmental sustainability and demonstrate a company's commitment to ESG principles.

The emphasis on reducing environmental impact extends to packaging and materials used in the export and import processes. This shift is a response to regulatory pressures and a direct result of growing consumer demand for environmentally responsible products. Companies are moving towards sustainable packaging solutions to minimize waste and enhance recyclability – driven by the very consumers they serve.

Discussion Questions

1. **Discuss the main challenges companies face when managing an international supply chain and how technology, such as e-business platforms, can help overcome these challenges.**

2. **Which of the following is NOT a commonly used incoterm in international trade?**
   A) EXW
   B) FOB
   C) CIF
   D) CIFAR

3. **What is the primary benefit of using export management companies (EMCs) for SMEs entering international markets?**
   A) Direct access to foreign buyers
   B) Complete control over product pricing and marketing
   C) Financial protection and market expertise
   D) Elimination of all exporting risks

4. **The terms "supply chain management" and "international supply chain management" are interchangeable and have no significant differences. True or False?**

5. **Exporting through a joint venture typically requires less initial investment than direct exporting methods. True or False?**

Recommended Readings

Aksoy, M., Yilmaz, M. K., Golgeci, I., Tatoglu, E., Canci, M., & Hızarcı, A. E. (2024). Untangling the Influence of Corporate Sustainability on Export Intensity: The Moderating Role of R&D Intensity. *Journal of International Marketing*, 1069031X231214233.

Dathe, T., Helmold, M., Dathe, R., & Dathe, I. (2024). Sustainable Supply Chain. In *Implementing Environmental, Social and Governance (ESG) Principles for Sustainable Businesses: A Practical Guide in Sustainability Management* (pp. 211–226). Cham: Springer International Publishing.

Dygas, R. (2024). The Overview of ESG Doctrine application in Business Management in Europe and Asia. Central and Eastern Europe in the Changing Business Environment, 24th International Joint Conference Central and Eastern Europe in the Changing Business Environment: Proceedings, SGH Warsaw School of Economics, World Economy Research Institute, Department of East Asian Economic Studies, Warsaw, Poland DOI 10.18267/pr.2024.vol.2512.4.

Khaire, F. (2024). Container Terminal Performance: System Dynamic Approach with Port Capacity Constraints and ESG Integration. *JJMIE*, 81(1).

Lou, S., You, X., & Xu, T. (2024). Sustainable Supplier Evaluation: From Current Criteria to Reconstruction Based on ESG Requirements. *Sustainability*, 16(2), 757.

Marano, V., Wilhelm, M., Kostova, T., Doh, J., & Beugelsdijk, S. (2024). Multinational firms and sustainability in global supply chains: scope and boundaries of responsibility. *Journal of International Business Studies*, 1–16.

Quaranta, D. (2024). Strategies to improve the carbon footprint of industrial zones and their competitiveness: Implications of the adoption of an ESG framework to measure performances of industrial zones and identify potential interventions. A study of two industrial zones in Morocco.

Shamsi, H. (2024). *Global Supply Chain Vulnerabilities: Assessing Firm Risk, Environmental Commitments, and Information Channels in the wake of COVID-19*. Indian Institute of Management Ahmedabad.

List of Figures

https://doi.org/10.1515/9783111510286-013

List of Tables

https://doi.org/10.1515/9783111510286-014

Appendix – Answers

Chapter 1

Discussion questions

1. Possible answer: Cultural sensitivity is crucial in international business as it affects how a company communicates and operates in foreign markets. A lack of cultural understanding can lead to marketing blunders, communication breakdowns, and overall business failures. For example, the chapter mentions how Pepsi and Electrolux faced significant challenges in China and the U.S. due to translation and cultural misunderstandings.

Multiple-Choice Questions

2. A) Currency exchange rates (This is considered an external force affecting international business.)
3. B) Language and cultural barriers
4. False (Political and legal factors, such as regulations and trade tariffs, critically influence how international businesses operate within foreign markets.)
5. True (Governance and compliance with international laws are essential for maintaining legitimacy and stability in global markets.)

Chapter 2

Discussion questions

1. Understanding cultural dimensions such as power distance, individualism vs. collectivism, and uncertainty avoidance can help managers adapt their strategies to align with local customs and expectations, improving communication, negotiation, and management practices in different cultural settings.
2. B) The perception that one's own culture is superior to others.
3. D) Profitability vs. Sustainability
4. False (Sustainability in international business also encompasses social and economic dimensions, ensuring long-term viability and ethical practices.)
5. True (Recognizing and overcoming ethnocentric views is essential for effectively interacting and conducting business in culturally diverse global markets.)

https://doi.org/10.1515/9783111510286-015

Chapter 3

Discussion questions

1. Geopolitical dynamics, such as political stability, government policies, and international relations, significantly influence legal frameworks in international trade by shaping regulations, tariffs, and intellectual property rights. This affects global business operations by dictating the terms of trade, investment opportunities, and the protection of intellectual property across different jurisdictions.
2. A) To reduce foreign dominance in the domestic economy.
3. B) Design patent
4. True (Privatization generally aims to reduce government intervention by transferring ownership and management of enterprises from the public to the private sector, promoting efficiency and competition.)
5. True (Copyrights protect the expression of ideas through mediums like books, music, and art but do not protect the ideas, systems, or operational methods themselves.)

Chapter 4

Discussion questions

1. Changes in the international monetary system, such as the transition from the gold standard to the Bretton Woods system and then to floating currency exchange rates, significantly influence global trade and investment. For instance, adopting floating exchange rates allowed more flexibility in currency valuation, affecting how countries engage in international trade and manage economic policies in response to global market dynamics.
2. B) To stabilize national currencies and provide a predictable monetary environment.
3. C) It allowed currencies to be valued based on supply and demand market forces.
4. True (This system was established to provide stability by pegging global currencies to the U.S. dollar, which was convertible to gold at a fixed rate.)
5. False. (Under the gold standard, a country's ability to circulate money was directly tied to its holdings of gold, thus limiting its ability to print money freely.)

Chapter 5

Discussion questions

1. International institutions like the UN and WTO provide a framework of rules and guidelines that can influence multinational corporations' strategic planning. These organizations facilitate trade, regulate international norms, and provide platforms for dispute resolution, which can help companies navigate the complexities of global markets and enhance their competitiveness globally.
2. C) To offer financial assistance and policy advice for economic development
3. B) Domestic exporter strategy
4. True (The IMF was created to stabilize international exchange rates and facilitate global monetary cooperation.)
5. False (A multinational strategy emphasizes adapting products and operations to local markets rather than strictly focusing on minimizing costs.)

Chapter 6

Discussion questions

1. The choice of organizational structure influences the efficiency and effectiveness of implementing global strategies and controlling operations across different markets. Structures like matrix, functional, or divisional have distinct implications on decision-making, communication, and resource allocation, which can either enhance or hinder the corporation's ability to respond to global market demands and integrate operations across geographies.
2. C) Difficulty in scaling operations internationally
3. C) Matrix structure
4. True (Hybrid structures combine elements of multiple organizational designs, which can lead to role ambiguities and conflicts over resource allocation and decision-making authority.)
5. False (A WOS is 100% owned and thus typically offers the parent company complete control over its operations, unlike a joint venture where control must be shared with other partners.)

Chapter 7

Discussion questions

1. Global leaders can manage diverse challenges by developing cultural intelligence, enhancing their understanding of local and global business environments, and adapting leadership styles to meet the specific needs of different cultures. Effective strategies include fostering open communication, encouraging collaboration, and being sensitive to cultural nuances. This approach helps build trust, promote innovation, and ensure organizational goals align with local expectations.
2. C) Transformational leadership
3. C) Understanding and integrating into local cultures
4. True (Transactional leadership involves rewards and penalties, focusing on the direct interactions between leaders and employees.)
5. False (Global leaders need to adapt their leadership styles to fit cultural differences and local business practices to manage international teams effectively.)

Chapter 8

Discussion questions

1. The most critical factors include assessing market potential, understanding the legal and political environment, analyzing socio-cultural influences, and evaluating the level of competition. These factors are crucial as they provide insights into the feasibility of market entry, potential barriers, and the competitive landscape, which help minimize risks and formulate effective entry strategies.
2. B) Government economic reports (These are secondary data sources.)
3. C) They help assess the competition and establish business contacts.
4. False (Secondary data refers to existing data not explicitly collected for current research needs.)
5. True (Trade missions allow firms to understand the foreign market environment firsthand and make informed decisions about entry strategies.)

Chapter 9

Discussion questions

1. Companies can balance global brand consistency with localization by maintaining core brand values and messaging while adapting their marketing strategies to fit local cultural norms, consumer behaviors, and market conditions. For example,

Starbucks maintains its global brand image but adapts its menu to include local favorites like Dragon Dumplings in Hong Kong. Similarly, Nike's global campaigns emphasize inclusivity and equality but are tailored to resonate with local audiences through culturally relevant content and endorsements.

2. B) It ensures compliance with local regulatory requirements. (Adapting products to meet local tastes and regulatory standards increases their chances of success in diverse markets.)
3. D) Positioning (The 4 Ps of marketing are Product, Price, Promotion, and Place. Positioning is a broader strategic concept.)
4. False (While consistency is important, the primary goal is to balance standardization with localization to meet different markets' specific needs and preferences.)
5. True (Digitalization reduces costs and increases the reach of SMEs, allowing them to develop international marketing strategies and engage customers worldwide effectively.)

Chapter 10

Discussion questions

1. The main challenges include cultural adjustment, family relocation issues, cost management, and effective communication across borders. These can be addressed through comprehensive pre-departure training, providing support for families, implementing clear communication strategies, and offering competitive compensation and benefits packages that account for the cost of living and other expatriate-specific needs.
2. B) No language barriers and a better understanding of local markets
3. C) Long-term stock options
4. False (The ethnocentric approach involves hiring employees from the parent country to manage the subsidiaries.)
5. True (Effective repatriation programs ensure that expatriates are well-prepared before their assignment and maintain strong connections with the home office throughout their tenure abroad.) These activities and questions are designed to help students understand the complexities of international human resource management and the specific challenges related to managing a global workforce.

Chapter 11

Discussion questions

1. Managing foreign exchange risk is crucial for international companies to protect against the financial impact of currency fluctuations. Strategies include forward contracts, futures contracts, options, swaps, currency invoicing, and natural hedging. Hedging helps stabilize cash flows and financial statements, allowing companies to budget and plan more effectively. It also protects against potential losses from adverse currency movements, ensuring more predictable financial performance.
2. B) To provide a consistent and transparent framework for financial reporting across countries
3. D) Technological
4. False (GAAP is primarily used in the United States, while many other countries adopt the IFRS.)
5. True (The functional currency is the primary currency used in the economic environment in which the company operates.)

Chapter 12

Discussion questions

1. Challenges include managing longer and more complex transportation routes, dealing with multiple regulations and customs procedures, currency exchange rate fluctuations, and building trustworthy relationships across different cultures. Technology and e-business platforms can help overcome these challenges by providing real-time tracking and management of shipments, facilitating smoother transactions across borders, ensuring compliance with local regulations through automated systems, and enhancing communication and collaboration among global partners.
2. D) CIFAR (CIFAR is not an incoterm; it stands for Canadian Institute for Advanced Research.)
3. C) Financial protection and market expertise (EMCs provide financial protection and extensive market expertise, which helps SMEs navigate the complexities of international trade.)
4. False (While both terms share similar principles, international supply chain management involves additional complexities such as managing long distances, multiple regulations, and currency exchange rate fluctuations.)
5. True (Joint ventures often require less initial investment as they involve partnering with a local company that shares the costs and risks.)

Index

https://doi.org/10.1515/9783111510286-016

www.ingramcontent.com/pod-product-compliance
Lightning Source LLC
Chambersburg PA
CBHW080936240926
51849CB00004BA/473
* 9 7 8 3 1 1 1 5 1 0 0 4 0 *